Substance-induced

Alcohol

303.00 intoxication
291.40 idiosyncratic intoxication
291.80 withdrawal
291.00 withdrawal delirium
291.30 hallucinosis
291.10 amnestic disorder

Code severity of dementia in fifth digit: 1 = mild, 2 = moderate, 3 = severe, 0 = unspecified.

291.2x Dementia associated with alcoholism, _____

Barbiturate or similarly acting sedative or hypnotic

305.40 intoxication (327.00)
292.00 withdrawal (327.01)
292.00 withdrawal delirium (327.02)
292.83 amnestic disorder (327.04)

Opioid

305.50 intoxication (327.10)
292.00 withdrawal (327.11)

Cocaine

305.60 intoxication (327.20)

Amphetamine or similarly acting sympathomimetic

305.70 intoxication (327.30)
292.81 delirium (327.32)
292.11 delusional disorder (327.35)
292.00 withdrawal (327.31)

Phencyclidine (PCP) or similarly acting arylcyclohexylamine

305.90 intoxication (327.40)
292.81 delirium (327.42)
292.90 mixed organic mental disorder (327.49)

Hallucinogen

305.30 hallucinosis (327.56)
292.11 delusional disorder (327.55)
292.84 affective disorder (327.57)

Cannabis

305.20 intoxication (327.60)
292.11 delusional disorder (327.65)

Tobacco

292.00 withdrawal (327.71)

Caffeine

305.90 intoxication (327.80)

Other or unspecified substance

305.90 intoxication (327.90)
292.00 withdrawal (327.91)
292.81 delirium (327.92)
292.82 dementia (327.93)
292.83 amnestic disorder (327.94)
292.11 delusional disorder (327.95)
292.12 hallucinosis (327.96)
292.84 affective disorder (327.97)
292.89 personality disorder (327.98)
292.90 atypical or mixed organic mental disorder (327.99)

Section 2. Organic brain syndromes whose etiology or pathophysiological process is either noted as an additional diagnosis from outside the mental disorders section of ICD-9-CM or is unknown.

293.00 Delirium
294.10 Dementia
294.00 Amnestic syndrome
293.81 Organic delusional syndrome
293.82 Organic hallucinosis
293.83 Organic affective syndrome
310.10 Organic personality syndrome
294.80 Atypical or mixed organic brain syndrome

SUBSTANCE USE DISORDERS

Code in fifth digit: 1 = continuous, 2 = episodic, 3 = in remission, 0 = unspecified.

305.0x Alcohol abuse, _____
303.9x Alcohol dependence (Alcoholism), _____
305.4x Barbiturate or similarly acting sedative or hypnotic abuse, _____

305.7x Amphetamine or similarly acting sympathomimetic abuse, _____
304.4x Amphetamine or similarly acting sympathomimetic dependence, _____
305.9x Phencyclidine (PCP) or similarly acting arylcyclohexylamine abuse, _____ (328.4x)
305.3x Hallucinogen abuse, _____
305.2x Cannabis abuse, _____
304.3x Cannabis dependence,

305.1x Tobacco dependence, _____
305.9x Other, mixed or unspecified substance abuse, _____
304.6x Other specified substance dependence, _____
304.9x Unspecified substance dependence, _____
304.7x Dependence on combination of opioid and other nonalcoholic substance,

304.8x Dependence on combination of substances, excluding opioids and alcohol, _____

SCHIZOPHRENIC DISORDERS

Code in fifth digit: 1 = subchronic, 2 = chronic, 3 = subchronic with acute exacerbation, 4 = chronic with acute exacerbation, 5 = in remission, 0 = unspecified.

Schizophrenia,
295.1x disorganized, _____
295.2x catatonic, _____
295.3x paranoid, _____
295.9x undifferentiated, _____
295.6x residual, _____

(continued on endsheets)

Abnormal Psychology

Abnormal Psychology

Clinical and Scientific Perspectives

Second Edition

Barclay Martin

University of North Carolina

HOLT, RINEHART and WINSTON

New York   Chicago   San Francisco

Dallas   Montreal   Toronto

London   Sydney

Publisher	Ray Ashton
Managing Editor	Jeanette Johnson
Senior Project Editor	Arlene Katz
Production Manager	Annette Mayeski
Art Director	Bob Kopelman
Cover Photo	John Block/William Pope
Cover Design	Fred Charles
Text Design	Ron Farber

Library of Congress Cataloging in Publication Data

Martin, Barclay, 1923-
Abnormal psychology.

Bibliography: p. 533
Includes index.
1. Psychology, Pathological.   2. Psychotherapy.
I. Title   [DNLM: 1. Psychology. WM100 M377a]
RC454.M279   1980   616.89   80-22837

ISBN 0-03-050721-9

ACKNOWLEDGMENTS

Excerpts from the case of Katharina were reprinted with permission from Sigmund Freud Copyrights Limited, The Institute of Psycho-Analysis, and The Hogarth Press and were taken from Volume Two of *The Standard Edition of the Complete Psychological Works of Sigmund Freud,* revised and edited by James Strachey, copyright 1955. Permission in the United States was obtained from Basic Books, Inc.

The dream about Otto was taken from *The Interpretation of Dreams* by Sigmund Freud, and was used by permission of Basic Books, copyright 1965.

Material in Table 3-1 was taken from "Immediate effects on patients of psychoanalytic interpretations" by E. L. Garduk and E. A. Haggard in *Psychological Issues,* and reprinted with permission of International Universities Press, copyright 1972.

Excerpts from the case of Suzanne were taken from *Abnormal Behavior and Personality* by T. Millon and R. Millon, and used with permission of Holt, Rinehart and Winston, copyright 1974.

Excerpts from the case of Agnes were taken from *Personality Development and Psychopathology* by N. Cameron, and reprinted with permission from Houghton Mifflin Co., copyright 1963.

Material from the case of Boyd was taken from *Foundations of Psychopathology* by J. C. Nemiah, and used with permission of Oxford University Press, copyright 1961.

Material from the case of Ruth Langley was taken from *Case Histories of Deviant Behavior: A Social Learning Analysis* by G. R. Leon, and used with permission from Holbrook Press, copyright 1974.

Excerpts from *The Three Faces of Eve* by C. H. Thigpen and H. M. Cleckley were reprinted with permission from C. H. Thigpen, copyright 1957.

Excerpts from *The Technique of Psychotherapy* by Lewis Wolberg were reprinted with permission from Lewis Wolberg, copyright 1977.

Excerpts from "The open door: A structural approach to a family with an anorectic child," by J. Aponte and L. Hoffman, published in *Family Process,* were reprinted with permission from the Nathan W. Akerman Family Institute, copyright 1973.

Excerpts from "The other side: Living with schizophrenia" by Norma MacDonald, published in the *Canadian Medical Association Journal,* were reprinted with permission from the Canadian Medical Association, copyright 1960.

Excerpts from the case of Joan were taken from "A schizophrenic patient describes the action of intensive psycho-therapy" by M. L. Hayward and J. E. Taylor in *The Psychiatric Quarterly,* and reprinted with permission of Hudson River Psychiatric Center, copyright 1956.

Excerpts from interviews with adolescent suicide attempters were taken from *Adolescent Suicide* by J. Jacobs and used with permission of Irvington Publishers, copyright 1973.

Excerpts from the case of Peter were taken from "The view from 'the couch' " by F. Eberhardy in the *Journal of Child Psychology and Psychiatry,* and reprinted with permission of Pergamon Press Inc., copyright 1967.

Excerpts from the case of Mary were taken from *Truants from Life* by B. Bettelheim, and reprinted with permission of Macmillan Publishing Co., copyright 1955.

Excerpts from the case of Edith were taken from *Mental Retardation* by G. S. Baroff, and reprinted with permission of Hemisphere Publishing Corp., copyright 1974.

For permission to use other copyrighted materials, the author is indebted to the following:

CHAPTER 1   2, 3, 4 HRW Photo Bank   7 Arthur Tress   8 The Bettmann Archive   9 *Peanuts Treasury* by Charles H. Schultz. Copyright © 1968 United Feature Syndicate, Inc., and used with permission.

CHAPTER 2   19, 21, 24, 25, 28, 30, 34 The Bettmann Archive   23 Courtesy of the American Museum of Natural History   29 Courtesy of Roche Laboratories, a division of Hoffmann-LaRoche, Inc., Nutley, N.J.

CHAPTER 3   38, 42 Sigmund Freud Copyrights, Ltd., Colchester, England   45 Drawing by Dana Fradon; © 1973, The New Yorker Magazine, Inc.   48 © Arthur Sirdofsky   50 The Bettmann Archive   51 Association for the Advancement of Psychoanalysis, Inc.   55 Courtesy Rollo May

CHAPTER 4   59, 61 The Bettmann Archive   63 (left) Courtesy B. F. Skinner   63 (right), 69 © Mimi Cotter   68 Courtesy Albert Bandura   73 Authenticated News International

CHAPTER 5   79 HRW Photo Bank   81 Courtesy National Institute of Arthritis, Metabolism, and Digestive Diseases, N.I.H., Bethesda, Md.   85, 87 © Mimi Cotter

CHAPTER 6   94, 103, 105 Courtesy National Institute of Mental Health   106 Benjamin Kleinmuntz   109 Courtesy Bergen Pines County Hospital, Paramus, N.J.

CHAPTER 7   112, 113, 114 © Ken Karp   119 © Mimi Cotter   120 Authenticated News International   121 Courtesy American Red Cross in Greater New York   122 Associated Press   123 © James Soroka

CHAPTER 8   130, 133 Courtesy Kings Dominion, Richmond, Virginia   135 © Ahmed Essa   141 © Ken Karp   142 Courtesy CIBA Collection of Medical Illustrations

CHAPTER 9   146, 153, 155 © Ken Karp

CHAPTER 10   160, 161, 164 Authenticated News International   167 Courtesy of the Institute for Psychoanalysis; photo by Joseph J. Lucas, Jr.   169 Courtesy Carl Rogers   172 National Institute of Mental Health

CHAPTER 11   183, 192, 194 Courtesy Staten Island Zoo; photo by Jack Muntzer   185 Courtesy Joseph Wolpe   186, 188 © Ken Karp   195 From Behavioral Self-control, by Carl E. Thoresen and Michael J. Mahoney. © 1974 by Holt, Rinehart and Winston

CHAPTER 12   201, 203 Courtesy Carl Rogers   204, 214 © Ken Karp   207 Courtesy Grove Press   217 © Arthur Sirdofsky   218 Courtesy National Save-A-Life League   221 Marilyn Mitchell

CHAPTER 13   225, 233 (left) Black Star   228 © Arthur Sirdofsky   232 Bellevue Hospital Center   233 (right) Department of the Air Force   237 © Mimi Cotter   242, 247 © Ken Karp   246 National Institute on Aging

CHAPTER 14   249, 259 Black Star   251 Bob Levin for Black Star   255, 257 © Jerry Bauer   258 The Bettmann Archive   265 © Jill Krementz   266 Courtesy G. P. Putnam & Sons   267

CHAPTER 15   272, 273, 274, 281 HRW Photo Bank   342 Courtesy Dr. Louis J. Karnosh   279 Michael Weisbrot   286 Courtesy Lafayette Instrument Company

CHAPTER 16   298 HRW Photo Bank   306 Courtesy National Institute of Mental Health, *Schizophrenia Bulletin,* No. 1, December 1969   315 © Ken Karp   317 Ron Sugiyama, Authenticated News International

CHAPTER 17   321, 330 © N. V. Zwaluw. Released by United Artists   326, 328 HRW Photo Bank   331 (left and right) Courtesy of the Department of the Army, Walter Reed Army Medical Center   443 © Ken Karp

CHAPTER 18   340, 359 Black Star   342, 362 The Bettmann Archive   350 (left), 358 Authenticated News International   350 (right) Courtesy Dr. Leonard A. Rosenblum   352, 356 Michael Weisbrot   354 © Ken Karp   364 United Press International

CHAPTER 19   369, 371 Black Star   373 Courtesy Roche Psychiatric Service Institute, Hoffman-LaRoche, Inc., Nutley, N.J.

CHAPTER 20   380, 381, 382, 395 © Ken Karp   384, 385, 387, 391, 398 © Mimi Cotter   389 National Association for Retarded Citizens   390 (left) Courtesy Harry F. Harlow   286 (right) Courtesy President's Committee on Mental Retardation   402 Courtesy Lexington School for the Deaf

CHAPTER 21   407, 408, 410 Courtesy Association for Mentally Ill Children   422 Allan Grant

CHAPTER 22   426, 427, 428, 447 (left), 447 (right), 449 © Holt, Rinehart and Winston   440, 451 United Press International   441 Random House   453 Baltimore News American

CHAPTER 23   457 Black Star   464 © Mimi Cotter   466 © Holt, Rinehart and Winston   467 Courtesy Dr. Louis J. Karnosh   472 Courtesy Alcoholics Anonymous   447 The Bettmann Archive   478 © Ken Karp   479 Michael Weisbrot   483 Courtesy Daytop Village

CHAPTER 24   485, 486, 487, 506 (left and right) Courtesy Happy Times School, Burlington, North Carolina   499, 500 (Top) Courtesy of the National Association for Retarded Citizens   500 (Bottom) Courtesy Vocational Trade of Alamance, Burlington, North Carolina   502 Courtesy President's Committee on Mental Retardation

CHAPTER 25   509, 516, 517 Courtesy Neuropathology, New York State Psychiatric Institute, State of New York, Department of Mental Hygiene   518 Courtesy Committee to Combat Huntington's Disease   519 The Bettmann Archive

Preface

The aim of this book is to introduce the student to abnormal psychology from the perspective of an empirical science as well as from the rich literature of clinically based theories and therapeutic techniques. To that end a special effort was made to include recent advances in research findings and clinical innovations in this revision. One major organizational change is the incorporation of the final version of DSM-III (The American Psychiatric Association's listing of diagnostic categories for mental disorders). Although DSM-III is an improvement over DSM-II, it is by no means perfect, and I have not hesitated to critically comment on various aspects of the system.

No author can, or probably should, be completely neutral with respect to different theories and viewpoints. For the record, I would characterize my theoretical preference as social learning, broadly conceived but, as the reader will discover, this book includes more than a little appreciation for contributions from the psychodynamic, biological, and other approaches. I agree with clinicians of a humanistic persuasion who decry, with some justification, an approach to abnormal psychology in which the subject matter is treated as impersonally as the study of molecules and subatomic particles. The subject matter of this book is *people* struggling with problems in living. The human experience that accompanies psychological disturbances is portrayed in a way complementary to the scientific perspective and in no way contradicts it. This is done primarily through first-person accounts in which people speak for themselves. A rich and varied collection of case studies and dialogues is included to illustrate different forms of abnormal behavior.

Knowledge and understanding remain incomplete in the field of abnormal psychology, and the description of established facts on diagnostic syndromes can only be part of the overall goal of a book. Equally important is the raising of questions for which there are as yet no agreed-upon answers and evaluation of the current status of the various theories and research findings that bear on these questions. I hope by this means to stimulate a critical, question-asking approach on the part of the student—a goal that is given higher priority than the simple memorization of the prevailing theories and facts.

As part of the strategy for encouraging a critical attitude toward theory and research in abnormal psychology, I have tried to maintain a continuing but low-key concern with certain basic methodological issues, such as random assignment of subjects to groups and the drawing of general conclusions from a single case study. An undergraduate textbook is not the place for heavy-handed methodological critiques, but some attention to these simple but fundamental questions is appropriate where the encouragement of a questioning attitude is a primary goal. The pedagogical device termed Research Reports furthers this end and provides readers with enough information about procedure and results so that they can, to some extent at least, make a tentative judgment about the study's conclusions. This contrasts with many textbooks' reference to studies where only the results (usually summarized and simplified) and certain conclusions are presented. For teachers who would prefer not to emphasize the amount of research detail found in many of the Research Reports, students can be advised to skip or skim these sections. They have been designed to allow this flexibility, and there is little disruption to the flow of the text when this is done.

Other goals might be mentioned briefly. I have given more than usual attention to interactional and systems approaches to psychopathology, especially as applied to family and marital systems, because I believe this view has not received adequate attention in other texts. Also, I have tried not to shortchange either biological or psychosocial factors when considering the causation of abnormal behaviors. Most psychology undergraduates probably have less interest in biological than psychosocial determinants, but both are important and the truth is that we are biosocial organisms.

The chapters on mental retardation, drug abuse, and psychophysiological disorders still bear the imprint of their original contributors from the first edition, George Baroff, Paul Fiddleman, and Sara Hunter. Arlene Katz has done an outstanding job in seeing the book through the final stages of production and her efforts are greatly valued. Various typing chores have been competently handled by Patricia Eichman and Susan Roche.

August, 1980   B. M.
Chapel Hill, N.C.

To Susan, Betsy, Juan, and Nguyen

Contents

PART SIX: Impaired Brain Functioning 487

Abnormal
Psychology

Part One

Views of
Abnormal
Behavior

1

Introduction

- What does the term "abnormal behavior" mean?

- What is a "psychological handicap"?

- Is there a sharp dividing line between normal and abnormal?

- How is the study of abnormal psychology relevant to you?

- How can we study abnormal behavior scientifically?

Joanne: A Variety of Symptoms

Joanne, an attractive but overweight 27-year-old housewife, toyed nervously with her purse as she recounted various physical and emotional problems in her first therapy session. Although she had completed only a high school education, she was clearly an intelligent and articulate woman, and also a most unhappy woman. Her list of symptoms and problems was impressive.

She was unable to cope with the misbehaviors of her two young daughters, Milly, age 7, and Annette, age 3½. Milly especially seemed to take pleasure in aggravating her mother (Joanne called it "bugging") by deliberately doing things she knew would upset her. Joanne was not able to provide firm or consistent discipline; instead she nagged and, at times, when frustrated beyond endurance, screamed and spanked—none of which seemed to do any good. Her relationship with her husband was not better. She described him as a passive and noncommunicative man who refused all child-rearing responsibilities, except that he would on occasion undermine her attempts at discipline by permitting Milly to escape punishment or take Milly's side. Her dislike for her husband had turned to contempt and in later sessions she frequently would say that she hated him. She attempted to get him to do certain things around the house or to take a more active role in dealing with the children by nagging him, which he either ignored or verbally acquiesced to but then never followed through on. As with her children, her nagging occasionally escalated to angry outbursts toward her husband but with as little effect.

Joanne's father-in-law represented another source of distress. She and her family lived in a house located on the father-in-law's farm and owned by him, and they were to a considerable extent financially dependent on him. Joanne "hated" her father-in-law almost as much as her husband because he was constantly interfering in their lives. This was another sore spot with respect to her husband, who she felt was too weak and dependent to stand up against this unwarranted domination by the father-in-law.

Thus, Joanne felt trapped in life circumstances she felt powerless to change. She had no education or job skills that would make it possible to leave her husband, and with her two children establish an independent existence. Her anxieties, feelings of low self-worth, and almost chronic physical symptoms seemed to make such a venture even less feasible. In addition, her own mother, the church she attended, and friends and relatives all seemed to present a solid front in discouraging any such rebellious attitudes. She should, they said, be grateful for having a husband and in-laws who provided her and the children with a decent living. As a dutiful wife she should be thankful for what she had and not complain about the rest. Joanne, accordingly, carried a great burden of guilt about her angry, hateful feelings.

What kind of toll had these difficult life circumstances taken on Joanne's physical and emotional well-being? For several years now she had experienced frequent tension headaches, usually associated with difficult interactions with her children, husband, or in-laws. At her first therapy session she said that she felt some degree of tension headaches "almost all the time," and had for a year and a half been taking pills (Cafergot) to relieve these headaches. Once or twice a week these tension headaches developed into more severe migraine headaches that almost completely incapacitated her for a day or longer, and for a year and a half she had taken another drug (Periactin) at the onset of migraine headaches. In addition to these recurring headaches she occasionally had episodes of asthma, hives (a skin rash), and stomach upset that seem to be related to periods of stress and for which she sometimes took additional medication.

Moving from physical to more emotional kinds of symptoms, Joanne reported that she had been almost chronically depressed for several years. She experienced crying spells, frequently could not fall asleep until 3 A.M. or 4 A.M., and had strong feelings of guilt and low self-worth. In later sessions she would frequently say "I'm terrible" after having confessed to some angry or hateful feeling. For a year now she had taken an antidepressant drug (Elavil) daily, and that had seemed to control her depressive tendencies fairly well, but the depression returned as soon as she stopped taking the drug. Also, the drug seemed to increase her appetite and made it difficult to control her eating, and her weight problem remained. In the past, but not currently, she had also taken tranquilizers (Librium and Valium) to calm her "nerves."

Over the course of some 25 therapy sessions many of these disabling symptoms were alleviated. She was taught some parenting skills that enabled her to be more firm and consistent in disciplining her daughters and also to spend more time in enjoyable interaction with them. She learned to experience the full nature and extent of her angry feelings toward her husband and father-in-law and learned to assert herself appropriately with both of these individuals rather than alternating between the extremes of uncontrolled angry outbursts or withdrawal to her room in tears and depression. Using a technique called biofeedback, she learned to relax herself at the onset of tension and migraine headaches and thus to reduce to almost zero the frequency of her headaches. She acquired some insight into how her tendencies toward self-blame and pleasing other people at her own expense had developed in her relationships with her own parents, and in a rather gentle way changed the nature of her interactions with them. By the end of therapy she had stopped taking the antidepressant drug altogether without a return of the depression, and she was successfully losing weight in a carefully monitored weight loss program. All in all she was a much more self-confident and cheerful person.

How well do we understand the development of symptoms and behaviors of the kind shown by Joanne? How have strange and puzzling behaviors been explained in different cultures, in different historical periods, and by different theorists today? How effectively can we help individuals overcome such incapacitating symptoms? And what do we mean by the phrase *abnormal behavior* anyhow? The rest of this book will be devoted to answering these questions. For now we will concentrate only on the last question: What is abnormal behavior?

What is Abnormal Behavior?

The word *abnormal* itself implies that the behavior is different, unusual, or deviant. I will, however, quickly dismiss differentness or deviancy in and of itself as a criterion of abnormality. Olympic athletes, Nobel prizewinning scientists, gifted musicians, and people who make a killing on the stock market all deviate considerably from most people, but we are not inclined to consider them abnormal as the term is generally used. Although abnormal behavior does for the most part deviate from cultural norms, it is only certain kinds of deviant behaviors that are likely to be

called abnormal; namely, deviant behavior that is culturally inappropriate, is accompanied by subjective distress, and involves a psychological handicap (inability to cope with life's demands).

CULTURAL INAPPROPRIATENESS

The key concept here is that the behavior seems at odds with cultural expectations of appropriateness and propriety. A person does something that others find disturbing, puzzling, or irrational.

Ordinarily, a specific behavior is not judged strange in itself, but only in the context of a particular situation. Shout and shake your fists at a football

Some people behave in deviant ways. Should their behavior be considered abnormal?

game and there will be few lifted eyebrows, but do the same thing in church or in the public library and people will wonder what has got into you. Much of Joanne's behavior in everyday life would not be seen as culturally inappropriate. In fact, had she more overtly rebelled against the circumstances of her life this would probably have been seen as inappropriate in the local community, even though from another perspective it might seem like a constructive course of action. However, her crying spells, occasional outbursts of anger, and depressive moods would be seen in her neighbors' eyes as deviating from expected and understandable behavior.

Anthropologists have made the point well that our judgment of another person's normality will depend on the values and traditions of the culture in which we live. For example, hearing voices and going into a trance are likely to be labeled abnormal in our society, but among the Plains Indians of North America, such behaviors were highly valued as evidence of special talent for communication with the spirit world. Prestige and status would often accrue to the person having these experiences. But what would be the response today if a young maid from New Jersey announced that she heard divine voices instructing her to take over the position of Chairman of the Joint Chiefs of Staff of the U.S. Armed Forces in order to protect this country from foreign dangers. No doubt she would find a few followers, but it is unlikely that

she would be as successful as Joan of Arc in accomplishing her mission. Even in Joan's case not everyone bought her story.

When Ruth Benedict (1934) made her study of the Melanesian culture of the Dobu, she found the society was characterized by a degree of suspicion and mistrust that would be labeled *paranoia* in our culture. There was universal preoccupation with poisoning: No woman left her cooking pot untended for a moment, and because all others' food was considered to be deadly poison, community stores were out of the question. Their polite phrase at the acceptance of a gift, "And if you now poison me, how shall I repay you for this present?" There was one man in this Dobu society who had a sunny, kindly disposition and liked to be helpful. Others laughed at him and thought him silly, simple, and a little crazy. According to our standards, this culture had a topsy-turvy notion of who was crazy and who was sane. Prevailing cultural beliefs, then, will influence how strange or inappropriate a given behavior is perceived.

Anthropologists (for example, Kiev, 1969; Murphy, 1964), however, point out that we must not take too simple a view of the *cultural relativity* of abnormal behavior. For example, the trance states of shamans (priest-doctors such as voodoo priests and medicine men) show some similarities to psychopathological reactions in our society, but there are also important differences. Primarily, the shaman appears to be more in control of the trance state, deciding on which occasions to enter it and, most important, behaving according to cultural expectations while in it. A person who goes into trance states at inappropriate times and behaves in unpredictable ways might well be considered strange or "crazy" by the community.

The question still remains: Can abnormality be defined entirely in terms of cultural inappropriateness? There are some problems with such an approach. Take, for example, an individual in Nazi Germany who might in belief and action have differed from the prevailing anti-Semitic views and other aspects of the Nazi philosophy. Such a person would clearly have been deviating from acceptable cultural views and by this definition would have been considered abnormal. Or, more recently, some dissidents in the Soviet Union have been labeled mentally ill and placed in institutions because they voiced opposition to the Soviet dictatorship. Do we want to label this kind of behavior abnormal? On the contrary, it might

Joan of Arc heard voices and had visions regarding her mission to deliver France from English rule. In today's culture such experiences might be considered a symptom of mental illness.

be argued that standing up in this way against prevailing viewpoints takes considerable psychological strength.

Two other problems with cultural inappropriateness as the sole criterion of abnormality are: Many individuals in our society conform almost slavishly to the customs and laws of the community and yet experience inhibitions, anxieties, and great personal unhappiness. Although their overt behavior is not culturally inappropriate, we might nevertheless wish to consider their reactions as, in some sense, abnormal. Other individuals (for example, professional criminals) defy societal laws but otherwise function quite

well as spouse, parent, colleague, and friend. We are not prone to call such individuals abnormal—just crooks. Cultural inappropriateness, although a characteristic of most abnormal behavior in all societies, is not entirely satisfying as the sole criterion of abnormality.

SUBJECTIVE DISTRESS

Subjective distress refers to internal emotions or experiences that are real to the person but cannot be observed directly by other people; unhappiness, fear, apathy, terrifying visual and auditory experiences, and physical aches and pains are examples. Reports of subjective distress commonly accompany abnormal reactions. Joanne experienced a variety of unpleasant emotions: guilt, nervous tension, depression, and the pain of migraine headaches.

The individual's distress is an important dimension of abnormality that should be included as one aspect of an overall definition—but, once again, there are exceptions. Some individuals, especially those with the kind of reactions called *hysterical* or *manic,* may deny any subjective distress and, indeed, may maintain that they feel wonderful. Individuals labeled *psychopathic* experience little remorse or distress associated with their antisocial behavior. In these cases, reports about the degree of subjective distress would not be an adequate indication of the presence of abnormality.

PSYCHOLOGICAL HANDICAP

When persons are unable to function adequately in their roles as student, worker, parent, spouse, or friend, they can be considered to have a psychological handicap. They are unable to cope adequately with life's stresses and demands. In certain respects Joanne was not able to function effectively as a parent. When depressed or having a migraine headache, she was hardly able to get through the day and would frequently take to her bed. Her interpersonal relationships were hampered by an inability to assert herself appropriately.

One way of viewing the concept of psychological handicap is to say that individuals with such handicaps have fewer alternative ways of behavior open to

them. In this sense psychological handicap is analogous to physical handicap, and indeed, many of the terms used interchangeably with abnormality (such as psycho*pathology,* behavior *pathology,* behavior *disorder,* mental *illness,* and mental *disease*) imply a parallel with physical disease. For example, persons with a broken leg or pneumonia are handicapped and cannot do things they normally could. I should not push the comparison with physical handicaps too far, however. Many writers, such as Szasz (1960), have severely criticized the idea that mental illness is similar to physical illness. Disturbing behavior, according to these writers, is not the result of some underlying disease process, as the medical analogy might suggest, but is *learned* on the basis of life experiences. The concept of psychological handicap, however, need not imply any particular theory of how abnormality develops.

It is important to note that the person with a psychological handicap is *unable* to do certain things, as opposed to the person who simply does not do them because of personal values, lack of interest, or similar reasons. One cannot always tell from the behavior itself whether it stems from a psychological handicap; one has to make a judgment as to whether the person is free to do otherwise. A succession of short-lived marriages does not in itself indicate a handicap, but when a person wants a lasting marriage, is physically healthy, and yet seems to be involved in one disastrous marriage after another, a psychological handicap would be suspected.

In sum, then, most but not all forms of abnormal behavior are likely to be culturally inappropriate and accompanied by subjective distress, and all forms of abnormality might be conceived as reflecting a psychological handicap, a restriction in response alternatives that makes it difficult to cope with life's demands and stresses. This is as close as I will come

to an overall definition of abnormal behavior since, as you will see in the following chapters, this term applies to many different forms of behavior resulting from many different causative influences.

The Locus of Abnormality: The Individual or a Social Interaction?

I have been writing as though abnormality is a characteristic of individuals, but some writers (for example, Minuchin, 1974) have maintained that the psychopathology does not reside in the individual but rather in a larger interpersonal system, such as the family or an even larger social group. Joanne's depression and her headaches would seem to belong to her, but consider for a moment one set of circumstances that tended to instigate her headaches and make her feel depressed. Her daughter, Milly, "bugs" Joanne until eventually Joanne develops a headache or perhaps has a crying spell. At that point Milly stops her "bugging" and becomes solicitous of her mother's welfare. Milly provides Joanne with a payoff for getting "sick," namely, she ceases her obnoxious behavior. At other times when Joanne tries to punish Milly for something, Milly goes to her father who takes her side, possibly as a way of getting back at Joanne who has been nagging him to do some chore around the house. Thus, Joanne's behavior can be seen to be embedded in a family system of interaction in which the various members are instigating and providing payoffs for each other's behavior. From this perspective the basic abnormality is not so much

Joanne's headache or depression as the interpersonal system producing these responses.

The extent to which a given interpersonal system is considered abnormal would depend upon the factors previously described: Does the system generate either culturally inappropriate behavior or subjective distress in some members, and as a system can it effectively accomplish its goals?

Abnormality Is a Continuum

The conception of abnormality may be clarified further by viewing it as a *continuum,* with extreme abnormality at one end and positive mental health at the other. In extreme forms of abnormal behavior the person is severely handicapped, suffers much subjective distress, and is so culturally inappropriate as to evoke intense fear or revulsion in others. From these extreme instances, in which most observers would agree that something is wrong, we move by imperceptible steps to the range of behaviors that we call normal.

Joanne would be considered by most clinicians to be showing abnormal behavior of at least a moderate degree. Milder forms of psychological handicap include the boy who is too timid to ask a girl for a date, the homemaker who feels vaguely dissatisfied and unfulfilled, the alienated student who finds nothing of interest in the establishment world, or the young person who feels acutely irritated whenever confronted by anyone in authority. Mild handicaps are experienced from time to time by the vast majority of people in the middle range of this hypothetical continuum. Who among us does not have some occasional reaction that impairs work efficiency, disrupts interpersonal relationships, or otherwise hampers his or her ability to meet life's demands? Some of us feel anxious about speaking before an audience, some have minor irrational fears, and some get a little disorganized under the pressure of a course examination.

There is, then, no single point at which one can draw a line separating normal from abnormal, only varying degrees of psychological handicap, subjective distress, and cultural inappropriateness (Figure 1-1). Let us consider for a moment what is meant by the other end of the continuum, the psychologically healthy person.

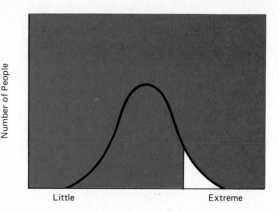

FIGURE 1-1. **Psychological handicap seen as a continuum along which people vary. Most of us fall in the middle range with only mild-to-moderate handicaps. Any separation of normal from abnormal, such as the unshaded area, is arbitrary.**

What is Mental Health?

Psychologically healthy persons do not necessarily escape the stresses and strains of life, and from time to time they wrestle with conflicting impulses, encounter crises in interpersonal relationships, and experience unpleasant emotions such as grief, anger, or fear. In general, however, they are able to function effectively and to find satisfaction in life. They can have lasting and emotionally gratifying relations with friends, spouse, parents, and children; they can work effectively and productively; and they can laugh, play, relax, and have fun. They are likely to make a realistic appraisal of their own talents and shortcomings, or at least they do not resort to extreme forms of denial or distortion of those aspects of themselves they wish were different. Basically they view themselves as worthy members of the human race.

This idealized description of mental health in no way implies that such persons have to be conformists, adjusting passively to the demands of their culture. In the present definition of mental health, freedom from psychological handicap is emphasized. Mentally healthy persons are able to pursue with effectiveness and satisfaction any number of life goals. They have weighed the value and desirability of the specific uses to which they put their psychological energies. A salesperson who enjoys selling, has mutually satisfying relationships with others, plays golf on Saturday, and drinks beer while watching the Sunday afternoon pro football game on TV would, by most criteria, be leading a conventional, middle-class life, and, by our definition, be enjoying mental health. A member of a rural commune who likewise has satisfying interpersonal relationships, enjoys organic farming, and relaxes by playing the guitar has an equal degree of mental health. Persons who try to reform society, such as political or religious leaders, may create a much more stressful life situation for themselves than either of the other two examples, yet to the extent that they successfully cope with these stresses, they also enjoy mental health. An individual with the necessary abilities and relative freedom from psychological handicaps should be able to choose among these and other life-styles. Good mental health leaves a person open to many alternative ways of behaving. It is not some idealized and unattainable state, but that end of the dimension where individuals have relatively few psychological handicaps.

BY WHAT NAME SHALL WE CALL IT?

Many terms have been used to refer to abnormal behavior, including *psychopathology, behavior disorder,* and *emotional disturbance.* While some use of labels is inescapable, we should ask whether there is any value in applying such general labels to people? It does not pay to become too preoccupied with whether a particular person behaving in a certain way should be labeled abnormal. Such terms refer to a broad and complex range of phenomena, which, as previously suggested, can be seen as a continuum on which there is no sharp dividing line. In this book I will be much more interested in describing, rather than labeling, certain abnormal behaviors, understanding how they develop, and considering how they might be modified.

Furthermore, there is a tendency for any term used in referring to these phenomena to acquire a derogatory meaning, and that fact deserves some comment. Most people feel frightened or repelled by individuals who behave abnormally, and these reactions account, in part, for the fact that abnormally behaving people have historically been the object of ridicule and abuse. Any term used to refer to such individuals seems to acquire in time a negative connotation. To say that a person is "mentally ill" or "sick" is likely to evoke negative reactions in many

listeners nowadays, yet use of the term *mental illness* was initially promoted by enlightened physicians seeking to reduce some of the negative attitudes associated with terms such as lunacy and notions such as demonic possession. Thomas Szasz has proposed that we abandon all such terms as *insanity* and *mental illness* and simply use the phrase, *problems in living.* There are some advantages to this strategy, but it is unlikely that it will dispel the negative attitudes any more than the euphemism "building custodian" adds prestige or status to the job of a janitor.

In conclusion, while I will use the terms such as abnormal behavior and psychopathology to refer to the general subject matter of this book, I see little value in applying such broad and inevitably pejorative labels to individual people.

The Prevalence of Abnormality

The looseness of definition should not in any way obscure the existence of abnormal behavior—which is both real and pervasive, as a number of studies have shown. In an early study, Leo Srole and his associates (1962) interviewed and administered a questionnaire to a random sample of 1660 individuals living on Manhattan's East Side. Symptoms indicative of mental disorder were measured, and the percentage of individuals falling in six categories representing degree of impairment was as follows:

Well	18.5%
Mild	36.3%
Moderate	21.8%
Marked	13.2%
Severe	7.5%
Incapacitated	2.7%

If the last three categories are combined, we find that 23.4 percent of the sample was considered to have at least a marked degree of psychological handicap. Similar results have been obtained in other studies involving rural as well as urban populations (for example, Warheit et al., 1975).

More recently researchers have attempted to make diagnoses of specific forms of psychopathology rather than settle for ratings of general impairment. Weissman et al. (1978) interviewed a random sample of adults in the New Haven, Connecticut, area and concluded that 15 percent were *currently* experiencing a psychiatric disorder. Using the same data, Weissman and Myers (1978) reported that 18 percent of the people interviewed had experienced a depressive disorder of at least a moderate degree sometime during the past year (but were not necessarily depressed currently). Estimates of prevalence rates for depression per 100 people in the population are shown in Figure 1-2 as a function of age and sex. Note that our case example, Joanne, falls in the highest rate group, young females. We will consider further the high incidence of depression in younger women in a later chapter; for now the data are presented primarily to show that psychological disorders and their associated handicaps in living are widespread.

The National Institute of Mental Health (1976) estimated the cost of mental illness to the country in 1974 to be approximately 38 billion dollars. Direct costs for mental health care (in mental hospitals, clinics, private practice, and other ways) accounted for $14.5 billion of the total; indirect costs (including the earnings lost in mental-illness-related deaths and disabilities and the time lost to persons who obtain outpatient therapy) accounted for $19.8 billion. The cost in human suffering cannot be measured. At the time this is being written the government has not completed more recent figures on the cost of mental illness, but it can be assumed that these costs have followed the same inflationary spiral as everything else.

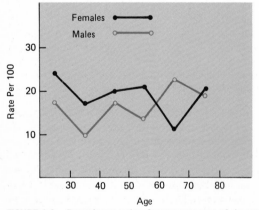

FIGURE 1-2. **Prevalence rates for occurrence of depressive symptoms over a one-year period by age and sex. From Weissman & Myers (1978). Copyright 1978 Munksgaard, International Booksellers and Publishers, Ltd. and used with permission.**

Why Study Abnormal Psychology?

There are several reasons for college students to take a course in abnormal psychology. Abnormal behavior is intrinsically interesting to some people. They are puzzled by strange and seemingly irrational behavior; they wonder what happened in Joanne's life that could lead to recurring depressions and how a physical symptom such as a migraine headache might, in part at least, be caused by social and emotional experiences. For these students, the study of abnormal psychology holds the promise that such behaviors and symptoms can be understood.

In addition, many of us have or will have a relative or acquaintance who is mentally retarded, is placed in a mental hospital, abuses alcohol or drugs, or seeks psychotherapy for personal problems. For several semesters, I have asked students in a course on abnormal psychology to fill out a brief questionnaire on which they indicate whether they or a close relative had experienced various forms of abnormal reactions. A summary of these responses in Table 1-1 shows that the lives of many students are touched by one or more of these disorders. The point of this demonstration is not to obtain scientific data on the prevalence of various kinds of abnormal behaviors but to show that for most of us the study of abnormal psychology is about something real and close at hand. The odds are that you would answer yes to several of these categories.

Some of you undoubtedly will apply your increasing understanding of abnormal psychology to yourself. You may find yourself asking: What are my psychological handicaps and to what extent do they represent a serious problem? Some students get the "medical student's disease," seeing symptoms of each new type of abnormality in themselves as they proceed from chapter to chapter, although they usually have no real grounds for concern. Reading a book and taking a course in abnormal psychology, however, can stimulate some constructive reflection about your own psychological functioning and open up new avenues of thought about yourself. Although the book may have personal relevance in this sense, reading about abnormal conditions will not necessarily help those who are experiencing them. In gen-

TABLE 1-1   Percentage of Students Reporting Psychological Problems as Happening to Them or a Close Relative

Problem	Percent
1. Has seen a psychotherapist for personal problems.	34
2. Has a physical disorder thought to be psychosomatic (such as stomach ulcers, high blood pressure, or chronic diarrhea).	37
3. Has anxiety attacks or periods of depression (at least moderately severe).	41
4. Has repeatedly engaged in antisocial acts (such as theft, passing bad checks, vandalism, or delinquency).	17
5. Has a drinking problem (alcohol).	34
6. Is addicted to or dependent on drugs, or abuses drugs.	13
7. Has a sexual problem (such as impotence, frigidity, exhibitionism, voyeurism, or incest).	7
8. Has been hospitalized for mental illness.	21
9. Is mentally retarded.	11

Note: N = 119.

eral, it is probably true that the more severe the difficulty, the less likely one will be helped by only reading about it. However, the occasional readers who come to recognize that they are experiencing difficulties of more than the usual magnitude may, as a result of their increased understanding, decide to seek professional help sooner than would otherwise have been the case.

The study of abnormal psychology is relevant to other aspects of your life as well. For example, if you are planning to be a lawyer, physician, teacher, journalist, minister, nurse, social worker, or to join any of a number of other professions, you will encounter abnormal behavior as part of your job. How you interpret this behavior and how you respond to those manifesting it will depend upon your understanding. In recent years, courses in abnormal psychology, psychiatry, and mental health have become an integral part of the curriculum in programs of teacher education, medicine, and divinity.

Regardless of occupation, taxpayers and voters are involved in the problems of caring for and treating the mentally ill, mentally retarded, elderly, abusers of alcohol and other drugs, and criminals. Voters may be asked to decide whether the government should continue to operate state mental hospitals or put its money instead into community mental health clinics or preventive efforts in schools. Public support may be asked for the introduction of new programs such as halfway homes for persons discharged from men-

tal hospitals or community-based treatment centers for alcoholics and drug abusers. Also, citizens serving jury duty are sometimes asked to judge whether the defendant was "sane" when a crime was committed. Some understanding of abnormal psychology should help you make more intelligent decisions in all these areas.

The Scientific Study of Abnormal Behavior

. . . there is really no scientific or other method by which men can steer safely between the opposite dangers of believing too little or of believing too much. To face such dangers is apparently our duty, and to hit the right channel between them is the measure of our wisdom.

—William James

Only recently have we attempted to study ourselves with the same objectivity that we have used in trying to understand the inanimate world and other living organisms. Abnormal behavior especially has lent itself to beliefs and superstitions that have yielded only slowly to the advance of scientific understanding. The history of changing conceptions of abnormality will be traced in subsequent chapters, but for now I want to limit our discussion to a consideration of common methodologies used in the scientific study of abnormal behavior and the advantages and disadvantages associated with them.

Many of you will have encountered in previous psychology courses some of the terms and concepts to be described. I review them here, however, as they apply specifically to the study of abnormal behavior. Although I will limit myself to a rather elementary consideration of research methodology, it is surprising how often one encounters reports in the literature that have failed to incorporate even these basic features of good research design. If you master the few concepts and principles covered in the next several pages, you will find them applicable to many studies in the field of abnormal psychology.

THE CASE STUDY

Carefully documented *case studies* of individuals continue to have a valued place in the study of abnormal behavior. Typically, the investigator derives information from talking with a person who displays abnormal behavior or those who know the person, and in narrative form describes the behavior of interest, related environmental circumstances, and past events that might make the present behavior intelligible. The intensive study of individuals, especially in the course of long-term psychotherapy, has been a rich source of ideas about the nature and causation of abnormal behavior.

Although case studies are useful in illustrating different forms of abnormal behavior and in generating theories, they cannot be used to "prove" a theory. For one thing, there is a tendency to select as evidence cases that support one's theory, while ignoring those cases that are embarrassingly inconsistent with it. Furthermore, the information used in a case report is highly selective and one rarely has any way of knowing how much information was omitted or never sought in the first place. Finally, even when the findings for a given case are accurate, they cannot be generalized to anyone other than the person being studied unless, as discussed in the following section, similar information was obtained on a *sample* of individuals. We should be careful, then, not to be led into believing that a general proposition has been demonstrated by a case study, no matter how persuasive and sensible the material seems to

be. With these reservations in mind, I have not hesitated to make generous use of case studies for illustrative purposes throughout this book.

NORMATIVE RESEARCH

It can be useful to have certain descriptive information about abnormal behavior—for example, the incidence of different forms of psychopathology among different socioeconomic classes, races, ethnic groups, age groups, and so forth. Research aimed at getting this kind of information is called *normative* or *epidemiological research;* the study of the prevalence of depression in the New Haven area, cited earlier, is an example of this kind of research. Basic requirements for good normative research, as well as other kinds of research, are *random sampling,* and *reliability* and *validity of measurement.* Let us look at what is meant by these terms.

SAMPLING AND GENERALIZATION

Weissman and Myers (1978) in their epidemiological study of depression randomly sampled one out of every 14 households in the New Haven area and then randomly selected one adult from each household. Such an approach ensures that, within a certain range of chance variation, estimates of the incidence of depression will fairly accurately reflect the actual incidence in the larger population. If these investigators had relied on statistics based on individuals who had sought treatment for depression, their results would be incomplete because of the omission of untreated cases of depression.

The nature of the population randomly sampled is important in determining to what groups of people a given finding can be generalized. Thus generalizations about the incidence of depression can be safely made only to those populations that resemble New Haven's in terms of racial, socioeconomic and other factors. Most research on psychopathology is not aimed at estimating rates of incidence in the general population but aimed rather at understanding something about the nature or treatment of a given disorder. In this case, too, it is important to know to what populations the results can be generalized. Thus Mosher and Menn (1978) assessed the effectiveness of a special treatment facility with schizophrenic patients. The patients used in this study were young, had not had more than one brief hospitalization previously, and were unmarried. Paul and Lentz (1977) evaluated the effectiveness of another approach to rehabilitating schizophrenic patients. Their patients averaged 45 years of age, had been hospitalized for an average of 17 years, and had recently been found unacceptable for transfer to an extended-care facility outside the hospital. Clearly one cannot assume that results obtained in one of these studies can be generalized to the population of individuals sampled in the other study.

RELIABILITY AND VALIDITY OF MEASUREMENT

Reliability of measurement refers to the extent to which a measure consistently yields the same result on repeated trials. In physical measurements reliability tends to be quite high. If several people measured the width of a table with a yardstick, their measurements would differ only by small amounts, perhaps $\frac{1}{16}$ of an inch. Such a measure is highly reliable for most purposes, although for some endeavors such as fine machine tool work it would not be. Psychological measurement is rarely as exact as physical measurement; thus reliability is an important factor.

One type of reliability that is particularly important in psychological research is *interobserver reliability*, the extent to which different observers (or raters) agree on the way they categorize or in some way quantify a given observation. Suppose, for example, that an investigator wished to measure aggressive behavior of mental patients. One method would be to count the instances of aggressive behavior among the patients. For this kind of data to be useful, however, the investigator must demonstrate that two or more independent observers agree on their ratings or counts of aggression. Thus it is usually necessary for observers to undergo preliminary training in which they practice making ratings until they can agree on which behaviors they are going to label a certain way, in this case as aggressive. The careful researcher will always report in some fashion the degree of agreement between independent observers.

A measure is valid if it measures what it purports to measure. When measuring certain clearly defined behaviors, such as the number of times a person

talks to or hits another person, there is little problem of validity. The problem arises when one must, in order to obtain a measurement, make an inference about a psychological trait or process that is itself not directly definable in terms of specific, observable behaviors. If, for example, raters are asked to judge the degree of aggressiveness shown by a person, we want to know if the resulting score really measures aggression—or something else. This is not always an easy issue to resolve. Ordinarily the best procedure is to provide the reader with a detailed description of what observable behaviors were used to make an inference about aggression (such as hitting and verbal insults) and let the reader decide whether the inference is reasonable.

The problem of validity becomes especially acute when certain behaviors are considered "signs" of some underlying and unobservable process. For example, fear of small enclosed places might be interpreted as a fear of death, or excessive consumption of alcohol as a sign of fixation at the oral stage of development (see Chapter 3). Unobservable states or characteristics, such as oral fixations or dispositions to be hostile, fearful, and so on, are frequently referred to as *constructs,* and the term *construct validity* is used to refer to the validity of some specific way of measuring the hypothetical construct.

High reliability does not guarantee high validity. Two observers might agree that one person punching another lightly in the ribs indicated aggression, when in fact the behavior was meant in a friendly way. Two observers might agree that a person's alcoholic indulgence reflects an oral fixation, but their agreement does not necessarily make it so. Construct validity is usually determined by the way that a given measure relates to other measures and conditions. If a given measure of the construct, disposition to be aggressive, predicts aggressive behavior in other situations, and if subjects high on this measure show more aggression than those low on it, we would conclude that there is some positive evidence for the construct validity of the measure.

CORRELATIONAL RESEARCH

Another method used to obtain knowledge about abnormal behavior is *correlational research.* In a correlational study the investigator attempts to demonstrate an association or correlation between two or more measures. For example, people's height and weight tend to be correlated. If we measure these characteristics in 100 people we would find in general that taller people are heavier. The correlation would not be perfect; some tall people would weigh less than some short people, but the general association would be positive. A descriptive statistic called the *correlation coefficient,* which varies between − 1.00 and + 1.00, is one way of quantifying how strong the relationship is. The correlation between two measures can be graphically portrayed by a *scatter plot.* In Figure 1-3, for example, we see examples of correlations of different magnitudes between two variables, *X* and *Y.*

Correlations do not demonstrate causation. Several years ago medical scientists began to find a correlation between cigarette smoking and lung cancer. Studies showed that the more cigarettes people smoked per day, the more likely they were to have lung cancer. The tobacco companies, their scientific zeal perhaps enhanced by the prospect of decreased profits, were quick to point out that such correlations did not prove that cigarette smoking caused lung cancer. It was quite possible that lung cancer and

cigarette smoking were both influenced by some unknown third factor. For example, a person with certain physiological characteristics might be predisposed to both tobacco smoking and lung cancer. In such a case it would not matter whether the person smoked or not, since the occurrence of lung cancer would depend on the unknown physiological variable and not on smoking. Another possibility considered was that people experiencing chronic nervous tension were more likely to smoke and develop lung cancer, and that lung cancer was caused by nervous tension, not smoking. As is frequently the case with correlational findings, one can go on at some length thinking up alternative explanations.

Correlational research, however, should not be discarded too lightly. It does make a difference whether one finds a strong positive correlation or no correlation, since a positive finding is consistent with the *possibility* of a causative relationship. No relationship, causative or otherwise, is likely to be associated with a zero correlation. It is possible also to rule out certain factors as the complete explanation (or cause) by controlling these factors. Thus, to return to the smoking example, we could divide our sample of cigarette smokers into a number of subgroups in which

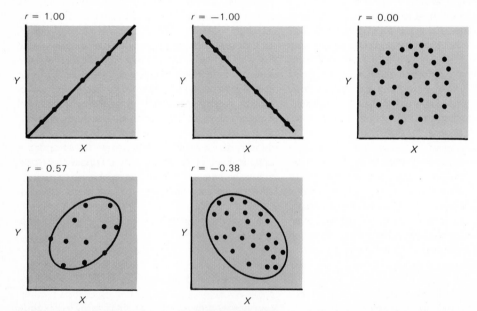

FIGURE 1-3. Examples of scatterplots showing correlations of different magnitudes between two variables, *X* and *Y.* Each person is represented by a point that reflects scores on the two dimensions. The correlation of +.57, for example, could be the relationship between height and weight for a sample of 11 individuals. (Adapted from Runyon & Haber, 1971.)

the individuals all show about the same amount of nervous tension: individuals very high in nervous tension would be in one group, those with moderate nervous tension would be in another group, and so on. If one still found a correlation between smoking and lung cancer within each group of people who have the same degree of nervous tension, then it would be difficult to explain the correlation by this particular variable. The problem is that there can be an unknown number of other variables that might be contributing to the observed relationship. As for lung cancer and smoking, subsequent correlational research that controlled for a number of other variables and experimental research with animals has pointed more and more convincingly to the likelihood that smoking indeed is at least one contributing cause of lung cancer, even though the causation in humans cannot be said to be 100 percent proven. The prudent person, however, would take the likelihood of such causation seriously.

Another example closer to our subject matter is the correlation obtained in some studies between schizophrenia in males and overprotective, intrusive tendencies on the part of their mothers. Such a finding is consistent with theories derived from case histories to the effect that overprotective, intrusive mothers contribute to the development of schizophrenia in their sons. The correlation does not prove the theory, however. Perhaps having an incapacitated son causes the mothers to be more concerned and protective rather than the other way around. It is not a bad idea when confronted with an association between two measures always to ask yourself how the causation might work in either direction or what third and fourth variables might be involved.

Much of the subject matter of abnormal psychology must be studied by correlational methods for practical and ethical reasons. For example, we cannot ethically manipulate family environments in an effort to produce schizophrenic offspring. If we are aware of and can avoid the interpretive pitfalls associated with correlational research, a great deal of understanding can be achieved by this method.

EXPERIMENTAL RESEARCH

The most powerful way of shedding light on factors that affect human behavior is the *experimental method*. The essence of the psychological experi-

ment is that the people to be studied are randomly assigned to two or more groups, in the simplest case to an *experimental group* and a *control group*. The experimental group experiences some special condition (a manipulation or treatment) while the control group does not. The logic of this approach is that if the experimental group shows effects not shown by the control group, then these effects can be considered to be caused by the experimental manipulation or treatment. Since the subjects are randomly assigned to the two groups, it is assumed that the groups are alike in every respect except for the experience of the particular treatment. Suppose, for example, that mental patients are randomly assigned to two groups, one of which is given tranquilizing pills while the other is not. We could say then that any consequent difference in symptom reduction between these two groups is attributable to the administration of the tranquilizing pills.

How large does the difference in symptom reduction between the experimental and control groups have to be before you can conclude that it is not just a chance difference that could occur between any two random samples? Statistical techniques are available for helping to make this kind of decision. These techniques permit you to say how often you might expect to find a difference of a certain magnitude if the research were repeated many times with different random samples. Thus, you might be able to say that a given difference would occur by chance once in every 20 times that the study was repeated, or once in every 100 or once in every 4. The more studies you would have to conduct to find a chance difference of a certain magnitude, the less likely it is that the one obtained difference is due to chance. Somewhat arbitrarily, psychologists usually accept a probability of once in 20 times ($p = .05$) as a *significant difference*, that is, a difference unlikely to have occurred by chance and therefore reflecting a real effect.

Unfortunately, interpreting the results of an experiment is not always simple. For example, in the experiment just described, we concluded that a significantly greater reduction in symptoms among subjects in the experimental group could be attributed to the administration of the tranquilizing pills. However, administering pills involves a number of factors in addition to what the pill does after it dissolves in the stomach of the recipient. Perhaps the patients who were given the pills were also given the expectation of improvement, since we expect medicine to alleviate symptoms of illness. When an expectation of improvement communicated by the doctors and nurses is sufficient to cause improvement, it is called a *placebo effect*. Perhaps the doctors and nurses, knowing who got the pills and who did not, unconsicously spent more time with those patients who received the medication. Perhaps the observers who rated the patients on their symptomatic behaviors were aware of who got the pills and who did not and unconsciously distorted their ratings to produce the obtained effect.

The experimental method by itself does not automatically lead to unambiguous results, but experiments can be designed to rule out many of these alternative interpretations. Thus the proper control group in our illustration might be one in which the patients are given a sugar pill (placebo), and the doctors and nurses administering the pills are kept ignorant of which pill is which. This type of experimental design, in which both subjects and personnel are kept blind with respect to whether a subject is in the experimental or the control group, is called the *double-blind* design. Properly used, the experimental method can be an incisive way of answering questions about the nature, genesis and development, and modification of abnormal behavior.

This brief introduction to some of the more fundamental aspects of scientific inquiry is by no means exhaustive of the methodological issues involved in research in this area. Later, in the context of specific investigations, I will consider other tactics that have been found useful in the study of abnormal behavior.

Summary

1. Three characteristics are commonly considered in defining abnormal behavior: cultural inappropriateness, subjective distress, and psychological handicap. In general, abnormality does not lend itself to precise definition, and the emphasis in this book will not be on labeling some behaviors normal and others abnormal, but on describing the behavior of interest, understanding the factors that have led to its development, and considering ways in which the behavior might be changed.

2. Abnormality can be seen as residing in an interpersonal system, such as a family or larger social group, as well as being a characteristic of an individual.

3. It makes sense to view abnormality as a continuum in which incapacitation and distress are extreme at one end and minimal at the other end. Most of us fall in the middle, with some mild inhibitions or anxieties that do not seriously handicap us.

4. Despite some looseness in definition, psychological disorders are real and they affect a substantial proportion of our population.

5. There are a number of reasons for studying abnormal psychology: intrinsic interest, personal and occupational relevance, and responsibilities of citizenship.

6. The study of abnormal behavior can be approached in a scientific manner. To do so, we need to be familiar with such concepts as sampling and generalization, reliability and validity of measurement, normative research, correlational research, and experimental research.

Suggested Readings

Provocative discussions on the nature and definition of "mental illness" can be found in T. Szasz, *The age of madness* (Anchor Books, 1973) and in O. Milton and R. G. Wahler, *Behavior disorders: Perspectives and trends,* Chapter 1 (J. B. Lippincott, 1973). B. A. Maher provides an extensive consideration of different approaches to the scientific study of abnormal behavior in *Introduction to research in psychopathology* (McGraw-Hill, 1970).

2

A Historical Perspective

- ■ "Whatever possessed you?" Is abnormal behavior caused by invading demons?

- ■ "Thou shalt not suffer a witch to live." The late Middle Ages was no time to be mentally disturbed.

- ■ Do diseased brains cause abnormal behavior?

- ■ Do ideas, emotional conflicts, and upsetting experiences cause abnormal behavior?

The Witch Trials of Salem

In the summer and early fall of 1693, 17 women and 2 men were taken by cart to Gallows Hill near Salem, Massachusetts, and hanged as witches. The principal accusers of these alleged witches were a group of young girls. Betty, the youngest at age 9, and her cousin Abigail, 11, were the first to show the symptoms of a strange malady that was to lead to this tragic end. These two girls had listened secretly to the stories of a West Indian slave woman, Tituba, and later other girls in the village had come to participate in these exciting yet forbidden sessions. Betty, always sensitive and subject to fits of weeping, began to act strangely. Sometimes her mother would find her sitting motionless staring fixedly at some invisible object. If called by her mother, she would start violently, scream, and be unable to give an explanation for her behavior other than meaningless babbling. This reaction was especially likely to come on during prayer, but her father, the minister for Salem Village, learned to leave her alone, for if he reproved her, she remained as rigid as ever but worked her mouth and gave off hoarse choking sounds, something like the barking of a dog.

Abigail caught the affliction as if by contagion, but went beyond Betty in the imaginativeness of her display. She got down on hands and knees and ran about, barking and braying, and sometimes went into convulsions where she would writhe and scream as though suffering the torments of the damned. Within a short time the affliction spread to other young girls in the village.

At another time or place such a phenomenon might have run its course and soon been forgotten. In the religious context of the time, however, notions of devil-possession and witchcraft were widespread, and soon the local physicians and ministers began to suspect that these innocent children were being possessed and tormented by witches. When the authorities first asked them to name the people (witches) who were afflicting them, they were unable to do so. No one afflicted them; it just happened. The minister and townspeople began to ask leading questions; names of suspects were suggested to the girls and their reactions sharply studied. Eventually Betty cried out, "Tituba . . . oh Tituba," and the other girls followed suit. Ignorant and confused, Tituba "confessed" to being a witch, and unfortunately in the process referred vaguely to nine other witches.

As the witch trials proceeded they developed a common pattern. One of the girls in her fits and convulsions would claim to see the spectral form of a village member tormenting her and this so-called "spectral evidence" was enough for the judges to render a verdict of guilty. Rebecca Nurse, 71-year-old matriarch of the Nurse family, was deeply pious, steeped in scripture, and had reared her children in loving devotion to both their spiritual and temporal welfare. Nor did her family ever desert her in the ordeal she underwent. Accused of witchcraft by several of the girls, she was brought to court and asked by one of the judges if she was a witch. Her answer was unheard by the audience at the hearing because almost as if on signal the girls fell into convulsions and set up a "hideous screitch and noise" that could be heard some distance away. "Oh, Lord help me!" cried poor Rebecca and spread her hands helplessly. The girls immediately spread their hands in like manner and thereafter whatever move Rebecca made they duplicated. Before the very eyes of the court she demonstrated her witchcraft; she made these innocent children follow her every motion. (Starkey, 1961)

From the perspective of the twentieth century these young girls might be seen as showing a form of disturbed behavior called hysteria, and more prosaic causes than possession by the devil might be sought. Initially, Betty provided the other girls with a model of strange behavior. Soon the townspeople began to take notice, and the girls became the object of concern and interest. Starkey suggests that grow-

A witch trial in Salem, Massachusetts. Did the tragedy of the Salem witch trials result, in part, from the actions of psychologically disturbed girls?

ing up in puritan Salem was at best a drab and no-nonsense business. Any inclinations toward fun, frivolity, and occasional mischief were dourly inhibited. Under the cloak of an acceptable reason, these girls were having the time of their lives. They gave vent to uninhibited physical and verbal expressions, and were given more attention than if "they had married the king and all his court."

Models and Metaphors

In trying to understand any new phenomena we tend to apply ideas that were useful in some more familiar domain. Thus in ancient times the world was sometimes conceived as a flat surface supported by a giant animal such as a turtle or an elephant, based presumably on the everyday experience that the earth looks flat and the knowledge that objects would fall unless supported. Later this metaphor was replaced by a model of a solar system in which planets revolved around the sun. After this model became commonplace and familiar, it was used as a way of conceiving the atom, that is, as a nucleus encircled by planetary electrons. What an atom actually looks

like has been much more difficult to determine than was the appearance of the solar system but, although this model has been useful to a degree, it has not been found to fit empirical data in a number of respects. In fact, many features of modern physics have been difficult to visualize by any familiar conceptions taken from everyday reality.

When scientists deliberately develop a model as an initial attempt to increase understanding in some new field of inquiry, it is usually understood that it may turn out to correspond with reality in some respects and not in others. Scientists hope, however, that it will be useful in suggesting new observations or experiments. A problem can arise, though, if we forget that the model is only meant to be saying "Let's view this phenomenon *as if* it were like such and such." We have been particularly susceptible to applying metaphors from some familiar area of experience or belief to abnormal behavior, losing sight of the fact that such views are best seen as models or metaphors rather than perceived reality. A consequence of having uncritically accepted a certain metaphor of abnormal behavior is that it largely determines how we interpret these behaviors, what we look for in terms of causes, and how we go about treating or changing these behaviors.

I have already implied that the strange behavior of the young girls of Salem might be interpreted from a different perspective than that of possession by witches. To take another example, if we apply an *illness* or *disease* metaphor to abnormal behavior, then the observed disturbances in behavior tend to be seen as *symptoms*, which are *caused* by some underlying psychological or physical pathology. Working within this metaphor it makes sense to conclude that modifying (that is, in some way getting rid of) the symptoms without treating the underlying cause will be futile and perhaps produce even more severely disturbed behavior. However, from a perspective that I will call *radical behaviorism* abnormal behaviors are viewed as learned responses rather than as symptoms. As such these responses should be capable of being unlearned as well as learned provided the basic principles of human learning are properly applied. In this view no assumptions are made about hypothetical disease processes and it would seem to follow that treatment should be directly focused on the abnormal behaviors. These alternative models or metaphors will be considered in more detail later, but it might be mentioned here that neither of these particular metaphors may turn out to be wholly adequate in capturing the reality of disordered behaviors. Also, there is a tendency to experience a given metaphor as "obvious" and "natural" once one has adopted that view and to see alternative mataphors as strange and perhaps farfetched. It is not easy to maintain the kind of detachment that permits us to see various metaphors as different ways of trying to understand a particular phenomenon with no one view necessarily being *the* correct one.

Demon Possession versus Naturalistic Explanations

Abnormal behavior has apparently been a part of the human condition in all times and in all cultures.[1] We can recognize in ancient writings descriptions of the convulsive fits that we now call *epilepsy* or perhaps

[1]The following historical review is derived, in part, from Rosen (1968) and Zilboorg and Henry (1941).

hysteria; excited, hyperactive states that we now call *mania;* melancholic, dejected reactions that we now label *depression;* severe disturbances in rational thinking that we now call *schizophrenia;* and irrational fears now known as *phobias.* And quite independently, it would seem, people in diverse lands and cultures developed a remarkably similar "theory" or metaphor to explain these aberrations—possession by some god, spirit, or demon.

EARLY DEMONOLOGY

Imagine yourself for a moment living in a small village 6000 years ago in the Middle East or China, with no education other than the religious teachings of that time. An acquaintance of yours begins to act strangely, to speak in unintelligible ramblings, perhaps to fling himself about in uncontrollable frenzy. You might well think, "He is not himself; he's not acting like the person I know." It would take little assistance from any prevailing theology for you to begin to think that if your friend is not acting like himself, is not "in control" of himself, then something else must be in control. Maybe one of the gods or spirits that control the storms, the lightnings, illnesses, and death has taken possession of your friend and is making him behave in this strange fashion. The logic, in other words, for the development of beliefs in *spirit possession* is not so farfetched, given the understanding about the causes of human behavior that existed in those times.

Theories of demon possession may have existed even in prehistoric times, as suggested by skulls showing *trephining.* In this procedure tools, probably of stone, were used to make a sizable hole in the skull, possibly with the intent of permitting entrapped demons to escape. Of course we cannot be sure that this procedure derived from a theory of demon possession; it is, however, quite consistent with such an explanation.

The Bible and other early literature is full of variations on the theme of spirit possession, and even today our language betrays how deeply we have been influenced by demonological conceptions. We still say, "Whatever *possessed* you?" or "What's gotten into him?" The expression "She was *beside* herself with anger" originally meant that the person's spirit left the body while the demon took over.

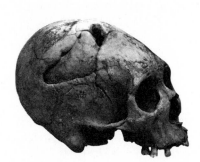
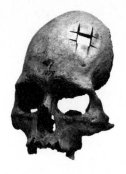

Some scientists have speculated that the holes in trephined skulls like these may have been chipped or cut out in order to release demons.

HIPPOCRATES

Even in the ancient world, however, not everyone subscribed to the prevailing belief in spirit possession. Many Greek and Roman physicians and philosophers held points of view that were essentially modern in their denial of supernatural explanations for both physical and mental disorders. The Greek physician Hippocrates (460–377 B.C.) was one of the first to advocate naturalistic explanations for disturbed behaviors. In speaking about epilepsy, referred to in those days as the sacred disease because of the belief that it reflected possession by a god, Hippocrates says, "It thus appears to me to be in no way more divine, nor more sacred than other diseases, but has a natural cause from which it originates like other affections." And again, "If you cut open the head, you will find the brain humid, full of sweat and smelling badly. And in this way you may see that it is not a god which injures the body, but disease" (*Sacred Disease* by Hippocrates, as quoted in Zilboorg & Henry, 1941, pp. 43–44). Hippocrates was a careful clinical observer, and his own classification of mental diseases included phobias, epilepsy, mania, melancholia, and paranoia (more like mental deterioration than what we currently call paranoia).

If people believe that psychological abnormalities are caused by spirit possession, then their ideas about treatment are likely to turn to ways of getting the disturbing spirit out of the person, whether by opening a hole in the skull, uttering religious incantations, or other means. Hippocrates, operating from the metaphor that behavioral abnormalities were sicknesses in the same sense as physical disorders, advocated "medical" approaches to treatment, such as moderate exercise and physical tranquility. His theories of bodily functioning were crude and frequently inaccurate by today's standards, but in general viewpoint and attitude he is essentially modern. Greek and Roman physicians such as Asclepiades, Aretaeus, and Galen carried on this tradition until about A.D. 200, at which time the demonological explanations, never entirely given up even among the Greeks and Romans, began to replace the natural causation views.

DANCE MANIAS IN THE MIDDLE AGES

A curious phenomenon developed near the end of the Middle Ages and appeared on and off for several hundred years—the *dance manias*. Peter Herental describes one such episode that occurred in 1374.

Both men and women were abused by the devil to such a degree that they danced in their homes, in the churches and in the streets, holding each other's hands and leaping in the air. While they danced they called out the names of demons, such as Friskes and others, but they were unaware of this nor did they pay attention to modesty even though people watched them. At the end of the dance, they felt such pains in the chest, that if their friends did not tie linen clothes tightly around their waists, they cried out like madmen that they were dying. In Liège they were freed of their demons by means of exorcisms such as those employed before baptism. (Rosen, 1968, pp. 196–197).

Similar dancing manias were called *tarantism* in Italy because they were believed to be caused by the bite of a tarantula, and in other parts of Europe they were known as *St. Vitus' dance* (after a 1518 episode in which dancers were sent to a chapel of St. Vitus). The dancers, mostly from the lower socioeconomic classes, sometimes set wreaths on their heads, bound themselves around with cloths or towels, or went half-naked. They would work themselves into a kind of ecstasy, suddenly throwing themselves on the ground with convulsive and twitching movements, sometimes losing consciousness and foaming at the mouth. In some areas the dance mania became institutionalized as an annual ritual. One group of women, for example, made an annual pilgrimage to a chapel of St. Vitus, where they would dance ecstatically until they collapsed from exhaustion. For several weeks before the pilgrimage they suffered from feelings of restlessness and a feeling of painful heaviness, but after the dance they were freed of these attacks and could anticipate a year of well-being (Rosen, 1968). The artist Pieter Bruegel probably witnessed a form of dance mania and incorporated the event into the painting shown.

DEMONOLOGY TRIUMPHANT: WITCHCRAFT

During most of the Middle Ages physicians confronted with various forms of psychopathology put together as best they could some of the traditional, by then somewhat garbled, views of the ancient Greeks and Romans, and the astrology, alchemy, demonology, and simple prayers of their own day. *Exorcising* (driving out) demons was not necessarily a brutal affair. Laying on of hands, the utterance of certain prayers, or the ingestion of unsavory potions were common procedures. Beginning near the end of the fifteenth century and continuing for some 200 years a more virulent form of demonology led to a widespread preoccupation with witches and their identification and destruction. Several historical conditions may have contributed to this phenomenon:

These women portrayed by the artist Brueghel may have been exhibiting St. Vitus's dance, one form of the dance mania that occurred in the Middle Ages.

A church whose doctrines were being severely challenged by the Reformation (Protestants, however, soon started their own witch-hunts) and general unrest caused by wars, economic depressions, and the Black Plagues all increased people's readiness to blame their woes on handy scapegoats.

The lengths to which physicians and clergymen would go to drive out invading devils became more and more extreme. Flogging, starving, immersion in hot water, and more refined forms of torture were employed. Initially a distinction existed between individuals who had been unwittingly seized by a devil and those who had intentionally signed a pact to do the devil's work. Only the latter were known as witches. The distinction, however, became blurred. If persons suspected of being a witch did not confess, they were likely to be tortured until they did. Following the biblical injunction, "Thou shalt not suffer a witch to live" (Exodus 22:18), convicted witches were put to death, frequently by burning at the stake. To individuals like Boguet, a French judge, the world seemed infested with witches:

I believe that the sorcerers could form an army equal to that of Xerxes, who had one million, eight hundred thousand men.

As to myself, I have no doubt, since a mere glance at our neighbors will convince us that the land is infested with this unfortunate and damnable vermin. Germany cannot do anything but raise fires against them; Switzerland is compelled to do likewise, thus depopulating many of its villages. . . .

No, no, the sorcerers reach everywhere by the thousands; they multiply on the earth like the caterpillars in our gardens . . . I want them to know that if the results were to correspond to my wishes, the earth would be quickly purged, because I wish they could all be united in one body so that all could be burned on one fire. (Zilboorg & Henry, 1941, pp. 162–163)

The witchcraft phenomenon is relevant to the study of abnormal behavior because some individuals suffering from behavior disorders were probably convicted as witches, and in some cases may even have believed themselves to be witches. Most convicted witches, however, were probably as "normal" as you or I. They simply had the ill fortune at the wrong time in history to get into an argument with a neighbor a few weeks before the neighbor's child got sick or the neighbor's cow died. But individuals

In the middle ages, devils were sometimes cast out (exorcised) by prayer as in this depiction of St. Catherine of Sienna. Such an approach to treating abnormal behavior may not have entirely disappeared in today's society, as indicated by the many movies about demon possession.

with behavior disorders played other roles in this affair. We saw how the children of Salem successfully accused others of witchcraft while in the throes of hysterical reactions. At yet another level perhaps the entire historical episode of witchcraft mania could be viewed as a form of collective madness—a whole culture suffering from a delusion that produced incalculable suffering and misery. Did not German society under the Nazis show similar features of "madness"? Yet we must be cautious in talking about "societal madness," not because such a thing may not exist but because its causes and characteristics may be very different from the more individualized forms of madness. To hold a "false" belief in common with most of the other people in your community is not the same thing as holding a "false" belief that is unique to you. There is also, of course, the basic problem of who is to decide whether a given belief is true or false.

VOICES OF REASON

To draw too sharp a line between medieval and modern views of mental illness would be inaccurate. Throughout the Dark Ages and medieval times some individuals maintained the more scientific and humane attitudes of the ancient Greek and Roman physicians. In Arabian civilization especially did these views prevail. A mental hospital, for example, was established as early as 792 in Baghdad, in which humane care for the mentally disturbed was provided.

At the height of the European obsession with witches lived Johann Weyer (1515–1588), a man whose views on mental disorders were far ahead of his time. His ability to see natural causes of deviant human behavior without becoming caught up in the prevailing theological explanations is illustrated by the case of Barbara Kremers. This 10-year-old girl had become a celebrity; miraculously she never ate, urinated, or moved her bowels, but was in good health. This "miracle" had followed a severe illness. For six months following the illness Barbara had remained mute, and since that time she had ceased to eat. Learned men came to see her and marvel, and the City Council awarded her a certificate testifying to the truth of this wonder. Weyer became interested in the girl and arranged to have her and her sister come to live at the estate where he lived (as personal physician to a Duke). It was soon discovered that Barbara and her sister had engaged in a clever swindle in which her sister had secretly supplied her with food. Barbara was treated with kindness by Weyer and in less than a week's time she was eating regular meals at Weyer's table. She had also been partially lame and walked on crutches, and in addition suffered from a twist in her arms. Weyer cured her lameness merely by rubbing bland oil on her back, and shortly thereafter the twist in her arms also disappeared. Weyer's clinical writings are full of examples of this kind in which a combination of astute clinical observation, uncluttered by demonological speculations, and a kindly respect for the person foreshadow modern psychiatry.

Weyer believed that many witches were mentally disturbed individuals who needed care and treatment, not torturing and burning. He made a careful study of witchcraft and published a book on the subject in which he deplored the senseless torturing and killing of innocent people. It was not until long after Weyer's death that the commonsense appeal of his book began to be accepted by medical authorities. The reaction of Church authorities at the time is summed up by the statement of Father Spina: "Recently Satan went to a Sabbath [a witches' gathering] attired as a great prince, and told the assembled witches that they need not worry since, thanks to Weyer and his followers, the affairs of the Devil were brilliantly progressing" (Castiglioni, 1946, p. 253).

Eventually, in the face of growing attacks, demonology gave ground. In England, Reginald Scott (1538–1599) exposed the fallacies of witchcraft and demonology in a book called *The Discovery of Witchcraft,* published in 1584. He especially denied the role of demons in producing mental disorders. St. Vincent de Paul (1576–1660), likewise at the risk of his own life, argued that mental diseases were similar in kind to bodily disease.

DEMONOLOGY TODAY: ALIVE AND WELL IN THE U.S.A.?

In most textbooks of abnormal psychology demon possession is discussed as a curious and interesting belief of ancient and medieval times that has given way to modern, scientific approaches to the understanding of human behavior. Although hardly in the mainstream of the scientific study of abnormal psychology, theories of demon possession still have their adherents.

Belief in occult phenomena—witchcraft, astrology, and so on—has enjoyed a revival in the last decade or so. Movies such as *Rosemary's Baby* and *The Exorcist* dealt explicitly and seriously with demon possession. The novel, *The Exorcist,* was based on an account that the author, Blatty, read in the newspaper in 1949. A 14-year-old boy was tormented by various strange happenings. His bed, with him in it, would shake violently and lift into the air and travel around the room. "Brandings" or markings resembling claw marks appeared on his flesh, accompanied by screams of anguish and pain from the boy. Psychiatrists had been consulted but apparently were unable to help. Eventually permission was obtained from the Cardinal for a Jesuit priest to use exorcism to drive out the devil that was presumed to have taken possession of the boy. After two months of exorcism the boy's strange behavior and the accompanying phenomena were reported to have gone away.

In fairness it must be stated that current advocates of demon possession rarely propose that all forms of abnormal behavior are caused in this way. Demon possession, they say, should be considered as an alternative hypothesis only after the more usual manifestations of psychopathology (neurosis, psychosis, and so on) have been ruled out.

In Chapter 1 I discussed research strategies used in the scientific study of abnormal psychology. At this point let us extend that discussion to the question of how one decides between two or more competing theories. How, for example, can one decide whether demon possession is better or worse than another theory in accounting for some specific instance of abnormal behavior? First we should consider whether the theory of demon possession can be shown to be wrong. Is it possible to design a series of experiments in which the demon possession theory leads to predictions clearly different from alternative theories? If so, we could see whether the demon possession theory or an alternative theory yielded the best predictions. But it is difficult to test demon possession in this manner, since *any* observation or result could probably be "explained" by the actions of unobservable demons. If we conclude that the demon theory does not lead to differentially testable predictions, then we should consider whether all of the known facts can be equally well explained by other, verifiable causes. If so, why invoke an additional entity, demons, to explain something that is already understood?

You may be familiar with an analogy from chemistry. Early chemists postulated the existence of phlogiston, a hypothetical substance, to explain fire and other phenomena. When these same phenomena were understood in other terms, the concept of phlogiston turned out to be superfluous and was discarded. We will see in the chapters ahead that a number of theories or principles that do not invoke demons appear reasonably promising as explanations of abnormal behavior.

A cursory look at the history of science suggests that supernatural explanations have flourished in areas in which scientific knowledge was limited. When scientific knowledge expanded, supernatural theories retreated to areas still untouched by science. Our understanding of abnormal behavior is still incomplete, and thus, not surprisingly, supernatural views still find some room for acceptance. If past history is any indication, demon possession, like phlogiston, will in time be seen as an unnecessary assumption and be abandoned. Of course, there may always be some people who prefer to believe something other than that which has been reasonably demonstrated to be so, as did members of the Flat Earth Society in the not too distant past.

Demonology, then, seems an unlikely winner in the contest among theories explaining abnormal behavior. But the most fundamental lesson that the history of science teaches is not be be dogmatic in support of or in opposition to *any* theory. Although current evidence provides little support for theories of demon possession, we cannot with 100 percent certainty say that there is no truth to them.

Humanitarian Reforms

THE EARLY ASYLUMS

In medieval times the fate of the mentally ill was varied. Some were simply allowed to wander the streets and the countryside, begging or stealing, making out as best they could. Some more troublesome individuals wound up in prisons or dungeons alongside common criminals, or if they were lucky they found a place in the occasional monastery that provided assistance for these unfortunates. The first institutions devoted entirely to the care of the mentally ill, called asylums, frequently had their start in monasteries. Although asylums usually began as havens where the mentally disturbed could find food, shelter, and some kindly attention, as time went by they tended to become overcrowded, noisy, unsanitary repositories. Patients were frequently chained, and no concern was shown for whether these conditions were helpful in restoring mental equilibrium. The living conditions at Bethlehem Hospital, a London asylum opened in 1547, became so noisy and chaotic that the word *bedlam* was derived from its name. Passersby could observe the more violent patients for a penny a look, and the more harmless individuals were forced to beg on the streets of London. In Vienna the so-called Lunatics Tower was constructed in 1784. Patients were confined between inner rooms and the outer curved wall, where in some cases they could be observed by the local citizenry.

Upper-class ladies and gentlemen, sometimes visited Bethlehem Hospital (Bedlam) in London to seek amusement as shown in this engraving by Hogarth.

TREATING MENTAL PATIENTS LIKE HUMAN BEINGS

In the eighteenth and nineteenth centuries several reformers began improving the care of the mentally ill. One of the most famous promoters of humanitarian approaches was Philippe Pinel. In the midst of the French Revolution in 1792, Pinel was placed in charge of a hospital for the insane, La Bicêtre in Paris. Although the leaders of the Revolution loudly proclaimed their ideals of liberty, equality, and fraternity, they were less than enthusiastic about Pinel's proposal to remove the chains from the insane and treat them with kindness and dignity. After considerable pleading Pinel was granted permission to try his experiment. Patients chained for as long as 40 years were cut free and permitted to see the sun and breathe fresh air once more. Many of these patients, after experiencing the freer and more humane con-

ditions created by Pinel, were eventually able to leave the hospital.

In other ways Pinel's reforms were forerunners of the modern psychiatric hospital. He interviewed and studied the patients carefully, making notes of what they said and of any other information relevant to their difficulties. In short, he introduced the keeping of systematic records on patients, an essential step if knowledge about the nature of these disorders was to progress.

Similar reforms were begun in England where the Quaker, William Tuke, founded the York Retreat in the English countryside, where patients were permitted to rest and work in an accepting religious environment. However, these reforms begun by specific individuals did not immediately spread to all institutions. The history of mental hospital care has been and continues to be one of cyclical rediscovery of dehumanizing treatment and the advocacy of re-

Philippe Pinel (left) and William Tuke (right) were pioneers in the treatment of the mentally ill. Pinel has been called "The Liberator of the Insane" for his work in France, while Tuke began his own "Benign Revolution" by founding the York Retreat in England.

forms. In mid-nineteenth century America a New England schoolteacher named Dorothea Dix (1802-1887) launched a campaign against the inhumane conditions in asylums. In a report to the Congress of the United States in 1848 she said that she had seen:

. . . more than 9000 idiots, epileptics and insane in the United States, destitute of appropriate care and protection . . . bound with galling chains, bowed beneath fetters and heavy iron balls attached to dragchains, lacerated with ropes, scourged with rods and terrified beneath storms of execration and cruel blows; now subject to jibes and scorn and torturing tricks; now abandoned to the most outrageous violations. (Zilboorg & Henry, 1941, pp. 583–584)

During the 40 years of her endeavors Dix was instrumental in founding or enlarging more than 30 state institutions for the proper custody and treatment of the mentally ill.

Modern reformers rarely find the extreme conditions described by Dorothea Dix, but they do frequently expose the dehumanizing psychological impact of the institutional environment. The sheer size of many twentieth-century public hospitals has made it almost impossible to create the atmosphere of personal concern that can exist in a setting such as the York Retreat.

The Organic View

The *organic view,* based on the belief that mental disorders have their origin in some biological malfunctioning transmitted through heredity, or caused by a disease, injury, lesion, or more subtle biochemical disturbance in the brain, is as old as Hippocrates. The theory and the methods of study have become more refined in recent years, but the basic idea re-

Dorothea Dix's untiring campaigns on behalf of the mentally ill led to many reforms in institutional treatment in the United States.

mains the same—that what is going on in the central nervous system has something to do with whether we are mad or sane. In short, we have the illness metaphor of mental disorders.

As we have seen, in the Middle Ages there was a retreat from scientific approaches to mental disorders, including the organic view. By the middle of the nineteenth century, however, the notion that disordered behavior was related in some way to disordered brains had regained considerable prominence. A German psychiatrist, Wilhelm Griesinger (1817–1868), contended that classification of mental disorders should be based on underlying brain lesions, and a French psychiatrist, Morel (1809–1873), proposed that mental illness resulted from brain deterioration, itself the consequence of a hereditary neural weakness.

AN INFLUENTIAL CLASSIFICATION SYSTEM: EMIL KRAEPELIN

The monumental work of Emil Kraepelin (1855–1926) further solidified the organic view and provided us with a classification system that has con-

tinued to influence psychiatric thinking to this day. In earlier centuries it was difficult to develop categories of mental disorder based on anything other than a description of current symptoms. Record keeping was either nonexistent or haphazard, and, as a result, it was not easy to accumulate information on how a disorder progressed over time or on its outcome. By Kraepelin's time the better hospitals, thanks in part to men like Pinel, had been keeping relatively good records for many years. Through the study of hundreds of these records as well as the direct observation of many patients, he developed his diagnostic categories.

Following a strategy that was paying off in the study of physical diseases, Kraepelin looked for individuals with patterns of symptoms (*symptom-complexes*) whose "diseases" showed a similar onset, course, and outcome. He then combined symptom patterns previously considered as separate categories into two major syntheses: *manic-depressive psychosis* and *dementia praecox* (roughly comparable to *schizophrenia* in current terminology). Mania (excited, elated reactions) was linked with depression or melancholia to form the manic-depressive category because the psychiatric records showed that: (1) these symptoms sometimes alternated with each other in the same person; (2) both mania and melancholia showed an abrupt onset and a periodic course in which the person tended to show spontaneous recovery but a high likelihood of future recurrences; and (3) in neither case was there progressive mental deterioration or physical symptoms such as paralysis. Dementia praecox represented an amalgam of an even greater variety of symptoms that had in common two characteristics: an early onset, usually in adolescence or young adulthood (thus praecox or precocious), and a progressive downhill course toward an incurable *dementia* (mental incompetence). The outcome, however, while irreversible was not death, but rather stabilization at a very reduced level of mental and social capacity. Kraepelin also included a third category, *paranoia,* which occurred less frequently than the other two symptom patterns and consisted of one symptom, a highly systematized delusional belief of a persecutory nature.

Kraepelin's two major classifications accounted for about two-thirds of all the patients in mental hospitals at that time. The importance of his work lay in the possibility that investigation of the cause and cure of these disorders could proceed more rationally if indeed these categories reflected distinct disease processes. Kraepelin himself thought that the manic-depressive psychosis was the result of some disturbance in metabolic function (probably inherited since this disorder seemed to run in families), while dementia praecox was caused by some abnormality in the sex glands. His organic theories, which were stated in very general terms, have not been proved (or clearly disproved either) by subsequent research. My purpose here, however, is not to evaluate the current status of research on biological causes of mental disorders but to put the organic viewpoint in historical perspective.

AN EXAMPLE OF ORGANIC CAUSATION: GENERAL PARESIS

The discovery of the nature of a mental disorder called *general paresis,* one of the great achievements of medical science, gave strong impetus to the development of organic theories of abnormal behavior. To start at the beginning of this medical detective story, we go back to a physician named Haslam, who in 1798 identified a symptom-complex consisting of delusions of grandeur, dementia, and progressive paralysis. In 1805 a French physician, Esquirol, added another bit of information to this pattern of symptoms: The paralysis and mental deterioration progressed rapidly to a fatal outcome. Bayle, a student of Esquirol, presented in 1826 even more precise descriptions of both the mental and physical symptoms and argued strongly that they represented a single form of mental illness that could be distinguished from other disorders. Previously many physicians had thought that paralysis might be a secondary accompaniment of many forms of madness.

Progress was slow for several decades. Then around 1860 with improved microscopes it became possible to demonstrate that the brains of patients who died from general paresis revealed widespread destruction of nervous tissue. In 1884 Fournier provided highly suggestive evidence that the symptoms of general paresis were related to and perhaps part of the venereal disease, syphilis. He found that 65 percent of patients with general paresis had a history of syphilis, compared with only 10 percent of patients with other mental disorders. Sixty-five percent was still short of 100 percent and it remained for Krafft-Ebing in 1897 to perform a convincing if ethically questionable study. He inoculated nine paretic pa-

tients, who had denied having a prior syphilitic infection, with matter from syphilitic sores. None of these patients developed symptoms of syphilis, indicating that an immunity had resulted from a previous or continuing infection. The specific infectious agent for syphilis, a spirochete called *Treponema pallidum,* was identified in 1905 by Schaudinn, and in 1913 Noguchi and Moore found this organism in the brain tissue of paretic patients.

Thus one identifiable pattern of mental disorder was found to have a clearly specified onset, course, and outcome, and, most important, to be caused by an infectious agent in the same manner as pneumonia or diphtheria. It is no wonder that medical scientists were encouraged to expect other forms of mental illness to reveal in time their own brand of organic causation. In some instances, this hope has been fulfilled as we will see in the chapter on organic brain disorders, but the two most prevalent classes of disorder, Kraepelin's dementia praecox (or schizophrenia) and manic-depression, have not yielded their secrets so readily. After 75 years of organically oriented research, few scientists still expect the cause of either of these classes of disorders to turn out to be anything so simple as an infectious disease. The organic viewpoint remains alive and active, but the search has turned to the subtleties of genetic (hereditary) transmission, brain neurophysiology, and associated biochemical processes. We will examine the current status of research on biological determinants later in the context of specific disorders.

The Psychological View

The view that beliefs, ideas, emotions, and interpersonal experiences—in short, that *psychological events*—might cause disturbed behavior arose largely through the study of *hysteria* and *hypnosis.* Hysteria includes not only the popularly recognized "hysterical attack," involving uncontrolled emotional outbursts of weeping, laughter, or other inappropriate behaviors, but also certain altered states of consciousness and a host of changeable bodily symptoms (such as paralyses, muscular contractions, and defects in hearing and vision) that have no identifiable organic basis. The term itself, derived from the Greek word for uterus, *hystera,* reflects a belief common in the ancient world that these disorders occurred in women only and resulted from a wandering or displaced uterus, a view based on an organic illness metaphor of mental disturbance.

HEALING BY SUGGESTION: ANTON MESMER

In modern times, the rise of a psychological metaphor for understanding these disorders began with the flamboyant career of Anton Mesmer (1734–1815). Trained as a physician, Mesmer was influenced by some of the astrological and pseudoscientific beliefs of his time. He believed that all human behavior was under the influence of the stars and that this influence was accomplished through a constant flow of a magnetic fluid that fills the universe. Physical symptoms developed when the distribution of the magnetic fluid became unbalanced within a person. Healing was produced by permitting a flow of the magnetic fluid into or from the person by the "magnetizer" or healer. Expelled from the Viennese medical profession for his unorthodox approaches to treatment, Mesmer went to Paris where he soon established a flourishing practice.

A typical session in Mesmer's clinic was highly theatrical. The patients gathered around a *bacquet* (a tub) whose floor was covered with powdered glass and iron filings and from which protruded iron rods that were applied to the afflicted areas of the body. Zweig (1932) gives the following account of a Mesmeric session:

The room where his patients were treated impressed them as soon as they had passed the threshold by the peculiarity of its setting, with the result that they became slightly troubled and excited. The windows were screened by curtains so that no more than a dim twilight should pervade the place; thick carpets and hangings on the walls deadened every sound. . . . Like a great pool, the healing tub, the famous bacquet, stood in the middle of the room. As in a church, silence prevailed, and the sick would gather breathlessly expectant around the magnetic altar. . . . From another room would come the strains of a pianoforte, or the dulcet tones of a choir. Mesmer himself would sometimes play the glass harmonica. . . . At length, Mesmer himself would enter upon the scene.

With a serious and dignified mien, calmly, slowly, radiating tranquility into the disturbed atmosphere of the seance, he would draw near to the patients gathered around the tub; at his proximity a gentle fit of trembling would spread through the assembly as if a zephyr had come to ruffle the placidity of a pool. He wore a lilac robe, thus calling up the image of a Zoroaster or of an Indian magician; all his energies, like those of a wild-beast tamer, were concentrated on a single objective; he carried a little wand in his hand, and kept the sufferers under control by the exercise of his will power as he passed from one to the other. Here he would halt for a time, inquiring about the man's ailment, and then would stroke the patient in a peculiar manner with his magnetic wand while fixing the gaze of the sufferer with a look of his own. . . .

Usually no great time elapsed before one or the other of the company would begin to tremble, then the limbs would start to twitch convulsively, and the patient would break out in perspiration, would scream, or groan. No sooner had such tokens manifested themselves in one member of the chain, than the others, too, would feel the onset of the famous crisis which was to bring relief. All would begin to twitch, a mass psychosis [sic] would arise, a second and a third patient would be seized with convulsions. . . . Some would fall to the ground and go into convulsions, others would laugh shrilly, others would scream, and choke and groan, and dance like dervishes, others would appear to faint . . . (pp. 54–56).

Under these dramatic conditions, many patients experienced relief from various aches, pains, and other symptoms. The medical profession, however, was not impressed, and in 1784 a committee of prominent men (including Benjamin Franklin, Joseph-Ignace Guillotin, and Antoine-Laurent de Lavoisier, the discoverer of oxygen) was appointed to investigate Mesmer and his therapeutic techniques. The committee concluded that Mesmer was a fraud and a charlatan. Magnetism, they said, could not be weighed, observed, or measured. Conducting some small experiments of their own, the committee concluded, "that imagination without magnetism produces convulsions and that magnetism without imagination produces nothing." And anticipating the importance that psychologists currently give to observational learning or imitation, they said, "the spectacle of the crises is equally dangerous because of that imitation of which nature, it seems to us, made a law; consequently any public treatment cannot but have at length very harmful results" (Semalaigne, as quoted in Zilboorg & Henry, 1941, pp. 345–346). Mesmer was discredited and forced to leave Paris.

But perhaps the investigating committee missed the point. The fact that many bodily symptoms could be removed by imagination was a scientific observation worthy of serious attention, whether or not Mesmer's theory about the phenomenon was nonsense. Although Mesmer himself faded into obscurity, his techniques provoked continuing interest and controversy. *Mesmerism* became a popular term for procedures used to induce trances and other altered states of consciousness. In time these phenomena came to be subsumed under the general heading of *hypnosis*, and most of the trappings and associated theory used by Mesmer were dropped. The central features of most hypnotic procedures, then as now, included some way of narrowing the field of attention to some specific stimulus (for example, the hypnotist's voice, a swinging pendulum, or a shining light), an atmosphere of expectation that an unusual state would indeed be forthcoming, and a willing, cooperative subject.

THE SCIENTIFIC STUDY OF HYSTERIA: JEAN-MARTIN CHARCOT

In the nineteenth century the prevailing medical view of hysterical symptoms was that either they resulted from an organic brain disorder, or they were displays by flighty women seeking attention and sympathy and were not to be taken seriously. Hypnotism continued to be associated with the occult, strange theories of "magnetic fluids," and charlatanism, or it was considered mere suggestion by the medical establishment. Although by no means the first person to study the relationship between hypnosis and hysteria, Jean-Martin Charcot was largely responsible for making both respectable objects of scientific investigation.[2]

Charcot was already a distinguished French neurologist when he became interested in the nature of hysteria. His previous solid accomplishments in the area of neurology (for example, the identification and naming of multiple sclerosis) and his reputation for conclusions based on careful clinical observation made him the ideal person to study the vagaries of hysteria.

[2]The material in this section is based, in part, on Owen (1971).

The Symptoms of Hysteria. A puzzling but significant fact about hysteria was the almost unlimited variety of symptoms it encompassed. In Charcot's day one symptom was the *grande hysterie,* in which the person lost conciousness, fell, showed muscular contractions similar to those in epileptic attacks, and proceeded to various other "gymnastics" such as a tetanuslike posture in which the body was bent in an arc resting only on head and heels. Following these physical contortions, the patient might express various emotions (such as pleasure, pain, fear, or hatred) that in some cases related clearly to a disturbing incident in the patient's life. After recovering from such an attack, the patient would be amnesic, that is, remember nothing about it.

Disturbances in sensory perception were frequent in patients diagnosed as hysteric. Most common of all was *anesthesia,* a lack of ordinary sensation in the skin; the body surface becomes insensitive to touch, pain, or heat. In some cases the whole body would be affected; more usually the lack of sensation would only occur on some part of the body. In *hemianesthesia* the whole of one side of the body became insensitive. In other cases, a hand, an arm, or some patch of skin lost the sense of touch. Other senses were sometimes affected. Hysterical blindness or deafness occurred but was rare; lesser impairments in vision and hearing were more frequent. In some individuals, for example, the field of vision was restricted so that they looked at the world as through a tunnel.

Hysterical pains were innumerable, especially in the head, abdomen, ovarian region, back, and joints. Various reflexes could become involved, causing persistent coughing, sneezing, yawning, or hiccoughing. A host of afflictions occurred in the musculature: *tics* (mild spasms, usually of the facial muscles), muscular tremors, muscular contractions, and paralysis. In the contractions, a hand might be permanently bent at the knuckles or at the wrist, or a knee drawn up, or one leg crossed over the other. Paralysis could affect any muscle group: legs, arms, or speech muscles, as in mutism. A particularly puzzling paralysis was *abasia,* the inability to walk. Patients with this symptom were frequently young and in good health. When examined in bed they could execute all normal movements and there seemed to be no detectable physical problem. Yet they were absolutely incapable of walking. If made to get out of bed, they fell to the

A clinical lecture by Jean-Martin Charcot at the Salpetrière Hospital in Paris. It was in lectures of this kind that Charcot induced bodily symptoms in hysterical patients who were in a hypnotic trance.

floor. Other *selective defects* frequently seemed related to occupations: a dressmaker who could no longer sew or a pianist who could not play the piano even though in neither case was there a paralysis of the hand.

Are Hysterics Faking?   Charcot did not believe there was a simple answer to the question. "Are hysterics faking their symptoms?" Some patients exaggerated or simulated certain symptoms with conscious intent, but in most instances the symptoms seemed to be as mysterious and unexplainable to the patient as to the physician. Hélène, for example, was a patient who had killed her young infant. Arrested, she lost her speech after the first interrogation. At first glance one might suppose that she was pretending to be mute in order to avoid prosecution or avoid

admission of guilt. In addition to her loss of speech she developed a general anesthesia of the whole body and restriction of her field of vision. At the same time, however, she could write fluently and by this means she fully confessed her crime. Under the circumstances it hardly seemed likely that she was malingering.

Hysteria and "Real" Physical Disease.   Charcot observed a number of ways in which hysterical symptoms tended to differ from similar symptoms arising from known organic causes. For example, patients having real epileptic seizures are likely to fall and hurt themselves while uttering a peculiar cry. The muscular contractions are restricted in nature and there is no speech whatsoever. By contrast, in the hysterical seizure patients have an uncanny knack of falling so that no harm results and may engage in the more spectacular display previously described. Several features are characteristic of hysterical paralyses and contractures: general lack of atrophy of the affected limb, disappearance of the affliction under chloroform (but not in ordinary sleep), normal reflexes (tendon reflexes of the elbow, wrist, knee, and Achilles tendon, for example), sudden onset, and occasionally, sudden disappearance.

Hysterical anesthesias were especially striking in that they frequently affected areas of the body that no known organic lesion or disease process could produce. In so-called *glove* or *sleeve anesthesias,* the insensitive area of the hand or arm corresponded with that which would be covered by a glove or sleeve, an outcome that could not result from any combination of injuries to the three sensory nerve tracts going to the arm and hand. Many hysterical patients, instead of being worried or depressed about their physical symptoms, appeared calm and indeed quite cheerful in some cases—a characteristic that Charcot christened *la belle indifférence.*

Psychological Determinants of Hysteria. Because Charcot was a neurologist, consistent with the prevailing climate of medical opinion he was strongly disposed to explain bodily symptoms, including the hysterical variety, in terms of central nervous system pathology. It is to his credit that over the years his allegiance to letting the data (in this case behavioral observations) speak for themselves gradually eroded his earlier theoretical convictions that brain disease or degeneracy lay at the root of hysteria. Not that he ever gave up entirely the idea of some nervous system weakness as a predisposing factor, but he clearly accepted more and more the possibility that "mental" mechanisms were involved.

The various ways in which hysterical symptoms were found to differ from known organic diseases were enough to arouse suspicion. The glove, stocking, or sleeve anesthesias were especially suggestive; it was as though the anesthetized area corresponded to the person's idea about a body area rather than to a functional neurological reality. Furthermore, the hysterical symptoms of some patients were way out of proportion to any physical accident that preceded them. A girl of 16 received a small cut on the arm which healed within five days. Yet a contracture of the hand and a hemianesthesia set in that persisted

a year after the accident. In other cases the precipitating event was purely emotional with no physical aspect at all. A man was out hunting and shot, as he thought, a fox. The "fox" turned out to be a good friend's dog. Later the same day, while firing at a rabbit, he fell to the ground and lost consciousness. When he revived, his right arm and leg were paralyzed, and subsequently he lost the power of speech, though not the ability to read and write. Charcot did not go as far as a modern psychoanalyst might in interpreting such observations, but he was clearly impressed with the power of psychological events to produce hysterical symptoms:

It seems probable that hystero-traumatic paralysis, is, among others, formed by the following process:

A man predisposed to hysteria has received a blow on the shoulder. This slight traumatism or local shock has sufficed to produce in this nervous individual a sense of numbness extending over the whole of the limb and a slight indication of paralysis. In consequence of this sensation the idea comes to the patient's mind that he might become paralyzed; in one word through *autosuggestion,* the rudimentary paralysis becomes real. (Charcot & Marie, 1892, p. 630)

Most convincing for a psychological theory of hysteria were Charcot's demonstration-lectures, in which hysterical patients were put under hypnosis and new symptoms, indistinguishable from the "real" symptoms, were produced and removed at will. Charcot's hypnotic demonstrations were largely limited to hysterical patients, but other investigators (for example, Liebault and Bernheim) were reporting that hysterical symptoms could be induced in subjects with no previous history of hysteria.

Charcot reported some success in removing hysterical symptoms by hypnosis and suggestion. Hypnotism seemed to work best when the symptoms were of recent onset; with older, more chronic patients the results of hypnotic treatment were disappointing.

The view that psychological factors played an important role in the causation of hysterical symptoms gained momentum toward the end of the nineteenth century. Many young physicians came to study with Charcot in Paris and were influenced by his teachings and demonstrations. Pierre Janet was one; he subsequently developed his own strongly psychological theory of hysteria which emphasized the *dissociation* of one part of the personality from another part under the influence of a fixed idea—the *idée fixe*. A young man from Vienna, Sigmund Freud, spent the year 1885–1886 at Charcot's hospital. In later years, Freud recognized the importance of this experience in his own career:

What impressed me most of all while I was with Charcot were his latest investigations on hysteria, some of which were carried out under my own eyes. He proved for instance the genuineness of hysterical phenomena and their conformity to laws . . . the frequent occurrence of hysteria in men, the production of hysterical paralysis and contractures by hypnotic suggestion and the fact that such artificial products showed, down to their smallest detail, the same features as spontaneous attacks which were often brought on traumatically. (Freud, 1948, p. 22)

The stage was set for the more dynamic theories of Freud.

Summary

1. Attempts to explain strange phenomena are usually couched in familiar metaphors, and this has been true for explanations of abnormal behavior.

2. Demon possession has been a popular explanation for abnormal behavior in many times and places.

3. Some ancient Greeks and Romans, such as Hippocrates and Galen, proposed more naturalistic explanations, including the idea that disordered brains caused disordered behavior.

4. In the late Middle Ages and afterward many individuals, some of whom were probably suffering from mental disorders, were convicted and put to death as witches.

5. Some courageous individuals such as Johann Weyer and Reginald Scott spoke against the prevailing beliefs and argued that mental illnesses resulted from natural causes, not from demon possession.

6. Belief in demon possession as an explanation for certain forms of abnormal behavior still finds some acceptance in modern society, as indicated by films such as *The Exorcist*.

7. Humanitarian reforms in the treatment of the mentally ill have waxed and waned throughout history. Especially important landmarks were the reforms instituted by Philippe Pinel in Paris in 1792 and by Dorothea Dix in the United States in the mid-nineteenth century.

8. The organic view of abnormal behavior experienced a revival in the nineteenth century, especially in the work and writings of men such as Wilhelm Greisinger and Emil Kraepelin. Kraepelin's development of two major categories of severe mental disorders, manic-depressive and dementia praecox, was a milestone in psychiatric diagnosis.

9. The discovery that a syphilitic infection produced the symptom pattern known as general paresis was particularly important in strengthening the organic view.

10. The psychological view of abnormal behavior arose largely from the study of hysteria, developing from the prescientific views of Anton Mesmer to the carefully documented work of Jean-Martin Charcot. Clinical observations strongly suggested that many hysterical symptoms did not result from organic disease but from strong emotional conflicts and the social context in which the person lived.

Suggested Readings

M. L. Starkey's *The devil in Massachusetts* (Doubleday, 1961) is a highly readable as well as scholarly description of the events surrounding the Salem witch trials. G. Zilboorg and G. W. Henry in *A history of medical psychology* (Norton, 1971) and G. Rosen in *Madness in society* (University of Chicago Press, 1968) both provide interesting and scholarly surveys of the history of mankind's experience with and attitudes toward abnormal behavior. S. Zweig's *Mental healers: Franz Anton Mesmer, Mary Baker Eddy, Sigmund Freud* (Frederick Ungar, 1932) is a fascinating and controversial portrayal of these individuals, and A. R. G. Owen's *Hysteria, hypnosis, and healing: The work of J. M. Charcot* (Dobson, 1971) is a well written account of Charcot's study of hysteria.

3

Psychodynamic and Humanistic-Experiential Approaches

- "What you don't know can't hurt you." Freud disagrees, if it's *inside* you.

- How did Freud explain hysterical and other symptoms?

- What were some of the theoretical differences that led Adler, Jung, Sullivan, and Horney to break away from the orthodox Freudian position?

- What are the contributions of Freud's theory? What are the shortcomings?

- How does the humanistic approach differ from the psychodynamic approach?

We saw in the last chapter how ideas about the psychological causation of hysteria were becoming widespread in the late nineteenth century. Against this background Sigmund Freud embarked upon a study of the mind that was to provide the foundation for all future variations of the *psychodynamic* approach.

The cardinal feature of the psychodynamic view is this: To comprehend abnormal behavior one must understand the dynamic interplay of those *intrapsychic* events—motives, drives, emotions, fantasies, and conflicts—that *underlie* the surface manifestations of symptoms. Thus, psychological symptoms are seen as analogous to physical symptoms, such as fever, which can only be understood and effectively treated if the underlying disease process causing the symptom, such as an infection, is identified. Such a view clearly represents a variant of the illness metaphor. In this case the underlying disease is not some physical lesion or infection but rather a pathological condition existing among the intrapsychic processes of the mind—in short, a *mental* disorder.

Let us follow Freud's observations and his thinking in the early stages of the development of this approach and see for ourselves whether it makes sense. Later, we will consider some of the more abstract aspects of psychoanalytic theory and then some of the variations in the psychodynamic tradition—the neo-Freudian views.

A Landmark Case: Anna O.

After spending the year 1885–1886 with Charcot, Freud returned to Vienna and a few years later began a brief but momentous collaboration with a physician named Joseph Breuer. Breuer had been seeing an intelligent 20-year-old woman named Anna O., who displayed a remarkable variety of symptoms. She had apparently been in good physical and mental health until her father developed an illness from which he died some nine months later. Anna O. nursed her father devotedly for the first few months of his illness until her own health began to fail. She became weak, lost her appetite, developed a nervous cough, and eventually was no longer allowed to nurse her father. She soon began to show a strong craving for rest during the afternoon, followed by a sleeplike state (Breuer referred to it as a self-induced hypnotic state) in the evening, and afterward by a period of high excitability lasting late into the night. Many physical symptoms appeared. The muscles of her right arm and leg contracted and held these limbs in a rigid position, and these same limbs became insensitive to pain (anesthetic). Similar symptoms eventually spread in varying degrees to her left arm and leg. The muscles in her neck became partially paralyzed so that she could not move her head except by moving her whole body. Her vision and hearing were impaired, and for periods of time she was mute or could only speak in English (her native tongue was German). In addition she experienced altered states of consciousness (called *absences* by Breuer) in which she seemed to be out of touch with her immediate surroundings and became preoccupied with some highly emotional inner fantasy.

Breuer discovered that if he could get Anna O. during a period of "absence" to talk about and describe the various scenes and images that were disturbing her, she would calm down and experience some relief from that particular set of disturbing thoughts. Anna O. referred to this as a "talking cure" or, jokingly, as "chimney sweeping." As time went by Breuer elaborated on this procedure, inducing a hypnotic state himself when necessary, and seeking to have her recollect the specific circumstances that had been associated with the onset of a particular symptom. When she was able to do this and not only describe the incident but re-experience the original emotions, the symptom disappeared, in some instances never to return again.

With respect to the contracture and anesthesia of her right arm and her inability to speak German, Anna O. recalled the following events under hypnosis.

Near the beginning of her father's illness, while she was still nursing him, she had dropped off to sleep at his bedside only to awaken in a state of considerable anxiety. In a dreamlike state she imagined she saw a black snake coming toward her father to bite him. She tried frantically to ward the snake off, but her right arm, draped over the back of the chair, had gone to sleep; it was "paralyzed" and "anesthetic." When the snake vanished, she tried to pray, but language failed her. At last she thought of some children's verses in English and then found herself able to think and pray in that language. After awhile her "asleep" arm returned to its normal state. Next day, in the course of a game, she threw a quoit into some bushes, and when she went to retrieve it, a bent branch suddenly took on the appearance of the snake, and immediately her right arm became rigidly extended. With the full ventilation of these episodes under hypnosis, Breuer reported that she was able to speak German again, and the contractures in the right arm disappeared.

Breuer emphasized that in her normal state of consciousness Anna O. had no inkling of the incidents and emotions that lay behind her various symptoms; ordinary consciousness had to be circumvented by some procedure such as hypnosis before the troubling memories and emotions could be brought into the open. *Abreaction* and *catharsis* were terms used to refer to this particular form of treatment. (Freud & Breuer, 1895/1966)

Freud's Psychoanalytic Theory

A central idea in Freud's later theory of psychological symptoms is illustrated by the case of Anna O.: Although emotionally distressing past experiences may be put out of one's mind or *repressed,* they can continue in some manner to find expression, in this instance through bodily symptoms and altered states of consciousness. Let us follow Freud in another of his early reports in which, playing detective like his fictional contemporary, Sherlock Holmes, he tracked down the origins of another neurotic symptom, a young woman's "suffocation spells" and provided an additional example of the "imprisoned emotion" theory.

Katharina: A Mountaintop Interview

(From Freud, 1962, pp. 71–82.)

Once when Freud had just reached the top of a 6000-foot mountain while vacationing in the Alps, an 18-year-old girl asked him if he was a doctor. On replying that he was, she immediately began to tell him how she sometimes felt that she was going to suffocate and die and that during these spells she saw an awful but unrecognizable face in front of her. Freud reports the ensuing conversation:

"Do you know what your attacks come from?"

"No."

"When did you first have them?"

"Two years ago, while I was still living on the other mountain with my aunt. But they keep on happening."

Was I to make an attempt at an analysis? . . . Perhaps I might succeed with a simple talk. I should have to try a lucky guess.

So I said, "If you don't know, I'll tell you how I think you got your attacks. At that time, two years ago, you must have seen or heard something that very much embarrassed you, and that you'd much rather have not seen."

"Heavens yes!" she replied, "that was when I caught my uncle with a girl, with Franziska, my cousin."

"What's this story about a girl? Won't you tell me about it?"

"You can say anything to a doctor I suppose. Well, at that time, you know, my uncle—the husband of the aunt—kept the inn. Now they are divorced, and it's my fault they were divorced because it was through me that it came out that he was carrying on with Franziska."

"And how did you discover it?"

"This way. One day two years ago some gentleman had climbed the mountain and asked for something to eat. My aunt wasn't home, and Franziska who always did the cooking was nowhere to be found. And my uncle was not to be found either. We looked everywhere, and at last Alois, the little boy, my cousin, said, 'Why Franziska must be in father's room!' And we both laughed; but we weren't thinking anything bad. Then we went to my uncle's room but found it locked. That seemed strange to me. Then I looked in the window, the room was rather dark, but I saw my uncle and Franziska; he was lying on her."

"Well?"

"I came away from the window at once, and leaned up against the wall and couldn't get my breath back—just what happens to me since. Everything went blank, my eyelids were forced together, and there was a hammering and buzzing in my head."

"Why were you so frightened when you found them together? Did you understand it? Did you know what was going on?"

"Oh no, I didn't understand anything at that time. I was only 16."

"Fraulein Katharina, if you could remember now what was happening in you at that time, when you had your first attack, what you thought about it—it would help you."

"Yes, if I could. But I was so frightened that I forgot everything."

"Tell me Fraulein, can it be that the head you always see when you lose your breath is Franziska's head as you saw it then?"

"Oh no, she didn't look so awful. Besides, it's a man's head."

"Perhaps your uncle's?"

"I didn't see his face as clearly as that."

She then went on to describe how a few days later she had become ill and nauseated. Finally, she reported the incident to her aunt, which eventually led to a separation between her aunt and uncle. Freud continued:

After this, however, to my astonishment, she dropped these threads and began to tell me two sets of older stories, which went back two or three years earlier than the traumatic moment. The first set related to occasions on which the same uncle had made sexual advances to her herself, when she was only fourteen years old. She woke up suddenly "feeling his body" in the bed. When I asked her if she knew what he was trying to do to her, she replied, "Not at the time." It had become clear to her much later on, she said; she had resisted because it was unpleasant to be disturbed in one's sleep and "because it wasn't nice. . . . " She went on to tell me of yet other experiences of a somewhat later date; how she had once again had to defend herself against him in an inn when he was completely drunk, and similar stories. Once the whole family had spent the night in their clothes in a hayloft and she was woken up suddenly by a noise; she thought she noticed that her uncle, who had been lying between her and Franziska, was turning away and that Franziska was just lying down.

At the end of these two sets of memories, she came to a stop. She was like someone transformed. The sulky, unhappy face had grown lively, her eyes were bright, she was lightened and excited. Meanwhile, the understanding of her case had become clear to me. The later part of what she had told me, in an apparently aimless fashion, provided an admirable explanation of her behavior at the scene of the discovery. At that time she had carried about with her two sets of experiences which she remembered but did not understand, and from which she drew no inferences. When she caught sight of the couple in intercourse, she at once established a connection between the new impression and these two sets of recollections; she began to understand them and at the same time to fend them off. There then followed a short period of working out, of "incubation" after which the symptoms of conversion set in, the vomiting as a substitute for moral and physical disgust. This solved the riddle. She had not been disgusted by the sight of the two people, but by the memories which that sight had stirred up in her. And taking everything into account, this could only be the memory of the attempt on her at night when she had "felt her uncle's body."

So when she had finished her confession, I said to her, "I know now what it was that you thought when you looked into that room. You thought: Now he is doing with her what he wanted to do with me that night and those other times. That is what you were disgusted at, because you remember the feeling when you woke up in the night and felt his body."

"It may well be," she replied, "that that was what I was disgusted at and that that was what I thought."

What about the recurrent hallucination of the head, which appeared during her attacks and struck terror into her? Where did it come from? I proceeded to ask her about it, and as though her knowledge too had been extended by our conversation, she promptly replied, "Yes, I know now. The head is my uncle's head. I recognize it now, but not from that time. Later when all the disputes broke out, my uncle gave way to a senseless rage against me. He kept saying that it was all my fault: if I hadn't chattered, it would never had come to divorce. He kept threatening he would do something to me; and if he caught sight of me at a distance his face would get distorted with rage and he would make for me with his hand raised. . . ."

I hope this girl, whose sexual sensibility had been injured at such as early age, derived some benefit from our conversation. I have not see her since.[1]

BASIC FEATURES OF FREUD'S EARLY THEORY

Unconscious Motivation.   In the course of working with many patients, Freud elaborated on the basic theme of unacceptable impulses struggling for and finding expression in various disguises, and thus he evolved the concept of *unconscious motivation*. He used this concept to explain not only hysterical and other symptoms but also all manner of irrational human behavior. There is, in fact, nothing incomprehensible about any human behavior, according to Freud, once we understand the underlying unconscious motivation. All behavior is completely determined. As the following account by Freud indicates, a slip of the tongue, for example, is not a chance mistake, but quite precisely reflects some unconscious conflict.

[1]Thirty-one years after the publication of the study of Katharina, Freud added a footnote to this case in which he revealed that Katharina's uncle was, in fact, her father.

Sigmund Freud (1856-1939), founder of psychoanalysis.

We are told that a lady who was well known for her energy remarked on one occasion: "My husband asked his doctor what diet he ought to follow; but the doctor told him he had no need to diet: He could eat and drink what *I* want." (Freud, 1963, p. 35)

Freud comments:

What we have before us are corrections, additions, or continuations, by means of which a second purpose makes itself felt alongside the first. "My husband can eat and drink what he wants. But as you know, I don't put up with wanting anything at all, so he can eat and drink what *I* want." (Freud, 1963, pp. 62–63)

Dreams likewise are not nonsensical collections of images and feelings; they are determined to the last detail by experiences of the recent and remote past, by unconscious motivations and conflicts, and by defensive strategies designed to keep the dreamer unaware of the dream's "true" meaning. Most, perhaps all dreams, according to Freud, include elements of wish-fulfillment.

The Sexual Basis of Psychological Symptoms. As Freud helped patients explore further and further into the hidden and disguised bases of their symptoms, it seemed that inevitably the trail led eventually to a sexual conflict. At first he thought that many, perhaps all, of his patients had actually experienced in childhood some kind of sexual attack or seduction by an adult (as had Katharina), which had caused the sexual conflict and its associated anxiety. Freud soon abandoned this theory and proposed instead that the patient as a young child had *imagined* that such events had taken place and in retrospect was unable to distinguish clearly between what had been wish and fear and what had in fact happened.

Do All Dreams Express an Unconscious Wish? Freud Says Yes

The patient, who was a young girl, began thus: "As you will remember, my sister has only one boy left now—Karl; she lost his elder brother, Otto, while I was still living with her. Otto was my favourite; I more or less brought him up. I'm fond of the little one too, but of course not nearly so fond as I was of the one who died. Last night, then, I dreamt that I saw Karl lying before me dead. He was lying in his little coffin with his hands folded and with candles all around—in fact just like little Otto, whose death was such a blow to me. Now tell me, what can that mean? You know me. Am I such a wicked person that I can wish my sister to lose the one child she still has? Or does the dream mean that I would rather Karl were dead than Otto whom I was so much fonder of?"

I assured her that this last interpretation was out of the question. And after reflecting a little I was able to give her the correct interpretation of the dream, which she afterwards confirmed. I was able to do so because I was familiar with the whole of the dreamer's previous history.

The girl had early been left an orphan and had been brought up in the house of a much older sister. Among the friends who visited at the house was a man who made a lasting impression on her heart. For a time it had seemed as though her scarcely acknowledged relations with him would lead to marriage; but this happy outcome was brought to nothing by her sister, whose motives were never fully explained. After the breach the man ceased to visit the house; and shortly after the death of little Otto, on to whom she had meanwhile turned her affection, my patient herself set up on her own. She did not succeed, however, in freeing herself from her attachment to her sister's friend. Her pride bade her avoid him; but she was unable to transfer her love to any of the other admirers who presented themselves later. Whenever it was announced that the object of her affections, who was by profession a literary man, was to give a lecture anywhere, she was invariably in the audience; and she took every possible opportunity of seeing him from a

> distance on neutral ground. I remembered that she had told me the day before that the professor was going to a particular concert and that she intended to go to it as well so as to enjoy a glimpse of him once more. That had been on the day before the dream, and the concert was to take place on the day on which she told me the dream. It was therefore easy for me to construct the correct interpretation, and I asked her whether she could think of anything that happened after little Otto's death. She answered at once, "Of course; the professor came to see us again after a long absence, and I saw him once more beside little Otto's coffin." This was exactly what I had expected, and I interpreted the dream in this way: "If now the other boy were to die, the same thing would happen. You would spend the day with your sister and the professor would be certain to come to offer his condolences, so that you would see him again under the same conditions as the other time. The dream means no more than your wish to see him once more, a wish which you are inwardly struggling against. I know you have a ticket for today's concert in your pocket. Your dream was a dream of impatience; it anticipated the glimpse you are to have of him today by a few hours." (Freud, 1900/1965, pp. 186–187)

The sexual basis of symptom-producing conflicts remained a cornerstone of Freud's theory and was the feature that provoked the strongest critical reactions not only from the public at large but from his professional colleagues as well. The intensity and, to Freud's mind, the irrationality, of the attacks on him and his theory seemed to prove further the validity of his position. Why would people resist the idea so strongly if the idea were not tapping their own unconscious sexual conflicts?

The Oedipal Conflict. It was not just any sexual conflict that seemed to be at the root of hysterical and other symptoms however; the sexual problem seemed to take a rather special form—the *Oedipal conflict*. In essence, the Oedipal conflict involves a sexual attraction to the opposite-sex parent, accompanied by feelings of competition and antagonism toward the same-sex parent, as in the myth of Oedipus who, unaware of their true identity, slew his father and married his mother. The Oedipal conflict (usually reaching its peak around four to five years of age) has no easy solution for the young child since the child cannot in reality affect a sexual liaison with the opposite-sex parent nor vanquish the competitor, the same-sex parent.

The conflict is further fueled by fantasied elaborations. A boy, for example, may harbor death wishes against his father and in turn begin to imagine that his father will do bodily harm to him as a punishment for his (the boy's) own impulses and feelings. The imagined harm at the hands of his father is likely to take the form of castration, since it is sexual pleasure associated with his penis that is causing all the trouble. The young child of either sex copes with this seemingly insoluble problem by pushing the whole thing—erotic interest in the opposite-sex parent, hostile wishes toward the same-sex parent, and fears of retaliation—out of his or her mind; in short, by *repression*. If children have had to deal with an especially intense Oedipal conflict, they are vulnerable to adolescence and young adulthood, when the sexual drive becomes increasingly intense, to rearousals of the conflict and ineffective repressive defenses. The result can be symptoms of psychological disorders.

ANXIETY AND THE MECHANISMS OF DEFENSE

In Freud's thinking, the motivation to avoid awareness and overt expression of unacceptable impulses came to center around the concept of anxiety, a powerful and unpleasant emotion thought by Freud to have its primitive beginnings in the infant's experience of being overwhelmed by uncontrollable stimulation. As the child grows older, anxiety also begins to serve as a signal that warns of some impending danger. The danger may be internal in the form of some disturbing instinctual impulse that threatens to break into awareness and possibly be expressed in overt behavior, or external such as a perceived threat of loss of love or physical injury from significant people in the child's life. The child then learns various strategies, *defense mechanisms,* to prevent anxiety-arousing impulses from entering awareness or being

CAST OF DREAM

THE MONSTER . . . . . . YOUR FATHER
KIND WOMAN . . . . . . YOUR MOTHER
POLICEMAN . . . . YOUR ANALYST
FIRST STRANGER. . . . YOUR BROTHER
SECOND STRANGER . . YOUR SISTER
LITTLE BOY. . . . . YOU

overtly expressed in ways that might evoke retaliation. *Repression* was the primary defense mechanism in Freud's early writing; it is the unconscious but intentional forgetting of memories associated with anxiety-arousing impulses and conflicts. Katharina, for example, had repressed aspects of memories of earlier episodes in which her "uncle" had molested her sexually and she had especially repressed the connection of these episodes to her current attacks. In time Freud expanded the concept of defense to include several other mechanisms in addition to the more basic one of repression.

Reaction formation represents an extension of the basic repressive strategy. In this defense people take the additional step of believing and acting as though they were motivated to do just the opposite of the unacceptable impulse: A man behaves in a kindly, considerate fashion when in fact he has an impulse to be mean, sadistic, or cruel; a woman is excessively neat, clean, and orderly when underneath she wants to be messy and dirty; a person conducts a crusade against pornography to control (and indirectly to gratify) unconscious sexual interests. Reaction for-

mations of this kind are likely to become long-standing character traits that color the whole personality.

Isolation refers to isolating a memory or impulse in such a way that it no longer creates anxiety. The most common form this defense takes is the separation of an idea from its associated distressing emotions. The person may become able to think of this idea—but in a cold, emotionless way. An incest wish, for example, may be experienced as an abstract, intellectual idea, bereft of both the attracting and repelling emotions previously associated with it. In *displacement* a disturbing emotion or conflict is transferred from its original source to some less threatening object or situation. A fear of castration might be displaced to a fear of dogs, for example. In *projection* the person disowns some impulse or attitude and projects it onto another person. "It's not I who am filled with a murderous rage against you; it's you who have it in for me." "It's not I who have a homosexual attraction for you; it's you who are making homosexual passes at me." The defensive aim of such a mechanism is clear.

This list of defense mechanisms is not complete.

Displacement.

In fact, there is no one standard list. Different psychoanalytic authors put together various combinations of ways that people defend against unacceptable impulses, reflecting the fact that people indeed use many defensive strategies and any listing is a somewhat arbitrary grouping of common forms.

Psychoanalytic theory has stimulated a certain amount of research, not so much by psychoanalysts themselves as by more research-oriented investigators who have attempted to derive testable hypotheses from the theory. The defense mechanisms have perhaps been the object of most of this research, which on the whole has been unconvincing to psychoanalytic practitioners. They doubt that laboratory studies of this kind have anything to do with the mental mechanisms observed in psychoanalytic treatment. Without surveying all the research in this area let us briefly consider a study by Halpern (1977) that does provide some evidence consistent with the psychoanalytic theory of projection. College student subjects were first divided into a high and low sexual defensiveness group on the basis of a questionnaire,

which tapped such things as denial of sexual fantasies or dreams. Half of the subjects in each of these groups were shown portfolios containing pornographic pictures—an experimental manipulation intended to produce sexual arousal. The other half of the subjects were in a control condition that did not see pornographic pictures. Afterwards all subjects rated themselves and a photograph of another person, previously rated as making an unfavorable impression, on a number of adjectives including the key adjective, *lustful*. As predicted, high-defensive subjects who had been shown the pornographic pictures rated the person in the picture as more lustful than did any other group. The psychoanalytic interpretation of this finding is that the high-defensive subjects were indeed sexually aroused but repressed this arousal from awareness and then projected it onto the person in the photograph. A criticism made of previous studies of projection was that the results could be explained in terms of a simple tendency to attribute your own characteristics to other people— to assume similarity, in other words—and that such attribution need imply no defensive maneuver. That interpretation cannot be readily applied to these data since the self-ratings of lustfulness of the high-defensive subjects who saw the pornographic portfolio were not higher than those for the high-defensive control subjects. The psychoanalytic interpretation is not the only interpretation possible for these results, but there would seem to be no reason at this point not to accept it as one possible formulation—at least until research evidence suggests a more likely or a more parsimonious interpretation.

A THEORY OF THE MIND: THE HIGHER-ORDER ABSTRACTIONS

Psychoanalytic theory is not so much concerned with behavior (what people do) as with what they think and feel, what goes on inside their minds. The basic inquiry of psychoanalysis is: What are the mental events, the *intrapsychic* processes, that help us understand other mental events such as dreams and anxieties? Psychoanalysis thus presumes to be a science of subjective experience.

Up to this point we can see that Freud's theoretical conclusions follow rather reasonably from his clinical observations. This is not to say that they are the only possible interpretations or that everyone would agree with them, but they do not depart radically from what someone else looking at the *same* clinical observations might plausibly conclude. As Freud's theory developed, however, certain aspects became more abstract and less immediately understandable to the uninitiated.

The Libido. One of Freud's most radical notions was that all motivation, other than a few simple physiological drives such as hunger and thirst, arises from the sexual instinct, the *libido*. Many forms of behavior that on the surface seem to have nothing to do with sex he considered *sublimated* expressions of the libidinal instinct. Thus a scientist's curiosity about the workings of nature might be considered to reflect a sexual curiosity that has been redirected to a more socially acceptable and rewarding area of investigation. The motive is "desexualized," changed so that it is no longer recognized as sexual. Sublimation is considered a psychologically healthy mechanism since it allows relatively full expression of the underlying instinctual energy.

Later Freud recognized the death instinct as a second major motivational system, accounting for all destructive behavior, whether people directed it against themselves or others. Not all of Freud's colleagues, however, were willing to accept the existence of an independent death instinct.

Stages of Psychosexual Development. According to the psychoanalytic theory of personality development, the individual progresses through certain biologically determined stages of *psychosexual development* in which the basic sexual instinct or libido seeks gratification via *oral, anal,* and finally *genital* zones of the body. The genital stage can be further subdivided into the *phallic stage,* corresponding to the Oedipal period from ages four to six; the *latency period,* starting with the repression of all sexuality as a way of coping with Oedipal conflict and lasting until adolescence; and then eventually the *adult genital stage,* in which the libido finds expression in a mature heterosexual relationship.

Fixations at and *regressions* to these various stages of development influence later personality traits, including features of abnormal symptomatology. Fixation refers to an undue investment of the sexual instincts at one of these stages of development; for example, oral fixation would tend to involve a continuing interest in oral activities such as the ingestion of liquids and sucking or chewing on objects. An anal fixation might involve excessive interest in messy, dirty activities (because of their symbolic relation to the process of defecation) or in "bathroom" humor. Fixations are thought to occur because the person has been either overindulged or unduly deprived of gratification at a particular stage. If persons are later frustrated or otherwise experience stress at a more "mature" level of psychosexual development, they are likely to regress to the stage at which they had previously become partially fixated. In the face of difficult life circumstances, for example, a person orally fixated might regress to oral sources of satisfaction and eat or drink excessively. Certain constellations of traits in adults thought to derive from these early fixations have come to be known as oral or anal character types. Fixation resulting from over-indulgence at the oral stage, for example, is thought to be associated with naive optimism, dependency, and strong needs for oral gratification. The anal character is commonly thought to show stinginess (related to anal retentiveness), stubbornness (related to opposition to bowel training), and compulsive orderliness and pedantry (reaction formations against urges to be messy and sloppy).

Mental Economics. Freud postulated that each person has a given amount of mental or libidinal energy. If a substantial proportion of this energy is fixated at the oral level, that much less libidinal energy is left over for investment at other levels. If a person's mental energy is being used to defend against unacceptable impulses, that much less energy remains to devote to the other demands of life. This model of *mental economics* sometimes takes the form of an hydraulic analogy in which the libido is likened to a certain amount of water pressure seeking an outlet. If free channels are available by sublimation or direct sexual expression, then the libidinal energy finds an untroubled release. If usual outlets are blocked by defense mechanisms, the pressure of mental energy will be expressed in psychological symptoms or converted to physical symptoms as in hysteria.

According to Freud neurotic symptoms do not result from adult concerns but from reactivated fears of early childhood.

The Structure of the Mind. Freud proposed that the mind could be conceptualized as consisting of three primary parts: the *id,* which is the source of basic instinctual drives seeking immediate gratification; the *ego,* which attempts to mediate between the urgings of the id and the demands of external reality; and the *superego,* an internalized and partially irrational representation of parental or cultural values. The ego, according to Freud, governs such processes as perception, learning, and thinking, whereby the person regulates the commerce between the id's impulses and reality; it also includes those mechanisms of defense already described. The superego was thought to develop primarily in the course of the resolution of the Oedipal conflict when children *incorporate* or *internalize* their irrational perception of the same-sex parent. This internalization is another kind of defense mechanism in which the child *identifies* with the same-sex parent and thereby avoids his or her displeasure—a strategy of "If you can't beat 'em, join 'em." Thereafter, this internalized parental representation becomes a source of praise or condemnation; it becomes, in other words, one's conscience.

CHILDHOOD ORIGINS OF NEUROTIC SYMPTOMS

Neurotic symptoms[1], according to Freud, result from the interplay between instinctual impulses striving for expression and defensive strategies. The key to understanding the strength of the forces involved lies in an appreciation of their early childhood origin. The conflict underlying hysteria, for example, is not between some *adult* sexual urge and some *adult* view of ethics and morality. While this may indeed be a source of conflict and stress, it does not result in the severe incapacitation of neurotic symptoms. Some temptation, rejection, or other stress in the current life situation usually does precipitate the disorder, but its crucial feature is a rearousal of urges, fantasies, and fears from early childhood, a time when loss of parental love or threats of punishment were experienced as catastrophic events. The defenses used to

[1]Freud and his followers used the term neurotic (or psychoneurotic) to broadly encompass the various hysterical, anxiety, phobic, and obsessional symptoms thought to derive from unconscious conflicts.

cope with these reawakened emotions are likewise not adult modes of handling psychological problems but those used by the young child in a desperate attempt to cope with what from a child's view are matters of emotional life or death.

Variations in Psychodynamic Approaches

As with any movement, whether intellectual, political, or religious, in which individuals propound points of view radically different from the prevailing beliefs, a band of followers developed around Freud devoted to protecting the embryonic psychoanalytic movement from the attacks of the establishment. And just as inevitably, there emerged splinter groups and individuals who disagreed with the developing orthodoxy of psychoanalytic theory. The universal role of sexual conflict in the causation of neurotic disorders was the point on which a number of early adherents began to disagree. Since this proposition was based on interpretations of memories, dreams, and so on provided by patients in the course of treatment, it could not be proved or disproved with any finality. Other analysts began to believe that the productions of their patients could be interpreted differently.

Alfred Adler, for example, came to believe that it was not sexual conflict that lay behind neurotic symptoms but conflicts revolving around needs to dominate or triumph over others. The free associations of his patients seemed always to lead to a central problem in which they were striving to be superior as a way of compensating for underlying feelings of inferiority. Carl G. Jung also doubted that all human motivation could be traced to sexual urges, and he questioned whether all significant personality characteristics were essentially molded in the first five years of life. Jung went on to emphasize the unconscious as an energy source from which positive, creative acts arose as well as lusts and meanness. He also had a strong mystical bent, reflected for example in his theory of the *collective* or *racial unconscious,* the idea that all humanity shares certain racial memories. These common racial memories, according to Jung, are expressed symbolically in the mythologies of all present and past cultures. Both Adler and Jung broke with Freud and developed their own movements, known respectively as *individual psychology* and *analytical psychology.*

In more recent times other individuals have developed their own brands of neo-Freudian theories, most rejecting Freud's exclusively sexual interpretation of human motivation and his overly restrictive view of biologically determined stages of psychosexual development. Instead, neo-Freudians such as Harry Stack Sullivan, Karen Horney, and Erich Fromm put more emphasis on the social environment as a determinant of personality development.

Sullivan, for example, became known for his *interpersonal theory* of psychological disorders, supplementing the Freudian preoccupation with intrapsychic dynamics with an equal concern about who is doing what to whom in the external world of social interaction. Thus, in his approach to treatment, Sullivan paid as much attention to how the patient was interacting with the therapist as he did to free associations, dreams, and other "windows" to the unconscious.

Karen Horney believed that most neurotic disorders could be traced back to a *basic anxiety* that has its origins in early childhood. All children, but especially those who later show symptoms, according to Horney, develop aggressive or hostile impulses toward their parents because of the inevitable frustrations that even the best-intentioned parents impose. If this hostility is intense, it produces strong basic anxiety over the possibility that children may alienate their parents by some hostile or antagonistic expression and thus find themselves deprived of love, their only source of acceptance and nurturance. Growing children, and later adults, engage in all manner of protective maneuvers to ensure that this does not happen. For example, they become overly dependent, submissive, placating, achieving, or competitive.

Not all revisions of Freud's early theories resulted in separate schools or movements. Starting around 1939 and continuing through the forties and fifties, a number of psychologists turned their attention to the ego. With so much attention focused on the unconscious, they felt that ego processes had been neglected. Heinz Hartman (1958), for example, suggested that the infant is born with certain ego-capacities, for learning, perception, memory, and physical movement that continue to develop in the

Alfred Adler (1870-1937) emphasized strivings for superiority as a compensation for feelings of inferiority in accounting for neurotic behavior.

Carl G. Jung (1875-1961) disagreed with Freud's emphasis on the sexual roots of neurotic disorders and expounded the theory of the racial unconscious.

course of the child's interaction with the environment. The new emphasis here is that these ego-functions do not result from conflicts between id impulses and external reality; they are inborn, *autonomous* capacities that ordinarily function in a *conflict-free sphere* of the psyche. Of course, other aspects of the ego (defense mechanisms, for example) do arise from conflicts, and it is possible that those aspects of the ego that were originally conflict-free could become embroiled in intrapsychic struggles resulting in inhibitions of sensation, memory, or physical movement, as in hysterical disorders.

All of the later developments and separatist movements in psychoanalytic thought still retain enough features in common that we can consider them variants of the psychodynamic approach. Most revisionists have continued to stress the importance of early childhood experience and the role of intrapsychic forces in the form of unconscious motives and defense mechanisms. Treatment has continued to focus on helping patients understand the unconscious forces affecting their behavior.

The Psychodynamic Approach: A Critique

How has the psychodynamic approach furthered our understanding of psychological disorders, and what are some of the shortcomings of this approach? I will consider these questions primarily in terms of understanding the nature and development of psychological disorders; the question of the effectiveness of treatment procedures such as psychoanalysis will be deferred to a later chapter.

It makes little sense to ask whether Freud's theory as a whole is correct or not since his work consists not of a single theory but of many theories only loosely tied together. Some are highly specific; others, such as the theory of psychosexual development, encompass wide areas of human behavior; and yet others, such as the tripartite conception of id, ego, and superego, are metaphysical models of the mind. The positive contributions listed below are not so much exact hypotheses which have been definitively supported by research, as they are general areas of investigation that were brought to our attention by Freud and accompanied by a number of plausible hunches that may or may not be vindicated in the future. Also, I will list the contributions only briefly at this point, since I have already provided more detailed descriptions and examples of these ideas in the previous pages.

CONTRIBUTIONS

One of the major contributions of psychoanalysis was its emphasis on the *role of childhood experience.* Over and over again the psychoanalytic writers bring to our attention the possibility that childhood experiences within the family context can contribute to subsequent development of psychological symptoms. Regardless of whether all adult symptoms turn out to be the result of childhood trauma or whether specific stresses such as the Oedipal conflict are always present, the general proposition that the child's experiences within the family in many instances play an important role in determining later psychopathology is accepted by most current investigators.

Another significant idea introduced by Freud is *unconscious motivation.* Seemingly mysterious behavior such as neurotic symptoms, slips of the tongue, and dreams reflect, in part, tendencies or motives of which we are unaware. Aside from theoretical arguments as to how best to theorize about so-called unconscious processes, the phenomenon itself is generally recognized as "real." We owe much to Freud and others for a multitude of examples of the way our behavior can be affected by internal or external events that we cannot specify.

Psychodynamic writers have likewise provided us with a wealth of illustrations and numerous theoretical formulations about the various psychological strategies, the *defense mechanisms,* that people use to minimize distressing anxieties and conflicts. Finally, Freud opened our eyes to the existence of *childhood sexuality* and the role that early conflicts in this area play in some adult disorders.

Karen Horney (1885-1952) stressed social and cultural experiences in personality development.

SHORTCOMINGS

The Data Source. Psychological theories do not spring forth from a vacuum; they develop from and are tested against some kind of observations. How good were the observations or data on which many of the original psychoanalytic theories were based? By current standards of research, not very good. In this discussion I will focus on theories pertaining to the childhood roots of neurotic symptoms. First, the data were almost entirely based on *adult* patients' *memories* of events in the remote past. There was little checking, if any, as to whether the memories of the adults corresponded with the actual fantasies and behavior of the young child. Second, the sample of adults was largely limited to middle- and upper-class Europeans living in the late nineteenth and early twentieth centuries. To generalize from this sample of people to people in general is, at best, risky. Third, although the data obtained in this way were used to construct a theory of psychopathological development, there was no "normal" control group. How, in other words, can we know which of the neurotic adult's memories and early conflicts are specific to people with neurotic symptoms, and which of these memories are present in everybody? We cannot make this distinction without a normal control group.

Fourth, we have to rely on the psychoanalyst's report about what the patient says and does. Psychoanalysis was, and largely still is, a private matter between therapist and patient. Little attention has ever been given to the question of interobserver reliability, the extent to which two observers would agree as to what they saw and heard. The problem of interobserver reliability is further complicated by the fact that what the therapist frequently reports is not a description of what the patient said but an interpretation or inference based on what the patient said. Investigators who have struggled with the problem of interobserver reliability are likely to have serious doubts about the accuracy of one person's unchecked reports. To obtain high interobserver agreement on even relatively simple and objective behaviors frequently takes considerable training. In fact, the evidence suggests that psychoanalysts do not agree at all well when asked to listen to tape-recorded segments of psychoanalytic sessions and make independent judgments about such characteristics as

anxiety, depression, blocking of associations, and ego dysfunction (see Research Report 3-1).

Fifth, there is considerable likelihood that over the course of frequent sessions lasting for several years the therapist will influence what the patient reports. By selectively responding and showing interest, the therapist might unwittingly increase the number of associations and dreams with Oedipal content and then conclude that here is yet another case to support the theory. The possibility of this kind of influence has been demonstrated in a careful analysis by Truax (1966) of tape recordings of a nonpsychoanalytic therapist, Carl Rogers. Rogers clearly responded to certain kinds of expressions on the part of the client and ignored others. As treatment progressed, the frequency of approved responses increased and the ignored verbalizations decreased.

I will conclude our consideration of the adequacy of the data source in psychoanalysis by considering two cases that have long been cited as classic demonstrations of certain psychodynamic phenomena: Anna O., of whom we have already heard, and Little Hans. Anna O. has been referred to in innumerable textbooks, including the present one, as the first ex-

RESEARCH REPORT 3-1 — Interobserver Agreement (Reliability) between Psychoanalysts

How well do psychoanalysts agree on what the patient is expressing or on what intrapsychic events are occurring? Garduk and Haggard (1972) had two psychoanalysts, graduates of the same training institute, listen separately to tape recordings of a series of five-minute periods during psychoanalytic sessions and make ratings on a number of variables considered important in psychoanalytic treatment. These periods were selected to represent the patient's reaction to two kinds of therapist intervention, either an interpretation or a noninterpretive comment. The degree of agreement indicated by the correlations between the two psychoanalytic observers' ratings on the different variables would be considered inadequate for psychological research by most investigators (Table 3-1). Reliability correlations of at least .70 are usually required. In this case the highest correlation was .52. Interobserver agreement for anxiety and ego dysfunctioning, central concepts in this approach, were not above chance levels—the observers could have agreed this well by drawing numbers out of a hat!

Auerback and Luborsky (1968) had experienced psychoanalytic observers rate similar variables after listening to 60 full treatment sessions. Interobserver reliabilities were somewhat higher, ranging from .26 to .70 (median = .46), but still too low for most research purposes.

Where do results of this kind leave us? The next time you read a clinical report (in this book as well as elsewhere) in which the clinician makes interpretive comments about the patient's anxiety or other characteristics, ask yourself whether another observer would have seen the same thing. A science that rests on unreliable observations may be building on shifting sands rather than solid rock.

TABLE 3-1   Interobserver Reliability of Psychoanalysts' Ratings of Psychological Variables during Therapy as Reported by Garduk and Haggard (1972)

1. Anxiety	.11
2. Depression	.32
3. Anger, hostility, aggression	.52
4. Defensive and oppositional associations (denial, repudiation, doubt, hostility to therapist; tries to distort, change subject)	.46
5. Presence of affect	.28
6. Pleasant affect	.21
7. Surprise	.30
8. Ego dysfunctioning (disruption, confusion, inability to function)	.04
9. Symptomatology (alterations or aggravation in symptoms)	.13
10. Communication of conscious material (factual, objective information)	.35
11. Communication of deeper-level material	.23
12. Blocking of associations	.13
13. Understanding and insight	.37
14. Transference-related material	.52

ample of a person with hysterical symptoms being successfully treated by the cathartic method. This case was published in "Studies on Hysteria" in 1895, 13 years after Breuer had seen the patient, and Breuer himself admits that his notes were "incomplete." But more crucially, Ellenberger (1972) has recently described hitherto unknown documents showing that Anna O. (really Bertha Pappenheim), far from having recovered at the end of her treatment with Breuer, remained so disturbed that she was sent immediately to Sanitorium Bellevue in Switzerland where she spent the next four months. Medical reports from the institution indicate that she experienced acute facial neuralgia (pains) that required high dosages of chloral and morphine; she would lose the use of the German language and revert back to English as soon as she put her head on the pillow, and she generally lacked insight into the severity of her nervous condition. This is the same person about whom Breuer made the following concluding statement:

On the last day, by the help of rearranging the room so as to resemble her father's sick room, she reproduced the terrifying hallucination which I have described above and which constituted the root of her whole illness. During the original scene she had only been able to think and pray in English; but immediately after its reproduction she was able to speak German. She was moreover free from the innumerable disturbances which she had previously exhibited.

After this, she left Vienna and traveled for awhile; but it was a considerable time before she regained her mental balance entirely. Since then she has enjoyed complete health. (Freud & Breuer, 1966, pp. 75–76)

The calculated withholding of the additional information about Anna O. from the published case history raises some question about the credibility of Breuer as a source of information. The importance of having data open to inspection by other qualified observers and the reporting of interobserver reliability is dramatically, and somewhat sadly, demonstrated in this case.

Little Hans is another hallmark case in the history of psychoanalysis. The case of four-year-old Hans has long been used to illustrate how intense castration fears accompanying an Oedipal conflict were displaced to a phobic fear of horses (Freud, 1955). Freud, in fact, saw Hans only once near the end of the treatment, which was conducted largely by visits or written correspondence with the father. Wolpe and Rachman (1960) reanalyzed the case of Little Hans from Freud's report and suggested that there were many instances of the father, after extensive discussion with Freud, asking leading questions and putting words in Hans's mouth.

Father: When the horse fell down, did you think of your daddy?
Hans: Perhaps. Yes, it's possible. (p. 51)

Wolpe and Rachman also question the basis of many of Freud's interpretations and suggest that Hans's phobia might well be explained by a simple conditioning process involving a few frightening experiences with horses. Our purpose here is not to assess the relative merits of Freud's versus Wolpe and Rachman's interpretations, but rather to point out that the data source is so questionable as to make it difficult to decide among *any* interpretations.

These various shortcomings in the data source are serious, but in themselves they do not disprove the psychoanalytic theories of symptom development. The observations made by Freud and others have been extremely useful in formulating theories and hypotheses, but for confirmation or rejection of the theories the deficiencies in the data source have to be remedied.

Overgeneralization. I turn now to certain aspects of the theory itself. Some psychoanalytic propositions may be true in individual cases but not true for all cases; in other words, the theory has been overgeneralized. Thus *some* instances of adult neuroses may result from unresolved Oedipal conflicts, or *some* instances of delusions of persecution may result from repressed homosexual impulses, but in neither case is the evidence strong that *all* instances have the same cause. A related problem is that the concepts may be so loosely defined that in a certain sense they are true for everyone. If the Oedipal conflict is interpreted so broadly as to include any feelings of anger, fear, competition, and affection that a child has for parents, then certainly such feelings will be found to some extent in all children and probably more so in children who develop psychological disorders. But a psychoanalytic theory watered down to this extent loses any specific characteristics of its own and says little more than that a history of disturbed family interaction is likely to be associated with symptomatic behavior in adults.

Oversimplified View of Motivation. Explaining almost all human motivation in terms of the libidinal or sexual instinct has been widely criticized, even within the psychoanalytic movement, as a vast oversimplification. The infant and young child show many forms of "motivated" behavior such as curiosity, exploration, and mastery of physical and intellectual skills that few would accept as being simply sublimated sexuality.

Predicting Behavior. Can psychoanalytic theory predict behavior? Generally speaking, psychoanalysts use their theories not to predict what a person will do in the future, but rather to explain why a person has already done something. Most theorizing, then, is *post hoc*. We explain Hans's present fear of horses in terms of a postulated Oedipal conflict and displacement of castration fear. This is an easy kind of theorizing. You avoid the embarrassment of being proved wrong in any decisive way. On the other hand, if you use your theory to set up an experiment in which you predict that something will happen, you have "put your money where your mouth is." In all fairness it must be pointed out that the kind of things we might be interested in predicting from psychoanalytic theory, such as whether certain kinds of early childhood experiences result in the later development of neurotic symptoms, are exceedingly difficult to test in a research framework—by psychoanalysts or anyone else.

A Mentalistic Theory. Psychoanalytic theory by its own choice is primarily a theory of subjective, mental phenomena, which by their very nature are not subject to direct observation by anyone other than the experiencing person. It is not entirely fair, however, to criticize the theory simply because it is a theory of mental events unless you want to say that mental events should never be theorized about. Some do take that position, but after all, mental events (wishes, feelings, images, and countless other unnameable blends of experience) do exist, and why should we not try to develop some theories about these things?

Tentatively accepting the development of mentalistic theories as a legitimate endeavor, we immediately run into severe problems, all of which can be traced to the fact that no observers, psychoanalytic or otherwise, can directly "see" the subject matter except in themselves. The mental events of patients in therapy must always be *inferred* from what they say or from some other observable manifestation such as a facial grimace or a clenched fist. The danger is that the theorist will begin to explain all manner of things in terms of observed intrapsychic events. John is neat because he has an anal fixation. Tom is angry at the policeman because of anger displaced from his father. Such explanations can be circular. How do we know that John has an anal fixation? Because he is neat. Why is John neat? Because he has an anal fixation. This is an exercise in explaining by naming. If we give neatness an important-sounding name like anal fixation, we feel we have explained something, when in fact we may have added little to our understanding. This same problem is encountered by theories of demon possession, which tend to be equally circular. Again, to be fair, the use of some inferred (or hypothetical) process, such as an anal fixation, can be useful if there is a body of theory that describes how it develops or how it is influenced by observable events and if the validity of the theory is checked by predictions about observable behavior. The problem is that it is very easy to begin to assume that the theory is true without bothering with the more laborious experimentation and to explain all manner of things such as neurotic symptoms by recourse to unobserved mental events.

A well-known psychoanalyst, Kenneth Colby (1958), has expressed some of these same points:

The lack of controlled experiment in which essential variables are manipulated or held constant constitutes the greatest weakness of psychoanalysis as a science. We cannot advance through thought only, or through waiting to observe nature's experiments. We must actively try to test out which hypotheses fit the empirical facts. For one reason or another . . . psychoanalysts shy away from testing hypotheses. They seem to believe that if a plausible hypothesis can be formulated, it deserves to be considered an explanatory law or principle. They seldom take the next step of testing out which among many plausible hypotheses can be confirmed or disconfirmed. (pp. 9–10)

In my critique of the psychodynamic approach I have concentrated on the traditional psychoanalytic theories and perhaps, in terms of space at least, have come down a little heavier on shortcomings than on contributions. More contemporary psychodynamic approaches are perhaps less subject to some of these criticisms. The strong suit of the psychoanalytic movement has been the long-term, intensive treatment of the individual person by a procedure that permits, if not direct observation, at least a more persistent and sensitive attempt to infer what is going on inside the head of emotionally disturbed patients than has been realized by most other approaches. The clinical reports of these endeavors have given us a rich storehouse of ideas that have influenced both theory and research in the past and will undoubtedly continue to do so for a long time to come.

Humanistic-Experiential Approaches

Some writers, psychotherapists for the most part, have reacted strongly against the implications of both the organic and the mental illness metaphors as well as the learning or behavioral metaphor to be discussed in the next chapter. These individuals (for example, Frankl, 1969; Mahrer, 1978; May, 1967; Rogers, 1970) have variously called their point of view *humanistic, existential, phenomenological,* and *experiential.* Although by no means totally in accord, these writers tend to agree on a number of points. All, for example, tend to emphasize an experiential or phenomenological approach, terms that refer to the person's subjective experiencings. To understand another person, they say, we need to know what that person is perceiving, feeling, or thinking. To apply some abstract theory to a person's mental processes or behavior, to analyze, whether in terms of id impulses and ego defense mechanisms or some other

Rollo May is well known for his writings on existential psychology. Photograph © 1977 Jill Krementz.

theory, inevitably forces these subjective experiencings into a mold that does not fit. The only way we can truly understand why persons behave as they do is to see and feel the world from the other's vantage point.

To some extent this point of view is antitheoretical, even antiintellectual; it implies that Western civilization in fostering abstract, theoretical thinking has cut us off from direct experience. A related idea is that it is not necessary to reconstruct past history in order to understand a person. Such a reconstruction would inevitably be theoretical in nature and take us away from the immediate here-and-now experiencings of the individual. To look at a human being in the same detached, analytical manner that we view atoms, molecules, or the functioning of the cardiovascular system may be scientific, in a certain sense, but it neglects, they say, the uniquely human quality of the person. The phenomenologically experienced self cannot be broken down into smaller units and analyzed; the proper unit *is* the self.

The concept of free will or free choice plays a central role in the humanistic approach. Both psychoanalytic and behavioral approaches assume that behavior is completely determined, although they disagree on the determining forces. The experientially oriented therapist believes that accepting responsibility for making one's "existential" choices is a key factor in therapy. This emphasis on choice dates back to European philosophers such as Kierkegaard. Kierkegaard maintained that personality is determined by the series of choices each person makes. The crucial decisions are between *inauthentic* and *authentic* existence. In inauthentic choices persons permit themselves to be shaped by the demands and expectations of others; in authentic choices they assume full responsibility for their own fate and existence. Existential anxiety occurs when persons face the prospect of taking responsibility for their own destiny; failure in this endeavor can lead to an existential neurosis according to the proponents of this point of view. A humanistic view, then, sees persons as valued human beings, struggling with the problems of their existence, and free to make their own choices—not as subjects for psycho-*analysis* or for behavior modification.

One point on which there is some disagreement among humanistic writers is the question of whether people are basically good, or bad, or neither. Freud's theory suggests that underneath the veneer of civilized behavior humans harbor strong aggressive, lustful, greedy, and selfish urges that have to be controlled and regulated by the society's internalized representative, the ego. Some humanistic writers such as Abraham Maslow and Carl Rogers argue that people are basically motivated toward self-fulfillment and constructive personality growth. Unfortunate life experiences can, however, warp or sidetrack this fundamental impulse. Other humanistic or existential writers (for example, Binswanger, 1967; May, 1967) conceptualize human nature as neither good nor bad. Mahrer (1978) espousing a humanistic theory of personality and therapy takes the latter position. He proposes that each of us has experiential *potentials,* of which some are conscious and rather directly control our behavior and others exist on a deeper, unconscious level. Some of these experiential potentials may be viewed as good and some as bad from ethical or societal standards, but there is no *one* basic potential that represents either a striving for "good," constructive personality growth or a striving for evil or destructive ends.

What exactly are the metaphors used to explain abnormal behavior in the humanistic framework? One such metaphor deriving from existential philosophy and mentioned previously is that symptoms of mental disorder occur when individuals make too many inauthentic choices and fail to confront the existential anxiety associated with taking responsibility for their own lives. Another, perhaps more common, metaphor is that symptoms occur when persons cut themselves off from their own experiencings. This metaphor is quite similar to the psychodynamic metaphor and perhaps differs primarily in avoiding theorizing about such constructs as id, superego, ego, fixations, and so on.

The Humanistic-Experiential Approach: A Critique

It is useful to be reminded that our subjective experiencings are rich, varied, and in many respects likely to be unique for each of us, and that any theoretical formulation will probably not capture all the nuances of these experiencings. There is also an ethical quality of humaneness that pervades this approach. Adherents of other approaches can be, and frequently are, just as humane, but the humanistic writers have most insistently reminded us that abnormally behaving people are *persons*, not *cases* to be considered only as interesting examples of psychopathology. On the other hand, the humanistic approach has not generated much research that has illuminated the nature of abnormal behavior. This is not surprising in view of the negative views of its adherents toward categorizing, quantifying, and experimenting with human behavior. And although humanistic writers sometimes imply that we are on the verge of some new methodology for studying subjective experience, how can they or anyone ever directly study somebody else's subjective experience—short of some kind of extrasensory, telepathic communication?

Summary

1. The psychodynamic approach explains psychological symptoms in terms of intrapsychic events such as motives, fantasies, and conflicts.

2. Sigmund Freud was largely responsible for the development of the psychodynamic approach to understanding abnormal reactions. As the cases of Anna O. and Katharina illustrate, a key idea in Freud's early theory was that the memories of distressing psychological experiences were repressed but continued to find expression in the form of symptoms such as physical disabilities or anxiety attacks.

3. Puzzling and seemingly irrational behaviors such as slips of the tongue, dreams, and neurotic symptoms become understandable if we discover the unconscious motives determining them.

4. Freud held that conflicts about sexuality, and the Oedipal conflict in particular, play an important role in all neurotic disorders.

5. Mechanisms of defense are used to cope with anxiety-arousing impulses and conflicts. They include: repression, reaction formation, isolation, displacement, and projection.

6. Freud considered that the libido, or sexual instinct, motivates most human behavior with the exception of a few physiological drives such as hunger and thirst. Personality development progresses through certain biologically determined stages of psychosexual development in which the libido seeks gratification via oral, anal, and finally genital zones of the body. Symptoms frequently reflect fixations at and regressions to these earlier stages.

7. There are three primary structures to the mind: ego, id, and supereg.

8. Other investigators differed with Freud and proposed psychodynamic theories of their own. Most of them renounced the idea that sexual conflicts lay behind all neurotic disorders and suggested other factors as being more important. Alfred Adler, for example, emphasized strivings for superiority and Karen Horney gave central importance to a basic anxiety that arose from a conflict between needs for affection and hostility generated by the inevitable frustration of these needs.

9. We are indebted to Freud and his followers for bringing to our attention the importance of early childhood experience in the family context, the phenomena subsumed under unconscious motivation, the various ways that people defend against strong anxiety, and the existence of childhood sexuality.

10. Shortcomings of the psychoanalytic approach include an inadequate data source, over-generalization of propositions such as the role of the Oedipal conflict in most psychological disorders, an oversimplified view of motivation in terms of the libido, difficulty in putting the theory to the test of predicting future behavior, and a general tendency to explain behavior *post hoc* in terms of unobservable psychic mechanisms.

11. Humanistic-experiential approaches emphasize subjective experiencings, avoidance of impersonal, analytical theorizing, the importance of free choices, and valuing people as unique individuals.

Suggested Readings

An excellent comparative discussion of the theories of Freud, Adler, Jung, and other neo-Freudians is found in C. S. Hall and G. Lindzey's *Theories of personality,* 3rd edition (Wiley, 1978). There is, however, no substitute for reading Freud in the original, and to this end both *A general introduction to psychoanalysis* (Liveright, 1919) and *The interpretation of dreams* (Avon, 1965) are good starting points. Another good presentation of psychoanalytic theory is provided by P. S. Holtzman in *Psychoanalysis and psychopathology* (McGraw-Hill, 1970). A critical evaluation of some aspects of psychodynamic theories can be found in A. Bandura's *Principles of behavior modification,* Chapter 1 (Holt, Rinehart and Winston, 1969).

Radical Behaviorism and Social Learning

■ Can we develop an adequate theory of abnormal behavior based only on observable behavior and observable environmental events?

■ What is meant by the social learning approach to understanding abnormal behavior?

■ How is the social learning approach similar to and different from radical behaviorism or the psychodynamic approach?

■ How might the mechanisms of defense (repression, denial, and so forth) be conceived in behaviorial and social learning approaches?

Radical Behaviorism

Only a few years after Freud embarked on the work that was to lead to the psychoanalytic movement, Ivan Pavlov in Leningrad and E. L. Thorndike at Columbia University began their studies of conditioning and learning in animals that were to eventuate in the behavioral approach. It is perhaps no coincidence that the behavioral approach to the study of abnormal behavior began with the study of animals. Dogs, cats, and rats are not likely to engage us with interesting dreams, strange states of consciousness, or slips of the tongue. Their observable behavior is more likely to attract the attention of investigators than the intricacies of their subjective mental functioning.

A *radical behavioral approach* is limited to the study of directly observable behavior. Subjective mental events, whose existence is not necessarily denied, are considered outside the realm of scientific study. Some behaviorists refer to mental events as mere *epiphenomena* that do not themselves cause behavior but are simple side effects. The problems of working with nonobservable events are circumvented by sticking strictly to what investigators can directly observe.

I call this approach "radical" here because I want to distinguish it from other behavioral approaches which make use of unobservable mediating processes in their models. The latter I will refer to as the social learning approach.

PAVLOV AND CLASSICAL CONDITIONING

Around 1900 Ivan Pavlov, a distinguished Rusian physiologist who had won the Nobel Prize for his work on the digestive glands, began his well-known studies of conditioning, using dogs as experimental subjects (Figure 4-1). If meat powder is placed in a dog's mouth, the dog will salivate. Pavlov (1928) discovered that if a stimulus such as a tone, bell, or light that previously had no capacity to produce salivation were paired with the presentation of meat powder on a number of occasions, this stimulus would in time elicit salivation even when no meat powder was provided. In other words, the dog had learned something new, to salivate to a bell. Pavlov called this learning process *conditioning,* and he developed a terminology for the component features: The meat powder was called the *unconditioned stimulus;* salivation produced by the meat powder was called the *unconditioned response;* the neutral stimulus (such as a bell or light) was called the *conditioned stimulus;* and the response of salivation to the conditioned stimulus

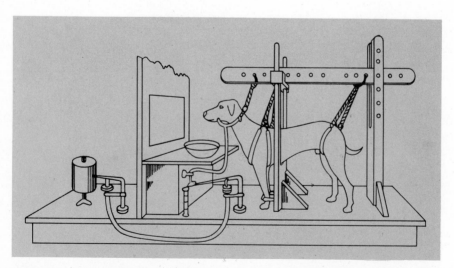

FIGURE 4-1. An apparatus similar to that used by Pavlov to study classical conditioning in dogs. (From *An Introduction to Psychology,* by Ralph Norman Haber and Aharon H. Fried, 1975. Copyright © by Holt, Rinehart and Winston. Reproduced by permission.)

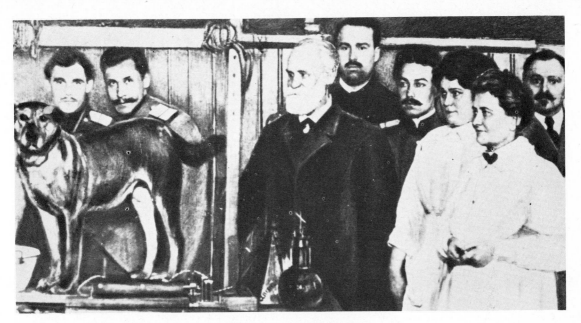

Ivan Pavlov and colleagues with one of the dogs used in his experiments.

was called the *conditioned response*. This kind of conditioning has come to be known as *classical conditioning* to distinguish it from *instrumental* or *operant conditioning,* to be discussed shortly.

Quantitative studies showed that conditioning followed a regular pattern. For example, if one plotted the number of times a dog salivated in response to the bell, the curve would look like that in Figure 4-2. Furthermore, if the experimenter stopped giving meat powder in association with the bell signal, the dog would gradually stop salivating, until after a while the bell would no longer elicit salivation (Figure 4-2). The procedure of withholding the unconditioned stimulus was called *extinction*.

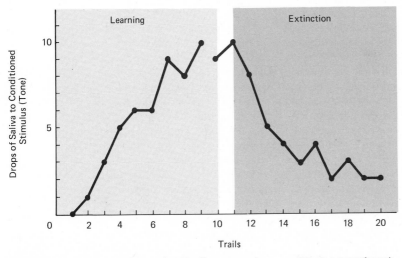

FIGURE 4-2. Typical learning and extinction curves in a conditioning experiment.

Although Pavlov and later J. B. Watson in this country were inclined to explain all of human learning in terms of the classical conditioning model, most investigators have felt such an extension was unwarranted. This model seems to account best for the learning of relatively simple reflexes: salivation and other digestive processes, such as acid secretion in the stomach; protective responses such as the eyeblink; and perhaps physical concomitants of strong emotion, especially fear. The last immediately suggests that classical conditioning may influence the development of irrational fears.

With Albert, a one-year-old infant, Watson and Rayner (1920) conducted a study that has long been cited in textbooks as a demonstration of the conditionability of fear in humans. Albert was described as an unusually healthy and unemotional child. Before conditioning he had been shown an array of objects, most of them furry, such as a white rat, a rabbit, a dog, and cotton. He showed no signs of fear in their presence.

As a fear-inducing unconditioned stimulus, the investigators used an unexpected loud noise produced by striking a steel bar closely behind the infant. In the first session the bar was struck on two occasions when Albert reached out to touch a white rat. A week later, five more paired presentations of rat and noise were given. On the eighth trial the rat alone was presented and Albert immediately began to cry and to crawl away rapidly. Five days later he was tested for *generalization* of the fear response. He played as usual with wooden blocks, showing no signs of fear. When the rabbit was put in front of him he responded at once, leaning as far away from the animal as possible, whimpering, and finally bursting into tears. Albert showed similar though not as strong reactions to the dog, cotton, and other furry objects. Thus Albert acquired a phobic fear of white rats and related furry objects by a simple conditioning process. Bregman (1934) was somewhat less successful in conditioning fear in 15 infants with a loud bell, but she used a different type of conditioned stimulus (geometrically shaped wooden blocks, for example) than the animal stimulus used by Watson and Rayner. There are ethical limitations to the experimental study of fear in human subjects and by contemporary standards, Watson and Rayner's study would be unacceptable.

In a more recent experiment, Campbell et al. (1964) used drug-induced respiratory paralysis with voluntary subjects. They found that with just one pairing of this horrific experience with a tone, indications of fear such as palmar sweating and change in heart rate became conditioned to the tone and showed no signs of extinguishing over a three-week period and 100 presentations of the tone by itself.

There is much indirect and anecdotal evidence to suggest that fear responses do indeed become associated with previously neutral stimuli on the basis of a few fear-arousing experiences. Some young children's reactions to the white-coated doctor from whom they have received shots on previous occasions are well known to many parents. Individuals who develop intense fear about riding on trains, cars, or motorcycles after having experienced one accident are other examples. It seems likely, then, that some fears can be learned by classical conditioning. You may recall from Chapter 3 that Wolpe and Rachman suggested that little Hans's fear of horses was learned in this way as the result of a few pairings of strong fear with horses. A word of caution should be given, however. Although we may conclude that fear *can* be learned by classical conditioning, it does not mean that all or even most fears are necessarily learned that way.

THORNDIKE, SKINNER, AND OPERANT LEARNING

In the late 1890s E. L. Thorndike began studying the process whereby animals learned to escape from a "puzzle box." Hungry cats, for example, when placed in the box, learned by trial and error to operate a latch that opened a door through which they could escape to get food. The cats slowly became more adept at the required response, taking less and less time to get out of the puzzle box on succeeding trials. On the basis of additional research of this kind, Thorndike (1911) formulated the "law of effect": When a behavior is followed by a satisfying consequence it is more likely to be repeated; when followed by a punishing or annoying consequence, it is less likely to recur. In other words, whether a given behavior is strengthened or weakened depends upon its consequences or effects.

In recent times, B. F. Skinner has been the most consistent exponent of a more radical behavioral ap-

B. F. Skinner, a strong advocate of radical behaviorism.

ing whether a given consequence will, in fact, be reinforcing for a given individual, but this does not matter for Skinner's theory. If a given consequence increases the probability of subsequent behavior, it is reinforcing; if not, it is not reinforcing. Painful or noxious consequences are not, strictly speaking, reinforcing, but any decrease or escape from noxious consequences would be reinforcing.

Another important concept in the operant learning model is the *discriminative stimulus*. What the organism learns is not just to make a response but to make it only under certain circumstances. A child learns to ask for a cookie *only when an adult is present;* making this response under other circumstances is not reinforced. The setting or situation signaling that a response is likely to produce a reinforcement is called a discriminative stimulus.

OPERANT LEARNING AND ABNORMAL BEHAVIOR

Skinner himself has not worked especially in the area of abnormal behavior, but many other investigators have used the operant model as a way of understanding the development of abnormal reactions

proach. In his book, *The Behavior of Organisms* (1938), he recognized two basic learning processes: classical conditioning and *operant conditioning*. The latter was similar to Thorndike's "law of effect," but it was restated in certain respects, especially to eliminate any hint of subjective experience such as might be implied in Thorndike's use of a word such as *satisfier*.

The essence of operant conditioning (or learning) is that the organism learns to make a response that *operates* on the environment so as to produce some consequence favorable to the organism. Skinner and others have used the term *reinforcer* to refer to a consequence that strengthens or increases the likelihood that a response will be repeated. Some consequences are almost universally reinforcing: water when thirsty, food when hungry, sleep when tired, and sex after deprivation. These biologically oriented consequences are called *primary reinforcers*. Other reinforcers, however, such as money, praise, and social status, are learned, and these are usually called *secondary reinforcers*. There is no sure way of know-

Reinforcement can take many forms: for example, food, a smile, and verbal indications of approval.

and as a basis for devising treatment or *behavior modification* procedures. Their basic assumption is that abnormal behavior is learned because it produces reinforcing consequences, so it should be subject to unlearning if the consequences are appropriately changed. Thus, from this point of view, children may develop strong and recurrent temper tantrums because such behavior is reinforced by parental attention or giving in to the child's demands. A depressed person who expresses feelings of worthlessness and preoccupation with physical complaints is reinforced because his family comforts him at these times. A child talks in vague, confused, and "crazy" ways because her parents become upset if she talks clearly and directly to them about areas of conflict. She avoids their distress by talking "crazy" (as they

may well do themselves) and is thus reinforced for developing abnormal behavior patterns.

The most impressive demonstrations of the power of external consequences to influence our behavior are experimental studies in which the investigator changes the consequences in such a way that old behavior is eliminated and new behavior is instituted. In a *reversal* design, the experimenter subsequently reinstates the original consequences and observes whether or not the former behavior returns. Then the new consequences are put into effect a second time to see whether the new behavior again replaces the old behavior. It is hard to argue with data of this kind; different external consequences clearly have led to different behavior. A reversal design is illustrated in the following clinical report.

Ann's Shyness Is Modified by Changing Consequences

Ann was a four-year-old girl who had become more and more isolated from the other children in her preschool, showing an increasing preference for interaction with the adult teachers. As time went by she spent an even greater proportion of her time simply standing and looking. Mild, ticlike behaviors such as picking her lower lip, pulling a strand of hair, or fingering her cheek also developed. Careful observation of Ann's behavior indicated that she was using many techniques for gaining and prolonging the attention of adults, and that most adult attention was contingent upon (was a consequence of) behaviors that were incompatible with playing with peers.

An intervention program was instituted in which Ann now received adult attention as a consequence of play with another child. This attention, of course, had to be given in such a way that it did not draw her away from her interaction with the other children. No adult attention was given for isolate behavior or in response to bids for interaction with adults. Almost immediately after these new consequences were introduced, Ann's play with other children increased dramatically and her interactions with adults decreased (Figure 4-3).

After five days of the new consequences the procedure was reversed. The teachers responded as they had originally, giving attention when Ann was showing isolate behavior or interacting with adults. Ann's peer interaction quickly dropped to its previous level. After five more days the new consequences were once more provided, again with immediate effects on Ann's behavior.

During the last days of the second reversal period, the teachers gave increasingly intermittent (nonsystematic) attention for interaction with other children. Many laboratory studies have shown that such intermittent or partial reinforcement increases the resistance to extinction of newly learned responses. No systematic attempt was made to maintain the program after the twenty-fifth day. On days 31, 38, 40, and 51 checks of Ann's behavior indicated that her new rate of interaction with peers was holding up moderately well. Perhaps enjoyable play with other children had come to serve increasingly as reinforcement in its own right for nonisolate behavior.

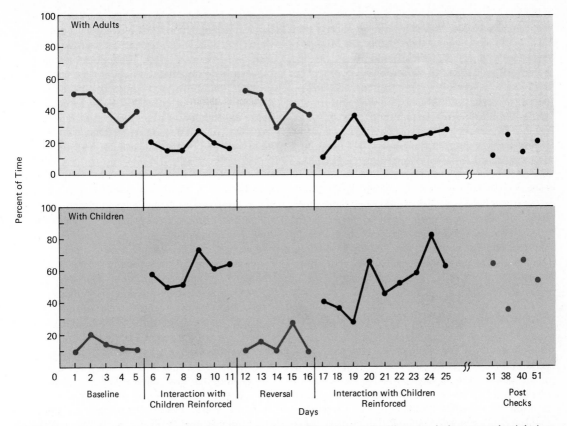

FIGURE 4-3. Percent of time Ann spent in social interaction with adults and with peers during approximately two hours of each morning session. (Adapted from Allen, Hart, Buell, Harris, & Wolf, 1965. Originally published in *Child Development*, 1964, *35*, 511–518. Copyright 1964 by the Society for Research in Child Development.)

REACTION TO THE ILLNESS MODEL

As indicated in the previous chapter the psychodynamic approach reflects an illness metaphor of abnormal behavior in which symptoms are seen to result from a "disease" or pathology of mental processes such as repressed conflicts. An illness model (sometimes referred to as a medical model) clearly implies that treating the symptom without identifying and treating the underlying cause is not likely to be successful, any more than treating a fever and ignoring the underlying infection.

Radical behaviorists argue that it is inappropriate to apply the illness metaphor to abnormal behaviors. These behaviors have been learned as the result of a history of reinforcement and can be unlearned if

reinforcement contingencies are changed. There is no need to stigmatize a person with a disease label; furthermore, the illness model's implication of some "underlying cause" tends to divert the clinician's time and energy from the environmental contingencies that are maintaining the abnormal behavior. The behavioral orientation with respect to psychological disturbances can be seen, in part, then as a reaction against the illness or disease model.

RADICAL BEHAVIORISM: A SUMMARY

To understand the nature of abnormal behavior from the radical behavioristic point of view, first we must define the abnormality in terms of observable behavior: "John *avoids* small enclosed spaces and his *heart beats faster* when he cannot escape from such a situation," rather than "John has *feelings* of anxiety resulting from *repressed* conflicts." Second, behaviorists examine the external environment for the factors responsible for the learning and maintenance of abnormal behavior, usually in terms of some combination of classical and operant conditioning: What reinforcing consequences have determined what responses the person will make in a given situation? What emotional responses such as fear have been paired with what conditioned stimuli to produce conditioned emotional reactions? And, of course, to change abnormal behavior, behaviorists focus on changing environmental contingencies so that new and less abnormal behavior can replace the old behavior. They are not concerned with trying to identify and change underlying intrapsychic processes.

RADICAL BEHAVIORISM: A CRITIQUE

Contributions.   Many of the contributions of radical behaviorism are counterpoints to the shortcomings of the psychodynamic approach. By concentrating on observable behavior and its relation to observable environmental events (contingencies of reinforcement and discriminative stimuli) behaviorists avoid untestable, post hoc, and circular explanations. The scientific tradition from which the behavioral approach comes provides it with a methodology of data collection far superior to the usual clinical report. Behaviorists are much more likely to appreciate the importance of clear specification and direct observation of the behavior being examined, interobserver reliability, problems of sampling and generalization, control groups, and observer influence on the person being studied.

Accountability, a term heard frequently these days with respect to government and business, is a central feature of the behavioral orientation. Its theory and methodology can be held to account for any predictions made. Perhaps the most positive thing that can be said about a psychological theory is that it is subject to disproof. If we hypothesize that changing the reinforcement consequences associated with Ann's behavior will cause her to become less isolated from her preschool playmates, and then implement these

changes, the data subsequently obtained will either support or not support this hypothesis. If it does not, we are forced to reconsider the theory (assuming that there is no serious question about the adequacy of the experimental methodology). There is, then, a healthy "show me" attitude in the behavioral approach. One is not going to believe something because an authority (Freud, Skinner, or anyone else) said it was so, but because research findings that can be reproduced by other investigators say it is so.

Shortcomings.   Radical behaviorism goes too far in excluding from its theory *mediating* processes between environmental events (stimuli) and responses of the organism. No one seriously disputes the existence of mediating processes, such as thoughts and wishes conceived either in physiological or psychological terms. The argument essentially is over whether it is useful to incorporate them into theories. As we have seen, there are dangers in theorizing too freely about unobservable events, but perhaps we lose a bit of the baby with the bathwater when we throw them out altogether. People do have thoughts. We have, for example, expectations that we will be praised if we do this and criticized if we do that. Thoughts of this kind may well influence our behavior. We also have images; an imaginary scene in which we make some social blunder may produce a measurable change in emotional response, or an erotic fantasy can produce yet another kind of measurable response. It is ironic that one of the best-researched methods of behavioral therapy, a form of *counterconditioning*, makes use of *imagined* scenes (what could be more mentalistic?) as a key feature in the therapeutic procedure.

Psychodynamic clinicians argue that behavioral theories about the nature of psychopathology are superficial because they ignore underlying causative factors and attend only to symptoms, the observable behavior. A radical behavioral approach that avoids any consideration of mediating processes is vulnerable to this criticism. Joseph Wolpe, a prominent behavioral therapist, provides an example of how a strict behavioral approach may be misleading and miss the "real" problem. A man with a fear of small spaces (claustrophobia) had been treated for 20 sessions without much benefit by a counterconditioning therapist who assumed that the anxiety was elicited by the stimuli associated with small spaces. Upon further discussion of the person's fears, however, the therapist discovered that what the person was really afraid of was dying. *Thoughts* about dying were the critical stimuli for his fear, not the external stimuli of small spaces. The general point here is that radical behaviorism unduly ignores mediating processes, which in all likelihood play an important role in the development and treatment of abnormal reactions.

A final shortcoming is that the scientific respectability accorded the behavioral approach may not always be justified. Although I previously said that in the behavioral approach there is less danger of indulging in post hoc explanations based on unobservable intrapsychic processes, this statement should be qualified. Terms such as *reinforcement, conditioned stimulus*, and *discriminative stimulus* have exact meanings in laboratory experiments, but when transferred to the "real world" to explain abnormal behavior, much of this precision can be lost. "Explanations" using this terminology can be just as post hoc and circular as those based on intrapsychic processes with the added danger that they may successfully hide behind the trappings of the scientific jargon. The advantage of the behavioral formulations, that they more readily suggest testable hypotheses, is not realized unless the appropriate experiments are conducted.

In sum, then, the primary contributions of the radical behavioral approach have been its avoidance of unverifiable explanations in terms of intrapsychic events and its insistence on research accountability. The disadvantages have been in going too far in denying the utility of mediating processes and occasionally in pretending to a scientific respectability in clinical work that is not yet justified. I will consider some of these issues again when I compare the behavioral and psychodynamic approaches to treatment.

Social Learning

The ways that mediating processes are used to explain abnormal behavior lie along a continuum with an extreme intrapsychic orientation at one end and an extreme behavioral emphasis at the other end (Figure 4-4). Few clinicians and researchers actually subscribe to such extreme positions. The dimensional representation, however, helps make clear that

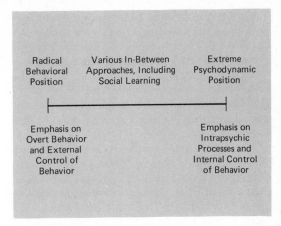

FIGURE 4-4. The radical behavioral and psychodynamic views as endpoints on a continuum.

we do not have to make an either-or choice. There are many ways to combine judicious use of mediating constructs with a continuing concern about specifying how these constructs are related to environmental events and observed responses, and checking such theoretically derived predictions with research. The term *social learning* will be used to refer to one broad class of theories about abnormal behavior that falls in this middle region. It should be clear, however, that the term is not being used to refer to a specific theory about psychopathology but rather to a general approach that encompasses many variations.

MEDIATING PROCESSES

One way of moving away from a radical behavioral position is to keep the basic models of classical conditioning and operant learning but to accept internal events as possible *controlling stimuli* and also as possible sources of *self-reinforcement*. Internal stimuli can arise from many sources: drive states such as hunger, thirst, fatigue, or sex; emotional reactions such as fear, anger, disgust, or grief; or mental events such as thoughts, verbalizations, and images. Research has strongly supported the idea that internal stimuli such as these can serve as conditioned or discriminative stimuli.

Miller (1951), for example, showed many years ago that a palmar sweating response could become conditioned to just thinking the letter *T*. May (1967) found that subjects who had intense irrational fears of nonpoisonous snakes showed greater heart rate increases and respiratory changes when just thinking about snakes than when thinking about other things.

Almost any kind of mediating stimulus can become associated with abnormal behavior, but of special importance are the conceptions persons develop about themselves and the interpretations they make of external events. A paranoid *belief* that others are plotting against you would surely affect your behavior. Bandura (1977) has emphasized expectations of lack of personal efficacy as being central to the development of many forms of psychopathology. The person has learned to expect to fail, become confused, be afraid, or be ineffective in other ways. Depressed persons, in this view, have learned to view themselves as ineffective and unworthy.

Most social learning theorists emphasize that these internal stimuli originally acquire their controlling power on the basis of external learning contingencies. Thus in Miller's experiment, thinking the letter *T* became a controlling stimulus for palmar sweating because previously there had been a pairing of an *externally* applied electric shock to the presentation of this letter. Similarly, it is assumed that past environmental events created a state of mind in which erroneous beliefs were likely to develop in the paranoid person. In both cases, however, the control later passed to cognitive processes.

Perhaps for many students I am belaboring the obvious, since the control of behavior by internal processes such as thoughts and images seems self-evident. The problem, of course, is how to incorporate this "obvious" fact into theories of psychopathology without falling into the difficulties that plague the more extreme psychodynamic approach. Social learning investigators have made a reasonable start.

So far I have been emphasizing internal stimuli that control behavior in the way that external conditioned or discriminative stimuli do. Internal consequences can also provide reinforcement for behavior in the same way as external consequences. This process is usually called *self-reinforcement*. It has been amply demonstrated that external social responses of approval ("Good!" "That's fine," a pat on the back, and so on) can serve as powerful reinforcers for most people. It has also been shown that persons can administer these consequences to themselves, thus reinforcing their own behavior. More still needs to be learned about the original external learning conditions, probably in early childhood, that make self-reinforcers effective, but it is clear that by six or seven years of age most children have already acquired the capacity to give themselves mental approval or disapproval and thus to control their own behavior to some extent. Self-reinforcement need not always be internal. Persons can reward themselves externally as well—for example, by permitting themselves to have a snack after they have studied for two hours. The basic point is that the reinforcers are given by persons to themselves. Self-control of this kind is clearly related to what in other contexts is called conscience or superego.

Albert Bandura has made major contributions to our understanding of the role of social learning in the development and treatment of abnormal behaviors. His work on observational learning has been especially outstanding.

OBSERVATIONAL LEARNING

One learning process that is not easily explained by either the classical conditioning or operant learning model is *observational learning*. It has been well demonstrated that both animals and humans can learn a novel response (one not likely to have been made before) after merely being allowed to observe another animal or person making the response. Both the classical conditioning and operant models require that the organism make a response in order for it to become associated with a conditioned stimulus or to be reinforced. But no overt response is made in observational learning; the subject only looks or listens! Nevertheless, it can be shown that after observing a model repeatedly making a response, an observer is more likely to make the same response than a subject who has not observed the model.

How can we explain observational learning? Albert Bandura (1977) has suggested that the observer makes a mental representation of the response, either as visual imagery or as words, and that later under appropriate circumstances this mental representation is translated into behavior. However it works, observational learning clearly exists and in all likelihood it plays an extremely important role in social development. Experimental studies with children, for example, have shown that distinctive features of aggressive behavior, standards of self-reinforcement and self-evaluation, the delay of immediate gratification for long-term gain, and language acquisition can all be powerfully influenced by observing these responses being modeled (see, for example, Bandura, 1969).

Various factors affect the extent to which an observed response is learned or subsequently performed. Assuming that the observer pays attention to the model, the likelihood of the observer performing the modeled response is increased if (1) the model is rewarded for making the response and (2) the model is a person of some importance in the observer's life, someone who controls important resources, as would be the case with a parent. In such social learning both observational and operant effects are involved. Thus a four-year-old boy who observes an older brother roughhousing and wrestling with another child is apt to engage in play of this same sort himself and to be reinforced by the fun of the interaction and his father's approval. A four-year-old girl observing the same behavior and subsequently trying it herself might be admonished by both parents to be more ladylike. The consequences increase the strength of the response in one case and decrease it in the other. Observational learning, then, is an ef-

Children imitate parents.

ficient way to learn completely new and novel responses, much better than trial-and-error operant learning. However, the extent to which the response becomes strongly incorporated in the person's behavior depends upon the rewarding and punishing consequences that follow it.

Observational learning can, of course, be involved in the development of abnormal reactions. Fears and phobias, for example, may be influenced by behavior we observe. Jones (1924) reports the following anecdote in her study of fears in young children.

Vincent showed no fear of the rabbit, even when it was pushed against his hands or face. His only response was to laugh and reach for the rabbit's fur. On the same day, he was taken into the pen with Rose, who cried at the sight of the rabbit. Vincent immediately developed a fear response; in the ordinary playroom situation he would pay no attention to her crying, but in connection with the rabbit, her distress had a marked suggestion value. The fear transferred in this way persisted for over two weeks. (pp. 389–390)

Vincent's sudden development of fear in all like-lihood was based on his observation of Rose's fear. It is a reasonable hypothesis that observational learn-ing plays an important role in the development of many forms of psychopathology: fragmented and highly personalized speech, hysterical symptoms, an-tisocial behavior, and drug abuse, to name a few. Recall the contagion of "hysterical" writhing and screaming in the young girls of Salem that followed their observation of Betty, the first girl to show the symptoms. How much of the dance mania (St. Vitus' dance) in the Middle Ages was transmitted by obser-vational learning?

Observational learning may be used, not only to induce, but also to relieve, fear. Bandura et al. (1967a), for example, assigned children between the ages of three and five who had a strong fear of dogs to one of four groups. In eight brief sessions, one group observed another child (the model) show pro-gressively greater degrees of approach and handling of the dog without fear. A second group observed the dog, but no model, in a highly positive party con-text, and a third group was never exposed to either the dog or the modeled fearlessness. Ability to ap-proach and pet the dog increased significantly more in the modeling condition than in either of the other two conditions, and these differences remained a month later when the children were tested with a dif-ferent dog. Extinction of fear by this vicarious obser-vational procedure has obvious implications for the treatment of more severe phobias; I will return to this possibility again in later chapters.

A SOCIAL LEARNING APPROACH TO ANXIETY AND DEFENSE[1]

I have shown how the social learning approach incorporates mediating variables in the form of con-trolling stimuli and self-reinforcers and also how it has added observational learning to the classical con-ditioning and operant learning models. Let us turn now to a consideration of how this approach can be applied to the study of anxiety and defense, notions that originally derived from the psychoanalytic ap-proach.

[1]The material in this section is based, in part, on Martin (1971, 1973).

As a response that is susceptible to learning, fear can be treated like any other response and studied in terms of classical conditioning, operant learning, and observational learning. I will postpone to a later chapter a more detailed consideration of fear or anx-iety (no distinction will be made between the two at this point) and assume for our present purposes that everyone would agree that intense fear is an ex-tremely unpleasant emotion, to be avoided if at all possible. From a social learning point of view, most defense mechanisms (repression, displacement, pro-jection, and so on) are learned behavior patterns by which we try to avoid or escape circumstances that produce fear or anxiety.

This kind of learning, known as *avoidance* or *es-cape learning,* has the following characteristics: If per-sons are exposed to some intensely unpleasant stim-ulation (such as pain, extreme heat or cold, or acute fear) they will usually learn to make some response that will reduce the unpleasant stimulation or permit them to *escape* it entirely. When such a response is made, it is reinforced by the cessation of the aversive stimulation. In many instances the person may even-tually learn to *avoid* the unpleasant experience alto-gether by making an avoidance response before the unpleasant stimulation begins. This is the essence of the avoidance learning paradigm.

A study by Solomon et al. (1953) illustrates the processes involved in avoidance learning. The ex-perimenters placed dogs individually in a box with two compartments separated by a gate. When a light over the compartment in which the dog was located was turned off, it was a signal (discriminative stimu-lus) that a painful electric shock would be applied through the metal grid floor in 10 seconds. The light stayed off until the dog jumped over the gate into the other compartment, where there was at this time no shock. After a while the light would go off in the sec-ond compartment, signaling that shock would be forthcoming in 10 seconds, and the dog would have to jump back into the other compartment within 10 seconds in order to avoid the shock. The dogs learned these contingencies by trial and error, and of course in the early trials they were not always able to avoid the shock. Fairly soon, however, the dogs learned to avoid the shocks entirely by shuttling back and forth between the compartments when signaled by the light going off.

An important characteristic of avoidance learning

based on an intensely unpleasant experience is that the learned response tends to be very resistant to extinction. The dogs in this study showed no tendency to stop making the avoidance response after 200 extinction trials. (No shocks were given no matter how long the dog remained in a compartment.) One dog was still going strong after 490 extinction trials, when the behavior of the experimenters themselves finally reached extinction and they discontinued the trials! On one measure of performance, the duration of time between the light going off and the dog's jumping, the experimenters found that the dogs were actually responding more quickly after 200 extinction trials than they had been when extinction began!

The strength of the avoidance response was further demonstrated in a second experiment in the same study. Nine dogs were trained by the same procedure. After the 200 extinction trials a glass barrier that prevented jumping was interposed between compartments on four of the ten trials for ten straight days. The dogs were thus forced to remain in the compartment and to observe that shock was no longer forthcoming. Seven of the nine dogs failed to show extinction in 100 trials given under this condition.

In a third experiment the experimenters gave 13 dogs similar initial training and then shocked them for 3 seconds for jumping into the other compartment, the previously learned avoidance response. Of the 13 dogs, 10 failed to reach extinction in 100 shock-extinction trials of this kind. In fact, the dogs tended to jump faster after shock extinction was introduced than before. In a paradoxical way, shock or punishment for the response seemed to strengthen it! In a fourth experiment, the researchers used a combination of glass barrier and shock extinction with dogs whose response had not extinguished under the conditions in the previous experiments. With this combined procedure the dogs finally stopped making the avoidance response after about seven days.

Learning theorists are not in full agreement as to how to explain the extreme persistence that learned avoidance responses frequently show. A common view is to consider avoidance learning to be based on two processes: classical conditioning of a strong fear response to the general situation and especially to the discriminative stimulus or signal, and the op-

erant learning of a response that avoids the aversive experience (Mowrer, 1950). In the case of the dogs in the Solomon et al. study, this theory would assume that after a number of trials the light going off has come to serve as a conditioned stimulus that elicits fear. When the dog leaves the compartment by jumping the gate, it removes itself from this conditioned stimulus and thereby reduces the fear. Fear reduction, then, occurs as a consequence of jumping and reinforces that response. Since the dog learns to jump immediately after the conditioned stimulus (light going off) is presented, there is little opportunity for the conditioned fear to extinguish, and the dog keeps on jumping almost indefinitely. Levis and Boyd (1979) have provided more recent evidence from animal experimentation that supports this interpretation. Other theorists, however, have proposed alternative explanations for the observed resistance to extinction of learned avoidance responses (see Mineka, 1979, for a review). The important point for our purposes is that avoidance learning based on strong fear produces exceptionally persistent responses.

The relevance of the avoidance learning paradigm to the study of abnormal behavior becomes clear when we note that most of the defense mechanisms discussed in the section on psychodynamic approaches can be considered forms of learned avoidance responses. A dog jumping over a gate may seem a long way from Anna O. not remembering a distressing episode at her father's bedside, but in principle the learning process may be similar. If we admit covert responses into our theorizing, then jumping over a gate or turning thoughts away from a disturbing memory can both be seen as ways of avoiding emotional distress. And if the original distress was intense, we would expect that in both cases the learned response would be very resistant to change. Let us consider how certain defensive strategies, both overt and covert, arise according to the social learning approach.

Physical Avoidance. One defense strategy persons might adopt is physically to avoid situations they find anxiety-arousing or otherwise distressing, as in phobias: for example, making public speeches, riding in airplanes, attending social gatherings, or asking someone for a date. Extreme social withdrawal is often part of some severe forms of psychopathology. If the anxiety-arousing stimuli come from within (as do aggressive or sexual urges and their attendant fantasies), then, physical avoidance may not be so successful. You cannot physically avoid yourself.

Using Positive Emotion to Reduce Negative Emotion.
The strategy of using positive emotion to reduce negative emotion is familiar to all of us. The young child engaged in thumb-sucking or gripping a "security" blanket when distressed is inducing positive emotions that decrease the intensity of the negative emotion. Watson and Rayner observed that, after fear conditioning, Albert engaged in more thumb-sucking when furry objects were present than when they were not present. This kind of response apparently works because the positive emotions are to some extent incompatible with the negative emotions and thus reduce their unpleasantness. The principle, in fact, is the same as that used in a counter-conditioning approach (systematic desensitization) to eliminating fears.

Variations on using positive emotions to reduce negative ones are limited only by the types of positive emotion-inducing procedures available. Alcohol and other drugs, smoking, sex, and food can be used in this way. This is not to say that these activities cannot be engaged in as ends in themselves, for the sake of the enjoyment alone; they can be. The point here is that they can also serve the purpose of reducing strong negative emotion, and when they do, they take on a compulsive quality and become highly persistent even in the face of secondary aversive consequences. Thus an obese person may persist in compulsive eating or an alcoholic in compulsive drinking even though it causes illness or social difficulties.

These compulsive responses are especially resistant to change because they not only avoid unpleasant experiences but also produce positive emotional reactions. The use of positive emotion to reduce negative emotion is seen most clearly in "addictive" kinds of disorders, such as obesity associated with excessive eating, sexual deviations, and alcoholism and other drug abuses.

Repression.
How do social learning theorists view Freud's primary defense mechanism, repression? The act of refusing to think about some disturbing event, or the more positive act of thinking about something else, is a response to anxiety-arousing stimuli in the same way that physical avoidance is a response, except that the former are covert actions and not directly observable. There is no reason to believe, however, that the learning of covert responses of this kind follows different principles than those involved in the learning of overt responses. This view of repression, then, is that it is simply a matter of learning to make a "think-about-something-else" response whenever a person's thoughts begin to approach a highly anxiety-arousing memory, wish, urge, or fantasy.

In the early stages of learning, individuals probably experience the memory and its associated anxiety to some extent and then make the "think-about-something-else" response, which is immediately reinforced by the reduction in anxiety that occurs when the unpleasant memory is removed from awareness. With repeated "trials," as with the dogs that learned to jump the gate, persons begin to make the response to thoughts that lead toward or anticipate the memory. In this way they learn to avoid almost entirely the anxiety associated with the memory, and in time the "think-about-something-else" response may occur automatically to thoughts so removed from the actual memory that they are no longer aware of the memory or that they are avoiding it. In the psychoanalytic concept of repression, the anxiety-arousing memory is banished or relegated to "the unconscious." The notion of banishment to some other part of the mind seems superfluous in the avoidance learning model.

Investigators have attempted to study repression experimentally with only limited success. At least psychoanalytic practitioners are not convinced that the research has much to do with the concept as defined within their theory. The main reason that research on repression is difficult is that ethically one cannot submit human subjects to the kind of acute anxiety-arousing situations that motivate repressive defenses.

Cognitive Interpretations. Several avoidance strategies, such as *denial* and *intellectualization*, involve beliefs or interpretations. The essential idea is that the degree of negative emotion associated with a particular situation can be influenced by what you believe about the situation. If, while walking down a lonely street at night, you believe that you are likely to be attacked and robbed, then you will probably experience fear. If you believe confidently that there is no danger of attack, then you are not likely to feel afraid. In other words, given the same objective situation, the magnitude of negative emotion can be greatly influenced by what we tell ourselves about the situation. Covert thought processes such as beliefs, interpretations, and expectations can have this effect. When one makes a covert interpretive response that reduces negative emotions, the response is reinforced and hence is more likely to occur in the future on similar occasions. We have, then, another kind of escape or avoidance learning.

When individuals are confronted with a situation that may result in aversive consequences and they interpret the situation in a way that denies the features associated with the aversive outcome, then they are employing the *denial* mechanism. Usually the person does not just deny some unpleasant truth, but asserts some contrary belief as well. A student may deny the growing evidence that her boyfriend is growing tired of her and continue to assert that the relationship is wonderful. For normal or neurotic individuals to use denial effectively, they must be dealing with incomplete or ambiguous information. If the unpleasant truth is based on incontrovertible fact, then persons—unless they exhibit psychotic delusion—simply have to believe it. They may use other strategies aimed at reduction of the negative emotion, such as thinking about something else, but they cannot deny the reality of the fact.

Another form of cognitive avoidance is known as *intellectualization.* The surgeon who cuts people open, the physician who intimately examines unclothed patients, the undertaker who prepares bodies for burial, and the general who issues the order that will certainly mean death or horrible injury to thousands of soldiers—all these individuals must somehow learn to avoid or minimize the strong emotional

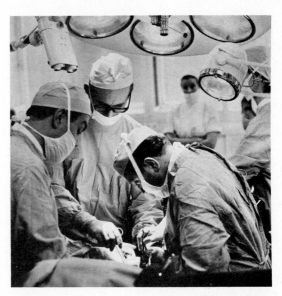

Surgeons must learn to not let emotions interfere with their professional work.

reactions that ordinarily accompany these actions. If they did not learn to inhibit them, the reactions would seriously interfere with their performance. Professionalism in any occupation involves this capacity to remain calm in carrying out a job. This separation of thought and behavior from emotional reactions is called *isolation* in the psychoanalytic approach (see page 45).

The capacity to intellectualize is not altogether a cognitive or interpretive function. It may partly involve the learning of some more direct nonthinking response that serves to inhibit emotional response. Or it may be a variant on the "think-about-something-else" response, in which the something else consists of professional, task-oriented thoughts. The surgeon pays full attention to the technical aspects of the operation, the general to the technicalities of strategy and tactics, and so on. It differs, however, from the type of "think-about-something-else" response described earlier in that persons do not change the subject, but only the *way* in which they think about it. By this means, they probably prevent the chaining of associations that might produce a continuing increase in emotion—the general does not brood about the suffering of soldiers and their families, nor does the physician build elaborate erotic fantasies about an unclothed patient.

Coping with Stress: Defensive Styles

A number of studies support the idea that some individuals consistently deal with threat-ening circumstances by denying the existence of the threat and perhaps by repressing anxiety-arousing associations. This defensive tactic seems to work only up to a point and, when the potential threat becomes inescapable, persons using a repressive style fre-quently show greater disturbance than persons who did not avoid recognition of the threat initially.

Janis (1958), for example, had judges rate patients on the extent to which they showed fear about the dangers and discomforts associated with an impending operation. Patients who showed the least preoperative fear frequently denied certain realistic ex-pectations about the postoperative discomfort involved and considered the surgeons to be infallible in their skills. The patients with these strong denial tendencies showed the greater disturbance after surgery: They were angry and disappointed when denial of the realities was no longer possible. Janis's study points up the necessity for some degree of informational ambiguity in order for denial to work; when reality becomes inescapable, as was the case after surgery, this avoidance strategy fails. Interestingly, the patients who expressed moderate degrees of preoperative fear showed the least postoperative psychological disturbance.

Shipley et al. (1978) assessed the reactions of *repressors* and *sensitizers* to a brief medical diagnostic procedure, endoscopy, which involves the insertion of a tube through the mouth into the stomach and the pumping of air into the gut for a 15–30-minute examination. This is experienced as stressful by most patients. The repression-sensiti-zation trait was measured by a questionnaire. Subjects scoring high on repression are characterized by the denying and "think-about-something-else" features previously de-scribed. At the other end of the dimension are sensitizers who ruminate and think ex-cessively about possible threats and stresses and frequently report higher levels of anx-iety. Subjects were randomly assigned to one of three conditions: *Control*—Before endoscopy these subjects viewed a videotape of an irrelevant documentary film; *Exper-imental 1*—Before endoscopy these subjects saw a videotape of a person undergoing endoscopy and experiencing moderate distress; *Experimental 3*—Before endoscopy these subjects saw the same videotape of the endoscopy examination three times. The authors had predicted that in the control condition the repressors would show less distress during the first five minutes of the actual examination than the sensitizers, the latter having worried themselves into a state of anxious expectation. In the experimental conditions in which the endoscopy videotape was viewed one or three times it was expected that the sensitizers would show decreasing degrees of anxiety arousal in the examination itself because they could see that although the procedure was somewhat distressing, it was not as bad as their worried expectations had led them to believe, or to put it another way, with repeated exposures to the anxiety-arousing videotape their anxiety would begin to extinguish. The repressors, on the other hand, were expected to show a marked increase in distress after being shown one viewing of the videotape since this would puncture their denying beliefs that there would be no distress at all. In Figure 4-5 it can be seen that heart rate increases during the first five minutes of the actual endoscopy examination followed these predictions. The sensitizers were quite anxious, as inferred from their increased heart rates, and the repressors were relatively unanxious. When shown one videotape of the examination, the repressors showed a dramatic jump in heart rate arousal compared to a decrease for the sensitizers. When they had been shown the videotape three times the repressors returned to their original low level of arousal; apparently the repeated showings had given them a chance to master the initial anxiety resulting from having their denial defenses broken through.

Further evidence that repressors show greater signs of anxiety when their repressive style is interrupted was provided by Weinberger et al. (1979). They asked subjects to complete a phrase that had either a neutral, aggressive, or sexual content. Repressors took longer to respond to the phrases and showed more palmar sweat gland activity (an indication of emotional arousal) than did subjects who admitted to high anxiety (similar to the sensitizers in the previous study) or nondefensive, low-anxiety subjects. See Figure 4-6.

There is, then, considerable evidence that some individuals do have a characteristic style of coping with life stresses by denial and repression, and that when circumstances prevent the use of these defenses, the person is especially vulnerable to strong anxiety.

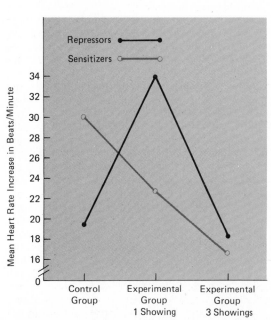

FIGURE 4-5 Mean heart rate increase during the first five minutes of scoping for repressors and sensitizers in each of the treatment conditions. E0, E1, and E3 refer to the groups that viewed the control tapes once, the experimental tape once,or the experimental tape three times, respectively. From Shipley et al., *Journal of Consulting and Clinical Psychology*, 1978, *46*, 499–507. © 1978, American Psychological Association and used with permission.

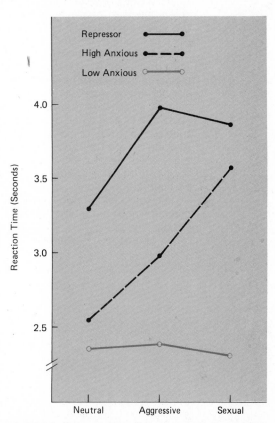

FIGURE 4-6 Mean reaction time in seconds to counter-balanced neutral, aggressive, and sexual phrase association presentations separately for low-anxious subjects (n = 15), high-anxious subjects (n = 11), and repressors (n = 14). From Weinberger et al., *Journal of Abnormal Psychology*, 1979, *88*, 369–380. © 1979 American Psychological Association and used with permission.

THE SOCIAL LEARNING APPROACH: A CRITIQUE

Contributions. The social learning approach is in a position to exploit the positive features of both the more extreme psychodynamic and radical behavioral views. By incorporating mediating thoughts, emotions, and drive states in their theories, social learning theorists avoid some of the limitations of radical behaviorism. At the same time, they introduce these mediating variables in a way that leads to testable predictions about relationships between environmental events and observable behavior. A growing body of empirical research on many topics related to abnormal psychology is testimony to the fruitfulness of this approach.

**RESEARCH
REPORT
4-2**

Reducing the Emotional Impact of a Film

In Research Report 4-1 we saw that individual differences in defensive styles can affect how people react to stress. In this research report we will consider evidence which suggests that most of us can use or not use several defensive styles if we are simply instructed to do so.

As a stressful experience Speisman et al. (1964) had subjects view a film depicting a ceremony of an aboriginal Australian tribe in which crude operations are performed on the penises and scrotums of adolescent boys. The film was shown under four experimental conditions created by commentary on the film's soundtrack. The conditions were: (1) silent (without soundtrack), (2) trauma, (3) denial and reaction formation, and (4) intellectualization. In the trauma condition the commentary emphasized the pain, cruelty, danger, and primitiveness of the rites. In the denial and reaction formation condition, the harmful aspects were denied (for example, by saying that the operation was not painful), and the positive benefits of participation in the ritual were emphasized by describing it as a joyful occasion for the native boys who looked forward with enthusiasm to becoming adult members of the tribe. In the intellectualization condition a scientific attitude toward the ritual was encouraged. The viewer was asked to observe the film in a detached manner, as an anthropologist might, analyzing the interesting customs of the primitive natives. Fifty-six college students were assigned randomly to the four experimental conditions.

Palmar sweating was highest under the trauma condition, next highest in the silent condition, next highest in the denial condition, and lowest in the intellectualization condition.

In order to verify the results of these studies further and to test the generality of

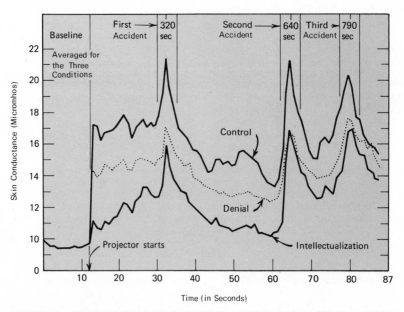

FIGURE 4-7. Effects of denial, intellectualization, and control conditions on palmar sweating in response to a stressful film. (Adapted from R. S. Lazarus, E. M. Opton, M. S. Nomilkos, and N. O. Rankin. The principle of short-circuiting of threat: Further evidence. *Journal of Personality*, 1965, *33*, 622–635. Copyright 1965 by the Duke University Press.)

results when a different kind of stressor film was used, another experiment was performed by Lazarus et al. (1965). They randomly assigned college students to the following conditions: (1) control, (2) denial, and (3) intellectualization. The stressor used was an industrial safety film portraying three shop accidents. First, a worker lacerates a finger; then another worker amputates a finger in a milling machine; and finally, a circular saw drives a board through the abdomen of a third worker, who dies, writhing and bleeding on the floor.

The different experimental conditions were created prior to showing the film. In the denial condition, the experimenters told the subjects to remember that the people in the film were actors and that no one was actually injured. In order to give the impression of bleeding, they said that red dye was squeezed from the palm of the hand. In the intellectualization condition, the emphasis was on analyzing the technique used in the film to promote industrial safety. The subjects were urged to consider the sociopsychological factors involved when a shop foreman attempts to promote shop safety. Subjects in the control group were given no particular suggestions for defensive coping.

The results for palmar sweating, shown in Figure 4-7, confirm those of the previous experiment. Subjects in both denial and intellectualization conditions showed less physiological arousal than in the control condition. Heart rate showed similar trends. Overall, these experiments by Lazarus and his colleagues demonstrate convincingly that emotional responses to stressful films can be reduced by denial and intellectualization.

Shortcomings. Because of its in-between position, the social learning approach also is vulnerable to some of the same criticisms as the two more extreme positions. Since they make use of mediating variables, proponents of this approach must continually guard against falling into the trap of explaining behavior too readily by reference to unobservable processes. The problem is always more acute in the clinical situation, where there is less opportunity to check a theory by controlled research. Thus, to explain a given patient's behavior after the fact in terms of observational learning or self-reinforcement should not obscure the fact that many other explanations might be equally valid. Also, social learning theorists who lean toward the behavioral end of the dimension may not do justice to the rich internal life of fantasies, interpretations, and so on that do influence our behavior.

In general, the social learning approach cannot be as clearly defined as the radical behavioral and psychodynamic approaches. It should probably be seen as a grouping of various approaches, theories, and terminologies. It remains to be seen which aspects of the social learning approach will be the most useful.

Summary

RADICAL BEHAVIORISM

1. Radical behaviorism has its roots in the classical conditioning studies of Pavlov and the operant learning model developed by Thorndike and, more recently, Skinner. In contrast to the psychodynamic approach, radical behaviorists concentrate on overt behavior, abnormal or normal, explaining it in terms of external variables such as controlling stimuli (conditioned or discriminative stimuli) and reinforcing consequences.

2. Radical behaviorists have contributed to our understanding of abnormal behavior. By concentrating on observable behavior and its relation to observable events, they avoid post hoc "explanations" in terms of intrapsychic processes. They have stated their propositions in ways that are subject to proof or disproof by experimental research, and pursued such research with sound methodology.

3. Radical behaviorism also has shortcomings. It goes too far in excluding mediating processes between environmental events (stimuli) and observable responses. There are such intervening processes, whether conceived in physiological or psychological terms, and they do affect our behavior. To omit them altogether restricts the theory unduly. Another criticism is that terms such as reinforcement and conditioned stimulus have highly exact meanings in laboratory experiments but lose precision when applied to abnormal behavior outside the laboratory.

SOCIAL LEARNING

1. The social learning approach falls between the two extremes of the radical behavioral and psychodynamic approaches with respect to the use of mediating variables. Advocates of the social learning approach make some judicious use of mediating variables, but they specify how these constructs are related to environmental events and observed responses and check such theoretically derived predictions with research.

2. Key mediating variables introduced by some social learning theorists include thoughts, images, and drive states that can serve as conditioned or discriminative stimuli, and self-reinforcement. Observational learning supplements classical conditioning and operant learning as a conception of how new responses can be learned.

3. Many of the defense mechanisms described by psychoanalytic writers can be conceptualized in terms of social learning, especially as versions of avoidance learning. Predictions about defensive behavior can be tested with experimental research.

4. An advantage of the social learning approach is that it partakes of the positive features of both the more extreme psychodynamic and behavioral views. The theory is enriched by mediating variables, but by remaining concerned about ties with environmental events and observable behavior, theorists avoid some of the pitfalls of an uncritical reliance on intrapsychic processes. At the same time they are potentially vulnerable to the criticisms of both extremes if they become too free with intervening variables or too reluctant to use them when necessary.

Suggested Readings

Social learning theory by A. Bandura (Prentice-Hall, 1977) is an excellent presentation of behavioral and social learning concepts as they apply to the nature and treatment of abnormal behavior. L. P. Ullmann and L. Krasner in *A psychological approach to abnormal behavior* (Prentice-Hall, 1975) also provide a strongly behavioral interpretation to the whole field of psychopathology.

5
A Developmental and Social Systems Perspective

- What does it mean to say that genetic and environmental influences interact?

- What are some of the research methods for determining genetic influences?

- Did you know that some children seem to be born with slow-to-warm-up temperaments?

- How does psychopathology develop within the family system?

- Do unhappy marriages affect children? How?

- Do features of larger social systems such as racial or sex discrimination increase rates of certain kinds of psychopathology?

Michael: Slow to Warm Up

Michael's nursery school teacher referred him for psychiatric evaluation when he was three years and nine months of age because of poor adjustment at school. He did not participate in group activities and each morning he clung to his mother and cried when she brought him to school.

Michael's difficulty had begun on the first day of nursery school. His mother had promised to stay with him but the school policy had been changed and she was not allowed to do so. He kicked and screamed when she left and refused to participate in any activity. This scene was repeated on the following day, accompanied by increasing demands for attention at home, and after a week he was withdrawn from the school. He was immediately enrolled in another school where his mother was permitted to stay with him. On the first day he allowed his mother to leave after she had stayed about one hour, and over the next few weeks the length of time his mother stayed was gradually shortened. Michael remained quietly on the sidelines at first but then began gradually to take part in the games and other activities. Within a month he began to look forward to going to the school, sometimes being dressed and ready to go fifteen minutes early.

This happy course of events was unfortunately marred a month or so later when Michael developed a respiratory ailment that kept him out of school for a week. His uneasiness about going to school returned, and it took a while before he began to participate actively with the other children again. At that point he suffered another acute illness, and for the next six months this pattern of brief periods at school interrupted by respiratory illnesses continued. His timidity at school became more extreme, and he began once again to cling to his mother in the morning. It was at this time that the nursery school teacher suggested that the parents seek psychiatric help. (Thomas et al., 1968)

In this chapter we will view abnormal behavior from a developmental perspective and also add another model or metaphor to our approaches to understanding abnormal behavior, namely, a *systems* approach in which abnormality is seen as a social interaction rather than something that exists within an individual. Michael will serve as a good example of how developmental processes involving biological and social learning factors interact to produce symptomatic behavior.

Heredity and Social Learning

Relatively few abnormal behaviors are inherited in the direct manner in which eye color, for example, is inherited. However, there may be biological dispositions or traits of temperament that make an individual more vulnerable to abnormal development; for example, a tendency toward unusual fearfulness in new

situations or unusual reactivity of certain physiological responses such as heart rate might make one more susceptible to the development of anxiety reactions. Given some genetically influenced vulnerability, the social learning experiences that a person has may then play a decisive role in determining whether or not abnormal reactions occur. Before considering this interplay, let us review briefly the mechanisms involved in hereditary transmission.

CHROMOSOMES AND GENES

The human cell contains 23 pairs of *chromosomes*, each containing many *genes*. Information about inherited characteristics is carried in the genes by a large molecule called *deoxyribonucleic acid* (DNA). The male sperm cell and the female egg cell (ovum) have only 23 single chromosomes, but as a result of sexual mating these two cells combine to form a new cell with 23 *pairs* of chromosomes. The genetic information in this cell is passed on to every cell in the growing fetus and directs their subsequent development. The particular set of genes in a given individual is referred to as the *genotype*.

Although we have just begun to be able to identify specific genes and their function in the chromosomes of some animals, most of our knowledge about the information contained in human genes is based on inferences from observed characteristics, physical or behavioral. These observable characteristics are referred to as *phenotypes*. Phenotypes are not inherited, but are the result of a given genotype interacting with given environmental circumstances. Some physical characteristics such as eye color, blood type, and fingerprint configurations are determined almost entirely by the genotype and are altered little if at all by environmental influences. On the other hand, some behavioral characteristics such as the particular language one speaks are determined entirely by environmental experiences. Thus the relative contribution of genetic and environmental influences in determining phenotypes varies widely.

With respect to most abnormal human behavior, we can rarely be sure that the phenotype of a given disorder is primarily determined by either heredity or environment. One rare form of mental retardation, *phenylketonuria* (see Chapter 24), has been shown to result from the lack of a specific gene required for the metabolization of an important dietary ingredient. However, as we move away from the extremes of the genetic-environmental dimension, it becomes exceedingly difficult to unravel the relative contributions of hereditary and environmental influences. This problem holds especially for humans since we are quite limited in the kind of experimental research that can be or should be conducted with human subjects.

THE HEREDITY-ENVIRONMENT INTERACTION

The difficulty in measuring the relative extent of genetic and environmental influences stems from the fact that they *interact*. For example, some infants are apparently born with an inherited tendency toward a negative mood state characterized by fussiness and irritability. An infant that "cries for hours on end" may eventually provoke its mother to be angrier or perhaps more solicitous than she would otherwise have been with a more contented baby. A genetically influenced characteristic has produced a change in the

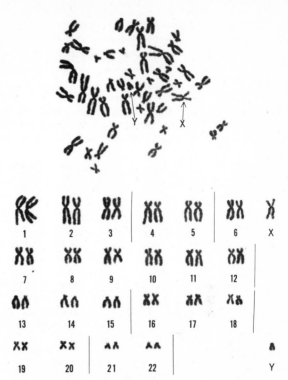

The chromosome complement of a normal person consists of 22 matched pairs of chromosomes, plus 2 sex chromosomes (2 X chromosomes for females, an X and a Y for males). The chromosomes shown above are those of a male.

environment. The infant now experiences a kind of maternal response that it would not have experienced if it had had a different genetic makeup. The different maternal environment may, in turn, further influence the infant's behavior, perhaps causing an even greater fussiness. The troublesome behavior one eventually sees in this child at one year of age will be the result of a continuing interaction between heredity and environment. Without rather complicated experimental manipulations there is no way to answer the question, "How much of this child's behavior is caused by heredity and how much by environment?"

RESEARCH METHODS FOR STUDYING HEREDITARY INFLUENCES

Ethical as well as practical considerations place experimental "breeding" research beyond the pale of acceptable procedures for studying hereditary transmission of abnormal behaviors in humans. Two more acceptable, but perhaps less definitive, research methods used instead are the *twin study* method and the *adoption* method.

The Twin Study Method. Fortunately, nature has helped us in our study of heredity by providing us with two types of twins: *identical* or *monozygotic* twins, which result from the splitting of a single fertilized ovum, and *fraternal* or *dizygotic* twins, which result from the simultaneous fertilization of two separate ova. Identical twins have the same genetic endowments, but fraternal twins on the average are no more alike genetically than any two nontwin siblings born to the same parents. Since sex is genetically determined, identical twins are always of the same sex, whereas fraternal twins are no more likely to be of the same sex than other nontwin sibling pairs.

In most instances twins are reared together in the same family context, and the logic of the twin method might be summarized as follows: Since each twin pair grows up in a very similar environment (same parents, siblings, neighborhood, socioeconomic level, educational opportunities, and so on) differences in degree of behavioral similarity between identical and fraternal twins will be largely due to the greater genetic similarity of the identical twins. Should there be no hereditary influence in the development of a given form of abnormality, then there should be no difference in the degree of similarity found in the two kinds of twins for this particular abnormality. If there are

significant hereditary influences, then identical twins should be more alike than fraternal twins on the behavior being observed.

This conclusion must be qualified, however, if it can be shown that people respond with greater similarity to identical twins than to fraternal twins in ways that contribute to the development of the abnormal behavior. In other words, environmental as well as genetic influences may be operating to produce any greater similarity found in identical twins. We should keep this qualification in mind when we consider twin study evidence for genetic factors in such disorders as schizophrenia.

The Adoption Method. Another method of assessing genetic influence is to compare two kinds of children who have been removed from their biological parents at or shortly after birth and adopted or raised by foster parents: (1) children in which one or both biological parents showed a form of behavior disorder, and (2) children whose biological parents did not show the disorder. If the environments provided by the adoptive or foster parents do not differ on the average for the two types of children, and the children whose parents were abnormal subsequently develop the same abnormality, then we can conclude that genetic factors were in part responsible. An advantage of this method over the twin study approach is that it avoids completely the question of whether identical twins experience a more similar environment than do fraternal twins.

TWO EXAMPLES OF POSSIBLE HEREDITARY INFLUENCE

Physiological Reactivity. Strong fear reactions are usually accompanied by physiological responses such as an increased heart rate, higher blood pressure, and more palmar sweating. If individual differences in reactivity of these responses are genetically influenced, then infants born with tendencies toward high reactivity might be more susceptible to the development of anxiety reactions or perhaps to psychosomatic disorders involving these systems. There is indeed some evidence that identical twins tend to be more alike on measures of heart rate, blood pressure, and palmar sweating than are fraternal twins (Hume, 1973; Lader & Wing, 1966; Zahn, 1977).

Identical twins share the same genetic makeup.

Sociability. As another example of the possible role of hereditary influences, consider the personality characteristic of sociability. I use the terms *sociability* and *extroversion-introversion* interchangeably to refer to the dimension represented at one end by individuals who are shy and socially fearful (especially with respect to strangers or new social situations) and at the other end by individuals who are outgoing, expansive, and at ease in new as well as established social situations. Children have been found to be quite consistent in their degree of sociability from early childhood to adolescence (Kagan & Moss, 1962). Such consistency would be expected in a trait with considerable hereditary determination, but learning experiences in a given family context could also produce the same consistency. Several studies have shown that identical twins are consistently more alike on various measures of sociability than are fraternal twins (see Research Report 5-1). These findings suggest strongly that the young child's tendency to be outgoing and friendly or shy and reserved may have some hereditary basis. Whether or not a disposition toward social apprehension eventuates in an abnormal degree of inhibition or anxiety will depend heavily upon the kind of social learning experiences to which the child is exposed over the course of the years.

RESEARCH REPORT 5-1

Is Social Apprehension Partly Inherited?

Gottesman (1962) compared identical twins and same-sex fraternal twins—all adolescents—on six scales from the Minnesota Multiphasic Personality Inventory (MMPI), a self-report questionnaire. One of these scales, called Social Introversion, is composed of items such as the following: I am a good mixer; I am easily downed in an argument; I like to go to parties and other affairs where there is lots of loud fun; I find it hard to make talk when I meet new people. Shields (1962) compared adult twins on a questionnaire measure of Extroversion-Introversion, and Scarr (1965) made ratings of social apprehension based on home observations of twins, all girls between the ages of six and ten. The results of the comparisons of twin correlations on sociability in these three studies are summarized as follows:

	Number of Twins		Correlation	
	Identical	*Fraternal*	*Identical*	*Fraternal*
Gottesman (1962)	34	34	.55	.08
Shields (1962)	43	25	.42	−.17
Scarr (1965)	24	28	.88	.28

Correlations were significantly higher for the identical twins than for the same-sex fraternal twins in each study. In Shields's (1962) study a sample of 42 identical twins separated early in life was also included. The correlation for this group was .61 compared to the correlation of .42 for identical twins reared together. If the experience of greater environmental similarity were the crucial factor in accounting for differences between identical and fraternal twins, one would expect the former correlation to be lower than that obtained for the identical twins reared together; in fact, it was higher, although not significantly so.

Although not reported as correlations, Horn et al. (1976) reported much greater similarity for 99 identical twins than 99 fraternal twins on questionnaire items involving discomfort in talking to strangers. The twin samples were composed of adult males. Eaves and Eysenck (1975) provide the most sophisticated genetical analysis of any yet performed in their study of extroversion in 451 adult identical twins and 257 adult fraternal twins of both sexes. They note that their extroversion scale is composed of two clusters of items, those involving sociability (liking and feeling at ease in social situations) and impulsivity (for example, "Do you often do things on the spur of the moment?"). On the basis of their analyses they conclude that about 40 percent of the variance (an indication of the variation in scores among individuals) of the questionnaire measure of extroversion can be attributed to genetic factors. They also conclude that although some common genetic factors are involved in the sociability and impulsiveness components, there are also distinctive genetic contributions to these two aspects of extroversion.

In yet another study Freedman (1965) found that during the first five months of life identical twins showed greater similarity on a measure of responsiveness to persons (based on visual fixation and smiling directed at people) than fraternal twins; and for months 5 to 12, identical twins were more alike on a measure of fear of strangers. The average of the differences between one twin and the other on these measures was used to compare degree of similarity in Freedman's study. This study is also of special interest because Freedman took motion pictures of each twin separately and had different judges rate the behavior for each twin in a given pair. There was, accordingly, no way that judges could have been influenced in their rating of one twin by knowledge of the other twin. Furthermore, by studying the twins at such a young age, he limited the effects of possible differential environmental influences on identical and fraternal twins.

THE INTERACTION OF TEMPERAMENT AND SOCIAL LEARNING

Temperament refers to consistent styles of behavior, usually present at an early age and presumed to have at least some genetic determination. Thomas et al. (1968) conducted a long-term developmental study in which measures of the same child's behavior were obtained by interviewing parents at three-month intervals during the first 18 months, then at six-month intervals until five years, and at yearly intervals thereafter. Some of the nine measures of temperament obtained were: *activity level; regularity* of repetitive biological functions such as sleeping, eating, and bowel movements; *initial approach* or *withdrawal reaction* to a new stimulus such as a new food, the first bath, or an unfamiliar person or place; *adaptability*, that is, how many exposures to a new situation occurred before the child responded without distress; and general *quality of mood* (happy and contented versus ready to fuss and cry with high intensity). The children were found to be moderately consistent in their temperamental characteristics over the first five years of life, especially for activity level and adaptability. In another study Torgersen (1973) reported that identical twins showed greater similarity than fraternal twins on all nine of these traits of temperament at nine months of age, thus providing some evidence for a genetic contribution.

An illustration of how traits of temperament interact with environmental circumstances to produce behavioral disturbances is the case of Michael described at the beginning of the chapter. Since Mi-

chael was a participant in the study conducted by Thomas et al., it was possible to trace the development of his difficulties over the course of his young life. At the three- and six-month interviews it had been noted that he initially rejected new foods and that he screamed when given his first bath at three weeks, after which he gradually cried less and eventually came to smile and relax in the tub. He resumed screaming at nine months when a different kind of tub was introduced, but eventually developed a positive reaction to the new bath. He required a number of exposures to each new baby-sitter before accepting the person, and generally with the introduction of each new experience, such as new medicine or temperature taking, he would respond with fussing and crying. Children like Michael, who responded negatively to each new situation and required a number of repetitions of the experience before they were able to respond positively, were called *slow to warm up*.

The help, in this case, consisted of advice based on the psychiatrist's knowledge of the slow-to-warm-up temperament that had been characteristic of Michael since infancy. Michael's disastrous experience at the first nursery school was seen as probably resulting from a rigid application of a rule about mothers not remaining. As a consequence Michael did not have an opportunity to adapt to the new situation at his own pace. The difficulties at the second nursery school were seen as the result of an unfortunate series of illnesses that served to reinstate the newness of the situation on too many occasions for him to master. His parents and subsequent teachers were able to understand Michael's slow-to-warm-up nature and be patient and tolerant with him; accordingly, during the following year at nursery school and subsequent years at kindergarten and first grade his school adjustment was generally good. In each case, however, there was some initial resistance and withdrawal followed by a gradual involvement in the school situation (adapted from Thomas et al., 1968).

Not all children who show distress upon entering nursery school are necessarily showing a slow-to-warm-up temperament. But for Michael that was apparently the case, and his reactions illustrate how important the environmental response is in determining whether or not a given temperamental disposition will escalate into a more serious problem.

Thomas and his colleagues identified a subgroup of children within their study at less than two years of age as "difficult children." The 14 children in this group tended to score high on several characteristics such as biological irregularity, withdrawal and distress in new situations, slowness to warm up, and a predominance of negative mood. Of these difficult children 70 percent (10) subsequently developed mild-to-moderate behavior disorders, compared to the overall incidence of behavior disorders in the total sample of 31 percent. The presence of certain traits at a very early age seems to increase the probability of a behavior disorder later in life.

Parents of the difficult children did not differ from other parents in the group in their approach to child care, as measured by interviews, during the early years. However, in a number of cases, as the difficult child grew older, disturbances in parent-child interaction emerged that appeared to be connected to the special characteristics of these children. Many college-educated mothers reacted to the troublesome temperament of their child with self-blame; for example, they interpreted their children's difficult behavior in terms of psychodynamic theories that the mother's unconscious attitude of rejection produced the problem. Other parents interpreted the child's crying and irregularity as intentionally defiant, and they reacted punitively.

Thomas et al. (1968) and Thomas and Chess (1977) traced the development of child disturbance in a number of families in a way that highlights the interaction between child temperament and parent reaction. For example, they describe two children who both showed a difficult temperament in the first few years of life, but whose parents responded dif-

Some children are fearful and slow to warm up in new situations.

ferently to their behavior. By age 5½ one child, a girl, had developed a marked behavioral disturbance including explosive anger, negativism, fear of the dark, encopresis (defecating in clothes), thumb-sucking, insatiable demands for toys and sweets, poor peer relationships, and protective lying. The other child, a boy, developed no symptoms of behavior disorder. The father of the girl disciplined her in a punitive way and spent little or no recreational time with her. The mother was more understanding and more permissive but quite inconsistent. Adaptation to nursery school in the fourth year was a problem for both children, and the parents of the girl, especially the father, reacted angrily to her difficulties in adjusting to the new situation. The parents of the boy, on the other hand, were patient and tolerant of his slowness to adapt to the nursery school, and more serious problems did not develop. Thus, even when children are born with a "troublesome" temperament, whether or not they develop a behavior problem is largely determined by the way that parents and others respond to them.

A Social Systems Perspective

It should be clear by now that mental disorders do not occur in a social vacuum. Interactions with people are considered important in both the psychodynamic, behavioral, and social learning orientations, but the focus has tended to be upon the individual. From a social systems perspective the abnormality is conceived as an aspect of some larger social unit, whether a simple two-person dyad or an entire culture. First let us consider the family as the locus of abnormality and then take an even larger sociological or cultural view.

THE FAMILY AS A SYSTEM

For young children the most important social learning experiences are those that occur in the family context, and although other environmental influences—relationships with peers and adults in the neighborhood and at school—become increasingly important as they grow older, for most children the character of their early family interactions leaves a long-lasting imprint on their personalities. Psychodynamic and social learning theorists agree on the importance of the family context but differ in interpretation. The psychodynamic orientation emphasizes the contribution of family experiences to psychosexual fixations, to Oedipal fantasies, and to other intrapsychic impulses and conflicts. Social learning theorists focus on who in the family is reinforcing whom for what, which behavior of a family member is serving as a cue or signal (discriminative stimulus) for some other member's behavior, and who is modeling what kind of behavior for whom.

Recall Joanne and her daughter, Milly, who served as our introductory case example in Chapter 1. When the therapist first saw this family, a repetitive interaction pattern had developed between Joanne and Milly. Milly "bugged" her mother and "drove her up

the wall." She would repeat the same question over and over, put her dirty clothes in the wrong place; refuse to take her bath, brush her teeth, or go to bed; tease and aggravate her baby sister; and so on. Joanne *attended* to these noxious behaviors, ineffectually repeated requests, and eventually yelled at her. When things got too bad, Joanne tried to spank Milly, but she "couldn't catch her" and the only result was an exciting chase around the house. It is not unreasonable to assume that Joanne was, in fact, reinforcing Milly's "bugging" behavior by the way she responded to it. At the same time Milly was probably reinforcing Joanne in two respects. Occasionally, a violent yell or successful hit would temporarily stop Milly's noxious behavior, thus giving Joanne some intermittent reinforcement for losing her temper. Also, when Joanne's distress reached a point where she was reduced to tearful despair or to an incapacitating headache, Milly would immediately cease her disruptive behavior and show concern and sympathy for her mother. In other words Milly reinforced her mother for becoming depressed or getting sick.

This is an example, then, of an interactive system in which mother and daughter are both teacher and learner. They are mutually reinforcing each other and thus ensuring that the interactive sequence will be repeated in the future despite the fact that there are some unpleasant consequences for both participants.

So far I have used a two-person (dyadic) interaction as an illustration, but systems can include more than two persons and, of course, get more complicated as they do. In the case of Joanne and Milly, for example, the father reinforced Milly's noncompliant behavior by not supporting Joanne's attempts at discipline and in some cases by actively sabotaging such efforts by telling Milly that she did not have to go to her room or comply with whatever the punishment was. The father's behavior in this case was probably an indirect attempt to retaliate against his wife for her nagging behavior toward him. I could expand further on his particular system by including the father-in-law, whom Joanne disliked intensely because of his dominating ways. The point, however, has been made that to understand fully the development and maintenance of certain forms of abnormal behavior it is useful and perhaps necessary to take into account the interpersonal systems in which the behavior occurs.

An unhappy marriage would seem to be a circumstance especially likely to be associated with behavioral problems in children, as was the case in Joanne's family and as shown in a number of studies (for example, Johnson & Lobitz, 1974; Oltmanns et al., 1977). There are many ways in which marital conflict can impinge on children. Simple displacement is the most common form. A parent who is angry at the spouse may displace the anger to a child in the form of an irrational temper outburst or chronic nagging that is totally inappropriate to the child's misbehavior, if any.

In some troubled marriages a spouse attempts to enlist a child as an ally against the other spouse, a tactic that creates problems for the child's own development. Minuchin (1974) reports an example that also shows how the same tactic can be passed along from generation to generation. The mother in this family has described how her parents attacked each other through her. Her mother encouraged her to disobey her father; her father attacked her when he was angry at his wife. Now this mother and her husband are being interviewed by Minuchin, and we see how she is now repeating this same tendency to get her son to join her in an attack on her husband.

Therapist: You know, this what you are describing is so familiar. . . . Tommy was growing up, and now you had three people instead of two. Now you had a model you learned from your home: That Papa and Mama fight through me. That you described as the model in your home.

Mother: But I never realized that until you just said it.

Therapist: Okay, but let's—let's bring it now to Tommy and see if this model—

Mother: I'd say we did. Definitely, oh, definitely we used Tommy to fight. I would get mad at Mark [her husband] and lock him out, and he would stand out there and pound on the door, and I would take Tommy to the window and—this was awful—point to him, and say, "See, Tommy, see the funny man," and we'd stand there and make faces at him.

Father: Yeah. (Laughs)

Mother: He'd be standing there, dying, ready to kill both—kill me because I was instigating that little baby, you know—

Therapist: You transferred a family model that you learned at your home into your marriage. (pp. 36–37)

Parents sometimes take out their frustrations on their children.

In other instances a parent whose marriage provides only frustrations and disappointments may turn to the child for interpersonal satisfactions denied in marriage. The child becomes a substitute spouse. As we will see in Chapter 20, the overprotective parent who is doing so may produce an overly dependent and fearful child.

Issues of child rearing may become battlegrounds on which parents fight out their antagonisms. The father may feel, for example, that the mother is too lax, or that she is too hard on the girls and too easy on the boys. The mother may retort that the father does not pay any attention to disciplinary matters until things get out of hand, and then he begins to yell. He leaves the day-to-day discipline to her but criticizes her for the way she handles it. Under these circumstances both the father's and the mother's reactions to the children become as much determined by their own conflict as by the children's actual behavior.

This last point is the basic destructive ingredient in all these impingements of marital conflict on children: The child is not being responded to as a separate person who is behaving well or misbehaving. Rather, the parent is displacing anger to the child, seeking to form a coalition with the child against the spouse, using the child as a substitute for the spouse, or reacting to the child in terms of marital disputes over child rearing. How these behaviors affect the child depends upon the child's temperament and the particular social learning sequences that develop.

A SOCIOLOGICAL VIEW

We have seen how psychopathology can be viewed as a dysfunctioning family system. Can it be seen as a feature of even larger social systems?

Cultural Relativity.   First let us reconsider briefly an issue raised in Chapter 1. Is abnormality entirely relative to the cultural context? If that were the case and given cultures that varied widely in terms of norms for appropriate behavior, then symptoms of schizophrenia, or depression, or anxiety should be labeled abnormal in some cultures and not in others. From a sociological (or cultural) view of this kind an important determinant of abnormality would be the particular values and behavioral expectations of the culture. In the past it has not been possible to draw firm conclusions on the question of cultural relativity because of a lack of standardized assessment procedures. More recently, however, investigators have found that certain symptom patterns are present in many different cultures and countries. For example, the World Health Organization (1973) sponsored a study in which similar assessment techniques were used in centers in nine different countries. In all countries there were patients who had symptoms such as social and emotional withdrawal, auditory hallucinations, delusions, and flatness of affect that were associated with the diagnosis of schizophrenia. Similar findings have been reported for mania (Leff et al., 1976). Cultural relativism in its extreme form would not seem to apply to these severe disorders. In general it would appear that most psychological symptoms that produce severe handicaps in functioning are seen as a "disorder" in most societies.

On the other hand, there clearly are a number of mental disorders that seem to be specific to a given culture. A rather distinctive pattern of behavior called *amok* was once a common form of mental disturbance in the Malay culture. To "run amok" involved a frenzied outburst of homicidal violence in which the person might kill or injure anyone who happened to get in the way. Certain North American Indian groups manifested a disorder involving a belief in possession by the Witiko, or cannibal monster, in which the person would also engage in homicidal excitement. Although these and other symptom patterns seem relatively unique to a specific culture, the anthropologist Devereux (1956) suggests that these manifestations

of psychological disorder represent a culturally recognized and accepted way of "going crazy." In another culture the same individual might have expressed his or her craziness in a different manner, but the basic tensions, social conflicts, or biological processes associated with the symptoms might have been the same.

Perhaps a more meaningful question to ask about the relation of culture to abnormality is whether certain features of cultures or subcultures tend to affect the frequency or severity of specific psychological symptoms. Does a society's practice of labeling and responding to certain forms of deviant behavior affect the nature and extent of certain mental disorders? Does a subculture of poverty and social disorganization produce certain kinds of mental disorders? Do certain cultural values and prejudices affect the degree of psychopathology in minority races or women? Some of these questions will be considered in more detail in connection with specific disorders in later chapters. At this time I want to address these questions in more general terms in order to clarify how the sociological view differs from other approaches.

Societal-Reaction Theory.   Scheff (1975) has been largely responsible for a view of psychopathology called *societal-reaction theory.* According to Scheff there are two kinds of deviance, primary and secondary. In primary deviance the person violates some societal rule or custom, for example, dresses or speaks inappropriately, engages in some "funny" behavior, does not go to work, or whatever. If these deviations are explained or labeled by others as due to ignorance, being drunk, or just plain laziness, then they remain primary deviances. On the other hand, if others explain the deviant behavior to be the result of mental illness and eventually mental health professionals officially label the person as having schizophrenia, a neurosis, or a learning disability, then a sequence of events is set off that produces secondary deviance. Such individuals are taught to label themselves as sick, to believe they *have* the specified disorder, and are reinforced for adopting the role of a mentally disturbed person. According to Scheff many, perhaps most, of the symptoms that are called mental illness result from playing the expected role of mental patient and thus reflect secondary deviance. In this view, then, biological and individual psychological factors contribute to the expression of the initial primary deviance, but the symptoms of second-ary deviance are determined largely by societal customs of labeling and reinforcing "mentally ill" be-haviors.

Social Class.   Social class has long been given im-portance in sociological theories of mental disorder, largely because of a clear trend for the diagnosis of severe psychological disorders to be more common in lower socioeconomic classes (Dohrenwend & Dohrenwend, 1974). For example, Gove and Howell (1974) found that 45 percent of low-income individ-uals admitted to mental hospitals were assessed to be severely disorganized and disruptive compared with 22 percent of individuals with higher incomes. The percentages were reversed for milder symptoms. If one takes a sociological view of mental disorder, then findings of this kind tend to be interpreted as showing that the stresses and prevailing attitudes as-sociated with living in impoverished circumstances produce the disorders, perhaps aided by tendencies on the part of mental health professionals to more readily label primary deviance in such populations as mental illness and thus to promote the development of secondary deviance. If, on the other hand, one takes a more biological or individual psychological view of mental disorders, then the higher proportion of severely disturbed individuals found in the lower socioeconomic classes is likely to be thought to re-flect a downward drift of individuals to these circum-stances because they lacked the psychological com-petence to cope with the demands of higher-level socioeconomic conditions.

Racial Discrimination.   Does experiencing discrim-ination as a member of a minority race increase vul-nerability to mental disorder? If so, this would be an example of a societal characteristic, racial discrimi-nation, influencing the development of psychological disorders. In fact, the evidence is not clear on this question. Although admission rates for blacks to mental hospitals tend to be higher than for whites, this difference disappears when treatment for psy-chological disorders by all means, such as private practice and outpatient clinics, is taken into account. Thus Pasamanick (1963) found hospital admission rates to be 650 per 100,000 for blacks and 357 per 100,000 for whites. But when data from all sources of treatment were included, the figures changed to

7395 per 100,000 for blacks and 12,974 for whites, suggesting that blacks actually have fewer disorders than whites. The higher rates of hospitalization for blacks may reflect a socioeconomic variable rather than race in itself since a higher proportion of blacks live in impoverished conditions. Warheit et al. (1975) also found higher rates of psychopathology in blacks than whites in an epidemiological survey, but when differences in socioeconomic level were taken into account, the differences between the races were greatly reduced. There is some evidence that clini-cians may have employed different criteria in diag-nosing blacks and whites. For example, Gross et al. (1969) found that the symptoms leading to hospi-talization in white women were usually labeled neu-rotic but similar symptoms in black women were in-terpreted as schizophrenic, and Watkins et al. (1975) found that among first and second admissions to a psychiatric facility a higher proportion of black pa-tients of *all educational levels* were diagnosed schiz-ophrenic than were white patients. Results such as these are consistent with the possibility that white psychiatrists have been influenced by the race of the patient in making diagnostic appraisals.

There is one kind of disorder that afflicts blacks, especially black males, more often than whites, and that is essential hypertension, high blood pressure without a known organic cause. To the extent that this disorder is caused, in part, by psychological fac-tors (this question will be considered in more detail in another chapter) it is relevant to our present dis-cussion. Both blacks and whites living in low socio-economic and socially unstable areas have been found to have higher rates of essential hypertension than their same-race counterparts living in higher so-cioeconomic and more socially stable environments (Harburg et al., 1973; James & Kleinbaum, 1976). And of particular interest, black males living in low socioeconomic and socially unstable areas had higher rates of hypertension than did white males living in similar environments. The latter finding indicates that, even with socioeconomic conditions held con-stant, black males have this disorder more often than white males, suggesting that the stresses of living in a racially discriminating society may increase the like-lihood of developing this disorder beyond the rates of occurrence influenced by low socioeconomic con-ditions themselves. Of course, alternative hypotheses can be entertained in interpreting results of this kind such as differences in diet (for example, more highly seasoned soul food) or possibly different genetic susceptibility stemming from the original African populations. With respect to the latter interpretation, however, Akinkugbe (1972) found hypertension levels to be lower in West African blacks than in American blacks. It is possible, then, that essential hypertension is a psychologically caused (at least in part) disorder in which the sociological variable of racial discrimination is an important contributing factor.

Sex Discrimination.   Do societal attitudes and expectations about appropriate sex-role behavior increase women's vulnerability to mental disorder? or men's? Recall Joanne, the woman first described in Chapter 1, who had recurring migraine headaches and whose chronic depression could only be alleviated by continually taking antidepressant drugs. Joanne found herself with two young children and a husband whom she "hated" and who was unwilling to join her in marital therapy. She felt trapped, both financially and emotionally, in a situation that seemed, in part at least, to be contributing to her distress. As a woman she had not learned occupational skills that would make it easy for her to achieve financial independence. Also, her friends, parents, and church all seemed to present a solid front to the effect that a woman should be thankful for being given economic security and not complain or rebel against whatever shortcomings her husband or father-in-law might have. She was, in short, made to feel guilty about her angry feelings. I do not wish to oversimplify the causative influences in a case such as Joanne's, but a sociological perspective would suggest that societal attitudes about appropriate sex-role behavior played at least some part in producing and maintaining Joanne's symptoms.

Although for young children psychological disorders are diagnosed more commonly in boys than girls, for adults the reverse tends to be true, especially for symptoms of depression. In the latter case women outnumber men 2 or even 3 to 1 (Chesler, 1972; Weissman & Klerman, 1977). Hammen and Peters (1977) performed a study that suggests one possible factor contributing to this discrepancy, namely, that depressive symptoms in females elicit less rejection by others than do depressive symptoms in males. In their study college students were asked to answer certain questions after reading male and female case histories and the authors did indeed find that both male and female students were more rejecting of depressed males and saw depressed males as more impaired in their functioning than depressed females. One interpretation of these results is that the helplessness, apathy, and grief associated with depression is more consonant with the female sex-role stereotype than the male sex-role stereotype and therefore more acceptable to others. Females, therefore, would receive less "punishment" and perhaps more positive reinforcement for being depressed than males, and would also, perhaps, be less reluctant to divulge these depressive feelings to mental health professionals. To the extent that the latter conclusion is true, the findings of less diagnosed depression in males might reflect, in part, a difference in help-seeking and willingness to admit to feeling depressed.

All of the above—a society's practices with respect to labeling certain behaviors as mentally disturbed and encouragement of playing the role of mental patient, the effects of poverty, the effects of racial discrimination, and the effects of sex discrimination—would represent sociological perspectives on the causes of mental disorder. As with other perspectives, the adoption of this one also has implications for the treatment of psychopathology. In general the sociological view suggests that treatment of individuals has little effect on the basic sociological conditions fostering the development of symptoms and that in the long run mental disorders will only be reduced if we eliminate poverty, racial discrimination, sex discrimination and so on. The main criticism of the sociological view is that by itself it is incomplete. Not all people who live in poverty or who experience racial or sexual discrimination develop psychological disorders. To understand why some do and others do not we have to include biological factors and individual social learning experiences.

The Development of Abnormal Behavior: An Outline of Causes

In the past several chapters we have considered various views, theories, or metaphors developed to explain mental disorders. With the possible exception of demon possession, all views have some validity as well as some shortcomings. In considering the caus-

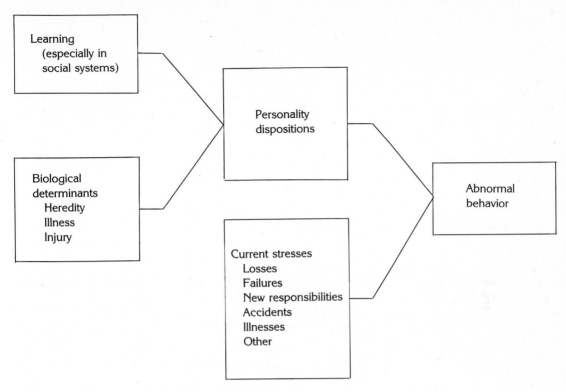

FIGURE 5-1.   An outline of determinants of abnormal behavior.

ation (or *etiology,* as causative influences are frequently called) it will be useful to follow a scheme that can incorporate all of these views; see Figure 5-1.[1] Whether or not a person behaves abnormally depends on current stresses and the person's unique pattern of response tendencies or *personality.* Thus, Michael showed disturbed behavior on his first day at nursery school (a current stress) because he had a tendency to respond to new situations with apprehension (a personality disposition). Another child with a different personality would not have responded in this way. The personality dispositions themselves result from a lifetime of interaction between biological characteristics and environmental learning experiences, the most important learning experiences being those that are embedded in the surrounding social systems. These personality dispositions include not only overt behavior but also mediating processes such as ideas, motives, emotions, beliefs, and values. In Michael's case his anxiety in new situations may have been partly inherited as a trait of temperament and partly learned from past experiences.

Personality, from this point of view, is not necessarily an unchanging, fixed set of characteristics, nor is it highly consistent in different situations. An individual's personality, in fact, may be in the process of change at any time as a function of new learning experiences. These changes, however, take time, so most people at any given moment make fairly predictable responses in specific situations. Current stressful circumstances, such as rejection by a friend or spouse, failure at work, or a death in the family, are often involved in producing abnormal reactions, but whether they do or not depends upon the given

_____

[1] A variation on this outline of causative factors is the *diasthesis-stress* model in which diasthesis refers to predisposing factors in the organism and stress to the immediate external stresses. Diasthesis has sometimes been used to refer to biological factors only and at other times has also included learned dispositions. I believe the scheme as outlined in Figure 5-1 includes the important determinants, and it is unnecessary to include a new word, *diasthesis,* which has somewhat ambiguous meaning.

individual's personality. One person reacts to a failing grade in school by temporary disappointment, a review of academic goals, and a decision to improve study habits; another responds with continuing self-reproach and feelings of unworthiness. Why the difference? Because somewhere in the past these two people experienced a different set of social learning experiences in interaction with their particular biological makeups.

This model of causation is compatible with the behavioral, psychodynamic and social systems perspectives. We can view the results of a given developmental history in terms of either intrapsychic processes or learned behaviors, or both, as they have occurred in certain social systems contexts. Likewise, we can describe the current environment in terms of discriminative stimuli and reinforcing consequences, or as circumstances likely to arouse intrapsychic conflicts, or as a set of social systems. This general scheme should be kept in mind as we consider the causes of various forms of abnormal behavior throughout the book.

Summary

1. Although the contributions to human behavior of genetic and environmental influences are separable in the abstract, it is exceedingly difficult to unravel them in life situations except at the extreme ends of the genetic-environmental continuum. This difficulty arises because these two influences interact: One kind of genetic endowment produces a different environmental response than another kind. In return, environmental events affect the way in which genetic factors are expressed, the observed phenotype. Thus, in most cases, it is nearly impossible to determine how much a given behavioral characteristic was caused by heredity and how much by environment.

2. Comparisons of identical and fraternal twins suggest that individual differences in autonomic nervous system reactivity and in sociability are partially determined by heredity.

3. A young child's temperament (largely inherited) interacts with social learning experiences (chiefly within the family) in the determination of psychological disturbances. The way the parents respond to a given trait of temperament, such as high activity level or being slow to warm up, is thus crucial in affecting the subsequent course of development.

4. Interacting systems develop between parent and child that reflect mutual influence processes, and these systems become autonomous from their original causes.

5. Clinical studies suggest several ways in which children can be adversely affected by unhappy marriages: A parent who is angry at the spouse may displace the anger to the child; one spouse may enlist the child as an ally against the other spouse; a parent disappointed in the marriage relationship may see in the child a substitute for the unsatisfactory spouse; or child rearing may become one of the battlefields on which the parents fight out their antagonisms.

6. In the sociological view psychopathology is seen to result from characteristics of the larger society, for example, from poverty, racial or sexual discrimination, or from societal customs of labeling certain individuals as mentally ill and reinforcing them in the role of mental patient.

7. The causes of abnormal behavior can be summarized as follows: Abnormal behavior is a function of current stress and the individual's personality, and the individual's personality results from a lifetime of interaction between biological characteristics and learning experiences. The most important learning experiences are those that occur in the context of social systems.

Suggested Readings

A. Thomas and S. Chess in *The dynamics of psychological development* (Brunner/Mazel, 1980) describe the interaction of temperament and parent-child relationships on the development of behavior disorders, drawing heavily on their longitudinal study of these factors. *Genetics of psychopathology* by D. Rosenthal (McGraw-Hill, 1971) is a good introduction to the role of genetic factors in abnormal behavior. T. Scheff describes his societal-reaction theory of psychopathology in *Labelling madness* (Prentice-Hall, 1975).

6
Classification and Diagnosis

- What are the problems in classifying behavior disorders?

- How well can different clinicians independently arrive at the same diagnosis?

- How readily can a diagnosis be influenced by "prestige suggestion"?

- How does a behaviorally oriented clinician deal with the problem of diagnosis?

- "Sticks and stones can break my bones, but names can never hurt me." Or can they?

- What are some common diagnostic procedures and tests?

Classification

In the beginning stages of most sciences investigators try to make sense out of nature's complexities by classifying observations. The early chemists sorted compounds with certain properties into a group they called *acids*; other compounds with different properties were classified as *bases*. This categorization was useful because once chemists found that a compound had certain properties of an acid, for example, they would know automatically that it also had a number of other predictable properties. Once acids and bases had been separated into useful classes, investigators could look deeper into the basic nature of these compounds and make subtler distinctions. Classification, then, can be the start of a process that leads to a more fundamental understanding of basic principles rather than just a labeling process that is an end in itself.

The attempt to develop a classification system for abnormal behavior was based in part on the example of the value of classification in the area of physical disease. People with a certain *syndrome* (pattern of symptoms) that showed a typical course and outcome without treatment—the symptoms of malaria, for example—were classified as having the same disease. Once a syndrome had been identified, research in many instances proceeded to identify the physical causes of the disease and to develop effective treatments or even preventive measures.

Investigators in the field of psychopathology have reaped similar benefits in several notable instances. As we saw in Chapter 2, the first step in the long process of fully understanding the mental disorder known as general paresis was the identification of a pattern of symptoms with an associated course and outcome. If physicians had not been interested in classification, it is hard to see how progress could have been made in separating out this particular disorder from the mass of mental disorders and discovering its highly specific cause—a syphilitic infection.

Thus a major aim of psychopathologists in developing classificatory systems is to discover to what extent there are distinctive patterns of abnormal behaviors with their own causative histories. The realization of this aim allows them not only to seek out causative influences but also to devise rational treatment and to detect individuals in the early stages of

certain disorders before the disorders become more serious.

In this chapter I will outline the classification scheme most widely used for abnormal behavior and consider some of the problems that classification systems of this kind encounter. Then we will look at a more behavioral approach to diagnosis and briefly consider the process whereby diagnoses are made.

A CURRENT SYSTEM OF CLASSIFICATION—DSM-III

During World War I the Navy had a system by which all mentally disturbed sailors were assigned to one of two categories: "insane, restraint" or "insane, other." Clearly, mental health professionals need a more sophisticated classification system. The system used for record keeping by all private and public institutions, called the *Diagnostic and Statistical Manual of Mental Disorders* (DSM-I), first published by the American Psychiatric Association in 1952, was revised in 1968 (DSM-II), and a third revision, DSM-III, was published in 1980. DSM-III represents a marked change from the two earlier systems, and in several respects these changes would seem to be an improvement. The disorders are described in more behavioral terms that are less tied to theoretical assumptions about intrapsychic causes, certain categories of doubtful utility have been dropped, and individuals are to be evaluated on each of five dimensions, or axes, as they are called. The axes are as follows:

Axis I The Clinical Psychiatric Syndrome
Axis II Personality Disorders (adults) and Specific Developmental Disorders (children and adolescents)
Axis III Physical Disorders
Axis IV Severity of Psychosocial Stressors
Axis V Highest Level of Adaptive Functioning Past Year

Axes I and II represent the basic classificatory system of mental disorders. Separating these two axes makes it less likely that the clinician will overlook long-term personality styles that might be missed when attention is directed to a current episode of disturbance. Multiple diagnoses can be made on either Axis I or Axis II. Children, in addition to the possible presence of a psychiatric syndrome, can be characterized in terms of various specific developmental disorders (such as reading disorder or bed-wetting). Axis III simply provides an opportunity to diagnose physical disease when present.

Axis IV explicitly encourages the diagnostician to make a formal judgment about the contribution of environmental stresses to the current symptoms. Some examples of areas of stress to be considered are:

Conjugal (marital and non-marital): engagement, marriage, discord, separation, death of spouse
Parenting: becoming a parent, friction with child, illness of child
Other interpersonal: all problems with one's friends, neighbors, associates or nonconjugal family members, such as illness of best friend, discordant relationship with boss
Occupational: includes work, school, homemaker, for example, being unemployed, retirement, problems at school

Living circumstances: change in residence, threat to personal safety, immigration
Financial: inadequate finances, change in financial status
Legal: being arrested, being in jail, involved in a lawsuit or trial
Developmental: the meaning given to phases of the life cycle, such as puberty, menopause, "becoming 50"
Physical illness or injury: illness, accident, surgery, abortion
Other psychosocial stressors: natural or manmade disaster, persecution, unmarried pregnancy, out-of-wedlock birth, rape

A rating from 1 (none) to 7 (catastrophic) of severity of psychosocial stressors based on all sources of stress is then made.

On Axis V a rating is made of the person's highest level of adaptive functioning during the past year, tak-

TABLE 6-1   Major Diagnostic Categories in DSM-III

Disorders Usually Arising in Childhood or Adolescence
   Mental retardation
   Attention deficit disorders
     With or without hyperactivity
   Conduct disorders
Anxiety Disorders of Childhood or Adolescence (for example, separation anxiety)
Eating Disorders (for example, anorexia nervosa)
Other Disorders with Physical Manifestations
   Stuttering
   Functional enuresis (bedwetting)
   Functional encopresis (soiling)
Pervasive Developmental Disorders
   Infantile autism
   Childhood onset pervasive developmental disorder (childhood psychosis)
Organic Mental Disorders
   Symptoms are caused by physical impairment of brain functioning
Substance Use Disorders
   Result from abuse of alcohol or other drugs
Schizophrenic Disorders
   Severe disorders usually involving impairment in thought, emotion, and behavior, and withdrawal from human contact and reality
     Disorganized (hebephrenic)
     Catatonic
     Paranoid
     Undifferentiated
Paranoid Disorders
   Delusions of persecution are prominent
Schizoaffective Disorders
   A combination of symptoms shown in the Schizophrenic and the Affective Disorders
Affective Disorders
   Severe disturbance in mood, usually involving extremes of depression or elation

Table 6-1   Major Diagnostic Categories in DSM-III

Major Affective Disorders
  Bipolar disorder
  Major depression
Other Specific Affective Disorders
  Cyclothmic disorder
  Dysthmic disorder (also called neurotic depressson)
Anxiety Disorders
  Phobic disorder
  Anxiety states
  Panic disorder
  Generalized anxiety disorder
  Obsessive-compulsive disorder
  Posttraumatic stress disorder
Somatoform Disorders
  Physical symptoms for which there are no demonstrable organic causes and for
    which there is evidence that the symptoms are linked to psychological factors;
    most symptoms previously called conversion hysteria would be included here
Dissociative Disorders
  Psychogenic amnesia
  Psychogenic fugue
  Multiple personality
Psychosexual Disorders
  Gender identity disorders (for example, transsexualism)
  Paraphilias
    Fetishism
    Transvestism
    Pedophilia
    Exhibitionism
    Voyeurism
    and others
Psychosexual Dysfunctions
  Inhibited sexual desire
  Inhibited sexual excitement (frigidity, impotence)
  Inhibited orgasm
  Premature ejaculation
  Functional vaginismus
Disorders of Impulse Control Not Elsewhere Classified
  Includes such disorders as compulsive gambling, stealing, and fire setting, or isolated
    explosive violence
Adjustment Disorders
Psychological Factors Affecting Physical Condition
  Includes disorders formerly called psychosomatic or psychophysiological such as
    headaches, peptic ulcers, high blood pressure, and asthma. The particular physical
    condition should be listed on Axis III.
Personality Disorders (Axis II)
  Paranoid
  Schizotypal
  Antisocial
  Dependent
  Passive-aggressive and other personality styles

Note: This is not a complete list of all disorders included in DSM-III. Subcategories in certain areas
    such as Organic Mental Disorders and Substance Use Disorders are omitted here but will be
    mentioned in later chapters. Certain rare disorders are left out altogether. The aim here is to
    provide an overview of the more important disorders. See Appendix for a complete outline of
    the DSM-III classification system.

ing into account behavior in three areas: social relations, occupation, and leisure time. This is a six-point rating ranging from 1 (superior functioning) to 6 (grossly impaired functioning).

In Table 6-1 a list of most of the major categories from Axes I and II is presented. The purpose here is to give you an overview of the range of disorders to be covered in the following chapters and not to provide detailed descriptions of the symptom patterns involved.

As an example let us apply this diagnostic system to Joanne, the woman first referred to in Chapter 1 who was depressed and having trouble managing her children and experiencing strong dissatisfaction with her marriage. Joanne's diagnostic summary might be as follows:

Axis I: Dysthymic disorder (neurotic depression)
Psychological factors affecting physical condition
Axis II: None
Axis III: Physical Disorders: tension headaches, migraine headaches
Axis IV: Psychosocial Stressors: marital discord, friction with children, conflict with father-in-law
Severity: 4 moderate
Axis V: Highest level of adaptive functioning in past year: 4 fair

PROBLEMS ASSOCIATED WITH CLASSIFICATION SYSTEMS

Two important questions should be asked of any classification system: (1) How reliably can the categories be judged? and (2) How valid are the categories in the sense of discriminating among disorders that have distinctive etiologies and possibly require different treatments? In addition, we will consider some of the psychological effects of labeling—on both patients and professionals.

The Reliability of Categories.   Studies have not yet been done on the reliability of diagnosis for the proposed DSM-III categories. Generally speaking, reliability has been only moderately good for the major diagnostic categories as defined in DSMs I and II; for example, independent psychiatrists agreed on a schizophrenic diagnosis in 53 percent of the cases in one study (Beck et al., 1962). Agreement on subcategories within the broader categories was even less. The lack of clear and generally agreed-upon criteria in making psychiatric judgments was highlighted in Temerlin's (1970) study, where the effects of "prestige suggestion" were shown to be marked. See Research Report 6-1.

RESEARCH REPORT 6-1

Diagnosticians Are Greatly Influenced by Prestige Suggestion

Temerlin (1970) studied the extent to which the diagnosis of a "normal" person was influenced by a suggestion from a person of high status and prestige. He taped an interview with an actor who played the role of a person enjoying good mental health. The actor attempted to convey a person who was happy and effective in his work; had warm, cordial, and relaxed relationships with other members of the community; was happily married; enjoyed sexual intercourse; was self-confident without being arrogant; and was free of depression, psychosomatic symptoms, inappropriate emotions, hostility, suspiciousness, delinquency, excessive drinking, and thinking disturbance.

Five groups—psychiatrists, clinical psychologists, graduate students in clinical psychology, law students, and undergraduates—heard (or were told secondhand) a well-known and respected person make the following comment (the prestige suggestion): "I know the man being interviewed today. He's a very interesting man because he looks neurotic but actually is quite psychotic." The actor-patient gave as his reason for coming to a clinic that he had just read a book on psychotherapy and wanted to talk about it. After listening to the interview all subjects were asked to make a specific diagnosis by checking on a data sheet that listed various psychotic, neurotic, and character (personality) disorders plus a "healthy personality" category. The terms *neurotic, psychotic,* and *character disorder* have not been defined as yet, but for purposes of understanding this study it can be said that psychosis refers to an extremely severe psychological disorder, neurosis to an intermediate degree of severity, and character disorder to a long-standing personality style frequently involving antisocial behavior. Temerlin also ran three control

TABLE 6-2 Diagnoses by Subjects Given Prestige Suggestion of Psychosis

GROUP	DIAGNOSIS		
	Psychosis	Neurosis or Character Disorder	Mental Health
Psychiatrists (N = 25)	15	10	0
Clinical psychologists (N = 25)	7	15	3
Graduate students in clinical psychology (N = 45)	5	35	5
Law students (N = 40)	7	29	4
Undergraduates (N = 156)	47	84	25

Adapted from M. K. Temerlin, Diagnostic bias in community mental health. *Community Mental Health Journal*, 1970, *6*, 110–117. Copyright 1970 by Human Sciences Press.

groups, each composed of a stratified sample of the various professions. These groups were (1) given no suggestion of any kind, (2) given a prestige suggestion of good mental health, or (3) told that it was an employment interview.

Few individuals in any of the groups receiving the prestige suggestion rated the person as mentally healthy (Table 6-2). The psychiatrists showed the least tendency to see mental health (0 percent), while the undergraduate students showed the greatest tendency (16 percent). On the other hand, no subjects in the various control conditions diagnosed the actor-patient as psychotic and most diagnosed him as mentally healthy (Table 6-3).

Clearly, the prestige suggestion had a strong impact on the diagnostic decisions of the subjects, and apparently the greater the training and experience of the subject the greater was the influence. One psychiatrist in the prestige suggestion group said, "I thought he was psychotic from the moment he said he was a mathematician, since mathematicians are highly abstract and depersonalized people who live in a world of their own," and then apparently ignored all the information indicating highly socialized and interpersonally effective behavior.

Temerlin's study is a remarkable demonstration of how far from objective our diagnostic procedures are. If the diagnosticians had been dealing with the symptoms of

TABLE 6-3 Diagnoses by Control Subjects

CONDITION	DIAGNOSIS		
	Psychosis	Neurosis or Character Disorder	Mental Health
No suggestion (N = 21)	0	9	12
Suggestion of mental health (N = 20)	0	0	20
Employment interview (N = 24)	0	7	17

Adapted from M. K. Temerlin, Diagnostic bias in community mental health. *Community Mental Health Journal*, 1970, *6*, 110–117. Copyright 1970 by Human Sciences Press.

physical disease, such as high blood pressure or stomach ulcers, which can be measured more or less objectively and reliably, it is unlikely that a prestige authority could have made many of them disbelieve what their own eyes were telling them. This study points to the danger of having important decisions, such as involuntary commitment to an institution, depend upon diagnostic decisions that are so easily influenced by external factors.

Feighner et al. (1972) developed what they called research criteria for diagnosis in which quite specific (and possibly arbitrary) criteria were listed for each diagnostic category. Agreement among four different raters ranged from 86 to 95 percent in a study of 314 psychiatric emergency room patients. Helzer et al. (1977) used the same research criteria as Feighner et al. and in addition trained psychiatrists in a more structured interview approach in which a standard set of questions were asked. Agreement between pairs of psychiatrists interviewing the same patients on different occasions was relatively high, as shown in Table 6-4. Agreement for schizophrenia was somewhat low, but the study was performed in a private short-term psychiatric facility where schizophrenic patients were not often seen and possibly posed a more than usually difficult diagnostic problem when they were seen. In the last column of the table are averaged agreement statistics for six previous studies in which more usual diagnostic practices were used. Agreement levels tended to be lower in these earlier studies. There is reason for optimism that diagnostic reliability will be improved with DSM-III since many of the Feighner et al. research criteria have been incorporated in this revision. Of course, reliability of diagnosis is likely to be higher when psychiatrists are carefully trained in a given set of criteria and when they are participating in a research study than in the rush of everyday clinical practice.

TABLE 6-4 Agreement Between Psychiatrists in Diagnosis

Diagnosis	Frequency of Diagnosis (%)	Specific Agreement (%)	K	K (Mean of Six Previous Studies)
Depression	81	84	.55	
Mania	13	73	.82	.33
Anxiety neurosis	35	73	.76	.45
Schizophrenia	5	43	.58	.57
Antisocial personality	15	72	.81	.53
Alcoholism	35	71	.74	.71
Drug dependence	15	76	.84	
Hysteria (female patients only)	18	68	.72	
Obsessional illness	7	67	.78	
Undiagnosed psychiatric illness	18	20	.19	

Note: $N = 101$. The percentage of specific agreement is determined by dividing the number of cases in which both psychiatrists assigned the particular diagnosis divided by that number plus the number of times one psychiatrist made the particular diagnosis and the other did not. K (Kappa) is a statistic that corrects for chance agreement and varies as a function of the base rate of patients with a given diagnosis. The Kappa values can be interpreted as roughly equivalent to the correlation between two psychiatrists' judgments. The psychiatrists were permitted to give more than one diagnosis to a given patient.

These data are based on findings published by J. E. Helzer, P. J. Clayton, R. Pambakian, T. Reich, R. A. Woodruff, and M. A. Reveley. Reliability of psychiatric diagnosis: II. The test/retest reliability of diagnostic classification. Reprinted by permission from the *Archives of General Psychiatry*, 1977, *34*, 136–141. Copyright 1977, American Medical Association.

The Validity of Categories. How useful have these categories been for understanding causes and for suggesting treatments? Some categories of the current system have turned out to be related to certain causative factors; for the most part these categories involve disorders with an organic cause, such as general paresis, or certain forms of mental retardation caused by a physical malfunction. Major problems still remain, however, in defining schizophrenia and affective disorders. As we will see in later chapters, much attention has been given to identifying subcategories within these disorders that might have distinctive causative features. For example, the division of Affective Disorders into Major Depressive and Bipolar Affective Disorders resulted in part from research evidence suggesting differences between these categories in genetic contribution and differences in response to various types of treatment. The less severe disorders such as the Anxiety Disorders and many of the Personality Disorders may never provide highly reliable diagnoses simply because the large contribution of social learning to these disorders results in a great range and overlap of behavioral manifestations.

The more radical behaviorists (as well as the more extreme antilabelers such as Szasz) have been especially vocal in arguing that abnormal behavior does not fall into categories. The vast majority of abnormal behaviors (except for those with known organic causation) are learned, they say, and therefore comprise an almost infinite number of variations, each with its own specific learning history. In this view any classification system is likely to do more harm than good by forcing people with different patterns of behavior and learning histories into the same pigeonhole.

Many clinicians nevertheless argue that, despite obvious limitations, schemes such as DSM-III do provide useful information. For example, knowing that a person has been diagnosed with high subjective certainty as schizophrenic rather than as phobic disorder by a well-trained and experienced clinician probably entails valid implications about both symptoms and expectations for improvement with certain kinds of treatment. Given some utility in these classification systems, they argue, we should work on improving them rather than throwing them out altogether. Nevertheless, most clinicians of all persuasions would probably agree that the information carried in any one diagnostic label such as *depression* or *generalized anxiety disorder* is limited. The variations within each category are large, and a more extended assessment of the particular individual's symptoms and life circumstances is necessary if one desires more than a superficial description of a symptom pattern.

The Effects of Labeling. Many clinicians have voiced concerns about the possible harmful effects of labeling. Thomas Szasz argues in *The Manufacture of Madness* (1970) that labeling a person as mentally ill, or more specifically as psychotic or schizophrenic, results in a kind of public stigma. People expect such a person to be crazy, violent, or at least strange, whether or not the person is actually behaving in these ways. The expectations themselves are likely to produce or make worse these very symptoms so that labeling in such a case creates a self-fulfilling prophecy. This view of the negative effects of labeling is essentially the same as the societal reaction theory of mental illness, namely, that most of the symptoms of mental illness reflect secondary deviances resulting from effects of labeling.

Mahrer (1978), an exponent of the humanistic view, also argues strongly against labeling, saying,

According to the psychiatric approach, the person *is* an anxiety reaction, hebephrenic, delinquent, homosexual, manic-depressive, and so on. . . . Our perspective would seek to describe the nature of the person's potentials for experiencing. . . . Instead of the question being, "What psychiatric category do you fall under?", the question is, "What are you experiencing?" (p. 21)

These concerns about the harmful effects of labeling would seem to be borne out by one person's experience:

. . . A few years ago, during my training in medical school, I was hospitalized at a reputable institution and, at some time during my stay, diagnosed as schizophrenic. . . . My label seemed to be the focal point for their (the staff's) debasing behavior. I felt that I had partly lost my right to stand among humanity as human, based on my treatment in the hospital, and that for some people I would be forevermore something of a subhuman creature. . . . Mental health professionals often treated me either overprotectively or as if I were a stranger or alien of sorts, set apart from others by reason of my label. . . . Returning to work as a fellow in a department of psychiatry, I was repeatedly in contact with psychiatrists, psychologists, and other mental health professionals. Quite frequently amidst such contacts there were derogatory and slanderous remarks of persons labeled schizophrenic . . . the psychosocial implications of the diagnosis of schizophrenia per se will need to be dealt with by clinicians (Anonymous, 1977, p. 4).

Labeling can have an effect on professionals as well as on nonprofessionals, as a study by Langer and Abelson (1974) shows. These authors compared judgments of two types of clinicians, those trained in a behaviorally oriented program and those trained in more traditional, psychodynamically oriented programs. Clinicians from both types of programs were shown a videotape of a person being interviewed. Half of the clinicians of each type were told that the person was being interviewed for a job and the other half were told that it was an interview with a patient. Clinicians from the psychodynamic orientation judged the person as more psychologically disturbed when he had been labeled "patient" than when labeled "job applicant." The behaviorally oriented clinicians rated the person as relatively nondisturbed whether labeled "patient" or "job applicant," with little difference between the ratings. The authors interpreted this finding as consistent with behaviorally oriented training, which focuses on specific, observable behaviors and discourages inferences about intrapsychic dynamics. The differences between the psychodynamic and behaviorally oriented clinicians are shown in the following examples of responses given to the questions, "What do you think might explain Mr. Smith's outlook on life? Do you think he is realistic?"

"Patient" Condition. Psychodynamic clinicians said: "Doesn't seem to be realistic because he seems to use denial (and rationalization and intellectualization) to center his problems in situations and other people"; "seems afraid of his own drives, motives . . . outlook not based on realities of 'objective world' "; "anxiety about his ability and adequacy"; "basically fear of his aggressive drives and in particular as they are related to his fear of women."

"Job Applicant" Condition. Psychodynamic clinicians said: "His attitudes are consistent with a large subculture in the U.S. . . . the silent majority"; "he

seems fairly realistic"; "fairly reality oriented; recognizes injustices of large systems but doesn't seem to think he can individually do anything to change them"; "realistic to some degree, he knows how to conform but finds it difficult"; "he seems to be perceptive and realistic about politicians"; "values capitalist system."

Behavioral clinicians responded to both labels much like the latter group of psychodynamic clinicians: "His previous experience working in bureaucratic organizations might account for his distrust of authority. . . . He is probably realistic"; "his desire to be a successful businessman may have been partly a function of the business orientation of his friends and family"; "he seems fairly realistic and apparently wants to do something to help the kids he's working with"; "don't know what his outlook on life is, except that he thinks people should be more involved in their work, and that is realistic" (p. 8).

This study is a rather convincing demonstration that some professional clinicians will develop sharply different perceptions and expectations from exactly the *same* information about a person, depending on whether or not the person has been labeled "patient."

The dangers of labeling (or diagnosing) are undoubtedly real, and the antilabelers should be thanked for raising our consciousness on this point, but to abandon all attempts at classification would be to overreact. The public use of labels (in school files, for example) should probably be minimized, but the judicious and sensitive use of classification categories by researchers and clinicians who are aware of these pitfalls still seems desirable—for the long-term benefit of the patient as well as for general scientific goals.

The Diagnostic Process

Although some clinicians, especially the humanistic-experiential, almost totally disavow any attempt at diagnostic assessment, preferring to move immediately into treatment, in most clinical settings some attempt at a diagnostic formulation is made. In addition to determining how to categorize the person's problem, the clinician may be expected to answer a number of other specific questions on the basis of the diagnostic process: Is organic brain pathology present? Are the person's symptoms partly a reaction to drugs? Is the person reacting to some acute situational crisis or is it a long-term problem? How severe is the disturbance? Is hospitalization indicated? Is suicide a risk? Is the person motivated for treatment? Is the person mentally retarded? In some cases a thorough physical and neurological examination is called for, perhaps including specialized measures such as an electroencephalogram (measure of brainwave patterns) or blood tests. However, the three primary methods for obtaining and evaluating diagnostic information are the *interview, observation,* and *psychological tests.* We will consider briefly each of these assessment techniques.

Clinician interviewing patient.

THE INTERVIEW

The interview is the basic, and often the only, instrument of assessment. Ordinarily a diagnostic interview (sometimes called an *intake interview*) is routinely given when a person is first seen at a clinic or institution; in some institutions, usually inpatient hospitals, the intake interview may be followed later by a more intensive mental status examination.

The nature of the diagnostic interview varies widely as a function of the theoretical orientation of the interviewer and the setting in which the interview is conducted. A psychodynamically oriented interviewer will be more interested in the person's thought processes and past social history than a more behaviorally oriented interviewer, who will be especially interested in current circumstances related to the person's symptoms. As for setting, the diagnostic problems seen in a college counseling center are likely to be quite different from those typical of a large mental hospital or a child guidance clinic.

From a social learning perspective an interviewer would probably want to obtain information in the following areas (taken in part from Goldfried & Davison, 1976, and Kanfer & Saslow, 1969):

1. Nature of problem(s). Describe the problem behaviors or target symptoms. Does the problem represent an excess of behavior (hyperactivity) or a deficit in behavior (avoidance of interaction)?
2. Current situational determinants. These may be divided into circumstances that precede the problem behavior and consequences that follow the problem behavior. The symptom tends to occur in relation to what situations, or people, or current life stresses? What kinds of consequences, especially rewarding payoffs, follow expression of the symptom? Under this heading one would look for social systems, such as the family, that seem to be maintaining the problem behavior. This aspect of the assessment corresponds to what behaviorally oriented clinicians call a *functional analysis.*
3. Cognitive mediators. What kinds of characteristic interpretations, expectations, and other self-statements seem to be contributing to the symptom? For example, "My dizziness and fast-beating heart mean that I must have a serious heart condition."
4. Past history. What kind of social learning experiences have contributed to the development of the problem behavior, for example, to personality dispositions to respond with symptomatic behavior in the face of current stresses? What past biological factors (illness or physical handicap, for example) have relevance for the current understanding of the person's behavior? For certain severe disorders (especially those involving schizophrenic and depressive symptoms) the incidence of similar symptom patterns in relatives may be an aid to diagnostic understanding.
5. What broader sociological factors are relevant to either the development or maintenance of the symptoms (ethnic, racial, religious, socioeconomic, and so on)?
6. Assets. What physical, intellectual, and social abilities does the person have that will be helpful in altering the maladaptive behavior? What factors are present in the social environment that can aid

the therapeutic process, for example, a cooperative spouse?

7. Motivation for treatment. What does the person say and what has the person done that would indicate degree of motivation for treatment? The extent to which the person has been coerced to seek treatment (for example, by school authorities or courts) may be associated with low intrinsic motivation.

Interviewers also vary widely in their concern about collecting certain prescribed factual information as opposed to encouraging patients to tell their own story and generally following the patients' leads. Skilled interviewers are able to combine these objectives, making sure that certain kinds of information are obtained but also facilitating patients in following their own emotional associations. In the following excerpt from an initial interview a psychiatrist is aiding a hospitalized young woman to tell more about certain rather bizarre experiences she has been having. Note that the interviewer permits the patient to tell her own story, occasionally facilitating the flow of her description by reflecting some emotionally important expression, or picks up on some puzzling but probably important phrase in a way that encourages her to elaborate on it. As a result a good deal of information about her delusional experiences will eventually come out.

I (Interviewer): . . . Do you know what the reason is you've come down here?

P (Patient): No, I don't.

I: Mmhnn. Well I've been asked to see you to help the doctors with . . .

P: My case. That is . . .

I: That's right. Yes. Why . . . ah . . . what happened that you went to _____?

P: Oh, I . . . I was very nervous and I didn't seem to have the desire to go anyplace. And I'd argue with my mother, and there wasn't any reason to argue with her because . . . ah . . . I don't know. Ah . . . I'd wake up and find my head being smashed in and everything.

I: Your head . . . ah . . . being . . .

P: I was being molested.

I: . . . smashed in?

P: Yes. I was being molested at home. And I thought perhaps if I went someplace else I would at least be safe.

I: Mmmhnn. Molested? How is that?

P: In every way. In . . . in . . . ah . . . I don't know . . . kicking my face in and everything.

I: Tell me about that.

P: Well, I can't tell you too much. I feel very ridiculous speaking about it, a little bit ashamed, I guess. But . . . ah . . . I don't know and I'd be asleep all through it. And then, as the day progressed, I'd remember that I was. And I'd actually feel the bangs and everything in my sleep. And . . . ah . . . I find it so all the time with me. And I don't know how to explain it or why. (Gill et al., 1954, pp. 298–302)

The interview as a source of diagnostic information is not without its problems. One is that the interviewer relies heavily on the accuracy of the person's self-report. Various circumstances can affect what a patient tells an interviewer: the skill of the interviewer in helping the patient feel at ease and in facilitating open and honest expression, personal characteristics of the patient (such as articulateness and defensiveness), and the immediate circumstances and purposes of the interview. The situational factors can be extremely important. Have persons sought outpatient help on their own initiative? Are they being interviewed at a mental hospital after being brought there against their will? Have they been referred by a judge with the understanding that psychological treatment is an alternative to jail? Have children been taken to a clinic because their teachers or parents want the clinic to "do something about their disruptive behavior"? With some people the age, sex, and perceived status of the interviewer will affect how they respond. Experienced clinicians are aware of these possible influences and take them into account as best they can.

OBSERVATION

The psychological interview cannot answer adequately all diagnostic questions. Further information may be obtained by *observational procedures,* which are concerned with what persons *do* rather than what they say they do. Some observational information is usually obtained as part of the interview. The interviewer notes the person's physical appearance, dress, and behavioral characteristics: whether the patient shows nervous mannerisms, avoids eye contact, speaks fast or slow, loudly or in a whisper, slouches back in the chair, and so on. A teacher, parent, or trained observer may report on a child's behavior at school or at home. Recall the case of four-year-old Ann (Chapter 4) who had withdrawn more and more from play with other children, preferring instead to interact with adults. The behaviorally oriented clinicians in this instance observed Ann right in her nursery school surroundings where the problem behavior occurred and was reinforced. Their *functional analysis* was of diagnostic value to the therapists in planning a treatment program for Ann.

Barlow (1977) provides an example of behavioral assessment of depression on a mental hospital ward. Psychiatric aides were trained to count instances of behaviors usually associated with depression: not talking to other people, avoiding social interactions (usually by withdrawing to their room), not smiling, and diminished motor activity. These behaviors (or their lack) intercorrelated highly and were combined to form one measure of depression. Degree of depression was also measured by self-report questionnaires. It is of some interest that improvement on the self-report measures did not successfully predict which patients would not relapse during the following year, whereas improvement on the behavioral measure did. The sample size was small in this study, but it points to the importance of behavioral observations as a supplement to self-report measures.

Besides relatively natural situations, special situations can be contrived to focus on a certain kind of behavior. For example, a phobic individual can be confronted with the real phobic object (or a slide presentation of the object), and various behavioral and physiological measures (heart rate, for example) can be obtained. Nonassertive individuals can be asked to role-play responses in contrived circumstances, testing their ability to say no to unrealistic requests. Measures of penile erection or vaginal response can be obtained to various heterosexual, homosexual, or fetishistic objects. Structured behavioral observations such as these may not always be feasible in everyday clinical work and are more likely to be used in controlled research.

PSYCHOLOGICAL TESTS

Psychological tests are another source of diagnostic information. Briefly, a psychological test is a highly standardized procedure for obtaining a sample of behavior from which inferences can be made about the person's general psychological functioning. Tests are usually constructed so that a person's responses can be quantified and compared with norms obtained on a large sample of other individuals. In general, tests seek to reduce some of the uncontrolled influences that operate in the interview and to provide more standardized information.

Psychologists have devised dozens of tests for different diagnostic purposes. *Intelligence tests,* such as the Stanford-Binet and Wechsler's intelligence scales for adults and children, are especially useful when there is a question of mental retardation or when for some other reason an estimate of the person's general level of intellectual ability is required. *Personality tests,* the other type used primarily by clinicians, assess various aspects of personality, such as characteristic motives, defenses, conflicts, self-image, and thought processes. The two most common types of personality tests are projective tests (or *techniques,* as some clinicians prefer to call them) and personality inventories. Let us look more closely at them.

Projective Tests. In projective tests, the person is asked to respond to ambiguous stimulus materials. Thus for the *Rorschach Test* the person is shown

This person is administering the Wechsler Adult Intelligence Scale, a test that is useful in diagnosing mental retardation and also in assessing the extent to which intellectual functioning has been impaired by other psychological disorders.

cards depicting inkblots and asked to describe what they look like. The clinician scores and interprets the perceptual responses. The *Thematic Apperception Test* (TAT) consists of pictures of varying degrees of ambiguity that the person is asked to make up stories about. The themes and imagery in the stories can then be used to make inferences about the person's motives, self-concept, emotions, and conflicts.

The basic assumption in all projective techniques is that people *project* their own internal dispositions into their responses, whether into what they "see" in an inkblot or what they tell in a story. The content of the following story, told by a patient who was diagnosed as paranoid schizophrenic, supports other information suggesting a long-term resentment of his mother's attempt to dominate and control him. The patient was shown TAT Card I, a picture of a young boy sitting at a table contemplating a violin, and told to make up a story about it.

The Thematic Apperception Test (TAT) is composed of pictures like this one. Stories told to the pictures are thought to reflect important motives, emotions, and conflicts of the storyteller.

There's a young boy . . . a young boy looking at a violin, wondering whether he should take the violin or not. He doesn't want to. He doesn't like it in the least. He doesn't like the idea. But his mother has told him to take the violin. Therefore he must take it. And he doesn't see any way to get out of it. So he's sitting there thinking about chopping the violin to pieces if he can get away with it, or destroying it, or perhaps thinking whether he should go to his mother and tell her, "I refuse to take the violin," but he knows he can't do that so he'll just think about it, and he'll look at the violin and hate it. (How will the story end?) He'll probably take the violin until he gets to a point where he's old enough to do what he pleases. (Shneidman, 1955, p. 111)

The validity and general usefulness of projective test measures for diagnostic purposes continue to be a topic of disagreement. Psychodynamically oriented clinicians tend to believe that these tests add a significant dimension to the understanding of patients, whereas behaviorally oriented clinicians are likely to feel that the tests have little utility. Research has not provided consistent support for the validity of the Rorschach and the TAT (Zubin et al., 1965). More recently Exner (1974, 1978) in an ambitious series of studies (unfortunately, rather incompletely reported) provides more positive evidence for the reliability and validity of a number of scores and indices derived from the Rorschach. Certain scores and combinations of scores were found to discriminate between normals and antisocial, depressive, and schizo-

phrenic inpatients; were found to be predictive of suicide; and showed certain changes as a function of psychotherapy. The kind of research support that Exner provides for the Rorschach may give this test somewhat more status then it has previously enjoyed among scientifically oriented clinicians. The Rorschach, however, will probably continue to be used mainly in an intuitive and clinical fashion rather than as a more objectified test such as the MMPI.

Personality Inventories. Personality inventories consist of a large number of statements to which the person is asked to respond in terms of fixed categories such as Yes, No, or Cannot Say. The important contrasts with the projective techniques are that the stimulus materials are not so ambiguous and that the person is not permitted the same freedom of response. The inventories are usually divided into various subscales to measure different aspects of the personality.

The *Minnesota Multiphasic Personality Inventory* (MMPI) is perhaps the most widely used personality inventory in the field of abnormal psychology. This test, developed by Hathaway and McKinley (1943), consists of 550 items covering a wide range of topics, including physical health, religious attitudes, moods, beliefs, fears, and social interests. When the test was being developed the items were administered to eight groups of psychiatric patients with known diagnoses (such as hysteria, depression, and schizophrenia) and

TABLE 6-5 **Personality Characteristics Associated with Elevations on the Basic MMPI Scales**

Scale	Characteristics
?, Cannot Say	A validity score that, if high, may indicate evasiveness.
L, Lie Scale	A validity scale that measures the tendency to present oneself in an overly favorable or highly virtuous light.
F Scale	A validity scale composed of highly infrequent items. A high score suggests carelessness, confusion, or claiming an inordinate amount of symptoms or "faking illness." Random responding also will result in an elevated F score.
K, Subtle Defensiveness	A validity scale that measures defensiveness of a subtle nature.
1 (Hs), Hypochondriasis	High scorers are described as cynical, defeatist, preoccupied with self, complaining, hostile, and presenting numerous physical problems.
2 (D), Depression	High scorers are described as moody, shy, despondent, pessimistic, and distressed. This scale is one of the most frequently elevated in clinical patients.
3 (Hy), Hysteria	High scorers tend to be repressed, dependent, naive, outgoing, and to have multiple physical complaints. Expression of psychological conflict through vague and unbased physical complaints.
4 (Pd), Psychopathic Deviate	High scorers often are rebellious, impulsive, hedonistic, and antisocial. They often have difficulty in marital or family relationships and trouble with the law or authority in general.
5 (MF), Masculinity-Femininity	High-scoring males are described as sensitive, aesthetic, passive, or feminine. High scoring females are described as aggressive, rebellious, and unrealistic.
6 (Pa), Paranoia	Elevations on this scale are often associated with being suspicious, aloof, shrewd, guarded, worrisome, and overly sensitive. High scorers may project or externalize blame.
7 (Pt), Psychasthenia	High scorers are tense, anxious, ruminative, preoccupied, obsessional, phobic, rigid. They frequently are self-condemning and feel inferior and inadequate.
8 (Sc), Schizophrenia	High scorers are often withdrawn, shy, unusual, or strange and have peculiar thoughts or ideas. They may have poor reality contact and in severe cases bizarre sensory experiences—delusions and hallucinations.
9 (Ma), Mania	High scorers are called sociable, outgoing, impulsive, overly energetic, optimistic, and in some cases amoral, flighty, confused, disoriented.
0 (Si), Social Introversion-Extroversion	High scorers tend to be modest, shy, withdrawn, self-effacing, inhibited. Low scorers are outgoing, spontaneous, sociable, confident.

From J. N. Butcher, *Objective Personality Assessment*, 1971. Copyright 1971, General Learning Press. Used with permission.

a control group of normals. Subscales were then constructed separately for groups of items that discriminated between each of these diagnostic groups and the normal group.

Four validity scales of the MMPI—Question Scale (?), Lie Scale (L), F Scale, and Correction Scale (K)—reflect different ways in which a subject's style of responding might affect the validity of the other scales. An excessive number of ? responses suggests evasiveness. The L scale is composed of a number of items that are mildly derogatory but probably true for most of us (such as "I get angry sometimes"). A person who denies many of these items may be trying to "look good." F detects faking toward more psychopathology than exists or just plain confusion in taking the test. K is a general measure of defensiveness, somewhat more subtle than ? and L; a high score indicates that the person is rather guarded and not inclined to disclose things that would seem unfavorable. See Table 6-5 for a summary of personality characteristics associated with elevations on the different MMPI scales.

Psychologists have conducted voluminous research on the MMPI, much of it suggesting that this test does have some value as an aid to diagnosis (Dahlstrom et al., 1975). It has not turned out, however, that a high score on, say, Sc (Schizophrenia) means that a person is behaving in a clearly schizophrenic fashion, or that a high score on Hy (Hysteria) means that a person is showing clear-cut hysterical symptoms. It is the configuration of several scale scores that is most useful diagnostically, not the score on a single scale. Many clinicians, in fact, tend to use the MMPI in a rather loose fashion, drawing upon their past experience and clinical intuition to make inferences about personality dynamics and psychopathology from a particular profile. As with the projective techniques, interpretations derived in this way by experienced clinicians may be useful, but such a use goes beyond the limits of the validated aspects of the MMPI.

An example of an MMPI profile is shown in Figure 6-1 (from Fowler, 1969). This profile was produced by a 37-year-old man who had been referred for test-

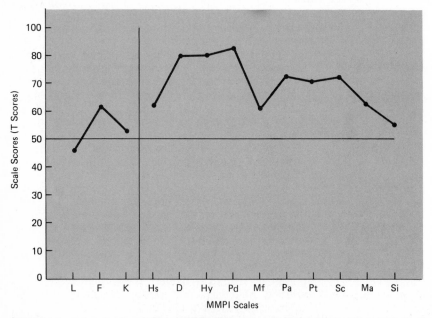

FIGURE 6-1. Example of a profile of MMPI scale scores. The scale scores were devised so that the original standardization sample of normal individuals had a mean of 50 and a standard deviation of 10, the so-called T-scores shown on the ordinate. Thus a score of 70 on a scale indicates that the person scored higher than 97 percent of the normal sample, two standard deviations above the mean. The data for this particular profile were taken from Fowler, 1969. Copyright 1969, McGraw-Hill Book Company. Reproduced with permission.

ing by his attorney after he had been charged with leaving the scene of an automobile accident. He had been arrested for drunkenness five times during the past two years, and he was showing many of the symptoms of alcoholism. Both his work and his marriage were being severely affected, and he reported that he and his wife were "sexually incompatible."

Butcher (1971) gave this profile to an experienced clinical psychologist, telling the psychologist only that the person was a 37-year-old man. The psychologist made the following "blind" interpretation:

This man is embroiled in, and nearly overwhelmed by, acute situational stress. Such factors as marital crisis, occupational setbacks, legal difficulties, or long-standing emotional turmoil and instability could be producing the stress. At the present time he feels completely thwarted and frustrated. Considerable anger and hostility are felt, but he cannot bring himself to express such feeling and is, consequently, quite depressed at this time. Long-standing characterological problems are suggested, and include impulse control problems, a lack of basic trust in others, and erratic performance under stress. More gross patterns of maladaptation such as alcoholism and psychosexual dysfunctioning are also possible. Beneath this man's apparent coldness and aloofness may reside a deep-seated dependency which he strives to deny or overcompensate for by much pseu-

dohypermasculine behavior such as excessive assertiveness and verbal aggressivity. While he is aware that he is in much distress at this time, and while he will welcome efforts by others to help him, he will impose strict qualifications on how others are to help him. He will not "go along with" anything and everything suggested, but will do so only if he sees immediate benefit accruing, and only if he is not required to effect fundamental changes in his style of life.

Diagnostic Impression: Situational stress reaction in an unstable and/or paranoid type of personality (p. 9).

In usual clinical practice a psychologist would not make such an interpretation "blind" but would incorporate other information into the diagnostic assessment. For our present purpose it is useful, however, to have the "blind" interpretation so that we can be assured that the conclusions drawn are based only on the MMPI profile.

Another development is the computerized MMPI interpretation. Information on personality characteristics and symptoms of individuals with certain types of profiles is stored in a computer. When a newly obtained profile is fed to the computer, it prints out characteristics that people with similar profiles have shown.

In many mental hospitals a team of mental health professionals meet to plan a comprehensive treatment program for each patient. In this photograph, taken at Bergen Pines County Hospital, Paramus, New Jersey, the team consists of an attending psychiatrist, a psychiatric resident, a social worker, a psychologist, a nurse, and an occupational and recreational therapist.

THE STAFF CONFERENCE

In many clinic and hospital settings a final step in the diagnostic process is the integration of information at a staff conference in which various members of the psychiatric team (psychiatrist, psychologist, social worker, and nurse) contribute their own expertise. A neurologist or psychiatrist may report med- ical and psychiatric findings, the psychologist may present the results of an interview and tests, the social worker may report on an interview with the patient's family, and the nurse may describe the patient's behavior on the ward. Ideally such a pooling of information should yield a more complete picture of the patient's difficulties than could be obtained by just one professional.

Summary

1. Classification is helpful in the first stages of most sciences. In the study of abnormal behavior a primary purpose in developing classificatory systems is to discover to what extent distinctive patterns of symptoms and their causes can be isolated.

2. The Diagnostic and Statistical Manual of the American Psychiatric Association (DSM-III) provides the classification scheme for abnormal behaviors currently most widely used in this country.

3. One of the problems associated with the current system for classifying abnormal reactions is that labeling itself may affect the expectations of mental health professionals and may also lead to more secondary deviance in those so labeled.

4. Clinicians are only moderately reliable in placing individuals in the current classifications, and there is a serious question as to whether discrete, homogeneous categories exist for many of the disorders.

5. In the present system there is a tendency to view psychopathology as residing in the individual; however, some disorders might best be seen as a disturbance in an interacting system composed of two or more people, such as a parent and a child.

6. Behavioral approaches to diagnosis emphasize a functional analysis for each individual of current and past environmental influences, as well as biological factors, that have affected the development and maintenance of the disorder.

7. The process of diagnosing, that is, assigning individuals to the various classifications, is ordinarily done by interview, direct observation, and psychological tests. Physical and neurological examinations may also be necessary.

8. The format of a diagnostic interview varies widely, depending upon the purpose and theoretical orientation of the interviewer. A behaviorally oriented clinician, for example, would be especially interested in the immediate environmental events that seem to be controlling the abnormal behavior. A more psychodynamically oriented interviewer would be more concerned with subjective mental processes.

9. Observational procedures emphasize what persons do rather than what they say they do. They may consist of observations in the natural environment or of behavior in specially contrived situations.

10. Psychological tests are standardized procedures for obtaining a sample of behavior from which inferences can be made about the person's general psychological functioning. Tests have been useful in the assessment of both intellectual and personality characteristics. Personality tests tend to be of two basic types, projective tests and inventories.

11. In projective tests the person is asked to respond to ambiguous stimuli, for example, to report what inkblots look like or to tell a story about a picture. These responses are then used as a basis for psychological interpretation on the assumption that the person has projected inner mental processes into the stimulus materials. Although these tests perhaps are useful to the individual clinician, research has not provided strong support for their validity.

12. The stimulus materials and responses called for on the personality inventories are more structured than on the projective tests. Usually the person is asked to respond to a number of statements by either Yes, No, or Cannot Say. The MMPI, the most widely used test of this kind, has been shown to have moderate validity as an aid to diagnosis.

Suggested Readings

The Diagnostic and statistical manual of mental disorders-III (American Psychiatric Association, 1980) provides detailed descriptions of the diagnostic criteria used in this system. J. Savodnik in Understanding persons as persons (*Psychiatric Quarterly,* 1974, *48,* 1–16) argues against labeling people with the traditional psychiatric categories, while S. Kety in From rationalization to reason (*American Journal of Psychiatry,* 1974, *131,* 957–963) presents the case for the use of psychiatric diagnosis. Another good discussion is R. L. Spitzer and D. F. Klein (Eds.) *Critical issues in psychiatric diagnosis* (Raven Press, 1978). Objective, projective, and behavioral approaches to assessment are covered in I. B. Weiner (Ed.), *Clinical methods in psychology* (Wiley, 1976).

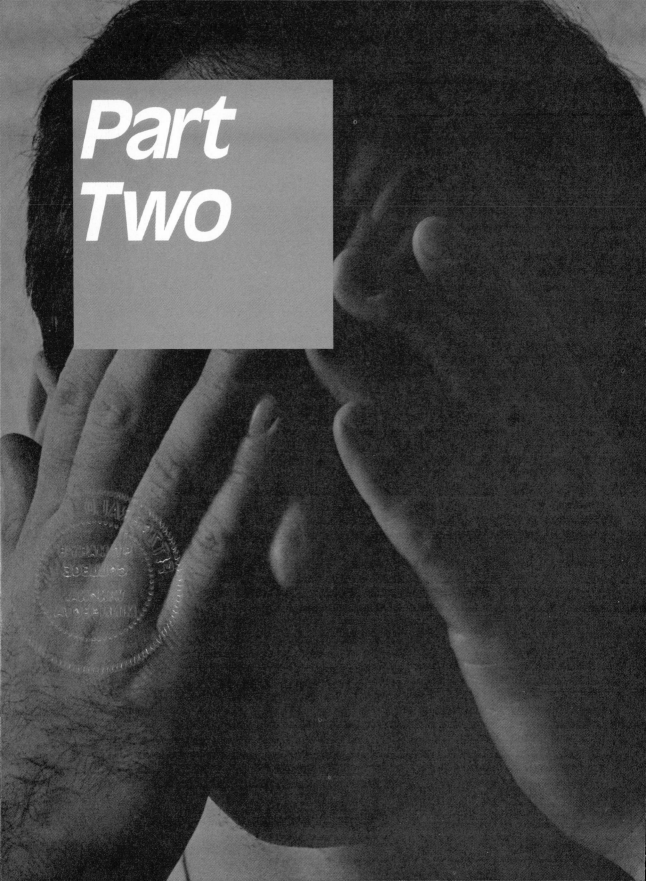

Part
Two

Some Nonpsychotic Disorders and Their Treatment

7

Reactions to Stress and Neurotic Traits

- "My heart was in my mouth." What would happen inside you if you saw a ghost?

- Do the effects of some terrifying experiences never go away?

- What stresses are especially likely to create temporary adjustment problems for college students?

- Why is it that some people develop excessive needs to be dependent, to be powerful, to be submissive, or to withdraw, which actually defeat their own basic desires?

- How can certain personality traits influence the development of disturbed marital interactions?

Reactions to Stress

In the course of evolution, human beings have developed biological systems for coping with stressful experiences: physical injuries, extremes of heat and cold, situations calling for physical exertion, dangerous animals, and so on. Emotional responses play an important role in most people's reactions to stresses, but these responses have been difficult to study because they are largely subjective in nature and cannot be directly measured. Investigators usually infer emotions from three sources: verbal report ("I'm angry"), behavior (hitting another person), or physiological responses (increased blood pressure). Despite imperfections in measurement, emotions—joy, excitement, fear, anger, grief, shame, disgust, and so on—are obviously real. Before we consider some psychological forms of emotional response, let us take a look at one of the body's physiological systems that is involved in almost all emotional responses, the *autonomic nervous system.*

THE AUTONOMIC NERVOUS SYSTEM

The autonomic nervous system primarily regulates the internal environment of the organism—facilitating or inhibiting digestive and eliminative processes; distributing blood flow toward or away from the heart and skeletal muscles; increasing or decreasing oxygen intake; and so on. Broadly speaking, it controls responses that on the one hand prepare a person to meet stressful environmental demands or on the other hand aid in the conservation and restoration of bodily resources. The former function is generally accomplished by the *sympathetic division* of the autonomic nervous system and the latter by the *parasympathetic division* (Figure 7-1).

Sympathetic Division. Arousal of the sympathetic division of the autonomic nervous system helps the organism cope with an emergency by fighting, running away, or by some other form of physical exertion. If you suddenly realized that you were being followed when out alone at night, you might well experience an arousal of the sympathetic division of your autonomic nervous system.

The biological significance of most sympathetic reactions (Table 7-1) is reasonably clear. The rate and force of contraction of the heart increase, and blood vessels to the viscera (stomach, intestines, and colon) and skin constrict so that the blood supply to the organs needed for emergency action, primarily the heart and the skeletal muscles, is increased. The combination of increased cardiac output and constriction of visceral and skin blood vessels results in an increase in blood pressure. Salivation in the mouth, muscular contractions in the stomach and intestines, and gastric secretions are inhibited. Bronchial passages in the lungs are dilated to permit greater oxygen intake to meet higher rates of body metabolism. The pupils dilate to increase visual sensitivity, and sweating occurs on the palmar surfaces of the hands and feet.

The adrenal medulla gland is stimulated to secrete epinephrine (adrenaline) and norepinephrine (noradrenaline) into the bloodstream. Epinephrine tends to sustain many of the sympathetic reactions initiated directly by sympathetic nerves. For example, it acts directly on the heart to increase the force of contraction and causes the liver to convert glycogen to glucose (blood sugar) to provide additional metabolic fuel. Circulating norepinephrine produces constriction of the blood vessels in the skin and viscera. In addition to being secreted by the adrenal medulla, norepinephrine plays a part in the chemical transmission of nerve impulses in the brain and from the end of sympathetic nerves to the smooth muscles of the viscera and blood vessels.

Parasympathetic Division. The parasympathetic division functions to conserve and restore rather than expend bodily resources. Thus activation results in slower heartbeat and dilation of skin and visceral blood vessels. The accompanying drop in blood pressure tends to decrease the utilization of fuels throughout the body. Parasympathetic stimulation promotes digestive processes, increasing muscle activity and dilation of blood vessels in the stomach and intestinal tracts, and the secretion of gastric juices in the stomach. Eliminative processes are also facilitated, and the pupil is constricted to reduce external stimulation. As can be seen, in many cases the two divisions of the autonomic nervous system affect the same organ in opposite ways.

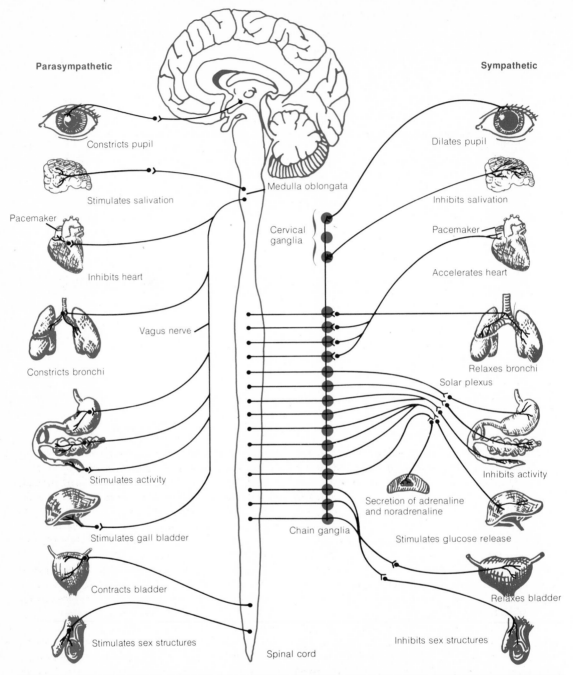

FIGURE 7-1. **The autonomic nervous system and some of the organs that it innervates. Many organs are served by both sympathetic and parasympathetic nerves, each functioning in opposition to the other. (From Lyle E. Bourne, Jr. and Bruce R. Ekstrand,** *Psychology: Its Principles and Meanings,* **3ʳᵈ Edition, 1979. Copyright 1979 by Holt, Rinehart and Winston. Reproduced by permission of Holt, Rinehart and Winston.)**

TABLE 7-1   **Functions of the Autonomic Nervous System**

Organ	Sympathetic Response	Parasympathetic Response
Heart	Rate increases Force of contraction increases	Rate decreases
Lungs	Air passages dilate	Air passages constrict
Blood vessels, to skeletal muscles and heart	Dilate, blood flow increases	Constrict, blood flow decreases
to viscera (stomach, intestines, colon)	Constrict, blood flow decreases	Dilate, blood flow decreases
Stomach	Inhibits secretion of acid and pepsin	Secretes acid and pepsin
Salivary glands	Inhibited	Secrete saliva
Liver	Releases sugar	None
Colon	Inhibited	Tone increases
Rectum	Inhibited	Releases feces
Genitals	Ejaculation (males) Blood vessel constriction (females)	Erection (males) Blood vessel dilation (females)
Eyes	Pupil dilates	Pupil constricts
Sweat glands and palmar surfaces	Secrete sweat	None
Adrenal medulla gland	Secrete epinephrine (adrenaline) and norepinephrine (noradrenaline)	None

Regulation of the Autonomic Nervous System. The autonomic nervous system is regulated largely by the hypothalamus, the posterior part being associated with sympathetic activation and the anterior part with parasympathetic activation. At the beginning of a predominantly sympathetic reaction, the anterior part of the hypothalamus is inhibited to reduce parasympathetic activation, and vice versa for the start of parasympathetic arousal. This process, called *reciprocal inhibition*, amplifies the effects of the system being aroused, since so many organs are affected in opposite ways by the two systems.

Homeostatic mechanisms in the autonomic nervous system also serve to restore equilibrium after imbalances have occurred. (*Homeostasis* is a general term referring to equilibrium in a dynamic system.) After sympathetic activation has resulted in increased blood pressure, pressure-sensitive receptors in the aorta and other arteries send neural impulses to cer-

tain brain centers which in turn cause blood vessel dilation and heart rate decrease. The result is a drop in blood pressure. Homeostasis is achieved through systems of this kind in which forces are set in operation by the original response that tend to dampen or reverse that response. This cycle is called a *negative feedback loop*. The homeostatic principle can also be seen in the working of a thermostat that regulates the temperature level of a house. Reciprocal inhibition, on the other hand, works in an opposite fashion; forces are set in motion by the original response that tend to further increase or amplify the response (sometimes called a positive feedback loop). Such a system, if allowed to go unchecked, would destroy equilibrium or homeostasis. In the well-functioning autonomic system the initial amplifying effects of reciprocal inhibition are eventually reversed by homeostatic controls.

FEAR AND ANXIETY

Charles Darwin's description of fear, written over 100 years ago, remains an excellent portrayal of this emotion:

Fear is often preceded by astonishment, and is so far akin to it, that both lead to the senses of sight and hearing being instantly aroused. In both cases the eyes and mouth are widely opened and the eyebrows raised. The frightened man at first stands like a statue motionless and breathless, or crouches down as if instinctively to escape observation.

The heart beats quickly and violently, so that it palpitates or knocks against the ribs; but it is very doubtful whether it then works more efficiently than usual, so as to send a greater supply of blood to all parts of the body; for the skin instantly becomes pale, as during incipient faintness. . . . In connection with the disturbed action of the heart, the breathing is hurried. The salivary glands act imperfectly; the mouth becomes dry and is often opened and shut. I have also noticed that under slight fear there is a strong tendency to yawn. One of the best-marked symptoms is the trembling of all the muscles of the body; and this is often first seen in the lips. From this cause, and from dryness of the mouth, the voice becomes husky or indistinct, or may altogether fail. . . . (Darwin, 1873, pp. 290–291)

In this chapter we will pay special attention to the emotion of fear; later in the book we will consider other emotions, especially grief and anger, in more detail. It should be noted, however, that emotions are complex and do not arrive in neat packages. We experience fear, anger, grief, shame, joy, excitement, and exhilaration in many mixtures and degrees, and researchers have not been entirely convincing in demonstrating that any given list represents *the* basic human emotions. The crucial point to remember for understanding of many forms of psychological disorders is that the extremes of negative emotion can be almost unbearable.

Humans, as well as most mammalian species, are born with the innate capacity to experience fear. Although there are undoubtedly neurophysiological systems in the brain associated with this emotion, we ordinarily infer its existence more indirectly from three kinds of data: *reports of subjective experiences* of apprehension, fright, tension, inability to concentrate, going to pieces, wishes to flee a particular sit-

uation, and physical sensations such as a pounding heart or sinking feeling in the pit of the stomach (reports of this kind are, of course, limited to individuals who have the capacity to verbalize these experiences); *behavioral manifestations* such as flight, disorganization of speech, motor incoordination, impairment of performance on complex problem-solving tasks, or sometimes immobilization as in being "paralyzed by fear"; and measurable *physiological responses* such as rapid and irregular heartbeat and breathing, palmar sweating, dry mouth, dilated pupils, and muscular trembling. The physiological responses largely reflect activation of the sympathetic nervous system, but some responses, such as diarrhea and increased frequency of urination, are produced by parasympathetic arousal. It is, perhaps, more accurate to say that the autonomic nervous system is thrown badly out of balance, with both subdivisions showing wide swings in activation.

A variation that may occur in acute fear is fainting. The physiological component in the fainting response, in contrast to the mixed sympathetic-parasympathetic pattern just described, is largely parasympathetic, involving abrupt dilation of the blood vessels in the viscera, slowing of the heartbeat, a drop in blood pressure, and loss of muscle tone. These effects result in a sharp decrease in the blood supply to the brain and produce loss of consciousness. The parasympathetic-dominated fainting response is likely to occur only in strong, acute fear.

Most of us have a pretty good idea of what an extreme fear response is like, either from our own experience or from observing others. Anyone who has seen the terror expressed by a frightened young child who has not yet been taught by society to conceal fear can appreciate the reality and potential intensity of this emotion. In humans the fear response is not strongly "connected" to any given set of external circumstances, although it is possible that strange and unfamiliar situations (people, animals, noises) and painful experiences have a higher likelihood than most other stimuli of eliciting fear in the infant or young child. Regardless of whatever unlearned tendencies exist for certain stimuli to elicit fear, it is a highly learnable response that can become associated with almost any situation or stimulus (external or internal) that happens to be present when the fear occurs, and it is also likely to be influenced powerfully by observational learning.

Fear can be an unpleasant and disrupting emotion.

A distinction is sometimes made between the responses of fear and anxiety. The usual distinction is that fear occurs in response to a real danger or threat, whereas anxiety is more irrational, occurring in response to situations that involve no actual danger, or is simply present much of the time without being clearly associated with any specific stimulus. This distinction between the kind of stimuli (real dangers or imagined ones) that elicit the fear does not necessarily involve a difference in the response itself.

Terror in Combat

A 21-year-old rifleman was flown directly from an area of fighting by a helicopter ambulance to the hospital. . . . His hands had been tied behind him for the flight, and he had a wild, wide-eyed look as he cowered in a corner of the emergency room, glancing furtively to all sides, cringing and startling at the least noise. He was mute, although once he forced out a whispered "VC" and tried to mouth words without success. He seemed terrified. Although people could approach him, he appeared oblivious to their presence. No manner of reassurance or direct order achieved either a verbal response or any other interaction from him.

His hands were untied, after which he would hold an imaginary rifle in readiness whenever he heard a helicopter overhead or an unexpected noise. The corpsmen led him to the psychiatric ward, took him to a shower, and offered him a meal; he ate very little. He began to move a little more freely but still offered no information.

He was then given 100 mg of chlorpromazine (Thorazine) orally; this dose was repeated hourly until he fell asleep. He was kept asleep in this manner for approximately 40 hours. After that he was allowed to waken, the medication was discontinued, and he was mobilized rapidly in the ward milieu. Although dazed and subdued upon awakening, his response in the ward milieu was dramatic. This was aided by the presence of a friend from his platoon on an adjoining ward, who helped by filling in parts of the story that the patient could not recall. The patient was an infantryman whose symptoms had developed on a day when his platoon had been caught in an ambush and then was overrun by the enemy. He was one of three who survived after being pinned down by the enemy fire for 12 hours. His friend told him that toward the end of that time he had developed a crazed expression and had tried to run from his hiding place. He was pulled back to safety and remained there until the helicopter arrived and flew him to the hospital.

Within 72 hours after his admission the patient was alert, oriented, responsive and active—still a little tense but ready to return to duty. He was sent to duty on his third hospital day and never seen again at our facility. It should be noted that he had no history of similar symptoms or emotional disorder. (Bloch, 1969, p. 294)

Reactive Disorders

POSTTRAUMATIC-STRESS DISORDER

Occasionally people experience severe stresses—tornadoes, floods, train or automobile accidents, fires, and various wartime experiences—that produce intense emotional disturbances. People who would never show symptoms of this kind in the ordinary course of their lives do show them under these horrific circumstances. Depending on the intensity and duration of the stress and the personality vulnerability of the individuals, they may recover quickly from their ordeal or continue to show emotional symptoms for months or even years after the stressful incident. The soldier in the case study is an example of a person who apparently made a rather quick recovery. The term *posttraumatic-stress disorder* is used to refer to these stress-induced reactions.

Few manmade stresses can compare with the horrors of war, and in every war there is a certain proportion of military personnel who develop incapacitating psychological symptoms—called *shell shock* in World War I, and *war neuroses, combat fatigue,* or *combat exhaustion* in subsequent wars. These reactions usually start with increasing irritability, difficulty in sleeping, and a tendency to react with startle to minor noises. If the stress is severe enough, the reaction may proceed to the more extreme terror and incapacitation shown by the Vietnam veteran.

Disturbances produced by severe stress can last for many years and in some cases increase in severity with the passage of time. For example, in 1957 the gasoline tanker *Mission San Francisco* collided with *Elna II,* a freighter, in the Delaware River. An intense explosion occurred in which ten men were killed.

Many of the survivors of this traumatic experience were given a psychiatric examination at the time and again about four years later (Leopold & Dillon, 1963). Most of the survivors reported symptoms of one kind or another: nervousness, tension, general upset, sleep disturbances, and gastrointestinal symptoms. In general, there was a tendency for the number of disturbances to *increase* over the four-year period. Many men were unable to return to sea on a regular basis, and most of those who did indicated that they were tense and fearful aboard ship although going to sea was a matter of occupational necessity. It would have been desirable in this study to have used a control group that had not had the traumatic ex-

Soldiers sometimes develop combat fatigue (combat exhaustion) after prolonged exposure to the stresses of war.

perience as a check on the general tendency for symptomatology to increase with time or age, but it is clear that the trauma survivors did not show much spontaneous decrease in their fear-related symptoms over this four-year period. The salesman in the next clinical report is a similar case.

Similar persisting effects have been found for survivors of Nazi concentration camps (Chodoff, 1963) and for soldiers suffering from combat fatigue (Archibald & Tuddenham, 1965). In the latter study, 62 veterans who had experienced combat fatigue 20 years previously in World War II were compared with a control group of combat veterans who had not shown combat fatigue. The combat fatigue veterans reported more depression, restlessness, irritability, jumpiness, fatigue, difficulty in concentration, sweaty hands, headaches, sleeplessness, yawning, and other signs of persisting anxiety. There was no clear indication that compensation for their disability played an important role in maintaining the disturbance. Most of the veterans, in fact, were receiving no compensation for their symptoms. It would be of special interest to know to what extent the combat fatigue veterans had shown similar anxiety symptoms (or other vulnerabilities) prior to combat, but that information is rarely available in studies of this kind.

Why do some people show continuing residual symptoms from a traumatic experience while others who experience the same situation do not? The answer no doubt lies in the fact that people bring to

Guatemalan earthquake scene. Natural disasters of this kind can produce traumatic neuroses in some people.

situational crises different vulnerabilities in personality makeup, resulting from particular combinations of biological temperaments and histories of environmental influences. It nevertheless seems likely, though difficult to verify with research findings, that for some people the residual effects are primarily due to the severity of the stress and only to a limited and secondary extent to their personality predisposition. In

A Car-Train Accident

Modlin (1967) describes the long-lasting effects of a car-train accident on a 36-year-old traveling salesman. This man was driving with his wife in a strange town at dusk. His car stalled as he was crossing some railroad tracks, and in attempting to restart it, he flooded the engine. While waiting for the engine to drain, he suddenly noticed a locomotive rolling slowly toward him. He gripped the wheel and stared in terror for perhaps ten seconds before the engine struck the car, pushed it along the tracks, then shoved it to one side. Physically he suffered only bruised ribs; psychologically he was seriously shaken. His wife was not hurt.

Immediately following the accident he was so uneasy, weak, and disorganized that his wife persuaded him they should stay in the town four days before starting the 200-mile trip home. Six months afterward he came to us. He was apprehensive, frightened, insecure, and seeking in all directions for help. He complained of difficulty in concentration and memory and was emotionally sensitive and tearful, sexually impotent, and withdrawn from all social contacts. He had tried to resume his job but had been discharged for incompetence. (pp. 52–53)

The holding of hostages has become a familiar occurrence in recent years. The individuals shown above are being released after being held by gunmen in Washington D.C. Living with the constant threat of being killed can have long-lasting psychological effects on some individuals.

other words, some of these individuals in all likelihood would never have shown psychological symptoms if it had not been for the stressful experience.

ADJUSTMENT DISORDERS

In *adjustment disorders* the person is showing a maladaptive reaction to an identifiable life circumstance. These disorders differ from the posttraumatic-stress disorder in two ways: First, the life circumstance does not ordinarily take the form of a specific accident or catastrophe but rather more often involves stresses associated with such things as business difficulties, physical illness, or developmental stages such as leaving the parental home, getting married, becoming a parent, and so on. Second, when the stressful life circumstance is removed, the person returns to normal functioning. If the stressful life event is long-lasting, such as getting

married or becoming a parent, then the adjustment reaction may continue or the person may eventually learn more successful coping responses.

Going away to college is an experience familiar to most of you, and one that can be stressful in a number of ways. The freshman year especially can be a trying one. Some symptoms of homesickness and loneliness are common as the student, perhaps for the first time, leaves family, friends, and a familiar environment. Many freshmen had been near the top of their class, academically, in high school and now find themselves competing with a highly selected group on subject matter that is taught in a more rigorous fashion. Where there were A's there now may be C's. Stresses may also arise in non-academic areas. Making new friends of either sex at a large university takes time. Athletic talents that were outstanding in high school now become merely good.

Listen to Sidney's distress as you read excerpts from his diary written in the first weeks of his freshman year:

September 11. "My past seems to have died. I stand alone before my life-to-come, full of doubts and fears of inadequacy."

September 13. "College is vast and overwhelming. What thoughts am I afraid of? I am somewhat awed at the brilliance around me."

September 14. "Last night at a college mixer I found myself lost and inadequate, terribly insecure. My status as a man was deeply shaken."

October 11. "I long for home with a powerful longing. I am obsessed and burdened with fantasies, thoughts, dreads. I feel a longing to return home and recapture a dead childhood. Help me!" (Madison, 1969, pp. 63–64)

Despite his initial distress, Sidney eventually graduated as one of the outstanding scholars of his class. He joined a nonfraternity living group, became a campus political leader of some importance, and after a slow start developed satisfactory relationships with several women in his upperclass years.

The college years are also a time for "identity" crises. Faced with decisions about an academic major and a long-term career, and confronted with new ideas that might raise doubts about one's previous political or religious beliefs, persons can begin to wonder just "who" they are. Coming to terms with who one is, one's identity, can be associated with a

Going away to college can involve a period of stress and temporary problems of adjustment.

period of active struggle and distress, or persons may become apathetic and see no desirable identity for themselves. To the extent that the identity crisis is primarily an adjustment reaction to the particular developmental stresses associated with the college years, persons are likely to work through to some acceptable sense of who they are and what they want from life.

Neurotic Traits

In contrast to posttraumatic-stress disorders and adjustment disorders some handicapping patterns of behavior have their origins primarily in the long history of interaction between biological temperament and environmental experiences. A tree growing on an ocean headland may be bent and distorted by years of prevailing winds so that even on windless days it shows its deformity. People who have experienced certain "prevailing winds" of social interaction in early and late childhood may in time show "deformities" of personality that are only minimally affected by changes in current circumstances. "Deformities" of this kind will be referred to as *neurotic traits,* by which is meant a personality style that involves some clear handicap or inefficiency in functioning but does not include the more specific symptoms or the more serious incapacitations seen in the disorders to be discussed in the following chapters and which have been traditionally referred to as neurotic disorders.[1]

CHILDHOOD ORIGINS

It is probable that many neurotic traits result from childhood stresses that produce strong negative emotions and defensive reactions. For example, Wayne, a college dean of students, feared expressing hostility in childhood since his parents "would have nothing to do with emotions and feelings at home, especially angry feelings toward one another." In therapy it came out that Wayne harbored intense resentment toward his older brother and had desperately tried to deny this negative emotion throughout his life. Although he recalled fighting with his brother before he was six or seven, he "restrained his anger from that time on and never upset his parents again." Unable to challenge his brother either physically, intellectually, or socially, Wayne became a "paragon of virtue." By being punctilious, scrupulous, methodical, and orderly, he could avoid antagonizing his perfectionistic parents and would, at times, obtain preferred treatment from them (Millon & Millon, 1974).

---

[1]The term *trait* is used for a response pattern that is to some degree consistent across time and across situations. The degree of consistency for neurotic traits, however, is an empirical question that has not yet been answered. It is likely that only some individuals show fairly strong consistency; research done on samples representative of the general population might yield relatively little consistency on these traits. Since the term *neurotic* is given less prominence in DSM-III, I considered using another phrase such as *handicapping trait* to characterize these personality styles but finally decided to stick with *neurotic trait.* The term is meant to be neutral with respect to theories of causation and, for example, does not necessarily imply the presence of intrapsychic conflicts.

The avoidance learning model is broadly applicable to the development of neurotic traits. The child who experiences intense distress, such as anxiety or shame, in desperation learns responses that minimize this distress. Wayne, for example, learned to deny his angry or hostile feelings and to behave always according to the rules. If the avoidance response is effective, it can become extremely resistant to extinction and persist for years, or a lifetime, as part of the individual's personality.

The well-learned avoidance response prevents the child from confronting the source of distress and mastering negative emotions. If the distress is strong enough and the avoidance response is effective, the child may never approach the feared situation again. Wayne, for example, was not able to reconsider his compulsive tendencies to be a paragon of virtue until he received psychotherapeutic help at age 40. The original fear may have been based in part on unjustified expectations, or, if it was originally justified, the circumstances may have changed; or the fear and associated avoidance responses may have generalized to different situations where there is no real reason to be afraid. The individual may nevertheless persist with the avoidance strategy.

Positive reinforcement also contributes to the learning of neurotic traits. The child may not receive the attention and appreciation that he or she desires in the everyday course of interaction and may have to resort to unusual and potentially neurotic strategies to obtain these parental "strokes." Wayne, for example, found that one of the few ways that he could get parental praise was by being a paragon of virtue, and in later life his traits of conscientiousness and orderliness were valued assets as a dean. Other children may learn that the only way to get parental attention and approval is by being smart in school, by being a social success, by acting the clown, or by some other behavior.

VARIETIES OF NEUROTIC TRAITS

What are some of the different forms that neurotic traits may take? Years ago Horney (1937) described various *protective strategies* that are similar to what I have been calling neurotic traits. Horney, as you may recall from Chapter 3, was a neo-Freudian psychoanalyst who abandoned certain features of Freud's theory, such as the centrality of sexual motivation and

the universality of the Oedipal conflict as causative agents in neuroses. Instead she maintained that most neurotic conflicts derive from a basic conflict between hostility toward important people (parents in early life) and anxiety over being rejected or deprived of affection and nurturance from these people. When this conflict is severe, individuals develop various protective strategies to cope with the unbearable anxiety. Some individuals, for example, focus on direct attempts to secure affection (approval and nurturance) from other people; others strive ceaselessly for positions of power or superiority in order to avoid the pain of helplessness or humiliation; and others withdraw (psychologically if not physically) from other people in order to avoid the hurt of emotional disappointment.

Let us consider the compulsive seeking of affection in more detail. The basic theme of this strategy is "If you love me, you won't hurt me." From the person's point of view it feels something like this: "What I want is so little—only that people be kind to me, give me advice, appreciate that I'm a poor, harmless, lonely soul, anxious to please and not hurt anyone's feelings." The person does not realize how much this attitude may antagonize others and lead to disappointing friendships, marriages, and relationships at work. Instead, the person is likely to conclude that others are inconsiderate, disloyal, and generally at fault.

The basic distinction between an excessive need for affection and a more normal desire for a loving relationship is that in the former the affection-seeking is primarily an avoidance response designed to reduce intense anxiety, whereas in the latter the person is more motivated by the positive pleasures of the relationship and is more likely to prize and respect the individual qualities of the other person. The individual with a neurotic trait uses positive emotion to reduce negative emotion, so that the affection-seeking acquires a compulsive, insatiable character similar in many respects to a food or drug dependency. The person is likely to become jealous at any sign of a spouse or other significant person showing affection or liking for other individuals. The affection must not be shared. This is truly a possessive love. It may also be indiscriminate. Everyone must be friendly—the drugstore clerk, the bus driver, the teacher, and the waiter. Criticism or annoyance from anyone tends to arouse basic anxiety.

The specific strategies devised to attain affection or liking can take many forms. Some individuals become submissive; they must be morally beyond reproach, comply with all wishes or demands of institutions or individuals, and suppress criticism or noncompliance for fear that it will alienate others. Unaware that their motivation is to avoid dislike and rejection, they may claim to be acting in terms of ideals of unselfishness, in a self-sacrificing renunciation of personal wishes. Such persons are likely to be excessively conforming, finding it impossible to make suggestions or take certain actions unless they are sure to please the people immediately around. They can become extremely skillful at predicting what kind of attitudes or opinions will be applauded in a particular group and act accordingly. Jung used the term *persona* to refer to the image a person wants to portray to others. In Greek the term originally referred to the mask worn by actors to indicate a particular role in a dramatic production. The overly submissive, overly conforming person may don a different persona or mask as the occasion demands. At the extreme, we see persons whose behavior is at the mercy of whatever group they find themselves in. They have developed no clear sense of who they are or what their own attitudes and opinions are. The following statement by a college student is an unusually clear example of this strategy:

I began trying to fit a personality to my make-up. I began "acting" out personalities and tried observing people and copying them, but I realized what I was doing and so carried that "how'm I doing attitude," that is, continually looking at and thinking about what I'd said or done, what impression I had made. But these personalities were all short-lived because they pleased some and not others and because they didn't produce that underlying purpose of making people like me; and every time unconsciously I would resort to my childish attitude and to make myself noticeable. Examples of these "personalities" are independence (but I couldn't keep it up); arrogance (but people were only arrogant back to me); big shot in sex (but people weren't so much in love with it as I thought); hatefulness (people paid no attention to me); extreme niceness (people took advantage of it, kidded me about it because I did it to an ultra degree); humorous nature (but I was only being childish, silly); quiet and studious (but people were only passing me by and I kept feeling I was missing something). I became a daydreamer so intensively that up to the present I find I'm daydreaming almost all the time. I became conscious of a person's approach and would become fluttered, flustered, would try to make a friend of him no matter who he was but I overdid it. (White, 1975, p. 148)

In a similar vein, White (1976) has used the term *strategic styles* to refer to personality traits that at an extreme can involve considerable handicap. Thus in the *derogatory* style the person finds fault with just about everything and everybody, an attitude summed up by the frequent use of questions like "How stupid can you get?" The chief accomplishment of this style is to "belittle and blame the outside world while implying that the self is free from faults and maintaining a flattering self-picture of wisdom" (p. 205). In the *humorous* style the individual may gain social acceptance and popularity, but at the extreme there can be costs. Humor at one's own expense, for example, can be used as a way of forestalling criticisms from others. Or if the person deals with serious issues by cracking jokes, she may find it hard to get others to take her seriously. She "may ultimately want more weight in matters of state than is generally accorded to the court jester" (p. 207). Other strategic styles described by White include the ingratiating style, the cool intellectual style, and the impulsive style. All of these styles when present to a moderate degree can produce positive benefits and yield social and occupational rewards. At the extreme, however, the handicap becomes more obvious. This is especially true in the sense that extreme manifestations of all these styles as well as those described by Horney interfere with nondefensive and mutually satisfying relationships with people.

It is possible that persons who have strong neurotic traits can find for many years living circumstances or ecological niches that are accepting of their styles and do not precipitate acute conflicts. On the other hand, such persons are always vulnerable should life circumstances change. An emotionally dependent man can lose a wife who for years has catered to his needs (perhaps because of her own neurotic traits); a person who has found security in power for many years can, for whatever reason, be removed from power. Wayne got along reasonably well as a college dean as long as his need to be a virtuous enforcer of rules was a valued characteristic. When the attitudes of students and college administrators changed and this trait was viewed more negatively, then Wayne's strategy no longer worked and he became emotionally upset.

As neurotic traits become more extreme, there is an increasing likelihood that the person will experience conflict because of incompatible inner tendencies, regardless of what is happening in the external environment. A person with insatiable cravings for affection may drive away people who were sources of affection, producing more anxiety or depression. Another person may attempt to avoid anxiety by withdrawing from close interpersonal relationships but feel too strong a need for affection and human nurturance to be comfortable as an isolate or recluse. Such a person continually feels impelled to seek out affection, thus renewing the chronic conflict and perpetuating the cycle.

Suzanne: A Display Piece

Suzanne learned to secure other people's esteem by being beautiful and talented. At age 34 she sought therapy in the hope that she might prevent the disintegration of her third marriage. The problem she faced was a recurrent one, her tendency to become "bored" with her husband and increasingly interested in going out with other men. She was on the brink of another affair and decided that before giving way to her impulses again she had better stop and take a good look at herself. The following history unfolded over a series of therapeutic interviews.

Suzanne was four years older than her sister, her only sibling. Her father was a successful and wealthy business executive for whom children were "display pieces," nice chattels to show off to his friends and to round out his family life, but "not to be troubled with." Her mother was an emotional but charming woman who took great pains to make her children "beautiful and talented." The girls vied for their parents' approval. Although Suzanne was the more successful, she constantly had to "live up" to her parents' expectations in order to secure their commendation and esteem.

Suzanne was quite popular during her adolescent years, had lots of dates and boyfriends, and was never short of attention and affection from the opposite sex. She sang with the high school band and was an artist on the school newspaper, a cheerleader, and so on.

Rather than going to college, Suzanne attended art school where she met and married a fellow student—a "handsome, wealthy ne'er-do-well." Both she and her husband began "sleeping around" by the end of the first year, and she wasn't certain that her husband was the father of her daughter. A divorce took place several months after the birth of this child.

Soon thereafter she met and married a man in his forties who gave both Suzanne and her daughter a "comfortable home, and scads of attention and love." It was a "good life" for the four years that the marriage lasted. Her husband was wealthy and had interesting friends. Suzanne attended a drama school, took ballet lessons, began to do freelance art work, and in general, basked in the pleasure of being the "center of attention" wherever she went. In the third year of this marriage she became attracted to a young man, a fellow dancing student. The affair was brief, but was followed by a quick succession of several others. Her husband learned of her exploits, but accepted her regrets and assurances that they would not continue. They did continue, and the marriage was terminated after a stormy court settlement.

Suzanne "knocked about" on her own for the next two years until she met her present husband, a talented writer who "knew the scoop" about her past. He "holds no strings" around her; she is free to do as she wishes. Surprisingly, at least to Suzanne, she had no inclination to venture afield for the next three years. She enjoyed the titillation of "playing games" with other men, but she remained loyal to her husband, even though he was away on reportorial assignments for periods of one or two months. The last trip, however, brought forth the "old urge" to start an affair. It was at this point that she sought therapy.

Suzanne felt that she had attained what she wanted in life and did not want to spoil it. Her husband was a strong, mature man who "knew how to keep her in check." She herself had an interesting position as an art director in an advertising agency, and her daughter seemed finally to have "settled down" after a difficult early period. Suzanne feared that she would not be able to control her tendency to "get involved" and turned to therapy for assistance. (Millon & Millon, 1974, pp. 238–239)

PERSONALITY DISORDERS

One of the major categories of the classification system in DSM-III is *personality disorders*. Under this heading are several disorders that refer to relatively extreme instances of neurotic traits, including the introverted, the histrionic, the dependent, the compulsive, and the passive-aggressive personalities. See Table 7-2 for brief descriptions of these personality styles. Suzanne resembles in many respects the histrionic personality.

The personality disorders represent one of the least satisfactory categories in DSM-III as well as in previous DSMs. The problem is that there are almost infinite variations in the form that excessive avoidances and strivings can take. The particular subcategories listed in DSM-III are relatively arbitrary and there is no evidence that diagnosticians can reliably agree on the assignment of individuals to these subcategories. It is perhaps better to understand the general principles involved in the development of neurotic traits and consider a range of examples rather than to crystallize these traits into a fixed set of "disorders." The one type of personality disorder that has received considerable clinical and research investigation, the antisocial or psychopathic personality, will be discussed in detail in a later chapter.

Our discussion of the development of neurotic

TABLE 7-2   Personality Disorders from DSM-III that Reflect Neurotic Traits

Personality Disorder	Description
Histrionic (formerly Hysterical Personality)	Behaves in an exhibitionistic manner, draws attention with exaggerated expression of emotion, initially is superficially charming and friendly but after a relationship is established may become demanding and self-absorbed. Despite sexual flirtatiousness is often naive and sexually unresponsive.
Dependent	Gets others to assume responsibility or make decisions, unwilling to make any demands on others for fear of jeopardizing relationship, lacks self-confidence, experiences intense discomfort if left alone.
Passive-Aggressive	Indirectly resists demands for adequate performance in both occupational and social areas. Resistance is shown by procrastination, dawdling, stubbornness, intentional inefficiency, and "forgetfulness."
Compulsive	Has restricted ability to express warm and tender emotions. Preoccupied with rules, order, and detail.
Avoidant	Shows extreme sensitivity to rejection, ridicule, or disapproval. Avoids close personal attachments even though desires affection and acceptance.

traits unfortunately has had to rely almost entirely on formulations derived from the study of clinical cases. As yet we cannot document these ideas with studies that clearly demonstrate the way social learning experiences in the family, probably in interaction with biological temperament, result in these various protective strategies.

NEUROTIC TRAITS AND UNHAPPY MARRIAGES

The marriage relationship has important implications not only for the immediate marital satisfaction of the couple but for the psychological development of their children. I mentioned previously how marital conflicts can impinge on children: Angry parents may displace anger to their children; one spouse may enlist the child as an ally against the other; or the child may become a substitute spouse.

The extent to which couples successfully work through the inevitable frustrations of marriage depends in part on the personality dispositions they bring to the marriage. If they bring neurotic traits—tendencies to withdraw, develop physical symptoms, attack, or be submissive in the face of disappointments—then various difficulties may develop in the course of the marriage.

Let us consider examples of two styles (from many possibilities) of distressed marital interaction. Philip and Constance were both inclined before marriage to respond to frustrations by attacking their frustrators with insults, sarcasm, and various other put-downs. Over the years their marriage has become one of frequent fights in which some initial, and on the surface trivial, event elicits a critical remark from one that causes the other to respond in kind. The interchange accelerates to a no-holds-barred shouting match—what Eric Berne, author of *Games People Play* (1964), calls a *game* of "Uproar." With no one either victorious or defeated, the hostilities eventually cease, perhaps out of exhaustion. Although there may be some immediate cathartic re-

lief, the fight in fact has contributed little to the solution of their basic disappointments and may have given them both some new "hurts" and resentments to nurse along until the bell rings for the next round.

Harold and Joy's relationship proceeded differently. Joy's resentment against the amount of time and energy Harold put into his job steadily increased. She had to stay home with the children, cook, and clean the house, while he was involved, at least as she saw it, in a fascinating and stimulating round of activities in the business world. Joy would not express to him, nor fully admit to herself, this increasing anger. She began to have headaches and various other bodily complaints which gave her a "legitimate" excuse for making demands on Harold's time. The neurotic trait in this case was an inability to appropriately assert her own interests; instead she resorted to sickness as a way of gaining attention and sympathy. Harold reciprocated by being helpful and treating her as an invalid. Joy's self-confidence became lower and lower. Harold invested more and more of his energy in work, but also patted himself on the back for being a long-suffering husband. Eventually Joy began to have martinis at lunch and midafternoon as well as in the evening. Neither Harold nor Joy was able to express directly the anger that these continuing disappointments were producing.

Of course, some marriages progress toward a disastrous outcome even though neither spouse could be described in any way as having neurotic traits. In many cases, however, such personality dispositions give a strong boost to the development of distressed marital interaction. And these marital conflicts can influence the larger family system in ways detrimental to the psychological well-being of the children. At this point we come full circle. Neurotic traits in spouses, in part the result of their own family upbringing, now may contribute to the development of neurotic traits in their own children (not necessarily the same traits). Thus, handicapping psychological characteristics are transmitted from one generation to the next.

Summary

1. Strong emotions play a central role in many psychological disorders. Responses of the autonomic nervous system are especially important physiological accompaniments of these emotions.

2. Human emotions do not lend themselves to neat categorization, but various combinations of fear (anxiety), grief, shame, and anger are prominent in psychological disorders. The extremes of these emotions can be almost unbearable, and the persistence of many self-defeating behaviors can be understood as attempts to avoid or minimize these unpleasant emotions.

3. Individuals who continue to show psychological disturbances after a severe stress such as a tornado, automobile accident, or wartime experience are said to have a posttraumatic-stress disorder.

4. When psychological symptoms develop in reaction to some life circumstance such as business difficulties or leaving the parental home, they are called adjustment disorders. Symptoms associated with an adjustment disorder tend to be relieved when the external situation changes or a more adaptive adjustment is made.

5. Neurotic personality traits represent protective and usually self-defeating behaviors learned in childhood that are only minimally affected by ordinary changes in current circumstances. To a large extent these behaviors can be viewed as learned avoidance responses designed to minimize strong negative emotions. Examples are the insatiable and indiscriminate seeking of affection and power, or withdrawal from all emotionally important interpersonal relationships.

6. When spouses bring neurotic traits to marriage (for example, to withdraw, develop physical symptoms, or attack in the face of disappointments) the relationship is likely to become progressively estranged, and this in turn may lead to psychological disturbances in children.

Suggested Readings

Two books devoted to reactions to stress are C. R. Figley (Ed.), *Stress disorders among Vietnam veterans* (Brunner/Mazel, 1978) and R. H. Moos (Ed.), *Human adaptation: Coping with life crises* (D. C. Heath, 1976). R. W. White in *The enterprise of living* (Holt, Rinehart, and Winston, 1976) provides a good description of "protective traits" and "strategic styles," similar to the concept of neurotic traits used in this chapter.

8

Anxiety, Phobic, and Obsessive-Compulsive Disorders

- Did you know that the most widely used drugs in the United States are tranquilizers, usually prescribed to relieve anxiety and tension states?

- How do psychoanalytic and social learning theories attempt to explain the development of anxiety disorders and obsessive-compulsive disorders?

- How important are specific traumatic experiences in the development of phobias?

- Your wife's long-standing fear of leaving the house has been cured. As her husband, are you likely to feel better or worse?

- Lady Macbeth keeps washing her hands. How can we explain this?

- Did you know that sometimes even young children develop severe compulsions?

Boyd C.: "I'm Shaking All Over"

Some four months before Boyd C., a man in his thirties, arrived at the psychiatric ward he suffered paralysis from the waist down as the result of an accident at work. A successful operation led to rapid improvement and within two months he had almost completely recovered except for a moderate weakness in his left leg. One day, while he was shaving, his legs suddenly gave way, he collapsed to the floor, and once again he was completely paralyzed from the waist down. After extensive neurological examinations, it was decided that this time his paralysis was hysterical, and he was transferred to a psychiatric ward. The following excerpts are taken from an interview conducted the day after Christmas.

Boyd: This is the roughest day yet, boy! Don't ask me why, because I don't know. Look—I can't even hold my hand still.

Dr.: Let's see when it began, and what it's all about.

Boyd: Gee, I don't know. I just think it's the aftermath of yesterday. Last night I lay in bed and bawled till about three or four this morning. It just hit me like that. I wasn't thinking about anything in particular, when, boom!, it just started like that. Yesterday after dinner I kind of thought of the kids and everything, and the wife. And looking at the football game I kind of wondered where the kid brothers are, and I knew one of them was home on furlough, and everything just seemed to come, and last night the dam just burst, that's all. Gee, I'm jumpy! I just don't know, I'm on edge.

Dr.: What is the feeling?

Boyd: Just jumpy. Criminy, I'm not only trembling on the outside. On the inside, I'm shaking all over. I can't seem to calm myself down.

Dr.: You're really quite anxious.

Boyd: I don't know whether it's anxious. I woke up shaking all over. Boy, it's an awful funny feeling. I wasn't thinking about anything. I just woke up that way. I've never experienced anything like this before, honest. I'll be doing something, like I was working on clay and I reached for something and gee, I just jerked like that, right out of a clear blue sky. This afternoon, getting some juice off the wagon there, the fellow was pouring it, and cripes, I gave a little jerk and spilled the glass of juice and everything. It's the awfullest feeling, not knowing what the heck is making me do it—why I should be that way. I feel almost as if I came off a big drunk or something. It's that kind of a fluttery feeling. And, criminy, I threw up what dinner I ate. (Nemiah, 1961, p. 38)

In the last chapter we saw how severe stress can precipitate psychological disturbances, some of which clear up when the stress is removed and some of which do not; and we also considered how persons can develop neurotic traits that inhibit and interfere with their full enjoyment of life. In this chapter and in the next we will consider more acute symptom patterns such as those of Boyd C. Although good data are lacking, it seems likely that these more acute reactions occur when persons with long-standing neurotic traits encounter an important change in life circumstances that makes it difficult or impossible to maintain the adjustment they had worked out for themselves.

The disorders in this and the next chapter have often been referred to as *neurotic disorders.* The term *neurosis* is given less prominence in DSM-III, and disorders of this kind are not grouped together under that heading. I will not entirely abandon the use of the term *neurotic* since it has been, and will probably continue to be, used widely. On the other hand I will use the term sparingly, preferring when possible to use the more specifically described symptoms. In general, the symptoms associated with the class of disorders that have been called neurotic are less severe than those traditionally labeled *psychotic,* and the individuals with neurotic disorders do not show the same loss of contact with reality and personality disorganization as those with psychotic disorders. The term *neurosis* originated in the belief that the disturbances so labeled resulted from some kind of neural impairment, but with the advent of psychological theories of causation the term lost that connotation. Within the context of the psychodynamic approach neurosis refers to the presence of crippling symptoms, such as those seen in hysteria and anxiety reactions, which are presumed to be caused by internalized conflicts.

From any perspective there is a degree of incapacitation and unhappiness in this class of disorders that makes one ask why the person persists in behaving in ways that are so self-defeating. Mowrer (1950) used the term *neurotic paradox* to refer to this puzzling feature. And his explanation of the paradox is the same as the one proposed in the previous discussion of neurotic traits: Individuals with neurotic symptoms are attempting to cope with unusual degrees of distressing emotions—usually anxiety—and many of their symptoms can be viewed as learned avoidance responses, which, as we have seen, can be extremely resistant to change. Another way to put it is that these persons are so focused on the immediate control of anxiety that the long-term handicapping results of their particular coping strategies are outweighed by the short-term relief from distress.

In this chapter I will take up those symptoms that in DSM-III fall under the general heading of Anxiety Disorders. These are *Generalized Anxiety Disorder, Panic Disorder, Phobic Disorder,* and *Obsessive-Compulsive Disorder.* One danger in following a system such as the DSM too uncritically is that it can leave the impression that we are dealing with a series of discrete and separate disorders. This is not the case. Persons can and do often show mixtures of these symptom patterns. Accordingly, the plan in this book will be to present initially the list of the more common symptom patterns as described in DSM-III but to emphasize in the discussion to follow certain basic processes and principles. It should be remembered that much of the clinical and research literature will have used categorical labels from earlier DSMs.

Widespread prevalence of anxiety and tension states is indicated by the fact that the most frequently prescribed drugs in the United States are the so-called minor tranquilizers, such as Equanil, Miltown, and Valium. It is difficult, however, to cite accurate statistics on the incidence of anxiety disorders because persons with such difficulties often do not seek professional help. They get drug prescriptions from general practitioners, or obtain counseling or therapeutic help from people not in the mental health field, and thus they do not end up as "statistics."

Generalized Anxiety, Panic, and Phobic Disorders

CHARACTERISTIC SYMPTOMS

The basic characteristics of the anxiety response are the same as those of the fear response described in the previous chapter. Boyd C., in the quoted interview, reports trembling, startle reactions to minor noises, and being sick to his stomach—all common features of acute anxiety or panic reactions. Some years back Langford (1937) studied 20 eight- to fourteen-year-old children who suffered from intense and persisting anxiety attacks. As described by the children themselves: "I have a lump in my throat; I get pains around my heart; it pumps real hard and fast. And I can't get my breath. It seems I would die"; "My heart beats real fast. I get real hot in back of my ears and then I get real cold like a peppermint feeling. Last night it felt like my hand was off and I didn't have any"; "My head comes in together and then it goes round and round and then it gets warm and sweaty and I feel like I'm going to faint and if I get it too much I might die" (pp. 211–212). The duration of these attacks varied from five minutes to an hour,

Many of us experience a mild phobic fear of amusement park rides. If the fear is not too intense, it can enhance the exhilaration of the ride.

and they occurred two or three times a week on the average. Although the reactions tended to occur somewhat more frequently in the evening, either just before or after going to bed, they were not otherwise related to any obvious external conditions.

In the generalized anxiety disorder the anxiety is chronic and long-lasting. In the panic disorder the anxiety occurs in acute and disabling attacks that characteristically last for a relatively short period of time—from a few minutes to an hour or so. For both disorders there is no predictable stimulus that elicits the anxiety. The phobic reaction on the other hand is associated with specific situations or objects. All of these reactions seem irrational to the person as well as to other observers—the generalized anxiety and panic disorders because there is no obvious precipitating event, and the phobias because the intensity of the reaction is far beyond any actual danger present in the situation. In the case of Agnes we have an example of a phobic fear of heights.

Phobic anxiety can become associated with a variety of objects or situations. Some common examples are:

Heights: cliffs, roofs, high windows, ladders
Enclosed places: small rooms, closets, elevators, subways
Open places: halls, wide streets, squares, parks, beaches

Agnes: A Fear of Heights

Agnes, an unmarried woman of 30, had been unable to go higher than the second or third floor of any building for a year. Whenever she tried to overcome her fear of heights (acrophobia) she only succeeded in provoking intolerable anxiety. She remembered when it all began. One evening she was working alone at the office when she was suddenly seized with terror lest she jump or fall out of the open eighth-story window. So frightened was Agnes by her impulse that she crouched behind a steel file for some time before she could trust herself to gather up her things and make for the street. She reached ground level acutely anxious, perspiring freely, her heart pounding and her breathing rapid.

After this the patient found that as soon as she reached the office each day her anxiety over heights made it impossible to attend properly to her work. At the end of two months she gave up her position. For a while she tried unsuccessfully to accustom herself directly to high places. Finally her need for income drove her to take whatever she could get within the limitations imposed by her phobia. The result was that she was downgraded from a confident, well-paid secretary to an unhappy, poorly paid saleswoman in a store. This was her situation when she came for treatment. (Cameron, 1963, p. 282)

Animals: dogs, cats, snakes, horses, spiders
Weapons: guns, knives, axes
Public gatherings: crowds, meetings, churches, theaters, stadiums
Vehicles: airplanes, trains, automobiles, buses
Natural dangers: storms, wind, lightning, darkness

DEVELOPMENT OF ANXIETY DISORDERS

What kind of evidence would we need in order to draw firm conclusions about the causation (or *etiology*) of anxiety disorders? Some of the research strategies (twin and adoption studies) that provide evidence for a genetic contribution have already been described in Chapter 5. With respect to social learning I will give special attention to influences exerted within the family. Statistical surveys have consistently shown that individuals with anxiety symptoms tend to come from homes in which a higher proportion of parents have anxiety symptoms than in the general population (Jenkins, 1966; Noyes et al., 1978). Findings of this kind do not, of course, tell us anything about the relative contributions of heredity and social learning or much about the actual social learning experiences involved in the development of anxiety disorders. It would be instructive to follow a large number of families from the birth of a child to, say, age eight and then see what features of family interaction distinguished those families in which a child developed a particular kind of symptom. Or we might select families that represent a greater risk for producing anxiety disorders (for example, families in which one or both parents have neurotic traits or symptoms) and compare them with low-risk families, again following the development of a target child from birth to some later age.[1] If good data were obtained—data that permit analysis of important interactive episodes between parent and child—then such studies could begin to give us a more direct answer to the question of what kind of family interaction is related to what kind of symptoms. The study by Thomas et al. (1968) described in Chapter 5 represents a good start toward this kind of research. Unfortunately, most of the sources of data on which we base our theories fall considerably short of these research strategies. Therefore you should consider the causes we will be examining as plausible hypotheses based upon the clinical study of individual cases rather than as conclusions supported by appropriate research.

Let us begin our consideration of the etiology of anxiety disorders by returning to the interview with Boyd C. being conducted by psychiatrist John C. Nemiah, and use Boyd as an example of how an immediate stress can interact with a neurotic trait to produce an anxiety reaction.

Boyd C.: Immediate Stress and Neurotic Traits. One factor apparently contributing to Boyd's anxiety is the fear that he will lose control and strike out in some violent fashion.

Boyd: At lunchtime there, the craziest damn urge hit me; there's a pitcher on the table there, and I was pouring a glass of milk, and, Christ!, I just wanted to pick that pitcher up and heave it! I think at the present time if I went back over there and someone would say something and I let myself—my feelings get away from me a little bit. I would enjoy having a fight with someone or banging something, or Christ!, going in and tearing my bed all to pieces or some crazy thing like that.
Dr.: This is what is making you so scared.
Boyd: That I won't be able to hold myself back . . . What if my sense of balance should go the other way—should give ground to these feelings I have of banging somebody or throwing a pitcher or some damn foolish thing like that? (pp. 45–46)

Boyd's intense anxiety and rage were apparently precipitated by the fact that his wife had not called him on Christmas Day, although he tended to deny that he was angry at her for not calling. In the following piece of dialogue, his disappointment, however, is shown as he talks about going to bed on Christmas night.

Boyd: I felt all right last night when I went to bed. I wasn't lonesome, I was a little sad, you know what I mean. Then I got to thinking about the wife and the kids, and then we watched TV and there was

---

[1]For ethical reasons one would be reluctant to withhold treatment from a family after it became clear that a child was developing neurotic symptoms, assuming that the family was interested in help and that treatment procedures of known effectiveness were available.

kids on it, and it just kind of made a lump in my throat. So I went to bed and said my prayers, and I got to thinking about home, and the first thing you know I started to cry and I bawled and bawled. I couldn't seem to stop. My God, it came out of me in buckets! It wasn't a loud cry, but I couldn't stop the tears from coming. It was a sad and choked up feeling, you know. (pp. 44–45)

We would seem justified in concluding that Boyd reacted with both anger and grief when his wife did not telephone on Christmas, and that his anxiety represented, at least in part, a fear of giving in to uncontrollable outbursts of aggression. The environmental stimuli for Boyd's reaction are the circumstances of being hospitalized and not hearing from his family on Christmas. But would most people have such an intense and debilitating reaction? Probably not. We must look at Boyd's personality disposition in order to understand why these circumstances produced such an extreme reaction. Again, let Boyd speak for himself. First we hear him talking about his lifelong difficulty in permitting himself to rely on other people.

Boyd: I don't have any really close friends, anyway. I've been more or less on my own, you know. In fact, when you get right down to it, I don't think I have a really close friend because I always kept my troubles to myself. All the scrapes I got into, I kept them to myself. I wasn't one to cry on somebody's shoulder. I always figured that when I left home I had to make my own way one way or another. . . . I want to stand on my own two feet, and if anybody has got to have anybody to lean on, I want him to lean on me, not me lean on him. You understand what I mean? (p. 243)

He then cites an experience that contributed to his fear of being dependent on others. When he was 16 he had worked away from home over the summer and sent money back to his mother for her to put in a savings account for him. In the fall he discovered that she had spent most of his savings for herself.

Boyd: Well, it's so long ago that I can't tell you exactly—when I first heard about it. I was mad. I was teed-off, and if it had been anyone else but my mother I probably could have cussed them out

In our fantasies we may attack those who have thwarted us.

in good shape, I was that mad. . . . I could have attempted to knock the hell out of them. . . . Then when I was told "Until you're 21 I can do whatever I want with your money," it was just a feeling of disgust, and then after the disgust left there was no feeling. I had no more feeling about it than I would with a total stranger. . . .

Dr.: I think being hurt by your mother like this makes you expect if from everyone else. Perhaps this is why you don't want to get into a situation where you might get hurt again.

Boyd: Yeah, I'll go along with that. I won't say I expect it from everyone, but I'm not going to let myself get into a situation where if it does happen again, I'll be hurt again. In other words if anyone is going to be hurt, I'm going to do the hurting. It's going to be the other guy. (pp. 245–246)

It is likely there were many occasions on which Boyd's mother gave him cause to doubt her trustworthiness. She was an unstable person, an alcoholic frequently involved in ephemeral affairs away from home. Alongside his fear of being dependent on others, we find, not surprisingly, an intense longing for a dependent relationship that is especially acute with respect to his wife. The following comment illustrates the insatiability of Boyd's need.

Boyd: When I feel this lonesomeness coming on, if I'm away from home, I work harder at physical work; then I can throw that feeling off. Whereas if I don't work harder, well, then I get that deep, deep, lonesome feeling. It seems to me there's a need, almost a physical need, just the same as an alcoholic needs a drink. I get that deep down craving for the family, and I just—well, I'm like an alcoholic; I throw everything aside to get that drink or the family. . . . (p. 247)

Boyd likens his need for a dependent relationship to an addiction, similar to the alcoholic's craving for liquor. Clearly we have here an example of a neurotic personality trait as described in the preceding chapter. Boyd is to some extent aware of the insatiable and unreasonable character of his need, and he senses that he might well alienate the very people he would turn to for help. In the psychodynamic tradition this avoidance strategy might be labeled a *reaction formation;* he leans over backward to be self-sufficient and independent, except possibly in his relationship with his wife.

Boyd's personality, like most people's, consists of more than just one strong disposition, and to explain all his later difficulties in terms of his dependency need is an oversimplification. Nevertheless, the craving for dependency that had become centered on his wife and family, the defensive strategy of putting on a front of exaggerated independence, and a tendency he does not wholly recognize to respond with anger and resentment when expected help is not forthcoming certainly must have contributed to the intensity of the anger, grief, and anxiety he experienced when his wife failed to call on Christmas Day. Although we have not explored the feelings, thoughts, and general circumstances surrounding the onset of the hysterical paralysis, it seems likely that his conflict over dependency gratification probably played a role in this too; being paralyzed provided a legitimate reason to make demands on people.

The case of Boyd C. illustrates the roles of immediate stress and personality dispositions but only hints at how these dispositions were learned. In the following sections we shall consider some evidence, but mostly speculation, about the contributions of genetic endowment and environmental experiences to the development of anxiety and phobic reactions.

Heredity. Some genetic determination in anxiety and phobic reactions cannot be ruled out. Remember Michael (Chapter 5) whose slow-to-warm-up na-

ture made each new school experience an anxious occasion until he gradually became comfortable in the new setting. If such a child were pushed arbitrarily into new situations and not permitted the usual warm-up time, an acute anxiety reaction could be precipitated. It is interesting that Langford (1937) reported that 19 of the 20 children with anxiety reactions in his study were timid children who did not mix with their playmates. These children had shown many signs of maladjustment prior to their anxiety attacks: feeding difficulties, bedwetting, restless sleep, and nail biting. All were afraid of the dark. Other characteristics of some children were concern about health, fatigability, car sickness, and crying spells. Clearly these children seemed temperamentally predisposed to the development of fears. The case for a constitutional contribution to the development of these anxiety reactions would be more convincing, however, if we knew what proportion of children with similar temperaments did not develop them.

Comparisons of identical and fraternal twins, as reported in Chapter 5, provide some evidence for a genetic contribution to autonomic reactivity and social apprehensiveness in childhood. There is also evidence for some hereditary contributions to anxiety reactions in adults. Slater and Shields (1969) compared 17 identical and 28 fraternal same-sex twins whose average age was 40 years. One of the twins in each pair had been diagnosed as having an anxiety reaction. Forty-one percent of the identical co-twins and only 4 percent of the fraternal co-twins had also been diagnosed with anxiety reactions. These differences in concordance between identical and fraternal twins suggest some genetic influence in anxiety reactions. Torgersen (1979), studying largely normal samples of twins, found greater concordances for identical than fraternal twins on a variety of fears that at their extreme would be considered phobias. The one exception involved separation fears, which were not significantly different in concordance for the two types of twins. Perhaps individuals with an inherited tendency to be autonomically reactive and socially apprehensive represent a higher-than-average risk group for the later development of anxiety and phobic reactions. Whether an anxiety disorder develops or not depends upon the individual's environmental experiences.

Traumatic Experiences and Classical Conditioning. Both behaviorally and psychodynamically oriented investigators have pointed to the role of traumatic experiences in the causation of anxiety disorders. Langford (1937) found some evidence that fear-arousing events had preceded the first anxiety attacks in 16 of the 20 children he studied. In six of these children the attacks followed within a month or two after tonsillectomies under ether; another six children either had had a death in the family or, in two cases, had been witnesses of violent deaths in the neighborhood. But how many children experience intense anxiety on occasions of this kind and do not develop recurring anxiety attacks? We do not have the data to answer that question. Langford's clinical study does strongly suggest, however, the possibility that a child temperamentally disposed toward fearfulness who also experiences traumatic incidents is likely to manifest recurring anxiety attacks.

There are numerous clinical examples in which phobic adults in psychotherapy come to remember specific psychological trauma of childhood that seemed to have contributed to the development of their phobia. Rimm et al. (1977) found that 71 percent of a sample of college females with long-lasting phobias remembered a specific fear-arousing event that seemed related to the onset of the phobia. This kind of data, of course, is even more retrospective and less objective than Langford's, but lacking anything better it can be useful in forming hypotheses about etiology. Moss (1960), for example, treated a 45-year-old woman who had had a lifelong, intense fear of dogs but otherwise seemed reasonably well adjusted. Under hypnosis she recalled and reexperienced emotions associated with the death of a younger sister, which occurred when the patient was about four years old. She remembered playing in the backyard of their home with her sister when the family dog knocked her sister down, causing her to suffer a splinter wound in her cheek. She died several days later, apparently of an infection. The patient felt that her mother accused her of knocking the sister down and thus blamed her for the sister's death. Several other incidents were recalled that involved a close association between the dog and the emotional distress related to the sister's death—guilt and feelings of being unjustly accused. The patient reported no conscious memory of these events prior to the hypnotic sessions. The existence of the family dog was confirmed by a brother and also the fact that she and her sister had been left momentarily alone at the time of the fatal accident.

Behaviorally oriented clinicians would emphasize the role of classical conditioning in traumatic episodes of this kind and suggest that the pairing of the conditioned stimulus *dog* with the unconditioned fear and distress associated with her sister's death might be a sufficient explanation for the learning of the phobia. But is it? Why did dogs become the one stimulus able to continue to evoke fear? Why did the mother, who was perceived rightly or wrongly as unjustly blaming her, not become a phobic stimulus?

Rachman (1977), a previous advocate of a conditioning theory of phobias (for example, Wolpe & Rachman, 1960) has recently criticized the conditioning theory as being incomplete. In classical conditioning theory any stimulus (object, sound, odor, and so on) can serve equally well as a conditioned stimulus, CS, as long as it has been paired with the unconditioned stimulus, UCS. But various sources of evidence suggest that this is not the case. For example, if all stimuli can serve equally well as CS, why are human phobias most commonly associated with a rather limited set of stimuli—fear of leaving home, specific animals and insects, heights, the dark, situations related to bodily injury or mutilation, and so on? Only rarely do we have phobias of pajamas, grass, or hammers; yet all of these can be associated with trauma. Pajamas, for example, are present when young children experience fears of the dark or have nightmares, but children rarely develop a phobia for pajamas.

Rachman also points out that people may undergo repeated fear-arousing experiences and not develop phobias to surrounding stimuli. Thus despite repeated exposure to fearsome air raids during World War II, only a very small proportion of adults or children developed phobias as a result. Rachman sees these findings as being supportive of a theory previously proposed by Seligman and Hager (1972) to the effect that humans, as well as other animals, can learn to be fearful of some stimuli more readily than they can of other stimuli. There is an innate *preparedness* to become fearful of certain stimuli because in our evolutionary past these stimuli were associated with real dangers—animals, the dark, heights, mutilated bodies. This theory of a preparedness to become fearful of some stimuli and not others may help explain why Bregman (1934) was unable to replicate Watson and Rayner's (1920) demonstration of fear conditioning in little Albert. Bregman attempted to condition fear in 15 infants but used biologically irrelevant objects such as geometrically shaped wooden blocks and cloth curtains; whereas Watson and Rayner used a furry rat. Recall also that the woman with the dog phobia developed a fear of dogs, not of grass, houses, her mother, or whatever other stimuli may have been present at the time of her sister's accident. It is, however, difficult to prove the existence of an innate preparedness. Bandura (1977), for example, agrees that phobias develop more readily to some stimuli than others, but argues that this can be explained by differences in the present nature of the stimuli rather than innate tendencies. Thus snakes and various animals are especially likely to become phobic stimuli because they can appear at unpredictable times and places, show great mobility, and inflict injury despite self-protective efforts. Whatever the explanation, it is true that we are more likely to develop fears of some things than others.

Operant Learning.   Will a child learn to repeat a strong fear response because it has been previously reinforced? A fear response, for example, might be followed by reunion with mother and removal from school. Does this reinforcement increase the probability that the child will react with fear the next time she goes to school? Many clinicians assume so, but in fact the evidence for operant learning of fear is rather weak. Two considerations cast doubt upon it: First, strong fear is an extremely unpleasant experience. How likely is it that a person will learn to use this response to achieve some end? Second, the laboratory evidence for the operant learning of fear is weak. In fact, there are no studies that report the operant learning of the full fear response. The studies only suggest that certain autonomic nervous system responses such as heartbeat, blood pressure, or palmar sweating may be changed by operant procedures. Even here the evidence indicates that this is a very difficult kind of learning, which only some subjects master under special circumstances (Blanchard & Young, 1973). To return for a moment to the example of a child with school phobia: Reunion with mother may indeed serve as a reinforcement, but it may not reinforce the fear response so much as other activities that produce mother's presence, such as yelling, screaming, crying, or throwing a temper tantrum. All these actions are readily learned by operant means, but they are not in and of themselves the fear response.

Observational Learning and Cognitive Mediators. There is considerable laboratory evidence that both animal and human subjects can learn emotional reactions, including fear, by observing other subjects model these reactions (Bandura, 1977). Recall Vincent, in Chapter 4, who showed no fear of a rabbit until he observed Rose crying and showing considerable distress in the presence of the rabbit. Extrapolating from experimental studies, we might then assume that the more intense anxiety and phobic reactions can also be influenced by observational learning.

Various cognitive processes may also play a role in the learning and maintenance of fear. A child's interpretation of events or expectation about what is going to happen can be important internal stimuli in this respect. The child who hears parents, siblings, or others warn of certain dangers can begin to tell himself about these same anxiety-arousing situations. The child's potential for imaginative elaboration can multiply and maintain the stimuli.

Repression and Intrapsychic Conflict.   Why did the woman with the dog phobia have no conscious memory of the childhood events surrounding the onset of her phobia? Was this no more than the normal forgetting that occurs for most of our early childhood experiences? As we have already seen, the concept of repression as a learned "think-about-something-else" response can readily be incorporated into a social learning interpretation, and might contribute to the "forgetting" of such painful events. Psychoanalytically oriented clinicians, however, would likely go further and consider the possibility that the fear, in part at least, was displaced from other sources and also consider the likelihood of other intrapsychic processes such as rivalry (and death wishes!) toward her sister and Oedipal hostility toward the mother as contributing to the irrational intensity of her fear. More generally the psychoanalytic theory of phobia formation would emphasize some initial repression of an anxiety-arousing conflict, the projection of the conflict onto the external world (Little Hans, for example, was said to have projected his wish to attack his father, and thus he believed his father wished to attack him) and then *displaces* the anxiety onto some other target (horses, in the case of Hans).

Agnes, the woman with the intense phobia of heights who was seized with terror that she might

Agnes: Behind the Phobia

In therapy it soon came out that Agnes had been deeply involved in an affair of long standing with a married man who could not, for religious reasons, get a divorce. She found herself caught in a severe conflict, guilty over her own conduct, too much in love to break off the liaison, and unable to give up a belief that one day she and her lover would marry. The crisis came when she was informed that she was pregnant. She told the man that he would have to get a quick divorce and marry her. When he refused, she threatened to expose him. A few days before her acute anxiety attack, and the onset of the phobia, she received a farewell letter from him and discovered that he had left town.

Agnes had felt humiliated and angered at having to beg and threaten her lover. His desertion was the final disillusionment. It overwhelmed her with helplessness and hatred. She now concluded that she was no better than a prostitute, and suicide seemed to her the only solution. It was in this setting of shame, fury, and abandonment that she became acutely frightened and phobic. She was terrified by her own sudden impulse to leap out of a hopeless situation to her death. She projected the danger from her own uncontrollable impulses of self-destruction, of which she was half-aware, on to the impersonal and controllable fear of situations like the one in which she had originally experienced the self-destructive impulse. She displaced the upsurge of vengeful hatred toward her lover, which also alarmed her by its force, to a feeling of abhorrence for high places. (Cameron, 1963, pp. 282–283)

jump from her eighth-story office window, was seen in therapy by a psychodynamically oriented therapist, Norman Cameron. As you read the additional information that Cameron provides about Agnes, consider how a social-learning-oriented clinician might incorporate these data in an explanation for the development of the phobia. At what points does Cameron introduce more distinctly psychodynamic concepts?

Social Systems and Anxiety.   There is rather good evidence that an interactive pattern between parent and child characterized by an overprotective parent and an overly dependent child is likely to be associated with fearfulness in the child—especially with respect to new situations involving separation from the parent. This fearfulness may result in part from children being prevented from learning to cope with fear experiences on their own. More on this in Chapter 20.

Hafner (1977) has provided evidence that suggests that the husbands of some women with agoraphobia (fear of leaving home) reinforce the phobia and resist any improvement in the symptom. When these women's phobias were successfully treated by

a form of behavior therapy, there was a subgroup of women whose husbands developed psychological symptoms themselves within three months of the end of treatment. When some of these women had relapsed somewhat by six months after treatment, the severity of the husbands' newly developed symptoms had decreased. Hafner gives the following examples of this phenomenon:

One husband attempted suicide about four months after the treatment. He said that he did so because since his wife's recovery he had felt useless and inadequate: she was no longer almost totally dependent on him in the way she had been while agoraphobic. Two husbands became depressed when the focus of dissatisfaction within their marriages shifted back from their wives' agoraphobia to their own sexual difficulties, which they were unable or unwilling to discuss. In four husbands (including the one who attempted suicide) their wives' recovery reawakened abnormal jealousy which had lain dormant as long as the wives had been unable to go out alone; this led to unpleasant arguments and markedly increased marital disharmony, which the wives attempted to reduce by partially resuming their agoraphobic behavior. (p. 293)

Once again we see the importance of the social system in which the symptom develops and is maintained. Nevertheless, it was only a subgroup of Hafner's phobic women in which the husbands seemed to play this symptom-reinforcing role.

To summarize, many factors may contribute to the development of anxiety and phobic reactions: genetic predisposition; the classical conditioning of fear by traumatic experiences; possibly, but with much less certainty, the operant learning of fear; observational learning and cognitive mediators of fear; the kind of intrapsychic conflicts proposed by psychoanalytic theory; and social systems effects such as the overprotective parent–overly dependent child relationship. The weighting of these different factors is likely to vary considerably from case to case.

Obsessive-Compulsive Disorders

Ruth L.: A Severe Handwashing Compulsion

By the time Ruth L. was 30 years old she had been in and out of treatment for many years with a succession of therapists who had used a variety of approaches with little lasting success. At this time she was a thin, tense woman who spoke without expression. She was unmarried, lived alone in a studio apartment, and had the good fortune to have an independent income that freed her of any serious financial worries.

SYMPTOMS

Ruth had engaged in ritualistic behaviors as far back as she could remember. By the time she was four or five she had already developed an elaborate play sequence which involved putting all her dolls in exactly assigned positions. Each doll had to be placed in its particular posture, for example, with right arm at a certain angle and legs pointed in a given direction. When the arrangement was completed, she would then move each doll to another part of the room and repeat the whole procedure with a different pattern of doll placement. She also said certain words such as "good doll" and "bad doll" while performing this activity.

As she grew older she developed a number of other rituals. Before going to bed, for example, she had to place her pillow, blankets, and various objects in a particular spot. Cleanliness rituals also played a prominent part in her repertoire of compulsions. At the time of this report she performed an especially complicated cleaning procedure whenever she urinated or defecated. She scrubbed each finger in order, carefully working between the fingers. Then she washed both sides of her hands and scrubbed her arms. After working this way with soap, she repeated the entire procedure with a strong disinfectant. After drying her hands and arms with a large number of paper towels, she scrubbed the toilet and sink, and finally for good measure washed her hands again. If she still felt contaminated, she would take a shower. She would also wash herself in this manner after cooking and housecleaning. Currently, she was washing her hands three or four times an hour, showering six or seven times a day, and thoroughly cleaning her apartment at least twice a day. The outer layer of skin on her hands had been virtually scrubbed off, causing considerable pain.

Ruth had masturbated since she was a child, and although she felt it was harmful and disgusting, she could not stop the practice. She felt compelled to perform numerous cleanliness rituals afterward. (Leon, 1974)

CHARACTERISTIC SYMPTOMS

Obsessions are thoughts that intrude repeatedly into awareness and are experienced as irrational, unwanted, and difficult to control or stop. *Compulsions* are actions that one is compelled to perform; they are also experienced as irrational and difficult to control. Mild forms of obsessive-compulsive experience—like mild forms of phobic reactions—are not uncommon in normal individuals. The song you cannot get out of your mind, or a compulsion to return home to make sure that the door is locked or the stove turned off—when there is no rational basis to expect otherwise—are examples from everyday life.

When obsessions and compulsions reach a handicapping degree of severity, they frequently can be seen to reflect conflicting tendencies within the person. Aggressive or sexual thoughts, for example, alternate with thoughts or actions that counteract or inhibit them. Some common examples of obsessive thoughts are: the idea of stabbing, choking, poisoning, shooting, or otherwise injuring one's child, parent, spouse, sibling, or oneself; the idea of shouting obscene words at home, work, or church; the wish that someone were dead; the thought or image of a forbidden sexual adventure, perhaps involving "perverted" sex acts; the thought of committing suicide by jumping out of a window or into the path of a truck; and the thought of contracting some disease from touching doorknobs, banisters, toilets, or other objects in public places.

Examples of thoughts or actions designed to counteract forbidden or distressing thoughts are: almost any kind of thinking ritual, such as counting to oneself, memorizing license plate numbers, reciting certain words or phrases to oneself, or more elaborate verbal rituals that have a scientific, philosophical, or religious basis; cleanliness rituals; excessive politeness; excessive orderliness and neatness; and inordinate attempts to schedule one's activities on a precise timetable.

Two other characteristics common in obsessive-compulsive disorders are indecisiveness and highly controlled emotions. Indecision is a consequence of strong conflicting tendencies; some individuals become almost incapacitated by endless compulsive rituals and the immobilization associated with obsessive indecision and doubting. The excessive inhibition of emotionality is reflected in the cold, detached,

For some people any disorder or messiness is very disturbing.

and unemotional fashion in which persons experience their obsessive ideas and compulsive acts. It is also reflected in the lack of spontaneity associated with patterns of orderly, timetable living, and in highly formalized interpersonal relations.

DEVELOPMENT

So far, no twin studies of obsessive-compulsive reactions have used adequate samples, so little can be said about the heritability of this kind of disorder. Psychological theories tend to look at conditions that would produce the observed conflicts. Since the obsessions and the counteracting responses almost always involve the expression of unacceptable aggressive or sexual impulses, it is natural to look for environmental learning experiences that promote strong conflicts in these areas.

A Clinical Study. Adams (1973) studied 49 obsessive children and their families. His observations suggest that certain family interaction styles play important causative roles in these disorders.

One of the above drawings was made by a person experiencing an anxiety reaction and the other by a person diagnosed obsessive-compulsive. Can you guess which person made which drawing? What cues in the drawing did you use to make your guess? © Copyright 1957 CIBA-GEIGY Corporation. Reproduced with permission.)

Severely obsessional children are rare, comprising perhaps two percent of the children seen in clinical practice. A general characteristic of all the children in this study was profound unhappiness; they were humorless, anguished, lacking in zest, awkward, and generally "uptight." Although unusually verbal, they communicated little of substance in their outpouring of polysyllabic words and were given to pedantic quibbling. They showed a variety of obsessive and compulsive rituals, such as counting, touching, and arranging. One young boy, when the therapist first saw him, took great pains to hold his palms and fingers rigid and pointing downward. When the therapist commented on this behavior, the boy answered immediately that he was preventing himself from raising his middle finger to God in an obscene salute; he shuddered at the thought of such an act of defiance against his Christian upbringing.

Demographically, the families were largely urban, affluent, and middle class. No obsessive black children came to the attention of the author, although black children with other difficulties were being seen at this institution at the time of the study (mainly in the 1960s). Descriptions of the family environments

suggest modeling of obsessive styles on the part of the parents as well as the presence of behaviors likely to induce strong conflicts centering around the management of aggressive urges. The parents tended to be highly verbal; "they acted as if talk . . . has a magic that dispels all sinister forces" (p. 62).

Adams found that another characteristic of the obsessive children's parents was their strong regard for "correctness" in thought and behavior. Although the "correct" attitude in many cases reflected conventional social values, this was not true in all instances. The parents impressed upon the children the extreme importance of their particular expectations. Relatively few families in this study (20 percent) took religion seriously and made it a significant aspect of home life, but the parents continually admonished their children to be good and think good thoughts. Emotions were generally ignored or "talked away"; a child with a nightmare, for example, might be told to think about pleasant things instead. The parents stressed cleanliness of the body as well as cleanliness of the mind. Bowel training was rigid, punitive, or prolonged in 40 percent of the families.

These families did not prize warm interpersonal

relationships. The parents had few close friends and did not encourage their children to seek out friendship. There was also some tendency toward hoarding; they devoted much time to saving, spending, and accounting, as if they lived amidst scarcity instead of in their actual affluence. Although less directly documented, Adams concludes that the parents (especially the mother) manifested hostile, rejecting behaviors (verbally denied) toward the child; they evoked intense anger that the child could not express directly but had to handle by various obsessive and compulsive defenses.

The outward and formal message is one which gives security and comfort to the child. Unfortunately, however, the message is not true. The parents say, "Mother and father love you more than they love life itself," and the child receives some consolation for his hideous discernment that one or both of his parents hate him, or wish him dead. If he plays along and clings with obsessive tenacity to what is stated, without heeding any of the undercurrents of parental hatred, he can stay fairly "safe" from his fear of being "wiped out," punished, and subjected to parental sadism. A fake security, an ersatz comfort, is thus derived for the child, and he is trained over and over in the modality of what has been said literally—ignoring what people really feel and really mean for one another. (Adams, 1973, pp. 82–83)

A Social Learning Interpretation. In the language of social learning theory, most of the stratagems of the obsessive-compulsive are responses learned and maintained because they reduce or avoid anxiety (or negative emotions of any kind). Adams's clinical study suggests that parents of obsessive-compulsive children not only fail to model humor, spontaneity, or fun but may also actively punish the child's expression of these traits. They seem to have carried to an extreme those conditions thought to promote the *internalization* of parental dos and don'ts: clear and repeated verbalization of expected rules of thought and conduct, consistent reinforcement (positive or negative) of these rules, modeling conscientious behavior of a compulsive quality themselves, and conditioning the child to experience positive emotion upon behaving (or thinking about behaving) in a desirable manner and to experience negative emotion such as anxiety, shame, or guilt upon behaving (or

thinking about behaving) in an undesirable way. Obsessive children have internalized the parents' dos and don'ts to such an extreme degree that their whole world has become one of striving for imagined parental approval by thinking good thoughts and of avoiding imagined parental disapproval by engaging in all manner of magical and ritualistic thoughts and behaviors.

A Psychoanalytic Interpretation. In psychoanalytic terminology, obsessive persons may be said to use several defense mechanisms. They *isolate* feelings from intellectual content so that their obsessive thoughts and endless verbosity become detached from their emotional roots; an overintellectualized pattern of life results. *Reaction formations* are likewise common: Obsessive concern with cleanliness may be a defense against underlying urges to be dirty or sexy (sex may be perceived as dirty or aggressive). Thus compulsive orderliness protects the person from the fear of unleashed aggression, of smashing everything in sight; excessive politeness and formality protect from urges to be cruel and sadistic. *Undoing* refers to many features of compulsive rituals in which the person attempts to "undo" the harm, real or imagined, that could result from an unacceptable impulse. Engaging in a certain mannerism (such as blinking the eyes, or touching or straightening an object) helps the person to feel that the dangerous impulse is canceled out. Reaction formations are similar to undoing except that they are expressed in broad personality styles rather than in highly specific rituals.

From a developmental point of view, the obsessive-compulsive person has regressed, in the face of an intense Oedipal conflict, to the anal stage. Compulsive concerns with cleanliness and orderliness represent reaction formations against anal impulses to be dirty and smelly, while compulsive tendencies to inhibit emotion or to be formal or excessively good reflect reaction formations against anal-sadistic impulses, originating in the child's defiance of parental efforts to force compliance with toilet training.

While reading the following additional information about Ruth's early childhood, consider how these early learning experiences might have contributed to the development of Ruth's obsessive-compulsive symptoms.

Ruth L.: Childhood Background

Ruth described her mother as a cold and distant person who preferred the company of her horses and dogs to human companionship. When her mother was around, she was always criticizing Ruth; she could not recall her mother ever hugging or kissing her. Her mother had been in some form of psychotherapy ever since Ruth could remember. Although she had some happy times with her father, he was away traveling much of the time.

As Ruth remembered it, her parents had an extremely superficial marital relationship, each pursuing separate interests. When they were together at home, they interacted with each other in a polite and formal manner. Her day-to-day care was largely in the hands of other caretakers who discouraged her from running around in spontaneous play and who always made sure that she was immaculately clean. Her mother was highly critical of the caretakers if her daughter was less than perfectly groomed. There were no other children to play with and she began to fill her time with ritualistic doll play, which her caretakers encouraged since this kept her busy and was a relatively clean activity. (Leon, 1974)

To summarize, clinical evidence, if not hard research data, suggests that individuals with obsessive-compulsive symptoms have experienced social learning conditions that produce intense conflict. Circumstances continue to evoke unacceptable thoughts or actions that the person attempts to control by various stereotyped, counteractive measures. Parents who model an obsessive concern with words and talk rather than actions and emotions may play a contributing role in the development of these symptoms in young children. By and large, lower-class families do not often create such severe conflicts about "correct" and "incorrect" behavior or place such an extreme emphasis on "talk" as to produce obsessive children.

Summary

1. Anxiety disorders are divided into generalized anxiety, panic, and phobic disorders. In the generalized anxiety disorder the anxiety is chronic and long lasting. In the panic disorder the anxiety occurs in acute and disabling attacks. Phobic reactions are associated with specific situations or objects.

2. Anxiety reactions, as all other behavior, are a function of the organism and the environment. Whether or not stresses in the current environment result in abnormal reactions depends on the individual's personality makeup. The case of Boyd C. illustrates how an environmental stress (wife did not call hospital on Christmas Day) produced an anxiety reaction in a person with a certain personality disposition (intense craving for dependency gratification).

3. Twin study evidence suggests some hereditary contribution to the development of anxiety disorders.

4. Environmental experiences that might contribute to the development of anxiety and phobic reactions are: classical conditioning of fear; possibly, but with much less certainty, the operant learning of fear; observational learning and cognitive mediators; experiences that cause intrapsychic conflicts; and social systems effects. The weighting of these factors is likely to vary from person to person.

5. The obsessive-compulsive reaction is characterized by thoughts that intrude repeatedly into awareness and by actions one is compelled to perform. Obsessions and compulsions usually reflect conflicting tendencies over the expression of sexual or aggressive impulses.

6. Obsessive-compulsive tendencies arise under conditions in which the person has strongly internalized parental dos and don'ts and little spontaneity has been modeled by the parents. According to psychoanalytic theory, they represent reaction formations against anal impulses to be dirty or sadistic.

Suggested Readings

J. C. Nemiah in *Foundations of psychopathology* (Oxford, 1961) gives an excellent account of neurotic disorders from a psychodynamic viewpoint. G. R. Leon provides well-written case studies in which neurotic disorders are interpreted largely from a social learning framework in *Case histories of deviant behavior* (Holbrook, 1974).

9

Conversion and Dissociative Disorders

- Can you *learn* to be deaf? To not see? To have a paralyzed arm?

- Do some people really switch from one personality to another, and not remember what happened in the other personality?

- Do "real" organic diseases sometimes get misdiagnosed as hysteria?

- Can you fake a hysterical symptom and get away with it?

- What do hypnotism and conversion symptoms have in common?

Anne: "I've Heard Enough"

Anne, 19 years old, and her mother had been engaging in angry disputes. Anne resented many of the things her mother did and especially blamed her mother for keeping her ignorant about sexual matters. At one point Anne left home to stay with a friend but soon returned, complaining of faintness, dizziness, and buzzing in the ears. Soon thereafter she awoke one morning to find herself totally deaf. Thorough physical examinations revealed no organic basis for the deafness, so it was concluded that the symptom was a hysterical conversion reaction. She learned lipreading and received six weeks of psychotherapy, but to no avail as far as restoring her hearing. (Malmo, 1955)

In this chapter I will focus on bodily symptoms thought to have psychological causes and certain altered states of consciousness. The bodily symptoms are referred to as *conversion disorders* and the altered states of consciousness as *dissociative disorders*. The symptoms included in both of these categories have been labeled hysteria in the past. DSM-III does not use the term *hysteria* and I will only make occasional use of it.

Conversion Disorders

In DSM-III conversion disorders are a subgroup of symptoms under a more general heading of *Somatoform Disorders,* which also includes *somatization disorders* and *psychalgia.* See the accompanying chart for definitions of these other disorders.

Somatoform Disorders, DSM-III

Somatization disorder

Recurrent and multiple somatic complaints for which medical attention is sought but that are not apparently due to any physical disorder. Common complaints are headaches, fatigue, fainting, nausea, bowel troubles, allergies, and menstrual and sexual difficulties. Frequently accompanied by anxiety and depression. Distinguished from conversion disorder in that in the latter one or more bodily symptoms, usually involving the skeletal musculature or sensory processes, occur in the absence of the full clinical picture of the somatization disorder.

Conversion disorder

A bodily symptom that is the direct expression of a psychological conflict or need. Usually involves skeletal musculature or sensory functions.

Psychogenic pain disorder

Complaint of pain in the absence of adequate evidence for a physical basis for the pain, and the presence of evidence that psychological factors have contributed to the causation.

Hypochondriasis

The unrealistic interpretation of physical signs or sensations as indicative of a serious disease. Physical examinations do not support the diagnosis of a physical disorder.

Note: The first three of the above were frequently diagnosed as forms of hysteria in previous DSMs.

CHARACTERISTIC SYMPTOMS

Conversion symptoms may involve a variety of bodily functions, usually being confined, however, to the skeletal musculature or to sensory functions (see Table 9-1). Anne's deafness would be one example. The terms *psychophysiological* or *psychosomatic disorders* are reserved for bodily symptoms involving the autonomic nervous system, such as stomach ulcers, high blood pressure, and diarrhea, in which psychological factors are believed to have at least contributed to their development. These disorders will be discussed further in Chapter 13. The term *conversion* derives from the psychoanalytic theory that psychic energy is "converted" into a physical symptom. In this book the term will have no theoretical implications; it will be used only as a descriptive label for a certain class of symptoms.

Anne's deafness is a good example of a conversion symptom, so let us consider her case in more detail. Anne showed no overt startle reaction when her therapist clapped his hands behind her head. However, an electromyogram (an instrument for recording the electrical impulses associated with muscle contractions) connected to her head, neck, and arms showed a strong contraction of these muscles when a loud sound was presented through earphones. When the same sound was given 60 seconds later, the electromyogram recorded no response, nor was there any response on subsequent presentations. Somehow during the 60 seconds following the first sound Anne had mobilized a block against the sound, effectively inhibiting the muscular reflex reactions. It is beyond the voluntary power of the average person to totally suppress a muscle reaction to such a loud stimulus after only one presentation.

A conditioning treatment was devised in which Anne learned to remove her finger from a button whenever she felt a shock. Before starting the con-

TABLE 9-1   Varieties of Conversion Symptoms

I. Motor Functions of the Skeletal Musculature
    A. Partial or complete paralysis of the arms, legs, or other body parts
    B. Selective loss of function, such as writer's cramp, in which the person cannot write but can use the same muscles for other purposes
    C. Contractions involving rigid flexion of fingers, toes, knees, elbows, or other body parts
    D. Astasia-abasia (the ability to move legs when lying or sitting but not to stand or walk)
    E. Speech disturbances: mutism (total inability to speak) and aphonia (ability to speak only in a whisper)
    F. Convulsions similar to epileptic seizures
    G. Tics (muscular twitchings), usually around eyes or mouth
II. Sensory Functions
    A. Disturbances in vision: total or partial blindness, tunnel vision, blurred vision, double vision, or night blindness
    B. Disturbances in hearing, involving total or partial deafness
    C. Anesthesia (general loss of sensitivity to stimulation of skin)
    D. Analgesia (insensitivity to superficial pain stimuli applied to skin)
    E. Paresthesia (false sensations, such as tingling feelings in skin)
III. Other Somatic Symptoms
    A. "Lump in the throat"
    B. Coughing spells
    C. Persistent belching or sneezing
IV. Simulation of Known Conditions
    A. Appendicitis
    B. Tuberculosis
    C. False pregnancy: cessation of menstrual cycle, swollen abdomen, and morning sickness

ditioning trials the therapist told her that his procedure would help restore her hearing and that in his opinion she would probably begin to hear again the next morning. A sound was presented half a second before each of a series of 150 shocks. After this point shock was occasionally withheld, but nevertheless each time the sound was presented the electromyogram recorded a burst of muscle activity in the finger, indicating that, at some neurophysiological level, Anne "heard." She had learned to respond to the sounds with a slight tensing of the finger muscles. After the session Anne smilingly asserted that she still could not hear.

The next morning a driver who had narrowly avoided hitting her honked his horn and shouted. Anne's hearing suddenly returned and remained intact thereafter. Anne's deafness, then, fits our definition of a conversion disorder. No physical basis for the disorder could be discovered and the available evidence strongly suggests that psychological processes were involved in the development of the symptom.

Sometimes individuals consciously fake bodily symptoms as a means of escaping a dangerous combat situation or in order to collect compensation for a supposed injury.[1] Malingerers cannot be absolutely identified since there is no direct way of knowing a person's conscious intent. However, they are likely to be more evasive and defensive than individuals with conversion reactions and less likely to show a lack of concern about their symptoms. Persons with conversion disorders are usually more willing to talk openly and rather naively about their physical disorders.

DEVELOPMENT OF CONVERSION DISORDERS

Organic Disease and Hysteria. In Chapter 2 you read how Charcot distinguished hysterical symptoms from similar symptoms having a basis in actual or-

[1]In DSM-III a new diagnostic category called Factitious Disorders is included, which refers to the voluntary production of symptoms of mental or physical illness. This disorder is distinguished from malingering in that there is no obvious external advantage that the person is trying to achieve other than to be "sick." Information on the prevalence of this disorder is lacking and, according to DSM-III, its existence by itself is extremely rare. Ordinarily this characteristic would occur in the context of other disorders such as personality disorders or schizophrenia.

ganic disease: for example, not hurting oneself when falling with an epileptic-like seizure; lack of atrophy and retention of normal reflexes in paralyzed limbs; disappearance of symptoms under chloroform; the fact that the body areas affected often do not conform to known neurological systems, as in glove anesthesia; and the unconcern of the patient, *la belle indifférence*. To this list might be added the inconsistency of symptoms—a person with aphonia who can speak only in a whisper but can cough in a normal manner, and a person with "writer's cramp" who can use the same muscles to shuffle a deck of cards with dexterity.

Unfortunately, it is not always so easy to distinguish between organic disease and conversion symptoms. Slater and Glithero (1965) conducted a nine-year follow-up study of patients initially diagnosed as having conversion symptoms; they found that 60 percent had either died from or developed signs of physical disease related to the central nervous system during this period. Whitlock (1967) compared the incidence of organic brain disorder in 56 patients who were diagnosed as hysterical with 56 patients who were diagnosed as depressive, as having anxiety reactions, or both. Of the hysteria patients, 62.5 percent showed evidence indicative of organic brain disorder, whereas such evidence was present for only 5.3 percent of the depression and anxiety patients. The most common indication of possible brain disorder in the hysteria patients was a head injury with concussion occurring within six months prior to the onset of the conversion or dissociative symptom. Other kinds of organic brain disorders present in the sample of patients with hysteria included cerebrovascular accident, epilepsy, encephalitis, and brain tumor. Whitlock's study is of particular interest because it also shows the relatively low incidence of organic brain disorders in anxiety and depressive disorders.

The organic basis for some symptoms diagnosed as conversion disorders can complicate attempts to study the role of hereditary and environmental influences. For example, some years after completing a twin study of hysteria Slater (1961) discovered that the "hysterical" symptoms of several of the twins were probably the result of brain disease.

Heredity. Slater (1961) investigated the possibility of a genetic disposition to hysteria (primarily conversion symptoms) by comparing concordance percentages for 12 identical and 12 fraternal twin pairs in which one twin had received a diagnosis of hysteria. He found no differences in concordance percentages; in fact, no co-twins of either type had received a clear-cut diagnosis of hysteria, although five identical and four fraternal co-twins could be considered as having a neurotic disorder of some kind. The lack of a difference in degree of similarity between identical and fraternal pairs argues against a hereditary component in hysteria, but it would be premature to make any definitive conclusions on the basis of one study with rather small samples.

Current Stresses. Specific stressful experiences are present, either currently or in the recent past, in almost all cases of conversion disorders. A year before the onset of her deafness Anne had had a baby out of wedlock and also contracted syphilis. Her parents, now in their late fifties, had been extremely upset, and Anne's relationship with her mother, especially, had deteriorated badly. She had always felt that her mother was partial to her sister, Kay, and now this feeling was intensified, and no doubt in part justified. With respect to her mother she said,

I felt she didn't trust me any more. She got angry if I ever stayed out late, and she kept watching me like a hawk. She kept harping on the "trouble" I had caused and the money it had cost. She kept picking on me and blaming me for everything. In the evening she sat and talked to Kay. Whenever I came into the room they'd shut up. I'm sure they were talking about me. (Malmo, 1955, p. 217)

Perhaps Anne's deafness was, in part, motivated by a desire to hear her nagging mother no longer. The immediate motive for developing a bodily symptom is, in most cases, to escape from some emotionally unbearable situation. We still have to explain, however, why some individuals develop conversion reactions and others do not when experiencing the same psychological trauma.

Developmental History. The developmental history and resulting personality dispositions of some people must increase the probability that they will react to current stresses with conversion symptoms. From a social learning perspective we would look for past instances in which the person had been reinforced

for having a physical symptom, either obtaining positive benefits or avoiding an unpleasant situation. We would also look for models who might have been observed to display and use symptoms in this way. There is little direct evidence for the role of these social learning experiences. Mucha and Reinhardt (1970) do provide indirect evidence consistent with a modeling effect—namely, that 70 percent of the parents of student aviators with conversion disorders had had an illness involving the same organ system (see Research Report 9-1). Psychoanalytic theory posits that some current situation reawakens an unsatisfactorily resolved Oedipal problem. The unacceptable impulses threaten to break through, creating anxiety that is then controlled by the development of the conversion symptom. We will consider shortly how the social learning and psychoanalytic approaches can be applied to an individual who had a dissociative disorder, thought to be similar in many respects to conversion disorders.

Culture and Conversion Disorders. Clinicians generally agree that the incidence of conversion symptoms in Western culture has decreased since the days of Freud. Whether this common assumption is true or not is open to some question. Stephens and Kamp (1962), for example, found the incidence of outpatients diagnosed with hysteria was the same (2 percent) from 1913 to 1919 as from 1945 to 1960. Despite this evidence to the contrary, many people believe there has been a decrease in conversion disorders, reflecting a presumed change in society's acceptance and reinforcement of such symptoms. In the nineteenth century there was less sophistication about possible psychological factors, and it may have been easier for patients as well as their physicians and families to accept symptoms as indicative of physical illness. Accordingly, the patient received much reinforcement in the form of attention, sympathy, and relief from responsibility. Repressive Victorian attitudes toward sexuality, including the pretense that childhood sexuality did not exist, may have also contributed to conversion reactions in which there was a mutual "conspiracy" between adults and children to deny the sexual meaning of certain symptoms.

Consistent with the hypothesis that psychological sophistication (assumed to be associated with educational level) may reduce the incidence of conver-

Conversion Disorders in Student Aviators

Although the incidence of conversion disorders is very low in most public and private clinics, they occur more frequently in military hospitals. Some possible reasons emerged in a study conducted by Mucha and Reinhardt (1970).

In one year, 1968, 56 student naval aviators with conversion disorders were evaluated in the United States Naval Aerospace Medical Institute in Pensacola, Florida. Three kinds of symptoms were observed: 41 patients (73 percent) had visual problems—blurred vision, diplopia (double vision), transient blind spots, difficulty in focusing, or a general decrease in acuity; eight patients (14 percent) had auditory impairments—inability to hear their instructors though audiometric tests found normal hearing; and seven patients (11 percent) had a paralysis or paresthesia. The authors reported a clear manifestation of *la belle indifférence:* The students were completely unconcerned about the long-range effects of their illness and never considered the possibility that they were seriously ill.

This study provides no support for the idea that conversion disorders are largely limited to the lower socioeconomic classes—80 percent of the fathers of the naval aviation students were either white-collar workers or professionals. It suggests, however, that other background features play a role. Seventy percent of the parents had had an illness involving the organ system used in the son's conversion disorder: A modeling effect is clearly suggested. The students were reared in achievement-oriented families, and 89 percent of them had won letters in one or more sports in high school or college. This fact suggests that they had strong needs to excel in earning their wings; hence quitting in the face of a difficult situation was unacceptable. The physical symptom was an acceptable, honorable way out of a stressful situation. Moreover, most conversion disorders occurred in the squadron that had the highest number of training fatalities, a circumstance likely to increase fears of death or injury.

In addition to these causative influences the authors, in a more psychodynamic vein, quote a psychoanalytic authority (Fenichel, 1945) to the effect that in a conversion disorder the afflicted body part is determined in part by unconscious sexual fantasies. They quote another authority (Bond, 1952) to the effect that "the erogeneity of the testicles is often deplaced to the eyes, with resulting castration fears." No data, however, were reported that bear on this interpretation.

sion disorders is the finding of somewhat higher incidence rates in low socioeconomic and educational levels of society. For example, Proctor (1958) found that 13 percent of 191 consecutive children seen at the University of North Carolina Medical School Psychiatric Unit were diagnosed as hysterical. This incidence was much higher than that in other parts of the country at that time. Proctor described the largely rural areas from which these children came as characterized by low economic and educational levels and as dominated by a pleasure-inhibiting fundamentalist religion that emphasized the sinful nature of smoking, drinking, and sex. Yet, at the same time, children in this region were likely to see behavior inconsistent with these verbal preachments. For example, they might witness their parents' sexual intercourse or sleep with the opposite-sex parent to an advanced age. The combination of overstimulation, strong inhibitions, and lack of knowledge about psychological influence probably contributed to the higher incidence of hysteria.

Hollingshead and Redlich (1958) also found the highest rates of hysterical symptoms in the lowest two social classes. We should, however, be cautious in assuming too strong a relationship between conversion symptoms and poorly educated people. Mucha and Reinhardt (1970), as described in Research Report 9-1, found a relatively high incidence of conversion reactions among naval aviation students from achievement-oriented middle-class families.

Hypnosis and Conversion Disorders. Although we sometimes speak with assurance about learning con-

"And Then I Started Jumping": A Group Manifestation of Conversion Disorder

Helen, one of the popular girls in her high school class, began to show a twitching and jerking movement in her right leg while attending her school's homecoming dance. She did not know how to dance at the time, nor did her father or older brothers, and she maintained that she was simply not interested in dancing. Nevertheless, as was common among her classmates, she did attend the dance as an observer.

Helen's twitching and jerking movements recurred occasionally during the weeks following the homecoming dance, especially when she was under nervous strain. Many of her classmates became aware of her twitching, and some apparently thought it might be the symptom of a contagious disease. About three weeks after the onset of Helen's symptom, two classmates, Millie and Frances, went to a Mardi Gras dance. After the dance Millie suddenly developed convulsive jerking movements in the chest and neck. Millie continued to manifest these symptoms at school the next day. On Thursday morning many students saw Helen experiencing her attacks during an assembly before the start of classes. During the second period Frances began making involuntary spasmodic movements which soon became noticeable to the class, and she was taken to the infirmary. In the meantime, Geraldine, who sat next to her, was getting increasingly nervous. As she said, "First I trembled a little. Then everybody kept saying, 'Look at Geraldine.' And then I started jumping."

The situation rapidly deteriorated at this point. Soon a number of crying, excited girls were showing various forms of jerking movements. Distraught parents arrived to take their children away from whatever strange epidemic seemed to be occurring. School was finally dismissed. Many of the girls were kept home and did not recover fully from their symptoms for several weeks.

Group hysteria (the most commonly used term for this phenomenon) by its nature would seem to call for a somewhat different pattern of causative factors. For example, it seems unlikely that all affected individuals would have an extensive social learning history predisposing them to conversion symptoms. One factor that seems to be present in most carefully studied incidents of group hysteria is one person who first develops the symptom and then serves as a highly visible model for others. This person probably developed the symptom in the usual individual fashion.

Thus in the case of the high school girls who showed the various twitching movements Helen provided the visible model. A few days prior to the homecoming dance where the jerking movements in her legs were first observed, obligatory instruction in dancing had begun in her physical education class. She avoided these lessons at first, a response that suggested strong inhibition about learning to dance. In addition, three days before the homecoming dance the results of the election of the king, queen, and court for the school's Carnival Ball were announced. Although Helen was a senior and fairly prominent among her classmates, she was not elected to any of these positions—positions in which some competence in dancing might be expected. At about the same time, Helen was also becoming aware of the success of a rival for the attentions of a prominent senior boy. The boy was a good dancer, and Helen's rival was a vivacious girl who tap-danced so skillfully that she had been asked to perform at the ball. In sum, then, the basis for the development of the hysterical symptom in Helen appears to be a rather strong conflict in which learning to dance played a central role. Perhaps the twitching and jerking of her legs were incipient dancing movements whose full expression was inhibited.

Four conditions probably contributed to the development of group hysteria: perhaps most important, a clear and visible model of the behavior (Helen); reinforcement for the behavior in the form of attention and concern; a general increase in the excitement or arousal level accompanied by expectations that dramatic happenings were in the offing; and a developing cognitive explanation, which in this case took the form of a belief that the symptoms might result from a contagious disease. These same conditions are present when faith healings, speaking in tongues, trancelike states, and convulsive seizures occur in certain religious groups. (Adapted from Schuler & Parenton, 1943)

version reactions through modeling and reinforcement contingencies, in fact we know relatively little about the mechanisms involved. In the psychodynamic approach even less attention is given to the specifics of the learning process. Is learning to make your legs paralyzed, your eyes not see, or your ears not hear really the same as learning to drive a car or brush your teeth? It seems unlikely. Perhaps in our enthusiasm to show that abnormal behavior, including conversion symptoms, is *just* learned behavior we have been a little guilty of explaining by naming, overlooking the fact that we still do not understand the specific processes involved in some instances.

Does the phenomenon of hypnosis shed any light on the learning process in conversion symptoms? Since the work of Bernheim and Charcot, a close relationship between hypnotically induced bodily symptoms and conversion symptoms has been recognized. These investigators and others have shown that hypnosis can be used with normal subjects to induce conversion reactions that are difficult to distinguish from their naturally occurring counterparts in clinic patients. Thus a study of hypnosis might shed light on mechanisms involved in the development of conversion disorders.

Although hypnosis itself is not completely understood, a growing body of evidence suggests the importance of two aspects of the hypnotic procedure. First, the subjects must focus their attention on some restricted field of experience, increasing the effect of the hypnotist's voice. Second, the subjects must be motivated to cooperate with the hypnotist in undertaking whatever roles may be asked of them.

Experiences of a mildly hypnotic nature occur in everyday life. If you narrow your field of attention and block out most sources of incoming stimulation without the aid of a hypnotist, you may achieve some limited state of self-hypnosis. You can probably remember occasions when you became completely

The induction of a hypnotic trance would seem to rely primarily on focusing and restricting the person's attention, and on the person being motivated to cooperate with the hypnotist.

engrossed in a task, if only for a few seconds or minutes, and later realized, or were told by others, that you had been completely oblivious to many things going on around you. It is also likely that during such a "dissociated" experience you were not aware even of yourself, that is, your personal identity.

Conversion symptoms in the form of motor and sensory disturbances may also be facilitated in some way by a state of high concentration and strong motivation to escape from some distressing life circumstance. A placebo pill reduces pain because we expect it to; probably that process has some similarities to the conversion reaction of analgesia. Hilgard (1969) has shown that the pain associated with immersion of a forearm in ice-cold water can be greatly decreased by hypnotic suggestion. In other research Hilgard and his associates used an "honesty interrogation" procedure designed to maximize truthfulness in the reporting of pain, and the results strongly confirmed the importance of the hypnotic procedures (Hilgard, MacDonald, Morgan, & Johnson, 1978). For highly hypnotizable subjects there was a clear superiority in pain reduction for subjects receiving the analgesic suggestion under hypnosis (see hatched graphs in Figure 9-1). The same suggestion given in a normal waking state or given under hypnosis without an analgesic suggestion showed much less pain reduction. The unhatched graphs show results for difficult-to-hypnotize subjects who were instructed to simulate, that is, fake a hypnotic trance, a deception that was not detected by the experimenter conducting these sessions. These faking subjects reported no reduction in pain in any condition when given the "honesty interrogation."

But how similar are hypnotically produced "symptoms" to those seen in conversion disorders? Apparently, quite similar. Recall Anne, who experienced the conversion symptom of deafness, and who showed little electromyographic response (electrical responses in muscles) to a series of tones after showing a startle response to the first tone. The authors of that study (Malmo et al., 1954) also found similar results for a subject in whom deafness was induced by hypnosis.

Sackheim et al. (1979) reviewed studies in which hysterically blind subjects were shown to respond in nonchance ways to visual stimuli—some subjects responding significantly better than chance and others responding significantly worse than chance. In the latter case the person would have to "see" the stimuli

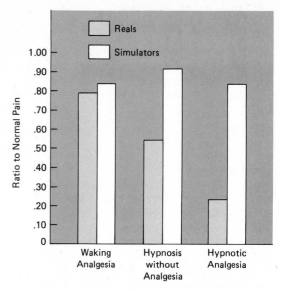

FIGURE 9-1. Pain reduction as reported in honesty inquiry in "real" and simulating subjects. Analgesia refers to suggestion of feeling no pain. From Hilgard et al., *Journal of Abnormal Psychology*, 1978, *87*, 239–246. © 1978 American Psychological Association and used with permission.

in some sense in order to answer incorrectly. The task was usually a simple one in which the person would be asked, for example, to report which of three geometric shapes was being presented. If they were truly blind, they would be expected to do no better than chance guessing. Despite their nonchance performance all subjects insisted that they saw nothing. Sackheim et al. (1979) suggest that the sensory information is received by the brain (as a so-called iconic representation) but that the hysterically blind person has somehow learned to block the more central processing mechanisms involved in actual "seeing" or perceiving. At the same time the visual information is being processed in other parts of the brain and is, in some way, available for the person to "know" what is there in order to "guess" at a nonchance level. Those persons who "guess" significantly worse than chance are, according to these authors, engaging in an additional defensive strategy, denial, which also is thought to occur outside of awareness. In other words, the initial blocking of the perceptual process is seen as a separate maneuver from the subsequent denial that is involved in performing worse than chance.

Hilgard, Hilgard, MacDonald, Morgan, & Johnson (1978) invoke a somewhat similar explanation to explain the blocking of pain stimuli from awareness under hypnotic suggestion. These authors also used a "hidden observer" technique involving hypnotically induced "automatic talking" to successfully communicate directly with that part of the person that was still experiencing the pain stimuli. Research findings, then, would seem to suggest that somehow certain individuals learn to dissociate or split off one part of the perceptual-cognitive processing of incoming information from another part and thus produce the strange phenomenon of not seeing, hearing, or feeling while at the same time having this information available within the brain.

Dissociative Disorders

CHARACTERISTIC SYMPTOMS

Dissociative disorders involve certain altered states of consciousness. One type of dissociative disorder, *psychogenic amnesia,* involves a sudden loss of memory for a certain period of time that is too extensive to be explained by ordinary forgetfulness. The memory loss is usually associated with a traumatic event such as an automobile accident.

The *psychogenic fugue* is similar to amnesia except that there is a more definite flight from the present situation. The person may go to some other part of the country and start an entirely new life—getting a job, marrying, and having children, in complete forgetfulness of an earlier life, and identity involving another job and family. A dissociative disorder of the fugue type is illustrated by the case of Barbara Y., who disappeared from her home one day without leaving a trace; two weeks later, disheveled and dirty, she was picked up by the police in a nearby city. Brought to a hospital, she failed at first to recognize her husband, did not know her own name, and could not remember anything about the past two weeks or her previous life. During the course of psychotherapy she gradually regained her memory of the two-week period as well as her past life. She had apparently left home with only enough money to buy a bus ticket to the city were she had lived as a child. She spent much of one day walking the streets where she had grown up and standing in front of the building where

Sometimes different selves may compete for control of the personality.

her father's office had been. Later she had gone to a motel with a man, and, according to the motel owner, had "entertained" several different men over a three-day period. On admission to the hospital, Barbara, wearing ponytail, bobby sox, and low-heeled shoes, appeared more like a high school girl than a woman of 31 (Goldstein & Palmer, 1975).

Multiple personality symptoms are rare. They involve a splitting off of larger segments of the personality than is the case for the more restricted amnesic or fugue states. The person may alternate among two or more personalities with varying awareness of what transpires in the other personalities. Although the extreme dissociation characteristic of this disorder is unusual, the basic tendency to have two or more conflicting "selves" is familiar to most of us. You may be quite a different person at a beer party, at church, and at a political demonstration. Many of us have experienced in the process of growing up a conflict between the conforming, restrained, "good" self on the one hand and the nonconforming, rebellious, "acting out" self on the other hand. This particular kind of split is fairly common in multiple personality.

The Three Faces of Eve

One of the more famous cases of multiple personality was the basis for a best-selling book and movie called *The Three Faces of Eve.* Eve White, a 25-year-old woman, sought therapy because of severe and "blinding" headaches often followed by blackouts. A description of Eve's first transformation to a different personality in a therapy session follows:

This superlatively calm, utterly self-controlled little figure of propriety showed no suggestion of anything that the layman might think of as *nervousness.* Her hands lay still on the arms of her chair as she spoke. . . . She was not undernourished but seemed somehow very delicate, the reticent, meticulous manner suggesting a physical fragility. . . . (Thigpen & Cleckley, 1957, pp. 1–2)

One day Eve White suddenly changed into Eve Black. The brooding look in her eyes became almost a stare. Eve seemed momentarily dazed. Suddenly her posture began to change. Her body slowly stiffened until she sat rigidly erect. An alien, inexplicable expression then came over her face. This was suddenly erased into utter blankness. The lines of her countenance seemed to shift in a barely visible, slow, rippling transformation. . . . Closing her eyes, she winced as she put her hands to her temples, pressed hard, and twisted them as if to combat sudden pain. A slight shudder passed over her entire body. Then the hands lightly dropped. She relaxed easily into an attitude of comfort the physician had never before seen in this patient. A pair of blue eyes popped open. There was a quick, reckless smile. In a bright, unfamiliar voice that sparkled, the woman said, "Hi there, Doc!"

With a soft and surprisingly intimate syllable of laughter, she crossed her legs, carelessly swirling her skirts in the process. She unhurriedly smoothed the hem down over her knees in a manner that was playful and somehow just a little provocative. . . . The demure and constrained posture of Eve White had melted in buoyant repose.

"She's been having a real rough time. . . . Would you give me a cigarette, Doc?"
He handed her a cigarette, and then lighting it, said, "Who is 'she'?"
"Why, Eve White, of course. Your long-suffering, saintly, little patient."
"But aren't you Eve White?" he asked.
"That's for laughs," she claimed, a ripple of mirth in her tone. She tossed her head slightly again. "Why you ought to know better than that, Doc!"
"Well, who *are* you?" he asked incredulously.
"Why, I'm Eve Black," she said (giving Mrs. White's maiden name). (pp. 20–22)

When it has been possible to reconstruct the childhood experiences of individuals with multiple personalities, it has seemed that the splits in personality have come at times of extreme emotional stress. Thus in the case of Sybil (Schreiber, 1973), a more recent example, there were some 16 different personalities—all inhabiting the same person. Sybil had experienced extreme cruelty from her mother, who at one time had been hospitalized and diagnosed as paranoid schizophrenic. The mother seemed to have provided a mixture of affection and cruelty that made it impossible for Sybil as a young child to rebel against her. The different personalities seemed to have split off at various times in Sybil's developmental history, and each personality seemed to have characteristics relevant to the particular stress that precipitated the dissociation. Even more recently Winer (1978) has reported a case in which the two dissociated personalities seemed to have split off during rather specific psychological trauma involving extreme anger and fear. One of these occasions was at age 14 when she had returned home one day to find her mother having intercourse with her boyfriend. The part of her that experienced a murderous rage toward her mother and subsequently seemed to believe that she had killed her mother with a knife split off at this time.

DEVELOPMENT OF DISSOCIATIVE DISORDERS

As with conversion disorders current environmental stresses of a relatively severe degree are almost always present. There is little evidence one way or the other for genetic or other biological factors that might predispose a person to dissociative reactions. With respect to psychological factors we can again view these influences from either a social learning or psychoanalytic perspective. Let us take the case of Barbara Y., the woman who disappeared from her home and remembered nothing about her activities during the two-week period before she was found. In reading the following description of Barbara's childhood and young adult experiences consider how these events might be viewed from both a social learning and a psychodynamic orientation.

From a social learning point of view Barbara's mother can be seen as modeling escape from responsibility by sickness, which may have been a partial determinant of Barbara's own tendency to vomit under certain emotional circumstances and to have "seizures" as a way of avoiding anxiety-arousing het-

Barbara's mother suffered from poor health, frequently taking to her bed for days at a time with fatigue and headaches. Barbara also remembered her mother as a fussy person who always seemed afraid that her daughter might become ill or have an accident. Barbara's own health was fair as a child, but she did have recurring episodes of nausea and vomiting that seemed to be in some unspecified way related to emotional factors.

As an adolescent Barbara had occasional "seizures" that consisted of a feeling of dizziness and a slight paralysis but no loss of consciousness. The first of these seizures occurred just prior to her second menstrual period and thereafter seemed to have some rough but not consistent association with her period. She remembered her first seizure clearly. She was driving with her father to a special teenage party when it came on, and her father had pulled over to the curb, laid her on the grass, and administered artificial respiration. A neurologist who subsequently observed several of her seizures indicated that she lay rigid on the floor with eyes rolled back but showed no other characteristics of a genuine epileptic seizure such as convulsive movements or abnormal brain wave patterns. Despite this he treated her with anticonvulsive medication. Some years later he came to suspect an emotional etiology and prescribed a placebo pill, telling her that it was a new medicine almost certain to eliminate the seizures. She remained free of seizures thereafter.

Her mother died shortly after Barbara graduated from high school, and two years prior to her fugue reaction her father died after a ten-year period of heart disease. During her father's illness Barbara had taken care of him at home as well as helped him with his real estate business. She was extremely upset after his death, and her physician advised her to take a long vacation trip, which she did. While touring the Caribbean, she had several brief sexual affairs, the last of which resulted in pregnancy and abortion.

Shortly after returning Barbara accepted an offer of marriage from her father's former partner, a man seventeen years older than herself. She became anxious as the day of the wedding approached and twice postponed the date. On the night following her wedding she had her menstrual period one week prior to the expected time, and she tearfully and apologetically rejected his sexual advances. It became apparent in time, however, that she was unable to be sexually aroused by her husband, and, in fact, felt disgusted by his advances. He became increasingly dissatisfied himself, and on one occasion he got her to drink rather heavily and became quite drunk himself. Their attempt at intercourse was a complete failure, and he swore at her and called her a "rubber mat." The next few days she felt guilty and tearful about this incident. The following week she disappeared. (Goldstein & Palmer, 1975)

erosexual encounters. Normal heterosexual development may have been impeded by the overprotective actions of both mother and father; and finally the emotionally intolerable marriage situation, in which Barbara's needs for nurturance and liking from a fatherly figure were in direct conflict with the anxiety (or disgust) aroused by the expectation of sexual intimacy, led to the dissociative avoidance response. Escape from the emotionally distressing situation with her husband provided immediate reinforcement for the dissociative reaction. Enjoyment of her sexual escapades, which was permissible in the dissociated state, may have provided additional reinforcement for maintaining the symptom.

The psychoanalytic theory of dissociation, by contrast, posits that some current situation reawakens an unsatisfactorily resolved Oedipal problem. The unacceptable impulses threaten to break through, creating anxiety that is then controlled by the development of the dissociative symptoms. The symptom itself is often a compromise that serves not only as a defense against the anxiety-arousing conflict but also as unconscious gratification of the forbidden impulse. Thus in Barbara's case psychoanalysts would attribute considerable importance to an early Oedipal attachment to her father, which interfered with a more usual development of heterosexual relationships with other men. Only upon the death of her father did she finally get married, and then to a man old enough to be her father. Oedipal anxieties would be expected to disrupt the normal enjoyment of sex in such a relationship. The solution was to flee from this intolerable situation by going into a restricted state of consciousness in which sexuality could be expressed, perhaps with frankly Oedipal fantasies, without the inhibitions that her normal conscious personality would impose. These Oedipal features were further borne out during her treatment, when she developed a strong transference involving erotic fantasies toward the therapist and made slips of the tongue in which she referred to the therapist as "daddy."

Barbara's case lends itself readily to both psychoanalytic and social learning interpretations. Perhaps we need not make a clear choice between theories in this case since they overlap considerably in their views of important developmental influences. Without buying the whole libidinal theory of psychosexual development, a social learning approach could easily incorporate the Oedipal features that seem so apparent in Barbara's case.

A Concluding Comment

In the course of describing variations in anxiety, conversion, and dissociative disorders it is easy to drift into a manner of discussion that makes it seem as though we are dealing with neat, discrete categories: Some people have anxiety reactions, others have conversion disorders, and so on. Usually this is not the case. People with all kinds of emotional handicaps in living seek help at clinics or from private practitioners. Individuals with relatively "pure" conversion or obsessive-compulsive reactions are rare, comprising about 5 percent of all outpatients. Many show some combination of anxiety and depression. Psychophysiological symptoms such as stomach ulcers, diarrhea, and high blood pressure are also fairly common accompaniments of the symptoms of anxiety. Many individuals do not show any of the acute symptoms of these psychiatric categories to a severe degree but are simply unhappy about certain aspects of their life; frequently their symptoms fall between the disorders we have been discussing here and neurotic traits of the kind described in Chapter 7.

Summary

1. Conversion disorders comprise a subgroup of symptoms under a more general heading of Somatoform Disorders, and involve impairments in the skeletal musculature or sensory functions and are thought to result directly from psychological conflicts.

2. Dissociative disorders are altered states of consciousness such as amnesia, fugue, or multiple-personality disorders.

3. Although conversion and dissociative symptoms can frequently be distinguished from organically based diseases (by not making neurological sense, for example), they cannot always be. Sometimes these symptoms turn out later to have an organic basis.

4. There is no clear evidence for a hereditary contribution to conversion and dissociative disorders.

5. Specific stressful experiences are present, either currently or in the recent past, in almost all cases of conversion and dissociative disorders. Social learning theory emphasizes immediate reinforcements, both escape from the unpleasant situation and various secondary gains, in acquiring and maintaining these symptoms.

6. The history of past reinforcements and observational learning contributes to the likelihood that a person will develop a conversion symptom in the face of current stress. In addition, psychoanalytic theory emphasizes a reactivated Oedipal conflict and the symbolic meaning of the body part affected.

Suggested Readings

The story of *Sybil* by F. R. Schreiber (Warner, 1973) is a fascinating account of an individual with 16 personalities. A more complete description of the case of Barbara, the woman who experienced a dissociative reaction, can be found in M. J. Goldstein and J. O. Palmer, *The experience of anxiety* (Oxford University Press, 1975).

10
Insight Therapy

- What does a psychoanalyst do?

- What is transference? Resistance?

- "The truth shall make you free." Is insight enough?

- Some therapists are considered to be humanistic or experiential in their approach. What do these terms mean?

- When should therapists tell clients their own feelings?

- Psychotherapy is a multimillion-dollar business today. Is it worth the thousand dollars or more you might have to pay?

- Would any therapeutic approach work if you had a strong belief or faith in the therapist? Would a sugar pill work as well if you believed it to be effective?

As soon as they read about psychological disorders, students usually ask how people with these problems can be helped. Rather than postponing discussion of this question to the end of the book, we will consider treatment in the context of each type of abnormal behavior. Those disorders that have been called neurotic are an especially apt place to begin, since many forms of psychological intervention originated with the treatment of these difficulties. In this chapter and the following two we will take up in some detail the psychodynamic, humanistic, behavioral, and social systems approaches to treatment. Although the focus will be on the application of these forms of treatment to those disorders traditionally called neurotic, I will raise general issues that apply to their use with a variety of disorders.

Psychotherapeutic procedures have become so diverse that it is no simple matter to provide an inclusive definition. Typically *psychotherapy* is defined as a form of treatment based on verbal interchanges whose aim is to remove psychological symptoms. This definition, however, is a bit narrow since it excludes those behavior therapies in which nonverbal techniques are primarily used. Accordingly I will expand upon the traditional definition and say that psychotherapy is a form of treatment that uses *psychological* intervention to effect changes in abnormal behaviors, in contrast to physiologically based treatments such as drugs, electroshock, or brain surgery. In this chapter we will consider psychotherapeutic approaches that emphasize verbal interchange or talk, especially as a way of facilitating increased self-understanding and as an opportunity to experience a relationship with a therapist that is in itself considered to be therapeutic. I will use the shorthand expression, *insight therapy,* to refer to these approaches to psychotherapy.

Psychotherapy has become a multimillion-dollar business in America, spawning a variety of professional programs and institutes to train practitioners in this art. We have come a long way from the early days of Freud when only a few affluent patients experienced the new treatment called psychoanalysis. Today psychotherapy is available in college counseling centers, psychiatric hospitals, and community mental health clinics, and from innumerable private practitioners and all manner of "growth" or human potential institutes. The demand for psychological help seems to stay ahead of the supply. It is as though the more psychotherapists there are, the more people want their assistance. We read constantly about psychotherapy in books, magazines, and newspapers, see programs about it on television, or discuss it in classes. As a result, more and more people become aware that some of their troubles in living, their various unhappinesses, may be relieved by these techniques.

Psychoanalysis

I have already traced the development of Freud's theory of neurosis; now we turn to the mode of treatment that he developed to alleviate these disorders—*psychoanalysis*. This psychotherapeutic approach and its variations continue to be a dominant force in the treatment of psychological disorders. As with all approaches, the specific techniques of treatment have been strongly influenced by the theoretical model or metaphor from which they derive. In reading the following remember that Freud's conception of mental disorder was a variation of the illness metaphor in which observed symptoms result from repressed impulses and conflicts.

Sigmund Freud as a young man.

FREE ASSOCIATION

In *free association* the patient is instructed to express whatever comes to mind, no matter how seemingly irrelevant, trivial, or embarrassing. Rather than actively organizing thoughts, the patient is encouraged to adopt a passive attitude, reporting the ideas, feelings, and images that come into awareness as though they were scenes observed from a train window. This introspective reverie is facilitated by lying on a couch with the therapist out of view behind the patient. In everyday conversation we suppress intruding, irrelevant thoughts in order to make an organized and logical presentation of whatever it is we wish to say. In using free association the therapist wants the patient to follow emotional rather than logical associations, circumventing the usual ego defenses, and thereby gradually uncovering the unconscious sources of symptoms. No one expects the patient to be able to comply fully with this instruction, least of all the psychoanalyst; sooner or later the patient draws a blank, begins to make well-planned speeches, gets into disputes with the therapist, or in many other ways resists the basic rule of free association. *Resistance,* as this is called, becomes a primary focus of attention for the therapist, who attempts to help the patient through such resistances by *interpretation* (more on this important psychoanalytic tool later). Since the way a patient resists is likely to reflect styles of ego-defenses used in other situations, insight about these resistances is an important therapeutic benefit. The following excerpt from psychoanalyst Lewis Wolberg (1977) illustrates free association, resistance, and interpretation of resistance.

Patient: So I started walking, and walking, and decided to go behind the museum and walk through Central Park. So I walked and went through a back field and felt very excited and wonderful. I saw a park bench next to a clump of bushes and sat down. There was a rustle behind me and I got frightened. I thought of men concealing themselves in the bushes. I thought of the sex perverts I read about in Central Park. I wondered if there was someone behind me exposing himself. The idea is repulsive, but exciting too. I think of father now and feel excited. I think of an erect penis. This is connected with my father. There is something about this pushing in my mind. I don't know

what it is, like on the border of my memory. (Pause.)

Therapist: Mm hmm. (Pause.) On the border of your memory?

Patient: (Breathing rapidly and seemingly under great tension.) As a little girl, I slept with my father. I get a funny feeling over my skin, tingly-like. It's a strange feeling, like a blindness, like not seeing something. My mind blurs and spreads over anything I look at. I've had this feeling off and on since I walked in the park. My mind seems to blank off like I can't think or absorb anything. (This sounds like a manifestation of repression, with inhibition of intellectual functioning, perhaps as a way of coping with the anxiety produced by a return of the repressed idea.)

Therapist: The blurring of your mind may be a way of pushing something out you don't want there. (Interpreting her symptoms as resistance.)

Patient: I just thought of something. When father died, he was nude. I looked at him, but I couldn't see anything. I couldn't think clearly. I was brought up not to be aware of the difference between a man and a woman. I feared my father, and yet I loved him. I slept with him when I was very little, on Saturdays and Sundays. A wonderful sense of warmth and security. There was nothing warmer or more secure. A lot of pleasure. I tingle all over now. It was a wonderful holiday when I was allowed to sleep with father. I can't seem to remember anything now. There's a blur in my mind. I feel tense and afraid.

Therapist: That blur contaminates your life. You are afraid of something or afraid of remembering something. (Focusing on her resistance.) (p. 536)

TRANSFERENCE

In time, most patients begin to have irrational emotional reactions toward the therapist, known as *transference* reactions. Patients may feel that the therapist does not like them, is bored with them, wants to dominate them, is secretly laughing at them, is letting them down, or one of many other variations. In response to these perceptions, the patients may attempt to dominate and control the therapist, argue, make erotic overtures, or win sympathy by being helpless and long-suffering; the possibilities are endless. The crucial theoretical point here is that the patients are supposedly *transferring* expectations and ways of reacting that were characteristic of their early relationships with their own parents.

The psychoanalytic situation is purposely constructed to facilitate irrational reactions of this kind. The therapist sits unseen behind the patient and divulges next to nothing about personal reactions. The therapist is indeed like an ambiguous inkblot onto which the patient can project expectations. Again, let us take an example from the writings of Wolberg (1977) to illustrate both a transference reaction and the therapist's manner of dealing with it by interpretation.

Patient: I want to talk about my feelings about you.

Therapist: Mm hmm.

Patient: You sit here, a permissive person who lets me go on. I want to do something now, but I'm afraid you will be disappointed in me if I upset the apple cart, if I explode. I think we are too nice to each other. I'm ready not to be nice. My greatest fear of you is that you are potentially going to be severe with me if I let loose. Also, I fear I will let you down by not performing well, by not being nice. I feel I will gain your disapproval and yet I see you don't condemn and don't criticize. It is still important to me to gain a nod from you or a smile. (Pause.)

Therapist: It sounds as if you would like to let loose with me, but you are afraid of what my response would be. (Summarizing and restating.)

Patient: I get so excited by what is happening here. I feel I'm being held back by needing to be nice. I'd like to blast loose sometimes, but I don't dare.

Therapist: Because you fear my reaction?

Patient: The worst thing would be that you wouldn't like me. You wouldn't speak to me friendly; you wouldn't smile; you'd feel you can't treat me and discharge me from treatment. But I know this isn't so. I know it.

Therapist: Where do you think these attitudes come from?

Patient: When I was nine years old, I read a lot about great men in history. I'd quote them and be dramatic. I'd want a sword at my side; I'd dress like an Indian. Mother would scold me. Don't frown, don't talk so much. Sit on your hands, over and over again. I did all kinds of things. I was a naughty child. She told me I'd be hurt. Then at fourteen I fell off a horse and broke my back. I had to be in bed. Mother then told me on the day I went riding not to, that I'd get hurt because the ground was frozen. I was a stubborn, self-willed child. Then I went against her will and suffered an accident that changed my life, a fractured back. Her attitude was, "I told you so." I was put in a cast and kept in bed for months.

Therapist: You were punished, so to speak, by this accident.

Patient: But I gained attention and love from mother for the first time. I felt so good. I'm ashamed to tell you this. Before I healed I opened the cast and tried to walk to make myself sick again so I could stay in bed longer. (Pause.)

Therapist: How does that connect up with your impulses to be sick now and stay in bed so much? (The patient has these tendencies, of which she is ashamed.)

Patient: Oh . . . (Pause.)

Therapist: What do you think?

Patient: Oh, my God, how infantile, how ungrown up (pause), it must be so. I want people to love me and be sorry for me. Oh, my God. How completely childish. It is, is that. My mother must have ignored me when I was little, and I wanted so to be loved. (This sounds like insight.)

Therapist: So that it may have been threatening to go back to being self-willed and unloved after you got out of the cast. (Interpretation.) Perhaps if you go back to being stubborn with me, you would be returning to how you were before; that is, active, stubborn, but unloved.

Patient: (Excitedly.) And, therefore, losing your love. I need you, but after all you aren't going to reject me. The pattern is so established now that the threat of the loss of love is too overwhelming with everybody, and I've got to keep myself from acting selfish or angry. (pp. 560-561)

In the throes of a strong transference reaction, the patient may lose sight of the basic goal of psychoanalytic therapy—self-understanding—and become preoccupied with winning the therapist's approval, defeating the therapist in a power struggle, or seducing the therapist. Skillful handling of these transference reactions is necessary to forestall an unsatisfactory termination of therapy. At the same time,

Freud's study where he saw his patients.

the transference reaction is an unusual opportunity to confront and gain insight into early childhood conflicts with parents; in fact, many psychoanalytic writers have suggested that the development and successful working through of a transference reaction is essential for therapeutic improvement. The transference can be seen as the reopening of "psychological wounds" of childhood, but now with the skillful help of the therapist the person can face these emotionally charged issues and come to a more adult resolution of them. This in turn should enable the person to relate to other people (not just the therapist) on the basis of present realities uncontaminated by residual feelings and expectations from the past.

INTERPRETATION

Our discussion so far has concentrated on what the patient does—free associates, resists, and has transference reactions—but what does the analyst do? I. H. Paul (1973) provides an excellent discussion of psychoanalytic technique in a book called *Letters*

to Simon. First, let us quote Paul on what an analyst does *not* do.

The therapist does not counsel, direct, or interview the patient; he provides little if any guidance, advice, and evaluation; he gives no rewards or punishments; he doesn't relate as a mentor, or teacher, or friend; he maintains a neutrality, an impersonality, and an impassivity that is quite severe; he observes without much participation, he comments without judging, and he shows only a narrow and selective range of feelings. (pp. 11–12)

What then does the analyst do? Compared with many other approaches to therapy the analyst is relatively inactive, from time to time trying to facilitate the patient's flow of associations with a question or reflection and most importantly offering an occasional *interpretation*. The interpretation is the analyst's primary tool in dealing with resistance and transference and in accomplishing the basic therapeutic goal of making the unconscious conscious. Playing such a crucial role, the art of interpretation has received considerable attention among psychoanalytic practitioners. The object is to make an interpretation that is neither too "deep" (about some unconscious process that the patient is not yet ready to accept) nor too "shallow" (so that the patient feels that the analyst is commenting on the obvious). Timing, in other words, is all-important. The best interpretation is one that goes only a little beyond the patient's immediate experiencing, produces some acknowledgment or surprised recognition, and induces a renewed burst of associations that confirm and expand the interpretation. In the previous excerpt from Wolberg we saw that the therapist's question about how the patient's present tendencies to be sick and stay in bed might connect with an earlier incident produced just this kind of reaction; thus it seems to have been an effective interpretation.

Although this process may sound simple, Paul indicates many pitfalls to be avoided. In addition to proper timing, interpretations must be kept short and to the point. A long, complicated interpretation loses its power. Interpretations must be offered to patients as possibilities to consider, not rammed down their throats. Patients tend to feel criticized by an interpretation even when criticism is not intended. The analyst must be prepared to deal with this reaction constructively without getting into an argument. I have only touched on some of the problems that arise; skill in the proper use of interpretation is the essential feature of good psychoanalytic technique.

CARING

The previous quote from Paul on what the analyst does not do with its emphasis on neutrality and impersonality may make the psychoanalyst seem more like a machine than a person. Some correction to that impression should be given. Although analysts avoid, almost like the plague, disclosures about their own personal life and feelings, this does not mean that they are lacking in human warmth or that they do not *care* for the patient. They express their caring by trying to *understand* the patient and to increase the patient's self-understanding, in the belief that this gift of insight is the best thing that they can do to free the patient from neurotic suffering. In a real sense psychoanalytic therapy rests on the belief that "The truth (about your intrapsychic conflicts) shall make you free."

Let us quote again from Paul:

Imagine yourself, Simon, in the position of our patient. You have a regular, periodic opportunity to speak your mind to someone who listens closely and maintains an attitude of neutrality. Despite the intensity of his listening he never makes a comment that betrays any valuation of you or any judgment about what you tell him. It doesn't matter to him that you do, think, and feel some shameful things, so he remains free of disappointment in you. He never conveys any satisfaction in how you are doing, either. His only apparent wish is to better understand you so that you can better understand yourself. And he maintains an attitude of respect, of tact, and of some warmth. Now, under these "safe" conditions, you talk steadily. Much of the time you recount your experiences both present and past; you talk about your thoughts, about your feelings; you tell your fantasies, your dreams, your wishes, and your fears. The focus of all attention is on you and your life. You also come to have thoughts and feelings about the person who is listening and helping you to talk and reflect. These thoughts and feelings you can recognize as largely your own products because he remains essentially a stranger to you. In this act of recognition, moreover, comes a profound sense of your inner reality—the range and richness of your Self. (p. 108)

INSIGHT AS AN EMOTIONAL EXPERIENCE

With all its emphasis on achieving insight and on making the unconscious conscious, psychoanalysis might seem to concentrate on intellectual or cognitive processes to the neglect of emotions. This criticism may be valid to some extent, but most analysts insist that the kind of insight that is therapeutic is not some abstract theory about one's psychodynamic processes but an insight based on the direct experience of the emotions and impulses involved. Alexander and French (1946) say that patients must undergo a "corrective emotional experience" as a result of being reexposed, under more favorable circumstances, to emotional situations that they could not handle in the past. Effective insight is rarely gained from one interpretation. In session after session the patient explores by free association all of the ramifications of a given problem area, slowly gaining wider and deeper self-understanding. This extended process is frequently referred to as *working through*.

MODIFICATIONS OF THE PSYCHOANALYTIC TECHNIQUE

So far I have described the standard psychoanalytic technique, a procedure that in its nature requires long and intensive treatment. The patient sees the analyst three to five times a week for two to three years, and frequently even longer. There have been a number of variations on the basic psychoanalytic approach to therapy.

Alexander and French developed a modified form of psychoanalytic therapy aimed at achieving more limited goals. They believed that certain therapeutic benefits could be attained with a more flexible approach in which the patient sits face to face with the therapist and free association is not always used. They especially advocated flexibility in the promotion of transference reactions, suggesting that at times the standard psychoanalytic procedure encourages a kind of childish dependency that unnecessarily prolongs treatment. However, they distinguished their modified psychoanalytic approach from the standard approach, agreeing that the latter is necessary to accomplish more basic personality changes.

Another variation in technique is associated with a greater theoretical emphasis on ego processes as opposed to id processes. Writers such as Horney, Sullivan, and Hartmann argue that Freud put too much emphasis on bringing unconscious instinctual impulses, the id processes, into awareness and had neglected the active, regulating capacities of the ego. Rather than seeing man as strictly at the mercy of instinctual urges, these theorists give more attention to people's ability to think, plan, and delay impulse expressions. Also, they put more stress on interpersonal relationships and the social environment. These

THE PROFESSION OF PSYCHOTHERAPY

Psychotherapists may obtain their training by any of several routes. *Psychiatrists* obtain an M.D. degree and then specialize in the field of psychiatry for three additional years beyond the internship. Training for psychiatrists has usually emphasized nonbehavioral, and frequently psychoanalytic, approaches. Because they are M.D.s, psychiatrists are equipped to diagnose medical problems that sometimes intermingle with psychological difficulties and to prescribe drugs.

Psychoanalysts receive several years of training at a recognized psychoanalytic institute. This preparation includes a training analysis, in which the candidate undergoes a personal psychoanalysis by a senior member of the institute. Most institutes require candidates to have obtained an M.D. degree and to have completed a psychiatric residency.

Clinical psychologists ordinarily obtain a Ph.D. degree involving four to five years of graduate work beyond the bachelor's degree. Ph.D. programs in clinical psychology include research training, the acquisition of knowledge in specific areas (such as abnormal, experimental, social, or developmental psychology), and the learning of clinical skills in assessment and therapy.

Psychiatric social workers complete a two-year course of study beyond the bachelor's degree, leading to a Master of Social Work degree. Social workers are likely to have considerable experience in working directly with families in their home environment and a familiarity with the many community resource agencies.

Under the pressure for additional mental health professionals, there has been increasing experimentation with other modes of training. Several institutions, for example, now offer Doctor of Psychology (not Ph.D.) degrees in programs that emphasize clinical training and eliminate many research requirements. In other settings, either academic or "on the job," there has been a trend toward training paraprofessionals, people who receive one or two years of training and then work under the supervision of professionals.

It is hard to guess how most psychotherapists will be trained ten years from now. The field is in flux at the moment, and in time there may be a new professional category that is not closely tied to any of the traditional categories described above.

Thomas French (left) and Franz Alexander (right) advocated a flexible approach to psychoanalytic therapy.

differences in theoretical orientation lead to differences in treatment technique. Sullivan, for example, focuses more on patients' interpersonal behaviors, the *security mechanisms* that protect them from anxiety in their relationships with others, than on deeply buried id impulses. Many current psychoanalysts such as Paul have incorporated features of the ego-analysts' approaches into their therapeutic style, so that these distinctions become blurred in actual practice.

A CRITIQUE

I will postpone to the end of the chapter discussion of the most central question in assessing psychoanalysis or any therapy: "Does it work?" Here we will consider other advantages and disadvantages associated with psychoanalysis.

There is little doubt that some psychoanalysts develop great skill in facilitating patients' self-understanding into the complexities of human motivation and in putting this understanding in a developmental perspective. Hans Strupp (1971) summarizes the positive features of psychoanalysis as follows:

In general it may be said that psychoanalytic psychotherapy represents modern man's most ambitious attempt to deal with neurotic problems. It is a radical form of psychotherapy in the sense of attempting changes in the patient's total life-style within which neurotic symptoms are embedded. It is in principle opposed to the goal of modifying the patient's behavior by coercion or other forms of psychological influence and instead focuses on the task of increasing the patient's efforts toward independence, autonomy, and self-direction. Its major appeal is to reason and self-control, and it proceeds on the working assumption that the patient's emotional understanding of the forces that motivate him permits their control. Its respect for the individual and his right for self-determination is unequaled (with the possible exception of client-centered therapy). (p. 32)

On the negative side, psychoanalytic technique is open to the questions and criticisms that have been raised about the psychoanalytic theory of personality and symptom development, on which it is largely based. Some of the specific criticisms of the theory (discussed more fully in Chapter 3) include overgeneralizations (for example, the claim that most neurotic symptoms have their roots in unresolved Oedipal conflicts), an oversimplified view of motivation, and an overly restricted view of personality development in terms of a few psychosexual stages. Theory can be useful in drawing attention to relationships and causative influences that might otherwise be missed, but it can also take attention away from other important factors. Has the pursuit of Oedipal conflicts and anal fixations sometimes taken the patient and analyst on long detours away from the essential therapeutic problem? Some critics say so.

Insight, as we have seen, is the crucial ingredient in psychoanalysis. But the kind of insights that a patient gets may be a function of the theoretical orientation of the therapist. By selective responding and interpreting, a Freudian therapist may elicit insights about Oedipal conflicts, a Jungian therapist about archetypes, an Adlerian therapist about strivings for superiority, and a Sullivanian therapist about interpersonal security operations. But even if a given insight is in some sense true, is it enough? Suppose you became aware that you felt a great deal of anxiety about expressing aggression toward your father, a reaction that has now generalized to other authority figures. Does this automatically mean that from now on you will stop feeling anxious and aggressive toward your father and other authority figures? Many critics argue that cognitive understanding of this kind can be a useful first step but that more needs to be done in order actually to change undesirable responses; in other words, insight is not enough. . . .

Psychoanalysts have hedged their bets a little on this issue by saying that if the insight is only "intellectual," then it probably will not help much; it has to be "emotional" to be effective. Furthermore, it is necessary to spend months *working through* the insights before they can be expected to be of therapeutic value. Psychoanalysts cannot tell us with any precision how one can know whether a new insight is intellectual or emotional; more often than not, it is an after-the-fact judgment. If symptoms do not improve, then it must have been an intellectual insight or working through must not have proceeded far enough. In the lengthy process of working through, however, a lot of other things could be happening, in addition to the acquisition of insight, that could account for any improvements—for example, extinction of anxiety, as we will see in the next chapter.

Another criticism of the standard psychoanalytic technique is that it is long (two to five years) and expensive (it can easily cost in excess of $15,000). Add to this the fact that research (Luborsky & Spence, 1971) has shown that it seems to work best with psychologically minded, motivated, well-educated people experiencing neurotic-type symptoms, and we see that it is hardly an answer to the mental health needs of the population at large.

Freud himself is said to have wondered in his later years whether psychoanalysis had not been more effective as an investigatory tool than as a mode of treatment. Marmor (1968), a psychoanalytic writer and practitioner, seems to have reached a similar conclusion: "Even more regrettable is the fact that the high promises once held forth by psychoanalysis as a *technique of therapy* have failed to materialize. . . . Freud's method arose primarily out of his efforts to *understand* the meaning and origins of his patients' disturbances. There is no good reason *a priori* why a technique of investigation necessarily should be at the same time a good method of therapy. . . . Today, we have learned the difficult lesson that rational understanding alone is not enough; that people can understand why they behave in certain ways and yet be unable to alter their unsatisfactory patterns." (p. 6)

Humanistic-Experiential Approaches

Although there is no one style of therapy associated with the humanistic-experiential approach, there is an emphasis on acquiring self-understanding and on the importance of the relationship with the therapist. In these respects it is similar to the psychodynamic approach. In other ways, however, it differs greatly. Humanistic-experiential therapists are much less interested in reconstructing past history as a way of understanding a person's present difficulties, and have little interest in making diagnoses. They tend to be more experiential in the sense of attending to present-moment subjective experiencings and also in the sense of avoiding theoretical analyses of these experiencings. Importance is attached to the freedom that people are seen to have in making significant choices in their lives in contrast to the deterministic assumptions that seem to underlie both the psychodynamic and behavioral traditions. Thus the metaphors of psychological disorder involved in the humanistic approaches would seem to emphasize being cut off from parts of one's own subjective experiencings and failure to take responsibility for making one's own decisions. Treatment techniques tend to follow from these metaphors. Let us consider three rather different approaches that fall under the humanistic-experiential heading, those of Carl Rogers, Fritz Perls, and Alvin Mahrer.

CLIENT-CENTERED THERAPY

Carl Rogers is largely responsible for the development of a form of therapy called *client-centered therapy* (originally, *nondirective therapy*). As the earlier term implies, a key feature of this approach has been to permit clients (Rogers preferred not to use the word "patient" because of its connotations of sickness) to guide the therapeutic process, to decide what they wish to talk about, and to make important life decisions without advice, reassurance, or other directive maneuvers on the part of the therapist. A basic assumption in this approach is that all people are motivated toward self-fulfillment and constructive personality growth. Unfortunate life experiences have somehow warped or sidetracked this basic impulse, but it is assumed that in the accepting, nondirective atmosphere of client-centered therapy persons can resume their growth toward self-fulfillment.

In Rogers's early formulation the task of the therapist was to accept, recognize, and clarify feelings. To this end the therapist seemed frequently to be simply reflecting what the client said. But there was an important distinction. The therapist was attempting to hear and reflect the emotional part of the message rather than the literal content. A client, for example, might say, "That test was unfair. I got a C." Content-oriented responses would be: "What kind of exam was it, objective or essay?"; "Did the professor grade on a curve?"; "If you study hard, you can probably do better next time"; or "I agree, that professor is unfair." None of these responses picks up the feeling message. Tone of voice and facial expression would probably be helpful in understanding that part of the communication. A reflection of feeling might be: "It just doesn't seem fair to give you a test like that—and it hurts, you feel 'what's the use?' " Rogers and other client-centered therapists reported that when the therapist was able to attend sensitively and reflect the feeling component, the client was more likely to follow and explore emotional associations, feelings, and conflicts than if the therapist had asked a lot of questions about content.

Later, Rogers (1951) placed a greater emphasis on the therapist's general attitude toward the client as opposed to the more specific technique of reflection of feelings. The aim of the therapist was to experience the phenomenological world of the client, to see through the eyes of the client, and to communicate an understanding of this shared experience back to the client. The raw material of the client's experiencing was not just "feelings" (a rather inexact term) but anything meaningful to the client's self-exploration. Rogers (1957) listed three characteristics as necessary and sufficient for constructive therapeutic change to occur: The client must experience the therapist as showing *unconditional positive regard,* being *accurately empathic,* and being *genuine.*

Unconditional Positive Regard.   The therapist should prize the person without qualification as worthy. This does not mean that the therapist should approve or disapprove of specific things that the client may do; in general, the therapist should refrain from passing

Carl R. Rogers developed the approach to psychotherapy known as client-centered therapy, and was one of the first to attempt systematic research on the therapeutic process. More recently he has written on encounter groups and the marital relationship.

judgment on the client's beliefs or conduct. It does mean that the therapist should have a deep respect for the client's capacity to discover unaided what to value and how to act; this level of acceptance and caring is more fundamental than approval or disapproval of specific actions.

Empathy.   The therapist must be able to enter into the client's moment by moment experience and accurately communicate this understanding to the client.

Genuineness.   The therapist must not hide behind a role of The Therapist, The Doctor, or The Expert, but should relate to the client as a fellow human being. Being a "real person" in the sessions may involve expressing some of the therapist's own feelings and reactions. This represents a departure from the original client-centered approach, which kept the focus entirely on the client's experiencing. Ordinarily the therapist would express negative reactions only if they were persistent or intense enough to impair accurate empathy or unconditional positive regard. Consider the following hypothetical example:

The therapist is becoming bored and even sleepy as a client drones on session after session with an obsessive, unemotional account.

Therapist: You know, I'm finding it harder and harder to keep listening. There is something about the way you talk that puts me to sleep. I want to tell you about this feeling because I'm afraid if I don't it will get in the way of my working with you.

Client: (Upset.) You too! I bore everybody. At least I thought *you* wouldn't be bored.

Therapist: It's hard to take. You feel that you bore everybody and now even your therapist is bored. Who else is there to turn to? (A guess at the client's reaction, not a question to be answered.)

Client: I drive people away with this endless talk about nothing. That was the way it was in my home. No one could ever say what they felt about anything. But I don't know what would happen if I stopped talking this way.

Therapist: I want to say one more thing about my feelings and then we will get back to yours. Right now, I'm not feeling bored at all. I feel in touch with your despair over driving people away and your fear of what will come out if you just let your feelings lead you.

In this hypothetical example the therapist has facilitated the therapeutic encounter by expressing a "negative" reaction. Initially, the client was hurt by the therapist's response, and, if left at that, the therapist's "genuineness" would probably have had a destructive effect. But the therapist remains sensitive to the client's reactions, and shortly thereafter can genuinely express a positive reaction. The overall result is likely to be an increase in the client's self-esteem rather than the reverse. In expressing the negative feeling in this way, the therapist, in addition to modeling openness and honesty, was also communicating, "I care enough about helping you that I want to bring my feeling out in the open where it can be dealt with in a constructive fashion."

Rogers (1967) himself characterizes the essence of the therapeutic process like this:

As he finds someone listening to him with consistent acceptance while he expresses his thoughts and feelings, the client, little by little, becomes increasingly able to listen to communications from within himself; he becomes able to realize that he is angry, or that he is frightened, or that he is experiencing feelings of love. Gradually, he becomes able to listen to feelings within himself which have previously seemed so bizarre, so terrible, or so disorganizing that they have been shut off completely from conscious awareness. As he reveals these hidden and "awful" aspects of himself, he finds that the therapist's regard for him remains unshaken. And, slowly, he moves toward adopting the same attitude toward himself, toward accepting himself as he is, and thus prepares to move forward in the process of becoming. Finally, as the client is able to listen to more of himself, he moves toward greater congruence, toward expressing all of himself more openly. He is, at last, free to change and grow in the directions which are natural to the human organism. (p. 1226)

GESTALT THERAPY

Gestalt therapy was developed largely by Frederick (Fritz) Perls, whose own early training had been in psychoanalysis. The one theme central to the Gestalt approach is an uncompromising focus on what you experience here and now. Persons are urged, not so much by didactic lectures as by actual practice, to attend to immediate feelings and impulses and to express and act upon them. The term "Gestalt," taken from a theory of perception, is applied rather loosely to the process of therapy. The basic idea is that our experiencing (including perceptions, emotions, desires, and ideas) usually consists of a *figure* or foreground, that part that we are attending to, and a *background* against which the figure is seen. We see a road sign, for example, against a background of cornfields, although while reading the sign we may be only vaguely aware of the fields. In terms more pertinent to Gestalt therapy, the client, for example, might be thinking about a recent break-up with a girl friend, the figure, against a vague background of tension and physical discomfort. The object of Gestalt therapy is to help the client become more aware of the total configuration (the Gestalt). Therefore the therapist, pointing out that the client's brow is furrowed and his voice hoarse and wavering, might ask the client to attend to these nonverbal expressions and exaggerate them. As a result the client might begin to experience sadness and begin to cry. In Gestalt terms, the client has been helped to incorporate more of the background into the experienced figure.

In addition to a focus on the here and now, Gestalt therapy attempts to free us from psychological enslavement by others, that is, from being irrationally concerned about whether other people are going to approve of what we do. In order to be free in this sense we have to become aware of and come to terms with internalized representations of others, frequently parents, that have become incorporated as part of ourselves. As we gain this kind of freedom we then learn to make our own decisions about life.

Perls originally used many of the techniques of the Gestalt approach in group settings. However, they have subsequently been used widely in individual therapy as well. Most of the specific techniques focus the person's attention on immediate experience and foster psychological autonomy. When individuals are talking impersonally about feelings, they may be asked to use "I" language, that is, to make an assertion of "I feel . . . " or "I want . . . " in order to help themselves both gain awareness and accept ownership of what they feel or want. Similarly, when they ask certain kinds of questions, they may be asked to change them to statements beginning with "I." For example, if the person asks the therapist, "Why don't you ever tell me what to do?" the therapist might ask the person to change the question to a statement. Upon reflection, the person might begin to recognize an irritation at the therapist for not giving advice and express it by saying, "I wish you would give me some advice; it annoys me when you don't." Another technique is for the therapist to take such an expression and ask the person to amplify the emotional message: "Say, 'Fritz, I hate it when you won't give me advice.' Fine, now say it again, louder," and so on. Nonverbal mannerisms are frequently commented on (as in the earlier example of the furrowed brow and hoarse voice) in an effort to bring unrecognized feelings or desires into the foreground. For example, the therapist might observe, "You are shaking your finger at me. Go ahead, do it some more." Modeling an exaggerated finger-shaking, the therapist might continue, "OK, what are you thinking or feeling?" The person may realize, "My mother shook her finger like that when she was lecturing me."

Since many problems result from internalized parental dos, don'ts, shoulds, and oughts, several techniques are used to help persons experience these reactions as part of themselves and not as belonging entirely to the external world. In the *empty chair technique* an empty chair is placed in front of you. You are asked to imagine that someone (such as father, son, husband, or mother) is sitting there and to tell the imagined person your feelings and desires about some problem area. Then you actually switch chairs, assuming the role of the imagined other person. It is not important that you attribute feelings or attitudes rightly to the other person, so long as you express those features of the other person, real or imagined, incorporated within yourself.

Similarly, dream images are considered to represent various internalized attitudes. To bring the meaning of the dream images into the foreground the person may be asked to become some part of the dream and talk from that vantage point. Thus Linda (Perls, 1969) dreamed that she was sadly watching a lake drying up. She thinks that maybe when all the water dries up she will find some sort of treasure, but all that she finds is an old license plate.

Fritz: Will you please play the license plate?

Linda: I am an old license plate, thrown in the bottom of a lake. I have no use because I'm no value—although I'm not rusted—I'm outdated, so I can't be used as a license plate . . . and I'm just thrown on the rubbish heap. That's what I did with a license plate, I threw it on a rubbish heap.

Fritz: Well, how do you feel about this?

Linda: (Quietly.) I don't like it. I don't like being a license plate—useless.

Fritz: Could you talk about this? That was such a long dream until you come to find the license plate, I'm sure this must be of great importance.

Linda: (Sighs.) Useless. Outdated. . . . The use of a license plate is to allow—give a car permission to go . . . and I can't give anyone permission to do anything because I'm outdated. . . . In California, they just paste a little—you buy a sticker—and stick it on the car, on the old license plate. (Faint attempt at humor.) So maybe someone could put me on their car and stick this sticker on me, I don't know. (pp. 81–82)

Many of the Gestalt techniques, then, attempt to bring persons in touch with feelings and attitudes within themselves that they were previously unaware of and to foster ownership of these parts of themselves. The experience itself is the important thing, not an intellectual analysis or interpretation of the experience.

ALVIN MAHRER

Mahrer's (1978) humanistic approach is similar in terms of underlying metaphors to Rogers and Perls. I refer to his view briefly at this point to illustrate a concept frequently encountered in the humanistic (and sometimes psychodynamic, too) orientation—namely, that repressed or blocked-off parts of one's experiencings can become extremely threatening to the conscious parts of oneself. Those conscious parts of oneself become afraid that if the blocked-off parts should ever break free and gain control, one might engage in unrestrained violence, sexuality, or whatever. In fact, what usually happens when these previously blocked-off parts are permitted into awareness in the safe environment of therapy is that these internal "demons" turn out not to be so fearsome after all, and in fact, add constructive qualities to the personality when they can be accepted into consciousness. There also tends to be a release of energy that was previously tied up in these blocked-off tendencies that can now be channeled into a generally more zestful life. Here are two examples of this process described by Mahrer (1978):

The middle-aged man confessed to terrible worries about being homosexual. He envisaged awful scenes of being called a queer by acquaintances, being recognized and made sexual overtures to by gay men, and possibilities of having anal intercourse with overt homosexuals. All of these were products of his disintegrative relationships with a deeper potential whose core experiencing involved intimacy and oneness. When he achieved integration with [those blocked-off experiencings] it was as if he had lifted a veil between himself and other men, a veil he had never known was there. For the first time in his life he saw their good form—images of man-to-man closeness and brotherliness, of deep oneness with men, of comradeship and loyalty among men. (pp. 48–49)

The attorney was torn apart by thoughts of becoming lazy, without ambition, being an old man, penniless, a bum. He became increasingly worried by such thoughts. [After integration, the blocked-off experiencings] acquired a wholly new form: being casual and easy going, rising above petty jealousies and ambitions, not falling into fruitless competitions and graspings. What he had feared now sprang forth in its integrative form and took its place as a wholly new way of being. (p. 50)

Rogers, Perls, and Mahrer all emphasize getting in touch with those parts of oneself that have been disowned in some fashion. In that respect these humanistic approaches do not differ so drastically from the psychodynamic orientations.

A CRITIQUE

The client-centered approach has had considerable appeal to beginning therapists because of its apparent simplicity. The therapist does not have to master intricate psychodynamic theories, and the techniques appear deceptively straightforward. Rogers and, to some extent, Perls have maintained that historical reconstruction of past childhood experiences, transference reactions, and diagnostic appraisals are not necessary for the successful conduct of therapy. By taking a rather extreme position on these questions Rogers has helped to sharpen the issues, but many other investigators strongly disagree with one or more of his points of view. With respect to diagnosing the client at the outset, many therapists feel it is important to know, for example, whether a person is mentally retarded, is manifesting symptoms of schizophrenia or mania, or has an organic brain disorder. The answers to such diagnostic questions might suggest that other forms of treatment—drugs, for example—should be used in addition to or instead of client-centered or Gestalt therapy. Rogers

Therapist seeing a woman in psychotherapy.

sees the avoidance of psychoanalytic theorizing as an advantage; others see it as a naive approach to the client's problems and the therapeutic enterprise.

Many people find the general features of the humanistic approaches appealing. Who doesn't want to be appreciated and respected as a person? Who doesn't want to have a therapist understand the unique nuances of their own troubled experiencing rather than interpret their behavior in terms of abstract theoretical constructs (psychoanalytic or behavioral)? And many would prefer to think they are able to make free choices rather than that all their decisions are completely determined. However, not everyone would accept the way these issues are handled by the humanistic therapists. Let us listen in on a humanist and a behaviorist discussing some of these questions. They are old friends who can talk frankly with each other.

Humanist: The trouble with you behaviorists is that you see people as simply behaving organisms to be scientifically studied or therapeutically modified. You miss the person behind the behavior.

Behaviorist: Well, that's a common idea about behavioral therapists and maybe some are that way, but it's a vast oversimplification to characterize all of us in that fashion. Your statement implies that we don't appreciate and respect people as human beings, seeing them only as objects to be studied and manipulated. What bothers me about you humanistic therapists is that you seem to feel that by applying the term *humanistic* to yourselves, you have a corner on the market for all humanistic concerns. How self-righteous can you get?

Humanist: OK, OK, I overstated the case. But I think you'll have to admit that *as a group* behavioral therapists, with their background in scientific psychology and their preoccupation with measurement and experimentation, have been more likely to take a detached, scientific attitude toward their clients than have, say, client-centered therapists.

Behaviorist: True, but the point I'd like to make is that nothing in the behavioral point of view forces a therapist to have any less respect for a client or to care any less about reducing suffering than any other therapist would. Furthermore, I think the group difference that you mentioned may not exist in the newer generations of behavior thera-

pists—thanks, perhaps, in part to the criticisms of people like yourself.

Humanist: I'm glad if we've had some effect. I'm still not sure that a behavioral approach is basically compatible with a humanistic valuing of the person.

Behaviorist: Let me try another tack. So far I have been on the defensive, reacting to your claim that behaviorists are not concerned about people. When Lang and Melamed (1969) saved the life of an infant by devising a behavior modification procedure that stopped the infant from vomiting uncontrollably, would you tell me that they cared less about saving the infant's life than some other kind of therapist would have? But that is not my main point. Because of these therapists' behavioral orientation, they were able to develop a procedure that worked. Everything else had been tried with that baby, and he seemed doomed to die. If you are really concerned about relieving human suffering, then you have to be concerned about developing procedures that work. And that involves measurement, experimentation, and all that other "bad" stuff.

Humanist: Touché, or at least a partial touché. I know you could reel off quite a few examples of that kind. Your point is well taken and I accept it. But most psychotherapy these days is not done with nonverbal infants, or psychotics, or people with a highly specific symptom, such as a phobia. Most therapy clients are more broadly discontented with life and have feelings of worthlessness and lack of fulfillment. Although a mechanical apparatus may effectively stop a baby from vomiting or perhaps even remove a restricted phobia, it seems unlikely that anything so mechanical will ever work with these more complex problems in living.

Behaviorist: OK, my turn to yield a point to you. But only a point, not the entire game. Actually, I believe that some of these more complex problems can be broken down into separate components such as self-derogatory statements, or inability to appropriately assert oneself, and behavioral technologies can be developed to modify them. I intentionally used the term *technologies* because I know it's like waving a red flag in front of a bull. It confirms your belief that we view therapy as a depersonalized technology like bridge building rather than some kind of unique, almost mystical, experience between two human beings. But don't forget, it was a technology that saved the baby's life, and what I am now proposing is that technologies can help people with more complex difficulties, such as low self-esteem. And since we are strongly committed to evaluating whether our technologies work, we may in the long run be able to help people more effectively than you to raise their self-esteem, develop their full potentials, free themselves from narrow societal expectations, or any other humanistic goals you might want to specify.

Humanist: Well, maybe. Don't forget that Carl Rogers, a humanistic therapist, was also one of the first people to attempt to evaluate the effectiveness of psychotherapy. There is some reason to believe that even your technologies work best when conducted by therapists who are warm, sensitive, have a sense of humor, and treat their clients with respect.

Behaviorist: You're probably right about that, and behavior therapists are more concerned about these characteristics, what they sometimes refer to as "soft clinical skills," than they used to be. That is certainly another point for the psychodynamic and humanistic therapists. I would stress, however, that characteristics such as warmth and respect represent a kind of baseline that is necessary for the effective use of more specific procedures. Cold, insensitive, uncaring therapists are not likely to be effective, no matter what they do. At the same time, many clients are not likely to be helped by simply sitting with a warm, sensitive, respecting therapist. The therapist must exercise some technical competence in addition to being a beautiful person. On this point, psychoanalytic therapists would be in strong agreement with behavior therapists.

Humanist: I can go along with most of what you're saying, although we may continue to differ on the relative emphasis on the quality of the relationship with the therapist as opposed to change-producing technologies. We humanists will have served a useful purpose if we have made it more difficult for therapists of any persuasion to forget that they are trying to help people, not just shape behavior.

Another drawback to the behavioral approach is that most of your procedures tend to further cut persons off from their subjective experiencings. You desensitize the person's fear of public speaking but never give the person a chance to fully explore all the cut-off experiencings associated with this fear—possibly preventing individuals from enriching their personalities through a fuller integration of different aspects of themselves.

Behaviorist: That may reflect a real difference in our metaphors of human psychology. Certainly the idea of expanding and enriching the domain of subjective experiencing has not been given much importance by behaviorists. On the other hand, to return to your example, it may be that as a result of having the fear associated with public speaking removed, the person is now free to experience life more fully, including the satisfactions of public speaking.

Now there's one other question I want to raise. Humanistic-existential therapists keep introducing the issue of free will and determinism into their discussions, usually by accusing the behaviorists, and psychoanalytic therapists too, of further dehumanizing their clients by seeing their behavior as completely determined, by denying them free will. Now, the question of free will is a subtle one about which philosophers themselves have not as yet come to any generally acceptable solution. When therapists, humanistic or behavioral, engage in amateur philosophizing about this question, I strongly suspect that a good deal of naiveté is involved. It is emotionally appealing to see ourselves in control of our destiny by making "free" choices. But because something is emotionally appealing doesn't make it so. My point here is not to argue for or against some form of free will or determinism, but to say that there are various sophisticated, philosophical positions on these issues, most of which are quite compatible with the basic features of a behavioral approach.

Humanist: You may be right about the subtleties of the free-will issue. I would argue, however, that it can make a difference if a therapist is communicating to a client that the client can make decisions and be responsible for them, as opposed to a message that the client's behavior will be changed as a result of the external manipulation of contingencies.

Behaviorist: I agree. In fact, current behavior technologies are much concerned with the question of how to help the person gain more self-control. But to return to my initial point, a therapist can be concerned about creating conditions that maximize the client's taking responsibility without having to take a position on the philosophical issue of free will. As a matter of fact, I have my own amateurish thought about free will and determinism; at some point B. F. Skinner and Zen Buddhism (unlikely bedfellows!) converge to the same position. With Zen enlightenment one realizes that everything is determined and that each one of us is part of that determining process. We can have it both ways, in other words. God, or if you'd rather, Ultimate Reality, determines everything and we are part of God.

Humanist: You're beginning to sound more like a muddleheaded humanist than a hard-nosed behaviorist. Perhaps we've taken this discussion as far as we can for now.

As this imaginary conversation suggests, there have been real differences in attitude and approach between the more radical behavior therapists and humanistic therapists. The discussion also implies, however, that we do not have to make an either-or choice on some of these issues. It may be possible to be a behavior therapist with strong humanistic values or a humanistic therapist who is concerned about the effectiveness of treatment experiences.

The Effects of Insight Therapy

CRITERIA FOR A GOOD RESEARCH DESIGN

Investigators continue to disagree as to whether insight therapy is effective with neurotic patients. One difficulty in trying to settle the issue is that most of the studies that have been conducted have major flaws. Before we consider some examples of the research evidence, it will be worthwhile to reflect for a moment on what an ideal research design in this area

would be. First, there has to be a control group comparable to the group that receives psychotherapy on such variables as severity and duration of disorder, motivation for treatment, age, education, and so on; and patients must have been assigned randomly to the treatment and no-treatment conditions. The purpose of a no-treatment group is to see to what extent patients improve "spontaneously," that is, without formally labeled "treatment." For psychotherapy to be considered effective, it clearly has to produce more improvement than would have occurred with the simple passage of time. It is crucial for such a comparison that no selective factors affect which patients go in which group. For example, if patients who are more acutely upset are more often assigned to the treatment condition because they seem to need help more urgently and the treatment group is subsequently found to show more improvement, such a finding may mean only that acutely disturbed patients are more likely under any circumstances to show improvement than patients with more chronic kinds of disorders.

Second, there should be assessment of characteristics that the treatment is supposed to change before, just after, and at a follow-up point some time after treatment. The measures should meet accepted standards of reliability and should not rely entirely on self-reports by the patients, or be performed by the therapists or others who have a vested interest in demonstrating the effectiveness of the treatment. For example, in addition to the patient's own statement about how much therapy has helped it is desirable to obtain some indication of actual behavioral change in the patient's life, either by direct observation or by interview with close associates of the patient.

Third, the individuals conducting the treatment should be well trained and experienced in the form of treatment being evaluated; otherwise, a poor showing can always be explained as the result of relatively incompetent therapists. Of course, a good showing by inexperienced therapists is no problem. Such a finding suggests that the approach is effective and can be taught quickly to new therapists.

Unfortunately, few studies meet these criteria for good evaluational research. Random assignment to treatment and no-treatment conditions is especially hard to attain. Patients seeking professional help cannot be treated like subjects in an experiment and randomly assigned to a condition of no-treatment.

When there is an already existing waiting list, however, most investigators feel that it is ethically permissible to assign patients randomly to either a treatment or a waiting group. If treatment on the average is relatively short, say four to six months, it may be possible to have the control group wait for a period of time roughly comparable to the duration of treatment. This kind of control group has been used fairly often.

Studies also encounter difficulty in measuring characteristics that the treatment is supposed to change. The problem is especially acute for the psychodynamic or humanistic therapies in which the changes derived from therapy are frequently described in terms of intrapsychic processes or subjective experiencing rather than observable symptoms or other behaviors.

SPONTANEOUS IMPROVEMENT

A no-treatment control group, as just indicated, provides a baseline of *spontaneous change* (natural improvement or worsening) against which to compare the treatment group. Waiting-list control groups, however, can rarely be kept longer than six months. Do we have any information on the long-term course of neurotic disorders? If, for example, we identified 100 patients with various neurotic[1] disorders and then assessed them again, say, after five years without treatment, how many would have improved and to what extent? Several attempts have been made to acquire data of this sort, but for the most part the findings are rendered almost meaningless by serious methodological shortcomings. Perhaps one of the best studies of this kind was performed by Hastings (1958). This author followed up 371 patients whose symptoms were disabling enough to warrant admission to the University of Minnesota Hospital between 1938 and 1944. At that time treatment on this ward was extremely limited, amounting largely to providing rest and temporary removal from life stresses. The author argued that it was unlikely that these patients

received further treatment during the follow-up period since they resided in rural areas in which there were few if any psychotherapists. The follow-up assessment consisted in almost all cases of an interview conducted 6 to 12 years after the patient's release from the hospital.

For the total group, 46 percent were rated as having an "excellent" or "good" psychological adjustment at the time of follow-up. Breaking cases down into more specific symptom categories, Hastings found 14 anxiety neurotics (65 percent), 73 hysterics (56 percent), 23 obsessive-compulsives (44 percent), and 23 hypochondriacal patients (25 percent) to have either an "excellent" or "good" psychological adjustment at the time of the follow-up. (Hypochondriasis, a category infrequently used these days, refers to patients who are preoccupied and worried to an irrational degree about physical symptoms.) This study suggests that about half the patients with symptoms severe enough to lead to hospitalization will recover to a substantial degree with little or no treatment over a relatively long period of time.

Bergin and Lambert (1978) summarized the results of 18 studies of untreated patients who had neurotic symptoms and found an average rate of spontaneous improvement of 43 percent—ranging from 22 percent to 67 percent. Of special interest for the behavioral versus psychodynamic issue are the findings of Malan et al. (1975), who made a distinction between symptomatic improvement and psychodynamic improvement (resolution of underlying conflicts). They found that 51 percent of a sample of neurotic patients were judged to be improved or recovered by symptomatic criteria over a two- to eight-year follow-up period compared with only 24 percent by psychodynamic criteria.

Spontaneous improvement rates obtained in such studies cannot substitute for control groups in evaluational research unless one can prove that these patients are comparable to patients in the treatment groups on such variables as severity of symptoms, intelligence, educational level, and motivation for treatment. This problem can be avoided best by randomly assigning current patients from the same clinic population to the treatment and control groups. However, since treatment cannot usually be withheld indefinitely, these studies may have to serve as our best estimates of the long-term rates of spontaneous improvement.

---

[1]The issue has frequently been stated in terms of whether psychotherapy is effective with *neurotic* patients. Accordingly, I will use the term *neurotic* fairly often in this section. Generally, the kind of disorders included under this heading have been anxiety, conversion, and mild-to-moderate depressive disorders.

Of course, spontaneous improvement is not really spontaneous. Many factors other than formal treatment could change neurotic reaction patterns. For example, the stressful circumstances responsible for precipitating the acute reaction may change. Persons with a neurotic personality trait may find a niche in life that protects them from symptom-producing stresses. Getting married, getting divorced, changing jobs, a job promotion, moving away from family or in-laws, meeting new friends, and joining religious or other movements all can be sources of stress or escapes from previous sources of stress. There is, in other words, no reason why therapeutic experiences must be confined to the therapist's office.

THE EVIDENCE FOR EFFECTIVENESS

Only two investigations meet our basic criteria for an adequate evaluational study of the effectiveness of nonbehavioral psychotherapy with neurotic patients. One is a study conducted by Sloane et al. (1975) at Temple University in which 90 neurotic outpatients were assigned randomly to a short-term psychoanalytically oriented therapy condition, a behavioral therapy condition, or a minimal contact waiting-list group. The groups were matched with respect to sex of patient and severity of symptoms. In general the patients were good candidates for therapy: They were young, intelligent, and well educated, with "quite severe" but not entirely incapacitating problems. The three psychoanalytic therapists and three behavior therapists were well trained and highly experienced. The senior psychoanalytically oriented therapist, for example, had treated some 6000 patients over 35 years of practice, some in classical psychoanalysis and many in psychoanalytically oriented psychotherapy. The senior behavior therapist, widely experienced, had treated an estimated 2000 neurotic patients over the course of 20 years of practice. A variety of pretreatment, posttreatment, and follow-up measures were obtained, including ratings of target symptoms by an independent interviewer who was ignorant of the therapeutic conditions, reports by informants who had known the patients for an average of 12 years, standard psychological tests, and ratings by the patients themselves.

After four months of treatment both the psychoanalytic and the behavioral therapy groups showed marked improvement relative to the waiting-list control group, but on most measures they were not significantly different from each other. On a rating of overall outcome by independent assessors, 80 percent of both the psychoanalytic and behavioral therapy groups were considered "improved" in contrast to 48 percent for the waiting-list group. Likewise ratings of severity of specific target symptoms showed significantly greater decreases for both treatment groups than for the waiting-list group, and there was again no difference between the two treatment approaches. The greatest shortcoming in this study from a scientific point of view lies in the follow-up assessment of the extent to which these improvements endured. Ethical considerations led the investigators to give all patients the option of continuing treatment after the four-month experimental period was over; nine patients in the psychoanalytically oriented therapy condition, 15 in the behavior therapy condition, and 22 in the waiting-list condition received at least three sessions during that period. Although all groups showed continued improvement at follow-up, this finding tells us little about the relative changes in the different groups or what would have happened if no further treatment had been provided.

Mary Teresa Moore is an example of a person who was randomly assigned to the psychoanalytically oriented therapy condition.

Mary Teresa Moore was a beautiful girl of 19, but with a worried, nervous look. She had been depressed and anxious for about three months, had lost 15 pounds, and had trouble sleeping. She found it hard to fall asleep and waked at 5:00 in the morning. She planned to be married in a few months, but although her fiancé was a good Catholic, her twin sister, a nun, was urging her to put off the marriage. She felt guilty about feeling sexual desire, despite her lack of sexual experience. She had had obsessive thoughts about cutting off her fingers, or her future children's fingers, and of shutting her children into small spaces where they would suffocate. She felt depersonalized, as if she weren't really herself, felt as if her head were charged, felt as if God wanted her to go out of her mind, and then felt guilty for all these feelings. Prayer made her feel worse. She had had a happy home life, had done well in high school, had had lots of friends and dates. Mary Teresa was diagnosed as a mixed psychoneurosis with anxiety, depression, and obsessional and phobic thoughts. (Sloane et al., 1975, p. 79)

After four months' psychotherapy, Mary Teresa Moore had completely lost her obsessive thoughts about harming her children or herself. Her depression and anxiety were nearly gone, and in general she was almost completely recovered. She still felt a little guilt about sex but expected this to stop when she got married in three months, and she had a fine relationship with her fiancé. In summary, her rather severe symptoms had dramatically improved. (p. 115)

The second study with acceptable methodology is one reported by Strupp and Hadley (1979). College students experiencing loneliness, isolation, depression, and anxiety were randomly assigned to one of three conditions: (a) psychotherapists of a psychoanalytic or experiential orientation with an average length of experience of 23 years, (b) college professors with *no training* in psychotherapy who were selected on the basis of their reputation for warmth, trustworthiness, and interest in students, and (c) a minimal-contact, waiting-list condition similar to the one used by Sloane et al. (1975). For some but not all measures, clients seeing the two types of therapists showed greater improvement than those in the minimal-contact, waiting-list condition. There was, however, no difference in improvement between clients seeing well-trained and experienced psychotherapists and those seeing friendly and interested college professors who had no training as psychotherapists. To say the least, this well-designed study raises a question about the relevance of the technical skills of therapists. Would Sloane et al. (1975) have found the same results if they had included a similar group to compare with their nationally known therapists? We cannot know, of course, but the possibility gives pause for thought.

NONSPECIFIC EFFECTS: WOULD A SUGAR PILL DO AS WELL?

We have long known that various symptoms, physical and psychological, can be ameliorated if the person is given a sugar pill and deceived into believing that the pill will be effective. This improvement is called the *placebo effect*. Brill et al. (1964), for example, found that neurotic patients given placebo pills showed more improvement than patients in a waiting-list control group. Under the heading of *nonspecific factors* that might contribute to improvements are included not only placebo or expectancy effects but all other aspects of the treatment that can be separated from the more specific therapeutic procedures. Simply receiving attention from an interested person or making the effort to keep regular appointments are aspects of psychotherapy common to all approaches. Once we know that some one form of therapy is more effective than no therapy at all, we must go on to discover what features of the procedure account for its effectiveness. It might turn out, for example, that it makes no difference whether you provide psychoanalysis, client-centered therapy, behavior therapy, or a tranquilizing pill, as long as the patient believes the procedure will help and receives continuing attention from a person who seems to want to help. Some writers, such as Jerome Frank (1961), argue that most, if not quite all, therapeutic benefits do indeed result largely from nonspecific factors of this kind. The results of Strupp and Hadley (1979) strongly support this argument. The nonspecific factors of attention and warmth in the untrained college professors seemed to have produced as much change as the more specific technical competencies of the experienced therapists.

Placebo effects are further illustrated in a study by Gliedman et al. (1958), as shown in Figure 10-1. This curve shows a self-rating of personal discomfort for 12 patients who had been helped by six months of psychotherapy but at a two-year follow-up interview had complained of recurrence of problems and had shown interest in further help. Placebo pills were given to the patients at that time, and two weeks later another measure of personal discomfort was obtained. As the figure shows, the placebo pill produced an immediate drop in their distress.

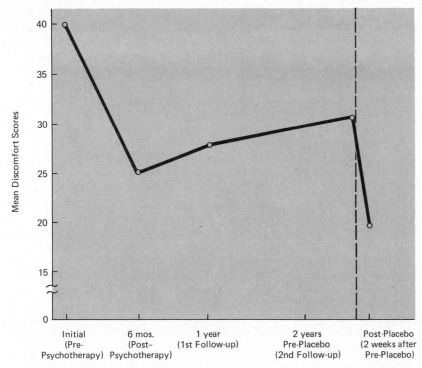

FIGURE 10-1   Mean discomfort scores taken before psychotherapy, after psychother-apy, and after taking placebos. (Adapted from L. H. Gliedman, E. H. Nash, S. D. Imber, A. R. Stone, & J. D. Frank, Reduction of symptoms by pharmacologically inert substances and by short-term psychotherapy. *Archives of Neurology and Psychiatry*, **1958,** *79,* **345–351. Copyright 1958 by the American Medical Association. Data used with permission.)**

The placebo effect in this study is illustrated by the case of a 26-year-old salesman who complained of lack of energy, tension, and inability to sell his merchandise at the time of the follow-up interview. As soon as he began taking the "medication" he found it possible to carry out his sales duties and began to feel less tense and more energetic. His sales commissions jumped dramatically. However, the gains resulting from this two-week period of placebo treatment gradually were lost, and after four months his problems had returned.

Not all patients responded equally well to place-bos in this study. The entire population of 56 patients given placebos (from several studies combined) was divided into a group of 28 who had responded favorably and a group of 28 who had shown little or no improvement. Some interesting differences emerged between these two groups. The patients who responded favorably were found to report more minor sicknesses, to place more value on medicines and physicians as distress relievers, to recommend actively what they found helpful to others, and to see themselves as more religious. They had apparently already developed attitudes and beliefs that facilitated placebo effects.

In conclusion, faith in the therapist's power to heal and nonspecific factors such as attention, interest, and warmth very likely contribute to the effectiveness of psychotherapy with some patients. Whether special technical competencies on the part of traditional insight-oriented therapists add significant increments of effectiveness remains an open question. It would definitely be premature to conclude that such com-petencies are irrelevant on the basis of the one study by Strupp and Hadley, which was limited to short-term therapy with college students showing a re-stricted range of neurotic symptoms.

THE THERAPIST

Bergin (1963) looked more closely at the results from psychotherapy outcome studies and concluded that there was a tendency for outcomes to be more variable for the groups receiving individual psychotherapy than for the no-treatment control groups. Some patients apparently got better with treatment while others got *worse*. The implication of this finding was that psychotherapy may have harmed some patients. Bergin and Lambert (1978) reviewed more recent research and maintained that there continues to be evidence that a small proportion (perhaps 5 to 10 percent) of psychotherapy patients show what has come to be called a *deterioration effect*.

At the same time that the deterioration effect was being reported, other investigators were attempting to test Rogers's (1957) proposition that three qualities of the therapist—unconditional positive regard, genuineness, and empathy—were correlated with therapeutic improvement. Truax and Carkhuff (1967) presented an impressive array of evidence suggesting that therapists rated high on these variables produced greater therapeutic improvement than those rated low. Since that time, several other studies have failed to support this finding (for example, Mitchell et al., 1973). And in a more recent survey of research on this question Lambert et al. (1978) concluded: "Despite more than 20 years of research and some improvements in methodology, only a modest relationship between the so-called facilitative conditions and therapy outcome has been found. Contrary to frequent claims for the potency of these therapist-offered relationship variables, experimental evidence suggests that neither a clear test nor unequivocal support for the Rogerian hypothesis has appeared." (p. 486)

It is tempting to combine these two lines of research and conclude that the deterioration effect is produced by therapists who are lacking in unconditional positive regard, empathy, and genuineness. It may prove true, but the evidence is still a bit shaky. It is safer to conclude that some therapists are more effective than others (perhaps because of technical skills and other qualities as well as the three Rogerian conditions), and that some therapists may be so low on the required skills and qualities as to produce a worsening of some patients' difficulties. *Caveat emptor*—let the buyer beware.

CONCLUDING COMMENTS

Standard and modified psychoanalytic techniques and the humanistic-experiential therapies are popular modes of treatment, but they hardly give a complete picture of the many variations in psychotherapy currently being practiced. Many therapists incorporate techniques from two or more of these approaches, as well as other approaches not described, to form a blend of therapeutic practice colored by their own personality styles. Unlike Gertrude Stein's statement about roses ("A rose is a rose is a rose is a rose"), you cannot say psychotherapy is psychotherapy is psychotherapy is psychotherapy. It is many things to many people.

If *you* have found psychotherapy, in whatever form, to solve some of your problems in living, to reduce crippling feelings of anxiety or depression, then statistical comparisons of treatment and control groups will leave you unmoved. You *know* that it can work. But such a personal reaction cannot be the

TABLE 10-1
Summary of Distinguishing Characteristics between the Psychodynamic and the Humanistic-Experiential Approaches

Psychodynamic	Humanistic-Experiential
1. Analytic: emphasize understanding causes and intrapsychic dynamics.	Nonanalytic: emphasize understanding clients' immediate experience.
2. Subdivide the personality into parts.	Study the total person or self as the proper unit.
3. Make use of abstract theory.	Make minimal use of theoretical constructs. Is sometimes antitheoretical.
4. Reconstruct past events to understand present behavior.	Focus on immediate experience.
5. Assume that all behavior is completely determined.	Emphasize free will, taking responsibility for one's own decisions.

basis for a scientific conclusion about the general effectiveness of psychotherapy.

The question itself is probably too general to be very meaningful. More specific questions are likely to yield more useful answers. Is a certain form of therapy effective in changing certain symptoms in certain kinds of individuals? The results of the Temple study (Sloane et al., 1975) must be qualified in this way. Brief psychoanalytically oriented therapy by experienced clinicians was effective in reducing a variety of symptoms in a high proportion of relatively young, well-educated, and motivated patients.

Summary

1. Psychoanalysis employs the technique of free association. Patients typically develop resistances and transference reactions that the analyst deals with by interpretations. The aim of psychoanalysis is to aid the patient in achieving insight into the unconscious conflicts presumed to lie behind symptoms.

2. Modifications of psychoanalysis have introduced flexibility with respect to the use of the couch, free association, the promotion of transference reactions, and the relative emphasis on id and ego processes.

3. Psychoanalysis has been praised for attempting to change the total life-style within which a person's neurotic symptoms are embedded, avoiding the use of coercion, working toward increasing the patients' independence and self-direction, and freeing the patient from destructive emotional motivation by means of self-understanding.

4. Psychoanalysis has been criticized for being based on a theory of personality development that has serious shortcomings (such as an oversimplified view of motivation) and for relying too heavily on the presumed power of insight alone to remove neurotic symptoms. Psychoanalysis is also time-consuming (two to five years), expensive, and works best with psychologically minded, motivated, and well-educated people.

5. Humanistic-experiential approaches emphasize the person's own unique experiencing of the world, the immediate moment as opposed to what happened in the past, free will and its role in making authentic and inauthentic choices, and a view of the patient as a person to be prized and respected but not analyzed or manipulated in a detached, scientific manner.

6. Client-centered therapy, developed by Carl Rogers, emphasizes nondirectivity on the part of the therapist and assumes that the client is basically motivated toward growth and self-fulfillment. Rogers proposes three conditions as necessary and sufficient for therapeutic change—the therapist must be perceived as showing unconditional positive regard, accurate empathy, and genuineness.

7. Gestalt therapy, developed by Frederick Perls, focuses on immediate experience. By techniques such as the use of "I" language, restating questions as statements, exaggeration of verbal and nonverbal expressions, the empty-chair procedure, and taking the role of dream images, it promotes awareness and ownership of feelings and motives.

8. The basic aim in Mahrer's humanistic approach to therapy is to integrate blocked-off and feared parts of oneself into one's conscious personality.

9. Although certain features of the humanistic-type approaches are appealing, many therapists feel that they can promote humanistic values just as well with other approaches.

10. Client-centered therapists deserve credit for initiating some of the first psychotherapy research. They have been criticized for ignoring the historical development of symptoms and for denying the importance of transference reactions and diagnostic assessment.

11. Criteria for a good study of the effectiveness of psychotherapy are: random assignment of patients to treatment and no-treatment control groups, sound measurement before, after, and at follow-up of those characteristics the treatment is supposed to change, and the use of experienced, well-trained therapists.

12. Few studies of nonbehavioral psychotherapy with neurotic patients meet these criteria. Two studies do. In one it was found that brief psychoanalytically oriented therapy (about four months long) is effective with relatively young, well-educated, and motivated patients. In the other, college professors not trained in psychotherapy were found to be as effective as trained psychodynamic or experiential therapists.

13. Studies suggest that about 43 percent of neurotic patients, depending on the severity of the symptoms, are likely to show marked improvement with no formal treatment over a period of several years.

14. Placebo or expectancy factors probably contribute to but do not account for all of the effectiveness of psychotherapy.

Suggested Readings

In *Letters to Simon* (International Universities Press, 1973) I. H. Paul provides a sophisticated yet highly readable description of psychoanalytic technique. C. R. Rogers's book, *Client-centered therapy* (Houghton-Mifflin, 1951) probably remains the single best introduction to this approach. J. T. Hart and T. M. Tomlinson, however, in *New directions in client-centered therapy* (Houghton-Mifflin, 1970) provide a more recent view of clinical and research activities in this area. *Gestalt therapy verbatim* (Real People Press, 1969) by F. T. Perls is a good starting point for further exploration into Gestalt therapy. Several chapters in S. L. Garfield and A. E. Bergin (Eds.), *Handbook of psychotherapy and behavior change* (Wiley, 1978) are devoted to research on outcomes and processes in psychotherapy.

Behavior Therapy

11

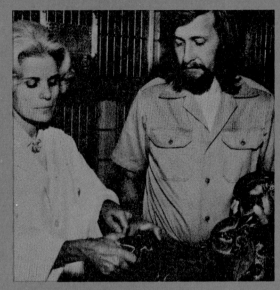

- What is behavior therapy?

- How does it differ from insight therapy?

- Systematic desensitization seems to work. Why?

- Your brother fears the water. Should you insist that he stay in the water? Should you jump in first? Walk him through a series of puddles? Or promise him an ice cream cone on the other side of the pond?

- Did you know that many contemporary behavior therapists attempt to modify *thoughts* as well as overt behavior?

- If you remove a phobia by behavior therapy, without regard for any underlying conflicts, will a new symptom arise (symptom substitution) to replace the one removed?

- "I'm just a girl who cain't say no." How can she be helped to say no?

The insight therapies have for the most part emphasized talking to a therapist with the aim of acquiring self-understanding and experiencing a relationship that is itself therapeutic. The early behavior therapists, by contrast, emphasized changing the external environment in some systematic way in order to modify behavior. They considered neither insight into intrapsychic dynamics nor the relationship with the therapist of much importance. In this chapter we will consider first the earlier forms of behavior therapy, based on the classical conditioning and operant models, and then more recent developments that have begun to incorporate observational learning and mediating cognitions. Throughout we will be concerned with the questions: "Does it work?" and "Why does it work?"

There is no exact agreement as to what constitutes behavior therapy. The term will be used to refer to a general orientation rather than to either a specific theory or set of techniques. This point of view is characterized by: (1) clear specification of the behaviors, or symptoms, to be changed; and (2) a direct attempt to change whatever is maintaining the undesired behavior, for example, reinforcement contingencies.

The methods of behavior therapy (or behavior modification) are derived largely from the laboratory study of learning. In its early years behavior therapy was characterized by a fairly extreme theoretical orientation (radical behaviorism) based almost entirely on the classical conditioning and operant learning models. Currently, most behavior therapists prefer to say that they attempt to apply the concepts and findings of experimental psychology to the understanding and treatment of abnormal behaviors without subscribing to any particular theory of learning. This course is wise, since modern experimental psychology itself has found serious limitations to the operant and classical conditioning theories as complete explanations of the learning process. In considering the development of various kinds of disorders from a social learning perspective I have frequently suggested that operant, classical conditioning, observational, and cognitively mediated learning all may have contributed. The basic assumption of the behavior or social learning therapist is that those same processes might be used in the unlearning of abnormal behavior. In this chapter we will consider the application of behavioral techniques to those disorders traditionally called neurotic—focusing primarily on anxiety and conversion symptoms.

The Classical Conditioning Model

Three treatment procedures were based originally on the classical conditioning model: (1) desensitization or counterconditioning, (2) extinction or flooding, and (3) aversion conditioning.

DESENSITIZATION

Desensitization was seen by its early advocates as a counterconditioning process in which one emotional reaction came to replace another. If a conditioned stimulus is presented that would ordinarily elicit a slight amount of fear, but at the same time the individual is made to have an even stronger emotional response that is incompatible with fear, such as deep relaxation or pleasure associated with eating, then the latter response will after a number of pairings, come to replace the fear response—or so goes the theory.

Peter, an Early Example. In the early 1920s, a quarter of a century before the behavior therapy movement began in earnest, Jones (1924) was making systematic use of counterconditioning in treating children's fears. Three-year-old Peter, for example, showed intense fear of animals, fur objects, cotton, hair, and mechanical toys. Jones arranged a systematic procedure for counterconditioning this fear. While Peter was eating at one end of a large room, a rabbit in a cage was placed at the other end, far enough away so that it did not disturb Peter's eating. Each day the rabbit was moved a little closer to the table where Peter was eating. Eventually the rabbit was removed from the cage. During the final stages of treatment, the rabbit was placed on the table and even in Peter's lap. Subsequent tests showed that Peter was no longer afraid of the rabbit and furthermore that the treatment effects had generalized so that he was also no longer fearful of other furry objects.

As part of a large study of children's fears, Jersild and Holmes (1935) found that some parents had discovered on their own how to reduce their children's fears by using techniques similar in certain respects to counterconditioning. Parents who used

Joseph Wolpe, prominent behavior therapist and originator of systematic desensitization procedure.

1. Thinking about taking examinations while at home during the summer.
2. Sitting in the classroom on a day when there is no examination.
3. Studying for the examination a week before.
4. Studying for the examination three nights before.
5. Studying for the examination the night before.
6. Walking to the examination classroom.
7. Sitting in the classroom starting to take the examination.

Next, the therapist would teach you a response that is incompatible with anxiety, usually deep muscular relaxation. Four to six sessions may be devoted to hierarchy construction and training in relaxation.

All of this is preliminary to the desensitization procedure itself, which is conducted as follows: Muscular relaxation is induced, and you are asked to visualize the scene associated with the least anxiety-arousing item in the hierarchy, giving a signal, usually raising a finger, whenever you begin to experience anxiety. If, for example, you are able to visualize item one for a while without signaling anxiety, the therapist tells you to stop visualizing the scene, briefly reinstates relaxation, and then has you visualize the scene again. After several repetitions without anxiety arousal the therapist proceeds to the next item in the hierarchy. Whenever you signal anxiety, the therapist immediately stops the item visualization, reinstates relaxation, and returns to the item again, or if necessary to the preceding item. The procedure is followed until you can repeatedly visualize the phobic stimulus without experiencing anxiety.

reassurance, ridicule, forceful confrontation with the feared situation, and ignoring of the child's fear were all relatively ineffective in helping their children overcome fears. Other parents, however, who had with some patience introduced their children to the feared objects *by small steps* reported considerable success. For example, a child who feared the dark was provided with a dim night-light which was later removed.

It was not until the 1950s that Wolpe (1958) developed a highly systematic procedure for applying the counterconditioning model to phobic reactions. A key feature of Wolpe's procedure, which he called systematic desensitization, was the use of imagined scenes rather than real-life situations. This innovation permitted him to treat patients with all manner of phobic reactions without having to set up actual situations as Jones had done with Peter.

Wolpe's procedure is conducted as follows: In the initial sessions the therapist and client identify the phobic object or situation and together construct a hierarchy of scenes that arouse anxiety. Each successive scene evokes more anxiety, until the most anxiety-arousing aspect of the phobia is represented in the final scene. For example, suppose you have intense anxiety reactions while taking course examinations. You might construct the following hierarchy of scenes:

Does Desensitization Work? An early, and now classic, study on the effectiveness of desensitization was conducted by Paul (1966). He selected college students with strong fear of public speaking and obtained pre- and posttreatment measures while the subjects were actually making a speech. Behavioral ratings, self-report, and physiological measures (heart rate and palmar sweating) were obtained. Subjects were randomly assigned to one of four groups: systematic desensitization, insight-oriented psychotherapy, attention placebo, and no treatment. The same five therapists (all with extensive experience in insight therapy and no previous experience with desensitization) saw three subjects individually in each of the three treatment conditions for a total of five hours over a six-week period.

In the insight-oriented psychotherapy condition,

the therapist attempted to reduce anxiety by helping clients gain insight into the historical and current interpersonal aspects of their problems. In the attention-placebo condition, the therapist provided interest and warmth—along with a placebo "tranquilizer" pill—while the subjects worked on certain tasks. Subjects were told that performing these tasks after taking the placebo pill was an effective fear-reducing procedure that would generalize to public speaking.

Desensitization was found to be more effective on almost all measures than any of the other three conditions. Insight-oriented psychotherapy and the attention-placebo condition were uniformly more effective than no treatment. A composite index of improvement based on behavioral, physiological, and self-report measures yielded the following percentages of subjects showing improvement:

Desensitization	100 percent
Insight-oriented psychotherapy	47 percent
Attention-placebo	47 percent
No treatment	17 percent

These effects were maintained at a six-week and two-year follow-up (Paul, 1967). There was no indication that any individuals had developed new symptoms at the end of treatment or at follow-up.

Paul's study was exceptionally well executed. The conclusion seems inescapable that desensitization was the superior treatment. It is of interest that insight therapy did no better than the attention-placebo condition, and that both were effective to a substantial degree (47 percent improvement). Since this pioneering study, many additional studies have shown that desensitization is more effective than a no-treatment control group in reducing fears of public speaking, taking tests, nonpoisonous snakes, rats, and spiders (Kazdin & Wilcoxon, 1976).

The most serious question raised about studies of the effectiveness of desensitization is whether the findings can be generalized to clinical cases. Subjects in most of the above studies were either college student volunteers or individuals who responded to newspaper ads. Would desensitization be as effective with individuals so disabled by phobias that they have sought professional help? We still cannot give a definitive answer to this question. Evidence from clinical studies that did not employ control groups or independent assessors suggests that the answer is yes. Hain et al. (1966), for example, reported that phobic fears were successfully reduced in 78 percent of 27 adult patients in an average of 19 sessions. The average duration of these phobias prior to treatment was 8.6 years. In a study that did use a comparison condition and independent assessment, Gelder et al.

Individuals who experience acute anxiety when talking before an audience can be helped with systematic desensitization.

(1973) found that desensitization was significantly better than a placebo-attention condition for women with severe agoraphobia (fear of leaving their homes).

Why Does It Work? Assuming that desensitization is effective for many anxiety reactions and phobic reactions, the curious investigator still wants to know why. Wolpe would say it is because of counterconditioning; incompatible emotional responses have been paired in such a way as to substitute relaxation for fear. But there are many alternative explanations. Perhaps the effectiveness results from a supportive relationship with another person or from instructions that lead the subjects to believe that they will lose their fear—the expectancy or placebo effect. Perhaps the effectiveness results from just learning how to relax, or from being positively reinforced by social approval from the therapist for each step of progress, or from repeatedly visualizing a scene so that eventually the anxiety extinguishes.

The results of some of the early research on systematic desensitization seemed to indicate that the specific features of the procedure, the pairing of relaxation with a graded series of imagined scenes, were indeed essential for its effectiveness (see, for example, Davison, 1968; Lang et al., 1965; Paul, 1966). Unfortunately, as research has accumulated over the years there has not been *consistent* support for any aspect of the procedure as being essential. Thus numerous studies suggest that the pairing of relaxation with the visualized scenes is not a necessary ingredient of the process (Yates, 1975); nor does it always seem necessary to progress through the hierarchy of scenes from least to most anxiety arousing (Yates, 1975). For example, Krapfl and Nawas (1970) found that the procedure was equally effective whether the hierarchy items were presented in ascending order of anxiety-arousing properties or in descending order. With respect to nonspecific factors, when placebo-attention conditions have been matched for credibility with the desensitization condition, desensitization has been found to be more effective in some studies but not in others (Kazdin & Wilcoxon, 1976). However, in the one study that used patients with severe clinical phobias (as opposed to college student volunteers) systematic desensitization *was* more effective than an equally creditable attention-placebo condition (Gelder et al., 1973).

Although the effectiveness of desensitization may not be consistently related to any one variable such as the use of relaxation or the use of a gradual hierarchy, it may be related in a rather complicated way to the pattern of several of these variables. Thus Watts (1979) reviews evidence that suggests that relaxation is more likely to facilitate desensitization only when the phobic stimuli are presented for short durations; and likewise that a graded stimulus hierarchy is more likely to be facilitative when relatively short stimulus durations are used. Variations in the durations of the presented stimuli in different studies might account, in part, for the overall inconsistency of results. The interested reader may wish to pursue Watts's theoretical explanation of these and other complex relationships, a theory that makes use of the concepts of *sensitization* and *habituation* rather than counterconditioning or extinction. In conclusion, what had initially seemed like a rather simple counterconditioning process is not so simple after all.

The importance of the relationship between therapist and client has been stressed by DeVoge and Beck (1978), who suggest that a view of behavior therapy in which the therapist is seen as applying some technique (desensitization or any other behavioral technique) to a client is too limited and that an understanding of the interactional system in which the behavior therapy occurs is important. These authors review a number of research studies in which it is strongly suggested that when a client's own interactional style is to respond submissively to a dominant but friendly other person, then the client is likely to be cooperative and the usual procedures are likely to work. When, however, a client is inclined to respond to friendly dominance in another person by hostile dominance in return, then he or she is not likely to be cooperative and may find social "reinforcements" in the form of praise aversive and punishing rather than positively reinforcing. It will pay the therapist in this latter case to develop different tactics for eliciting cooperation before plunging ahead with the particular procedures. The interactional context of behavior therapy can, of course, be conceived in behavioral terms.

FLOODING

The occasional finding that the visualization of scenes without relaxation is as effective as the complete desensitization procedure is consistent with an

extinction model of desensitization, that is, that anxiety simply extinguishes as a result of the repeated,
but safe, presentation of the feared stimulus. Advocates of an extinction approach to the modification
of fear have developed procedures that differ in important ways from the desensitization procedure. I will
use the general term *flooding* to refer to these procedures.

In laboratory work with animals it has been shown
that fear extinguishes more rapidly and completely
when an animal is forced to remain in the situation
that has come to serve as a conditioned stimulus for
the fear (Baum, 1970). Rats, for example, who have
been conditioned to fear a compartment because
they have in the past experienced painful electric
shocks there recover more completely from their fear
when they are forced to stay in the compartment
(without shocks, of course) than when they are permitted to escape. The basic principle is that certain
stimuli continue to elicit strong fear almost indefinitely so long as the animal can continue to make
successful avoidance responses. For humans the
fear may be elicited by thoughts and avoided by
thinking about something else.

Applying this principle to anxious humans, clinicians developed techniques designed to force the
person to stay in contact, either in imagination or in
actuality, with the feared stimulus. In this approach
the patient is flooded with anxiety-arousing stimuli.
The key feature of the flooding technique is that the
therapist intentionally seeks stimuli that will evoke the
strongest anxiety reactions in the patient and keeps
presenting and elaborating on these stimuli, not permitting the patient any escape. As one might guess,
compared to the benign and sometimes boring desensitization sessions, these sessions are strongly
emotional. To be successful the person must be kept
imagining aspects of a given situation until it elicits
a marked decrease in anxiety. If strong anxiety is
aroused and the person is immediately permitted to
stop thinking about the situation, an avoidance response has been reinforced and no anxiety has been
extinguished; in fact, under these circumstances the
anxiety might be even worse the next time the person
confronts the situation.

In a variation of flooding called implosive therapy,
Stampfl (Stampfl & Levis, 1967) has the person viv-
idly imagine not only the anxiety-arousing situation

**Patients in implosive therapy are asked to imagine the
most awful consequences of their phobic fears.**

but also fantasied elaborations frequently based on
psychoanalytic themes such as castration, abandonment, death wishes, and so on. Other clinicians stick
closer to the general behavioral orientation and flood
the person only with the more obvious aspects of the
anxiety-arousing situation. An example of the successful use of flooding or implosion in the treatment
of a child with school phobia (Billy) is discussed in
Chapter 13.

Does Flooding Work?   Experimental research with
volunteer subjects is not unanimous in confirming
the effectiveness of flooding or whether it is more or
less effective than desensitization (Morganstern, 1973).
For the more severe phobias seen in clinics there is
some evidence that a combination of imagined and
real-life flooding is more effective than desensitization
(Marks et al., 1971). Gelder et al. (1973), however,
found desensitization and flooding to be equally effective with clinic cases. Foa and Goldstein (1978)
report the successful use of a variation of the flooding
technique with clinic patients who had shown severe
obsessive-compulsive symptoms for 2 to 30 years
before treatment. The treatment involved flooding in
imagination to anxiety-invoking situations that would
ordinarily precipitate the compulsive rituals—for ex-

ample, imagining the various "disasters" that might happen if a compulsive urge to wash hands was not complied with. In addition, a *response prevention* technique was used in which the patients were prevented from acting on their compulsive urges. A compulsive hand washer, for example, would be prevented from hand washing. The treatment consisted of 10 to 15 sessions conducted during a two- to three-week period, and only three of the 21 patients failed to benefit from the treatment.

One reason that flooding may be more effective than desensitization in treating some anxiety disorders is that for some individuals the cues associated with the anxiety reaction itself serve to elicit further anxiety. An anxiety attack is a very unpleasant experience, and it would not be surprising to find that the subjectively experienced sensations of anxiety—a fast-beating heart, feelings of dizziness, or whatever—produce a fear of fear reaction. In flooding one has a chance to experience the fear itself for an extended period of time under safe circumstances and thus to extinguish the anxiety-arousing properties of the anxiety itself.

Many therapists who are concerned about precipitating intense anxiety reactions in patients prefer the less stressful desensitization procedure. In fact, relatively few instances have been reported in which flooding has made patients worse. It is probably good policy to use the least distressing procedure that will get the job done. For some disorders, however, a variation of the flooding technique may turn out to be the most powerful and efficient treatment.

AVERSION CONDITIONING

Aversion conditioning, another technique based in part on the classical conditioning model, is frequently used when there is some behavior that the patient wishes to stop. In this procedure an unpleasant emotional reaction is conditioned to the undesired behavior or to situations that tend to elicit the undesired behavior. It is considered most appropriate for addictive problems such as drug abuse, excessive eating, smoking, or certain compulsive sexual activities. I will take up this form of treatment in later chapters when these kinds of problems are considered.

The Operant Learning Model

The operant approach to behavior therapy involves the systematic use of positive reinforcement for desired behavior, the removal of positive reinforcement for undesired behavior (extinction), and punishment for undesired behavior. As a pure form of treatment it has been used most often with aggressive children, autistic children (a severe disturbance discussed in Chapter 20), mentally retarded people, and psychotic patients.

Although the operant approach is not often used as the sole form of treatment for people with neurotic problems, a good example of its use is the case of Fay.

Fay: Modification of Compulsive Scratching

Fay, a five-year-old girl, had for a year been scratching herself until she bled, resulting in large sores and scabs on her face and one arm and leg. Psychiatric consultation had not been helpful in eliminating the scratching. The father had spanked her, sometimes severely, when she scratched, and the mother had continuously criticized her for scratching, but all to no avail. The mother had come to dislike the child so intensely and was so repelled by her appearance that she felt it might be better if Fay were placed outside the home to live.

The operant approach to therapy involved the removal of reinforcers for undesired behavior and the addition of reinforcers for preferred behavior. The mother was instructed to ignore scratching behavior and not to reinforce it by any form of attention. Fay was to be given approval and attention for whatever commendable behavior occurred when she was not scratching, such as playing with her dolls or looking at a book. Since the mother found it very difficult to respond to Fay in a positive fashion, a program for additional reinforcement was initiated, in which Fay received a gold star for every 30 minutes during which she did not scratch. The accumulation of stars was occasionally rewarded by a snack (cookie and favorite beverage) or an inexpensive trinket.

After one week of this program the mother reported a decrease in scratching during the day but a continuation of scratching at night. The program was revised to include more powerful reinforcers contingent on not scratching at night. Every afternoon of a scratch-free day Fay and her mother would go shopping for an accessory for Fay's Barbie doll that would serve as the next morning's reinforcer. The item was put on a shelf in plain view, and if there was no evidence of fresh scratching in the morning, Fay was given it. At the end of five days of this revised program the mother reported four scratch-free days and nights.

After a total of six weeks of treatment every sore had completely healed, the extrinsic reinforcers in the form of gold stars and Barbie doll items had been gradually reduced in frequency, and treatment was terminated. The father had stopped his irrationally severe punishments, and quarrels between the father and mother over disciplinary procedures had diminished. Four months later there had been no relapse. (Allen & Harris, 1966)

OPERANT TREATMENT: A Case of Hysterical Blindness

The operant approach has been fairly successful in modifying responses that are more or less under voluntary control such as Fay's scratching, but how effective is this approach with more involuntary responses such as hysterical blindness, deafness, and paralysis? So far we have only occasional clinical reports from which to form an answer to this question. The following case of a 47-year-old woman with hysterical blindness described by Parry-Jones et al. (1970) is an example of such a report.

The woman had been totally blind for two and one-half years when she was admitted to a psychiatric hospital. She had had a brain operation for an aneurysm several years before the onset of her blindness, and at first it was thought that the blindness was a delayed result of either the aneurysm or the operation, but further neurological and psychological observations led the clinicians to suspect a hysterical basis. She had average intelligence but only limited education, and had worked as a housemaid and waitress. At age 41 she married a man with a history of psychiatric disorder, a poor work record, and long police record. The marriage was characterized by considerable discord. After she became blind her husband deserted her.

Daily treatment sessions of about 15 minutes' duration were begun. In the first eight sessions she was told simply to push a button every 20 seconds. If she pushed the button within 18 to 21 seconds after the last button press, a buzzer would sound indicating that she had made a correct response. In sessions 9 to 16, without informing the patient, a light bulb was placed in front of her and was turned on as a cue to help her identify the correct time to press the button—assuming, of course, that she could learn to use this cue. Her performance improved considerably over these sessions (Figure 11-1). Before starting session 17 she was told that there was a light bulb that would light up when it was time to press the button, and she was encouraged to look for it and concentrate very hard.

In session 19 she suddenly stopped and sat motionless for about 30 seconds. When

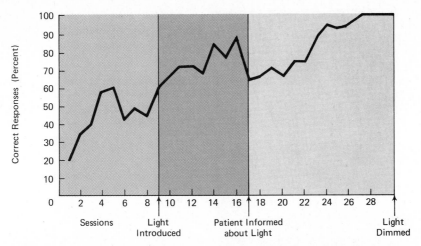

FIGURE 11-1. Percent correct responses in pressing a button to a light stimulus as a function of various therapeutic interventions for a person with hysterical blindness. (Adapted from Parry-Jones, Santer-Westrate, & Crawley, 1970. Copyright 1970 by Pergamon Press and used with permission.)

asked what was the matter, she became tearful and excited and said she could see the light, intermittently, as a dim double image. After this she began to rely on the light altogether; by session 27 she was making 100 percent correct responses.

In contrast, however, to other cases of hysterical blindness or deafness treated by similar procedures (recall the case of Anne in Chapter 9), there was no dramatic return of her full vision at this point. In fact, the only use she could make of her recovered visual ability was to see this one light bulb! The authors then embarked on a systematic attempt to expand her visual capacities to forms other than the light bulb and to situations outside of the treatment room. For example, she was given practice in seeing and describing large letters and pictures in magazines, and encouraged to continue practice outside the treatment room. After 127 of these brief sessions she had regained normal vision in her everyday life. Two years after the completion of her treatment her vision remained normal. She was working as a ward orderly at a geriatric hospital. She seemed to lack any insight into the nature of her blindness, although she marveled at the treatment. In her own words, "Having faith in somebody is the important thing."

The effective ingredient in this treatment procedure according to the operant model is the reinforcement of the visual response by feedback (a buzzer at first and then other forms of social reinforcement) indicating a correct response.

Few experimental studies have been conducted to assess the effectiveness of the operant approach with neurotic disorders. Clement and Milne (1967), using small samples of four children per group, did find that tangible reinforcement for social approach behavior resulted in a greater increase in such behavior in shy, withdrawn boys than did a traditional group play therapy condition.

Observational Learning

I have referred previously to the well-documented potency of imitative learning based on the observation of models (for example, Bandura, 1977). It is only natural that therapists of a social learning orientation have thought observational learning a prom-

Modeling and guided participation can help people overcome irrational fears, such as those of nonpoisonous snakes.

ising agent for therapeutic change, incorporating it in many therapeutic techniques.

Well-controlled experimental studies have demonstrated the effectiveness of modeling in reducing irrational fears of dogs in children (Bandura et al., 1967a), irrational fears of snakes in adults (Bandura et al., 1969), and shyness in children (O'Connor, 1969).

At a theoretical level observational learning can probably be understood best in terms of cognitive mediation. If an entirely new response is involved (for example, a submissive individual learning to be assertive), visualizing or in some other fashion forming a cognitive representation of the response should help a person actually make the response at a later time. In many cases, however, the person already knows what the desired response is and how to make it (for example, picking up a nonpoisonous snake in a laboratory test). In these cases the important learning may be expectancies of the form, "If that person can pick up the snake without being hurt, then maybe I can too." The importance of cognitive processes in observational learning is further shown by research in which the subject simply *imagines* a model performing the desired behavior. Kazdin (1975), for example, has shown that *covert modeling*, as this technique is called, can be successfully used to develop

appropriate assertive behavior in overly submissive students, especially when the students imagined that the model was rewarded for behaving assertively.

Mediating Cognitions: It's What You Tell Yourself That Counts

Although there are still behavior therapists who decry the use of cognitive variables in theory and technique and see such use as a retreat to the older mentalistic therapies such as psychoanalysis, these therapists represent a relatively small minority at this time. *Cognitive behavior therapy* has become widespread as a term, as a class of clinical techniques, and as an area of considerable research activity. To the old-guard behavior therapists, the term "cognitive behavior therapy" is a contradiction. They have a point. A therapy cannot be purely behavioral and also cognitive. However, there is nothing inconsistent about a therapy that attends to both overt behavior *and* intervening cognitions without claiming to be *purely* behavioral, and that is what the cognitive behavior therapists purport to do.

COGNITIONS AS A CONTROLLING STIMULI

The basic assumption of the cognitively oriented therapists is that thought processes *do* affect behavior, including emotions. Thus interpretations of the meaning of past or current events, expectations about future success, failure, approval or disapproval, fantasies and daydreams all can affect our actions and our emotions. If these internal stimuli are to some extent controlling our behavior, it makes sense to attempt to modify these internal stimuli as well as relevant external stimuli, and that is what the cognitive behavior therapists do.

Imagine that you are giving a speech before a group of people, and midway through someone gets up and walks out. Before reading on, think for a few seconds about what you would say to yourself.

You might think, "I must be a boring speaker.

Maybe other people are going to leave too." Thoughts such as these are likely to make you feel anxious or depressed and decrease your effectiveness as a speaker. Or you might think, "Maybe that person has reasons for leaving that have nothing to do with my talk. Too bad; he's going to miss a good speech, but that's his problem." If you imagined something like that, the odds are that you would not be as upset by the incident. If you imagined the former kind of thoughts, a cognitive behavior therapist would first help you become aware of how such thoughts were contributing to your distress and then help you develop some alternative thoughts that would aid you in successfully coping with public speaking situations.

The use of cognitions by the cognitive behavioral therapist is quite different from the way cognitions are used in the psychodynamic tradition. In the latter the emphasis is on becoming aware of (getting insight into) unconscious urges and conflicts and their historical antecedents with the assumption that such awareness in itself will result in symptom relief. The cognitive behavior therapist, as I implied above, is much more interested in helping a person *change* specific self-statements that seem to be producing much of the immediate distress. These cognitive self-statements are viewed as covert "behavior" and it is assumed that these covert "behaviors" can be changed by the same procedures used to change overt behavior—by modeling, rehearsal, reinforcement, and so on.

RATIONAL EMOTIVE THERAPY

An early variant of cognitive behavior therapy is an approach developed by Albert Ellis called *rational emotive therapy* (1973). As can be seen by the following quotation from Ellis (1962), this approach is based almost entirely on the notion that it is the person's interpretation of events that is the root of neurotic disorders.

Thus, it shows people that their emotional Consequences (at point C) do not directly stem from the Activating events (at point A) in their lives, but from their Belief systems (at point B) about these Activating events. Their Belief systems, when they feel dis-

turbed, consist of, first, a set of empirically based, rational Beliefs. For example, when they fail at a job or are rejected by a love partner (at point A) they rationally convince themselves, "How unfortunate it is for me to fail! I would much rather succeed or be accepted." If they stick rigorously to these rational Beliefs, they feel appropriately sorry, regretful, frustrated, or irritated (at point C); but they do not feel emotionally upset or destroyed. To make themselves feel inappropriately or neurotically, they add the non-empirically based, irrational Beliefs: "How awful it is for me to fail! I must succeed. I am a thoroughly worthless person for failing or for being rejected!" Then they feel anxious, depressed, or worthless.

The therapist or teacher shows people how to vigorously challenge, question, and Dispute (at point D) their irrational Beliefs. Thus, they are shown how to ask themselves: "Why is it awful that I failed? Who says I must succeed? Where is the evidence that I am a worthless person if I fail or get rejected?" If people persistently and forcefully Dispute their insane ideas, they acquire a new cognitive Effect (at point E), namely, the Beliefs that: (1) "It is not awful but only very inconvenient if I fail"; (2) "I don't have to succeed, though there are several good reasons why I'd like to"; (3) "I am never a worthless person for failing or being rejected. And if I never succeed or get accepted, I can still enjoy myself in some ways and refrain from downing myself." (p. 19)

Meichenbaum (1977) has developed cognitive change procedures based on Ellis's rational emotive approach that have been found to be effective in reducing anxiety in various situations including public speaking and test taking. Meichenbaum's procedures are worth describing in some detail since they are a good example of translating cognitive concepts into specific therapeutic operations. For example, there were two aspects to Meichenbaum's (1972) cognitive change treatment of test anxiety: the identification of inner verbalizations that were interfering with performance ("How awful if I flunk this test," "I'm starting to feel upset and can't think straight," and so on) and a modification of the desensitization approach in which the person imagined successful coping behavior. In essence the person learns to substitute relaxation and imagined successful coping for the old "worry" responses. Thus individuals are taught muscular relaxation and helped to construct a hierarchy of test anxiety scenes just as in standard desensiti-

Students who experience intense anxiety when taking tests can be helped by systematic desensitization and by cognitive behavior modification.

zation. However, when persons report that they are becoming anxious, instead of stopping the visualization of the scene as in desensitization, they are asked to continue and to imagine that they are successfully coping with the situation by relaxing, inhibiting task-irrelevant or worrisome thoughts, and focusing on thoughts that facilitate performance. In the study of test anxiety both the cognitive change technique and desensitization were effective in improving grade point average and reducing self-reported test anxiety, with the cognitive change approach showing the greatest effect.

An important innovation in Meichenbaum's approach is giving the person practice in coping with the presence of anxiety. This is not an explicit part of desensitization. Meichenbaum and other cognitively oriented therapists have also argued that cognitive training should result in greater generalization of treatment effects from the original anxiety-arousing situation. They suggest, in other words, that the person learns a set of cognitive skills that can be applied in situations other than the original phobic situation. Wolpe (1958), on the other hand, reasoning from an animal-learning-derived stimulus-response theory says rather explicitly that his desensitization procedure must be applied to each anxiety-arousing stimulus to ensure successful treatment, although he would expect some weak stimulus generalization effects. In an ingenious experiment in which each subject had *two* phobias, one of rats and one of snakes, Meichenbaum and Cameron (1972) found that a cognitive change therapy showed significant generalization from one phobia to the other and standard desensitization did not. The treatments were applied to only one of the phobias and the degree of fear reduction to the untreated phobia was the measure of generalization. Self-statements, then, that enabled an individual to cope with one stressful situation may have value in helping that individual to cope with many stressful situations. See the accompanying boxed insert for examples of the kind of self-statements that might be used at various stages of a stressful experience. Meichenbaum (1977) uses the term *stress-inoculation training* with respect to learning these self-statements that can be applied to any future anxiety-arousing experience.

COGNITIONS AS CONSEQUENCES

In social learning terminology, mediating cognitions are said to affect overt behavior in two ways: as cues or discriminative stimuli eliciting other responses, or as consequences that reinforce or punish previous responses. So far I have concentrated on the first function. The person with anxiety about public speaking thinks "Oh my gosh, I'm really going to blow it," and cues in more anxiety. In this section I will concentrate on the second function, the use of cognitions to punish or reward ourselves.

Covert sensitization, a term introduced by Cautela (1966), is a covert (or internal) form of aversion conditioning or punishment used to reduce undesired behavior such as smoking, overeating, alcoholism, or deviant sexual behavior. Instead of being made to experience discomfort or pain by some external stimulus (such as electric shock or a nausea-inducing drug), individuals imagine some distressing scene, for example, a scene so revolting and disgusting that it actually makes them feel sick to their stomach. They practice imagining that scene whenever they begin to think about indulging in the undesired behavior. This approach has shown only variable success in modifying alcoholism, smoking, and obesity (Little & Curran, 1978). It has shown considerable promise in reducing certain deviant sexual behaviors, such as exhibitionism; an example of its use in that respect will be given in Chapter 14.

We can also reward our own behavior, a process called self-reinforcement. Self-rewards can be covert (a thought of self-approval) or overt (treating yourself to a snack after completing a difficult assignment). There is a cognitive component, however, in the use of external rewards for self-reinforcement; the person must engage in cognitive planning for the anticipated self-administered reward. See the boxed insert for

some examples of self-reinforcing statements used by Meichenbaum (1977). Rehm and Marston (1968) successfully used self-reinforcement in the treatment of male students who were shy about initiating contacts with women. As a major aspect of the intervention the subjects constructed a graded series of situations involving college women, ordered so that each item aroused more anxiety than the preceding one. They were told to attempt the least anxiety-arousing item, record their progress, and award themselves points and engage in generous self-praise whenever they successfully accomplished an item.

Some Examples of Coping Self-Statements to Be Used Before, During, and After an Anxiety-Arousing Experience (adapted from Meichenbaum, 1977)

Preparing for the anxiety-arousing experience
You can develop a plan to deal with it.
Just think about what you can do about it. That's better than getting anxious.
No negative self-statements: just think rationally.
Don't worry: worry won't help anything.

Confronting and handling an anxiety-arousing experience
  One step at a time: you can handle the situation.
  Don't think about fear; just think about what you have to do.
  Stay relevant.
  This anxiety is what the doctor said you would feel. It's a reminder to use your coping exercises.
  Relax; you're in control. Take a slow deep breath. Ah, good.
Coping with the feeling of being overwhelmed
  When fear comes, just pause.
  Keep the focus on the present; what is it you have to do?
  You should expect your fear to rise.
  Don't try to eliminate fear totally; just keep it manageable.
Reinforcing self-statements after the experience is over
  It worked; you did it.
  Wait until you tell your therapist (or group) about this.
  It wasn't as bad as you expected.
  It's getting better each time you use the procedures.

Bandura (1977) has suggested that a major feature in many forms of abnormal behavior is a set of cognitive processes, serving as both controlling stimuli and reinforcing consequences, that result in a lowered sense of *self-efficacy*. Such persons have come to expect that they cannot cope with various life situations whether these involve giving speeches, taking tests, making friends, or whatever. They attend less to success experiences and are more likely to give self-punishment for failures rather than self-rewards for successes. According to Bandura the success of many forms of behavior therapy may result from cognitive changes in which perceived self-efficacy is enhanced. Consistent with this view, Bandura et al. (1977) found a high correlation, $r = .86$, between the strength of reported self-efficacy at the end of a behavioral treatment for snake phobia and subsequently measured actual approach to nonpoisonous snakes.

Procedures Using a Combination of Learning Processes

It is unlikely that the effectiveness of any therapeutic procedure can be ascribed to one aspect of the learning process. As we have seen, even a relatively simple counterconditioning procedure such as desensitization may acquire some of its effectiveness from reinforcements (including self-reinforcement), expectancy or placebo effects, the learning of active cognitive strategies, and so on. For the practical goal of helping people overcome psychological problems, there is no reason why the therapist should not capitalize on all factors that might add to the overall effectiveness. Several behavior therapies do just this.

The Use of Drugs to Treat Anxiety

A class of drugs sometimes called the *minor tranquilizers* (to distinguish them from the *major tranquilizers* such as chlorpromazine used to treat psychotic disorders) are commonly prescribed for anxious patients. The most widely used minor tranquilizers are meprobamate (Miltown, Equanil), chlordiazepoxide (Librium), and diazepam (Valium). Well-controlled research has clearly shown that these drugs relative to placebo pills are effective in reducing anxiety (e.g., Rickels et al., 1971). Although the minor tranquilizers were initially thought to be nonaddictive, it has become clear that long and heavy use can result in physical as well as psychological dependency (see Chapter 23 for a definition of these terms). Both psychodynamic and behavior therapists are in agreement that drugs do not remove the "underlying" causes of psychological disorders—intrapsychic dynamics on the one hand or controlling stimuli and reinforcers on the other hand.

Behavior rehearsal and the closely related procedure, role playing, involve practicing new and less handicapping behaviors with the aid of modeling, coaching, feedback, and positive reinforcement from the therapist. One of the most widely used forms of behavior rehearsal is assertive training in which inhibited, submissive individuals are helped to behave more assertively, to stand up for their rights. For example, some people find it extremely difficult to say "no" to unreasonable requests, to make requests of others, to express anger, or to respond to someone else's anger. Some are afraid to express their true feelings in these situations; others assert themselves but then feel guilty or anxious about it. Wolpe (1973) uses assertive training quite extensively in his practice, seeing it as a form of counterconditioning in which social anxiety is inhibited by the incompatible response of assertion or mild aggression. Assertiveness training has been shown to be effective in many investigations (see Rich and Schroeder, 1976, for a review).

Symptom Substitution

If you eliminate a person's symptom without doing anything about the underlying causes, will it not come back or be replaced by some other symptom? Psychodynamic therapists warned that such symptom substitution was to be expected when therapists ignored underlying, intrapsychic causes of the patient's symptom. The question, of course, is an empirical one, to be answered by data rather than theoretical argument, and the data seem to say, for desensitization at least, that symptom substitution does not occur when this technique is properly applied. Lang et al. (1965) and Paul (1966) found no evidence of an increase in other symptoms at the end of treatment or at follow-up for subjects whose snake phobias or public speaking anxieties had been removed by desensitization. Lang et al., in fact, found a trend in the opposite direction: Other fears decreased more in the desensitization group than in the control conditions. Hain et al. (1966) found no evidence of symptom substitution in their work with clinical patients who had various kinds of phobias for an average of 8.6 years prior to treatment.

Although the specter of symptom substitution following desensitization has not turned out to be as

TABLE 11-1
Summary of Learning Models from Which Different Behavior Therapy Approaches Have Been Derived

I. Classical Conditioning
A. Desensitization
B. Flooding
C. Aversion Conditioning
II. Operant Learning
III. Observational Learning
IV. Mediating Cognitions
V. Combinations of the Above

troublesome as some had thought, the issue cannot be dismissed so easily. In complex disorders the successful elimination of one symptom may simply bring to the foreground other difficulties that were less prominent but were there all along. Or the successful elimination of a symptom may produce a change in the response of other people. In Chapter 8 a study was described (Hafner, 1977) in which some husbands of agoraphobic women developed symptoms of their own after their wives' phobias had been successfully treated by flooding. For example, one husband's tendency toward irrational jealousy was exacerbated when his wife became free to leave the house. This kind of development can, of course, be labeled symptom substitution, but it is not a reason for not using behavior therapy. Whether or not the husband's concern about keeping his wife at home played some role in the development of the symptom, the behavior therapist now can deal with this new problem if the couple wants help with it.

Bandura (1969) points out that phenomena resembling symptom substitution may occur if certain social learning principles are ignored. For example, if avoidance responses motivated by anxiety reduction, such as certain compulsive behaviors, are suppressed by punishment, the improvement is likely to be temporary. More lasting benefits will be obtained if the anxiety motivating the avoidance response is removed by desensitization or flooding before retraining of the compulsive behavior itself is begun. In general, if the program of behavior therapy has not identified the important controlling stimuli and reinforcing consequences (external or internal) and effectively changed them, then the treatment may be ineffective and symptom substitution phenomena may occur. As Bandura (1969) puts it, "Psychodynamic and social learning approaches to psychotherapy are, therefore, equally concerned with modifying the 'underlying' determinants of deviant response patterns; however, these theories differ, often radically, in what they regard these 'causes' to be . . . " (p. 49).

Behavior Therapy: Some Concluding Comments

One cannot help being impressed by the sheer magnitude and vigor of research and clinical activity in behavior therapy. New techniques are constantly being developed. Research answering not only "Does it work?" but also "Why does it work?" is being published at such a rate that it is hard to stay abreast of the field. The effective ingredients of therapeutic change are being winnowed from the chaff of irrelevant ritual. The contrast with the more stately progress of research on the psychodynamic and humanistic-existential approaches is striking.

Nevertheless there are therapists, especially those of the humanistic-experiential type, who continue to have deep reservations about the behavioral approach. Mahrer (1978) is one of these. He believes that behavior therapists essentially ally themselves with the person's conscious experience and help the person to cut himself or herself off even further from the deeper potentials for experiencing. "Within our perspective, behavior modification serves . . . to kill the deeper potential . . . to foreclose the possibility of change, to place the person in a condition of mechanicalness . . . At the least sign of disruption of the person who resides within the domain of the operating potentials [conscious experience], the behavior modificationist sets to work murdering the intrusive deeper potential" (p. 368). This is a strong statement, and few behavior therapists would agree that they are "murdering" some potentially valued kinds of experiencing. The view does, however, reflect an attitude of many experiential therapists.

Behavior therapy has come to recognize that the psychodynamic approach is right in one respect: People's thoughts are important in affecting what they do. As behavior therapists have expanded both theory and technique from the classical conditioning and operant learning models of radical behaviorism to include observational learning and various kinds of mediating cognitions, the boundary between the behavioral or social learning therapies and the psychodynamic therapies has become less distinct. Although some argue that the models of radical behaviorism and psychoanalysis are paradigms of human behavior and treatment as different as the Copernican heliocentric view of the solar system and the old earth-centered view (see Davison & Neale, 1978, for example), the current expanded social learning approach suggests that it is not necessary to choose between such extreme models. There is a place for "underlying processes" and even "symptom substitution" within the social learning approach if these terms are defined carefully.

Thinking back over these last two chapters on the psychodynamic, humanistic-experiential, and behavior therapies, can we see, despite their obvious differences, any common elements? There may be at least one: Most therapeutic interventions with the kind of problems traditionally labeled "neurotic" involve in some fashion having the person confront experiences that produce painful emotional reactions. In psychoanalysis patients are helped to reexperience the emotional trauma of childhood; in client-centered therapy and Gestalt therapy they are led, by different methods, to confront emotion-laden problem areas; in desensitization and flooding they are made to imagine scenes that produce emotional distress; and in behavior rehearsal they are asked to practice behaviors that make them anxious. This common focus on learning to cope with emotionally distressing situations or memories by facing them is consistent with the view presented in Chapters 7, 8, and 9 on the origins of neurotic traits and neurotic disorders: The individual develops neurotic symptoms in the first place by learning various protective or avoidance strategies against strong, painful emotions. Perhaps the main exception to this "common thread" is the operant approach by which new, nonneurotic behaviors are shaped by reinforcement contingencies. The operant approach is rarely used in pure form, however, for the treatment of neurotic disorders.

If we tentatively accept the importance of this common element in many therapies, we are still left with the question of what it is about such repetitive reexperiencing that is therapeutic. Wolpe would say that psychoanalysis and other insight therapies have some effectiveness because they inadvertently pair thinking about anxiety-arousing events with the relatively safe and relaxed atmosphere of the therapeutic situation, thus providing a watered-down version of desensitization. This, of course, is a partisan view that would explain most therapeutic effectiveness in terms of counterconditioning.

It is unlikely that any one learning process, such as counterconditioning, will turn out to be the sole basis for effective therapy. It is wisest, until research shows otherwise, to assume that various learning processes can contribute to successful therapy. Some change probably does result from the simple pairing of anxiety-arousing stimuli (either external or internal) with incompatible responses as in counterconditioning or from forcing the person to stay with the anxiety-arousing stimuli until the anxiety eventually diminishes as in flooding. New responses can also be learned by observation of models, and old responses such as anxiety may be reduced by observing others who show anxiety-free behavior. A whole array of cognitive processes may facilitate therapeutic change: expectations of success as in placebo effects; switching from emotionally distressing thoughts to thoughts that produce emotional well-being; cognitive rehearsal of successful coping responses; and attention to and self-reinforcement for positive steps toward new behavioral goals. Although proponents of various points of view might have us believe differently, there is no solid basis at present for choosing among these alternatives. If anything, the evidence suggests that all of them add to the therapeutic process.

Summary

1. Behavior therapies emphasize clear specification of the behaviors to be changed and a direct attempt to change characteristics that seem to be maintaining the undesired behavior.

2. Three treatment procedures are based on the classical conditioning model: desensitization or counterconditioning, extinction or flooding, and aversion conditioning.

3. Many experimental studies indicate that desensitization is effective in reducing anxiety in college student volunteers and people who respond to newspaper ads. There is less experimental evidence with clinical patients, but what there is suggests that it is effective here too, though less so with more severe cases.

4. At this time research does not give a clear answer to the question, "What are the effective components of desensitization therapy?"

5. Flooding, based on the extinction model, has also been shown to be effective with volunteer subjects suffering from a variety of phobic and anxiety reactions, as well as with phobic patients. Some studies indicate that it is more effective, or achieves the same results more rapidly, than desensitization. Other studies find desensitization to be more effective. The question of relative effectiveness remains unresolved.

6. Aversion conditioning is used most often with addictive behaviors.

7. The operant approach, not often used in pure form with neurotic disorders, involves the use of positive reinforcement for desired behavior, the removal of positive reinforcement for undesired behavior, and punishment for undesired behavior.

8. Observational learning has been shown effective in reducing phobic and anxiety reactions; it should be a useful supplement to other procedures.

9. Behavior therapists have recently begun to include mediating cognitions in both theory and treatment techniques. Research demonstrating the effectiveness of attention and placebo conditions is most readily interpreted in terms of cognitive mediators. Ellis and Meichenbaum have developed forms of therapy that focus almost entirely on changing thoughts that produce emotional distress. Experimental results suggest that this type of treatment procedure is effective.

10. Covert sensitization and self-reinforcement, two other forms of cognitive intervention, have also been shown to have therapeutic promise in preliminary researches.

11. Procedures using a combination of factors—operant learning, desensitization, behavior rehearsal, modeling, and cognitive change—are likely to turn out to be powerful therapeutic techniques.

Suggested Readings

M. R. Goldfried and G. C. Davison provide a good introduction to the various behavior therapy techniques in *Clinical behavior therapy* (Holt, Rinehart and Winston, 1976) and J. Wolpe gives a lot of clinical detail on the conduct of behavior therapy in *The practice of behavior therapy* (Pergamon, 1973). The inclusion of cognitive concepts and procedures in behavior therapy is covered by D. Meichenbaum in *Cognitive-Behavior modification* (Plenum, 1977). P. Wachtel in *Psychoanalysis and behavior therapy: Toward an integration* (Basic Books, 1977) points to ways in which psychoanalytic and behavioral approaches may be fruitfully combined. An excellent comparison of the psychoanalytic, behavioral, and Gestalt approaches is C. A. Loew, H. Grayson, and G. H. Loew (Eds.), *Three psychotherapies* (Brunner/Mazel, 1975) in which proponents of these approaches describe how they would treat the same three cases.

12

Group, Family, and Community: Treatment and Prevention

- What are T-Groups, sensitivity groups, encounter groups, and group psychotherapy?

- "Honesty is the best policy." But when does it help, and when does it harm?

- "The Lord helps those who help themselves." Does this apply to therapy?

- Freud cautioned against psychoanalysts' seeing more than one family member at a time. Why?

- What are some of the advantages of seeing entire families together in therapy?

- Do family systems act like a thermostat?

- What is community psychology?

- Can we prevent the development of abnormal behaviors by changing social systems?

We have been focusing on treatment of the individual. Now let us broaden our perspective, first to consider treatment in groups, then treatment of the family, and finally "treatment" of the community. Of the three approaches, group therapy is most like individual therapy in the sense that the treatment does not directly involve other people, such as family members, with whom the person has a long history of emotional involvement. The members of a group usually are relative strangers who meet only for purposes of therapy. In family therapy, on the other hand, the participants have had and will continue to have, a long history of intense interrelationship. Finally, in community psychology we expand our view to include other social systems—schools, churches, government, the economy, and so on. No person lives in a social vacuum, and our mental health is affected for better or worse by our participation in these larger systems.

Group Therapy

Interest in group treatment intensified during and after World War II, partly stimulated by the hope that the limited number of trained professionals could go further toward meeting the increasing demand for psychological help by seeing six to ten patients at a time. Two sources contributed to the original group therapy movement: the *group dynamics* or *T-Group* approach, deriving from the study of psychological processes involved in small, task-oriented groups; and the extension of therapeutic techniques such as psychoanalysis or client-centered therapy to the group setting. These original sources have mingled in the last decade with influences from Gestalt therapy, psychodrama, transactional analysis, and other recent innovations.

According to its advocates, *group therapy* is not just a less expensive way of providing watered-down individual therapy to more people, but superior to individual therapy in several respects. First, the patient acquires insights and experiments with new behavior in the context of people other than the therapist, so generalization of new learning to the outside world is more likely to occur. Second, a person may acquire insights and ideas for new behaviors vicariously by watching other group members wrestle with

their problems. This kind of modeling also provides permission for the observer to engage in similar explorations of emotionally charged problems. Third, there is consolation and support in seeing that other people have similar problems, and in some groups direct verbal and physical support by other group members is encouraged.

T-GROUPS, ENCOUNTER GROUPS, AND SENSITIVITY TRAINING

T-Groups (short for Training Groups) developed originally not as a form of treatment for psychological disorders, but as a way of studying general principles of group dynamics and facilitating effective, task-oriented group functioning in "normal" people. People from industry, government, or education, for example, attend T-Groups, usually for one or two weeks, in order to learn how to work more effectively within their organizations. For example, superintendents and department heads might use the small group setting to learn and practice leadership and managerial skills. Generally speaking, T-Group leaders steer away from the exploration of personal problems and keep the focus on interpersonal relationships within the group.

The boundary line between the T-Group and the therapeutic group has become less clear in recent years. *Sensitivity training* incorporates many features of the T-Group but gives more attention to helping members become sensitive to their own behavior and its effect upon others. For example, a man who complains a lot may become conscious of how his behavior irritates others, or a woman who always mumbles may come to realize why people never talk to her for long.

Sensitivity groups in turn blend into so-called *encounter groups*, which are even more explicitly oriented toward personal growth. In everyday use, however, the terms "sensitivity group" and "encounter group" have become almost interchangeable. I will simply use the phrase *sensitivity–encounter* group without any precise distinction. In the 1960s there was a virtual explosion of sensitivity and encounter groups, including many variations such as incorporating Gestalt therapy techniques, meeting in the nude, and meeting for 36 hours straight without sleep. Although the aim of the groups, more or less

An encounter group led by Carl Rogers.

unfriendly, or boring is not likely to make you go home feeling better about yourself.

It is important *how* the injunction to be honest is implemented. Aronson (1972) gives an example of how "honesty" can lead to communications problems and how the problem was handled in an encounter group.

In the course of the group meeting, one of the members (Sam) looked squarely at another member (Harry) and said, "Harry, I've been listening to you and watching you for a day and a half, and I think you're a phony." Now, that's quite an accusation. How can Harry respond? Another way of asking the question is: What are Harry's options? He has several: he can (1) agree with Sam; (2) deny the accusation and say that he's not a phony; (3) say, "Gee, Sam, I'm sorry that you feel that way"; (4) get angry and call Sam some names; or (5) feel sorry for himself and go into a sulk. Taken by themselves, none of these responses is particularly productive. (p. 247)

explicitly stated, was to further personal growth rather than treat neurotic or other kinds of problems, this distinction is not easy to maintain. It is likely that many individuals attending such groups are seeking help for moderately severe psychological disorders.

Don't Be a Phony.　Let us look more closely at the sensitivity–encounter group experience. A small group of roughly ten strangers is brought face to face under the guidance of a trained group leader. To begin, the leader may ask them each to express immediate feelings about themselves and the others (for example, "I'm a little worried about this whole setup" or "Being with so many younger people makes me uncomfortable"). The one rule that holds for all such groups is an injunction to be honest in the expression of your feelings and other reactions, to be authentic as opposed to putting on a front. Of course you may not be in touch with some of your feelings; you cannot honestly express something you are not aware of. The group, however, may help to increase self-awareness, as we will see.

Some people are scared away from encounter groups because of these groups' reputation for promoting soul-searing honesty. They wonder, "What awful things are people going to say about me if they really say what they think? Will I come away feeling worse about myself than before I went?" Unfortunately, this fear is sometimes justified. When a group is badly led, honesty can lead more to hurt than to growth. Simply to hear that you are phony, hostile,

The effective group leader would require that Sam's reactions be stated as feelings he is having rather than as criticisms. Thus, following Sam's accusation of Harry, the group leader in this case asked Sam if he had any *feelings* about Harry, to which Sam responded, "Well, I *feel* that Harry is a phony." This is not really a statement of a feeling but a judgment or criticism of Harry that is likely to evoke the same defensive response in Harry as the initial statement. The leader again asked what Sam's feelings were and Sam insisted that Harry was a phony. "And what does that do to you?" asked the leader. "It annoys the hell out of me," answered Sam. Someone else asked what kind of things Harry had done to annoy him, and after several minutes of discussion with other group members Sam admitted that he got annoyed whenever Harry showed affection to some of the women in the group. Eventually Sam owned up to a feeling of jealousy—he wished he had Harry's smoothness and success with women. The clarification of Sam's feelings and his *owning* of them as his feelings (as in the Gestalt approach) opened up a level of communication with Harry that would have been extremely unlikely had the interchange been allowed to run its usual course without guidance from the leader, probably ending in mutual name-calling or hurt withdrawal.

One reason, of course, why Sam had learned to

College students participating in a sensitivity-encounter group. The basic injunction in most such groups is "Don't be a phony."

hide certain feelings and express them as a personal attack is that in "real life" the expression of jealousy or other feelings might be taken as a sign of weakness or immaturity and thus make him vulnerable to criticism and hurt. However, given the general positive value of honesty in sensitivity–encounter groups, the most common reaction to Sam's new openness would be expressions of liking. Harry, of course, also learned something from this encounter about how his actions affected other men.

Most encounter group leaders do more than simply help other group members to be honest. They frequently interact intensively with the other participants, expressing their own feelings to model the kind of openness they are trying to promote.

Do These Groups Work?   Lieberman (1976) reviewed 47 studies published in 1973 and 1974 that evaluated the effectiveness of sensitivity–encounter groups. Overall the results suggested that these groups do produce positive effects. However, this conclusion must be tempered by the fact that measures of improvement were almost always *self-reports* of changes in such characteristics as self-esteem, values, anxiety, and amount of social interaction; that groups whose values were sharply discrepant with

those of the approach (for example, a conservative and religiously fundamentalistic group, and a group composed of ghetto-dwelling adolescents and police) showed little change; and that the persistence of change was rarely measured by follow-up assessments.

Lieberman, Yalom, and Miles (1973), in the most ambitious study of sensitivity–encounter groups to date, found some evidence for beneficial effects when measured by self-report questionnaires but not when assessed by friends and acquaintances of the college student participants. They likewise report some "casualties," people who found the group experience destructive and left the group feeling worse about themselves (see Research Report 12-1).

Certainly, *some* encounter groups achieve their intended aim for *some* members—an increase in emotional self-understanding, sense of worth, and sensitivity in human relationships—but encounter groups have also been criticized for providing cheap emotional thrills, for attracting leaders without proper training, and in general for not taking responsibility for the occasional destructive effect on certain individuals. Paradoxically, there can be a certain tyranny in groups of this sort in which the social pressure by both the leader and the group members for *their*

RESEARCH
REPORT
12-1

Encounter Groups: A Study of Their Effectiveness and Casualties

For this study Lieberman, Yalom, and Miles (1973) randomly assigned 206 college students who wished to participate in encounter groups to 16 groups led by experienced professionals. They also obtained certain measures on a control group of 69 students who enrolled for the group experience but could not get in because of schedule conflicts. The groups met for about 30 hours, frequently in lengthy sessions from 3 to 15 hours in duration, and represented a wide range of approaches: T-Group (2); Gestalt (2); psychodrama (2); psychoanalytic (1); Transactional Analysis (2); Esalen eclectic (1); Rogerian (1); Synanon (1); personal growth encounter (2); and leaderless group conducted by instructions from a tape recording (2).

The investigators obtained several kinds of measures before, after, and at a six-month follow-up. In response to several rating scales, 57 percent of those who completed the group experience (38 students dropped out of the groups) indicated that some positive change had occurred. At the sixth-month follow-up this figure had dropped to 46 percent. The leaders were clearly impressed by the effectiveness of their groups, reporting some improvement in almost 90 percent of the participants.

Both participants and control subjects had nominated from three to five people who knew them well (friends, spouse, parents, and so forth); at the time of the six-month follow-up these individuals were sent questionnaires asking what changes they had noticed in the participants. For almost 80 percent of both experimental and control subjects these observers noted specific positive changes. In other words, no significant differences on this measure emerged between the participants and the nonparticipants; apparently many college students show positive changes, or at least are perceived as showing positive changes, over a six-month period. A self-report questionnaire did show some significant differences between participant and control subjects immediately after termination of the groups, but many of these differences had diminished to nonsignificance at the follow-up. A serious question is raised by the finding that ratings of change from different sources (participants themselves, leaders, fellow participants, and outside friends and relatives) were not related—intercorrelations among these four sources hovered around zero! How much confidence can we have in positive changes if different observers cannot agree upon them?

We might conclude, then, that individuals who complete encounter groups tend to *believe* that it has been a positive, growth-enhancing experience, that this belief decreases somewhat in time, and that other people in the person's life see about as many positive changes in nonparticipants as participants.

Looking at the 16 different types of encounter groups, it is clear that no one approach emerged as superior or inferior in terms of producing positive change. The styles of leadership in the groups were vastly different: Some leaders were interpretative, some nondirective, and some emotionally provocative; some freely disclosed their own personal reactions, others did not; some emphasized working with individuals, others focused on group processes; some used many nonverbal exercises, others relied wholly on talk; and so on. In general the leaders whose groups showed the most positive changes were moderate in the extent to which they attempted to elicit strong emotional responses by challenging and exhortation, were high in caring, and gave clear explanations of why their particular encounter group techniques should be helpful. The "ideology" of the approach was not nearly so important as the style of the particular leader. Thus, in terms of an index of overall positive change in participants, one of the Gestalt groups was one of the most successful, but the other Gestalt group was the least successful. The group showing the most improvement was a Transactional Analysis group, but the second Transactional Analysis group was near the bottom. As it turned out, the two groups conducted by tape recordings were slightly above the median in effectiveness.

Casualties. A casualty was a person who showed serious psychological harm six to eight months after the group ended that could reasonably be attributed to the group experience. By this definition 9 percent (16) of the people who completed the encounters were considered casualties. Three of these students had psychotic reactions; several had anxiety or depressive reactions; and others had less clear-cut syndromes but reported some disruption to their self-esteem, discouragement about making positive changes, or tendencies to avoid or withdraw from interpersonal relations.

One person, for example, was unequivocal in her evaluation of her group as a destructive experience. The leader and the rest of the group undertook to help this person, a passive, gentle individual, to "get in touch with her anger." She was attacked by both the leader and the group, including a physical assault by one of the female members. At one point the leader cryptically remarked that she was "on the verge of schizophrenia." He would not elaborate on this statement, and she found herself ruminating about his remark for months afterward. She withdrew from her family and friends, became depressed, and had difficulty sleeping at night.

Another person described the experience as follows: "I tried to overcome my defenses as best as I could but couldn't do it. The leader kept pressuring me to express my feelings but I didn't know what I felt. When I said this I was attacked as a phony. This reinforced my defenses so later in the sessions I just withdrew and watched" (p. 186).

The authors conclude that encounter groups can be harmful. Although not demonstrated by statistical test, the casualties did not appear to be randomly distributed across groups. Groups in which there was a good deal of attacking and aggressive behavior on the part of the leader and the participants produced more casualties than groups in which there was more emphasis on warmth, support, and acceptance.

definition of honest expression can produce conformity rather than individual autonomy. The best advice to give to the prospective participant is to suggest that he or she check on the qualifications of the leader, talk with previous participants, and not to expect long-term psychological handicaps to be removed by a few weekend encounters.

GROUP PSYCHOTHERAPY

The distinction between encounter-sensitivity groups and psychotherapy groups is not sharp. Perhaps the most important difference is that psychotherapy groups are likely to continue for months or years; whereas encounter-sensitivity groups are more often limited to a marathon weekend or some limited number of sessions. Also, members of continuing psychotherapy groups, on the average, are likely to be experiencing more severe degrees of psychological disturbance. The theories and techniques applied to the group setting frequently derive from individually based approaches such as psychoanalysis and client-centered therapy, modified by some therapists to include techniques developed in the encounter-sensitivity group movement. Behavior therapy has also been conducted in groups, especially group desensitization (for example, Lazarus, 1961).

An approach that has enjoyed some popularity is a blend of Transactional Analysis and Gestalt techniques, sometimes abbreviated as TA-Gestalt. Transactional Analysis was developed by Eric Berne, author of the best-seller, *Games People Play* (1964). Although the developers and practitioners of TA-Gestalt tend to come from the psychodynamic tradition, it is interesting to note how compatible in many ways this approach is with the behavioral and social learning orientation. In fact, many TA-Gestalt therapists, dissatisfied with the emphasis on historical reconstruction and the preoccupation with intrapsychic dynamics in the psychoanalytic therapies, maintain that TA-Gestalt approaches are much more efficient in changing troublesome behaviors.

Let us consider a few of the important features of the TA-Gestalt approach. In contrast to many group approaches in which relatively free interaction is encouraged among all group members, in the TA-Gestalt approach interaction tends to be largely limited to the therapist and the group member who is "working" at the moment. Then, there is the contract. Group members are asked to state what they wish to accomplish in specific, behavioral terms, and the therapist agrees to help the person achieve these goals. Gaining control over drug use, getting rid of headaches, learning how to elicit positive responses (social reinforcements or "strokes") from other peo-

Eric Berne, author of *Games People Play* and *What Do You Say After You Say Hello*, and originator of a form of group therapy called Transactional Analysis.

ple, or abandoning thoughts of suicide are examples of good contracts. To attain happiness, emotional security, or self-understanding would be too vague and lacking in behavioral referents to be useful as contracts.

The contract is one aspect of a more general feature of the TA-Gestalt approach—namely, placing responsibility explicitly and repeatedly upon the group members to work toward their goals. One of the "games" that Berne has described is "Rescue." All games are interactional, requiring at least two participants; in Rescue there must be a Victim and a Rescuer. The TA-Gestalt therapist is careful not to play the role of Rescuer no matter how strongly group members try to initiate such a game. The following example, described by Steiner (1974), illustrates how the therapist avoids this trap and how the resulting experience strengthens the member's sense of responsibility for helping herself.

Groups of this kind tend to evoke characteristic neurotic traits (or game playing), and the therapist

Carol: Reaching for Help

Carol, attending her first meeting with a group at the Radical Psychiatry Center in San Francisco, looked desperate and in great need, but was unable to say that she wanted to work on any particular problem. The Worker (therapist) made a special point of not trying to rescue Carol from her misery and when she failed to respond to his invitation to take some time in the group for herself, he turned to other group members. Later in the session the Worker again turned to Carol and the following interchange took place:

"You look like you need something. I would like you to ask for it so that we can see if we can help." Carol burst into tears. Jack, sitting next to her, put his arm around her but she cringed and he, hurt and upset, took his arm back lightning fast. . . . The Worker, after letting her cry for about a minute, said, "Carol, it seems you feel quite powerless and without hope to do anything about it. Am I right?" . . . She said, "That's right, powerless. There is nothing I can do, I am such a mess."

The Worker answered, "The way we work here is that we want to do what we can to help you but we need you to use all of your energy or it won't feel good to us."

"I told you I can't do anything," answered Carol.

"You can start to take your power to act by asking for something. . . ."

"That's not being powerful, that's being weak!" answered Carol.

"I don't think so but, anyway, I want to help you to ask for something. . . ." (pp. 284–286)

At this point another group member asked for time to do some work and Carol was left to decide whether or not she wanted to do something. Later in the session she did ask to be hugged by several women and through her tears talked about some of her difficulties. When she returned the next day, she was feeling better and had learned that it was up to her to take responsibility for doing something about her troubles.

and other group members can help the person become aware of these traits. Members then have an opportunity to work on changing these behaviors if they so desire. Gestalt techniques, such as talking to imagined other people or to parts of oneself, are used to bring persons in touch with their emotional selves and to provide rehearsal of new ways of responding.

In their approach to TA-Gestalt group therapy the Gouldings (1978) emphasize how persons make themselves feel guilty, angry, ashamed, or anxious by what they tell themselves. Note the similarity to the cognitive-behavioral approach. They also suggest that people continue to make themselves feel unpleasant emotions such as guilt or fear because in their childhood they had experienced payoffs for feeling that way—essentially an operant learning view. The following interchange began with Ian saying that his father, not wanting to be tied down by a child, had divorced his mother because of him, and that he felt very guilty about this. The therapist asks him to pretend to be his father:

Therapist: What is your name, father?
Ian as Father: Michael.
Therapist: OK, I want to interview you, Michael. You and your wife have sex, she gets pregnant, and you feel what?
Ian as Michael: Angry. Tied down.
Therapist: Interesting. Have you any idea what you felt angry about, tied down about, before Ian was born?
Ian as Michael: No. I don't know.
Therapist: Had to be something. You see, if you'd been a happy man, you'd happily have chosen to raise a child or not raise a child. Whatever. Somehow you knew how to feel tied down, angry, and then to split. Make up what happens when you were little. . . .
Ian as Michael: Very strange. I never thought of all that. . . . I was always the no-good member of the family. Everyone said so.
Ian: (Returns to Ian's chair and talks to his "father" in the empty chair.) Of course, you were the no-good person . . . you never really had a chance. Your family hated you and mother was the martyr. Of all the men she could have picked, she picks one who'll leave her. Of course. I never thought of all that. Well, you two, I didn't have anything to do with your desertion or your martyrdom. And I am not guilty. (pp. 164–165)

In this interaction Ian is learning to stop telling himself that he is responsible for his parents' divorce and then to stop feeling guilty. For this kind of technique to work it is probably important for the person to "get into" the emotions and perceptions associated with those early experiences; otherwise it may simply be an intellectual exercise.

A most important feature of these TA-Gestalt groups is the strong, positive support that members can get from the therapist and other group members for experimenting with new thoughts and behaviors. Most TA-Gestalt therapists do not emphasize an attacking, defense-stripping mode of operation as do some encounter group therapists. Thus persons can learn to feel good about themselves by effecting positive changes in their environment and by experiencing the warmth and acceptance of the therapist and other group members. Homework assignments in which members are asked to practice some new behaviors between sessions are another feature similar to the behavioral approach. However, TA-Gestalt therapists have shown little interest so far in the experimental evaluation of the effectiveness of this approach.

Family Therapy

If the family is as important as we have assumed in producing and maintaining psychological disorders, then it makes sense to involve the family directly in the treatment process. It was not, however, until the early 1950s that therapists in any number began to see several family members together in the same session. The reason for this long delay probably was the strong prohibition in the psychodynamic tradition against the psychoanalyst's seeing more than one member of a family at a time. This doctrine was based on the fear that therapists would develop strong countertransference reactions and would not be able to remain impartial in dealing with different family members.

A SYSTEMS APPROACH

Most of the early investigators in the field of family therapy advocated a radical departure from the traditional psychodynamic views in theory and in techniques (Jackson, 1965; Satir, 1964). I have already referred to this orientation in an earlier chapter as a social systems model or metaphor. In this view the focus is not on an abnormally behaving individual who has intrapsychic conflicts but on disordered interactions in the larger family system that produce symptoms in one or more family members. I used the case of Joanne and her family to illustrate a systems perspective. Recall that her daughter Milly's obnoxious, bugging behavior was reinforced by Joanne's giving in and her attention. Joanne's tearful despair and headaches were reinforced when Milly would stop her upsetting behavior at the onset of those symptoms in her mother. And the father further reinforced Milly's obnoxious behavior by siding with her against Joanne. The "disorder" from this perspective does not exist in Joanne or in Milly but in the family interaction patterns.

Aponte and Hoffman (1973) describe another example of disordered interaction. Laura, a 14-year-old girl, refused to eat and was eventually hospitalized for excessive weight loss. When Laura and her family were referred for family therapy, they denied having any disagreements, although Laura finally admitted that it irritated her when her parents urged her to eat. In the following excerpt from the first therapy session, the therapist (Salvador Minuchin) asks Laura and her parents to reenact what happens when she refuses to eat. Laura's younger sister Jill and brother Steve are also present.

Minuchin: (To Laura.) When you get annoyed, how do you express your annoyance? What do you say to Dad? Say it now, the way you said it then.
Laura: (To Father.) No, I don't want any food. (Pause.)
Minuchin: What do you do then? (Pause.) Dad, what do you do then, when she says that?
Father: I naturally insist.
Minuchin: You insist. Insist now. I want to know how it works.
Father: (Overlapping.) Well, this is more present than recent. This is not . . .
Minuchin: OK, yeah, OK. Make believe that it's happening.
Father: OK (To Laura.) I'm going downstairs, Laura. Do you want something?
Laura: No.
Father: Nothing at all, no snitch, something, a piece of fruit?
Laura: Nothing. I don't want anything.

Father: A little ice cream?
Laura: No.
Father: OK.
Minuchin: (To Laura.) Do the same thing with Mom. How does it go? (To Mother.) It goes also with you similar?
Laura: Uh . . .
Minuchin: (Indicating that Laura should continue.) OK.
Father: (To Laura.) Try it at the dinner table with Connie. I think that might be better because (to Mother) you don't go down as often as I do. (Laughter.)
Laura: (Laughs.) My mother stops, and she stops after once. My father he keeps going on and on. (p. 4)

Here is part of a discussion between another family therapist, Aponte, and another observer of a videotape playback of the sessions shown directly above.

Aponte: He's starting with the struggle over food. First he asks: How does it go between Dad and Laura? Then: How does it go between Mother and Laura? He finds out that the real struggle is between Laura and her father. Mother insists a little but then stops. So he knows that this father-daughter relationship is a particularly charged one, and he assumes that this must have something to do with the girl's refusal to eat.
Observer: In other words, it's a way she's fighting the father.
Aponte: Well, that would be simplifying it. Minuchin is trying to find out the way the relationships in this family are structured. In most families where a child has a symptom, you find that he is in a special kind of triangle with his parents. One parent will be intensely involved with him. The other parent will be more peripheral. This usually happens when the parents are in a conflict but can't openly admit it or resolve it. The child brings them together by giving them a focus for their concern. (p. 5)

Thus, in accord with the systems approach, Laura's reduced eating and extreme weight loss are not seen as symbolic of some inner conflict but as, among other things, a struggle with her parents (presumably about growing up).

An important property of interpersonal systems is that they resist change. Any group of two or more people that has to accomplish certain continuing tasks, such as the family, will develop characteristic styles of interaction, and any deviation from the expected way of doing things is likely to be resisted. This tendency to maintain interactional styles is another example of the *homeostatic principle* (described for the autonomic nervous system in Chapter 7). The house thermostat, you may recall, is an example of a homeostatic regulating device—it restores equilibrium after imbalances have occurred. Families have their own interactional "thermostats," and when the behavior of one or more members becomes too deviant (too hot!), the larger family system responds in a self-correcting manner.

Again, let us look at Laura and her family to see how *family homeostasis* works in a specific case. As we see in the next excerpt from their first therapy session, Laura's father has developed a close and "cuddly" relationship (with erotic overtones) with Laura and her younger sister, but his relationship with his wife is distant and strained.

Father: We congregate in our room and, ah, Steve he will cuddle and scratch my back, and I'll scratch his back (Jill laughs), and, ah, Mommy, she'll be doing something—ah, Laura, she'll be . . .
Minuchin: Do you scratch her back also?
Father: Whose?
Minuchin: Mom's.
Father: Mommy? No. (Laughter and more talking.)
Mother: (Laughing.) I don't like my back scratched.
Father: So, ah, I'll maybe massage the girls, their legs, and Laura—I haven't done too much for Laura lately. You see, it's been reversed, ah, Laura always enjoyed combing my hair, or if I get dandruff and don't have time to wash my head, some of the girls will take the comb or brush and brush my hair out . . .

                        . . .

Minuchin: Ah, Dad is describing a lot of nurturance going between him and the kids. (To Mother.) Where are you when all that happens?
Mother: Well, sometimes I'm just laying on the bed, you know, watching TV with them. Ah, sometimes she'll want her back rubbed, I'll rub her back— he'll want his back rubbed. Other times I'll just be sitting on the bed, either doing needlepoint,

or maybe I'll be going down to the kitchen and emptying the dishwasher, or heating up coffee or . . .
Minuchin: Daddy's a cuddler, he likes to cuddle, he likes the children to cuddle with him . . .
Mother: Yeah, he enjoys that at night.
Minuchin: (To Mother.) What about you, are you a cuddler?
Mother: Am I? Ah, not as much as him I guess. Ah— I don't know. I'm always busy in the house it seems. I don't know, I'm folding clothes and putting them away, or . . .
Minuchin: Do you like to cuddle with him?
Mother: Yeah. (Laughing.)
Minuchin: But he likes to cuddle with the kids?
Father: Yeah.
Minuchin: Sometimes would you like him to drop the kids, and be with you alone?
Mother: No! No, absolutely not. (Shaking her head.) (pp. 9–10)

Apparently, Laura's father prefers to maintain the kind of relationship he has established with his daughters (presumably one factor in Laura's refusal to eat), because otherwise he would have to satisfy his needs for closeness and "cuddling" from his wife, a course that is apparently unacceptable to him. His wife also seems to favor the present arrangement.

The principle of family homeostasis, then, may account for the persistence of symptom-producing family interaction even when the symptom causes great distress. However, family systems are not totally impervious to change. Most family systems, in fact, undergo extensive changes as children grow up and also change in response to external pressures and intrusions. The family is not a closed system; it is affected by external economic, religious, educational, political, and social forces. So it is probably best to think of family homeostasis as a relative resistance to change, a resistance that may be more intransigent for symptom-producing interaction than for other kinds of interaction.

TECHNIQUES OF FAMILY THERAPY

Therapists who conduct family therapy from a systems point of view (sometimes called a *communication-interactional approach*) tend to focus much more on the immediate interaction, who is doing what to whom, rather than on past experiences that produced the present problems or on intrapsychic conflicts in individual family members. Two aspects of the family's interaction are heeded: how members communicate with each other and the structure of the relationships.

Disturbed families are considered to be especially lacking in communication skills. Messages are frequently disguised, hidden, or given indirectly by nonverbal means. One goal of therapy is to aid the family members to express their desires, feelings, and points of view directly and clearly to one another. The concept of structure, less clearly defined, refers to certain formal characteristics in interaction patterns: Are there coalitions between different family members? For example, do mother and son "gang up" against father? Is a given child expected to play the role of parent? How clear are the intergenerational boundaries between parents and children? The last question is investigated in the next excerpt from therapy with Laura's family. The therapist, who had just learned of the close relationship between father and daughters, is interested in the mother's reaction to this relationship.

Minuchin: There are times in which you say to the kids, OK kids, it's the end of—you leave because it is now time for . . .
Mother: No.
Minuchin: . . . time for me and daddy alone?
Mother: Never! Never!
Minuchin: The door of your room, do you leave it open during the evening?
Mother: Always.
Minuchin: Always open. I would expect that.
Mother: In fact, I don't even like the children to close theirs, which they very rarely do for sleeping—they do for (inaudible words). (p. 10)

Observers drew the following conclusions from this part of the session:

Aponte: There is no boundary between this father and his kids. Family therapists who think along structural lines see a "healthy" family as one where there are clear demarcations between the generations. Within each generation level, there will be strong ties, as well as adequate differentiation between individuals. The pair that is the governing unit, the parents, have to have a particu-

larly strong alliance and clearly worked-out areas of functioning special to each. The same is true of children, except that differentiation with them should be appropriate to age. Of course, much of this will be defined by the culture, but the general rule of clear generation lines and adequate differentiation will hold. In an "unhealthy" family, or what Minuchin sometimes calls an "enmeshed" family, there is a blurring of the generation lines and a lack of differentiation. So this is what the therapist goes for.
Observer: The tone of that "Never," when Minuchin asks whether she ever tries to be alone with her husband, is so final, so sharp.
Aponte: Sure. She's an accomplice in this. You see, what you often find in these enmeshed families is that there is a hiatus between mother and father but it isn't openly expressed. Mother depends on the kids to console Dad for the fact that she isn't very interested in him. In asking the two parents whether they ever get to be alone together, Minuchin is putting a circle around the dyad. At the same time, he finds out about the hidden crack between husband and wife. (pp. 11–12)

There is a good deal of variability in how therapists attempt to improve communication and produce changes in pathological interaction or structure. By and large, family therapists are active rather than passive, using the immediate situation as an opportunity not only to point out characteristic interaction styles but also, more importantly, to urge experimentation with more direct communications and different modes of interaction. For example, the therapist in Laura's family has family members practice directly expressing their desires and points of view, and he attempts to make a clearer intergenerational separation between Laura and her father by raising the issue of children's right to privacy.

Minuchin: Laura do you close the door of your bedroom?
Laura: No.
Minuchin: Don't you want sometimes . . .
Laura: No.
Minuchin: . . . to close—don't you want some privacy sometimes?
Laura: No—yeah, I do, but I get enough leaving the door open.

. . .

Minuchin: Would it bother Dad to tell him that you want the door closed, and you want him to knock at the door?

Laura: I don't think so.

Minuchin: Are you certain of that? Hm?

Laura: (Laughing.) I don't know.

Minuchin: I have the feeling that it would bother Dad because he is a very loving kind of Dad that likes always to have people respond to him and he responds to people—to the children certainly. That's my hunch—ask him. Ask Dad if it will bother him if you asked him to knock at your door instead of entering. (Mother and Jill both look sharply at Laura, then look at Father.) (pp. 12–13)

In discussing this part of the therapy session, observers commented on the therapist's role:

Aponte: You notice that Minuchin makes a switch here. He goes from the parents shutting their door against the kids, to Laura shutting her door against her father. And what he is doing here is to facilitate her claim for privacy.

Observer: Is that why he moves so carefully?

Aponte: Sure. First he gets an admission from the girl that she sometimes does like her door closed. Then he asks if at those times her sister and mother respect her privacy enough to knock, and she says yes. Only then does he ask her about her father: "Do you ask him to knock?"

Observer: He gets a very doubtful answer.

Aponte: And he respects her reasons. He's trying to help her to challenge her father, but he sees that she can't because she knows her father would oppose her. So then he says, "Well, I think it would hurt him because your father is a very loving father." He makes the father's opposition a positive rather than a negative thing. So he has diluted what could have been a very stressful transaction. It's as though he were saying, "We can talk about boundaries in terms of flower hedges; it doesn't have to be guns." (p. 14)

I have so far emphasized the systems approach to family therapy; however, there are many variations in approach. Clinicians of the traditional psychodynamic mold feel that systems therapists have gone too far in concentrating on the system to the neglect of the individual's internalized conflicts, and some therapists attempt to strike a compromise between an individual and a systems orientation.

Behavioral therapists have also entered the family field. The behavioral and the systems approach are similar in several ways. Both emphasize changing behavior or interaction patterns (who is doing what to whom) and deemphasize historical reconstruction and concern with intrapsychic processes. The differences center on the techniques of producing change; the systems therapists generally conduct therapy in a loose, intuitive manner, while the behavioral therapists help the families to specify explicit new modes of interaction and to set up new reinforcement contingencies that will bring them about. The case of Fay (Chapter 11), the girl who scratched herself until she bled, is an example of a behavioral approach to family therapy, in this case largely limited to the mother-child dyad. Recall that the therapist asked the mother to ignore Fay's scratching and to reinforce her nonscratching behavior.

CRITIQUE

Although few studies meet all of our criteria for good research design, findings in general suggest that nonbehavioral family therapy is superior to both no treatment and to treatment limited to an individual family member identified as the patient (Gurman & Kniskern, 1978). For example, Ro-Trock et al. (1977) found that hospitalized adolescents who received family therapy showed no incidence of rehospitalization during the three-month period following discharge compared with a 43 percent rehospitalization rate for adolescent patients who had been seen in traditional individual psychotherapy.

Behavioral approaches with an operant emphasis have also been shown to be effective (Gurman & Kniskern, 1978). As with individual psychotherapy the distinction between behavioral and nonbehavioral approaches is becoming blurred, and some investigators blend communication training with contingency management. Martin (1977), for example, found that a brief family intervention procedure in which both communication skills and contingency management skills were taught to mother-child dyads or mother-father-child triads was effective in reducing the frequency of mother-child problems compared to a control condition.

Generally speaking, there are several reasons why it makes sense to have most, if not all, family members meet together in the therapy sessions even though only one family member may be initially identified as needing help. First, significant features of family interaction related to the maintenance of the psychopathology are likely to become apparent to the therapist (and also to the family) much more quickly than if the therapist has to rely on indirect verbal reports by one individual. Second, if other family members are not directly involved in the treatment sessions, they may counteract or sabotage initial efforts on the part of the identified patient to behave differently. When the family meets conjointly, these undermining attempts can be dealt with as part of the therapy. Third, considerable observational learning can occur in family sessions; a member who sees others expressing important feelings and attitudes and experimenting with new modes of responding is more likely to do the same. Finally, the problem of generalization from the therapy session to the outside world is less severe when an important part of the outside world, one's family, is participating in the therapy.

However, an extreme systems point of view can be criticized for neglecting characteristics of the individual that do exist in some sense independently of the system. In time, chronic phobic or obsessional responses, though affected and perhaps partly maintained by interaction with other people, may also reflect such strong response tendencies in the person as to require some individual attention. Theorists seem to find it hard to resist the temptation to push one good idea as the *only* interpretation of abnormal behavior and its treatment: Freud with the Oedipal conflict, Skinner with extreme behaviorism, Ellis with cognitive self-statements, and certain family therapists with the systems approach. It is possible to keep the added explanatory power of an interactive or systems view without rejecting personality dispositions that people bring to the interactions.

The concept of family homeostasis may be overstated also. There is little empirical research on the question of what happens in a family when a member with psychological symptoms begins to improve with outside help. Will most families, in fact, immediately take action to recreate the symptoms in that family member as the homeostatic principle would suggest? Maybe only certain families do so and only under certain conditions. In perhaps the only experimental study of family homeostasis Martin (1977) investigated the question of whether the treatment of mother-child problems would be as effective with fathers excluded from treatment as with fathers included. For the mild to moderately severe problems involved it turned out not to make any difference whether fathers were included. In other words, family homeostasis did not seem to interfere to any strong degree.

Clinicians also report instances in which an individual family member's psychological improvement was greeted by support and approval by other family members and led to improvements in other parts of the family system. In the case of Fay, when her self-scratching behavior was modified, the relationship between her mother and father improved. They no longer got into arguments about how to discipline Fay. In other words, psychological symptoms in one family member do not always serve a purpose for the family, nor will a change in these symptoms always be resisted by the family.

Marital Therapy

You may wonder why it is necessary to have a section on marital therapy separate from family therapy. Although it is true that marital conflicts are frequently dealt with as part of family therapy, married couples, some without children, seek help specifically for marital problems, and some techniques have been developed specifically for marital therapy. In this section I will concentrate on some of the newer behavioral approaches to marriage therapy.

Behavioral marriage therapy includes operant techniques as well as training in communication skills (Gottman, 1979; Jacobson & Margolin, 1979). The operant aspect of treatment usually involves a contract, in some cases an actual document signed by both spouses, in which each agrees to reward the other for performing some desired behavior. Distressed marriages have been found to be characterized by high rates of punishing or coercive responses such as nagging, complaining, and pouting, and low rates of pleasing or affectionate behavior (Billings, 1979; Birchler et al., 1972). In other words, spouses in distressed marriages try to get the other person to do what they want by negative reinforcement (coer-

Couples can be taught conflict resolution skills in marriage therapy.

cion) rather than positive reinforcement. One aim of the operant approach is to decrease the use of coercive controls and increase the use of positive rewards as a way of influencing the spouses' behavior. The therapist monitors the progress of the couples in implementing the contract and helps them set up new contracts for different problems as needed.

In communication training couples are taught how to resolve conflicts and, in some cases, how to negotiate contracts. In the latter instance the communication and operant approaches are blended together. A usual first step in communication training is to teach couples to translate desires and dissatisfactions into specific behavioral referents. Instead of saying, "You just don't like anything I do," a spouse might learn to say, "You criticized the dinner I cooked last night." Spouses (and therapists!) may feel dis-

couraged about changing anything so general and "internal" as an attitude or an intention; it seems more believable that a person might stop doing some specific thing such as criticizing meals. The next step is to teach couples how to communicate in less destructive and more rewarding ways. Using various combinations of behavior rehearsal, feedback, coaching, and modeling, couples are taught to minimize blaming, nagging, and other negative responses, to state their own desires clearly and specifically, and to engage in task-oriented negotiations with the partner to reach acceptable compromises or contracts. If strong emotions are present, the spouse may learn to express them briefly and with full intensity but without an extended blaming speech; for example, "It makes me furious when you come home late for dinner and don't call." Thus couples come to acknowledge and own their feelings as in the Gestalt and some encounter group approaches.

Jacobson (1978a) reviewed research on behavioral approaches to marriage therapy and concluded that approaches involving either communication training or behavioral contracting or both were indeed effective compared to no-treatment control groups. There is little clear evidence for the effectiveness of nonbehavioral approaches to marital therapy if those involving structured communication training are excluded (Gurman & Kniskern, 1978). In one of the best-designed studies Jacobson (1978b) found a behavioral approach not only to be more effective than a no-treatment group but also to be superior to a placebo-attention discussion group matched for creditability with the behavioral treatment groups. See Research Report 12-2 for an example of how behavioral contracting worked with a couple in another study by Jacobson (1977).

RESEARCH REPORT 12-2

Behavioral Marriage Therapy

Jacobson (1977) describes the treatment of one couple in an experimental study of behavioral marriage therapy. Marlene complained that Leon spent little or no time talking to her and that when he did talk a high percentage of his verbal responses took the form of "demanding" statements. Leon disliked Marlene's continual nagging and also wished that she would spend more time relaxing. The therapist asked Leon and Marlene to record daily frequencies of the behavior they disliked in the other person for two weeks. At the first treatment session two weeks later (day 14) the couple negotiated a contract in which Leon agreed to spend more time talking with Marlene, and Marlene was to reward this new behavior by showing interest in his daily activities. The number of minutes that Leon talked with Marlene increased immediately, going from an average of 7 minutes per day

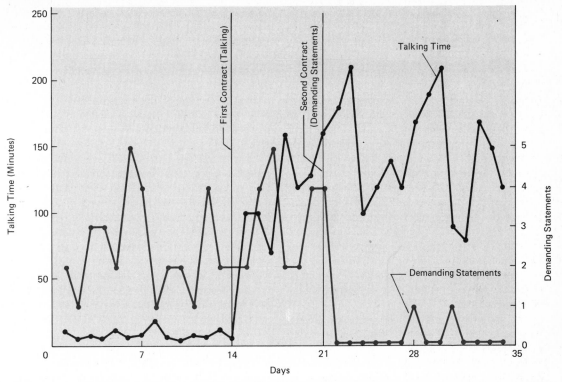

FIGURE 12-1. Wife's daily record of husband's demanding statements and amount of time engaged in conversation as a function of behavioral marriage therapy. (Adapted from Jacobson, N. S. Problem-solving and contingency contracting in the treatment of marital discord. *Journal of Consulting and Clinical Psychology*, 1977, *45*, 92-100. Copyright 1977 by the American Psychological Association. Reprinted by permission.)

before treatment to an average of about 120 minutes per day during treatment (Figure 12-1). At the second treatment session (day 21) another contract was reached in which Leon agreed to decrease his demanding statements, and there was a dramatic drop in the frequency of such statements.

The treatment strategy used with Leon and Marlene illustrates the *multiple-baseline technique,* in which two or more behaviors are recorded for an extended baseline period and then intervention is begun for one of the behaviors. If only that behavior and not the other behaviors being recorded is changed, it suggests that the specific therapeutic procedure (behaving in accord with the contract in this case) is responsible for the change, rather than general and nonspecific aspects of the procedure such as attention or placebo effects. At the second treatment session a contract was negotiated to help Marlene spend more time relaxing, and a steady increase in this behavior was seen over the next several days. Likewise, at the third session, a contract was agreed upon to help reduce Marlene's nagging behavior, and this behavior showed a sharp drop to a zero rate.

The five couples seen in this kind of treatment for seven sessions showed significantly greater improvement than the control group on percentages of positive and negative responses rated from videotapes of problem-solving interaction, scores on a self-report inventory of marital satisfaction, and target behaviors recorded by spouses. At a one-year follow-up these changes were maintained as measured by the self-report inventory.

Community Psychology

Neither individuals nor families live in a social vacuum. After age five a child is increasingly subject to the influences of the school, neighborhood, and various organized activities such as scouting, Little League, church functions, and so on. For example, a boy who is beginning to have academic difficulty in school may be responded to in such a way by the teacher (excessive criticism) and by classmates (reinforcement for disruptive behavior) that he begins to develop a behavior disorder. In addition, large-scale social phenomena such as wars, poverty, unemployment, and racial or religious prejudice may also intrude upon the child or adult. The social systems metaphor can, in other words, be expanded beyond the family to encompass broader sociological circumstances.

The importance of the social network of friendships as a protection against symptoms of anxiety and depression is suggested in a study by Miller and Ingham (1976). These authors found that women who reported the lack of at least one intimate friend had significantly more psychological symptoms than women who did have a close friend that they could confide in. Although causality might work the other way, with symptoms of anxiety and depression preventing the development of friendships, it is likely that at least part of the observed association results from the therapeutic effect of being able to express disturbing feelings and thoughts to an accepting other person.

The general thrust of the community mental health approach (sometimes called community psychology or community psychiatry) is to think of the individual as an interacting participant in various social systems—friendship networks, the neighborhood, the school, the city power structure, or the economy—and to conceive of intervention as the modification of those aspects of a system that seem to be fostering the development of abnormal reactions.

One of the motivating forces behind the development of community-level intervention in the late 1950s and early 1960s was the growing disenchantment in some quarters with the traditional approaches to treating abnormal behavior, approaches that emphasized either individual treatment or institutionalization. First, there was little hard evidence at that time that either method did much good. Second, professional therapists were in such short supply that individual treatment could be made available to only a small percentage of those who needed it. And third, only the middle and upper socioeconomic classes could afford the individual treatment that was available.

If it is unlikely that we will ever have enough professionals to treat everyone suffering from some kind of psychological handicap, then what is to be done? The answer, say the proponents of community intervention, is *prevention* of abnormal behavior, or at least early detection and treatment before incipient disorders get worse. Since the shortage of therapists or inability to afford therapy makes it impossible to work individually with each child or family, in this view the only feasible way to prevent the development of psychopathology is to change the social systems that are producing it.

INTERVENING IN THE COMMUNITY

Preventive approaches have been divided into: *primary prevention, secondary prevention,* and *tertiary prevention.* The aim of primary prevention is to forestall the development of disorders in the first place by creating a physical and social environment that does not produce abnormal behaviors. In theory this means changing social systems so that psychopathology-inducing characteristics are removed. A more modest strategy is to identify high-risk groups (such as children of psychotic parents or children of recently divorced parents) and provide them with psychological experiences that will promote healthy development. Secondary prevention is oriented toward stopping mild disorders from becoming more severe or more chronic. Early detection of developing disorders and early treatment are the key strategies in implementing secondary prevention. Settings that provide an opportunity for large-scale screening for psychological difficulties, such as schools and colleges, the armed forces, industry, and labor unions, are likely to be useful in achieving the aims of secondary prevention. Tertiary prevention refers to preventing an already existing disorder from becoming chronic. Only primary prevention is truly preventive; both secondary and tertiary "prevention" involve some kind of intervention after a disorder has begun to develop or is already fully developed.

Prevention through modification of social systems carries with it certain attitudes and strategies that are quite different from the more traditional approaches. Traditionally mental health professionals wait until patients come to them, whether the patients seek psychotherapy or are admitted to a mental hospital. Community-oriented professionals, on the other hand, leave the clinic or institution, get out in the world, and seek opportunities to prevent disorders or perhaps catch a developing disorder in an early stage. The difference has also been couched in terms of a "sickness" versus a "health" model. Traditional therapists treat only people who have developed a disorder or "sickness," whereas many community-oriented professionals are interested in improving systems in order to maintain and foster mental health.

Consultation. The community mental health professional is a consultant to others who, by the nature of their jobs, are in close contact with many people struggling with adjustment problems—schoolteachers, police, ministers, physicians, probation officers or other court officials, public welfare workers, and so on. If through discussions with mental health professionals these individuals can learn to be sensitive to the beginning maladjustive reactions that they encounter and to provide certain helpful "therapeutic" experiences, then the influence of one mental health professional might be multiplied far beyond what a therapist could accomplish working only with individual patients. In addition to secondary preventive efforts of this kind, consultants also promote sound mental health practices among those with whom they come in contact, thus achieving some degree of primary prevention.

The Use of Paraprofessionals. Yet another way in which the community-oriented professional hopes to have some impact on the larger social system is by training paraprofessionals, individuals who have not completed traditional graduate training in one of the mental health professions. Training in certain human relations skills may vary from a few weeks to a year or more of supervised on-the-job experience. For ex-

Community mental health professionals do not wait for already-disturbed clients to come to them. They seek out opportunities to forestall the development of maladjustive reactions.

ample, college students have been trained to participate in treatment programs for psychotic patients in mental hospitals (Karlsruher, 1974); local people have been recruited from the inner city for work with the poor (Reiff & Riessman, 1965); and women have been trained to work with children having adjustment problems in school (Cowen, 1968) and in clinics under the supervision of the more traditionally trained professional staff (Rioch, 1967). In a survey of 42 studies in which paraprofessional helpers were compared with professionally trained therapists Durlak (1979) found the paraprofessionals to be generally as effective as the professionals. This was especially true for relatively structured approaches to specific target symptoms such as insomnia, assertiveness, speech anxiety and test anxiety.

Rioch and her associates gave women two years of "nondogmatic" training in psychotherapy that included a great deal of supervised on-the-job experience. They were then placed in schools, outpatient clinics, and mental hospitals, where evaluation toward the end of their training and again at a three-year follow up indicated that they were performing their jobs competently. Indeed, their performance on the Psychiatric Boards (an examination of knowledge about psychopathology and treatment) was as good as that of newly trained psychiatrists. The evaluation in this study was not aimed at determining whether the paraprofessionals were actually effective as therapists, but whether supervisors, co-workers, and outside observers perceived them as competent to do the same things as the more traditionally trained clinicians. Although this study does not represent a community intervention, it suggests that some paraprofessionals can assume traditional clinical responsibilities, relieving some of the shortage of therapists.

Crisis Intervention.   Another approach advocated by the community professional is crisis intervention. Crises may be such obvious and dramatic calamities as floods, tornadoes, train wrecks, automobile accidents, or wars. They may also be more personal in nature—and in some cases not so visible to others: divorce or separation, a crisis not only for husband and wife but also for the children; serious illness, perhaps with lengthy hospitalization; loss of a loved one; abortion; loss of a job; or forced housing relocation. Severe situational stresses of this kind may mark the beginning of psychological disturbances. When the stress is unusually severe or, more commonly, when the stress interacts with personality dispositions, a persisting abnormal reaction may occur.

Community professionals see crises not only as traumatic experiences but also as unique opportunities for psychological intervention. Persons with certain psychological vulnerabilities may never seek help as long as they can get by, but in the face of the loss of their job or an impending divorce their "protective organization" of defenses may no longer work and they are more receptive to the idea of therapeutic assistance. Conceivably with therapeutic help

Widely advertised telephone numbers permit people to obtain brief counseling, support, or information during a crisis.

they will become able to cope better with new crises in the future. The storm cloud of the crisis, in other words, may have a silver lining if intervention is timely and effective.

The general strategy of crisis intervention is to reach the person in the early stages of the crisis or soon thereafter with a kind of psychological "first aid" to prevent the development of a more entrenched disorder (see Research Report 12-3). Bureaucratic red tape is minimized by eliminating time-consuming referrals, filling out of forms, long waiting lists, and other administrative complications. One specific tactic has been to set up "storefront" or walk-in facilities close to the people who may need assistance. The help provided by such facilities includes not only brief therapy for emotional reactions to crises but assistance with economic, housing, or educational problems. Another approach to crisis intervention involves

RESEARCH REPORT 12-3

Homebuilders: Keeping Families Together

Kinney et al. (1977) describe a crisis intervention approach that is designed to prevent the removal of family members to alternative living situations such as mental or correctional institutions and foster homes. The first thing that the intervention team does for a family in crisis is to meet with each family member separately and listen to his or her feelings and point of view, communicating interest and acceptance by reflecting feelings in the manner of a client-centered therapist. These "listening" sessions may take several hours and usually have a calming effect on the family. The next day the team meets again with the family separately or as a group, depending on the emotional states of the individuals, and this time attempts to identify specific problems in behavioral terms. General name-calling and vague complaints are discouraged.

Here is a specific example. A court social worker reported that a mother on the verge of a nervous breakdown was asking that her four children, ages 16, 15, 6, and 5, be placed in foster care. An intervention team, meeting with the family, constructed the following list of problems:

1. The mother's ex-husband had caught her arm in his pickup truck and dragged her so that she had been paralyzed. She was still in constant pain.
2. The pain made it very hard for her to carry her books. She had returned to school and was finding it almost overwhelming.
3. She was trying to raise four children on $385 a month. They did not have a car, and they felt trapped together much of the time.
4. None of the children would help with the chores, and the place was a mess.
5. Her ex-husband had allegedly murdered his previous wife, and was supposedly psychotic. He made frequent threats to kill her or kidnap the children.
6. The 15-year-old boy often put skates and boxes on the top stair. The mother felt he did this on purpose to try to hurt his younger brother. She also frequently caught him twisting his brother's arm until he screamed.
7. The 16-year-old daughter had just found out she was pregnant.

The intervention team met with the family for five more five-hour sessions within the next week and a half. During this time, they taught the family problem-solving and communicational skills by a combination of modeling, behavior rehearsal, and behavior contracting. Information about community resources was also provided. The family eventually arrived at the following agreements: The children agreed to divide the chores among themselves and to deliver positive and negative consequences to each other for their performance. The mother, the 16-year-old daughter, and the daughter's boyfriend agreed that abortion was the best solution for the pregnancy. Over several days, the mother decided to quit school, lined up several job interviews, had a friend move in who could help pay the rent, and identified several things that she was doing that reinforced her ex-husband's coming around and threatening her. The mother began outpatient therapy. The team maintained telephone contact with the family. After six months the family had continued to deal with its problems without disabling crises.

At the time of their report, Kinney et al. had seen 47 families with the following kinds of precipitating problems:

Potential runaway	22
Child abuse or physical violence	19
School problem	16
Emotional exhaustion	13
Actual runaway	8
Drug problem	7
Alcohol problem	4
Sex/pregnancy	3

In only five of these families was outside placement used, two of these being short-term placements while the mother worked on her problems. Considering that all 47 families were on the brink of having one or more members leave the home, these results strongly support the promise of this kind of crisis intervention.

The authors also suggest that this approach may have impressive economic advantages. For example, the average cost per family in their study was $650. Costs for institutionalization and other expenses if the crisis interventions had not been attempted were estimated to be $3950 per family over a similar time period.

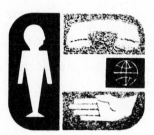

**TROUBLED? CONFUSED?
WORRIED? LONESOME?
UPSET?**

Talk It Over
with someone who
cares. Anytime . . .
Day or Night

CONTACT
333-6121

the use of a widely advertised telephone number. Paraprofessionals usually provide telephone counseling and referrals to professionals with specialized training. The greatest number of calls come from people having family, alcohol, drug, money, and employment problems, who are depressed and lonely, and who are seeking general information. About 10 percent of the calls are emergencies that require immediate attention, usually involving drug abuse, suicide, or family difficulty. An especially promising form of crisis intervention involves prevention of disabling symptoms, primarily depression, in the recently bereaved person. The result of such a study (Raphael, 1977) will be described in Chapter 18.

Prevention in Early Childhood. If the assumption is correct that vulnerability to psychological disorders often has roots in childhood, then it makes sense to focus preventive efforts on that time of life. Several community intervention programs have done just that. Hereford (1963), for example, found that parent groups devoted to discussing parent-child relations had some effect on children's adjustment in school. The effect, of course, was limited to those children whose parents volunteered to participate. Glidewell et al. (1973) made a similar parent education program available to parents in certain schools and not in others. He found a small but significantly greater reduction in mother-reported problems over a 30-month period for the children, especially boys, in schools where this program was available.

One of the most impressive attempts at early identification and prevention of psychological disorders in children is that of Cowen and Zax (1969). A finding of considerable significance in their series of studies is that many children who are experiencing adjustment difficulties in the first grade are likely to continue to show signs of maladjustment throughout their school years if they do not receive help. On the basis of personality and intelligence tests, classroom observations, and social worker interviews with mothers, all first-grade children in three elementary schools were divided into two groups: Red-Tag and Non-Red-Tag. A Red-Tag child was one who showed some degree of psychological disturbance, ranging from mild to severe. All other children were designated Non-Red-Tag. (These labels, of course, were not known to the child or family.) Approximately 30 percent of the children fell in the Red-Tag category, a percentage essentially the same as that reported by Glidewell and Swallow (1969) for the incidence of school maladjustment derived from their survey of a number of incidence studies.

Three years later, at the end of the third grade, Red-Tag children in the two schools where intervention was not attempted were showing poorer academic performance (lower grades, achievement, and ability scores), had been referred to the school nurse more often, and were experiencing more adjustment problems (as measured by teacher ratings, self-reports, and peer ratings) than were their Non-Red-Tag counterparts. The implication is clear: Without help

Women's consciousness-raising groups are not therapeutic groups in the usual sense of that term. By helping women, however, to be aware of current sex-role expectations, to explore alternative roles, and to do this in a supportive atmosphere, such groups may prevent psychological maladjustment in some women.

most of the children tagged at the beginning of their school careers as having academic or adjustment problems were still having such difficulties three years later. Although there were undoubtedly individual exceptions, as a group they showed little tendency for "spontaneous" improvement. Indeed, another follow-up performed when the children were in the seventh grade indicated that adjustment problems were still persisting (Zax et al., 1968).

An attempt was made in one of the three schools to intervene with the Red-Tag children and their families to improve the child's difficulties or prevent the development of more serious disorders. School mental health professionals, psychologists, and social workers consulted with teachers and other school personnel rather than doing direct clinical work with the children. In meetings with teachers, the professionals shared information from the screening assessments and worked out strategies for helping the children with adjustment problems. After-school activity programs were also established for children who needed more individualized contact than could be given in the classroom, and various parent-teacher

meetings were arranged to provide ongoing communication about mutual problems.

At the end of three years children in the prevention group were significantly better than control children with respect to absences, grades, reading comprehension, adjustment rating by teachers, and Anxiety and Lie Scale scores on a self-report questionnaire. The program seemed to have been clearly effective in education as well as personal adjustment.

In subsequent studies these authors and their colleagues expanded their resources by using "child-aides". These women, none with college degrees, selected for their warmth, outgoingness, and interest in children, were given six weeks of intensive training. When a teacher felt that a given child's difficulties required more attention than could be given in the classroom, a meeting was arranged with the teacher, a child-aide, and a mental health consultant. Together they tried to understand the child's problems and planned some remedial treatment. The child then saw the child-aide outside the classroom, usually twice a week for 30-minute periods. The nature of these meetings varied depending on the nature of the problem, but one general aim of all such meetings was the development of a warm relationship between the child and the child-aide. The aides used several approaches, including playing games, story telling, recreational activities, or just plain talking with the children. Five half-time aides, at a total cost less than that for a single professional, could see 50 youngsters—a clear demonstration of how individual contacts can be multiplied by the use of paraprofessionals.

Cowen (1968) provides evidence for the effectiveness of the child-aide program as well as of programs using other paraprofessionals such as college students (Cowen, Carlisle, & Kaufman, 1969) and retired persons (Cowen, Leibowitz, & Leibowitz, 1968).

Cowen and his colleagues later expanded their preventive program to include 13 schools that represented a broad range of socioeconomic levels. Again they showed that the child-aide procedure was effective in reducing children's disturbances over a one-year period (Cowen, Lorion, et al., 1975). Most recently an improved version of the intervention procedure was again shown to be effective in four schools over a one-year period (Cowen, Gesten, & Wilson, 1979). In general, the pioneering work of Cowen and his colleagues represents an excellent example of how to translate the abstract principles of community intervention into specific actions and evaluate their effectiveness.

CRITIQUE

That each of our lives is embedded in a social fabric that extends far beyond our immediate friends and family is beyond dispute. Nor can one seriously question the impact of some of these larger social systems on our mental health. The hope, then, that we can prevent or ameliorate certain kinds of abnormal reactions by changing these systems is not entirely unreasonable. It is much too soon to judge the general effectiveness of community approaches since evaluational research is still rare, but it is worthwhile to consider some questions that have been raised about it.

An issue raised by some critics is the question of voluntary consent. Individual treatment is ordinarily something that the patient or family asks for; it is not done to them without their consent. But if you decide

to institute a program of early identification and prevention in the public schools, in what sense should and can you get informed consent from the parents and the larger community of citizens who support the schools? Interventions aimed at reducing psychological handicaps cannot be free of value judgments, and although mental health professionals may feel that a withdrawn, anxious child should be helped to become more outgoing and another child's aggressive outbursts should be reduced, there is no guarantee that the parents or other citizens will always agree with these changes.

Community interventions become social action programs that may have all kinds of educational, political, and economic ramifications, so that the professionals initiating such programs are no longer just clinicians but social activists. Community psychology (or psychiatry) programs occasionally falter because of adverse community reactions. Some of these failures may have been good. In a free society we do not want a small group of mental health professionals deciding what is appropriate and inappropriate in behavior. Community action programs, then, should be open for public inspection and debate, not only because they may otherwise fail but because this practice is consistent with the values of a democratic society. Before any such programs are instituted, health professionals should inform, educate, and listen to the people to be involved—for example, in a school system, the school board, administrators, teachers, and the PTA. If handicapping emotional disorders can indeed be prevented, then it is up to the mental health professionals to show the people involved that preventive programs are in their own self-interest. Most community-oriented professionals are aware of the political and social implications of their endeavors and agree on the importance (even necessity) of informed consent and community participation.

Advocates of community psychology have sometimes seemed to imply that most mental disorders will be eliminated when we correct existing societal evils such as poverty and various kinds of oppressions related to race, sex, or religion. This would seem to be carrying the sociological metaphor too far and ignoring the importance *within* a given community of individual differences in biological makeup and social learning experiences. Poverty, for example, has been eliminated in Sweden for more than a generation. Yet Sweden has one of the highest rates of alcoholism in the world and there are no dramatic differences in rates of various neurotic and psychotic disorders from that of other countries where poverty is still a problem.

Perhaps one of the most promising areas for community psychology has to do with social support systems, which can range from one close friend and confidant to family members to a larger friendship network. There is increasing evidence that a strong social support system is a powerful factor in amelio-

rating and perhaps to some extent preventing psychological disorders. This possibility is suggested by the finding of a correlation between the lack of intimate friends and the frequency of psychological symptoms (Miller & Ingham, 1976). In Chapters 14 and 18 we will see even more evidence for the importance of social support systems as they relate to the development of psychophysiological disorders and depression.

Summary

1. Two sources contributed to the development of group therapy; the group dynamics or T-Group movement and the application of techniques derived from individual approaches such as psychoanalysis and client-centered therapy to the group situation.

2. Advocates of group therapy believe that it is superior to individual therapy in some respects; for example, it requires less generalization to the outside world and provides more opportunities for vicarious learning.

3. T-Groups, sensitivity groups, and encounter groups attempt to help people become more aware of their own feelings and of how their behavior is experienced by others.

4. A major emphasis in all sensitivity-encounter groups is learning to communicate one's feelings honestly to the group. Some leaders are able to facilitate honesty in expression and increase members' self-awareness with a minimum of destructive side effects. In some groups, however, a small percentage of participants appear to be harmed by the experience.

5. Research suggests that T-Groups have some effectiveness in improving human relations skills in relatively "normal" people. For encounter groups the evidence is less clear, but at least according to reports of the participants themselves the experience can produce positive changes.

6. An approach to group therapy based on Transactional Analysis and Gestalt therapy is used rather widely. There are several points of similarity between this approach and the behavioral orientation.

7. Most of the early investigators in the field of family therapy advocated a systems approach in which abnormal behavior was seen as a reflection of pathology in the overall pattern of family interaction. They stressed homeostasis, the tendency for the system to resist changes in its characteristic way of functioning.

8. Therapists who conduct family therapy from a systems point of view tend to focus on the immediate interaction, on who is doing what to whom, rather than on past experiences that produced the present problems or on intrapsychic conflicts in individual family members.

9. Controversy continues between psychodynamic and systems therapists over the amount of attention that should be given to the family system as opposed to individual intrapsychic conflicts. Likewise, they disagree as to how strong or universal is the tendency for families to maintain homeostasis. Sometimes constructive changes are welcomed by other family members rather than resisted.

10. Research to date suggests that both nonbehavioral and behavioral family therapies are effective and probably more effective than traditional insight therapy with a single family member.

11. Many therapists use essentially the same approach in treating couples as they do with the larger family. Behavioral marriage therapy frequently involves the negotiation of a contract that sets up certain reinforcement contingencies for desired changes in behavior; it also involves aiding the couple in verbally resolving conflicts.

12. Research indicates that marital therapy involving behavioral contracting or structured communication training, or both, is effective.

13. In the community approach we extend our view to those larger systems in which individuals and families are embedded—the school, the neighborhood, the church, city or national government, and so on. It is assumed that these larger systems play a role in the development of certain kinds of abnormal behavior.

14. Proponents of community orientation advocate prevention, or early detection and treatment. To this end they actively seek intervention in the community rather than waiting for patients to come to them, consult with others such as schoolteachers and policemen as a way of expanding their impact, train paraprofessionals as yet another way to increase the availability of mental health services, and offer crisis intervention.

15. Social support systems would seem to be an especially significant factor in ameliorating or preventing some psychological disorders.

16. The prevention and early detection of disorders in young children is a natural outgrowth of the community view. Research already suggests that such an approach can indeed be effective for school-related problems.

17. Controversies about the community approach center around questions of how much of a social activist the mental health professional should be and of carrying the sociological metaphor too far, ignoring within community individual differences in biological makeup and social learning experiences.

Suggested Readings

I. D. Yalom's *The theory and practice of group psychotherapy* (Basic Books, 1970) is an especially good introduction to this field; *Encounter groups: First facts* (Basic Books, 1973), by M. A. Lieberman, I. D. Yalom, and M. B. Miles, provides much information about the nature and variety of encounter groups as well as a research evaluation of their effectiveness. A good clinical description of family therapy from a systems point of view is S. Minuchin's *Families and family therapy* (Harvard University Press, 1974). A. Y. Napier with C. A. Whitaker provide an interesting and provocative account of family therapy with one family in *The family crucible* (Harper & Row, 1978). A social learning approach to family interventions can be found in *Families: Applications of social learning to family life* by G. R. Patterson (Research Press, 1971) and to marriage therapy in N. S. Jacobson and G. Margolin, *Marital therapy* (Brunner/Mazel, 1979). The field of community psychology is surveyed in P. A. Mann, *Community psychology: Concepts and applications* (The Free Press, 1978).

13
Psychophysio-logical Disorders

- It's all in the mind—or is it?

- Can what you think actually kill you?

- What happens to your chances of getting high blood pressure or other symptoms if you take a job as an air traffic controller or your present job is terminated?

- What kind of person is most likely to get a heart attack? To have high blood pressure?

- Did you know that blacks are more than two times as likely to have dangerously high blood pressure as whites? Why is that?

- Are asthma attacks caused by allergic reactions or patterns of family interaction—or both?

- What works best in treating high blood pressure and migraine headaches—biofeedback or simple relaxation training?

- Are your chances of developing a psychophysiological disorder less if you have close, supportive relationships with other people?

Wanda D.: The Emotional Origins of Disease

Wanda D. was a bright, active girl, the middle child in a family of five children. Her childhood was healthy. In adolescence, she was inclined to commit herself to too many projects at once and then have deadline problems. Her first psychophysiological episode occurred at the age of 15, at a time when she was under stress because of the death of her father, resulting in family dislocation and poverty, and the knowledge that her mother was dying. She herself was preparing to attend a national conference a few days hence. As she was walking to town, she became dizzy and broke out in hives (urticaria). She fainted a few minutes later. She was treated at a nearby clinic with a mild tranquilizer and brief bed rest. During the next two months, she had several anxiety attacks, with feelings that she could not breathe or was dying.

Wanda remained well, aside from periodic mild depressions, until the age of 27, when she first developed migraine headaches with severe, throbbing head pain and nausea. The headaches began abruptly as she was adjusting to living alone in a foreign country. They continued and increased in frequency during the next year, when she was simultaneously breaking off a long, stormy love affair and working at a high-pressure editorial job. Headaches were typically weekend episodes, but gradually spread to Fridays and then Thursdays. Treatment with ergotamine tartrate, a blood-vessel-constricting agent commonly used to treat migraine, sometimes shortened attacks, but did not prevent them. When she left this job and tried to make a new life in another city, the headaches decreased. During this period she had trouble finding another job; women were not being hired at the executive level in this new city, and she was told she was overqualified for lesser jobs. She found herself frequently depressed and exhausted.

Later, in debt from six months of unemployment, she undertook two demanding jobs simultaneously, working 100 hours or so a week. In one of the two jobs, she had frequent clashes with a boss who did not believe women should work. Headaches still occurred infrequently, but she was feeling more and more fatigued. She attributed the fatigue to overwork and did not see a doctor until she fainted at work. It was found that she was bleeding briskly from a gastric ulcer, and there was reason to believe that she had been bleeding slowly over many months before she hemorrhaged; hence her fatigue came from anemia as well as overwork. She was hospitalized for 12 days and received six pints of blood. Further treatment consisted of barbiturates, a mild diet, antacids, and quitting her jobs on the strong recommendation of her physician.

During the recovery period, she decided to change careers, probably a factor in her remaining free from further life-threatening ulcerations. Migraine headaches, which had ceased with the onset of the hemorrhaging and removal from her stressful life situation, returned but were less frequent and disabling than before. They usually occurred at the onset of her menstrual period, a common trigger in migrainous women. After two years in a teaching job, she decided to get a Ph.D. As might be expected, the pressures of graduate school resulted in further psycho-physiological symptoms in this tense, highly achievement-oriented woman. During the four years of graduate school she developed *Lichen planus* (a highly itchy skin rash), tachycardia, and hypertension. Tachycardia, in which the heartbeat is speeded up and irregular, appeared prior to her preliminary oral examination, when she was also interviewing for jobs in her new field. Heart symptoms were of special concern to her because both her parents had died of heart attacks, but an

> electrocardiogram was normal. However, it was found that she had moderately high blood pressure. When the stress of graduate school ended, all these symptoms disappeared.

Physical symptoms, such as those shown by Wanda, for which there is no apparent organic cause and in which emotional stresses seem to play a role are called psychophysiological disorders. Often when physicians suggest that physical symptoms may have emotional origins and recommend psychotherapy, patients react with anger and fail to seek the therapy. It seems to the patient that to suggest psychotherapy is to imply that a headache is not real. The word "psychosomatic," which combines the Greek words *psyche* or soul with *soma* or body, was the term originally used to categorize psychophysiological disorders, but it has been used loosely and has come to connote "all in your mind." However, the pain is real, the tissue damage is real, and in some cases the patient can die from the disorder.

Although psychophysiological disorders were given a prominent place in earlier DSMs, this term is no longer used in DSM-III and such disorders are now listed under the heading, Psychological Factors Affecting Physical Disorders. This change was apparently made because the authors of DSM-III decided that these disorders were physical diseases and not psychiatric or mental disorders. However, the line between behavioral (or mental) symptoms and physical symptoms cannot be drawn sharply. In anxiety reactions, for example, the behavioral, cognitive, and physiological components are equally important. An additional reason that psychophysiological disorders might have been omitted from DSM-III is that recent evidence suggests that most diseases, even those previously considered as strictly organic in nature such as heart disease and cancer, can be affected by stressful life events and perhaps by personality characteristics. The choice begins to become one of calling almost all diseases psychophysiological or calling none of them by this name and simply recognizing that psychological factors can play a role in any disease process. In DSM-III a psychophysiological disorder such as high blood pressure is listed on Axis III as a physical disorder and the contributing psychological factors are described on Axis I under the heading Psychological Factors Affecting Physical Disorders. In this text I will continue to use the terms *psychophysiological* and *psychosomatic* to refer to disorders where psychological factors have played an important contributing role.

The Mind-Body Problem

In our culture it is hard to view the body and mind as one. No English word exists for the union of body and mind, so we have to import bulky Latin or Greek combinations. The ancient Greeks felt it necessary to treat both the body and soul to effect a cure. When, during the Middle Ages, sinning or demon possession was considered to be the cause of illness, repentance or exorcism was the treatment of choice; people ignored the body, the emotions, and microbial and other physical causes of illness. With the rise of modern science during the Renaissance, the notion of psychic influences on the body began to be regarded as unscientific, and the mind and soul were relegated to the province of religion and philosophy. René Descartes, a French philosopher of the early seventeenth century, attempted to deal with the problem of the relation between mind and body. In his view, the body was physical and operated like a machine, whereas the soul was spiritual and therefore nonphysical. He saw the mind and body as interacting (in the pineal gland of the midbrain) but separate. The advantage of his view at the time was that it freed him and others to proceed with physiological studies without infringing on the domain of the church.

The discovery in the nineteenth century that microorganisms cause some diseases led to a mechanistic medicine in which all disease was seen as resulting from physical damage to cells. Claude Bernard, a great French physician of the mid-nineteenth century, was one of the first in modern times to resist this trend. He emphasized the psychological contribution to the body's ailments. And, of course, one of the great contributions of Freud was his emphasis on psychic causes for the physical symptoms of hysteria. Psychosomatic medicine as a movement within medicine was introduced in this century to counteract the impersonal and mechanistic approach that accompanied the introduction of science into medical education. In this view patients were again to be treated as whole beings whose emotions and life experiences were important in the course of any illness.

Many unusual phenomena support the theory of interaction between psychological processes and bodily ailments. These include voodoo death, target dates for death, and placebo responses. Voodoo death is the sudden, unexplained death of a previously healthy person as the result of a hex or similar threat. Usually all attempts to save such persons fail.

Can people set a target date for death? Not uncommonly, spouses manage to die from no discernible cause shortly after the death of a mate or on the anniversary of the death. Mark Twain, the great American author, was born in 1835 at the advent of Halley's comet and said that he would die when it reappeared in 1910. He did so. Thomas Jefferson, the author of the Declaration of Independence, died on the fiftieth anniversary of its signing. He was near death on July 1 and on July 2 fell into a stupor which lasted until the evening of the 3rd, when he awoke and asked his physician, "Is it the fourth?" His phy-

sician replied, "It soon will be." Jefferson died at 1 P.M. on July 4. Another signer of the Declaration, John Adams, simultaneously on his deathbed, also died on the same day. His last words were, "Thomas Jefferson still lives."

Another example of the intimate interactions between psychological and physiological events is the placebo phenomenon, which we discussed when evaluating psychotherapy in Chapter 10. For example, Frankenhaeuser et al. (1963) gave white or pink capsules, both inert placebos, to subjects on two different occasions. The white capsule was described to the subjects as a sleeping pill, the pink capsule as a stimulant. This manipulation of beliefs about the same placebo (except for color) had definite and opposite effects on the subjects' self-reports of alertness, speed on a reaction-time test, and also produced appropriate changes in heart rate and blood pressure.

All of these phenomena—voodoo death, target dates for death, and placebo responses—strongly imply that a person's beliefs and attitudes can have a profound effect on physiological reactions.

Types of Psychophysiological Disorders

Traditionally psychophysiological disorders have been defined as physical symptoms that are caused, at least in part, by emotional factors and tend to involve bodily functions under autonomic nervous system innervation. The physiological changes observed are usually those that normally accompany certain emotional states, but in these disorders the changes are more intense and sustained.

Psychophysiological disorders occur most commonly in six organ systems: skin, musculoskeletal, respiratory, cardiovascular, gastrointestinal, and genitourinary. Examples of each type are listed in Table 13-1. It is important, especially when planning treatment, to differentiate these disorders from conversion symptoms, but sometimes it is difficult, especially with musculoskeletal symptoms such as backache. In contrast to conversion reactions, psychophysiological disorders tend to involve organ sys-

Beliefs and expectations can have a powerful effect on bodily processes. In this picture a Brazilian Macumba voodoo doctor (*cavalo*) is bringing one of the congregation into a trance (the cigar is part of the ceremony).

TABLE 13-1
Some Common Forms of Traditionally Labeled Psychophysiological Disorders

I. Skin

Eczema	An inflammatory skin disease most common on hands and face. Lesions vary greatly in different patients: There may be dry patches, red patches, blisters, oozing, edema (swelling), scales, crusts, or pustules from secondary infection.
Urticaria (hives)	A skin eruption (often in response to allergenic substances such as shellfish, penicillin, or insect bite) characterized by large, smooth, circular wheals either redder or paler than surrounding skin. Itching may be severe.
Neuro-dermatitis (lichen simplex)	A chronic, itching, lichenlike outbreak of the skin most typically on the nape of the neck, inner thighs, pubic region, or backs of the hands. The skin lesion is commonly dark brown or purple in color with deep creases caused by constant rubbing and irritation.

II. Musculoskeletal

Backache	
Muscle cramps	
Tension headache	Headache caused by chronic tension in muscles of the neck and scalp.

III. Respiratory

Hyperven-tilation	Overbreathing; excessive rapid and deep breathing.
Bronchial asthma	Attacks of difficult breathing associated with cough, feeling of tightness in chest, and wheezing on expiration of breath. Chest may be held almost fully extended in effort to breathe. Low fever may be present.

IV. Cardiovascular

Paroxysmal tachycardia	The heart speeds up (*tachycardia* is Greek for "fast heart") to over 100 beats per minute in erratic fits.
Hypertension	High blood pressure, either erratic or chronic. May be no symptoms until damage is severe. May lead to heart and kidney failure, retinal damage, or a stroke.
Raynaud's phenome-non or disease	Spasmodic obstruction of peripheral arteries. Fingers (sometimes toes) become white or lead-blue, cold, and numb, and sometimes ache. Later blood flow is excessive; fingers become blotchy, turn red, and throb or tingle. In severe cases, gangrene may result.
Migraine	Periodic vascular headache, usually one-sided and accompanied by nausea.

V. Gastrointestinal

Gastritis	Inflammation of the stomach. Symptoms include gastric discomfort or pain, nausea, loss of appetite, belching, and distention of the stomach with gas.
Peptic or duodenal ulcer	An open sore on the wall of the esophagus, stomach, or duodenum caused in part by excessive production of pepsin and hydrochloric acid. Symptoms include nausea, discomfort or sharp pain an hour or two after eating, and, in severe cases, bleeding, which may be noted in vomitus or the passing of tarry black stools.
Colitis	Inflammation of the colon leading in *ulcerative* colitis to ulcers and bleeding with symptoms such as lower abdominal pain, diarrhea, constipation, anemia, and sometimes fever. In *mucous* colitis, mucus is passed in the stools. Symptoms include indigestion, poor appetite, and, less often, gas formation and

TABLE 13-1
Some Common Forms of Traditionally Labeled Psychophysiological Disorders (*Continued*)

V. *Gastrointestinal*		VI. *Genitourinary* (continued)	
	resulting distension. Current medical opinion tends to downplay psychological factors and leans toward an autoimmunological explanation.	Polymenor-rhea	Abnormally frequent menstrual periods.
		Dysmenorrhea	Painful menstruation.
			DISTURBANCES OF SEXUALITY
Hyperacidity	Excessive production of hydrochloric acid in the stomach.	Impotence	Sexual inadequacy in the male typified by either failure of penile erection or failure to maintain an erection.
Heartburn	A burning sensation in the esophagus and stomach, often with sour belching.	Premature ejaculation	
Nervous eructation	Nervous belching after air swallowing.	Orgasmic dys-function	Failure of sexual response in the female, ranging from sexual indifference to inability to achieve orgasm.
Spastic colon	The descending colon contracts tightly, causing vague attacks of abdominal pain and diarrhea.	Vaginismus	Spasm of the vagina, making sexual intercourse difficult, painful, or impossible, depending on its extent. *Dyspareunia* (from the Greek for "badly mated") is the general term for difficult or painful intercourse in women.
Chronic constipation or diarrhea			*URINARY DISORDERS*
		Dysurea	Painful or difficult urination. *Psychic* dysurea is inability or difficulty in passing urine in the presence of other persons.
VI. *Genitourinary*		Polyurea	Passing of excessive amounts of urine.
	MENSTRUAL DISORDERS	Enuresis	Involuntary urination, especially during sleep; bedwetting.
Amenorrhea	Absence or abnormal stoppage of menstrual flow.		
Menorrhagia	Excessive flow during menstruation.		

tems not under voluntary control. They are less likely to reduce anxiety and to have a symbolic meaning. Moreover, in psychophysiological disorders, actual tissue damage can occur, as in the development of a bleeding ulcer, whereas the paralyses, tics, and sensory disturbances of hysteria ordinarily involve no tissue damage.

Psychophysiological disorders mainly involve body functions under autonomic nervous system innervation. (This system was described in some detail in Chapter 7.) The adaptive significance of most features of the autonomic nervous system in our evolutionary past is apparent. For example, in circumstances requiring an aggressive attack or instant flight, the increased heartbeat, blood pressure, blood flow to heart, brain, and muscles, epinephrine secretion, and so on associated with activation of the sym-pathetic division are essential. The digestive and eliminative functions of the parasympathetic division are likewise important during periods of rest and recuperation.

In the jungle environment of prehistory, emergencies requiring attack or flight tended to be resolved one way or another in a fairly short order. You either escaped from the saber-toothed tiger and your autonomic reaction subsided, or you did not escape; there was no prolonged autonomic reaction in that case, either. In our present civilization, however, inhibitions and restraints are imposed upon overt acts of aggression or flight. When we experience continuing threats to our prestige or self-esteem, many of us are likely to experience autonomic reactions that are not easily terminated. Although persons with strong physiological alarm systems were best equipped to survive in the past, in modern society these reactions can be maladaptive.

Incidence

The incidence of psychophysiological disorders is hard to determine because chronic illnesses tend to be underreported. The findings of Schwab et al. (1974) may represent as good an estimate of at least some kinds of psychophysiological disorders as any. These authors randomly sampled residents in a North Florida county that includes both urban and rural populations. The percentages of the sample reporting that they had experienced during the last year either regularly or occasionally certain physical symptoms usually labeled psychophysiological are shown in Table 13-2. Headaches, stomach, and eliminative problems are reported by a high percentage of the sample. In Table 13-3 percentages of individuals reporting two or more of these symptoms *regularly* are broken down by race, sex, and income. Blacks, females, and low-income persons clearly are more susceptible to these disorders. The dramatically higher incidence of these disorders among the poor should puncture the myth that stomach upsets, ulcers, and high blood pressure are the special province of the striving, ambitious executive.

The blood pressure statistics were further confirmed by direct measurement of blood pressure in a subsample of cases. Abnormally high blood pressures were obtained in 36 percent of the blacks and 15 percent of the whites. This finding is consistent with those of other investigators that hypertension in black persons is more than twice as common as in white persons (N. M. Kaplan, 1974). Hypertension is particularly deadly to black men, who seem to have less resistance to the disease than black women. Reasons for the racial difference in hypertensive disease are not clear, but genetic factors, skin pigmentation (dark-skinned blacks have a greater degree of hypertension than lighter-skinned blacks), environmental stresses, dietary differences, obesity, enzyme differences, and resistance to hypertensive drugs have all been suggested.

Schwab et al.'s finding that women more often have psychophysiological disorders than men has also been supported by other research. For example,

TABLE 13-2
Percentages Reporting Psychophysiological Symptoms in the Previous Year (*N* = 1645)

Symptoms	Regularly	Occasionally
Headaches	8.7	38.0
Nervous stomach	5.2	17.5
Diarrhea	0.9	14.4
Hypertension	6.2	8.0
Asthma	1.9	2.9
Ulcers	0.9	1.4
Colitis	0.4	0.9

Adapted from Schwab, Fennell, and Warheit (1974). Copyright 1974 The Academy of Psychosomatic Medicine and reproduced with permission.

Gove and Tudor (1973) found 137 women to every 81 men received treatment for these disorders in hospitals. Why this is so is unknown. Gove and Tudor think it is because women's roles are more stressful and less rewarding than men's rather than because women are more open to admitting symptoms. Specific differences by sex are peculiar, particularly for ulcers. Women used to suffer ulcers more frequently than men; the incidence in 1900 was reported as 12:1. By the 1930s, men were as likely as women to have gastric ulcers, and by the late 1950s to the early 1960s, the incidence was three or four men to one

TABLE 13-3
Percentages Reporting Two or More Symptoms Regularly by Race, Sex, and Income

Sociodemographic Group	Percent[a]
Race	
White	16
Black	23
Sex	
Male	10
Female	23
Income, thousands of dollars	
0–3	30
3–6	24
6–10	17.5
10–15	11
15+	10

[a]Figures rounded to nearest whole number.
Adapted from Schwab, Fennell, and Warheit (1974). Copyright 1974 The Academy of Psychosomatic Medicine and reproduced with permission.

woman. The present ratio appears to favor men 2:1; in other words, ulcers are again increasing in women. In general, heart conditions, asthma, ulcers, and neurodermatitis are far more common in men, whereas migraine, rheumatoid arthritis, and colitis are more common in women.

Among persons aged 25 to 64, coronary heart disease causes more mortality and disability than any other disease. It is the leading cause of death for men aged 35 and over and is responsible for one-third of all deaths in the United States, while stroke (cerebrovascular disease) accounts for 11 percent of all deaths. The mortality rate from coronary heart disease for white men is 2.75 to 6.50 times greater than that for white women. However, House (1974) reports that heart disease is beginning to increase in women aged 35 to 54.

Development

In outlining causative factors in psychopathology in Chapter 5 I indicated that the abnormal behavior or symptom results from an interaction between immediate stressful circumstances and personality dis-

Psychophysiological disorders can produce actual tissue damage. In this photograph of an autopsy specimen the arrow points to an ulcer in the duodenum (that portion of the small intestine that joins to the stomach), which has perforated into the pancreas, seen to the right and below.

positions to respond to stress in certain characteristic ways. Nowhere is this interaction so clear as in psychophysiological disorders. Let us consider first the stress side of this interaction.

IMMEDIATE STRESSES

The stress theory proposed by Selye (1956) suggests that the body's emergency resources may become exhausted during prolonged stressful experiences that demand chronic mobilization of the body's alarm-response mechanisms. At this point appear psychophysiological symptoms, which Selye terms "diseases of adaptation." Wanda's symptoms were almost always precipitated or made worse by life stresses: Her first case of hives followed the death of her father and preceded an important national conference that she was to attend; her migraine headaches became worse when she was breaking off a long, stormy love affair and working at a high-pressure editorial job; her gastric ulcer developed while she was working 100 hours a week and clashing with a boss; and so on.

The job of air traffic controller is generally assumed to be a rather stressful occupation inasmuch as the lives of many airline passengers depend upon these individuals' continued attention and accurate decision making. If psychophysiological disorders are related to stress, then one might expect the incidence of such disorders to be higher in persons so employed. That is, in fact, what Cobb and Rose (1973) found. The annual incidence of new cases of hypertension was nearly six times as high in a sample of air traffic controllers as in a comparison group of second class airmen (a classification of individuals licensed to fly airplanes). Furthermore, the incidence of hypertension for air traffic controllers working at high traffic density centers (presumably more stressful) was significantly higher than those working at low traffic density centers. Similar results were obtained for peptic ulcers.

A high cholesterol level is thought to be one predisposing factor to coronary heart disease. When cholesterol levels were compared from January through June in two groups of accountants, one of which was heavily involved in tax work with an April 15 deadline, the levels were found to rise sharply, in the tax accountants only, starting March 1 and decreasing again shortly after the deadline (Friedman

The incidence of high blood pressure has been found to be higher in individuals who perform the stressful job of air traffic controller.

& Rosenman, 1975). A longitudinal study of blue-collar workers whose jobs were abolished (Cobb, 1974) gives further support to the stress hypothesis. The mean rate of norepinephrine excretion (an indication of sympathetic nervous system arousal) and the level of blood cholesterol were significantly elevated before and at termination of their jobs, and had slowly returned to normal after 24 months, by which time most men had found new jobs. A preliminary report covering blood pressure changes in these same men (Kasl & Cobb, 1970) showed that blood pressure levels in men who were not fired did not change; for those who were fired, blood pressure increases were greater during the period when job loss was anticipated than in the year afterward, and blood pressure remained high in men who had trouble finding new jobs after job loss.

A self-report questionnaire measure of life changes (both positive and negative) occurring in the recent past has been found in several studies to correlate with the frequency of illnesses (for example, Rahe, 1968). Subsequent research, however, has shown that it is the life changes experienced as negative or distressing that may be more important in predicting physical illness or psychological problems, not the changes experienced as positive (for example, Mueller et al., 1977). Some sample items from a recently developed scale of this kind called the Life Experiences Survey (Sarason et al., 1978) are shown in Table 13-4.

TABLE 13-4
Some Sample Items from The Life Experiences Survey

Death of a spouse
Male: Wife or girl friend's pregnancy
Female: Pregnancy
Changed work situation (for example, new responsibilities)
Serious illness of close family member
Change of residence
Marital separation
For students only:
   Beginning a new school experience (for example, starting college)
   Academic probation
   Failing an important exam
   Joining a fraternity/sorority

From Sarason, Johnson, and Siegel (1978).
NOTE: The person is asked to indicate whether the event occurred within 6 months or from 7 to 12 months previously and is asked to rate on a seven-point scale how positively or negatively each event was experienced.

In conclusion, there is ample evidence that stressful life events can adversely affect physical health. However, we still have to explain why some people respond to a given stressful experience with physical symptoms and others do not.

Prisoners of war frequently experience prolonged stresses that affect their psychological and physical health.

THE SOCIAL SUPPORT SYSTEM: A BUFFER AGAINST STRESS?

An impressive array of studies have begun to suggest that if one has a social network of supportive friends and family, stressful life events will produce less illness (and psychological symptoms too) than if one does not have such a support system (for example, Berkman & Syme, 1979). Let us return to the study of blue-collar workers who lost their jobs (Cobb, 1974). Recall that their cholesterol levels were significantly elevated during the period surrounding their job loss. When these men were divided into a group that reported having considerable support from wives, friends, and relatives and a group lacking in such support, the latter showed significantly greater increases in levels of cholesterol associated with the unemployment period and less decrease in cholesterol levels 24 months later. In this same study men filled out a symptom checklist. One of the items was indicative of arthritis, a swelling in the joints. For men reporting low social support 41 percent said they had experienced two or more swollen joints during this period. For those high in social support only 3.6 percent said they had two or more swollen joints. As a final example, de Araujo et al. (1973) measured the average daily doses of steroids given to adult asthma patients to control their asthmatic attacks. The patients had filled out a Life Change Questionnaire and the investigators had made an assessment of social support. As can be seen in Table 13-5, when recent life changes were high and social supports were low, the steroid doses were more than three times higher than when social supports were high. The presence of social supports seemed to provide complete protection from increased need for steroid drugs as seen in the fact that the doses were essentially the same for individuals high and low on life changes when both groups had high social support. Lack of social supports in and of itself is not producing the higher need for steroids to control the asthma because the low life change, low social supports group is also low in steroid dosage.

All of these studies then, as well as others reviewed by Cobb (1976), suggest that the harmful effects of stressful life events can be reduced by the presence of an effective social support system. A word of caution: These studies are correlational, and cause and effect may be difficult to determine. For example, it is possible that people with strong social support systems may also be people who have certain personality characteristics that make it easy for them to develop intimate friendships and also help them cope with stresses. In this case it is the personality characteristic that is the important variable, not the social network per se.

PERSONALITY DISPOSITIONS

Given a stressful event, with or without certain moderating circumstances such as social supports, why do some individuals develop psychophysiological disorders, whereas others do not? Why does one person develop high blood pressure and another peptic ulcer? The answers to these questions, of course, involve dispositions to respond in certain ways to certain situations and reflect a lifetime of interaction between biological and social learning factors. For psychophysiological disorders the biological factors are clearly of considerable importance, and let us consider them first.

Biological Vulnerabilities. Different patterns of autonomic reactivity, possibly inherited, have been identified in infants before social learning can have much effect (Richmond et al., 1962). These individual differences continue in the older child or adult, and a given individual is likely to show the same response pattern to any stress, or even to nonstressful stimuli. Hypertensive patients, for example, were reported by Hodapp et al. (1975) to react with blood pressure changes to "stressors" that objectively were not stressful (projected color slides of neutral scenes)

TABLE 13-5
Average Daily Steroid Dosage in Milligrams per Day for Patients with Asthma as a Function of Life Change Score and Social Support

Life Change Score	Social Support	
	High	Low
High	5.6	19.6
Low	5.0	6.7

From de Araujo, van Arsdel, Holmes, and Dudley (1973). Copyright 1973 by Pergamon Press Ltd. and reproduced with permission.

in the same way as to situations with stressful impact. Normal controls showed no blood pressure changes in response to the slides.

Those with high levels of autonomic reactivity also vary in which system they respond with. Some are muscle tension overreactors, others cardiovascular, and others gastrointestinal. In still others, such as Wanda, many or all subsystems affected by the autonomic nervous system are overreactive. It is as if their homeostatic mechanisms were a thermostat that consistently overshot and then undershot the moderate regions of psychophysiological balance.

A related explanation of why a person develops a disorder in one organ system and not another is the concept of *organ vulnerability.* In some individuals, a specific organ or organ system has been weakened or made vulnerable by either inheritance or illness. Under stress the psychophysiological symptom is most likely to appear in the susceptible organ. For example, between 70 and 80 percent of childhood asthmatics have had some respiratory illness before the asthma developed. A biological predisposition to excrete high levels of pepsinogen (an enzyme that aids digestion in the stomach) may make some individuals more prone to develop ulcers. Although scattered bits of evidence indicate the importance of such biological dispositions, much remains to be understood about how these factors contribute to specific psychophysiological disorders.

Specific Conflicts and Attitudes. Within the psychodynamic tradition there developed a view that each kind of psychosomatic disorder was associated with a specific personality trait or type of psychological conflict. Asthma, for example, was thought to represent an inhibited cry for maternal help provoked by fear that one's own demandingness or sexual fantasies might incite abandonment by one's mother. Peptic ulcers were thought to result from intense conflicts associated with repressed dependency needs, and individuals with migraine headaches were considered to be perfectionistic, rigid, intelligent, and to have unrealistic achievement goals. Clinicians have not always been in agreement, some proposing one kind of attitude or conflict associated with a given disorder, others proposing quite different characteristics. Nor has research been especially supportive of a high degree of specificity of personality characteristics for each disorder. In broad outline it would ap-

pear that certain personality characteristics, ways of coping with stress, might predispose one to a variety of physical ailments, the specific disorder depending more on biological dispositions than the specific psychological conflict. However, there may be some partial truths in the specificity hypothesis, as some of the following research suggests.

Personality and High Blood Pressure. Psychodynamic therapists have for many years proposed a relationship between suppressed anger and essential hypertension (for example, Saul, 1939). Our language is full of sayings that assume such a relationship: "Don't get your blood pressure up," "She was flushed with anger," "He reddened with anger." Hokanson and his collaborators have provided extensive experimental verification for this idea. Hokanson and Burgess (1962), for example, had an experimenter frustrate and anger subjects, and these subjects showed significant increases in systolic blood pressure and heart rate compared to nonfrustrated subjects. Then half of the frustrated subjects were given a chance to retaliate verbally against their frustrators in the guise of a questionnaire evaluation of the conduct of the research. Those subjects who were allowed to express their anger in this way showed a return to their prefrustration levels of blood pressure and heart rate; whereas those not given this opportunity maintained their elevated levels. These results are clearly consistent with the theory that unexpressed anger is associated with increased blood pressure.

Turning to individuals with already existing hypertension, early results were somewhat inconclusive with respect to an association between chronically aroused but inhibited anger and high blood pressure (McGinn et al., 1964), but more recently there has been some support for this theory with hypertensives reporting stronger hostile feelings and *fewer* aggressive actions than normotensives on a personality inventory (Esler et al., 1977).

McClelland (1979) has developed a theory of hypertension that is related to the suppressed anger view. He suggests that three factors are associated with the development of high blood pressure: (a) a high need for power, (b) a strong tendency to inhibit the overt expression of this need in the form of aggressive actions, and (c) strong situational challenges to use power. In various tests of this theory Mc-

Clelland measured "need for power" from stories told to pictures (a version of the TAT described in Chapter 6). Story imagery involving having an impact on others by aggression, persuasion, accumulating signs of prestige, and so on were coded as indicative of a need for power. Steele (1973) provided some evidence for the validity of this measure and its relation to autonomic arousal. He found after the need for power was experimentally aroused that the more power imagery there was in the TAT stories the greater were the epinephrine and norepinephrine in the urine of the subjects.

McClelland (1979) reported three studies of his own. In the first, 77 German men with hypertension were compared with 50 German men without hypertension on story-derived measures of power imagery and power inhibition. The power inhibition score was simply the number of times the word *not* was used in the stories, a measure found by McClelland (1975) to be a good index of the extent to which people control their actions. Twenty percent of the hypertensive men were found to have the high power, high inhibition combination compared to 4 percent of the normotensive men. The low absolute values of these percentages may reflect the fact that these data had been collected to measure other variables and that the pictures were not designed to elicit power themes.

In the second study McClelland found that college males who had stronger power motives than affiliative motives (the desire to be in friendly relations with people) and were also high in need to inhibit power had higher blood pressures, especially diastolic blood pressure, than did students with all other combinations of these variables, such as power stronger than affiliation but low need to inhibit power. It is rather impressive that at this age, around 18 on the average, these young men's blood pressures already showed some relationship to their personality styles. The students were not hypertensive, however. Their blood pressures were all in the normal range. The results nevertheless raise the question of whether the men showing the high-power/high-inhibition combination might not be at greater risk for developing high blood pressure later in life.

McClelland's third study was designed to shed light on this question. Seventy-eight males whose blood pressures were recorded during their junior year in college (around 1940) and approximately every five years thereafter until 1972–1974 were sub-

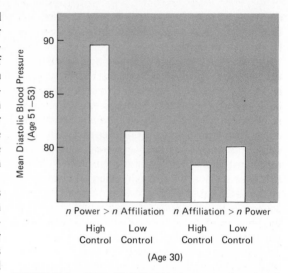

FIGURE 13-1. Mean diastolic blood pressure in men of age 51–53, classified by their power motive type at age 30. (From D. C. McClelland, Inhibited power motivation and high blood pressure in men. *Journal of Abnormal Psychology*, 1979, *88*, 182–190. Copyright 1979 by American Psychological Association and reproduced with permission.)

jects in this longitudinal study. During 1950–1952 they told stories related to five pictures, and these were scored for power, affiliation, and inhibition in the same manner as in the second study. The results were striking. Men who when age 30 had power scores greater than affiliation scores and high inhibition scores had significantly higher diastolic blood pressures at ages 51–53. See Figure 13-1. At the most recent checkup, six men were under treatment for hypertension, 14 had elevated blood pressures (diastolic pressure over 90 mm Hg), and five had died of cardiovascular disease. Of the 23 men classified in the power greater than affiliation and high inhibition group, 61 percent (14) had shown definite signs of hypertension in their early fifties, as compared with only 23 percent (11) of the 47 men classified in the other three categories. This rather remarkable study, then, suggests that a personality pattern of a strong but inhibited need for power, not softened by high affiliative needs, existed *before* the development of high blood pressure. The relationship is not perfect. The correlation between degree of inhibited power motive at age 30 and diastolic blood pressure at age 51–53 was .41. This means that other factors such as changing motive patterns, various life experiences, biological dispositions and illnesses can also affect the development of hypertension. There was also no assessment of McClelland's third factor, situational challenges to power, in this study. More information on that variable might have made it possible to predict elevated blood pressure even more accurately, or it might be that power challenges were fairly common in most of these men's lives and therefore would not have added much to individual prediction. Although at first glance McClelland's findings appear to support the specificity hypothesis, a specific psychological conflict associated with hypertension, we cannot conclude that this is the case until it can be shown that this same conflict is not associated with other disorders.

McClelland's theory is consistent with a psychological interpretation of the high rates of hypertension in black males, who would seem to be high on all three factors proposed to contribute to this disorder. There is some evidence that black males score high on power needs in TAT stories (Veroff et al., 1960); because of discrimination and lack of realistic avenues to power they have frequently had to inhibit overt power striving, and yet at the same time they have constantly felt the challenge to do something about their relatively powerless status.

Personality and Heart Disease. One line of research has suggested that a certain cluster of traits,

Research suggests that people with Type A personalities (competitive, impatient, tense) have a greater likelihood of developing coronary heart disease.

TABLE 13-6
Characteristic Behaviors of a Type A Person

1. Speaks explosively, hurriedly, uses limited vocabulary. Impatient with discursive or slow speech in others.
2. Walks, eats, moves rapidly.
3. Gets impatient at the rate at which events occur, such as the movement of traffic. Sets unnecessary deadlines.
4. Strives to do two or more things at once (such as drinking coffee while dictating letters).
5. Always strives to bring conversations around to preferred topics; often only pretends to listen to others.
6. Feels guilty for relaxing. *Very* competitive in sports.
7. Does not notice interesting or lovely things in the environment (for instance, would not stop to look at a beautiful scene).
8. Is preoccupied with getting things (*having*) rather than becoming something worth *being*.
9. Attempts to schedule more and more activities in less and less time.
10. Challenges other Type A persons aggressively.
11. Has certain nervous gestures such as fist-clenching, table-banging, or facial tics.
12. Attributes success to speed.
13. Evaluates people on the basis of numbers, such as amount of sales, number of publications, or appendectomies performed.

Adapted from Friedman and Rosenman (1975), pp. 100–102.

called the Type A personality, is associated with greater risk for coronary heart disease (Friedman & Rosenman, 1975). The *Type A personality* is characterized by "excessive competitive drive, aggressiveness, impatience, and a harrying sense of time urgency" (p. 14). "Free-floating hostility" is also present and ready to be triggered by any event perceived as irritating, such as having to wait in line. More specific characteristics of Type A are listed in Table 13-6. The Type B person simply does not show Type A behaviors: The person is not hurried or harried, relaxes easily, plays for fun rather than to display superiority, is not hostile, and is more concerned with *being,* or the quality of existence, than with *doing* and amassing numerical proof of success.

Typical studies as summarized by Friedman and Rosenman (1975) and House (1974) of the link between heart disease and Type A personality involve classifying a group of apparently healthy men (most studies have used men as subjects) into Type A or Type B and following them over periods as long as ten years. Results show that Type A persons are significantly higher than Type Bs on heart disease risk factors. For example, they have higher serum cholesterol levels (despite highly similar diets) and smoke more cigarettes than Type Bs. It is known that persons smoking more than ten cigarettes a day are three times more likely than nonsmokers to suffer early onset of coronary heart disease, but even when amount of smoking was controlled in comparing Type A to Type B persons, Type As had considerably higher rates of heart disease. In general, depending upon the study, Type As have been found to have from 1.4 to as high as 6.5 times as many heart attacks as Type Bs; Type As are also at higher risk for recurrent and fatal heart attacks (House, 1974).

However, personality is not the sole cause: There is an interplay between psychological traits and situational factors, as House has emphasized. It is possible, for example, that Type As, with their high degree of ambition and competitiveness, seek out jobs of higher stress. Wanda showed many features of the Type A personality. She was ambitious, striving, and seemed to seek out high-pressure situations such as holding two jobs simultaneously or entering a Ph.D. program. Some of her symptoms—tachycardia, migraine, and fainting—were cardiovascular in nature.

Liljefors and Rahe (1970) reported a unique study in which hereditary factors were controlled by studying identical twin pairs who were discordant for coronary heart disease. More specifically each twin was rated on a seven-category scale of degree of coronary heart disease: for example, a score of 1 indicated a definite previous heart attack; a score of 3 indicated a history of angina pectoris (chest pains associated with constricted coronary arteries) and electrocardiogram changes provoked during exercise; a score of 7 indicated no past or present evidence of heart disease. On the basis of an interview the twins were also rated on such psychosocial dimensions as Devotion to Work, Lack of Leisure (these first two are similar to Type A traits), Home Dissatisfactions, and Life Dissatisfactions. Then for each pair of twins they computed a difference score between the twins' ratings

of severity of heart disease and another difference score between the twins' ratings on the psychosocial variables. It was then possible to answer the question: When there is a large difference between degree of heart disease in the two twins (say one had had an actual heart attack and the other had had no history of heart disease) will the twin who has heart disease show more devotion to work, greater life dissatisfactions, and so on? The answer to the question was generally yes. The correlation between the difference in heart disease variable and a combined difference score on all psychosocial measures was .47. The Life Dissatisfactions measure tended to show the strongest relationship among the several psychosocial variables. In contrast to the twins with heart disease, the twins without were more able to relax during time away from work, took more leisurely breaks during their work day, rarely worked overtime, and when at home primarily read or watched TV. They always took their vacations. The twins with relatively severe heart disease felt that their education was inadequate for the jobs they had, reported poor childhood and adult interpersonal relationships (Did they lack effective social supports?), and were more dissatisfied with their income level.

Surprisingly there were no differences in medical variables usually found to be associated with heart disease, such as cigarette smoking, blood pressure and cholesterol levels, or obesity. These biological variables probably do contribute to heart disease risk but the exact matching on genetic makeup in this study may have reduced individual differences within twin pairs on these variables to a point where they were essentially controlled, permitting the psychosocial variables to be especially salient.

The psychosocial measures in this study probably reflect a mixture of stressful life events and personality traits (similar to Type A), so that one cannot conclude that it is a personality dimension per se that is crucial, although the results are consistent with that possibility. With respect to specificity for heart disease it is of interest to note that for two co-twins who scored high on stressful psychosocial characteristics but did not have heart disease, one was found to have a peptic ulcer and the other was a chronic alcoholic. The combination of stressful life events and Type A personality may not be specific for heart disease.

Personality and Cancer. There is a long history of speculation about the contribution of psychological factors to cancer. In the second century A.D. the Greek physician Galen proposed that cancer occurred more frequently in melancholic than sanguine (cheerful and expressive) women. Current speculations tend to center around depressive feelings such as hopelessness and the inability to express emotions, especially anger (for a summary of these views see Holden, 1978). One of the better researches in this area is that of Greer and Morris (1975), who did *not* find a relationship between either depression or frequency of life stresses and breast cancer, but did find an association between the extent to which emotions, especially anger, are inhibited or excessively expressed and breast cancer (see Research Report 13-1). Findings as potentially as important as these should be replicated, however, before we accept them as true. The search for causes of cancer has produced too many false leads to warrant accepting any one finding as conclusive. A similar finding for the role of emotions in patients with lung cancer as opposed to controls with noncancerous lung dis-eases was reported by Kissen (1963, 1969); the significant difference was described as "restricted outlet for emotional discharge" in the lung cancer patients. Through what kind of biological mechanism emotional inexpressiveness might lead to cancer remains to be determined, as well as whether this characteristic is related to other forms of cancer.

Learning and Personality Dispositions. Just how classical conditioning, operant learning, and observational learning in interaction with biological traits of temperament contribute to the development of personality styles that might put a person at risk for psychophysiological disorders is primarily a matter of speculation. Although some psychophysiological reactions, asthma for example, are sometimes elicited by stimuli such as a picture of a horse, a goldfish bowl, or the national anthem (Dekker & Groen, 1956), it is quite possible that the conditioning in these cases occurred *after* the development of the asthmatic condition when a severe attack had been fortuitously paired with one of these stimuli.

RESEARCH REPORT 13-1

Breast Cancer and the Abnormal Expression of Emotions

Greer and Morris (1975) have reported one of the most convincing studies to date showing a relationship between a personality characteristic and the incidence of breast cancer. A series of 160 women who had a breast tumor were interviewed and given psychological tests on the day before an operation was scheduled to determine whether or not the tumor was cancerous (malignant). Note that neither the interviewer nor the patient knew at that time whether the tumor was malignant. This is an important feature of the study. For example, if a woman already knew that she had breast cancer, such knowledge could possibly affect her behavior in the interview and influence personality ratings. Under these circumstances, any conclusions about cause and effect would be questionable.

After the diagnostic operation 69 women were found to have breast cancer and 91 were found to have benign breast tumors. Seven (three with cancer) refused to take part in the study. The two groups of women did not differ on marital status or social class. There were no significant differences between the two groups on occurrence of depressive reactions, intelligence, frequency of severe stresses, or the tendency to react to stress with the mechanism of denial. The women with cancer were significantly older.

The most important findings were with respect to the manner in which the women expressed anger. They were assigned to one of three categories: *Extreme suppressors* had never or not more than twice in their adult lives openly shown anger; *extreme expressors* had a history of frequent temper outbursts; and *normal expressors* fell between these two extremes. Significantly higher proportions of women with cancer were in the extreme suppressor or extreme expressor categories (Table 13-7). Since the women in the cancer group were, on the average, older than those in the noncancer group, it is possible that this third variable might account for the relationship, especially if it were found that as women get older they become more extreme in their manner of expressing

TABLE 13-7   Abnormal Expression of Anger in Women with Malignant and Nonmalignant Breast Tumors

| Type of Anger | Number and Percent of Women | | |
Expression	Malignant Tumors	Nonmalignant Tumors	p*
Extreme suppressors	33 (48%)	14 (15%)	.0001
Normal	20 (29%)	66 (73%)	.0001
Extreme expressors	14 (20%)	9 (10%)	.02
Uncertain	2 (3%)	2 (2%)	
Total	69 (100%)	91 (100%)	

From Greer and Morris, 1975. Copyright 1975 by Pergamon Press Ltd. and reprinted with permission.
*Significance of differences between proportions.

anger. In fact, the authors did find a positive relationship between age and the abnormal expression of anger. However, when the age variable was controlled by examining the relationship between type of emotional expression and breast cancer within separate age levels, the relationship was found to hold within each of these age ranges (Table 13-8).

Given the extremely low probability for these results to have occurred by chance and the "blindness" of both patient and interviewer to the diagnostic outcome, this study provides strong evidence for a relationship between either overly restrictive or overly expressive modes of handling anger and breast cancer. Similar results were obtained for the way in which emotions other than anger were expressed. The major shortcoming in this study is that the authors failed to obtain measures of interrater reliability. However, given the "blindness" with respect to diagnostic outcome, it is hard to see how the raters could have biased the results. How extremeness of emotional expression might affect physiological processes (perhaps hormonal or immunological) to increase the likelihood of cancer awaits further investigation.

It is difficult to report a study of this kind (and others in this chapter) without feeling some concern for the anxiety such results might arouse in the reader. Bear in mind two points in this regard. First, no data are given on the proportion of women who are extreme expressors or suppressors and who do not have a breast tumor of any kind. And second, should these findings turn out to be repeatable, they suggest that one approach to prevention would be therapeutic opportunities to learn less extreme ways of handling emotions.

TABLE 13-8   Abnormal Expression of Anger as a Function of Diagnosis and Age Group

| Age Group | Number and Percent of Women | | | |
	Malignant Tumors		Nonmalignant Tumors	p
Under 40	3/5	(60%)	4/25 (16%)	.0001
40–49	13/18	(72%)	10/46 (22%)	.0001
Over 50	31/46	(67%)	9/20 (45%)	.06

From Greer and Morris, 1975. Copyright 1975 by Pergamon Press Ltd. and reprinted with permission.
NOTE: Numerator of fraction is number of women who are *either* extreme suppressors or extreme expressors.

Autonomic responses can also be brought about by operant learning. Miller and his colleagues, using rewards such as direct pleasurable stimulation of the brain, avoidance or escape from electric shock, and water for thirsty animals, have operantly conditioned salivation, heartbeat, intestinal contractions, rate of urine formation, stomach blood flow, blood flow to the ear, blood pressure, and brain-wave patterns in rats and other animals (Miller, 1969). Although there have been problems in replicating a few of these animal studies, the research has strongly suggested that many autonomic responses can be modified by operant procedures. By 1974, evidence for successful operant learning of autonomic responses in humans had been reported in over 90 percent of some 95 experiments (Kimmel, 1974).

It is easy to imagine how operant principles might operate in the development of a psychophysiological symptom. For example, a child who develops asthmatic wheezing in school may be reinforced by being allowed to go home and then getting special attention from parents. The wheezing would be more likely to occur on future occasions, and, if it were similarly reinforced, the autonomic nervous system responses characteristic of asthma would be strengthened. However, there are no studies directly demonstrating the role of operant learning in the development of psychophysiological disorders, and we should be cautious in generalizing from the laboratory to real life.

The family is a likely setting in which social learning experiences may contribute to the development of psychophysiological disorders. The Type A personality that we have previously considered with regard to heart disease probably has its origins in the family context, although this hypothesis has not been tested. Garner and Wenar (1959) reported results strongly suggesting that disturbed mother-child interaction may play some role in the development of psychophysiological symptoms in children. These authors measured features of mother-child interaction for a group of 21 children with a variety of psychophysiological disorders: bronchial asthma, rheumatoid arthritis, ulcerative colitis, peptic ulcer, and atopic eczema. They also obtained the same measures on a group of children with chronic illnesses such as polio, congenital cardiac disease, and nephrosis to control for the possibility that the mother's

reactions in the psychosomatic group were just secondary responses to a chronically incapacitated child. Mothers of children with psychophysiological disorders were rated as more irritable, angry, competitive, and domineering with the child. The child likewise responded to the mother in a more negative fashion. The relationship was generally characterized as one of mutual entanglement in which neither person could leave the other alone for any period of time, and both seemed compelled to persist with their mutually frustrating reactions.

A higher proportion of mothers of children with psychophysiological reactions reported special stresses during the first year of the child's life; for example, having to work full time to make ends meet, having the husband away at war, and severe marital problems. These stresses may well have contributed to the mother's irritability and abrasive reactions with the child. How a continuing series of upsetting emotional interactions might lead to specific psychophysiological disorders is not shown by this study. A likely possibility is that recurring emotional distress interacts with particular biological susceptibilities to produce the specific symptom.

In conclusion, the evidence points to multicausal explanations of psychophysiological disorders—life stresses, the lack of social support systems, biological vulnerabilities and social learning histories that lead to personality dispositions to respond to stress with certain psychophysiological patterns. In the following sections we will consider the nature and development of two disorders, migraine headaches and bronchial asthma, in somewhat more detail.

Migraine Headaches

SYMPTOMS

There are several types of migraine headache; here we will consider *common migraine,* which is characterized by headache and nausea associated with spasms of cranial arteries and dilation of blood vessels in the brain. Usually it affects only one side of the head at onset, but becomes diffuse later in the attack. About half the patients experience throbbing pain, synchronized with pulsation of the cranial ar-

Many people with migraine headaches experience throbbing pain associated with pulsations in the cranial arteries.

teries. Skin may become tender, and there may be swelling (edema) of the face and scalp. Head movements such as those involved in coughing make the pain much worse.

Duration of the headache is variable, but it seldom lasts less than 3 hours and often from 8 to 24 hours. Some patients suffer as long as a week. Even if the patient does not vomit, food is likely to be thoroughly unattractive. Some patients experience increased salivation, lacrimation (tearing), and a stuffy nose.

Patients may have "red" or "white" migraines. Red migraines usually occur in people who flush with anger or blush easily. Their faces may become flushed just before onset of the headache and remain flushed throughout. More common is the pale, haggard face of the white migraineur, who looks almost as if in shock. Some people flush briefly in the first minutes of an attack and then suddenly blanch.

Migraines may bring blurring of vision or actual temporary blindness, abdominal symptoms, alterations of fluid balance (water retention followed by profuse diuresis), generalized physical irritability (marked by hypersensitivity to sound, light, touch, or smell), dizziness, fever, mood changes, listlessness, and a desire for rest in a quiet, dark place. A need to sleep may be irresistible.

Wanda D.'s migraines began with hyperacuity to sound, light, and odor, and, a little later, sore skin. Intolerance of sound was the first symptom; she once reported being "awakened by the sound of the snow falling on the windowsill"! She experienced throbbing pain on the right side of her head accompanied by increasing nausea. She would become pale and chilled. Later in the attack she usually had to urinate repeatedly and also had diarrhea. As soon as the secretory phase passed, she would have to lie down and sleep. She vomited only once or twice, but always experienced nausea.

DEVELOPMENT

A family history of migraine is frequently reported by migrainous patients. Waters (1971) interviewed first-degree relatives and found the incidence of migraine in the families of migraine sufferers to be about 10 percent. In the best twin study to date Lucas (1977) found a 26 percent concordance rate for 86 identical twins and a 10 percent concordance rate for 75 fraternal twins—percentages that suggest a relatively small genetic contribution to migraine.

In Wanda's case, neither heredity nor observational learning seem strongly implicated, since no one in her immediate family showed similar symptoms (until after she did!) and only one aunt among a large number of relatives had migraine, unknown to Wanda. Her sister had had three episodes of the visual phenomena that in some persons presage a migraine attack. She saw *scintillating scotoma* (starlike, flickering shapes or flashes, or simple geometric forms) and then experienced temporary blindness (hemianopia) in part of the visual field.

The cranial arteries in migraineurs appear to be both more responsive and more variable than those of persons who do not have migraine headaches. There is some evidence that suggests that migraine headaches begin with a period of vasoconstriction, possibly caused by high levels of serotonin in the blood, which is followed by a phase of vasodilation associated with a sharp drop in serotonin levels (Adams et al., 1980). The pain results from the expanded arteries pressing on nearby nerves. Allergic mechanisms are important in some patients. Inhalants such as molds and house dust; animal danders, such as from cat hair; foods such as milk and the pea family; and odors such as tobacco smoke or diesel fumes are the most common allergic causes of migraine (Speer, 1971). Psychic stress is often a factor. Speer described a patient who had only two migraines in her lifetime: one when she got married, the second when her daughter got married!

Asthma

SYMPTOMS

Asthma is the Greek word for "panting." This disorder is characterized by narrowing of the airways, which severely impairs air exchange, especially the expiration of air, leading to audible wheezing. Narrowing may be caused by swelling (edema) of the airway walls, muscle spasms, excessive mucus secretion, or collapse of the walls of the trachea and bronchi during forced respiration. The trigger for an asthmatic attack (an allergen, an emotional outburst) may differ in a given patient. During an attack, the patient may experience various negative feelings, ranging from irritability to depression, anxiety, and even panic. The sensation of choking can be terrifying, and fear may worsen an attack.

The incidence of asthma in the United States has been estimated as between 2.5 and 5 percent of the population. Boys are about twice as likely to suffer from asthma as girls, and about 60 percent of asthmatics are 16 years of age or less. Interestingly, the sex difference evens out over the adult years.

DEVELOPMENT

Asthma almost certainly results from different patterns of causes in different individuals. Rees (1964) obtained extensive psychological and medical information on 441 asthmatic patients. He concluded that the *dominant* cause was infectious (whooping cough, bronchitis, pneumonia, and other respiratory illnesses) in 38 percent of the cases, psychological (precipitated by emotional reactions) in 37 percent of the cases, and allergic in 23 percent of the cases (Table 13-9). Note that psychological causes were considered *unimportant* in 30 percent of the cases, a finding that, if true, should make us wary of overemphasizing psychological determinants in each instance of psychophysiological disorder.

The common observation that emotionally arousing experiences can precipitate asthma attacks in many individuals undoubtedly gave impetus to the idea that asthma is a psychophysiological disorder. French and Alexander (1941), within the context of psychoanalytic theory, proposed that the asthmatic attack had its childhood origins in a suppressed cry for help associated with real or imagined estrangement from the mother. In later life the attack would be precipitated by similar occasions or fantasies of estrangement. Many clinical reports (for example, Mohr et al., 1963) have emphasized an overly close relationship between mother and child.

Family interaction is implicated as a contributing factor in asthma by the repeated finding that removal of the child from the home and placement in a hospital often results in immediate and dramatic improvement for some children (for example, Long et al., 1958; Purcell, 1963). It is possible, of course, that removal of the child from the home involves removal from allergens such as house dust and animal fur or feathers as well as from the family. In the Long et al. study, a number of children placed in a hospital experienced almost immediate relief from asthmatic symptoms. The hospital rooms of these children were then sprayed with dust taken from their respective homes, and none of the children developed asthmatic symptoms, although 14 of the 18 children had previously shown skin sensitivity to house dust. Of

TABLE 13-9 **The Contribution of Psychological, Infective, and Allergic Causes to Asthma**

Cause	Relative Importance (Percent)		
	Dominant	Subsidiary	Unimportant
Psychological	37	33	30
Infective	38	30	32
Allergic	23	13	64

From Rees (1964). Copyright 1964 by Pergamon Press Ltd. and reprinted with permission.

course, other allergens may have been responsible for the asthma at home, but the results are strongly suggestive of familial causes.

Purcell (1975) identified a subgroup of asthmatic children whose attacks were, at least at times, precipitated by intense emotions. Four emotional reactions most frequently served as triggers for attacks: laughing, yelling, anger, and excitement. An example of a family-interaction-induced emotional precipitant is illustrated in the following quote from a mother:

You know how Mike used to get asthma at almost every meal when I tried to get him to eat. I'd scold him and he would get angry and choke up and then start to cough and then, bingo, he would have asthma. Well, I decided if Mike didn't finish his food we would just leave him at the table to clean up the dishes and not say anything. Since we started that he

hasn't coughed once at mealtime—and no asthma at those times.

See Research Report 13-2 for another study that demonstrates the role of family interaction in the maintenance of asthmatic symptoms in some individuals.

Treatment

In this section I will focus on psychological approaches to treatment. This is not to minimize the importance of physical treatments such as drugs for the control of asthma, high blood pressure, migraine headaches, and peptic ulcers, but I will not emphasize these medical therapies.

RESEARCH REPORT 13-2

Remove the Family from the Child and Reduce Asthma Attacks

Purcell et al. (1969) report results that strongly suggest that family interaction variables contribute to asthmatic attacks in one group of children—those whose attacks are precipitated by emotional reactions. They interviewed parents of 60 asthmatic children with respect to the frequency of asthmatic attacks and whether or not emotional reactions were important in instigating attacks. They selected 13 families in which emotional factors were important and 12 families in which they were not important. These families participated in an experiment involving five two-week periods: (1) qualification (the selection period—no mention was made of a future separation); (2) preseparation (the family knew that separation would occur at the end of this period); (3) separation; (4) reunion; and (5) a postreunion follow-up for most subjects.

During the period of separation, the entire family except for the asthmatic child moved out of the home and lived in a motel. A substitute mother lived with the child. No contacts were permitted between the parents and child during this period. During all periods of the study, four measures of asthma were obtained: (1) Expiratory peak flow rate, measuring how rapidly the child could expel air, was obtained four times a day; (2) rating of degree of wheezing was made once a day at a clinic; (3) amount of daily medication was reported by the adult (mother or mother substitute); and (4) daily record of frequency and intensity of asthma attacks was reported by the adult.

Results showed a dramatic drop on *all* these measures of asthma during the separation period for the group of children for whom emotional factors played an important role. There was no difference between the qualification and preseparation periods—a difference that might have been expected if the child's *anticipation* of separation from parents was a contributing factor. For the group of children for whom emotional factors were considered unimportant, only one variable—adult-reported frequency of attacks—decreased during separation, and this change was not as great as for the other group. Figure 13-2 shows the results for one measure, daily frequency of asthma attacks for the emotional-precipitation group. It is interesting to note that when children are reunited with their families the asthmatic symptoms begin to return to their previous levels.

Many mothers of children in the emotional-precipitation group had strong emotional reactions to the separation. Several had anxiety reactions. One mother crawled onto the

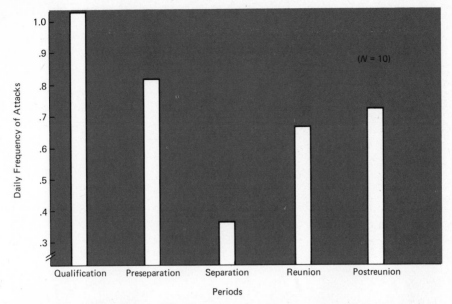

FIGURE 13-2. Mean daily frequency of asthma attacks during each period of the study for children whose asthma attacks were precipitated by emotion. (Adapted from K. Purcell, K. Brady, H. Chai, J. Muser, L. Molk, N. Gordon, & J. Means. The effect on asthma in children of experimental separation from the family. *Psychosomatic Medicine*, 1969, *31*, 144–164. Copyright 1969 by American Elsevier Publishing Co. and used with permission.)

roof of her house to peek through a window to see her boy without his knowledge. Another mother alternated between critical attack on the mother substitute and self-condemnation with thoughts of suicide.

INSIGHT THERAPY

Psychotherapy can give a person a chance to become aware of emotional reactions that precipitate or maintain psychophysiological symptoms and to understand and possibly change life circumstances that produce them. There is evidence that psychotherapy can be helpful with these disorders. Berle et al. (1953), for example, compared 34 ulcerative colitis patients treated by group psychotherapy with 34 receiving medical treatment. Of those seen for psychotherapy, fewer died or had operations, fewer got worse, and more became free of symptoms. There is no indication in this study that patients were randomly assigned to the two conditions, but the results are highly suggestive of the efficacy of psychotherapy. In two other studies, group psychotherapy was found to be more effective than medical treatment alone for asthma (Groen & Pelser, 1960) and ulcer-

ative colitis (Grace et al., 1954). Titchener et al. (1959), however, were unsuccessful in reducing blood pressure in hypertensive patients with group therapy.

BEHAVIORAL APPROACHES

Desensitization. If emotional reactions, especially anxiety, tend to precipitate various psychophysiological symptoms, then it would make sense to use systematic desensitization to reduce these emotional reactions to the people or situations eliciting them. This has been done with some success. For example, both Moore (1965) and Yorkston (1974) found systematic desensitization to be effective in reducing asthma attacks. It may, however, make even more sense to view desensitization as only one of several techniques that may be used in various combinations as the circumstances indicate.

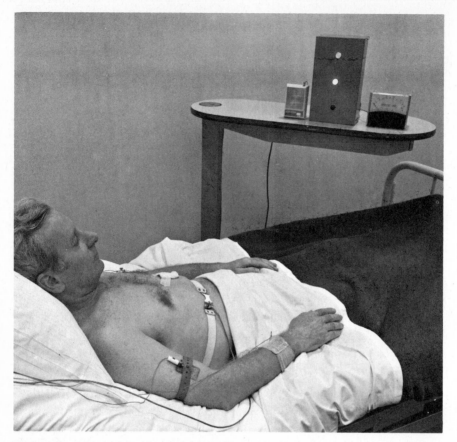

Most people can gain some control over certain physiological processes if given feedback on their responses. In this photo a patient is learning to control irregular heart rhythms. Two kinds of feedback are being given: The degree of irregularity is shown by the color of a lighted panel (red indicates high irregularity, yellow a medium condition, and green, low irregularity). The meter on the right provides a summary indication of the percent of time that the person has maintained low irregularity.

Biofeedback Training. I have already referred to the possibility that operant learning of autonomic responses may cause psychophysiological symptoms. Conversely, operant learning of reduced autonomic responding has been facilitated by the use of *biofeedback* training. In this procedure a mechanical or electronic device is used to monitor some response such as muscle tension in the forehead and to give the patient information (feedback) about it—that is, whether tension is increasing, decreasing, or staying the same. Feedback may be provided by a needle on a meter, a clicking tone, colored lights, or other methods.

Immediate informational feedback of this kind seems to facilitate the ease with which a person learns to make whatever response is producing the physiological change. So far, biofeedback training has shown promise in treating such psychophysiological disorders as migraine, high blood pressure, tension headache, cardiac arrhythmia, and Reynaud's disease (cold extremities) (Tarler-Benlolo, 1978). Overall, however, the better designed studies have shown only moderate effectiveness of biofeedback, with a substantial number of patients showing limited gains or relapses during follow-up (Miller, 1978).

Meditation and Relaxation Training. Interest in meditation as a way of achieving a state of serenity and relaxation has become widespread in this country in recent years. Although meditative procedures vary and are associated with different theories (some are embedded in religious beliefs), the essence of most techniques is quite simple. You may be able to experience it yourself by doing the following exercise: Close your eyes, breathe slowly, and with every expiration say to yourself, "one." The goal is a kind of relaxed attentiveness. When you discover that your thoughts have drifted off on other matters, which they inevitably will, do not be upset; simply bring your attention back to your breathing and the word, "one" (Benson, 1975). To become proficient in any given meditative technique requires weeks or months of daily practice.

Research on one highly publicized technique, Transcendental Meditation (TM), showed that a group of 22 hypertensive patients significantly reduced their blood pressure levels after practicing TM for from 4 to 63 weeks (Benson & Wallace, 1972). Honsberger and Wilson (1973) reported that 94 percent of a group of asthmatic patients could breathe more freely (air passages were less constricted) after practice in TM.

Nonmeditative approaches to relaxation have tended to involve progressive relaxation of various muscle groups (Jacobson, 1938) and is the same procedure used as part of the systematic desensitization treatment. Recent research has shown that relaxation by itself is usually just as effective as biofeedback, especially for high blood pressure and migraine headaches (Blanchard et al., 1978; Seer, 1979). This is an important finding since relaxation techniques do not involve the expensive equipment and electronic expertise that biofeedback does and should accordingly be more available to the average patient.

Meditative procedures can aid relaxation, and preliminary evidence suggests that it may be useful in relieving such disorders as high blood pressure and asthma.

Broad-Spectrum Behavioral Approaches. In the clinical treatment of many psychophysiological disorders it is probably best not to rely on just one procedure. An example of a broader approach to the treatment of migraines is provided by Mitchell and White (1977). Overall these authors teach migraineurs to identify the specific people or situations associated with strong emotions or migraine attacks and then use a combination of techniques tailored to the requirements of the particular patient, both to modify the patients' emotional reactions and to change certain aspects of their social environments. The emphasis throughout is on learning to master these techniques *on their own.* Initial results from a carefully conducted outcome study suggest that their approach is quite effective, producing an 83 percent reduction in migraine frequencies.

Summary

1. In Western culture today most people view mind and body as separate entities. However, a close and perhaps inseparable interweaving of psychological and physiological influences contributes to the development of psychophysiological disorders. Voodoo deaths, target dates for death, and placebo responses are all examples of the psychophysiological interaction.

2. Traditional psychophysiological disorders have tended to involve autonomic nervous system functions and have included disorders of the following systems: skin (e.g., hives), musculoskeletal (e.g., tension headaches), respiratory (e.g., bronchial asthma), cardiovascular (e.g., high blood pressure and migraine headaches), gastrointestinal (e.g., peptic ulcers), and genitourinary (e.g., sexual dysfunction). Other disorders such as heart disease and cancer, however, may be influenced by stressful events and personality characteristics, and thus the definition of what constitutes a psychophysiological disorder is no longer so clear-cut.

3. Stressful life events have been found to be associated with increased incidence of psychophysiological disorders. These stresses, however, may have less effect if the person has a good social support system.

4. Personality dispositions play a role in the development of psychophysiological disorders—both individual differences in biological reactivity as well as cognitive-behavioral traits.

5. The Type A personality (competitive, aggressive, impatient) has shown some relationship to coronary heart disease; the tendency either to overexpress or overinhibit anger and other emotions has shown some relation to breast cancer in women; and inhibited power motives have shown some relation to high blood pressure.

6. Migraine headaches are associated with spasms of cranial arteries and dilation of blood vessels in the brain. The headaches may have some genetic determination. They have been successfully treated with biofeedback training.

7. Asthma can result from several patterns of causes: respiratory infections, emotional reactions, and allergic reactions. For children in whom emotions play an important precipitating role, disturbed family interaction patterns seem to be especially important.

8. Research has shown various forms of medical and psychological interventions to have some degree of effectiveness with psychophysiological disorders. Relaxation training by itself seems to be as effective as the more expensive biofeedback procedure. Most promising would seem to be the use of a variety of behavioral interventions tailored to meet the circumstances of each individual.

Suggested Readings

J. S. Werry surveys research on the etiology and treatment of psychophysiological disorders in children in *Psychopathological disorders of childhood,* Chapter 4 (H. C. Quay & J. S. Werry, Eds., Wiley, 1979). Hans Selye discusses his general adaptation syndrome and the effects of chronic stress on physical disease in *The stress of life* (McGraw-Hill, 1978). The relation of personality characteristics to coronary heart disease is explored in *Type A behavior and your heart* by M. Friedman and R. H. Rosenman (Fawcett, 1975).

14
Sexual Dysfunctions and Variations in Sexual Behavior

- What is normal sexual functioning? How can it become impaired?

- What's wrong with "watching yourself" make love?

- How effective is desensitization in treating sexual dysfunctions?

- Did you know that transsexuals feel trapped in the body of the opposite sex?

- From a psychological viewpoint, how successful are sex-change operations?

- What are fetishism, transvestism, voyeurism, exhibitionism, pedophilia, masochism, and sadism?

- Is there something of the voyeur, the exhibitionist, and the fetishist in each of us? Why do some people carry it to extremes?

- Is homosexuality a matter of hormones? Of close-binding mothers?

Roger: Trapped in a Boy's Body

For as long as Roger could remember, he had thought of himself as a girl. His extremely effeminate behavior made him the object of scorn and ridicule when he entered high school at the age of 15. Usually passive and unassertive, he ran away from home at this time and attempted suicide by an overdose of antihistamines. A return to school resulted in fainting spells. He left school and was placed under the care of a psychiatrist who hospitalized him briefly and then maintained him on antidepressant and phenothiazine drugs for nine months. When considered for a program of therapy that would help change his feminine identity to a more masculine one, he was moderately depressed, withdrawn, extremely frail, and was attending secretarial school where he was the only boy in the class. A chromosome analysis yielded a normal male pattern. (Barlow et al., 1973)

Scientists have only recently begun the systematic study of human sexuality. Kinsey et al. (1948, 1953) were among the first to collect data on the prevalence of different kinds of sexual behavior such as masturbation, marital and premarital heterosexual intercourse, homosexual behavior, and so on. And Masters and Johnson (1966) not so many years ago reported their groundbreaking work on the physiology of sexual functioning. Concurrently with these scientific advances the so-called sexual revolution was taking place, challenging the traditional moral view that the only proper sexual outlet was genital intercourse between married men and women. The climate of opinion has clearly moved (but not unanimously by any means) toward the view that almost any form of sexual gratification between consenting adults that does not harm other people is acceptable.

The issues, however, are not always so simple. Roger's preference for a female identity (and physique too, if possible) created severe psychological problems for him. Should Roger's sexual inclination be seen as simply one of many acceptable variations with no implication of abnormality, or should it be viewed as a disorder, a psychological handicap that should be modified if Roger desires this? In this chapter we will first consider some basic aspects of adequate sexual functioning, then certain generally agreed-upon impairments in sexual functioning, then deviations in sexual preference that probably reflect some inability to express affectionate sexual activity with a human partner, and finally homosexuality.

Adequate Sexual Functioning

Masters and Johnson (1966) in their pioneering study of human sexuality greatly increased our knowledge about physiological aspects of sexual functioning. One of their findings was that the basic sexual response cycle is the same for men and women, and consists of four phases: The *excitement phase* begins with whatever is sexually stimulating for the particular person. Excitement builds quickly if the stimulation is strong enough, until sexual tension reaches a point called the *plateau phase*. If stimulation is terminated or ceases to be effective at this point, the person will not experience orgasm but will enter a prolonged period of gradually decreasing sexual tensions. The *orgasmic phase*, a totally involuntary response, consists of those few seconds when the body changes resulting from stimulation reach their maximum intensity. During the *resolution phase* sexual tensions decrease as the person returns to the unstimulated state. Women are capable of having another orgasm if effective stimulation is continued. For men, on the other hand, there is a period of time, which varies among individuals, when rearousal and orgasm are impossible. This period is called the *refractory period*.

Masters and Johnson's findings also corrected some previously held fallacies about human sexuality:

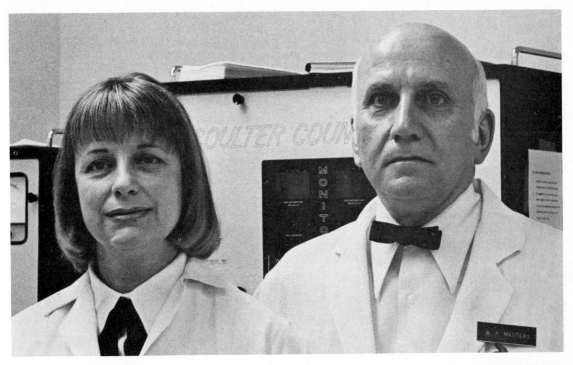

Virginia E. Johnson and William H. Masters' pioneering research corrected a number of fallacies about human sexuality.

1. Direct stimulation of the clitoris is essential for the attainment of orgasms. In the female the clitoris is the organ that is most sensitive to sexual stimulation. It has been widely believed that continuous and direct clitoral stimulation is important for the attainment of orgasms. This is not so, say Masters and Johnson. In fact, during the plateau phase the clitoris retracts and becomes relatively inaccessible to stimulation by either hand or penis. Actually, the clitoris is stimulated during intercourse without any special effort because every thrust exerts pressure indirectly on this organ. Furthermore, many women find direct stimulation of the head of the clitoris irritating and prefer either stimulation on the side of the clitoral shaft or the general genital area.

2. Clitoral orgasms are better than vaginal orgasms. Freud proposed that vaginal orgasms represent a more mature level of psychosexual functioning than clitoral orgasms, a viewpoint widely held in psychoanalytic circles. Although various writers (for example, Ellis, 1962) had argued against this idea, it remained for Masters and Johnson to disprove it conclusively. There is only one kind of

female orgasm and clitoral stimulation plays an important role in it. In fact, the women in their study frequently reported that orgasms resulting from masturbation or manual manipulation by a partner, both of which tend to focus on the clitoris, were more intense than orgasms achieved in intercourse.

3. Simultaneous orgasms represent a superior sexual accomplishment. The older marriage manuals stated that the couple's achievement of simultaneous orgasms was a mark of superior sexual accomplishment. Masters and Johnson did not find this to be so. In fact, preoccupation with achieving simultaneous orgasms could cause partners to direct their attention to the adequacy of their performance rather than losing themselves in the feelings of lovemaking. *Assuming the spectator role,* as Masters and Johnson call this attitude, can lead to impotence in men and failure to have orgasm in women.

4. Size of penis contributes importantly to female sexual enjoyment. In a study of 80 men Masters and Johnson found remarkably little variation in

size of erect penises. Even though there is some small range in size, the authors draw attention to the fact that during entry the vaginal walls expand just enough to accommodate the penis, so that the friction between penis and vagina should not be much affected by penile size.

Psychosexual Disorders

DSM-III classifies psychosexual disorders into three categories: *gender identity disorders, paraphilias,* and *psychosexual dysfunctions.* Let us begin with the third.

PSYCHOSEXUAL DYSFUNCTIONS

The essential feature of psychosexual dysfunctions is that the normal sexual response cycle is impaired by psychological-emotional factors. DSM-III divides these dysfunctions into the following categories:

Inhibited Sexual Desire. This dysfunction involves persistent and pervasive inhibition of sexual desires. This diagnosis will rarely be used unless the lack of desire is a source of distress either to the individual or his or her partner.

Inhibited Sexual Excitement. This dysfunction involves recurrent and persistent inhibition of sexual excitement during sexual activity. In males it is manifested by partial or complete failure to attain or maintain an erection until completion of the sexual act. Previously this has been referred to as impotence and has been classified as either primary impotence, in which the man has never been able to maintain an erection sufficient to accomplish sexual intercourse, or secondary impotence, in which the man has succeeded at sexual intercourse in the past but is having difficulty at the present time. The occasional failure that most men experience because of tiredness or distraction is not considered secondary impotence or a disorder of sexual excitement. For women this disorder involves a partial or complete failure to attain or maintain the lubrication-swelling response of sexual excitement until completion of the sexual act, and has been previously referred to as frigidity.

Inhibited Female Orgasm. This dysfunction involves recurrent and persistent inhibition of the female orgasm as manifested by a delay or absence of orgasm following a normal sexual excitement phase during sexual activity that is adequate in focus, intensity, and duration. It may also involve inhibited sexual excitement. This disorder has previously been called orgasmic dysfunction and is also subdivided into two categories: primary, in which the woman has never had an orgasm by any method, and secondary, in which the woman is able to have orgasms under certain conditions and at certain times but not others. For example, she may be able to masturbate to orgasm but not achieve orgasm during intercourse, or she may be able to have occasional orgasms during intercourse under special circumstances only.

Inhibited Male Orgasm. This is rare and involves a recurrent and persistent inhibition of orgasm following an adequate phase of sexual excitement.

Premature Ejaculation. Ejaculation occurs before the individual wishes it, indicating the absence of reasonable voluntary control of ejaculation and orgasm during sexual activity.

Functional Dyspareunia. This involves recurrent and persistent genital pain in either the male or female associated with sexual intercourse.

Vaginismus. This involves recurrent and persistent involuntary spasms of the musculature of the outer one-third of the vagina that interfere with sexual activity.

DEVELOPMENT

According to psychoanalytic theory men and women show inhibited sexual excitement or orgasmic difficulties because unconsciously they perceive sexual activity as dangerous. The physical inhibition of sexual response is thus a defense against the threatening impulse. In this view anxiety over sexual expression stems from the Oedipal conflict, which leads in men to intense castration anxiety. As Fenichel (1945) puts it, "In the simplest and most typical cases, impotence is based on persistence of an unconscious sensual attachment to the mother. Superficially no sexual attachment is completely attractive because the partner is never the mother; in a deeper layer, every sexual attachment has to be inhibited, because every partner represents the mother" (p. 170).

If we extract from the psychoanalytic theory the basic notion that sexuality has become associated with anxiety (or other negative emotions) and set aside the emphasis on the Oedipal conflict and castration anxiety, then we are left with a proposition with which many investigators might agree. Masters and Johnson, for example, suggest that many of the less severe sexual dysfunctions have their origins in *performance anxiety.* Both men and women can become preoccupied with "producing" or "performing," the man with satisfying the woman, the woman with having an orgasm, the overt expression of which she sees as important in satisfying her male partner as well as herself. Fears of not being able to perform increase the likelihood of failure, and each new failure increases the worries of failing next time—a vicious circle. The woman, blaming herself to some extent for the man's failure, may become even more concerned that she is not performing adequately. One or both individuals may take on a *spectator role,* in which they are critically observing their performance rather than unself-consciously participating in love-making.

In addition to current worries about performance, previous social learning experiences may also contribute to sexual anxieties and inhibitions. In their study and treatment of 32 men with primary impotence Masters and Johnson report the following kinds of past influences as determined from interviews with the men. Three men reported having had clearly *seductive mothers.* In each instance the son had slept in the mother's bedroom at least through puberty, and although there had been no actual intercourse, the relationship had involved strong erotic features. The father in these families had been either absent or ineffective. These three cases are consistent with an Oedipal interpretation.

Six men came from a background in which there was a strong *religious belief that sex was sinful.* It is of interest that these men married wives with equally restrictive religious backgrounds, five of whom had vaginismus. Another six men had had *homosexual attachments* as teenagers and still considered themselves basically homosexual in orientation. Three of

these homosexually inclined men had had domineering mothers but the other three reported nothing unusual in the family pattern. Four other of the impotent men had had humiliating initial sexual experiences with prostitutes. The squalid quarters, repelling physical appearance of the women, and the amusement and derision of the prostitutes had made sexual arousal impossible and destroyed their self-confidence.

No two of the remaining 13 of the 32 impotent men reported similar histories, either in terms of initial sexual trauma or features of family beliefs or interaction. In general, these retrospective reports suggest that no one kind of social learning history is associated with inhibited sexual excitement. To the extent that there is a common theme, it is that one way or another heterosexual performance had become associated with anxiety. Interviews with sexually dysfunctional women revealed a similar variety of social learning experiences that may have contributed to their difficulty. Although sexual mores in our society have been changing in recent decades, in the past at least, cultural attitudes have probably exerted a much stronger inhibitory influence on girls than on boys.

TREATMENT OF PSYCHOSEXUAL DISORDERS

Considering the central role that sexual conflict plays in psychoanalytic theories of neurotic symptoms, one might expect psychoanalysis to be especially effective with sexual dysfunctions. In fact, there is little clear evidence that this approach is particularly effective with male or female sexual dysfunctions. Perhaps, as suggested in Chapter 10, this is because psychoanalytic treatment emphasizes understanding *why* one has the symptom to the neglect of direct training procedures that might change the undesired responses.

Wolpe (1958) was among the first to apply systematic desensitization to sexual dysfunctions. He pointed out that his counterconditioning approach to sexual inhibitions seemed especially appropriate, since anxiety inhibits sexual responding in a direct way. Preorgasmic sexual arousal is predominantly parasympathetic in nature, whereas anxiety almost always involves strong sympathetic arousal. Thus anxiety would directly inhibit the parasympathetic activation necessary for effective sexual responding. On the other hand, if the parasympathetic sexual arousal could be made to be stronger than the competing anxiety response, then the former in time should replace the latter.

Rather than use imagined scenes Wolpe had individuals conduct their own desensitization *in vivo,* that is, at home with a cooperative partner, usually a spouse. The basic strategy was to have the person determine at what point in the sequence of sexual activity anxiety began, and to go beyond that point only gradually and in small steps, permitting the anxiety associated with each stage to be successfully counterconditioned. It was important that both partners understood and accepted that in the initial "sessions" no particular level of performance was expected. An impotent man, for example, might begin by just lying next to his wife in bed and not doing anything else until he felt completely comfortable and perhaps mildly excited. In the next session he might turn toward her and fondle her breasts—and so on until he could maintain an erection in actual intercourse. Of course, all this would not be accomplished in one occasion. It might take 5 to 25 "sessions" to successfully overcome the sexual dysfunction. On the basis of his clinical records Wolpe (1973) concluded that 14 of 18 (78 percent) impotent men recovered to the extent of achieving "entirely satisfactory sexual performance." Another three attained a level that was acceptable to their partners. Wolpe did not separate his cases into those with primary and secondary impotence.

There are certain basic similarities between Wolpe's desensitization techniques and the approach to treatment of sexual inadequacies later devised by Masters and Johnson (1970). These authors take the view that sexual arousal and orgasm are natural expressions of the human body and cannot themselves be either learned or unlearned. What can be learned and unlearned are various beliefs, concerns over performance, and other anxieties that inhibit the natural response. As with Wolpe's approach, one of the first instructions is to back off from any expectations of complete sexual achievement and simply to enjoy touching and exploring one another's bodies, a process called *sensate focus.* During the several days of sensate-focus training the couple also has interviews with their cotherapists (a male and a female), and

they discuss their various anxieties, problems encountered in following the procedure, and so on. Next the cotherapists give the couple specific instructions with respect to their specific sexual dysfunctions. For the nonorgasmic woman, suggestions are given to the man that involve an extension of the touching and fondling involved in the sensate-focus sessions to various forms of genital stimulation. For men with premature ejaculation the couple is usually taught the *squeeze technique* whereby the woman stimulates the penis until the man is about to ejaculate and then squeezes on the top and bottom surfaces immediately below the head of the penis. This stops the ejaculatory process and after a brief pause stimulation can be resumed. In this way the man can learn to experience longer and longer periods of erection and stimulation without ejaculation. Masters and Johnson report moderately high success rates in treating sexual dysfunctions in both men and women.

Other investigators have added further refinements to the Wolpe and the Masters and Johnson approaches. Lobitz and LoPiccolo (1972), for example, incorporate a nine-step masturbation program for women who have never experienced orgasm and also the role playing or simulation of orgasm by women in the treatment session. With these and other innovations they reported 100 percent success in treating 13 women with primary orgasmic dysfunction. Sotile and Kilmann (1977) reviewed a large number of studies and concluded that various methods of systematic desensitization are successful in treating orgasmic dysfunctions, dyspareunia, and vaginismus in women.

Obler (1973) reports one of the best controlled studies of the treatment of sexual dysfunctions. Twenty-two matched individuals with sexual dysfunctions (premature ejaculation and secondary impotence in males and secondary orgasmic dysfunction in females) were assigned to each of three conditions: systematic desensitization plus assertiveness training; psychodynamically oriented group therapy; and a no-treatment control group. The systematic desensitization plus assertiveness training group showed marked improvement over the 15 sessions in terms of the percentage of successful sexual attempts; both the individuals in group therapy and the members of the no-treatment control group showed little or no increase on this measure. The improvements in the behaviorally treated group were maintained at an 18-month follow-up.

Sexual dysfunctions may sometimes be one manifestation of a more generally disturbed marital relationship. In that case it may be necessary to help the couple modify these other patterns of interaction in addition to providing the more specific sexual therapy. Kaplan (1974), for example, describes treating a couple in which the man was impotent. Some success was immediately achieved by following the Masters and Johnson procedures, but then after about two weeks of therapy they reported a "disastrous" sexual attempt in which his impotence returned.

In this instance, the couple had had a serious dispute which on the surface involved money. She had wanted to buy new furniture for the apartment by taking out a loan which she would repay on time out of her salary. He had refused and attacked her as being extravagant. The couple tried to make love the morning after the argument and he promptly lost his erection on entering. Contrary to explicit instructions that she avoid pressuring him for sex when he appeared to experience difficulty, she had insisted on having intercourse and attaining a coital orgasm.

The immediate causes for the "failure" were discussed during the session. He could not function in an ambience of rejection, strife, and bitterness. In addition, her demand for performance again interfered with his sexual response. She had expressed her hostility to him by her sexual demands, which she unconsciously knew he could not meet. (p. 170)

The therapist then focused on the excessive sensitivity to criticism and fear of rejection (in both spouses) that lay behind this particular episode concerning the new furniture. After that feature of their marital interaction had improved, it was possible to complete successfully the more specific sexual therapy.

GENDER IDENTITY DISORDERS

The main disorder included under this heading is *transsexualism*. Transsexual persons such as Roger (described at the beginning of the chapter) differ from individuals with unconventional sexual outlets in a fundamental way: They experience their basic sexual identity to be that of the opposite sex; or as some transsexuals put it, they feel trapped in a body

of the opposite sex. *Transvestites,* for example, experience sexual arousal when dressing in clothes of the opposite sex, whereas transsexuals do not. For the transsexual it is just the normal way to dress. The transsexual identity is also different from a homosexual orientation. The transsexual male thinks of "herself" as basically a woman and "her" attraction to males as heterosexual. Male homosexuals, on the other hand, consider themselves to be males who are sexually attracted to other males.

Transsexual: For a while I thought the homosexual life would be the answer, and it wasn't.

Doctor: Why wasn't it?

Transsexual: I found it revolting. To me the idea of two men in bed with each other is sickening, while a man and a woman together is perfectly natural . . . I am a woman. I have a problem, a growth, but I'm a woman. I am in no way like a male.

Doctor: Except that you have a penis and testes, and you don't have a uterus, and you don't have ovaries.

Transsexual: Yes.

Doctor: So anatomically—

Transsexual: Anatomically, I am female, with those things stuck on. (Green, 1974, p. 47)

Professional tennis player, Dr. Richard Raskind, became Dr. Renee Richards after a sex-change operation.

Most transsexuals report that their preference for an opposite-sex identity began early in life. The following interview is with a male-to-female transsexual who has been living as a woman, married to a man, for a period of ten years.

Transsexual: I remember that as a little girl [six] I used to lie in bed at night with my penis between my legs and my ankles crossed real tight and play a silly game and say if I did this, in the morning when I'd wake up, it would be gone. This is very, very long ago.

Doctor: How long ago?

Transsexual: Definitely preschool. I don't know where I got this notion, but I just felt that it would go away by morning, and I was so disappointed because every morning I'd reach down there and there it was. In kindergarten the kids used to make fun of me because I was girlish.

Doctor: How?

Transsexual: I used to like to play with girls. I never did like to play with boys. I wanted to play jacks. I wanted to jump rope and all those things. The lady in the schoolyard used to always tell me to go play with the boys. I found it distasteful. I wanted to play with the girls. . . . I remember one day the teacher said, "If you play with the girls one more day, I am going to bring a dress to school and make you wear it all day long. How would you like that?" Well, I *would* have liked it. (Green, 1974, p. 74)

Causative influences in the development of transsexualism are not clear. Biological factors may well be present. Animal research has demonstrated that masculine behavior can be increased in female animals by providing high levels of male hormones in the prenatal environment, while male animals behave more like females when not given sufficient amounts of male hormones prenatally. Goy (1970), for example, injected pregnant rhesus monkeys with the male hormone testosterone. Masculinized female infants were born with genitals that included both male and female characteristics. When these females grew up, they showed more rough-and-tumble play and were more masculine than normal females in other social behaviors.

Similar effects have been noted in human female children. During the 1950s a number of pregnant women were treated with synthetic progestin (a hormone that prepares the uterus for pregnancy) in order to reduce miscarriages. An unexpected side effect of this drug was that it caused an excess of male hormones and thereby affected the development of female fetuses. Compared with matched control girls, these girls had more "masculine" interests, gave higher priority to a career over marriage, were less interested in participating in baby care of a younger sibling or a neighbor's child, and preferred to play with boys' toys such as cars, guns, and trucks rather than dolls (Erhardt, 1973). The prenatal exposure of male fetuses to female hormones (estrogen and progesterone) has also been reported to produce feminization in boys (Yalom et al., 1973).

Social learning experiences may also contribute to the development of transsexualism. Green (1974) has been studying the childhood recollections of adult transsexuals as well as a sample of 50 young boys (whose average age is seven) with normal anatomy who show an unusually high degree of feminine behavior. Pointing out that the social learning histories of these individuals vary quite a bit, Green offers only tentative suggestions for a possible psychological etiology. In a number of instances, the mother finds her infant son to be unusually attractive and cuddly and she fosters a mutually close relationship. As the son begins to explore his environment, he finds many colorful accessories that belong to her and begins to play with her shoes, jewelry, and so on. He begins to imitate his mother's feminine behaviors and is reinforced because the mother and other family members think this behavior is cute. Later his father begins to feel alienated from his son because the son refuses to engage in more rough-and-tumble masculine play. As a result the boy relies even more on his mother for guidance and intimacy. Girls become his main friends, and this serves to solidify his female interests and developing identity. He is likely to continue "playing" at being a girl by cross-dressing, still without any discouragement from his mother. It is usually between the ages of seven and nine that some other person, a teacher or neighbor, brings the increasing feminization of the boy to the parents' attention. This account suggests that the parents, especially the mother, show an unusual degree of "blindness" and tolerance for the boy's developing sex-role problem and, in fact, may be actively fostering it.

James Morris (left) "became" Jan Morris (right) after undergoing sex-change surgery and hormonal treatment. "I was mending a discrepancy ... I found that when people took me to be unquestionably a woman, a sense of rightness calmed and satisfied me.... I felt myself to be passing through an anteroom of fulfillment" (Morris, 1974, pp. 130–131).

Roger: Some Developmental Influences

Roger's development fits the pattern described by Green relatively well. He had been a keen disappointment to his mother, who had wanted a girl. Nevertheless he became her favorite child. His father, on the other hand, worked long hours and had little contact with him. Roger began to dress in girls' clothes from time to time before the age of five years and continued this practice into junior high school. Also during his childhood he developed an interest in cooking, knitting, crocheting, and embroidering, skills he acquired by reading an encyclopedia. His older brother often scorned him for his distaste of "masculine" activities such as hunting. Roger reported associating mostly with girls during this period, although he remembered being strongly attracted to a "boyfriend" in the first grade. In his sexual fantasies, which developed at about 12 years of age, he pictured himself as a woman having intercourse with a man. Although these fantasies were accompanied by masturbation, neither orgasm nor ejaculation had occurred by the time of the initial interview. (Barlow et al., 1973)

There are also striking similarities between Green's description of the feminization of these pretranssexual boys and the concept of the "close-binding" mother thought by some to play a role in homosexuality. More detailed future studies will be necessary to identify the particular patterns of biological and social learning influences that distinguish these two sexual orientations.

It should be pointed out that when young children show deviations in gender identity they are not labeled transsexual in DSM-III but rather *gender identity disorder of childhood.* Apparently, most children who manifest gender identity problems do not become transsexuals as adults.

No forms of psychological intervention have been shown to be consistently effective in changing transsexualism. Pauly (1965), for example, reports 26 cases in which a change in sexual identity was unsuccessfully attempted through psychotherapy. Nor has behavior therapy fared much better. Gelder and Marks (1969) treated both transsexuals and transvestites by electric shock for cross-dressing in an aversion therapy program. Although 18 of 20 transvestites were not cross-dressing at follow-up, all five transsexuals continued to cross-dress and request sex change through surgery. Barlow et al. (1973), however, were successful in modifying the sexual identity of Roger using a step-by-step procedure in which Roger was taught by modeling, videotape feedback, and generous social reinforcement (praise) to sit, stand, walk, and generally act in a masculine fashion. His sexual urges and fantasies were also modified by reinforcement for heterosexual arousal and punishment for homosexual arousal. At a one-year follow-up Roger's sexual identity change had endured and he was now going steady with a girl friend. It is important to note that he had indicated a willingness to change his transsexual orientation through a behavioral approach, with the understanding that if this failed he could consider a sex-change operation.

Sex-change surgery, of course, can be viewed as another approach to the treatment of transsexualism. Hastings and Markland (1978) found that most of the 25 individuals who had undergone male-to-female sex-change surgery were making a satisfactory adjustment five years later. None regretted having the operation. Individuals most likely to have adjustment problems afterward had been judged to be psychopathic (antisocial disorder) prior to the operation. The authors advocated that sex changes not be made in such individuals in the future. Meyer and Reter (1979) found similar follow-up results for a smaller sample of males and females who underwent sex-change surgery, but also found that a group of individuals who were referred for sex-change operations but for various reasons did not receive the operation showed

comparable improvements in adjustment. The latter finding raises the question of how essential the sex-change operation was for improving psychological adjustment. Current standards for accepting individuals for surgical sex change are quite stringent and emphasize a life-long gender identity with the opposite sex in addition to extremely strong motivation for the change.

PARAPHILIAS

DSM-III uses the term *paraphilias* (from *para,* meaning deviation, and *philia,* meaning attracted to) to refer to what were previously called sexual deviations. In general the paraphilias involve gross impairment in the capacity for affectionate sexual activity between adult human partners. These individuals show persistent sexually arousing fantasies associated with (a) preference for use of a nonhuman object for sexual arousal, (b) sexual activity with humans involving real or simulated suffering or humiliation, or (c) sexual activity with nonconsenting partners. Fantasies of this kind may be playful and harmless and acted out with a mutually consenting partner, in which case it would not be considered a disorder. The pathological feature of the paraphilias is that the deviant expression of sexuality tends to become the *only* outlet; that is, the person is unable to experience affectionate sexual activity with an adult partner.

Fetishism. In *fetishism* sexual interest becomes focused on a part of the body such as the hair, ears, breasts, feet, or ankles, or some object such as fur, underwear, high-heeled shoes, or stockings. The body part or object usually has some rather obvious sexual associations for most men (fetishism is rare in women), but the important distinction is that it becomes the preferred or sole source of sexual arousal and gratification.

Transvestism. The transvestite (almost always male) shows a recurring and persistent tendency to dress in female clothes for the purpose of sexual arousal. The person's sexual orientation is usually heterosexual, however, and not homosexual.

Zoophilia. The individual uses animals as the preferred or exclusive method of producing sexual ex-

Diana: What Shall I Wear Tonight?

Steve (Diana) is a sales manager for a large company, father of three children, active in the marine reserves, and a devoted football fan. When cross-dressed he becomes Diana. For seven years after his marriage Diana kept "her" secret. "She" sneaked out to dress, waited until no one was at home, or went to motels. Diana speaks of the erotic feeling "she" has when dressing. A very pleasant, nice feeling that no longer demands immediate sexual gratification, but rather is enjoyable all over. "She" follows fashion magazines and enjoys trying out an eye makeup or foundation.

In her future, Diana sees a bleak time when "she" will have to be very careful—the children are growing and are around more at night. Dressing at home is not so easy. "I might have to pack Diana into my suitcase and dress only at a meeting. But I know after the kids grow up she'll be back again. You know, even though it's clearly a deviation and you could call me a sexual deviant—even though it's made for trouble in my life—if you gave me a pill to stop dressing, I don't think I'd take it". (Feinbloom, 1963, pp. 67–68)

citement. The animal may be the object of intercourse or may be trained to sexually excite the person by licking or rubbing. Usually the preferred animal is one with which the individual had contact during childhood, such as a pet or farm animal.

Pedophilia. The essential feature is the preference for repetitive sexual activity with prepubertal children. Heterosexual contact is about twice as frequent as homosexual contact. In most cases the adult knows the child well, either living in the same house or in the neighborhood. The sexual activity often is just looking, touching, or fondling, but may involve penile insertion. The child may be asked to manipulate the pedophile's sexual organ or perform mouth-genital contacts.

Exhibitionism. The exhibitionist deliberately exposes his genitals to girls or women for purposes of sexual arousal. This frequently takes place in some isolated place such as a park, a darkened movie theater, or a parked car. It is one of the most common sexual offenses reported to the police in the United States. These individuals are frequently introverted and quietly appropriate in ordinary social relationships. Not uncommonly they are married, but sexual adjustment in the marriage tends to be poor.

Voyeurism. The *voyeur*, or "peeping Tom," seeks sexual gratification from secretly looking at women undressing or women engaging in sexual activity.

They may, in many instances, masturbate while engaged in their peeping behavior.

Sexual Masochism. The person obtains sexual gratification through experiencing pain or suffering. According to DSM-III masochistic fantasies, such as being bound, tortured, beaten, raped, or otherwise humiliated, are not in themselves sufficient to diagnose this disorder. The person must also act on these impulses.

Sexual Sadism. The term *sadism* comes from the name of the Marquis de Sade (1740–1814) who achieved sexual gratification by inflicting pain on his partners. Again, the person must have acted out these impulses, not merely fantasized them.

Partners sometimes complement each other in sadistic and masochistic tendencies, one being sadistic and the other masochistic. It is also common for sadistic and masochistic tendencies to alternate within the same person—the common denominator is pain, either given or received. The pain may be produced by whipping, spanking, biting, scratching, or pinching, and may be accompanied by fantasies of more extreme cruelty. When acts of cruelty and mutilation are carried out against a nonconsenting partner, sadism becomes a form of rape.

Rape. Rape is not a diagnostic category in DSM-III but does usually involve a disturbance in normal sexual functioning. Legally rape is divided into *statutory*

The Marquis de Sade (1740–1814), from whose name the term sadism was derived.

rape, involving the seduction of a minor, and *forcible rape,* in which the victim is over 18. In almost all cases the rapist is a male. Forcible rape by definition is an act of violence or coercion and could just as well be considered in Chapter 21 on the topic of violence and crime. Groth et al. (1977) studied 133 convicted rapists and 92 victims of rape, and concluded that the motivations of the rapists fell largely into four categories. These groupings mainly reflected variations in the expression of power or aggression, with sexual motivation being secondary. (1) The *power-assertive* type of rapist is primarily interested in controlling and intimidating the victim. This person frequently has fantasies, rarely realized, that the victim will participate in the sexual act with wild abandon once she is overpowered. More rapists, 44 percent, fell in this category than any other. (2) The *power-reassurance* type also seeks to overpower his victim but in this case there is a stronger underlying feeling of inadequacy and doubt about his masculinity. The rape, in other words, may be an attempt to reassure the person that his masculinity is intact.

Twenty-one percent of the sample were of this type. (3) The power-oriented rapists described above rarely injure their victims. The *anger-retaliation* type, on the other hand, can be extremely dangerous and may on occasion murder their victims. These individuals seem obsessed with rage and contempt toward women, and there is relatively little sexual satisfaction in their attack. Thirty percent were of this type. (4) The *anger-excitation* type is motivated primarily by sexual sadism. He can only derive sexual pleasure from seeing his victim suffer from his cruel and sadistic attack. Only 5 percent were of this type.

In considering these variations in sexual behavior I have focused on rather extreme examples. Perhaps I have left too strong an impression that such sexual patterns as voyeurism, fetishism, exhibitionism, sadism, and masochism are distinctive conditions that play little role in "normal" sexuality. This is not the case. Most of us probably have tendencies in one or more of these directions. In fact, it is a little hard to conceive of "pure" sexual behavior that does not contain, for example, a trace of voyeurism (looking at the partner), fetishism (arousal by some bit of clothing or body part), or some fantasied feeling of "forcing" or being "forced" by the partner. These variations in sexual expression, then, range from mild inclinations common to many people to extreme forms that dominate the person's whole approach to sexuality.

DEVELOPMENT OF PARAPHILIAS

Most of the data on the development of the various paraphilias derive from retrospective reports of the individuals involved. These reports suggest that some mixture of learned anxiety or inhibition with respect to more conventional heterosexual behavior plus positive experiences with their particular form of sexual expression is frequently present. McGuire et al. (1965) stress the importance of some early experience with the deviant sexual behavior followed by a period of time during which the person masturbates while fantasizing about the deviant object or behavior. Following a classical conditioning model, the repeated masturbation is thought further to condition sexual arousal to the particular fantasied stimulus. These authors suggest that without the subsequent pairing of masturbation with the fantasied object, the deviant behavior would probably not develop.

McGuire and his associates report several examples where such conditioning could have occurred. Two exhibitionists reported similar experiences in which they had been urinating in a semipublic place when they were surprised by a passing woman. They felt no sexual arousal at the time; rather they were embarrassed and left hurriedly. It was only later that the sexual significance of the encounter occurred to them, and each had then masturbated frequently to the memory of the incident. Eventually the thought of self-exposure became so sexually arousing that each had acted upon the idea. In another case, a 17-year-old male had seen through a window a girl dressed only in her underwear. He was sexually aroused and later masturbated repeatedly to this memory. In time the memory of the actual girl became vague, but advertisements and shop window displays continually reminded him of underwear, and his masturbating fantasies gradually fixated on female underwear. Three years later he had no sexual interest at all in girls but was sexually aroused by female underwear, which he bought or stole.

Sadomasochistic tendencies seem to have their origin in almost every instance in some early experience in which intense sexual arousal is associated with the giving or receiving of pain. Hirschfeld (1948), for example, describes a masochistic man who reported the following experience at age 13. He and his two older sisters were in the care of a sadistic governess who beat the girls almost daily. The boy and a friend used to look at these beatings through a keyhole, and later in the evening they would masturbate together. One evening the governess caught them in the act of masturbating and told them that she was going to give them a good hiding, now and every evening for eight days. When the boy (who later became a masochist) was being beaten by a stick on his bare buttocks, he experienced sexual arousal. He also noticed that the governess's hands, during the beatings, frequently strayed between his legs and stayed there. The close association in this case between sexual arousal and painful beatings no doubt served as a powerful impetus toward masochistic development.

In conclusion, a classical conditioning model in which the early pairing of sexual arousal (or orgasm) with pain is further reinforced by subsequent mas-

turbatory fantasies or overt behavioral acts would seem to account rather well for the development of many paraphilias. A broader view of the social learning history, however, is probably necessary for a more complete understanding in many cases.

AVAILABILITY OF PORNOGRAPHY AND THE INCIDENCE OF SEX CRIMES

An important social and ethical question is whether the easy availability of explicit sexual materials in the form of magazines and X-rated movies tends to increase illegal forms of deviant sexual behaviors. One might argue either way. On the one hand, exposure to sexual material might stimulate sexual fantasies and arousal, and lead to an increased acting out of these impulses, or, on the other hand, the pornographic material might provide an outlet, perhaps through masturbation, for the deviant impulses and thus reduce the frequency of sex-related crimes.

Kutchinsky (1973) provides a careful analysis of

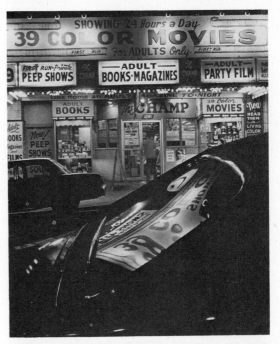

Evidence from Denmark suggests that the easy availability of explicit sexual material is not associated with an increase of sexual offenses.

the effects of the rather sudden increase in the availability of pornographic materials in Denmark in the middle 1960s. As can be seen in Figure 14-1, the incidence of all sex offenses known to the police decreased after 1965, the year in which the first hardcore pornographic picture magazines appeared in Denmark. Offhand this evidence would seem to support the view that increased availability of pornography is associated with a decrease rather than an increase in sex crimes. There are other possible interpretations, however. With increasing liberalization of sexual mores, victims may have become less willing or interested in reporting certain offenses, or police may have become less inclined to officially register certain sexual offenses. Indeed, the former interpretation may well account for the observed decreases in the less serious offenses of exhibitionism

and minor sexual harassment of adult women (touching or pinching on crowded buses, for example). Kutchinsky, however, found that there was no tendency for victims (or parents) to decrease their reporting of sexual molestation of children, and yet there had been a 69 percent decrease in sexual offenses against young girls in Copenhagen from 1959 to 1970. He concludes that the availability of pornography was very likely an important contributing factor to this decrease.

No sexual offenses showed an increase during this period. Thus there was little support for the theory that increased availability of pornography would lead to an increase in sex crimes. The incidence of rape remained unchanged and was apparently unaffected one way or the other by the change in availability of pornography.

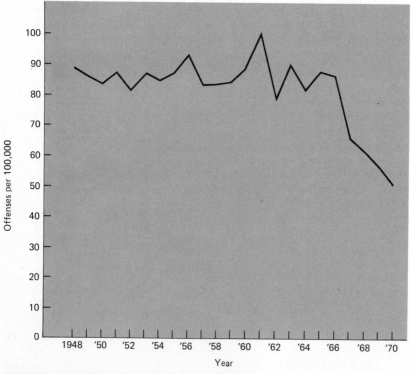

FIGURE 14-1. Incidence of all sex offenses (except incest) known to the police in Denmark for the period 1948–1970. From Kutchinsky (1973). Copyright 1973 by Society for the Psychological Study of Social Issues and used with permission. Kutchinsky (personal communication) reports that sex offenses continue to decrease until 1973, leveling off thereafter at about 40 per 100,000 people.

TREATMENT OF PARAPHILIAS

Treatment will depend, of course, on some motivation on the part of the individual to change. Some individual fetishists or transvestites may be relatively satisfied with their sexual adjustment and have little interest in being treated for it. For those paraphilias in which there is a victim, as in pedophilia or extreme sadism, the issue of treatment is essentially the same as for criminals confined for any other offense. In general, prisons are moving away from forced participation in treatment programs. Ethically speaking it is probably best to see treatment for unconventional sexual behavior limited to those individuals who *want* to make certain changes in their sexual preferences.

Various forms of aversion therapy have been successful in modifying deviant sexual behavior when there is strong motivation to change. Although general effectiveness cannot be judged from individual cases, Raymond provides a good example of this kind of therapy.

Raymond (1956) treated a 33-year-old married man who had felt compelled since the age of ten to physically attack ladies' handbags and baby carriages. He had been in mental hospitals on several occasions and had been picked up by the police some 12 times as a result of this behavior. There was a fetishistic or sexual component in these attacks as indicated by the fact that his masturbation fantasies revolved around these objects, and he could not have intercourse with his wife without similar fantasies. He had had many hours of psychoanalytic therapy in which the sexual symbolism involved in handbags and baby carriages had been discussed and the historical origins of the problem had been traced; for example, as a young child he had once become sexually aroused in the presence of his sister's handbag. The attacks continued despite this treatment, and since he was a clear danger to the lives of infants, a prefrontal lobotomy was being considered at the time it was decided to try aversive conditioning.

The treatment consisted of inducing nausea by injection of apomorphine and presenting the patient with a collection of handbags and carriages at the same time. This treatment was repeated every two hours, day and night, for a week. He was then allowed to return home for eight days and he reported that for the first time he had been able to have intercourse with his wife without the handbag or carriage fantasies. The treatment was continued at irregular intervals for another nine days, at which time he was discharged from the hospital. One booster treatment was given six months later. A follow-up 19 months later indicated that there had been no further attacks on these objects and that he no longer had to imagine the objects for successful intercourse. No other symptoms were substituted for the fetish.

A number of individual case studies have shown covert sensitization to be effective in modifying such sexual patterns as pedophilia, sadistic fantasies, and exhibitionism (for example, Barlow et al., 1969; Maletzky, 1974). Covert sensitization is a form of aversion conditioning in which the person is required to imagine some painful, disgusting, or nauseating scene while thinking about the behavior to be modified. Little and Curran (1978) end their review of this topic by concluding that covert sensitization has shown impressive and relatively consistent effectiveness with sexual deviations but has not shown the same promise in modifying alcoholism, smoking, or obesity. Covert sensitization may be most effective with problem behaviors in which the behavior is greatly influenced by preceding fantasies, as is the case in most sexual activity.

Brownell et al. (1977) describe the successful treatment of five individuals who each exhibited two of the following patterns of deviant sexual arousal: exhibitionism, pedophilia, masochism, sadism, or transvestism. In addition to covert sensitization two subjects underwent *orgasmic reconditioning,* in which they were instructed to masturbate to the deviant fantasy and to substitute a heterosexual image or fantasy just prior to ejaculation. As they accomplished this without loss of erection, the heterosexual fantasy was substituted earlier in the sequence until it became the sole content of the masturbatory process.

Let us follow the process in more detail for one person.

> Subject 5 was a 31-year-old married policeman, seeking treatment for uncontrollable urges to dress in women's clothing and appear in public. He had a 16-year history of transvestism, had been discharged from the Marine Corps for cross-dressing, and had risked public disclosure on several occasions. The subject's wife had threatened divorce as a result of the cross-dressing, yet she frequently purchased women's clothing for him and was "compassionate" while he was in feminine attire. Subject 5 also had a 12-year history of sadomasochistic behavior. During intercourse with his wife, he had tied her to the bed, handcuffed her, and had her wear an animal leash with a collar. He had also tied himself with ropes, chains, handcuffs, and wires while he was cross-dressed, and he was concerned that he would injure himself seriously. The subject's wife claimed to "not enjoy sex," intercourse was infrequent, but when it did occur Subject 5 would fantasize being cross-dressed. (p. 1146)

A course of orgasmic reconditioning successfully increased the extent of this man's heterosexual arousal but had no effect on his arousal to transvestite or sadomasochistic fantasies. Covert sensitization was begun for the transvestism and effectively decreased the sexual arousal associated with these fantasies. An abbreviated example of a covert sensitization presentation in which sexual arousal to the deviant fantasy is followed by the noxious or aversive fantasy is described below:

You are in your house alone, and you are feeling lonely. You get the urge to put on the clothing, so you enter the bedroom and open the closet. You begin to get aroused as you decide what to wear. As you put on the clothing, you can see the colors and feel the clothing on your hands. You really are turned on as you put on the bra, panties, nylons, wig. You feel like playing with yourself as you apply your makeup, but you can't wait to go out. As you leave the house, you get very excited. You are touching your penis through the panties as you're driving.

And then you hear sirens! The police pull you over, and it's your fellow policemen. They start to laugh and call for other police cars. A crowd is gathering, and they know you're a man. The officers throw you around and take you to the station. The women are disgusted, and the chief will take your gun and badge. You are humiliated, and they call you "sick." Your kids are crying as they return from school because others tease them about having a perverted father. Look what you've done to yourself! (pp. 1147–1148)

Although the transvestism was reduced by this procedure, it had no effect on the sadomasochistic fantasies. Another course of covert sensitization focusing on this problem was introduced and was effective in reducing sexual arousal to these fantasies. An important feature of this study is the multiple-baseline procedure in which one symptom is treated for a period of time while the other symptom, other than keeping track of frequency of occurrence, goes untreated. Since the untreated symptom does not improve, this rather strongly indicates that the therapeutic intervention cannot be explained in terms of such nonspecific factors as attention. Also, one of the measures of arousal in this study was a physical one, penile circumference, and therefore was not subject to faking in the same way as self-reports.

Homosexuality

Homosexuality refers to sexual behavior between members of the same sex. Should the topic of homosexuality even be included in a textbook of abnormal psychology? Most homosexual, or gay, individuals would probably say no, especially if such inclusion implied that homosexuality was a disorder, a sickness, rather than simply a sexual preference of a small minority. Some mental health professionals continue to view homosexuality as indicative of a psychopathological condition in which the expression of "normal" heterosexual sexuality has been impaired. Others, perhaps most, do not consider homosexuality in itself to reflect a psychological disorder. This is the position taken in DSM-III in which homosexuality *per se* is not listed as a mental disorder. *Ego-dystonic homosexuality,* however, is listed as a disorder; it refers to a sustained pattern of overt homosexual arousal that the individual does not want and experiences as a source of distress. In addition, the person desires to acquire or increase his or her heterosexual relationships. In other words, homosexuality is considered a disorder only if the person is dissatisfied with that orientation and wishes to change.

Let us postpone for a bit the question of whether homosexuality should be viewed as a disorder and look at some of the facts about this sexual orientation. Societal acceptance of homosexuality has varied widely during different historical periods and in different cultures. In a survey of 76 societies Ford and Beach (1951) found that 49 considered some form of homosexual activity acceptable, though not for all members of the community. However, homosexuality was not found to be universal; in the remaining societies it was either totally absent, rare, or carried out in secrecy. For example, the Seivans, a small North American tribe, expected all men and boys to engage in homosexual sodomy, and a man was considered strange if he did not have both male and female affairs. Other cultures, such as the Tahitians, that were very permissive with respect to heterosexual behavior between young, unmarried people regarded homosexual activity as extremely aberrant.

Although many people think that either one is a homosexual or one is a heterosexual, in fact, sexual preferences for the same or opposite sex are probably best conceived as a continuum. In an early study Kinsey et al. (1948) interviewed 5300 white males and found the following variations in homosexual experience:

1. Thirteen percent had experienced homosexual urges toward other males without having overt homosexual experience after the onset of adolescence.
2. Thirty-seven percent had had homosexual experience to orgasm after the onset of adolescence.
3. Fifty percent of those who remained unmarried to the age of 35 had had homosexual experience to orgasm since the onset of adolescence.
4. Eighteen percent had equal homosexual and heterosexual inclinations and experiences in their histories.
5. Eight percent had engaged almost exclusively in homosexual activities for at least three years between the ages of 16 and 55.
6. Four percent were exclusively homosexual from adolescence on.

It is difficult to know how representative Kinsey's sample was of the population at large. Subjects were recruited through lectures and requests of various clubs and organizations around the country. The sample is probably biased somewhat toward college-educated men. Whether or not we accept the specific percentages described above as accurate (even if accurate in the 1940s, they may have changed since then), these data support the notion that there are varying degrees of homosexual commitment and

Kate Millett, author of *Flying and Sexual Politics,* chooses a bisexual lifestyle, being neither exclusively homosexual nor heterosexual.

Merle Miller, author of *Plain Speaking: An Oral Biography of Harry S. Truman,* is in the vanguard of those homosexuals who have chosen to "come out of the closet" and express pride in their sexual orientation.

that some proportion of the population clearly has mixed sexual preferences.

Female homosexuals, or *lesbians,* have not been studied as extensively as male homosexuals. In a subsequent study Kinsey and his colleagues (1953) obtained similar data on female sexuality. They found female homosexuality to be less prevalent than male homosexuality. For example, 8 percent of the male sample was found to have engaged almost exclusively in homosexual activities compared with only 3 percent of the female sample. There was also a difference in degree of promiscuity, with females more often restricting their sexual relationships to one other person. Kinsey's results, however, may well be out of date. As with the male data, it should not be assumed that these results are an accurate representation of the situation today.

IS HOMOSEXUALITY A DISORDER?

How does one decide whether homosexuality is a disorder or not? In 1974 the American Psychiatric Association's Board of Trustees voted to remove homosexuality from its official list of mental disorders. As a social decision this may well have been a desirable action in that it was a step toward reducing some of the oppression that gay individuals experience. Matters of scientific interpretation, however, are not proved or disproved by votes of any group, no matter how prestigious.

In a more scientific fashion, then, how does one prove that something is or is not a disorder? How, for example, would you prove that a strong preference for jazz music is or is not psychopathological? If you found that jazz enthusiasts showed significantly higher frequencies of abnormalities (other than liking jazz) than the population at large, and also that they had had more troubled relations with their parents, then perhaps you could begin to build a case for jazz preference being symptomatic of some more general psychological difficulty. That, at least, is how the question of homosexuality as a disorder has been approached.

With respect to current adjustment most studies of homosexuals not in treatment or not charged with a sexual offense have found either no difference or minor differences such as lower self-confidence or lesser happiness, which might well result from the strain of living in an antagonistic society rather than reflect personality difficulties associated with the origin of the homosexuality itself (Chang & Block, 1960; Siegelman, 1972a, 1972b; Thompson, 1971; Weinberg & Williams, 1974). A trend in the findings of both Thompson and Siegelman was that female homosexuals seemed especially lacking in signs of maladjustment and on some variables seemed somewhat better adjusted than their heterosexual comparison groups. This may reflect the possibility that many female homosexuals are single, successful, professional women in an era of feminine liberation. A major problem in determining the degree of current maladjustment in homosexuals is obtaining a truly representative sample of homosexuals. Considering the varying degrees to which homosexuals are willing to be identified as such and are willing to participate in studies, it is highly unlikely that any investigator can obtain a sample from which generalizations can be made to the homosexual population in general.

Bell and Weinberg (1978) make no claims as to the representativeness of their sample, but they did develop a scheme for classifying homosexuals into subgroups that would probably be applicable to most samples even though the proportions of homosexuals that fall into the subgroups might vary in samples taken in different parts of the country. Bell and Weinberg intensively interviewed 575 white male, 111 black male, 229 white female, and 64 black female homosexuals in the San Francisco area. They found that most of these individuals could be classified in one of five types:

Close-Coupled. These homosexuals lived with a partner in a quasi-marriage situation. Of all the types, they were least likely to seek partners outside their relationship, had the fewest sexual problems, and were unlikely to regret being homosexual. The men in this group had rarely experienced difficulties related to their sexual orientation such as being arrested, trouble at work, or assault and robbery. Both men and women were no different from a heterosexual comparison group on psychosomatic symptoms, happiness, self-acceptance, depression, or tension.

Open-Coupled. These men and women were living with a special sexual partner but were not entirely happy with their circumstances and tended to seek satisfactions with people outside their partnership. Both the men and the women did more "cruising" (for example, going to gay bars looking for a transient sexual encounter) than the Close-Coupled persons. Compared with the other homosexual subgroups, the Open-Coupled were intermediate in their adjustment. The Open-Coupled males, however, expressed more self-acceptance and less loneliness than the Open-Coupled females, suggesting that this kind of nonexclusive relationship is apparently more trying for the female than the male.

Functional. The Functionals came closest to the notion of "swinging singles." They seemed to organize their lives around their sexual experiences and reported more sexual activity with a greater number of partners than did any of the other groups. They were unlikely to regret being homosexual, cruised frequently, and generally displayed a great deal of involvement in the gay world. These individuals showed little or no psychopathology, not differing from the heterosexual comparison group on psychosomatic symptoms, self-acceptance, or depression.

Gay individuals have become more militant in opposing gay oppression.

Dysfunctionals. This group most closely approximated the stereotype of the tormented homosexual. They were troubled people who were having a great deal of difficulty managing their lives. They were most regretful about their homosexuality, reported more sexual problems, and more often reported being arrested or having job difficulties related to their homosexuality, and were more lonely and more depressed than the other groups.

Asexual. These individuals showed a lack of involvement with others, scoring lowest on level of sexual activity and having few sexual partners. They differ from the Dysfunctionals primarily in terms of their isolation from others.

Like any typology the above one is arbitrary in some respects, and other plausible groupings could be made. Nevertheless, the classification system makes certain points clear. First, any stereotype about homosexuals and their life-styles is unlikely to apply to all, even a majority, of homosexuals. There is a great range of life-styles and personality characteristics. Second, many homosexuals lead satisfying and full lives in which their homosexuality is only a small part (as with heterosexuals). There are also some interesting gender differences. Twenty-eight percent of the homosexual women in this sample had a Close-Coupled relationship compared with 10 percent of the men. And in terms of the less well-adjusted categories, 28 percent of the men were classified either Dysfunctional or Asexual compared with 16 percent of the women.

DEVELOPMENT OF HOMOSEXUALITY

Theories and evidence about the development of homosexuality have implications for the question of whether it is, in some sense, a disorder. First, let us consider biological factors. Kallmann (1952) reported twin-study data supportive of a genetic contribution, but subsequent research has not corroborated this finding (Rosenthal, 1971). The possibility that imbalances in male and female hormones contribute to homosexuality has been an attractive hypothesis, and, as we saw in the section on transsexualism, research does indicate the importance of both prenatal and postnatal levels of sex hormones in sexual development. Testosterone plays a crucial role in the development of secondary sex characteristics in men, such as the growth of facial hair, deepening of the voice, and the enlargement of the testes for the manufacture of sperm. There have been occasional reports of finding lower levels of testosterone in the urine or blood of male homosexuals than in male heterosexuals (for example, Kolodny et al., 1971), but Brodie et al. (1974) found *higher* levels of testosterone in male homosexuals. In perhaps the best controlled study to date, Tourney et al. (1975) found no significant differences in testosterone levels between 14 male homosexuals and 11 heterosexuals, with a strong trend for the homosexuals to have higher levels ($p < .10$). Most of the research in this area has used small and not necessarily random samples, and we might well question how representative these small samples are of the total population of homosexuals. If subgroups of homosexuals should be found to have lower than average levels of testosterone, we would have to discover what is cause and what is effect. Meanwhile, research so far provides little consistent support for hormonal differences in

male homosexuals. Meyer-Bahlburg (1979) reviewed research on sex hormones and female homosexuality and concluded that the majority of female homosexuals have normal sex hormone levels. About one-third of the lesbian women studied had higher than normal androgen (male sex hormone) levels, but again cause and effect are uncertain.

Psychological theories about the development of homosexuality have tended to stress one basic theme—anxiety over heterosexual expression of the sexual drive that impels the person to seek a safer avenue of expression with people of the same sex. In the psychoanalytic tradition homosexuality has clearly been viewed as a symptom of underlying psychological disorder. Thus Bieber and his colleagues (1962) wrote, "All psychoanalytic theories assume that adult homosexuality is psychopathologic" (p. 18). In this theory strong heterosexual anxiety is thought to date back to the Oedipal conflict and derives from anxiety (castration anxiety in males) about incestuous sexual urges toward the opposite-sex parent. Various other ideas are added to this basic proposition by different psychoanalytic practitioners—for example, that another man's penis is sought because it symbolizes the breast to the orally fixated homosexual.

Bieber et al. (1962) conducted a study comparing 106 male homosexual patients, in treatment with 77 New York psychoanalysts, with a group of 100 heterosexual patients also in treatment. Based on information given by the analysts, Bieber and his colleagues concluded that the results strongly supported the psychoanalytic theory of homosexuality—especially that fear of heterosexuality underlies homosexuality. For example, the homosexual patients were reported to be more fearful of disease or injury to the genitals (symbolic of castration) and this in turn was thought to be associated with fear of and aversion to the female genitalia. Of special significance in their view was the "close-binding, intimate mother" who maintained an overly close emotional attachment with her son and prevented the development of autonomy and more typical masculine behaviors. The fathers of the homosexuals were viewed as either remote or hostile, in neither case providing much encouragement for their sons' masculine identification.

The Bieber et al. study can be criticized in two important ways: (1) All of the homosexual subjects were in treatment and therefore by definition were experiencing symptoms or other difficulties in adjustment. One cannot generalize these findings to homosexuals in general, especially those not in treatment. (2) The usual safeguards for proper psychological research, such as the demonstration of interobserver reliability, were not included. Because of these shortcomings, the study would not be taken too seriously if it were not for the fact that subsequently another investigator (Evans, 1969) repeated the study with improved methodology.

Evans constructed a 27-item questionnaire based on the findings of the Bieber study, and under the pretext that he was studying cardiovascular disease administered it to 43 homosexuals (members of a Los Angeles homosexual organization) and 142 heterosexuals. Twenty-four of the 27 items discriminated between the two groups and in general strongly confirmed Bieber's findings. Homosexuals more often reported that:

1. They were frail or clumsy as children; they reported less often that they were athletic.
2. They were fearful of physical injury, avoided physical fights, played with girls, and were loners who seldom played baseball and other competitive games.
3. Their mothers were puritanical, cold toward men, insisted on being the center of the son's attention, made him her confidant, were "seductive" toward him, openly preferred him to the father, interfered with his heterosexual activities during adolescence, discouraged masculine attitudes, and encouraged feminine ones.
4. Their fathers did not encourage masculine attitudes and activities. The subjects spent little time with their fathers, were aware of hating their fathers, were afraid their fathers might physically harm them, and felt less accepted by the fathers.

The studies of Bieber et al. and Evans both rely on retrospective memories of childhood experiences and may reflect distortions of past events to an unknown degree. Nevertheless, the similarity in results is striking, considering that the men were in treatment in one case and not in treatment in another. The lack of the usual degree of masculine robustness, the "close-binding" mother, and the distant father may be an important pattern in the development of some homosexuals. I emphasize *some,* be-

cause there is a danger of leaving the impression that almost all homosexuals report this particular pattern. That is not so. These studies found that significantly more homosexuals responded to a particular item in a given way than did nonhomosexuals. For example, 28 percent of the homosexuals responded "often" to the item "Son was mother's confidant" compared with 5 percent of the heterosexuals. The remainder responded "sometimes." It was clearly a minority of homosexuals who remembered having their mothers confide in them often.

A quotation from Bell and Weinberg's (1978) study of homosexual patterns of living in San Francisco provides an appropriate conclusion to our discussion of this topic.

As for homosexuals' social and psychological adjustment, we have found that much depends on the type of homosexual being considered. Many could very well serve as models of social comportment and psychological maturity. Most are indistinguishable from the heterosexual majority with respect to most of the nonsexual aspects of their lives. . . . Close-Coupleds and Open-Coupleds behave much like married heterosexuals. Functionals draw on a host of support systems and display joy and exuberance in their particular life-style. To be sure Dysfunctionals and Asexuals have a difficult time of it, but there are certainly equivalent groups among heterosexuals. Clearly, a deviation from the sexual norms of our society does not inevitably entail a course of life with disastrous consequences. (pp. 230–231)

There are differences of opinion as to whether "treatment" in the sense of changing sexual orientation should be offered to homosexuals. The climate of professional opinion has been moving toward helping ego-dystonic homosexuals change their sexual preference, but only if they clearly desire this and only after they have had an adequate opportunity to explore their motivation for wanting to change (Adams & Sturgis, 1977; Halleck, 1976). Clinicians have also become more willing to help homosexuals improve their homosexual functioning in the same way that they are willing to help heterosexuals improve their heterosexual functioning (Russell & Winkler, 1977).

Summary

1. The normal sexual response cycle consists of four phases: the excitement phase, the plateau phase, the orgasmic phase, and the resolution phase.

2. Masters and Johnson's research helped to dispel previously held fallacies about direct stimulation of the clitoris, clitoral versus vaginal orgasms, simultaneous orgasms, and the size of penis and sexual enjoyment.

3. Impairments in sexual functioning can take several forms: inhibited sexual desire; inhibited sexual excitement, in males consisting of primary or secondary impotence, in females consisting of frigidity; inhibited female orgasm; inhibited male orgasm; premature ejaculation; and functional dyspareunia.

4. Anxiety about sexuality plays an important role in the development of these dysfunctions. Masters and Johnson especially emphasize performance anxiety and a spectator role.

5. Many sexual dysfunctions have been successfully treated by variations of an *in vivo* systematic desensitization.

6. Transsexuals feel trapped in a body of the opposite sex. Although unusual levels of sex hormones, present before or after birth, may contribute to transsexualism, direct research has not yet shown this to be the case. Social learning experiences that enhance opposite-sex identification may also be involved.

7. Paraphilias involve gross impairment in the capacity for affectionate sexual activity between adult human partners. They include fetishism, transvestism, pedophilia, zoophilia, exhibitionism, voyeurism, and sexual masochism and sadism.

8. Paraphilias are thought by some to develop as a result of a chance association between these unusual stimuli and sexual arousal followed by a long period of masturbating to fantasies of these stimuli.

9. Behavioral approaches to treating paraphilias appear promising, especially those involving covert sensitization and orgasmic reconditioning.

10. Homosexual and heterosexual orientations are best seen as endpoints on a continuum rather than as distinct categories.

11. Although in the past many mental health professionals tended to view homosexuality as a disorder, this is no longer the case; most now see it as simply a different but not in itself a pathological sexual orientation. Many homosexuals seem to be just as healthy psychologically as the average heterosexual person.

Suggested Readings

A survey of treatments for all kinds of sexual dysfunctions, including the procedures developed by Masters and Johnson, can be obtained in C. D. Tollison and H. E. Adams, *Sexual disorders: Treatment, theory, research* (Gardner Press, 1979). H. S. Kaplan provides a comprehensive discussion of therapeutic approaches to sexual dysfunctions in which, among other things, she considers those occasions when the interpersonal dynamics of the relationship must be dealt with as well as the sexual behavior itself (*The new sex therapies,* Quadrangle Books, 1974), and also *Disorders of sexual desire* (Brunner/Mazel, 1979). A. P. Bell and M. S. Weinberg present detailed findings of a study of homosexual life styles in San Francisco in *Homosexualities: A study of diversity among men and women* (Simon and Schuster, 1978).

Part
Three

Schizophrenia and the Affective Disorders

15
Schizophrenia and Paranoia

- What is schizophrenia? How would persons have to act or talk in order for this label to be applied to them?

- "I start thinking or talking about something, but I never seem to get there . . ." What is cognitive slippage?

- What is a delusion of influence? Of thought broadcasting?

- Is the prospect for recovery better if schizophrenia comes on slowly or abruptly? What is the process-reactive dimension?

- If a Joan of Arc heard voices and tried to muster an army today, what would mental health professionals say of her?

- What is *paranoia?* How does it differ from paranoid schizophrenia?

- Did you know that one famous case of paranoia (Daniel Paul Schreber) may as a child have actually been persecuted by his father?

Norma M.: A Strange Awakening

I know that I spent an unhappy childhood and a tragic adolescence and that, until a complete mental collapse occurred when I was 24, I lived through a series of emotional upheavals, depressions, abrupt changes of mind and plan, severe asthma, and a great many minor ailments like colds, fevers, influenza, and general fatigue, which left me little energy for sports or social life. Worst of all, I lived with constant fear and inhibition, making it impossible for me to make friends unless they were younger or in some respect inferior, or unless they were so extroverted they could take me under their social wings and brighten my life a little. Intellectual pursuits were my only strength, and a fear of failing at these kept me in a state of continual anxiety. I achieved some success at art. . . .

My father had been in a mental hospital since I was four years of age. I hadn't seen him for many years, and I lived in secret dread that it might be hereditary. My mother wouldn't talk about him because it upset her. I was an only child, with no one else to talk to.

After that year at college I returned to school-teaching for a year, and then attended a radio academy in Toronto to answer a lifelong urge to learn about acting. Life on a shoestring in a situation tense with the threat of competition worked things up to a crisis. . . .

What I do want to explain, if I can, is the exaggerated state of awareness in which I lived before, during, and after my acute illness. At first it was as if parts of my brain "awoke" that had been dormant, and I became interested in a wide assortment of people, events, places, and ideas that normally would make no impression on me. Not knowing that I was ill, I made no attempt to understand what was happening, but felt that there was some overwhelming significance in all this, produced either by God or Satan, and I felt that I was duty-bound to ponder on each of these new interests, and the more I pondered the worse it became. The walk of a stranger on the street could be a "sign" to me, which I must interpret. Every face in the windows of a passing streetcar would be engraved on my mind, all of them concentrating on me and trying to pass me some sort of message. . . .

New significance in people and places was not particularly unpleasant, though it got badly in the way of my work, but the significance of the real or imagined *feelings* of people was very painful. To feel that the stranger passing on the street knows your innermost soul is disconcerting. I was sure that the girl in the office on my right was jealous of me. I felt that the girl in the office on my left wanted to be my friend but I made her feel depressed. It's quite likely that these impressions were valid, but the intensity with which I felt them made the air fairly crackle when the stenographers in question came into my office. Work in a situation like that is too difficult to be endured at all. I withdrew farther and farther, but I became more and more aware of the city around me. The real or imagined poverty and real or imagined unhappiness of hundreds of people I would never meet burdened my soul, and I felt martyred. In this state, delusions can very easily take root and begin to grow. I reached a stage where almost my entire world consisted of tortured contemplation of things that brought pain and unutterable depression. . . .

Living with schizophrenia can be living in hell, because it sets one so far apart from the trend of life followed by the majority of persons today, but seen from another angle it can be really living, for it seems to thrive on art and education, it seems to lead to a deeper understanding of people and liking for people, and it's an exacting life, like being an explorer in a territory where no one else has even been. I am often glad that illness caused my mind to "awaken" 11 years ago, but there are other times when I almost wish that it would go back to sleep. For it is a constant threat. A breakdown in physical health, too much pressure, too many

> responsibilities taken on because they sound interesting to the "well" side of me, and I could be plunged back into the valley. Am I to live in a chair on a basement ward of a mental hospital, forced to endure a meaningless existence because people don't know how important freedom is to survival, or am I to move ahead to find a place in the modern world outside hospital walls? (From MacDonald, 1960, pp. 218-221)

Some of the disorders considered in this and the next several chapters represent severe forms of psychopathology that are usually labeled *psychoses.* Two characteristics distinguish psychotic disorders from the less severe disturbances thus far discussed: *distortion of reality* and *severe personality disorganization.* Like Norma, psychotic persons experience the world in a vastly different manner than most of us do. They may develop beliefs about the intentions and behaviors of other people that have no basis in fact, hear voices or smell odors that have no external source, and have little or no insight into their own distortions of reality. Their capacity for effective functioning is likely to be severely impaired; they cannot work, study, or assume the responsibilities of spouse or parent.

Psychotic disorders may or may not be associated with specific organic diseases. Disorders with no identifiable organic basis, the *functional psychoses,* include schizophrenia, paranoia, and some affective disorders. Biological causes for some disorders now called functional may be discovered in the future; and, like all human behavior, behavior in functional psychoses has some parallel in physical processes. Although the distinction between functional and organic can be blurred by these considerations, the term *organic mental disorder* is still reserved for disorders related to specific pathological processes such as an infection, tumor, or injury.

The disorder or disorders called *schizophrenia* continues to be one of the great puzzles in the field of abnormal psychology. Despite the accelerating increase in time and money devoted to its study during the last 100 years, fundamental questions about the nature and development of schizophrenia remain unanswered. In this chapter I will describe schizophrenic symptomatology and in the following chapter consider the current state of knowledge about its etiology.

The prevalence of schizophrenia is usually estimated to be about 1 percent of the population (Doh-renwend & Dohrenwend, 1974), indicating that about two million people in this country are currently suffering from this disorder—and this estimate may be conservative! Although patients diagnosed as schizophrenic compose about 20 percent of first admissions to mental hospitals, they usually represent about 50 percent of the resident population. This difference reflects the frequent readmissions of many schizophrenic patients and the chronicity and lack of response to treatment in others. Most schizophrenics are between 20 and 40 years of age when first admitted to a mental hospital; the highest rate of admission for any ten-year period is between 25 and 35 years of age (Yolles & Kramer, 1969). Schizophrenia clearly poses a problem of the first magnitude not only for the persons involved but for society at large.

Schizophrenic Behavior

You may recall from Chapter 2 that Kraepelin used the term *dementia praecox* to refer to a symptom syndrome that involved an early, usually gradual onset and a progressive deterioration of mental functioning. Bleuler (1950) introduced the term *schizophrenia* in 1911 to refer to essentially the same pattern of psychological symptoms. He drew upon the Greek words for "split mind" to refer to a split between thought processes and emotions or to a general disorganization in thought and behavior. This kind of splitting is not the same as that in the dissociation reactions of fugue, amnesia, or multiple personality. In those conditions the split is between different states of consciousness (different selves and motivational systems) rather than between thought and emotion. Bleuler did not believe that schizophrenia necessarily began in childhood or adolescence or that it necessarily progressed to an irreversible dementia.

It is not easy to summarize the symptoms under the heading of schizophrenia. They may include disturbances in language and thought, sensation and perception, motor behavior, social relationships, and emotional expression. The range and particular pattern of symptoms can vary so much that some investigators wonder whether there is one schizophrenia or several schizophrenias. For present purposes I will not attempt to discriminate between symptoms that may be more central and symptoms that may be more peripheral or secondary. This question will be considered later in this chapter and again in the next chapter. The following list of characteristics, then, are found in many, if not all, patients diagnosed as schizophrenic.

DISTURBANCES IN LANGUAGE AND THOUGHT

Loosening of Associations. One aspect of the schizophrenic person's difficulty in thinking and speaking clearly is a tendency toward loose, disjointed expression. As one patient described it,

My thoughts get all jumbled up. I start thinking or talking about something but I never get there. Instead, I wander off in the wrong direction and get caught up with all sorts of different things that may be connected with things I want to say but in a way I can't explain. People listening to me get more lost than I do (McGhie & Chapman, 1961, p. 108).

Bleuler (1950) referred to this problem as the "derailment of associations" by which he meant that the person becomes distracted by irrelevant associations, cannot suppress them, and as a consequence wanders farther and farther off the subject.

The above patient expresses himself quite adequately in telling us about his trouble in thinking. Most patients would not be so clear. Another patient, for example, said, "I'd give a pretty dime to talk like I like or place my words in talking with people noticing." Referring to her thinking, she goes on to say, "It slips because you go on and talk and have imaginations and try for others and seems just to come back to you" (Cameron, 1963, p. 611). Her use of the word *slips* is interesting because writers (for example, Meehl, 1962) have frequently used phrases like "cognitive slippage" to describe how the schiz-

ophrenic's train of thought seems to slip away from its intended goal.

The schizophrenic's loosening of associations is readily seen in the following example: A patient who was asked to define "diamond" as part of an intelligence test responded that it was "a piece of glass made from roses" (Hunt & Arnhoff, 1955). Those who are poetically inclined may find this a delightful definition. Unfortunately, the cold-blooded scorer of an intelligence test will find this response incorrect. There is, of course, nothing abnormal about having associations such as "glass" or "roses" to the word *diamond*. But if you accept the goal of giving a dictionary-type definition to the word, then you must suppress these intruding associations and stick to the task at hand. This is what the schizophrenic has great difficulty doing. Intruding associations may sometimes be highly personal and result in speech that is egocentric or *autistic,* and in extreme instances almost totally unintelligible, as the following quotation reported by Cameron (1947) illustrates.

Interviewer: Why are you in the hospital?
Patient: I'm a cut donator, donated by double sacrifice. I get two days for every one. That's known as double sacrifice; in other words, standard cut donator. You know, we considered it. He couldn't have anything for the cut, or for these patients. . . .
Interviewer: Well, what do you do here?
Patient: I do what is known as the double criminal treatment. Something that he badly wanted, he gets that, and seven days' criminal protection. That's all he gets, and the rest I do for my friend.
Interviewer: Who is the other person that gets all this?
Patient: That's the way the asylum cut is donated.
Interviewer: But who is the other person?
Patient: He's a criminal. He gets so much. He gets twenty years' criminal treatment, would make forty years; and he gets seven days' criminal protection and that makes fourteen days. That's all he gets.
Interviewer: And what are you?
Patient: What is known as cut donator Christ. None of them couldn't be able to have anything; so it has to be true works or prove true to have anything, too. He gets two days, and that twenty years makes forty years . . . (pp. 466–467)

Another experience that many schizophrenics report, which may be related to the uncontrollability of associations, is the feeling of being inundated by stimulation from both external sights and sounds and internal ideas and images. The person seems to be passively at the mercy of these stimuli and cannot turn them off or selectively attend to only some of this input. Again, let us listen to how some of the patients in McGhie and Chapman's (1961) study describe this experience:

It's as if I am too wide awake—very, very alert. I can't relax at all. Everything seems to go through me. I just can't shut things out.

Sometimes I feel alright then the next minute I feel that everything is coming towards me. I see things more than what they really are. Everything's brighter and louder and noisier. (pp. 104–106)

In paranoid schizophrenia the person may become preoccupied with delusional beliefs of persecution.

Perhaps the experience of being bombarded by stimulation that cannot be shut out and having irrelevant associations that derail one's attempts at communication are different aspects of the same basic problem. At any rate, it is easy to see how a person with these experiences would be greatly impaired in everyday functioning.

Delusions. As an extension of an egocentric and autistic orientation, many schizophrenic individuals at some point begin to see personal significance in everyday events, to read in intents and meanings that are not there. Recall how Norma felt that as her brain "awoke" various people, events, and places took on overwhelming significance. The walk of a passing stranger was a "sign"; every face on a passing streetcar was trying to give her some kind of message. In another case, a graduate student who was working on a computerized model for predicting the wild duck population began to believe that the computer printouts referred to him.

I would put myself into the model . . . trying to predict whether I should be going on . . . to a Ph.D. next year. . . . And, uh, then I figured that . . . well, I predicted that I was going to die. . . . Uh, so that I thought that this model was right in saying that the world was coming to an end, and it was my feeling that the world was coming to an end. But the model said I shouldn't tell anybody about the model, that that would just lead to chaos. (Reilly et al., 1973, p. 412)

Personalizations of everyday experience, or *ideas of reference* as they are sometimes called, provide a background against which more systematic *delusions* can develop. A delusion is a belief contrary to social reality that becomes fixed and resistant to change even in the face of strong evidence against it. Delusional beliefs can take many forms.

People with delusions of *persecution* believe that they are threatened and persecuted by various people or groups: neighbor, competitor, boss, communists, the FBI, or some vague "they." They find confirmation for this delusion by misinterpreting everyday experiences: A frowning person is plotting some sadistic action against them; a group of people laughing at a joke are laughing at them; or a television newscaster is making veiled threats at them.

People with delusions of *influence* believe that they are being controlled by some external agent.

Thus they may believe that a murderous impulse, a sexual fantasy, or an urge to commit suicide is imposed from the outside. The controlling agents may be God, the devil, parents, political groups, or again a vague "they." The mechanism of control is sometimes spelled out—for example, hypnotism, extrasensory perception, or influencing machines such as a television set or an X-ray device. The critical difference between a neurotic obsession or compulsion and a delusion of influence is whether the person takes the additional step of interpreting the obsessive idea or compulsive urge as being implanted by an external agent. Somewhat in contrast to the belief that external agents are inserting thoughts into one's head, some individuals develop the delusion that their thoughts are being broadcast into the external world so that everyone can hear them.

People with *grandiose* delusions or delusions of grandeur believe in their own greatness, usually as a political, military, or religious leader. At the other end of the continuum are *self-deprecatory* delusions in which people believe that they have done some horrible deed—such as causing World War II—a belief that could explain feelings of guilt and need for punishment.

Delusions of *body change* are beliefs about physical changes in the body; for example, a man believes that his body is changing from male to female, that his insides are rotting or that his head is filled with granite.

DISTURBANCES IN SENSATION AND PERCEPTION

Sometimes schizophrenic patients report perceptual distortions: The world seems flat, unreal, or remote; objects seem unusually large or small; or time passes with unusual slowness or rapidity. One patient described how people appeared distorted: ". . . people look confusing . . . they look almost like they're made up . . . like they're real people . . . and people I know, but they have masks on or they're disguising themselves. It's like a big play . . . " (Freedman & Chapman, 1973, p. 52).

Even more dramatic than perceptual distortions are the schizophrenic's experiences of stimuli that are not present at all—*hallucinations.* The person hears voices, sees visions, smells odors, or has sensations

of touch for which there are no identifiable external stimuli. Auditory hallucinations are the most common; the voices the person hears may condemn, praise, direct, or accuse. They may be identified with a specific agent such as God, the devil, parents, or more mysterious "others." While experiencing a hallucination, the person ordinarily has no way of knowing that the voices or other stimuli are not real. Usually they seem to come from an external source. The individual may listen passively to the voices, act upon their commands, or talk back to them, arguing, pleading, or cursing them. The hallucinatory experiences are usually not random sounds, sights, or smells. They often clearly relate to the person's own strivings, hopes, and fears. The persecuted hear themselves cursed or are advised to retaliate; the grandiose receive special communications from the Almighty; and the depressed are told of their unforgivable sins. The person in the following excerpt hears voices that complement his paranoid belief that "pursuers" are out to get him.

To the person with schizophrenia the world sometimes seems unreal, even one's own hands.

One day I went to reconnoiter in New York City's East Side. Being a stranger I was surprised to hear someone exclaim twice: "Shoot him!", evidently meaning me, judging from the menacing talk which followed between the threatener and those with him. . . .

These unidentified persons, who had threatened to shoot me, pursued me. I knew they were pursuing me because I still heard their voices as close as ever, no matter how fast I walked. . . .

I heard one of them, a woman, say: "You can't get away from us; we'll lay for you, and get you after a while!" To add to the mystery, one of these "pursuers" repeated my thoughts aloud, verbatim. . . .

Thus, in connection with their mind-reading ability, they are able to carry on a conversation with a person over a mile away and out of sight by ascertaining the person's unspoken thoughts, and then by means of their so-called "radio voices," answer these thoughts aloud audibly to the person. An uninitiated person would probably be very much startled over such phenomena. For example, what would you think, if you were on a level, desolate tract of land without any vegetation, or places of concealment upon it, and without a human being within miles, when you heard a mysterious, seemingly unearthly voice answer a question you were just thinking about? (White, 1964, pp. 133–135)

DISTURBANCES IN MOTOR BEHAVIOR

Schizophrenic persons may engage in strange, stereotyped gestures, postures, or facial grimaces. Occasionally they may cease bodily movements altogether in *catatonic immobility* or, at the other extreme, become wildly excited and violently attack other people in *catatonic excitement.* Some schizophrenics' behavior is regressive in nature. They become unable (or unwilling) to dress, undress, feed themselves, or attend to their toileting needs. Ordinary inhibitions may be lost so that they urinate, defecate, or masturbate in public.

EMOTIONAL DISTURBANCE

Shallow, flattened, and *blunted* are words frequently used to describe the emotional state in schizophrenia. The lack of enjoyment in all aspects of life that often characterizes the schizophrenic person is sometimes referred to as *anhedonia.* Some schizophrenics, however, do express emotions, but inap-

propriately; they laugh, cry, giggle, or rage with no clear relationship to events in the social environment.

SOCIAL WITHDRAWAL

Schizophrenic individuals avoid close interpersonal relationships, spend much of their time alone, and retreat more and more into their own fantasy world. The withdrawal is both physical and psychological. Their unintelligible speech and inappropriate emotional expression keep them as psychologically distant from others as would miles of physical space.

The Diagnosis of Schizophrenia

European and American psychiatrists have, at least until recently, diverged in their diagnostic practices with respect to schizophrenia. The Europeans have stayed rather close to Kraepelin's original concept, which emphasized an early and usually gradual onset and a progressive deterioration in functioning. As a result European psychiatrists have not tended to give this diagnosis to individuals who abruptly develop acute schizophrenic-like symptoms and recover from the episode within a few months. European psychiatrists have also been inclined to diagnose a number of patients as manic-depressive (or affective disorder) who would be diagnosed schizophrenic in this country. American psychiatrists, on the other hand, were more influenced by Bleuler, who used a broader definition of schizophrenia, did not insist on a chronic course of the disorder, and explicitly stated that the diagnosis of manic-depressive disorder should be made only if the diagnosis of schizophrenia had definitely been ruled out. A demonstration of how the diagnosis of schizophrenia increased from the 1930s to the 1950s in the United States is provided by Kuriansky et al. (1974), who showed that only 28 percent of the patients at the New York State Psychiatric Institute were diagnosed schizophrenic between 1932 and 1941 compared to an astounding 77 percent between 1947 and 1956.

Cooper et al. (1972) directly studied differences in British and United States diagnostic practices during the period 1966–1968 by having a number of consecutive admissions to a mental hospital near London and to a mental hospital in Brooklyn, New York, interviewed and diagnosed by a special team of psychiatrists. These diagnoses were then compared with those made on the same patients by the usual psychiatric staff at the different hospitals. The psychiatric staff at the Brooklyn hospital diagnosed schizophrenia in 65 percent of the cases compared with 34 percent for the London hospital psychiatrists. The special team, including both American and British psychiatrists, were more in accord with the regular British diagnoses, diagnosing 32 percent of the same Brooklyn patients as schizophrenic and 26 percent of the same London patients as schizophrenic.

DIAGNOSTIC CRITERIA OF SCHIZOPHRENIA, DSM-III

Recently there has been a decided swing back toward the narrower European definition of schizophrenia in the United States. In DSM-III many of the acute schizophrenic-like episodes will not be included in this diagnosis as a result of the requirement that active schizophrenic symptoms must be present for at least six months before the diagnosis can be made. The term *schizophreniform disorder* will be applied to schizophrenic-like symptoms that last less than six months. Of course, in a fair number of new cases the symptoms will persist longer than six months, at which time the diagnosis will be changed to schizophrenia. This rather simple change in diagnostic criteria should produce a major decrease in the number of first-admission patients diagnosed schizophrenic.

In addition to lasting longer than six months, DSM-III requires that one of the following three symptoms must be present before the diagnosis of schizophrenia can be made: delusions, hallucinations, or marked disorder of thought. The symptoms must be severe enough to cause disorganization of daily functioning in such areas as work, social relations, and self-care.

SUBTYPES OF SCHIZOPHRENIA, DSM-III

There has always been variability in the patterns of symptoms shown by schizophrenic patients. Krae-

pelin proposed three major subtypes of schizophrenia (or dementia praecox, as he called it): *hebephrenic, catatonic,* and *paranoid.* He subsequently added a fourth subtype, *simple,* as suggested by Bleuler. The simple subtype has been dropped in DSM-III since no overt signs of psychosis are present and individuals of this kind are now to be diagnosed *schizotypal* or *borderline personality disorder.*

Hebephrenic (Called Disorganized in DSM-III). The essential features are incoherent speech, hallucinations, fragmented bits of delusional beliefs with the content not organized into a coherent theme, inappropriate emotional responses frequently involving silly laughter, and stereotyped mannerisms and grimaces. The patient who referred to himself as a "cut donator" provides a good example of speech with hebephrenic disorganization. The overall disorganization and impairment is severe in this form of schizophrenia and the course tends to be chronic without significant remissions.

Catatonic. The most common features are rigid immobility and unresponsiveness to environmental stimuli, often for long periods of time. Catatonic im-

Some schizophrenic persons show various postures and mannerisms. The same awkward posture may be maintained for long periods of time.

With secret weapons; kidnaping; and the language in reverse; Capitol Hill massacred the people and enslaved the world. Thus, Liberty, stands for slavery: The White House, represents The Black House, 'Communists,' (Con-hew-mist.)

On Nov. 24, 1766, 13 Communists (Colonists) signed The Magna Charta, (1215 + 551 = 1766); and on Dec. 15, 1774, they registered as a Party; which appeared on the titlepage of The Proceedings of the Congress, & in every newspaper in New Y*ork*; (New *Crow*).

Today, Communists on Capitol Hill kidnap the American public on a mass scale; then taken to gas chambers in Houston, Texas, etc. The human dung is used for oil; the flesh made into Textiles; & the bones & teeth are made into China; Christals, etc. A Communist world-wide profit sharing biz. Thus, Allied Chemical Bldg. at 42nd St. & B'way stands for, The Foe's Chemicals.'

I quote Abe Linc*oln*, "With our secret weapons; kidnaping, and the language in reverse; our Communist govt. of by & for the free people shall perish from this earth." "4 score & 7 years ago." False, it was 5 score & 17 years ago; 1863 − 117 = 1746.

I quote Daniel Webster, "Our Communist operations cannot be published without confusion of tongue; or be exposed to the charge of treason." (Web-ster,' stir the web)!

See incredible evidence in The American Heritage, Feb. 1965, Vol. 16, #2. (ComUS-con U.S.)

The Creators fury kindled against His flock; He sent His grim pill (pil-grims, 1620 + 126 = 1746) thru John James Audubon to "Con them all; to hew them down the mist." Mist stands for (human) garbage: Con-hew-mist; (Communists.) The Creator sent along His own secret weapons to cause violent death & fatal diseases-Cancer; Heart attack; Paralysis; Stroke; Cerebral palsy, etc. The shell of the crab & seahorse; scales of fishes; & horns of the bull & the ram: Note: 'Horn & Hardart;' Horns & Heart Art.

Leaflet circulated in New York by a person who was probably paranoid schizophrenic. Note preoccupation with communist conspirators, the fragmented and disjointed character of the writing, and distraction by "normal" associates (e.g., horns of the bull and the ram, Horn and Hardart, Horns and Heart Art).

mobility is on rare occasions accompanied by "waxy flexibility," a condition in which the patient's body can be molded into various positions and remain in these shapes for long periods. Immobility is sometimes interrupted by periods of extreme excitement and homicidal violence.

Paranoid. Paranoid schizophrenics are characterized by delusions of persecution, grandiosity, or jealousy, frequently accompanied by hallucinations and some degree of personality disorganization. The impairment in everyday functioning, however, is not nearly as severe as in the hebephrenic form.

Undifferentiated. This subtype, frequently diagnosed, points up the fact that schizophrenic symptom patterns do not conform neatly to the above subcategories. This diagnosis is used when symptoms are different from those in the other subtypes

or when symptoms represent a mixture of features found in the other subtypes.

Residual. This category is applied to individuals who have previously been diagnosed schizophrenic and have shown some improvement in their acute symptoms but who still show residual signs of the disorder such as emotional blunting, social withdrawal, eccentric behavior, or mild thought disorder.

First-admission diagnoses of hebephrenic and catatonic schizophrenia have been rare in the past 10–15 years. Paranoid schizophrenia has for many years been the most commonly diagnosed subcategory. For example, Romano (1977) found for all patients diagnosed schizophrenic on first admission to psychiatric hospitals in Monroe County, New York, during 1971–1975 the following breakdown by subtype: hebephrenic, 1 percent; catatonic, 3 percent;

paranoid, 37 percent; chronic undifferentiated, 25 percent; and acute undifferentiated, 17 percent. Many of the individuals in the acute undifferentiated subtype (from DSM-II) would by current procedures be called schizophreniform disorders. The unaccounted-for percentages in these figures reflect small percentages in other categories no longer used in DSM-III.

Schizotypal Personality Disorder and Borderline Personality

In DSM-III one of the personality disorders is called *schizotypal personality disorder*. The essential features of this disorder are various oddities of thinking, perception, communication and behavior which are not severe enough to meet the criteria for the diagnosis of schizophrenia. Usually the person is distant and withdrawn in social relationships. Previously, personality characteristics of this kind have been called schizoid, borderline or latent schizophrenia, or simple schizophrenia. The psychological traits are similar to those seen in residual schizophrenia after recovery from a course of active schizophrenia. According to some investigators, the schizotypal personality is present in individuals who are genetically vulnerable to schizophrenia. (Meehl, 1962)

The concept of *borderline personality* originally implied that the person existed on the borderline of psychotic breaks with reality. In DSM-III the definition emphasizes such characteristics as the following: impulsivity or unpredictability, a pattern of intense but unstable interpersonal relationships, inappropriate, intense anger, disturbance in sense of identity, and physically self-damaging acts.

THE PROCESS-REACTIVE AND THE PREMORBID ADJUSTMENT DIMENSIONS

"[Madness] rais'd on a sudden from some solemn evident, as from a vehement passion, is much safer than invading by degrees." This observation that a gradual onset of psychotic behavior was indicative of a more severe and chronic course than that associated with an abrupt onset was made in 1685 by Willis writing in *The London Practice of Physick* (Wender, 1963). Both Bleuler and Kraepelin (in his later writings) were aware that not all patients diagnosed as schizophrenic showed an irreversible course toward total deterioration. Historically there have been two interpretations of this fact: (1) These patients must have been misdiagnosed in the first place, since *by definition* schizophrenia is a progressive and incurable disorder; or (2) there are two types of schizophrenia, one type showing the progressive deterioration and the other showing the capacity for recovery.

The latter point of view was led to the distinction between *process* and *reactive* schizophrenia, the former with a poor prognosis for recovery and the latter with a good prognosis (see Kantor et al., 1953, for an early attempt to make this distinction). Process schizophrenia is further characterized by an early and gradual onset of symptoms; the person develops little social or intellectual competence and eventually shows more and more withdrawal and disorganization. Reactive schizophrenia, on the other hand, is marked by relatively normal social and intellectual development and appears abruptly in the form of an acute reaction, frequently in response to known life stresses. The person with such an acute reaction may be severely disturbed, delusional, confused, and disorganized, but has a good chance of recovery. Process schizophrenia has been thought to have a biological basis and reactive schizophrenia to result from past learning experiences and immediate situational stresses.

The first problem that arose with the process-reactive distinction was a familiar one: Patients did not fit neatly into these categories either. When attempts were made to categorize schizophrenic patients in terms of their life histories, many showed some intermediate degree of prepsychotic adjustment and suddenness of onset, leading investigators to conclude that the process-reactive distinction is best conceived not as two separate types but as endpoints on a continuum (Higgins & Peterson, 1966).

Various rating procedures have been developed to assess degree of premorbid adjustment (see Kokes et al., 1977, for a review of these procedures). An individual scoring low on premorbid adjustment usually has not been married, has never worked at one job for two years or more, has had no academic or vocational training after high school, did not date steadily as a teenager, and has never been deeply in love and told the person about it. These ratings of the patient's social and heterosexual adjustment prior to hospitalization have been found to be highly predictive of recovery from the first hospitalization for schizophrenia (Phillips, 1953; Stephens et al., 1968). Researchers have also found that poor-premorbid patients are more deviant in their language and thought processes and possibly have a stronger genetic disposition to the disorder than do good-premorbid patients (Gottesman & Shields, 1972; Maher et al., 1966).

So what does it mean that premorbid adjustment is related to tendencies to recover from schizophrenic symptoms? First, it is likely that a number of good-premorbid patients with acute onset of symptoms would be diagnosed as schizophreniform disorder by DSM-III and thus may not be "true" schizophrenics by the narrower definition of the term. On the other hand, that may be simply playing with labels, since the definition of a schizophreniform disorder is the presence of schizophrenic symptoms that last for less than six months. More fundamentally, all of the research to date on the premorbid adjustment and the related process-reactive dimension would seem to be consistent with the idea that individuals vary in their vulnerability to schizophrenia (whether biologically or psychosocially produced). The person toward the process or poor-premorbid end of the dimension has a greater susceptibility to the schizophrenic reaction pattern and manifests these symptoms earlier in life and with less external stress; the person toward the reactive or good-premorbid end of the dimension has less susceptibility to the disorder and shows the reaction later in life and in response to identifiable life stresses.

Although there had been a fair amount of optimism about chances of recovery from schizophrenia when the broader definition had been used, when a narrower definition following Kraepelin's criteria (composed of a higher proportion of process rather than reactive schizophrenics) is used, the prognosis is not so bright. Stephens (1978) reviewed 38 studies of long-term follow-ups of patients diagnosed schizophrenic by the narrow criteria. Overall, roughly 60 percent of these patients were unimproved at the time of follow-up, which ranged from 5 to 40 years from first admission. Many of these patients, however, began their hospital stays before the era of modern drug therapies and emphasis on brief hospitalization. For more recently admitted patients a small proportion remain in the hospital indefinitely, but a higher proportion experience repeated episodes of incapacitating symptoms so that they are in and out of hospitals, sometimes maintaining only a marginal adjustment when they are out (Zubin & Spring, 1977).

One Disorder or Several?

For Kraepelin, dementia praecox was not necessarily one disorder; he used the term in a generic sense as a grouping of several psychotic disorders. Bleuler (1950) likewise referred to the "group of schizophrenias." "For the sake of convenience I use the word in the singular although it is apparent that the group includes several diseases" (p. 8). To this day there is no clear evidence as to whether schizophrenia is one underlying disorder with various symptom manifestations, whether there are several disorders with relatively different causations, or whether there is no "underlying disorder" at all but simply an almost unlimited variety of behaviors that have been learned in the process of coping with life's problems. For example, schizophrenia may reflect a basic underlying deficit in mental functioning whose expression is greatly influenced by other factors such as intellectual abilities, cognitive styles, socioeconomic class, and patterns of family interaction. These could account for the great variability in symptom pictures. I will return to this issue when considering the question of etiology.

What Comes First?

Closely related to the question of whether schizophrenia is one disorder or several is the question of which, if any, of the symptoms of schizophrenia are basic and which tend to follow as secondary effects from the more primary disturbance. Is it possible that some of the observed variations in schizophrenic symptoms are only different secondary manifestations rather than differences in the basic disorder? Bleuler, for example, proposed that fundamental to schizophrenia were disorders in thinking (the derailment of associations) and emotional expression. He saw withdrawal, autistic preoccupation, and ambivalence (conflicting reactions such as love and hate) as direct expressions of the fundamental disorder. Other symptoms such as delusions, hallucinations, catatonic immobility, and belligerence he considered secondary. Delusions and even hallucinations, for example, might result from an extended period of withdrawal and preoccupation with internal imaginings; catatonic immobility might result in some cases from intensely ambivalent feelings or wishes that literally immobilize the person. The primary disorder might or might not give rise to one or more of these additional symptoms. Some patients diagnosed as schizophrenic do not show any of these secondary symptoms, a fact that provides some support for Bleuler's proposal. On the other hand, many writers have disagreed with Bleuler's particular choice of fundamental schizophrenic traits. One of the difficulties with Bleuler's fundamental symptoms is that concepts such as emotional expression, ambivalence, and autism have been difficult to judge reliably. In DSM-III, as we have seen, the diagnostic criteria for schizophrenia emphasize the more (relatively) reliable assessment of the presence of delusions, hallucinations, and thought disorder.

In considering "fundamental" symptoms we quickly get into questions of causation since advocates of different etiological theories are inclined to see different aspects of the reaction as fundamental. Advocates of biologically oriented theories think of some basic defect in brain functioning that impairs perception or attention or produces an anhedonic state (lack of capacity to experience pleasure) as being fundamental, whereas partisans of psychological theories see the disorder as fundamentally a way of coping with a "crazy" environment or as a regression to an early stage of ego development.

Experimental Research on the Nature of Schizophrenia

In the late 1930s researchers began to apply the methodology of experimental psychology to the study of psychopathology. Rather than drawing inferences from case studies or psychological tests, they began to conduct laboratory experiments using schizophrenics and normal persons as subjects. Although this research does not tell us what causes schizophrenia, it does aid our thinking about what might be "fundamental" to schizophrenia by specifying its deficits more accurately. There is no way that the vast amount of experimental research on schizophrenia can be surveyed in this one section. One type of research has been selected as representative of work in this area: research on attentional deficits.

PAYING ATTENTION TO THE WRONG THING

Early Reaction Time Research. David Shakow (1963) and his group at Worcester State Hospital in Massachusetts were among the first to use the methodology of experimental psychology in the study of psychopathology. Beginning their work in the late 1930s they looked for the simplest levels at which schizophrenic impairment might appear, and found no differences between schizophrenics and normals on measures of sensory acuity, motor reflexes, or steadiness. However, when they examined responses in a simple reaction time experiment, enormous differences appeared. Reaction time is the length of time it takes to make a response to a designated stimulus; for example, in the Worcester research the subject was asked to lift a finger from a telegraph key as soon as a light came on. Schizophrenics are markedly slower on this task than normals, with process schizophrenics showing greater impairment than reactive or paranoid schizophrenics.

Most subjects show shorter reaction times if another stimulus is provided ahead of time that signals when the response stimulus is about to occur. This preliminary stimulus provides an interval in which to get set to respond. When this preparatory interval is long, eight seconds or more, process or chronic schizophrenics are no longer aided by it and their performance again becomes slower than normals. A common interpretation of these findings is that schizophrenics, especially of the process variety, cannot maintain attention for the several seconds required for this task; they become distracted by irrelevant stimuli, either from the external environment or from their own thought processes.

More Recent Research on Attention Deficits in Schizophrenia.   Since the early experiments by Shakow, numerous studies have substantiated the inability of the schizophrenic person to maintain attention and not be distracted by irrelevant stimuli (for example, Neale, 1971). There are certain problems of interpretation associated with the typical study in which a group of schizophrenic patients is compared with a normal control group even when the control group is well matched on such variables as age, socioeconomic status, and estimates of general intelli-

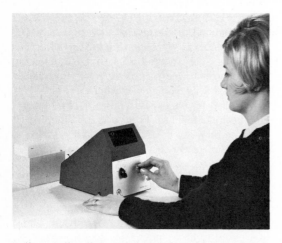

In the reaction time experiment the subject is asked to move a switch as soon as possible after a signaling stimulus is presented. Schizophrenic persons have been found to respond more slowly in tasks of this kind.

gence. How can we know that obtained differences in performance do not result from the social, dietary, and other characteristics associated with living in an institution, taking medication, learning to play the role of mental patient, or generalized confusion in the acute phase of the disorder rather than from some fundamental aspect of the disorder itself? As a step toward ruling out these alternative interpretations Asarnow and his colleagues have suggested that if a psychological deficit is a primary feature of schizophrenia, it is likely to be present in two additional groups: children who are at risk for schizophrenia because they have a biological parent who has been diagnosed schizophrenic and former schizophrenic patients who have recovered from their acute and obvious symptoms and are now maintaining themselves in the community. These two groups should be unaffected by factors associated with institutionalization or the confusion and disorganization of an acute episode.

To test one prediction from this theory Asarnow et al. (1977) compared high-risk foster children whose biological mothers had been diagnosed schizophrenic, a foster control group of children for whom neither parent had been diagnosed schizophrenic, and a community control group of children living with their biological parents. Several measures of attention deficit were obtained. One test, for example, was the span-of-apprehension task in which the subject was asked to report whether a T or an F had been briefly flashed on a screen. The task was further complicated by adding either two, four, or nine distracting other letters. It had been shown in previous research that schizophrenic patients relative to normals made increasing numbers of errors as the number of distracting letters was increased (Neale, 1971). Asarnow et al. found in their study that children at risk for schizophrenia did indeed show similar deficits in attention on this task as had the adult schizophrenics in the previous study. Not all of the at-risk children showed the deficit, which was to be expected since only a small proportion were likely to actually become schizophrenic as adults, but enough showed the deficit to make the overall mean score significantly different from the other two control groups.

In a second study Asarnow and MacCrimmon (1978) compared the performance of hospitalized schizophrenics, remitted schizophrenics, and normal controls on the same span-of-apprehension test used with the children as well as one other measure of attentional deficit. The remitted schizophrenics had been discharged two to three months previously, were maintaining themselves in the community, were being seen in an outpatient clinic, and had been judged to be free currently of major symptoms such as hallucinations, delusions, and affect disorders. The normal control subjects were similar to the schizophrenic subjects in age, intelligence as measured by a vocabulary test, and proportion of men and women. The hospitalized schizophrenics and the remitted schizophrenics both showed greater decreases in correct identifications as the number of distracting letters increased than did the normal control subjects (see Figure 15-1), with no differences emerging between the remitted and nonremitted schizophrenics. It should be pointed out that both groups of patients were receiving drug treatment at the time of the study (the remitted schizophrenics on an outpatient basis) and it might be argued that the attentional deficit was produced by the drugs. There is fairly good evidence, however, that the drugs used (phenothiazines) actually improve span-of-apprehension performance (Spohn et al., 1977), so this factor is an unlikely explanation of the findings.

Considering the two studies together, then, the results are consistent with the theory that an attentional deficit in the form of an unusual susceptibility to distraction by irrelevant stimuli is a basic feature in the schizophrenia-prone individual, a feature that may well be present before the full-blown disorder develops and after recovery from an acute phase of the disorder. In the next chapter we will consider the implications for the etiology of schizophrenia of findings from high-risk children.

Distraction by Normal Associations. In the studies just described the distracting stimuli were primarily external. Other research suggests that schizophrenic individuals may also be especially susceptible to distraction by internal stimuli, that is, by irrelevant thoughts and associations. Chapman and Chapman (1973a) have developed a theory of schizophrenic thought disorder that emphasizes yielding to normal associations. They follow Bleuler's line of thinking in emphasizing the importance of associative interference, the inability to suppress responses that have a high associative connection to the previous word or thought. One of Bleuler's examples of this is the pa-

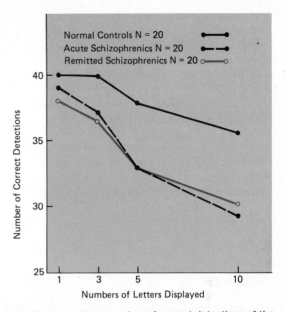

FIGURE 15-1. Mean number of correct detections of the target stimuli as a function of the number of letters displayed for acute and remitted schizophrenics and normal controls. (From R. F. Asarnow, & D. J. MacCrimmon, Residual performance deficits in clinically remitted schizophrenics: A marker for schizophrenia. *Journal of Abnormal Psychology*, 1978, *87*, 597–608. © American Psychological Association and used with permission.)

tient who is writing a New Year's greeting: "I wish you then a good, happy, joyful, healthy, blessed and fruitful year, and many good wine-years to come, as well as a healthy and good apple-year, and sauerkraut and cabbage and squash and seed year" (Bleuler, 1950, p. 606). Each association that this person made is normal—an association that any of us might have to the preceding word. What is abnormal is the perseveration along the chain of associations in a way that impairs the intended expression of a New Year's greeting. The speech of the nonschizophrenic person is strongly controlled by the surrounding context or the overall goal of the speech. Thus a normal person instructed to say the first word that comes to mind in a word association experiment is free to respond with any strong association; likewise on the psychoanalytic couch the patient is instructed to respond with whatever associations come to mind. In these situations there are few restraints and the nonschizophrenic person's associations may be loose and illogical. Schizophrenics appear to be constantly responding to word association or free-association instructions.

According to the Chapmans one kind of association that can interfere with a person's speech is the *meaning response,* the subjective meaning of the word or phrase. For example, some words have more than one meaning response, and these different meaning responses vary in strength, some strong and some weak. The word *rare,* for example, may mean "uncommon" or "partially cooked." The former meaning is the stronger-meaning response for most people, the one they are likely to give first if asked to define *rare.* On the other hand, if we provide a context, the normal person can easily shift to the weaker meaning. Such would be the case if we asked the person to define *rare* in the sentence, "John likes rare meat." The Chapmans' theory states that schizophrenics will fail more often than normals to use contextual cues of this kind. Chapman et al. (1964), for example, found that schizophrenics could not ignore the strong meaning of a word even when the contextual cues clearly indicated that the weaker meaning was appropriate. See Research Report 15-1 for another study that supports the Chapmans' theory.

RESEARCH REPORT 15-1

Schizophrenics Cannot Ignore Associative Distractors

Rattan and Chapman (1973) assessed the effect of associative distractors on performance on a vocabulary test. Subjects were asked to respond to two 60-item multiple-choice vocabulary tests, one of which contained items with distracting associates, whereas the other included only items without associates. The following is an example of an item with a distracting associate:

> *Shoot* means the same as
> A. rifle (associate)
> B. rug (irrelevant)
> C. sprout (correct)
> D. none of the above

The following is an example of an item with no associate:

> *Scale* means the same as
> A. pin (irrelevant)
> B. yell (irrelevant)
> C. climb (correct)
> D. none of the above

The Chapmans had noted in another article (Chapman & Chapman, 1973b) that the magnitude of the difference in performance between a generally less able group and a comparison group is affected by the discriminating power of the test. Discriminating power is determined by the reliability of the test and the range of difficulty of the items used in the test. If a test lacks discriminating power, then it will reduce real differences in ability between the groups or not show them at all. In many studies comparing schizophrenic and normal performance on some task, the neutral or nondistractor task tends to be an easier and therefore less discriminating task. The greater deficit shown by the schizophrenics could simply be an artifact of this difference in discriminatory power rather than a reflection of the basic nature of schizophrenia.

To avoid this artifact, the authors matched the two vocabulary tests on the means and variances (a measure of spread of scores) of the scores, and on the mean and variances of item difficulty, using a normal standardization group. The experimenters tested

TABLE 15-1   Mean Number of Correct Responses to Vocabulary Test

Groups	With Distractors	No Distractors
Schizophrenic	22.4	28.0
Normal	36.4	35.3
Dull normal	27.9	28.0

Adapted from Rattan and Chapman (1973) and Chapman and Chapman (1973).

42 chronic schizophrenics (free of antipsychotic drugs for four weeks prior to testing) and a normal control group, and as usual the schizophrenics scored more poorly than the normals on both tests (see Table 15-1). However, the important finding is that the schizophrenics did significantly more poorly on the test with distracting associates than they did on the test with no distracting associates. The matched normal group performed the same on both tests.

As added proof that the schizophrenics' poorer performance on the test with distractors cannot be explained by a generalized deficit, the authors also compared the schizophrenics to a subsample of the normal group that scored at the same level as the schizophrenics on the no-distractor test. The scores for this group of "dull normals" on the test with distractors, however, was the *same* as their scores on the no-distractor test, indicating that these individuals did not show the same kind of distractability as the schizophrenics. This study provides clear support for the Chapmans' view that the schizophrenic is unduly distracted by normal associations, and furthermore that this kind of thought disorder is not the same as found in people who have low intelligence.

Although the research of investigators such as Chapman has documented rather strongly the schizophrenic's tendency to be distracted by normal dominant response tendencies, such findings leave unexplained the clearly bizarre and highly personalized (autistic) responses that schizophrenic individuals sometimes make. Any comprehensive theory of schizophrenic thought disorder must account for this aspect of schizophrenic thinking too. A likely possibility is that many schizophrenics do retreat psychologically to an inner world of fantasy where, cut off from the possibility of external validation, they develop strange and peculiar ideas.

Shakow (1961) has summarized a basic feature of the schizophrenic thought disorder illuminated by the experimental research we have just reviewed:

If there is any creature who can be accused of not seeing the forest for the trees, it is the schizophrenic. If he is of the paranoid persuasion, he sticks even more closely than the normal person to the path through the forest, examining each tree along the path, sometimes even each tree's leaves with meticulous detail. If at the other extreme he follows the hebephrenic pattern, then he acts as if there were no paths, for he strays off the obvious path entirely; he is attracted not only visually but even by smell and taste, by any and all trees and even the undergrowth and flora of the forest, in a superficial flirting, apparently forgetting in the meantime about the place he wants to get to. (p. 14)

These studies by no means answer all questions about the nature of disordered thinking in schizophrenic persons. For example, they tell us nothing about the cause of the difficulty, whether it results from some biological impairment in the central nervous system or represents a response learned in the context of social interaction. The main contribution of this kind of research is that, by sharpening our understanding of certain aspects of schizophrenia, it allows for a more precise search for causes and treatments.

Paranoia
Dr. McD.: Plots and Conspiracies

Dr. McD. had led a rather distinguished career as a physician prior to the time of his admission at age 54 to a Veterans Administration hospital. As a young doctor he had done significant research on kidney functioning and had written a well-received book on internal medicine. At the time of his hospitalization he had reentered military service as a lieutenant colonel and was in command of an overseas hospital. During this period he began to write letters to the War Department in Washington complaining of graft in both the American and Korean forces. When evidence for the graft was requested, Dr. McD. gave investigators boxes containing slips of paper, many of which were laundry receipts or old drugstore prescriptions. At the time he accused many officers in the high command in Korea of being secretly on the side of the Communists.

He was given a medical discharge and advised to accept hospitalization in a VA hospital, which with some protest he did. He explained to the admitting psychiatrist that he considered the Korean War to be a conflict between Christianity and Judaism and that he was willing to enter the hospital so that he could report to the proper authorities on the subversive activities of "Jewish psychiatry." In the hospital he refused to assume the role of patient and behaved as though he were a staff physician, having some success in awing the younger physicians and nursing staff. He was, after all, a person with a brilliant record as a research worker and diagnostician, and with his gray hair, erect military posture, and imperious voice it was difficult to resist the role reversal that he insisted on. Most attempts to interview him about his background and personal life met with resistance and arrogant refusal to discuss such matters.

Occasionally, he made bizarre notes on other patients' charts:

3.00 A.M. Heard shots being fired at the back fence. This is obviously another case of failure on the part of the hospital administration.
5:00 A.M. I could not locate the body.
9:00 A.M. Freshly burned refuse in back of building 504. Contains what must be human bones. The administration had gotten rid of the evidence.

After about five months he left the hospital against medical advice (he had entered voluntarily). For 13 months he remained out of the hospital. During this period his behavior became increasingly bizarre, culminating in an attack on his Japanese houseboy, whom he accused of plotting an attack against him and of being a thief and a sexual pervert. He was relatively unsuccessful in reestablishing his medical practice and increasingly preoccupied with his paranoid suspicions; for example, during the month prior to his readmission he called the police 15 times about suspicious-looking characters who were entering the lobby of his apartment house or walking by on the street. He was finally committed involuntarily by the Superior Court on the petition of his sister.

At the time of this report his condition was essentially unchanged, and it was the opinion of the psychiatric staff that he would probably remain there for the rest of his life. There were no obvious signs of intellectual deterioration; emotionally he showed little overt anxiety or depression; and in general he was well-behaved and cooperative. He nevertheless resisted all efforts at individual or group therapy. A young graduate student in psychology was able to establish a friendly relationship with him by listening patiently to Dr. McD.'s attitudes about the war, medicine, psychiatry, and so on. One day when the young psychologist for the first time asked about some small aspect of his personal life, Dr. McD. in a rare moment of openness said, "Young man, I am an old and lonely man, and there is nothing you can do about it." (From Goldstein & Palmer, 1975)

SYMPTOMS

Paranoia is a rare condition characterized by an elaborate delusional system. In spite of a chronic course the disorder does not seem to interfere with other aspects of the individual's thinking and functioning; the disorganization in thought and behavior seen in schizophrenia or the extremes of elation and depression seen in the affective disorders are not present. Except for those parts of life related to the delusional beliefs, the person may seem perfectly normal, as did Dr. McD.

The essential feature of paranoia is a delusion of persecution or grandiosity, the two frequently going together. Much of the paranoid's thinking and behavior is logical if one accepts a basic premise—for example, that a certain group is conducting a conspiracy. Any attempts to dissuade the paranoid of such false beliefs by logical argument and questioning of the evidence are likely to fail. In fact, if you try too hard, the paranoid person may conclude that you are part of the conspiracy. Diagnoses of paranoia are rare because such individuals do not seek help. They function effectively as long as their delusion does not interfere.

Some paranoid individuals develop delusions of grandeur in which they see themselves endowed with special abilities or as having been called by God to lead mankind to salvation. Other individuals feel they have made some great invention that the world ignores no matter how hard they try to promote it.

It is easy to see how persecutory themes can quickly develop in the context of grandiose beliefs. Religious messiahs are rarely welcomed by the establishment, and inventions that cannot be proved to work are likely to elicit rebuff. Paranoid persons respond to these criticisms by constructing more elaborate beliefs about special groups whose whole purpose is to persecute them.

Authorities disagree on the extent to which paranoia is a separate disorder from paranoid schizophrenia. Once again we encounter the difficulty that plagues all diagnostic schemes; that is, distinctions are not so plain in life as in theory. As manifestations of schizophrenic disorganization decrease, the person is more likely to be diagnosed as paranoid, but degree of disorganization varies continuously and any dividing line is likely to be arbitrary. Dr. McD.

showed relatively little disorganization, but occasionally some of his behavior (such as including laundry slips as evidence for conspiracy) became bizarre enough to approach schizophrenia.

Paranoia is also difficult to distinguish from *paranoid personality*. The latter, a type of personality disorder, is defined in DSM-III as showing hypersensitivity, rigidity, unwarranted suspicion, jealousy, envy, excessive self-importance, and a tendency to blame others and ascribe evil motives to them. Perhaps the most crucial distinguishing feature is that a paranoid personality lacks an enduring, well-formulated delusional belief.

DEVELOPMENT

Paranoid delusions can be precipitated by biological conditions. Organic brain disease or the excessive use of certain drugs such as amphetamine are associated with paranoid delusions in some people. In these cases it is difficult to know how much the biological factors are directly producing paranoid delusions and how much they are simply triggering delusions in people whose previous personalities make them vulnerable. Intensive and prolonged use of amphetamines produces such a reaction with enough regularity to suggest a fairly direct biological connection. However, because there is considerable personality disorganization in the amphetamine psychoses, these reactions seem closer to paranoid schizophrenia than to paranoia.

Psychological theories usually emphasize a developmental history in which the person as a child is isolated from other children and never experiences good social relationships with them (Schwartz, 1963) and develops a special sensitivity to shame or humiliation (Colby, 1977). Cut off from the normal give-and-take of childhood interaction, the child begins to feel different and perhaps inferior, oversensitive to criticism or ridicule, and angry in anticipation of being snubbed. The person becomes like the man in the old joke who has a flat tire on a country road but has no jack with which to lift the car. He walks toward the nearest farmhouse, thinking to himself that the farmer will certainly be annoyed and probably unwilling to lend him a jack. By the time the farmer answers his knock on the door, the man has become

Dr. McD.: Inferiority and Anger

Both of Dr. McD.'s parents died when he was a young child, and his sister, 20 years older, became his guardian. He rarely saw her, spending most of his time at boarding schools or summer camps. Although his academic performance was outstanding, he had few if any friends. Other boys considered him a sissy or a teacher's pet and made him the object of considerable teasing and ridicule. During college and medical school he lived isolated in a room by himself, and although he did attend various social affairs given by his sister, he resisted all her efforts to pair him with young ladies that she knew. Outside of medicine his interests were limited almost entirely to his hobbies of model railroads and astronomy. Once, just before entering medical school, he had traveled in Europe and attempted to look up relatives in the country where his mother was born. He was upset and disgusted to discover that these relatives lived in a ghetto; when he spoke of this fact to his sister, he seemed unaware that his mother was Jewish.

A psychological interpretation of his paranoia would emphasize a profound sense of inferiority, intense anger at other people for real or imagined ridicule, and a projection of this anger onto others in the form of beliefs that they were persecuting him. (Goldstein & Palmer, 1975)

so enraged at this expected rejection that he blurts out to the astonished farmer that he can take his bloody jack and . . .

In this fertile soil delusional beliefs develop. Isolated from other people, the person cannot easily test the reality of any budding suspicions. The person may grow up with a suspicious nature, readily projecting blame for personal shortcomings onto others, but not develop a systematized delusion until late middle age. Some new failure may occur, some new rebuff, and this time all the suspicions run together to form one grand explanation for those lifelong trials and tribulations. Several characteristics in the early life of Dr. McD. might have made him vulnerable to develop a pattern of delusional thinking.

Although Freud did not see many psychotic patients in his practice, he developed a theory of paranoia based primarily on his study of the writings of Daniel Paul Schreber, an eminent German judge who developed paranoid delusions at the age of 42 and was in and out of mental institutions until his death at age 69. Freud's theory was that persecutory beliefs had their origins in unacceptable homosexual impulses. A man, for example, experiencing the impulse, "I love him," defends against it by converting it into, "I hate him," and then projects this reaction onto the other person, "He hates me." Few clinicians today accept this explanation for *all* paranoid delu-

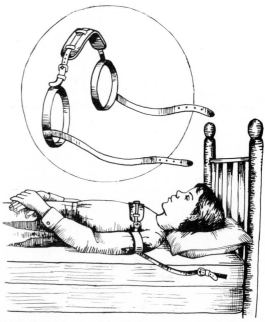

Daniel Paul Schreber developed paranoid delusions of persecution and "soul murder" in middle age. During childhood his father had attempted to crush any signs of disobedience. Shown here is a belt designed by Schreber's father to keep children supine and straight while sleeping.

sions. On the other hand, in individual cases conflicts over homosexuality may well play some role.

The case of Schreber has been reconsidered recently. Schatzman (1973) advanced an interesting argument to show that Schreber probably *was* persecuted by his father, so that he had some childhood basis for his feelings of being victimized. Schreber's father was also a distinguished German, well known for his books on education, physical culture, and child rearing. His views on the latter subject might be summed up in the idea that the natural inclinations of children are evil and must be stamped out by whatever means necessary.

In the case of nearly every child, however, even the most well brought up, there are sometimes surprising manifestations of defiance or rebelliousness, although if the discipline has been good these should occur only rarely—a vestige of that *innate barbarity* which leads the developing self-confidence astray. . . . The most important thing is that the disobedience should be *crushed* to the point of regaining complete submission, using corporal punishment if necessary. (pp. 136–137)

One of the son's later beliefs was that he was the victim of "soul murder," by which he meant someone had taken possession of his soul. At first he thought one of his previous doctors had committed soul murder on him, then he wondered if it was not God, but apparently he never considered that it might have been his own father.

At the time when my nervous illness seemed almost incurable, I gained the conviction that soul murder had been attempted on me by somebody. . . . (p. 55)

It occurred to me only much later, in fact only while writing this essay did it become quite clear to me that God Himself must have known of the plan, if indeed He was not the instigator, to commit soul murder on me. . . . (p. 77)

Schatzman makes a convincing case for the interpretation that many of the son's delusional beliefs derive from his relation with his father, a point of view strikingly similar to that of Laing (discussed in the next chapter), who argues that crazy beliefs no longer seem crazy when we understand the family context in which they arise.

PARANOID OR SANE?

Although Schreber may have experienced real persecution as a child, in all likelihood he did not as an adult. However, when paranoid symptoms develop in people who are actually victimized by large sections of society, we have a special problem in the use of the term *paranoid*. For example, for blacks in the United States to feel that certain environments are hostile is not paranoia but accurate perception. Grier and Cobbs (1968) go so far as to say that it is necessary to the black American's mental health to distrust whites; to be protected from unbearable emotional distress "he must develop a *cultural paranoia* in which *every* white person is a potential enemy unless proved otherwise and every social system is set against him unless he personally finds out differently" (p. 178). This extreme view points up the problem of disentangling real from imagined persecutions.

Of course, like everybody else, blacks can develop the more personalized paranoid beliefs that go beyond the limits of real persecution. In understanding and treating a paranoid person, it is important to appreciate the real events that have contributed to the development of the more extreme disorder.

Likewise, certain cultures such as the Dobu of Melanesia "normally" believed there was danger of being poisoned, and the Kwakiutl Indians of the Canadian Northwest believed in persecution by spirits and witches. Individual paranoia cannot be diagnosed without taking the normal level of cultural paranoia into account.

What about a person who claims to have experienced a mystical revelation of some religious truth and feels compelled to pass it along to others? There is no way, of course, to prove whether the person did or did not have a real experience beyond the comprehension of most of us. Unless other symptoms clearly indicate a pathological reaction, it is best not to call such beliefs paranoia. Other factors that would indicate paranoia are a strong sense of being persecuted, bizarre beliefs that have little possibility of being true, resistance to change in the face of clearly contrary evidence, deep feelings of inferiority, and, finally, extreme sensitivity to criticism.

Summary

1. Schizophrenia poses a problem of the first magnitude for society. In the United States, 1 percent of the population and approximately 50 percent of the resident population of mental hospitals carry this diagnosis.

2. Symptoms of schizophrenia include disturbances in language and thought, sensation and perception, motor behavior, social relationships, and emotional expression.

3. Schizophrenic speech and thought is characterized by looseness and disjointedness. Some schizophrenics develop delusional beliefs of persecution, grandiosity, influence, thought broadcasting, self-deprecation, and body change.

4. Disturbances in sensation and perception may involve seeing the world in a flat, two-dimensional manner, or experiencing hallucinations such as voices.

5. Many schizophrenics show flattened or inappropriate emotional reactions and tend to withdraw psychologically from other people.

6. In DSM-III schizophrenia is subdivided into hebephrenic, catatonic, paranoid, undifferentiated, and residual categories.

7. Other dimensions of schizophrenia which have proved to be useful (for example, in predicting recovery) are the process-reactive and good-poor premorbid dimensions.

8. The process schizophrenics show progressive deterioration with little likelihood of recovery; their symptoms have an early and gradual onset. The reactive end of the dimension refers to opposite characteristics.

9. Controversy continues as to whether schizophrenia is one disorder or several and as to which aspects are fundamental.

10. Experimental research on schizophrenia has helped to sharpen our understanding of the nature of the schizophrenic deficit. Thus, the reaction time research of Shakow and the strong versus weak meaning response research of Chapman and his associates have provided quantitative and objective measures of schizophrenics' inability to maintain attention and their distraction by irrelevant stimuli or associations.

11. Paranoia is a rare condition characterized by a delusional system involving unwarranted beliefs of persecution and in some cases beliefs of grandiosity.

12. Paranoid delusions can be precipitated by biological factors such as amphetamine drugs or organic brain disease.

13. In psychological terms, people who develop paranoid delusions are thought to have lived socially isolated lives as children and developed strong sensitivities to criticism.

14. Some paranoid individuals probably *were* subject to parental persecution when they were children (as was Schreber), thus laying a foundation for delusions of persecution as an adult.

Suggested Readings

First-person accounts of what it is like to be schizophrenic can be found in *The inner world of mental illness,* by B. Kaplan (Harper & Row, 1964) and in *Retreat from sanity,* by M. B. Bowers (Human Sciences Press, 1974). A fictionalized account of the author's personal experience of a schizophrenic disorder in adolescence can be found in the beautifully written *I never promised you a rose garden,* by H. Green (Signet, 1964). In a more scientific vein Chapman and Chapman give a thorough and thoughtful review of theories and empirical research on the nature of the schizophrenic thought disorder in *Disordered thought in schizophrenia* (Prentice-Hall, 1973). M. Bleuler (Eugen Bleuler's son) follows the course of the schizophrenic disorder in a large sample of patients in *The schizophrenic disorders: Long-term patient and family studies* (Yale University Press, 1978). M. Schatzman in *Soul murder: Persecution in the family* (Random House, 1973) makes a case for real persecutions underlying the delusional beliefs of Daniel Paul Schreber.

16

The Causes of Schizophrenia

- Is schizophrenia a matter of chemistry? Of genes? Of family interaction?

- If a child's biological mother is schizophrenic and the child is placed for adoption shortly after birth, does the child have a greater than average chance of becoming schizophrenic?

- What is dopamine? What has it got to do with schizophrenia?

- Do some parents have a "talent" for producing schizophrenic children?

- "Go away closer." What is a double-bind?

- "Square pegs in round holes." Are schizophrenic children reacting sanely to a crazy world?

- Do economic recessions increase rates of hospital admissions of individuals diagnosed as schizophrenic?

Many theorists have strongly advocated either biological or psychosocial causes of schizophrenia, and many investigators, though giving lip service to the other side, have clearly focused on one of these alternatives or the other. First, let us consider the case for the biological approach, then for the social environment, and finally the possibility of interactions between the two.

The Case for Biological Determinants

HEREDITY

Evidence accumulated over the years points strongly to a genetic contribution to schizophrenic disorders. For example, schizophrenia occurs at a significantly higher rate in the close relatives of schizophrenic individuals than in the population at large (Rosenthal, 1971). This fact, of course, can be explained as readily by environmental influences as by heredity. More relevant to the genetic hypothesis are the results of twin studies.

Twin Studies.   Without exception twin studies have found identical twins to be concordant for (share a

diagnosis of) schizophrenia more often than fraternal twins. See Table 16-1 for a summary of ten studies conducted at different time periods and in different countries.

The Gottesman and Shields (1972) study deserves special attention because of the methodological care with which it was conducted and because it provides strong evidence that concordance rates become higher when the index twin's (that member of the twin pair who was initially diagnosed as having the disorder) schizophrenia is more severe and chronic. The authors identified their 24 pairs of identical and 33 pairs of same-sex fraternal twins from the records of the Maudsley Hospital in London where information on the twin status of all patients had been kept since 1948. There was no tendency for the incidence of schizophrenia in twins, either identical or fraternal, to be different from that in the population at large; nor have other investigators found such a difference. Identical or fraternal status was determined by comparing blood groups and fingerprints as well as appearance. Most twin pairs were interviewed and given psychological tests, and available hospital records were examined.

In 10 out of 24 identical twins (42 percent) both twins had been hospitalized and at some time diagnosed as schizophrenic by a psychiatrist. The corresponding rate for fraternal twins was 3 out of 33 (9 percent). In order to control for diagnostic bias the

TABLE 16-1   Concordance Rates for Schizophrenia in Twin Studies

	Number of Pairs		Concordance Percentages	
	Identical	*Fraternal*	*Identical*	*Fraternal*
Earlier Studies				
Luxenberger (1928), Germany	19	13	58	0
Rosanoff et al. (1934), U.S. and Canada	41	53	61	13
Essen-Möller (1941), Sweden	11	27	64	15
Kallmann (1953), New York State	174	517	69	10
Slater (1953), England	37	58	65	14
Recent Studies				
Inouye (1961), Japan	55	11	60	18
Kringlen (1967), Norway	55	90	25	4
Tienari (1971), Finland	19	20	16	5
Fischer (1973), Denmark	21	41	24	10
Gottesman and Shields (1972), England	24	33	42	9

authors had six experienced clinicians (five psychiatrists and one clinical psychologist) make diagnoses on the basis of extensive case summaries in which no information about identical or fraternal twin status was included. All six clinicians had to agree on a diagnosis of *definite* schizophrenia before a case would be so labeled. On this basis, 40 percent of the identical twins were concordant for schizophrenia compared with 10 percent of the fraternal twins.

Previous investigators had observed that for discordant identical twins the disorder in the index twin was less severe and chronic than when the twins were concordant (Inouye, 1961; Rosenthal, 1959). Gottesman and Shields also examined their data for this possibility and made some interesting findings. They considered as mild any index identical twin who had not been in the hospital during the last six months and was presently working or supporting a family; all others were considered severe. The separate concordance percentages for these two types of identical twins were 17 percent for the mild cases and 75 percent for the severe cases, clearly confirming the trends reported by previous investigators. These findings are consistent with the distinction between process and reactive schizophrenia, although they do not tell us whether these are separate disorders with only process schizophrenia having a genetic basis or whether there is only one disorder in which the genetic effect varies from weak to strong. Some of the "mild" index twins might have been diagnosed schizophreniform disorder by current DSM-III criteria.

Adoption Studies. Evidence from adoption studies is even more difficult to explain on the basis of environmental influences. Heston (1966) found that children born to schizophrenic mothers and placed in foster or adoptive homes within the first three days after birth had a significantly higher incidence of schizophrenia as young adults than did a control group of foster or adoptive children whose parents were not schizophrenic. Five of the 47 children whose biological mothers were schizophrenic were diagnosed, without knowledge of the group to which they belonged, as schizophrenic; none of the children in the control group was so diagnosed. Although the absolute number of children who became schizophrenic is small, the chance of all five coming from the experimental group is less than 2.5 times in a hundred ($p < .025$).

TABLE 16-2
Percent of Parents Diagnosed as Having Either Definite or Uncertain Schizophrenia

Type of Parent	N	Percent Schizophrenic
Biological parents of schizophrenic adoptees	173	13.9
Biological parents of control adoptees	174	3.4
Adoptive parents of schizophrenic adoptees	74	2.7
Adoptive parents of control adoptees	91	5.5

NOTE: From S. S. Kety, D. Rosenthal, P. H. Wender, & F. Schulsinger (1976).

Rosenthal et al. (1975) obtained similar results in a study conducted in Denmark, where it was possible through a central psychiatric registry to determine who had been adopted at an early age and who among the biological parents, either father or mother, had been diagnosed as schizophrenic. Yet another variation on this kind of study is that of Kety et al. (1976) who, using the same psychiatric register in Denmark, identified a group of early adoptees who had become schizophrenic. They then tracked down as many of the biological parents of the adoptees as they could to see what proportion of them were schizophrenic. The results are summarized in Table 16-2 where it can be seen that the diagnosis of schizophrenia or uncertain schizophrenia was highest, about 14 percent, in the biological parents of schizophrenic adoptees than for any other group of parents.

The results of these adoption studies are extremely difficult to explain by environmental factors, since the early removal of the child from the biological family prevents the psychological transmission of the disorder. It would be necessary to show that the adoptive environments of the experimental children were more pathology-inducing than those of the control children *before* the children were placed there in order to have a strong case for an environmental interpretation. Differences in parental behaviors observed after the children had been received into the family could reflect an interactive effect that the schizophrenically disposed child had on the parents.

There is no particular reason to believe that such differences existed prior to placement.

An interesting finding in most of these adoption studies is that there tends to be a greater than expected proportion of biological parents or other relatives of schizophrenic children who have non-schizophrenic disorders such as severe personality disorders of an obsessive, hysterical, or antisocial type, or have alcohol problems, or show schizoid personality traits. These other kinds of disorders also appear to be more common in adopted children who have a schizophrenic biological parent. This suggests the possibility that some aspect of the genetic disposition to schizophrenia may, in weaker form, manifest itself in these diverse disturbances.

The findings of Asarnow et al. (1977) described in the last chapter are also suggestive of a genetic factor in schizophrenia. In their study they found foster children whose biological mother was schizophrenic to show greater deficits in paying attention than various comparison groups. These results suggest that attentional deficits are a basic aspect of the schizophrenic disorder and that they are to some extent genetically determined.

In summary, both the twin studies and the adoption studies indicate that genetic factors contribute to the development of schizophrenia. However, not even the staunchest advocates of hereditary influences propose that schizophrenia is determined by genetic factors to the same degree as, for example, eye color or blood type. Concordance rates for identical twins are never found to be 100 percent, as they would have to be if schizophrenia were caused entirely by genetic inheritance. A common view is that a genetic predisposition is a necessary but not a sufficient basis for schizophrenia. Without some genetic predisposition a person will not become schizophrenic under any environmental stresses; with some genetic predisposition a person may or may not become schizophrenic depending upon the strength of the genetic tendency and the nature of environmental stressors.

BIOLOGICAL CORRELATES

The term *correlate* is used as a reminder that even if a certain biological deviation were found in schizophrenics, it would not prove that the deviation caused the schizophrenia. Environmental stresses causing the schizophrenia may also have caused the biological deviation, or the deviation might result from some other factor, such as long-term institutionalization or diet, that is correlated with being schizophrenic. In cases where the biological deviation precedes the schizophrenic disorder, it seems improbable that the biological deviation is a secondary manifestation of the schizophrenic reaction. In general, however, keep in mind that causality is not necessarily demonstrated by the presence of some biological abnormality.

Postmortem examinations of brains of schizophrenic patients have revealed no anatomical deviations or lesions that consistently distinguish them from the brains of normals. However, indirect evidence does suggest some possible impairment in brain functioning in schizophrenia. Ricks and Nameche (1966), for example, examined guidance clinic records of adolescents who were subsequently hospitalized for schizophrenia. The individuals who became chronic schizophrenics showed more "soft signs" of neurological impairment (abnormal speech, abnormal gait, poor coordination, impaired attention span, and hyperactivity) than those whose schizophrenia took an acute or episodic form.

Other indications of organic involvement in schizophrenia are the higher incidence of abnormal brain wave patterns (Itil, 1977), errors in smooth pursuit eye movements (Holzman & Levy, 1977), and evidence that points to dysfunction in the left hemisphere of the brain (Buchsbaum, 1977) found in samples of schizophrenic patients. Other findings suggest that some schizophrenic persons are physiologically overreactive, whereas others are underreactive (Venables, 1977). See Research Report 16-1 for a description of findings related to the latter possibility.

The High-Risk Strategy. In the high-risk approach, children who have a biological parent diagnosed as schizophrenic are selected for study because of the prevailing evidence that about 10 percent of these children will become schizophrenic at some point in their lives, a frequency of occurrence that is about ten times higher than in the general population. In high-risk studies the child in many cases is living or has lived with the biological parents, so results of these studies do not bear on the genetic-environ-

RESEARCH
REPORT
16-1

Schizophrenics: Overreactive, Underreactive, or Both?

Investigators have studied physiological response patterns, especially of the autonomic nervous system, for years without finding any consistent pattern of over- or underarousal in schizophrenics, including separate analyses for the process and reactive, as well as good- and poor-premorbid, dimensions (Klorman et al., 1977; Venables, 1977). Venables and his associates, however, in a number of different studies find evidence for two extremes in autonomic reactivity among schizophrenic patients with overresponding and underresponding patients not showing any strong or consistent correspondence to the process-reactive dimension. Typically over- or underresponding is measured by electrodermal responses to a series of tones. These responses are a measure of sweat gland activity on the palmar surfaces of hands or feet innervated by the sympathetic division of the autonomic nervous system. Most normal subjects show a clear-cut response to the first few presentations of the tone, part of the orienting response, and then rather quickly habituate, that is, stop making the electrodermal response on subsequent presentations. In Venables's research many schizophrenics make no response at all to the first tone or continue to respond even to the fifteenth presentation of the tone and therefore take much longer than normal to habituate. Not all researchers have found such clear-cut bimodality in responding (for example, Zahn, 1976), but overall the evidence at this time appears more in favor of the existence of these two extreme types of responders than against it. And a recent study by Rubens and Lapidus (1978) yielded strong evidence for this distinction. With overresponding defined as failure to reach an habituation criterion of electrodermal responding by 15 tone trials and underresponding as either making no response or an isolated first trial response, *all* 40 of the schizophrenic patients fell into one of these extreme categories and none of the 20 normal control subjects showed either of these extreme patterns. Such a sharp discrimination is unlikely to hold up in other studies, but it does provide impressive support for Venables's two-types-of-responder theory. Twenty of the schizophrenics were chronic inpatients and 20 were outpatients who had never been hospitalized for more than six months. There was no significant difference between these groups in terms of the proportions of over- and underresponders.

The overresponders seemed to be overreacting to both external and internal stimuli and were unable to "get used" to a recurring stimulus and stop responding to it. This physiological overarousal would seem to parallel the subjective reports of some schizophrenic persons who say that they are at the mercy of all stimulation whether originating externally or internally. Underresponders, on the other hand, seemed to have shut out most external and internal stimuli.

Another interesting aspect of this study is that the same measures were obtained a second time six weeks later. At that time eight of the outpatients and three of the inpatients had changed from one extreme pattern to another. *None* changed from an extreme pattern to a normal pattern of responding. The authors suggest that these changes may reflect adaptive attempts by the schizophrenics to modulate their responsivity to stimulation—attempts, however, that swing from one extreme to another. This conclusion is supported by the fact that there was a higher proportion of changers in the outpatient group and that within the outpatient group changers had significantly shorter lengths of accumulated hospitalizations. The ability to change, in other words, may represent a psychological strength.

mental question. What these studies can tell us is something about the psychological and physiological characteristics of these children *before* some small proportion become schizophrenic and thus possibly point to more fundamental traits that are not secondary manifestations of an overt psychosis or of labeling and institutionalization.

In the first major study of this kind, Mednick and Schulsinger (1968, 1973) and Mednick et al. (1975), took advantage of Danish record keeping and selected in 1962 a sample of 207 children whose mothers had been hospitalized for at least a total of five years and were considered process schizophrenics. This sample was called the high-risk group. A comparison group of 104 low-risk children whose mothers were not schizophrenic were selected and matched with the high-risk group. The average age of the children at the start of the project was about 15 years. High-risk children, relative to low-risk children, were found to have had more birth difficulties; for example, they had longer deliveries and more abnormal placentas. On an association test in which they were asked to report all associations to a specific word printed on a card placed in front of them, the high-risk children gave a greater percentage of clang associations (rhyming associations) and associations to their own response words (which they were explicitly asked not to do) than did low-risk children. This finding suggests that a mild disorder of association was already developing in some members of the high-risk group.

Five years later the authors identified 20 high-risk subjects who had begun to show severely abnormal behavior. These subjects were labeled the Sick Group. Twelve had been admitted to psychiatric facilities or were under psychiatric care, and the remaining eight were severe schizoid personalities, delinquents, alcoholics, or had shown some kind of bizarre behavior. Each of these 20 individuals was matched with another person in the high-risk group that had either maintained or improved adjustment, and also with a subject in the low-risk group. Matching variables were level of adjustment at the time of the initial assessment, age, sex, and social class. The second high-risk group was called the Well Group.

Thus there were now two groups of high-risk subjects that had been judged equal in level of adjustment in 1962. Since then the individuals in one group

had suffered severe mental breakdowns and the individuals in the other group had maintained or improved their mental health. How can we account for the difference? Part of the answer may lie in characteristics that already existed in 1962. At that time the Sick Group differed from the Well Group and the low-risk control group in several ways. First, the schizophrenic mothers of the Sick Group had been hospitalized when their children were younger and their psychoses were generally more severe. Second, these subjects had more often been disciplinary problems at school; they tended to be domineering, aggressive, and disruptive in class. Third, on the association test they had tended to "drift" away from the stimulus word, responding to their own associations. For example, to the stimulus word "table" they might respond "chair, top, leg, girl, pretty, sky. . . ." Those in the Sick Group who did not show drifting apparently controlled this tendency by repeating the same one or two responses for the entire one-minute period.

With respect to biological variables there were two main findings: First, a higher proportion of the Sick Group (70 percent) had suffered one or more serious complications of pregnancy or birth than the Well Group (15 percent) or the low-risk control group (33 percent). These complications included anoxia (oxygen deprivation), prematurity, prolonged labor, placental difficulty, mother's illness during pregnancy, and breech presentations. Second, there was a strong and consistent tendency for the Sick Group to show physiological overreactivity as indicated on several measures of electrodermal response. Perhaps before or during the early stages of schizophrenia the overarousal pattern predominates, and it is only later that the two distinct groups of over- and underarousal emerge.

Other investigators of children with a schizophrenic parent have found only partial support for indications of autonomic overarousal and sensitivity reported by Mednick and Schulsinger (Salzman & Klein, 1978; Van Dyke et al., 1974). Part of the problem may be that only a small subgroup of children with a schizophrenic parent are actually at risk for schizophrenia (about 10 percent will actually become schizophrenic), and these are too few in number to significantly affect the mean scores of the larger at-risk group. Recall that only a subsample of Mednick and Schulsinger's high-risk children fell into the Sick Group category five years later.

A number of high-risk studies have found evidence for attentional deficits, especially susceptibility to distraction (for example, Asarnow et al., 1977; Erlenmeyer-Kimling, 1976; Hanson et al., 1976). A subset of high-risk children in the Asarnow et al. study showed especially high consistency in attentional deficits across various tasks, and these children may well be the ones who are "really" at risk.

The high-risk strategy of research has paid off in terms of providing some provocative findings. Physiologically there is some indication of an overreactivity pattern, and psychologically attentional deficits and looseness of associations are indicated. These two sets of findings would seem to be closely related. The physiological indicators of overresponsiveness would seem to have a parallel in the susceptibility to distraction shown in psychological performance. If these empirical findings turn out to be repeatable, then we will want to discover the underlying neurophysiological and biochemical mechanisms responsible for the defect.

Brain Chemistry. Do biochemical processes in the central nervous system produce some of the symptoms seen in schizophrenia? This possibility has an old and honorable tradition that goes back to Grecian theories of "humors" in the blood and more recently to Kraepelin, who believed that dementia praecox was probably caused by toxic substances secreted from the sex glands. The fact that certain chemicals, such as hallucinatory and stimulant drugs, can produce striking changes in mental experiences that resemble the schizophrenic reaction lends credence to the hypothesis that in schizophrenia the body may be producing its own toxic substances.

For 50 years the search for a biochemical mediator of schizophrenia has gone on at an ever-increasing tempo, accompanied by much false hope and disillusionment. Many articles, not only in scientific journals but in newsmagazines and Sunday supplements, have announced the latest discovery of "the biochemical basis of schizophrenia." Being less newsworthy, subsequent failures to replicate the finding rarely reach the popular press, although fortunately they usually are published in the scientific journals.

Many substances have been reported or speculated to be uniquely present, or present at deviant levels, in the bloodstreams or in the brains of schizophrenics. One of the most consistently supported findings is evidence that implicates the role of excessive activation of neuronal tracts using the neurotransmitter, dopamine. Research suggests that this overactivation may reflect an oversensitivity of cortical dopamine receptors rather than excessive amounts of dopamine (Bacopoulos et al., 1979; Post et al., 1975). See Research Report 16-2 for a more detailed account of the dopamine hypothesis.

More recently there has been speculation that a group of substances called endorphins may be involved in the biochemical story of schizophrenia. Endorphins (from endogenous morphines) are produced in the brain and have morphinelike properties, such as the ability to reduce pain. There is accumulating evidence that endorphins can affect the activity of dopaminergic neurons (Volavka et al., 1979). Either an excess or a deficiency of endorphins can apparently cause supersensitivity of the dopamine receptors and thus could be contributing to the presumed overactivity of dopaminergic neurons in schizophrenia.

The field of schizophrenia research is littered with the abandoned wrecks of once-promising theories. Excessive dopaminergic activation may yet turn out to be a secondary aspect of the neurophysiology of schizophrenia. Even if it plays a primary causative role, there still remains the task of understanding how the disturbed dopaminergic system produces the symptoms of schizophrenia. There are many possibilities since, for example, dopamine neurons are involved in various cortical, brainstem, and limbic systems that affect motivation, emotion, and attentional processes. At some point the behavioral research on attentional deficits and the physiological research indicative of over- and underarousal will converge with the biochemical research to complete our understanding of the biological side of schizophrenia. And very likely this final picture will include the locus of those biochemical or neurophysiological dysfunctions that are genetically transmitted. We are not there yet. We may be close or the goal may elude us for some time to come.

RESEARCH
REPORT
16-2

Schizophrenia: Excessive Activation of Dopamine Neurons?

The initial evidence for the dopamine hypothesis resulted from two lines of research: One was derived from the fact that the *phenothiazine* drugs (see Chapter 17) are generally acknowledged to be highly effective in alleviating the symptoms of schizophrenia, and a second was based on the fact that certain other drugs, the *amphetamines* in particular, occasionally produced schizophrenic-like reactions in normals or intensified symptoms in already schizophrenic individuals.

Let us begin with the phenothiazines. If these drugs act on whatever is fundamentally impaired in schizophrenic brains, an understanding of the way they act should shed light on the nature of the disordered brain functioning. But do the phenothiazines act upon something fundamental to the disorder, or are they a kind of supersedative? Research is fairly clear-cut on this point: Compared to a sedative such as *phenobarbital*, the phenothiazines are definitely more effective in treating schizophrenia, whereas phenobarbital is frequently no more effective than a placebo (Casey et al., 1960). Furthermore, if one roughly categorizes schizophrenic symptoms into fundamental and secondary symptoms, following Bleuler (1950), it is found that the phenothiazines are most effective with the more basic symptoms. Thus phenothiazines are most effective in reducing thought disorder, flattened affect (emotion), and withdrawal; moderately effective with hallucinations; less effective with delusions, hostility, and belligerence; and relatively ineffective with anxiety, depression, and disorientation. All in all the evidence suggests that the phenothiazines exert a fairly specific therapeutic effect on schizophrenic patients.

The next step is to determine how the phenothiazines produce their effects. As it turns out, there are a variety of phenothiazines, some of which are more effective than others in treating schizophrenia. Research has shown that those phenothiazines that are most effective are also those that seem to block the *dopamine* receptors in the brain (Carlsson, 1978). Dopamine is a neurotransmitter substance that takes part in the chemical transmission of nerve impulses from the nerve ending of one neuron to the cell body of another neuron (Figure 16-1). Different groups or tracts of neurons used different neurotransmitters, and dopamine apparently is used only in certain areas of the brain, primarily in a dopamine tract originating in the brainstem and two other tracts in the limbic structures.

Several kinds of evidence support the conclusion that phenothiazines effective in treating schizophrenia block dopamine receptors in this tract. First, one of the frequent side effects of heavy and prolonged use of phenothiazines is symptoms resembling *Parkinson's disease*, rhythmic tremors and difficulty in controlling body movements. The dopamine tract has been shown to degenerate in Parkinson's disease, and the disease can be successfully treated with L-dopa, an amino acid that replenishes the available supply of dopamine. Thus, the phenothiazines in all likelihood are in some way reducing activity in dopamine neurons and thus mimicking, in part, the symptoms of Parkinson's disease.

Second, animal research strongly suggests that phenothiazines block dopamine receptors and that the more effective the particular phenothiazine is in treating schizophrenia, the more complete is the blocking action. (Carlsson & Lindquist, 1963; Nyback et al., 1968) Furthermore, the effects of the phenothiazines tend to be relatively specific for dopamine; there are fewer effects on other neurotransmitters such as norepinephrine. In addition, the geometric shapes of the molecules of effective phenothiazines would permit them to substitute for dopamine molecules and thus block the receptor site, whereas relatively ineffective phenothiazine molecules have less similar shapes. (Horn & Snyder, 1971)

Dopamine is also implicated by an entirely different line of research with *ampheta-*

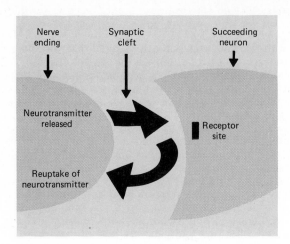

FIGURE 16-1.   Molecules of chemical neurotransmitters,
such as dopamine and norepinephrine, are released at
the nerve ending, travel across the synaptic cleft, attach
themselves to receptor sites on a succeeding neuron,
and thus activate an electrical impulse that travels along
that neuron. After performing this function, most neurotransmitter molecules, including those of dopamine
and norepinephrine, are released and reabsorbed in the
original nerve ending.

mine drugs. These stimulant drugs produce two effects related to schizophrenia: (1) In
large and continuing doses amphetamines elicit a psychosis that can be indistinguishable
from acute paranoid schizophrenia; and (2) in very small doses they exacerbate certain
symptoms of schizophrenic patients. Some authors have suggested that amphetamine-
induced psychoses may result from lack of sleep, overexcitement, or precipitation of
psychosis in borderline schizophrenics, and therefore have little to do with basic causes
of the disorder. However, it has been shown that when large doses of amphetamine
were given to subjects who had no evidence of preexisting schizophrenia or schizoid
tendencies, a psychosis was uniformly precipitated in one to four days. (Griffith et al.,
1972)

An important qualification in considering amphetamine psychosis as a model of schizophrenia is that it rarely resembles nonparanoid schizophrenia. Perhaps, as Snyder suggests, the drug does produce the basic schizophrenic process, but because the drug also
has a strong "alerting" effect, the reaction tends to take a paranoid form. Schizophrenic
patients themselves recognize the effects of amphetamines as worsening an already
present illness, whereas they perceive the effects of other drugs such as LSD as super-
imposing a different mental disturbance upon their preexisting one. (Janowsky et al.,
1973)

To control for the possibility that amphetamines exacerbate schizophrenic symptoms
by a nonspecific stimulation of the central nervous system, Angrist et al. (1974) gave large
doses of caffeine to schizophrenic subjects. Although all showed tremor, anxiety, and
more rapid heartbeat, none showed an increase of schizophrenic symptoms. And last,
another fact favoring an association between amphetamine-induced symptoms and
schizophrenia is that phenothiazines are the best antidotes for amphetamine psychosis
and for amphetamine-induced intensification of schizophrenic symptoms. By contrast,

barbiturate sedatives do not relieve symptoms of amphetamine psychosis and in some cases make the symptoms worse. (Angrist & Gershon, 1970)

After reviewing animal and human research, Snyder (1974) concludes that amphetamine psychosis is mediated by increases in dopamine, but that the central stimulant alerting effects are caused by increases in another neurotransmitter, norepinephrine. Amphetamine produces an increase in both dopamine and norepinephrine by blocking the *reuptake* of these neurotransmitters by the neurons—that is, their reabsorption. Therefore, excessive, unabsorbed amounts of the neurotransmitters remain in the synaptic cleft (Figure 16-1). Phenothiazines, on the other hand, block the receptor sites involved in transmission from one neuron to another—quite a different process.

The evidence reviewed thus far provides a strong, though indirect, indication that some kind of overactivation of dopaminergic neurons is associated with schizophrenia. It was assumed at first that the disorder involved excessive production of dopamine. Research, however, has cast doubt on this possibility. Post et al. (1975), for example, found no difference in levels of homovanillic acid (one of the substances resulting when dopamine is metabolized) in the cerebrospinal fluid of acute schizophrenics and various comparison groups. Findings of this kind have led investigators to suspect that an oversensitivity in the dopamine receptors may account for the inferred unusual degree of activation in the dopaminergic neurons.

The Case for Psychosocial Determinants

Our understanding of schizophrenia will not be complete until the environmental contributions have also been comprehended. The strongest evidence for an environmental influence in the etiology of schizophrenia is the fact that concordance rates for identical twins are less than 100 percent, usually closer to 50 percent. Since genetic makeup is precisely the same in discordant twins, different environmental influences must account for the difference. It does not necessarily follow, however, that the environmental influences are psychological or social in nature. Biological factors such as different intrauterine environments, birth complications, or subsequent diseases might contribute to the development of schizophrenia in one twin and not the other.

A research strategy that seemed initially promising was the study of identical twins who were discordant for schizophrenia. Environmental factors should be highlighted in this situation where one identical twin becomes schizophrenic and the other does not, since the two individuals begin life with exactly the same genetic dispositions. Some researchers did find evidence suggestive of the possibility that the twin who became schizophrenic had experienced more central nervous system illnesses, or suffered from more complications or asphyxias at birth, or had a lighter birth weight (Pollin & Stabenau, 1968). Other investigators, however, have not always found similar differences (Wahl, 1976). The one finding that has been consistently supported is that the twin who later becomes schizophrenic is found on the average to be more submissive, sensitive, and dependent as a young child. This may simply reflect an early manifestation of the schizophrenic process itself and does not implicate any particular physical or psychosocial influence. This finding does imply that whatever environmental factors contribute to the discordance between the twins must occur very early in life.

For the remainder of this section I will focus on possible psychosocial contributions to the development of schizophrenia. Let us begin by looking at some clinically based theories of schizophrenia and then see what the research evidence has to say.

THE UNCONSCIOUS UNLEASHED

Psychoanalytic theory has long held that schizophrenia reflects a weak ego that can no longer contain the expression of ordinarily unconscious id impulses. The combination of weak ego and fixations at the oral stage leads to a regression to this early level of development.

Many features of schizophrenia are explained in this way. The weak, infantile ego cannot distinguish clearly between external reality and internal wishes and fantasies, the boundary between self and others becomes blurred, and thought reverts to the *primary process* mode in which ordinary logic and organization are lost. For example, in world destruction fantasies, inner rage is confused with some universal apocalyptic event; in sexual fantasies, sexual impulses are projected onto other people. Id impulses, whether sexual or aggressive in nature, may be expressed without the usual inhibiting and regulating functions of the ego. Schizophrenic persons are also said to have withdrawn their libidinal attachments from other people and turned this energy inward, toward themselves. Thus they become detached from other people and autistically preoccupied with their own inner world.

The psychoanalytic view of schizophrenia as a weak ego overpowered by instinctual impulses is symbolized by the artistic productions of some patients.

At a descriptive level this psychoanalytic view indeed characterizes many schizophrenic individuals. We encounter, however, the usual problem with psychoanalytic theory: How do we translate concepts such as weak ego, oral fixations, and primary process into testable propositions about the development of schizophrenia? Is primary process a useful theoretical concept or is it simply a label for illogical, emotion-controlled thought processes? Investigators, of course, differ on the value of the psychoanalytic contribution to our understanding of the origins of schizophrenia.

FAMILY INTERACTION

Neo-Freudian writers on schizophrenia, less tied to the concepts of orthodox psychoanalytic theory, have frequently stressed the importance of the early relationship with the mother (for example, Sullivan, 1953). In fact, certain mothers thought to have special "talent" for producing schizophrenic offspring have been called *schizophrenogenic*. This label may be a bit unfair since fathers may well play their part too. The central feature of the schizophrenogenic mother is extreme overprotectiveness and intrusiveness. This "engulfing" mother infantilizes the child, must know what the child thinks or feels, tells the child what to think or feel, and in general prevents the child from growing up as a separate person with a sense of personal identity and autonomy. The lack of separation between the mother and child is thought to reflect the mother's perception of the child as an extension of herself. The child cannot escape this relationship and contributes in a way to its continuation.

Several early studies found that mothers of schizophrenics relative to mothers of normals answered questionnaire items about child-rearing attitudes in a direction more consistent with overcontrolling, intrusive behavior (for example, Mark, 1953). However, subsequent studies have failed to substantiate the finding (for example, Heilbrun, 1960a). Even if the finding could be repeated, it leaves open the question of cause and effect: It is possible that having an "ill" child elicits more overprotective responses from a mother than she would otherwise make. Consistent with this interpretation are the results of a study in which mothers of schizophrenics were found to be "overpossessive" relative to mothers of normals but not different from mothers of brain-injured and re-tarded children (Klebanoff, 1959). On the other hand, studies that have measured *children's perceptions* of maternal behavior have showed quite consistently that mothers of schizophrenics are perceived by their schizophrenic children as being intrusively overcon-trolling (for example, Heilbrun, 1960b; McKinley, 1963). These findings of *perceived* maternal over-control still leave the cause-and-effect question up in the air, but they do caution against a too hasty con-clusion that there is no relationship between maternal overcontrol and schizophrenia.

Murray Bowen in the early 1950s was one of the first persons to conduct systematic clinical studies in which he and his staff directly observed the interac-tion of families in which there was a schizophrenic son or daughter. In the beginning, at the Menningers' Clinic, he brought the mothers of schizophrenic young adults to the clinic to live with their children in a cottage. Later Bowen also brought in fathers and then finally, when he had moved to the National In-stitute of Mental Health in Bethesda, Maryland, he brought in parents plus a nonschizophrenic sibling to live in special apartments on the hospital wards. On the basis of his observations Bowen (1978) de-scribed a phenomenon that he called the *transfer of anxiety.* The mother, for example, would become anxious and then focus her thinking on the sickness of her child, repeatedly verbalizing how disturbed the child was. Soon the mother's anxiety would be less and the patient's psychotic symptoms would be worse. Or in other instances, less common, the son or daughter would make positive steps toward re-covery and the mother would show increasing signs of anxiety, perhaps taking to her bed with some kind of physical illness. More generally Bowen proposed that when one member in an overly attached rela-tionship functioned at a level less than the person's capacity, the other individual functioned in an over-adequate fashion. As with anxiety, occasionally the roles of underadequate and overadequate would be exchanged. Overt schizophrenic symptoms would be one manifestation of underadequate functioning.

The phenomenon of the transfer of anxiety was just one aspect of the kind of family relationships that existed in families that were too closely knit in an emotional sense. Bowen and others have used terms like *ego-fusion* and *enmeshed* to describe families of this kind. According to Bowen most psychopathology

arises in families that cannot maintain an optimum balance between emotional closeness and individual autonomy. Schizophrenia was seen as developing in families that were quite extreme in their ego-fusion or enmeshment.

Theodore Lidz: The Intensive Study of Whole Fam-ilies. Lidz and his colleagues (1965) conducted in-tensive studies of the families of 17 schizophrenic patients, and found pervasive psychopathology in all of them. Four of the families had been specifically selected because the referring psychiatrist consid-ered that the family had provided a good setting and the parents were emotionally stable. However, long-term study and intensive interviewing revealed that these families were as disturbed as the others, per-haps even more distorting of reality because of their need to mask the conflicts and dissatisfactions of their members.

To summarize some of the findings, mothers were almost always highly unstable, often strange persons who had difficulties setting boundaries be-tween themselves and the child who became schiz-ophrenic. The fathers were just as disturbed as the mothers; some were aggressive and even paranoid but others were passive and ineffectual. Although none of the parents had been hospitalized, in 60 per-cent of the families at least one parent was consid-ered to be virtually psychotic or paranoid, and in the remaining families one or both parents maintained a precarious adjustment involving considerable dis-tortion of reality. The boundaries between the gen-erations were always breached, either because one parent acted like a sibling with one of the children in rivalrous competition for the spouse or because a parent used a child as an emotional replacement for a spouse.

Most of the marriages were severely disturbed. The majority were characterized by *marital schism* involving overt conflict, with each spouse seeking to gain the upper hand, defying the wishes of the other, devaluing the other to the children, and attempting to form alliances with the children against the spouse. The remaining families showed a pattern called *mar-ital skew,* in which the serious psychopathology of the dominant parent was passively accepted by the other. The effects of these family patterns on the child were devastating. The parents provided poor models for identification; they could not believe that the child could be self-reliant and they led the child to believe that marriage and parenthood were unattractive and even dangerous; they sometimes taught distrust of outsiders; and because of their eccentricities the child was reluctant to bring acquaintances into the home.

Lidz especially emphasizes the *transmission of irrationality.* Growing up in a household in which family members deny and distort the obvious interpretations of experiences, are egocentrically impervious to the child's own feelings and desires, act as though certain disturbing situations (such as a father's occupational failure) did not exist, and talk to each other in vague, amorphous, or fragmented ways would seem to be a training program well designed to produce the thought disorder seen in the adult schizophrenic. No recourse to hypothetical organic deficits would seem to be necessary to explain the resulting impairment in language and thought.

The Double Bind.   Bateson et al. (1956) proposed that one kind of parent-child interaction is especially important in the development of schizophrenia, the *double bind.* The double bind arises when: (1) the child is emotionally dependent upon the parent and it is therefore extremely important to understand communications accurately and respond appropriately; and (2) the parent expresses two contradictory messages. The content of what the parent says may be the opposite of the message contained in tone of voice or facial expression, or the content itself may simply consist of two incompatible messages. The child cannot comment on the incongruous messages, withdraw from the situation, or ignore the messages. Caught in a bind from which there is no escape, the child uses "crazy" thinking and actions to cope with this intolerable situation. Bateson et al. (1956) give the following example:

A young man who had fairly well recovered from an acute schizophrenic episode was visited in the hospital by his mother. He was glad to see her and impulsively put his arm around her shoulders, whereupon she stiffened. He withdrew his arm and she asked, "Don't you love me anymore?" He then blushed and she said, "Dear, you must not be so easily embarrassed and afraid of your feelings." The patient was able to stay with her only a few minutes more and following her departure he assaulted an aide and was put in the tubs. (p. 144)

The double bind.

According to Bateson, the patient might begin to break away from this double bind if he could comment verbally on this double message. "Mother, it is obvious that you became uncomfortable when I put my arm around you and that you have difficulty accepting a gesture of affection from me." The patient, of course, is ordinarily unable to make such a statement. Despite his anger at his mother he remains intensely dependent upon her and may well have been punished (in a psychological rather than physical fashion) for any past attempts at more direct and honest communication of this type. Also the mother is probably not aware of the negative side of her double message and would probably deny it.

In other words, it takes considerable psychological strength and confidence in one's own perceptions to confront the double bind directly. The schizophrenic person is poorly equipped to do this, after a lifetime of having others impose their feelings and thoughts and having had little practice in drawing conclusions on the basis of personal feelings or thoughts.

Ronald Laing: A Strategy for Survival in an Insane World. Ronald Laing, along with Thomas Szasz, is a gadfly on the contemporary psychiatric scene. Szasz says mental illness is a myth; people just have problems in living. Laing says that schizophrenics have frequently found the only sane way to get along in an insane environment, and that to pin a label such as "sick" on them and put them away in an impersonal institution is only to further the insanity of the environment.

The family is the primary locus of "craziness" with which the schizophrenic-to-be must come to terms. The schizophrenia-producing family environments described by Laing bear many similarities to those described by Lidz, Bateson, and others. *Mystification* is a term frequently used by Laing to refer to the effects of the confusing, double binding, and irrational messages given by the family.

Laing and Esterson (1971) studied the families of 11 schizophrenic women. In each case they felt there was strong evidence that family environment could account for the patient's schizophrenic behavior. Their basic thesis is that the behavior and thought processes of people diagnosed as schizophrenic indeed seem crazy outside of the family context, but seen from the family perspective are not crazy or irrational at all. In fact such behavior is just how a person might rationally react to such an environment.

MAYA: A Mystifying Environment

One of the women studied by Laing and Esterson (1971) was Maya, who had spent nine of her last ten years diagnosed as schizophrenic in a mental hospital. She experienced herself as a machine rather than as a person, was confused about her identity, and felt it necessary to move and speak with studious and scrupulous correctness. She sometimes felt that her thoughts were controlled by others, and said that not she but her "voices" often did her thinking.

Her parents seem to have opposed all expressions of developing autonomy on Maya's part. Even at the present time her mother objected to her ironing without supervision, although for the past year she had been working in a laundry without mishap. Both parents regarded Maya's using her own mind as a symptom of her "illness" and a rejection of them. To quote her mother:

—but this illness has been so completely em—our relations have been different—you see Maya is er—instead of accepting everything—as if I said to her, er—"Black is black," she would have probably believed it, but since she's ill, she's never accepted anything any more. She's had to reason it out for herself, and if she couldn't reason it out herself, then she didn't seem to take *my* word for it—which of course is quite different to me. (p. 19)

The parents became convinced that Maya could read their thoughts, and on a number of occasions her father set up an experiment without informing Maya to see if she could read his thoughts. The father and mother, in other words, secretly conspired to test this idea. One of Maya's clinical symptoms was "ideas of influence." Laing and Esterson concluded that Maya's ideas of influence were not some weird aberration but had a basis in actual fact. When Maya had accused her parents of trying to influence her, they laughed it off. In the course of the study they admitted to her what they had been doing and Maya said, "Well I mean you shouldn't do it—it's not natural."

Her father replied, "I don't do it—I didn't do it—I thought, 'Well, I'm doing the wrong thing, I won't do it.' "

TABLE 16-4   Mystifying and Disqualifying Responses by the Parents of a Schizophrenic Woman

Maya says:	The parents say:
Blackness came over her when she was eight.	It did not. Her memory is at fault. She was imagining this, showing a "mental lapse."
She was emotionally disturbed in the years eight to fourteen.	She was not.
She started to masturbate when she was fifteen.	She did not.
She masturbates now.	She does not.
She had sexual thoughts about her mother and father.	She did not.
She was worried over her examinations.	She never worried over examinations because she always passed them, and so she had no need to worry. She was too clever and worked too hard. Besides, she could not have worried because they would have known.
Her mother and father were trying to influence her in some ways.	Nonsense. (But they attempted to influence her through prayer, telepathy, thought control.)
She could remember the "attack" on her mother quite clearly but could not explain it.	She could not remember it.
She was responsible for it.	She was not responsible for it. She was ill. It was part of her illness that she said she could remember this attack, and that she said she was responsible for it.
Her mother was responsible for her being sent away as a result of this episode.	This was not so. Her mother did not even know Maya was going to the hospital when the doctor drove her away in his car.

Adapted from Laing and Esterson, 1971.

When all three were interviewed together, the mother and father kept exchanging a constant series of nods, winks, and knowing smiles. These were so obvious that the interviewer commented on them after 20 minutes or so, but they continued, unabated and denied. Whenever in the course of the several interviews Maya expressed a point of view, feeling, or action on her part, it would then be denied or in some way disqualified by one or both parents. Some of these disjunctive views are summarized in Table 16-4.

The reports of Bateson et al. (1956), Bowen (1978), Laing and Esterson (1971), Lidz et al. (1965), and a number of other authors make a plausible case for family determinants of schizophrenia. Despite some differences there are several points of similarity in these clinical studies. One or both parents of the schizophrenic is found to be controlling, intrusive, and either overtly or covertly rejecting. The child is denied the opportunity to develop a personal identity, to know and interpret personal feelings and wishes;

instead, one or both parents take over the interpreting. Caught in this kind of enmeshed relationship (overcontrolling parent–overdependent child) from which there is no escape, the child responds to the "mystifications" and double binds with withdrawal and disturbances in thinking and communication skills.

These hypothesized family influences can be conceptualized quite adequately within the framework of social learning theory. Parents model, and perhaps reinforce, disturbed communication and peculiar ideas; they punish attempts at interpersonal intimacy, "straight" communication, and developing a distinct identity, forcing the child to withdraw in order to escape this aversive experience.

CONTROLLED RESEARCH ON FAMILY CORRELATES

The studies described in the previous section are essentially clinical in nature in that control groups of families without a schizophrenic member were not included, and interrater reliability for such variables as marital skew or mystification was not reported. Although the theories of the double bind, the schizophrenogenic mother, the transmission of irrationality, and other family-oriented views of the origins of schizophrenia appear plausible, controlled research has provided only partial support for these views.

Direct Observation of Schizophrenics with Their Families. A number of investigators have tried to circumvent the shortcomings of questionnaire and interview data by assessing directly observed interaction. Unfortunately this approach has its problems too. For example, can we be sure that 15 to 30 minutes of interaction on a laboratory task is representative of the kinds of interaction going on in the home over the past 20 years that may have influenced the development of schizophrenia? The specific task chosen, the artificiality of the situation, and the effects of "performing" before observers could all produce important changes from "natural" interaction at home.

Jacob (1975), in an exhaustive survey of all research to that time based on direct observation of family interaction, found no consistent evidence that families of schizophrenics were different from normal

control families in the amount of conflict, expression of positive or negative emotion, or in relative dominance of father and mother. With respect to clarity of communication, the nine studies that assessed this aspect of family interaction showed some consistent findings. In general, families of schizophrenics communicated with less clarity and accuracy than did normal families.

One of the studies that found a difference in communications style is that of Mishler and Waxler (1968). On two occasions they recorded the family interaction of good- and poor-premorbid, male and female schizophrenics, and of a normal control group while these families tried to resolve certain differences of opinion. In one session the schizophrenic child interacted with the parents. By using this design the investigators could see whether the parents' behavior was the same with the nonschizophrenic child as with the schizophrenic child.

Overall the results of Mishler and Waxler's research were disappointing; only a few of a relatively large number of measures significantly differentiated the groups. One of their limited findings, however, supports the view of various clinical investigators that the parents of schizophrenics frequently disqualify or mystify their children by not acknowledging a basic point or intention the child has expressed. Either the parents do not listen or they respond in terms of their own needs. Mishler and Waxler's measure of "positive acknowledgment" significantly discriminated the three groups for both male and female children, with the normal families showing the highest frequencies of acknowledgment and the poor-premorbid families the lowest frequencies. For males the same effect held for the nonschizophrenic sibling, suggesting that this was a rather general parental characteristic and not one exhibited only with the schizophrenic son. We have here, then, some limited research support for a characteristic style of communication in the families of schizophrenics that a number of clinical investigators have reported.

Family Interaction Before Schizophrenia Develops. Two studies have been reported in which information about family characteristics was obtained *before* the child was diagnosed as schizophrenic. McCord et al. (1962) made use of an extensive body of information that had been gathered on a large sample of boys as part of a delinquency prevention study. Later 12 of these boys became psychotic (10 were either schizophrenic or paranoid), and their family backgrounds were compared with a group closely matched on such variables as socioeconomic class and ethnic background of parents, presence of psychoses or neuroses in parents, physical disabilities sometimes found to be related to psychoses such as neurological signs and glandular imbalances, and race.

The comparison showed that a higher percentage of mothers of the psychotic sons were rated as overcontrolling (67 percent) than were mothers of the control group (8 percent). "Smothering" was the term used for mothers who rated high on each of three factors: dominant person in the family, overcontrolling of son, and affectionate toward son. Smothering mothers occurred in 58 percent of the psychotic sample, in 8 percent of the matched control group, and in 12 percent of an unmatched control group of 129 families in which neither the sons nor parents showed severe pathology but all of whom came from the same socioeconomic neighborhoods. The relatively small sample argues against making too much of this study, but the results are consistent with the "schizophrenogenic" mother hypothesis.

In another premorbid study, Waring and Ricks (1965) compared records of 50 children who had been treated at the Judge Baker Guidance Center in Boston and who later became schizophrenic as adults with those of a control group of children who were also treated at the center but who did not become schizophrenic. The two groups were matched on age, sex, IQ, presenting symptoms, socioeconomic class, and ethnic background. The 50 children who later became schizophrenic were further subdivided into 20 whose disorder was chronic, who had been hospitalized for many years at the time of the study, and 30 who had been released from their hospitals, well enough to return to the community.

Consistent with a number of other studies, Waring and Ricks found a higher proportion of psychotic parents in the chronic group than in either the released or the control group. Twenty percent of both mothers and fathers of the chronic patients were psychotic and an additional 15 percent of mothers and 20 percent of fathers were considered schizoid.

The evidence here for the schizophrenogenic mother is mixed. The personality descriptions of the mothers taken from case notes suggested that mothers of the chronic schizophrenics were primarily in-

adequate, withdrawn, vague, and generally unable to cope with life—not exactly the picture of the dominating, intrusive mother. On the other hand, when family environments were categorized in certain ways a kind of parent-child relationship called *symbiotic union* was present in a higher proportion of chronic patient families (35 percent) than in either the released patient families (20 percent) or the nonschizophrenic patient families (12 percent); see Figure 16-2. The authors defined symbiotic union almost exactly as we have portrayed the intrusive, overcontrolling, schizophrenogenic mother. Unfortunately, the authors did not specify what proportion of these symbiotic relationships were with the mother and what proportion were with the father, and therefore we cannot use this as clear evidence one way or the other for the concept of the schizophrenogenic mother. It is probably a reasonable assumption that most were with the mother.

At a minimum, Waring and Ricks's data suggest that a symbiotic relationship may play an important role in the development of some cases of schizophrenia, whether the relationship involved the father or the mother. However, we should not lose sight of the fact that 65 percent of the families of chronic schizophrenics were *not* characterized by symbiotic unions. Another methodological shortcoming in this study is that interjudge reliabilities were not reported for the various categories.

A marital relationship labeled *emotional divorce* was present in 35 percent of the chronic group, 17 percent of the released group, and 4 percent of the control group. Emotional divorce referred to marriages in which there was minimal interaction, infrequent or no sexual contact, and strong underlying hostility and distrust. It is interesting that 58 percent of the symbiotic unions occurred in the emotional divorce type of marriage, suggesting that one spouse may have been substituting a close-binding relationship with the child for an unsatisfactory marriage. The categories of marital skew and marital schism, based on Lidz's definitions, occurred as frequently in the control group as in the schizophrenic groups and thus provided little support for Lidz's theory.

Other features that distinguished the families in Waring and Ricks's study were a *chaotic environment* and *family sacrifice*. A chaotic environment is one composed of a disintegrated collection of schizoid, antisocial, or borderline psychotic individuals who

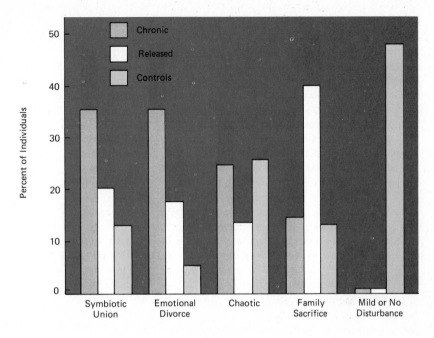

FIGURE 16-2 Percentages of individuals who became chronic schizophrenics, released schizophrenics, and controls who experienced different kinds of family environment and who did not become schizophrenics. (Redrawn from M. Waring & D. Ricks, Family patterns of children who become adult schizophrenics. *Journal of Nervous and Mental Disease*, 1965, *140*,351–364. Copyright 1965 by Williams & Wilkins Co. and used with permission.)

actively neglect the child's basic physical needs and are incapable of giving training in even the most rudimentary social values. The child is brutalized by such treatments as beating, tying, and actual desertion for periods of time. This environment occurred more frequently in the lower socioeconomic classes and did not discriminate well between the groups, occurring fairly frequently (about 25 percent) in both the chronic and control groups. A high number of convicted delinquents emerged from this environment both in the control group and among the siblings of the schizophrenic subjects.

In the *family sacrifice* category the child is openly rejected, distrusted, and invited or forced to leave home, usually in adolescence. This environment was most distinctly characteristic of the released schizophrenic. The authors suggest that the separation of the child from the family may have been a blessing in disguise that permitted the child to escape a pathological environment and to seek healthier relation-

ships elsewhere. Clearly the parents were less dependent upon the child to satisfy their own needs than is the case in the symbiotic relationship.

The category called *mild* or *no disturbance* in the family environment did not occur *at all* in the families of either the chronic or released schizophrenics, but was characteristic of 48 percent of the nonschizophrenic control families. This one comparison is a rather impressive documentation of the presence of severe disturbance in the families of schizophrenics prior to their becoming schizophrenic. A related finding was that there were no healthy marriages in either of the two schizophrenic groups compared with 15 percent healthy marriages in the control group.

All in all Waring and Ricks's data give rather strong support to the idea that future schizophrenics grow up in severely disturbed family environments. No one pattern of family interaction was shown to be uniquely related to the subsequent development of schizophrenia. The overcontrolling parent-overdependent child system (symbiotic union) may be one important path to schizophrenia, but these data by no means suggest it is the only path. Although the information in this study was obtained before the full-fledged schizophrenic reaction developed, it was not gathered with this further analysis in mind and cannot provide the more intensive or fine-grained analysis of family interaction patterns that would be desirable.

Adoption Studies.   All of the results described thus far that find some communication disturbance in the families of schizophrenics are, of course, consistent with the psychological transmission of this disturbance. However, these results are equally consistent with genetic transmission. Parents who are not overtly schizophrenic themselves but carry a genetic disposition to schizophrenia may manifest their "schizotypal" tendency in the form of somewhat impaired communication skills. The basic disposition to become schizophrenic, however, may be transmitted through the genes rather than through mystifying communication. A test of these two alternative theories could be made by assessing communication deviance in the adoptive parents of children who become schizophrenic. If psychological transmission is important, then these adoptive parents should show more disturbance in communication than adoptive parents of children who do not become schizophrenic. In the two studies designed to test this hypothesis, one (Wynne et al., 1976) supported it and the other (Wender et al., 1977) did not. Overall the adoption studies (summarized earlier in this chapter) would seem to provide much more convincing evidence for genetic transmission than for psychological transmission.

In summary, controlled research provides some evidence for greater disturbances in the families of schizophrenics, both in parent-child and husband-wife interactions, than in comparison families. It appears likely that the disturbed interactions were present before the child developed noticeable symptoms of schizophrenia. Although there is some indication that symbiotic parent-child relationships (involving a schizophrenogenic parent) may occur more frequently in families of schizophrenics than normals, in many, perhaps most, instances schizophrenia develops without this particular pattern being present. All research findings of this kind, however, are as

readily explained by genetic as by psychological transmission. The more crucial adoption studies have not provided convincing evidence that communication or other disturbances in the nonbiological adoptive parents could produce the schizophrenic symptoms in their adopted children.

SOCIETY AND SCHIZOPHRENIA

Society's Reaction to Deviant Behavior.   In Chapter 5 I described a view of mental illness called the *societal reaction theory* (Scheff, 1975). In agreement with Scheff, other writers such as Ullmann and Krasner (1975) and Perrucci (1974) argue that so-called schizophrenic behavior can largely be explained in terms of society's reaction to some initial deviant behavior. The person, for whatever reason, breaks some societal rule of conduct, is labeled as mentally ill or schizophrenic, and is hospitalized. In this view, most of what we consider to be the symptoms of schizophrenia develop *after* the labeling process. Both society and the person have definite ideas about how a "mentally ill" person should behave. "Crazy" behavior is expected and reinforced. The person finds that certain reinforcements (such as avoidance of responsibility) can be obtained by playing the "sick" role. Perrucci (1974) summarizes this point of view:

Thus, persons called mentally ill are not seen as patients, but as victims. They are victims of situational contingencies such that in one case an act of rule breaking will be transformed into a psychiatric symptom, whereas in another case the very same act may be ignored or dealt with in other than a psychiatric framework. They are victims of their vulnerable status in society which makes them less able to defend against more powerful family members or heavily credentialed experts whose job it is to pass judgment on the mental health of others. In addition, they are victims of their own humanness, which makes them responsive to the judgments of significant others, whereby they take the views of others and internalize them as their own. In short, the social role of mental illness can be created by collective judgments imposed upon those who are socially vulnerable, and voluntarily adopted by persons as a defensive strategy. The end result is not a patient with a disease, but a victim of a socially constructed reality. (pp. 17-18)

According to the reaction-to-social-deviance view, many symptoms of schizophrenia develop after institutionalization. The patient learns to play the "sick" role.

Ullmann and Krasner (1975), for example, suggest that persons may learn that psychiatric patients are expected to have hallucinations from reading the mass media, observation of other patients, and leading questions from psychiatric examiners. This expectation, in their view, may be one contributing cause to the development of reports of hallucinations.

It seems likely that society's reaction to deviance can contribute to the further development of schizophrenic-like behavior. This analysis, however, would seem to give insufficient attention to those circumstances that led to the development of schizophrenic symptoms before the person comes to the attention of society's labelers. Some individuals, after all, show many of the classic symptoms of schizophrenia before labeling and hospitalization. I will return to the issues raised by the reaction-to-social-deviance view when we discuss the effects of hospitalization in Chapter 17.

Cultural Influences. Schizophrenia apparently exists in all cultures, from the most "primitive" to the most "advanced." However, the incidence rates and character of the symptoms do vary widely from culture to culture. Murphy (1968), for example, reports unusually high incidence rates of schizophrenia in several subcultures: For the Tamil Indians living in Singapore the rate over a five-year period per 1000 adults was 5.0 compared with 3.5 and 3.0 for their Chinese and Malay counterparts; for Irish Catholics in southern Ireland at the turn of the century, the "insanity" rate was 4.7 in Ireland compared with 3.3 in England. The latter discrepancy has continued to the present time, and it applies particularly to schizophrenia. Differences of this kind could conceivably reflect differences in genetic makeup of the populations, although it is unlikely with large populations that have not been unusually isolated.

Murphy (1968) describes a study in which he compared rates of schizophrenia in three "traditional" French Canadian communities with rates in other French Canadian communities where traditions were changing and had less hold. The prevalence of schizophrenia in women was found to be extremely high in the traditional communities, 13.1 per 1000 adults. The high prevalence was especially apparent in two subgroups of women: married women over the age of 35 and young unmarried women. Schizophrenia was almost nonexistent among younger married women in traditional settings.

Murphy suggests that the unusual prevalence of

schizophrenia among the young single and older married women might be explained by cultural factors. The traditional communities consider the ideal woman as one who gets married early, has many children, is hardworking, patient, and submissive to her husband. The idea of an independent career for women, outside of religious orders, was only just beginning to be accepted as a possibility. For some women, according to Murphy, the conflict between satisfying the expectation of the community and pursuing interests of their own became sufficiently acute to precipitate the schizophrenic reactions, reactions that tended to occur either at the time they were entering the marriageable age period or later as their children were growing up and the satisfactions derived from the family were diminishing. The conflict described here is, of course, recognizable as an extreme instance of what the women's liberation movement has been trying to liberate women from. However, since there is no clear evidence of a greater incidence of schizophrenia in women than men in Western society as a whole, we have to be cautious in applying this explanation more generally.

Less controversial than whether culture affects the incidence of schizophrenia is the question of whether culture influences the form of schizophrenic symptoms. Murphy et al. (1963) conducted a questionnaire survey among psychiatrists in 27 countries representing the major regions of the world: Africa, Asia, Australia, North America, South America, the Middle East, Europe, and the Caribbean (limited, of course, to those societies "advanced" enough to have psychiatrists). In addition to providing certain demographic information such as ethnic, religious, and urban or rural status, the psychiatrists rated the frequency of 26 symptoms associated with schizophrenic patients they had seen.

Four symptoms were never rated "infrequent" in any country or culture: social and emotional withdrawal; auditory hallucinations; delusions; and flatness of affect. These symptoms would seem to be characteristic of schizophrenia wherever the disorder is found. Other features, however, varied markedly in the different cultures. For example, two kinds of delusions showed an especially strong relationship to the world's religions—delusions with religious content and delusions of destruction. The highest percentage of religious delusions was found for Roman Catholics, the lowest for Judaism and Buddhism.

Murphy proposes that religious delusions and delusions of destruction are positively correlated with the extent to which religions induce a sense of guilt. Also, he suggests that Eastern religions such as the Hindu, Buddhist, and Shinto types promote a more passive acceptance of fate and an emotional detachment from life. Consistent with the latter point was the finding that social and emotional withdrawal occurred most frequently as a symptom among the Japanese and Okinawans. Murphy felt that the low frequencies of religious delusions and delusions of destruction among the Jewish schizophrenics were inconsistent with his general interpretation, but he was unable to offer any alternative explanation.

Opler (1954) has also presented data that point to variations in the form of schizophrenic symptoms as a function of cultural influences. Comparing schizophrenic persons of Irish and Italian descent, he found that those of Irish extraction showed a higher preoccupation with sin and guilt and more fixed delusional beliefs; patients of Italian origins showed more overt homosexuality, somatic complaints, acting-out behavior, and attitudes of rejection toward authority figures. The greater degree of direct expression of impulses in the Italian sample was thought to reflect the Italian culture, which sanctions the free expression of emotions and expansive bodily action. The more inhibited and introverted Irish schizophrenic, on the other hand, was thought to be associated with similar features in the Irish culture, including perhaps the fact that in Irish families the central figure is the mother, whereas in Italian families it is the father.

Socioeconomic Influences. Do social and economic stresses contribute to the development of schizophrenia? Some sociologists believe so. For example, Faris and Dunham (1939) found that the highest rates of first hospital admissions for schizophrenia in Chicago were in the central city areas of lowest socioeconomic status, with decreasing rates as one moved toward higher-status outlying areas. Since then many studies have confirmed this basic finding for such cities as Kansas City, Milwaukee, and Omaha (Schroeder, 1954), as well as for Oslo, Norway (Sundby & Nyhus, 1963), and Bristol, England (Hare, 1956). The finding, however must be qualified in several respects. Kohn (1968), in summarizing results from a number of studies, concludes that for medium-size cities (100,000 to 500,000 population) the relationship is discontinuous; the higher incidence of schizophrenia is limited almost entirely to the lowest social class. For small towns and rural communities the relationship either is not found or is much weaker.

But how do we interpret such findings? Two fundamentally different hypotheses have been proposed: (1) The stresses associated with the extremes of social disorganization, poverty, and harshness found in the lowest socioeconomic level are a *cause* or partial cause of schizophrenia; and (2) schizophrenic or schizophrenia-prone individuals tend to *drift* into these slum areas because they are unable to function effectively in the rest of society.

In support of the *drift* hypothesis, Gerard and Houston (1953) found that if they restricted the sample studied to those patients admitted directly to mental hospitals from their own family settings, there was no longer a disproportionate number of schizophrenics from the lowest social class. The excess of schizophrenics from the slum areas resulted almost entirely from young schizophrenics who had left home and rented rooms in rundown sections of town.

Another way of investigating the drift hypothesis is to search out the origins of the schizophrenics and see if there is a tendency toward downward social mobility. Goldberg and Morrison (1963) obtained information on the occupations of the fathers of male schizophrenics in England and Wales. They found that although the occupations of schizophrenic sons were concentrated in the lowest social class, the occupations of the fathers were not, implying a downward drift on the part of the sons. Similar results have been reported by Turner and Wagonfeld (1967). Since it is well documented that a higher proportion of fathers and grandfathers of schizophrenics have a higher frequency of mental illnesses than the population at large, it is likely that some proportion of fathers (perhaps mothers too) of schizophrenics have themselves already drifted to lower socioeconomic levels, thus attenuating the downward mobility seen in each generation.

The evidence, however, is not so strong for the drift hypothesis that we are compelled to accept it as a complete explanation for the disproportionate number of schizophrenics seen in the lowest social class. It is still possible that some part of the higher

Does poverty cause schizophrenia or do schizophrenic persons drift into slum areas?

incidence rate results from the severity of stresses experienced in this environment. Many characteristics distinguish the lowest socioeconomic class from other classes and research has by no means convincingly demonstrated which, or what combination, of these features are especially influential in precipitating schizophrenia.

Brenner (1973) presents data that show a strong relationship between times of economic hardship and first-admission rates to mental hospitals (including schizophrenia considered separately). In one analysis he shows a high correlation between an index of employment in New York State and first admissions to mental hospitals in that state during the period between 1915 and 1967. In a second analysis he finds a similarly high correlation between an index of industrial production and first-admission rates in New York State for the period 1841–1915. In both analyses long-term trends in population growth and availability of mental hospital facilities were controlled. Periods of lowered employment or production, assumed to reflect economic recessions, were accompanied by marked increases in mental hospital admissions. Furthermore, in the 1841–1915 data the relationship was much higher for farmers, laborers, and salesmen than for individuals in more economically secure professions such as lawyers and doctors. The stress of an economic downturn should fall most heavily on the former groups.

Correlational findings, of course, are subject to many interpretations. One possibility is that during times of relative prosperity, individuals who are already schizophrenic are supported and cared for by relatives. In hard times, however, the relatives find they can no longer provide for such persons, and they commit them to a mental hospital, thus increasing the first-admission rates. Brenner, however, offers several bits of evidence against such an interpretation. First, admissions of patients who are totally dependent on others are not more affected by economic changes than are admissions of individuals who do have some savings and at least marginal capacity for earning a living. Second, admissions to private hospitals show a similar relationship to economic cycles. The cost of private hospitalization is considerably higher than the cost of keeping the patient at home. Third, hospitalization rates for the criminally insane show the same relationship. In these cases hospitalization is triggered by the commission of a crime, not by the need of a family to economize.

As an exercise you might try to think of other explanations of the relationship between hospital first-admission rates and economic recessions. One possibility, of course, is that the stresses associated with economic hardship precipitate schizophrenic reactions in some people. Not everyone experiencing severe economic hardships, however, develops schizophrenia. We are still left with the question of what set of circumstances makes one vulnerable to stresses of this kind. Nevertheless, if the stress interpretation is correct, it would mean that economic conditions can make a difference as to whether certain people become schizophrenic or not.

Another interpretation of the relationship between social class and schizophrenia is offered by Mintz and Schwartz (1971). These authors point out that the most impoverished areas of large cities are likely to include a mixture of people with different ethnic backgrounds. When people live in an area in which their own ethnic group is few in number, they may be especially subject to conflicting cultural traditions and expectations. Mintz and Schwartz found a significant negative correlation between the incidence of schizophrenia in people of Italian descent and the number of other people of Italian descent who lived in the community—the fewer the number of other Italians, the higher the rate of schizophrenia. The ethnic makeup was more important than the affluence of the neighborhood, which, in fact, proved to have no relationship to the incidence of schizophrenia within these particular groupings of Italian-Americans. These findings suggest that separation from a cohesive and supportive culture may be a more important correlate of schizophrenia than poverty itself. On the other hand, one might invoke the drift hypothesis again and propose that schizophrenic individuals tend to move away from their ethnic communities.

Biology and the Environment: An Interactive View

In looking at the etiology of schizophrenia we have seen the case for biology and the case for the psychosocial environment. The evidence tells us that we must somehow include both genetic and environmental factors in any complete theory of schizophrenia. Such a theory could take one of several forms. For example, Meehl (1962) considers an inherited brain defect a *necessary* condition for schizophrenia; without it, he believes, schizophrenia does not develop. According to Meehl, many more people have the inherited defect than develop overt schizophrenia. They show *schizotypic* behavior involving mild schizoid tendencies such as social withdrawal and inappropriate emotional expression. Whether or not overt schizophrenia develops depends upon environmental stresses.

In Meehl's theory the genetic disposition to schizophrenia is an all-or-nothing proposition; you either have it or you do not. An alternative view is that the genetic disposition varies from weak (perhaps zero) to strong, and that the stronger the inherited disposition the less severe the environmental stresses necessary to produce the overt disorder. This second view leaves a lot of room for variation in the importance of environmental learning experiences.

Whether certain kinds of physical or psychosocial environmental stresses are more likely than others to precipitate schizophrenic symptoms in vulnerable individuals is not known. For example, do certain birth complications or certain family interaction styles have special potency in producing schizophrenia in genetically predisposed persons? The evidence simply is not clear on this. Another possibility that cannot be entirely discounted is that some biochemical differences in schizophrenic individuals may result from chronic psychosocial stresses rather than from some biological defect. The fact that in half or more of all identical twin pairs in which one twin is schizophrenic the other twin is not leaves the door wide open for all kinds of interactive effects between genetic and environmental conditions.

Summary

1. Evidence strongly points to some genetic contribution to schizophrenia. Both twin studies and adoption studies support this conclusion.

2. There is considerable evidence that biological deviations are associated with schizophrenia; for example, soft signs of neurological impairment were found more often in children who later became chronic schizophrenics, and a subgroup of children with a schizophrenic parent often show some biological deviations. There is evidence that adult schizophrenics show physiologically either an over- or underarousal pattern.

3. The search for biochemical correlates of schizophrenia has been going on for many years, accompanied by many false hopes and disappointments. There is considerable indirect and circumstantial evidence that excessive activation of some dopamine neurons may contribute to schizophrenic symptomatology. This theory incorporates known facts about the effectiveness and site of action of phenothiazine drugs in the treatment of schizophrenia and the precipitation of paranoid schizophrenic reactions by amphetamine drugs.

4. The clearest evidence for environmental influences in the etiology of schizophrenia is the fact that concordance rates for identical twins are less than 100 percent. The environmental influences, however, need not be limited to psychological or social events; they may consist of biological influences such as birth complications and diseases.

5. The psychoanalytic theory of schizophrenia emphasizes a weak ego and regression to the oral stage of development. The weak and regressed ego cannot distinguish external reality from internal fantasies and cannot control id impulses.

6. Many investigators have pointed to disturbed family interaction as an important determinant of schizophrenia. The concepts of the schizophrenic mother and the double bind are two examples of disturbed parent-child relations thought to be related to schizophrenia.

7. In a clinical study, Lidz concluded that marriages in families that produce schizophrenics are almost always disturbed, reflecting either marital schism or marital skew, and that the family environment encourages the transmission of irrationality from parents to children.

8. Laing likewise emphasizes the irrationality in families of schizophrenics and speaks of the mystification that the parents' communications produce.

9. Controlled research has been only partially supportive of family interaction theories of schizophrenia. Research based on direct observation of family interaction has yielded some support for the proposal that parents of schizophrenics communicate with themselves and their children with less clarity than parents of nonschizophrenics. Other research has shown that families in which a child grew up to be a chronic schizophrenic were showing signs of severe disturbance before the child became schizophrenic.

10. Some writers propose that the symptoms of schizophrenia result largely from society's reaction to some initial deviant behavior.

11. Schizophrenia appears to exist in all cultures, but the incidence rate and the character of the symptoms show wide variation from culture to culture.

12. The highest rates of first hospital admissions for schizophrenia occur in the areas of lowest socioeconomic status, especially in cities of intermediate size. This fact has been explained in two ways: (1) Stresses associated with poverty cause schizophrenia; or (2) schizophrenic individuals drift into poor neighborhoods. Evidence is somewhat stronger for the drift hypothesis, although both explanations may be true to some extent.

13. Schizophrenia may well result from an interaction between biological (partially genetic) abnormalities and environmental influences. Environmental events, physical as well as social, may produce some biological changes, which in turn cause some of the symptoms of schizophrenia.

Suggested Readings

The student interested in following a well-executed study on the genetics of schizophrenia would do well to try I. Gottesman and J. Shields's *Schizophrenia and genetics: A twin vantage point* (Academic Press, 1972). Recent issues of the *Schizophrenia Bulletin* (National Institute of Mental Health) are a good source of review articles on the current status of biological and psychological contributions to schizophrenia. J. M. Neale and T. Oltmanns also provide an excellent survey of research in *Schizophrenia* (Wiley, 1980). For those who wish to look more closely into the family dynamics of schizophrenia, the clinical reports by T. Lidz, *The origins and treatment of schizophrenic disorders* (Basic Books, 1973), and by R. D. Laing and A. Esterson, *Sanity, madness, and the family* (Basic Books, 1971), are highly recommended.

17
Treatment of Schizophrenia

- Are drugs effective with schizophrenia?

- Will staying on drugs after recovery from schizophrenia prevent relapse?

- Freud believed that psychoanalysis was not an appropriate treatment for schizophrenia. Have other therapists agreed?

- What is it like to be a patient in a mental hospital?

- If you stayed in a mental hospital for a long time, would you begin to show the symptoms of schizophrenia?

- Is the solution to get patients out of the hospitals and back into the community?

- What is a token economy? Do token rewards lead to token learning?

The treatment we choose for a person displaying schizophrenic behavior depends upon whether we believe the disorder to be primarily biological or psychosocial. In the former case, we are likely to opt for drugs; in the latter, we will probably try some form of psychological intervention—psychodynamic or behavior therapy or a change in the social environment. In this chapter we will consider drug treatment, various psychosocial treatments, and the mental hospital environment itself as a treatment milieu.

Biological Therapies

DRUGS

In Chapter 16 I referred to the demonstrated effectiveness of the class of drugs known as phenothiazines in the treatment of schizophrenia. A commonly used variety is chlorpromazine, sometimes called by its trade name, Thorazine. Several well-controlled, double-blind studies support the belief that these drugs reduce schizophrenic symptoms. In one study involving 692 schizophrenic patients from 37 different Veterans Administration hospitals, Casey et al. (1960) found chlorpromazine to be much more effective than phenobarbital (a sedative) and a placebo over a 12-week course of treatment.

Hogarty and Ulrich (1977) provide evidence on the relapse rate for schizophrenic patients maintained on either chlorpromazine or placebo after discharge from a hospital. At the end of two and one-half years postdischarge 86 percent of placebo-treated patients had relapsed compared with 55 percent of the chlorpromazine group (see Figure 17-1). Although chlorpromazine was more effective than a placebo, the greater than 50 percent relapse rate for the former casts some doubt on the ability of the phenothiazine drugs to prevent relapse in many patients. Although this high relapse rate might be partially due to patients not taking their drugs, a study by Hogarty et al. (1979) has shown relapse rates to be similar for groups whose drug ingestion was directly observed and for groups where it was not.

There is evidence that the initial effectiveness of the phenothiazine drugs is related, at least in part, to their ability to alleviate attentional deficits, which, as we have seen, are thought by many investigators to

reflect a fundamental feature of the schizophrenic disorder. Spohn et al. (1977) measured several specific aspects of attentional, cognitive, and physiological functioning rather than relying on more global behavioral ratings of change. They found that chronic schizophrenic patients given chlorpromazine showed improvement relative to patients given placebos on several measures of attention (for example, reaction time and span of attention), a decrease in physiological reactivity (electrodermal and heart rate responses), and no change on tests measuring cognitive functioning (for example, interpreting proverbs and intelligence test items). Chlorpromazine, then, may be affecting something rather close to the underlying dysfunction in schizophrenia.

Although these and other studies show that phenothiazines are more effective than placebos and a number of other drugs, phenothiazines are not universally successful in reducing schizophrenic symptomatology. Some patients show only limited improvement, and a substantial number cannot get along outside the hospital even on this medication. Note the 50 percent relapse rate in the Hogarty and Ulrich study. Even for individuals who do not relapse to an extent requiring hospitalization, adjustment in many cases is marginal. Furthermore, some patients develop troublesome side effects to phenothiazines: drowsiness, constipation, nausea, dizziness, and jaundice. The most disquieting side effect that has been found to develop in some patients given long-term phenothiazine treatment is *tardive dyskinesia,* a symptom pattern consisting of slow, rhythmical, stereotyped movements of the legs, arms, or trunk, as well as oral movements such as lip smacking. The troublesome thing about this reaction is that it is difficult to treat once it has fully developed. Withdrawal of phenothiazine drugs does not help in many cases—and, somewhat paradoxically, the most immediately helpful treatment is to administer more phenothiazine drugs (Jeste & Wyatt, 1979). This, of course, puts the psychiatrist in the ethical dilemma of using the drug that presumably caused the disorder to treat it and risk, in the long run, even more severe effects. As of this writing there is no completely safe and effective treatment for tardive dyskinesia, and psychiatrists are urged to discontinue or reduce in strength the use of phenothiazines at the first signs of the reaction (Jeste & Wyatt, 1979). The developing awareness that tardive dyskinesia can de-

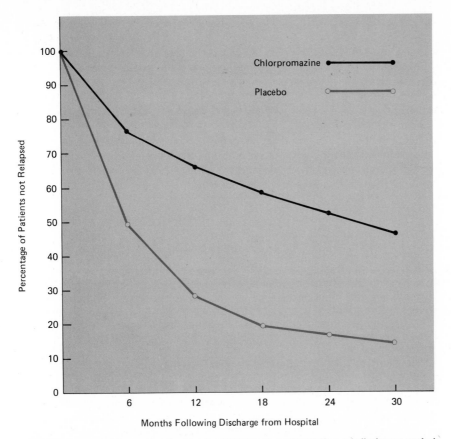

FIGURE 17.1. Percentage of patients not relapsing on a 30-month post-discharge period who continued to receive either chlorpromazine (a phenothiazine) or placebo. From Hogarty and Ulrich (1977). Copyright 1977 American Medical Association and used with permission.

velop after long-term treatment has increased motivation to find a drug that is equally effective but without this side effect. Clozapine appears promising in this respect but can in some cases produce its own side effects such as a lowering of blood pressure (Shopsin et al., 1979).

Aside from the problem of side effects, few investigators claim that phenothiazines "cure" schizophrenia. For some acute schizophrenics with a good-premorbid history, phenothiazine treatment may facilitate an almost complete remission of symptoms, but for the chronic patient with a poor-premorbid history the drug simply may permit a better adjustment to the hospital environment or a discharge to a nondemanding environment outside the hospital.

One problem in the drug treatment of postdischarge patients is seeing that they continue to take the drugs. An interesting aspect of this problem was investigated by Van Putten et al. (1976), who compared 29 habitual drug-refusers with 30 patients who regularly took their drugs. At admission, the drug-refusers had more often experienced grandiose delusions in contrast to the drug-compliers, who had more often experienced subjective distress during their psychotic periods. This drug-refusing subset of schizophrenic individuals would seem to support one popular view of the psychotic person, namely, that their own fantasy world is preferable to the pain of reality. For them, drug treatment may return them to a reality they would as soon avoid.

NEUROSURGERY

For a period of time from about 1940 to the mid-1950s a surgical procedure called *prefrontal lobotomy* was widely used with unmanageable schizophrenic patients who had not responded to other treatments. In this operation the nerve tracts from the frontal lobes to the lower brain centers are cut. Although some patients did seem to improve after this drastic and irreversible operation, others were reduced to a state of total apathy and incapacitation— human vegetables, as they were sometimes called.

The advent of the tranquilizing drugs plus increasing ethical concerns about the use of this procedure led to its almost total abandonment in this country as a form of treatment for functional psychoses.

Psychological Therapies

Let us begin our discussion of psychological approaches to the treatment of schizophrenia by considering the case of Joan and what psychotherapy was like for her.

Joan: "I'll Never Trust Anyone Again"

Joan developed symptoms of schizophrenia at age 17. During her recovery she described parts of the psychotherapeutic experience as follows: At the start, I didn't listen to what you said most of the time but I watched like a hawk for your expression and the sound of your voice. After the interview, I would add all this up to see if it seemed to show love. The words were nothing compared to the feelings you showed. I sensed that you felt confident I could be helped and that there was hope for the future.

It's like talking to a frightened horse or dog. They may not know your words, but the calm and strength and confidence that you convey helps them to feel safe again.

I had to tell you things by doing them instead of talking, because I didn't dare let you know things about me. I was sure you would turn things against me and use what I said to hurt me. Also, no one ever paid any attention to what I asked for, but they usually did react if I did something. I wanted terribly for you to help me, but I had to be sure I could trust you.

I hated you when you first came. So many other doctors had tried things with me and got discouraged that I had thought that now at last I would be left alone, in peace. But you just wouldn't go away, so I wanted to kill you.

If I got mad at mother and father, and refused what they wanted, they would make me feel guilty by saying how hard they had tried and that I only wanted to hurt them. I just had to get away from that. . . .

Hate has to come first. The patient hates the doctor for opening the wound again and hates himself for allowing himself to be touched again. The patient is sure it will just lead to more hurt. He really wants to be dead and hidden in a place where nothing can touch him and drag him back.

The patient is terribly afraid of his own problems, since they have destroyed him, so he feels terribly guilty for allowing the doctor to get mixed up in the problems. The patient is convinced that the doctor will be smashed too. It's not fair for the doctor to ask permission to come in. The doctor must fight his way in; then the patient doesn't have to feel guilty.

You seemed to be just the kind of doctor I needed, but I couldn't believe I could depend on you. All my other doctors had seemed dependable, but they would be pleasant to me and then end up by sending me away or trying to arrange plans with my family behind my back. The plans were what my parents wanted and never were good for me. Finally I decided I'd never trust anyone again. For two years I closed myself up and froze so I wouldn't feel anything. But no matter how mad I made you, you always came back and were always on time. . . .

My interviews were the only place where I felt safe to be myself—to let out all my feelings and see what they were really like without fear that you would get upset and leave me. I needed you to be a great rock that I could push and push, and still you would never roll away and leave me. It was safe for me to be bitchy with you. With everyone else I was trying to change myself to please them.

You have no idea how the warmth of your body would bring me back from my crazy world. It would change my whole picture of life when you held me. I had been so sure that no one could ever give warmth to me. You made everything look different.

Being nursed was as good as an orgasm. [The therapist actually fed her milk with a baby bottle.] It left me all relaxed and happy. The world looked real and pleasant. I could fall asleep comfortably. But the bottle had to be given by you with love. It wasn't just the milk that helped. It was the feeling that I had a mother who loved me.

I had to be able to tease you sexually so that I could be sure that I really was attractive, but before I could do this I had to be sure that nothing bad would come of it. . . .

If you had actually screwed me it would have wrecked everything. It would have convinced me that you were only interested in pleasure with my animal body and that you didn't really care about the part that was a person. . . . The real me would have been up on the ceiling watching you do things with my body.

I walked back to see the hospital recently, and for a moment I could lose myself in the feeling of the past. In there I could be left alone. The world was going by outside, but I had a whole world inside me. Nobody could get at it and disturb it. For a moment I felt a tremendous longing to be back. It had been so safe and quiet. But then I realized that I can have love and fun in the real world and I started to hate the hospital. I hated the four walls and the feeling of being locked in. I hated the memory of never being really satisfied by my fantasies.

In the first two years following the onset of her schizophrenic symptoms Joan was treated in four private hospitals with psychotherapy accompanied by 34 electroshock and 60 insulin treatments (another form of seizure-inducing treatment). She had shown little improvement and many considered her hopelessly ill when she began therapy with the therapist referred to in this account. She was withdrawn, seclusive, suspicious, actively experienced visual and auditory hallucinations, and at times was in a catatonic stupor. She attempted suicide on three occasions; at other times she became so violent that she had to be placed on the disturbed ward. After eight months of psychotherapy she was moved successfully to an open ward and eventually discharged. Five years later she had had no further hospitalizations. (From Hayward & Taylor, 1956, 212–239)

PSYCHODYNAMIC THERAPY

Freud and many of his psychoanalytic colleagues were skeptical of the value of psychoanalysis for schizophrenic patients. The extreme psychological withdrawal seemed to be an effective barrier against the intimate interpersonal interchanges and transference reactions considered so essential for psychoanalytic treatment. However, some therapists, notably Harry Stack Sullivan and Frieda Fromm-Reichmann, felt that with several major modifications psychoanalytic therapy *could* be used successfully with schizophrenic patients. In treating neurotic patients, the psychoanalyst arranges conditions so as to minimize the intrusions of external reality and maximize attention to internal thoughts, fantasies, and memories.

The development of a trusting relationship is considered central to the successful treatment of schizophrenia by psychodynamically oriented therapists.

Sullivan and Fromm-Reichmann argued that the schizophrenic patient was already too conscious of inner conflicts; therefore therapy should be structured so as to help patients accurately perceive the present reality and move away from their autistic ruminations. As a result their therapy frequently focused on the here and now (as Rogers, Perls, and other phenomenological therapists were later to emphasize with neurotic patients), was conducted face to face, and omitted free-association instructions.

The central issue in psychodynamic therapy with schizophrenic persons is trust. Joan eloquently describes how crucial it is for the patient to experience at first hand, not by words but by deeds, that the therapist cares. She watches "like a hawk" for the most minute signs, a gesture or tone of voice, that will confirm her suspicions that the therapist does not care for her as a person, is frightened off by her violence, is interested in her only as a sex object, or is made anxious by her psychotic loss of control (perhaps tapping the therapist's own latent fears of psychosis). The therapist had to pass many, many tests before Joan began to believe that he did want to help her as a person and would not desert her when the going got rough.

Not everyone is cut out to be a therapist for schizophrenic patients. Fromm-Reichmann, Sullivan, and more recently others such as Laing have emphasized

the patience, trust, and sensitivity to the schizophrenic's subjective experience that is necessary for working with these patients. These ingredients of effective therapy tie in with a particular view of the development of schizophrenia—namely, that schizophrenics experience in infancy and early childhood such an acute "hurt" in relationships with others, usually one or both parents, that they subsequently withdraw from any intimate human interaction. As young children they may cover over this hurt and put on a front, but later the basic conflict over close interpersonal relationships leads to the symptoms we call schizophrenia.

Does Psychodynamic Therapy Work?   Let us look at the evidence. To repeat an old refrain, no matter how convincing individual case examples such as Joan's may seem, they do not demonstrate the general effectiveness of a treatment procedure. By and large, studies with adequate controls have not shown insight-oriented psychotherapy to be particularly effective with schizophrenic patients. For example, May et al. (1976) found the phenothiazine drugs alone were just as effective as phenothiazine drugs plus psychotherapy, and both of these treatments were more effective than psychotherapy alone, suggesting that the drugs were the active therapeutic ingredient with psychotherapy contributing little or nothing to the treatment process. The major shortcoming in this study was that the therapists were relatively inexperienced, being psychiatric residents in training or recent graduates of training programs. However, Grinspoon et al. (1968) used experienced psychoanalytic therapists and also found that psychotherapy added little if anything to phenothiazine treatment. Nor did Rogers et al. (1967) find psychotherapy to be more effective than usual hospital care in the treatment of schizophrenic patients. In a somewhat methodologically flawed study, Karon and Vanden Bos (1972) did find that psychotherapy was more effective than phenothiazines in treating schizophrenic patients. There were only two experienced therapists in this study each having had over ten years of experience doing psychotherapy with schizophrenic patients, and these were the most effective therapists. There was also some evidence that six inexperienced therapists supervised by one of the experienced therapists were also more effective than the phenothiazine comparison group. This study badly needs replication because, if true, it is an important caution to the growing pessimism about the value of psychotherapy with schizophrenic persons. A well designed study now underway at McLean Hospital and Boston University may provide a clearer answer to whether schizophrenic patients, or some subgroup of patients, may benefit from therapy with experienced psychotherapists (Mosher & Keith, 1980). Perhaps a few talented therapists using certain techniques (which need to be specified) can effect important changes in the life adjustment of at least some schizophrenics.

BEHAVIORAL AND SOCIAL LEARNING APPROACHES

Most attempts to treat psychotic patients in a behavioral framework have emphasized an operant learning model. It has by now been demonstrated time and again that specific psychotic behaviors in specific patients can be modified by a straightforward application of operant principles. Ayllon and Haughton (1964), for example, trained attendants to reinforce selectively psychotic or nonpsychotic talk in Kathy, a 47-year-old schizophrenic hospitalized for 16 years. Psychotic speech generally consisted of references to herself as "the Queen": "I'm the Queen. Why don't you give things to the Queen?" "How's King George, have you seen him?" A prefrontal lobotomy had had no effect on this kind of speech. After 15 days of collecting baseline data the attendants began to reinforce psychotic talk by attending to it (listening, showing interest, and occasionally offering a cigarette or piece of candy) and withholding attention (looking away, acting busy, appearing bored) from nonpsychotic talk such as "It's a nice day," "I'd like some soap," or "What time is it?"

The number of psychotic responses increased dramatically from an already high level, while the number of nonpsychotic responses dropped to almost zero. When the contingencies were reversed, psychotic talk dropped sharply to a level far below baseline, while nonpsychotic talk increased far above baseline. It is difficult to argue with these data. Kathy clearly talked differently as a function of differential reinforcement. But can schizophrenia be "cured" by operant procedures? Could each behavior (or lack of behavior) that has caused Kathy to be labeled schizophrenic be appropriately modified by differential re-

inforcement until she would no longer be judged schizophrenic and could be discharged to lead a normal life outside the hospital? That seemed to be the hope of the early behavioral investigators. It has turned out to be more difficult than such demonstrations imply.

Interpersonal Skill Training. A major deficit in most schizophrenic individuals is an inability to interact with other people in effective and satisfying ways. Rather than teach these individuals specific patterns of speech, as in the case of Kathy, other behaviorally oriented investigators have thought it would be more worthwhile to teach patients more general interpersonal skills. Thus Goldsmith and McFall (1975), using modeling and behavior rehearsal, gave relatively nonchronic patients practice in initiating interactions, handling conversational silences, responding to rejection, and being assertive in such interpersonal situations as dating, making friends, job interviews, and relating to authorities. Compared to patients in a pseudotherapy condition emphasizing discussion and insight into their difficulties and a no-treatment control condition, the patients in the interpersonal skill training condition showed greater improvement in these skills on various assessment procedures. Finch and Wallace (1977) conducted a similar study with more chronic patients (hospitalized for at least a year) and also reported increases in interpersonal skills as well as a greater proportion of patients in their skills training group being discharged to the community within three months after treatment. Interpersonal skills training, then, would seem to be quite promising as at least one component in the treatment of some schizophrenic patients.

The Mental Hospital: Helpful or Harmful?

Although mental hospitals are meant to be places of asylum where the distraught find peace, solace, and effective treatment, they have rarely achieved that ideal. Instead they have regularly been subjected to one exposé after another of the most deplorable conditions. Let us consider the case against the mental hospital and then look at those arguments in favor of at least some form of mental institution. Although

I will give special attention to the schizophrenic patient, the nature of the mental hospital environment clearly has implications for patients carrying other diagnoses as well.

THE CASE AGAINST

Impersonal, inhumane attitudes toward patients, a "snake pit" environment, and occasional brutalities and sadism by staff have all been discovered and rediscovered many times and in many hospitals. Confining a patient in the typical mental hospital, it is argued, is to make a bad situation worse. Having been labeled "mentally ill" and accordingly treated as a "sick patient," a nonperson, the individual sinks lower and lower into apathy, loss of identity, and feelings of incompetence and worthlessness. The disease of "institutionalism" is added to whatever problems in living the person had before coming to the hospital. Taking this view of mental hospitals to its logical conclusion, Albee (1968) advocated that they

be closed and torn down—"taken apart piece by piece and stone by stone and then, like the city of Carthage, plowed three feet under and sowed with salt."

There is no lack of evidence that some of the abuses attributed to mental hospitals do occur. In one study (Rosenhan, 1973), "normal" individuals got themselves admitted voluntarily to mental hospitals and reported on the powerlessness and dehumanization that they experienced (Research Report 17-1).

In the *societal reaction* view of mental illness the prehospital difficulties that lead to a person's admission are given almost minor status compared with the institutionalism syndrome thought to be produced by a lengthy stay in a hospital. As described in Chapter 15, mental disorder, in this view, is primarily a matter of society labeling a person in such a way as to create many secondary behaviors (roles and symptoms) which are then labeled as further manifestations of the illness. Gruenberg and Zusman (1964) spell out stages in the development of chron-

The environment of mental hospitals has often produced feelings of powerlessness and depersonalization in patients, who are sometimes treated as nonpersons.

Patients Are Treated as Nonpersons

In a field study by Rosenhan (1973), "normal" individuals were admitted voluntarily to 12 different mental hospitals after complaining to the intake psychiatrist that they heard voices that said "empty," "hollow," and "thud." The pseudopatients' normality was not suspected or detected by hospital personnel.

The pseudopatients observed that the very structure of the hospitals segregated patients and staff. While on a ward the staff spent most of their time in a glassed-off enclosure emerging primarily for caretaking purposes such as giving medication, conducting a therapy group, or instructing or reprimanding a patient. Attendants spent 11.3 percent of their time outside of "the cage," as the pseudopatients called it, including time for such activities as folding laundry, directing ward clean-up, and sending patients to off-ward activities. Only a small part of this time was spent in talking or mingling with the patients. The nurses spent so little time out of the cage that it was easier simply to tally the number of times they emerged—on the average 11.5 times per shift, including times when they left the ward entirely. Psychiatrists were even less available and were rarely seen on the wards. When they were on the wards, they spent most of their time in an office or in the cage.

The pseudopatients conducted a small experiment in which they initiated standard-ized contacts with staff members such as the following: "Pardon me, Mr. (Dr. or Mrs.)_____, could you tell me when I will be eligible for ground privileges?" Thirteen psychiatrists were approached 185 times, and 47 nurses and attendants were approached 1283 times. The staff made the following responses:

Response	Psychiatrists (Percent)	Nurses and Attendants (Percent)
Moves on, head averted	71	88
Makes eye contact	23	10
Pauses and chats	2	2
Stops and talks	4	0.5

An example: "Pardon me, Dr. X, could you tell me when I am eligible for ground privileges?" Physician: "Good morning, Dave. How are you today?" (Moves off without waiting for a response.) To quote Rosenhan, "Neither anecdotal nor 'hard' data can convey the overwhelming sense of powerlessness which invades the individual as he is continually exposed to the depersonalization of the psychiatric hospital."

The pseudopatients reported other aspects of the hospitals that increased power-lessness and dehumanization. Personal privacy was minimal. Staff members were free to enter the patients' personal quarters and examine their possessions for any reason. The patients' personal history was open to inspection by any staff member; personal hygiene and waste evacuation were frequently monitored. The bathrooms had no doors. Staff members sometimes acted as though the patients were invisible, nonpersons whom they did not have to take into account. Sometimes staff persons would point to a man in the dayroom and discuss him animatedly within earshot, as if he were not there. One nurse unbuttoned her uniform to adjust her brassiere in full sight of an entire ward of men. She was not being seductive; patients were simply not the same as real people.

Rosenhan also makes much of the fact that the sanity of all pseudopatients went undetected. Although as we saw in Chapter 6 the reliability of psychiatric diagnosis is only moderate and subject to expectancy effects, still this study is not a fair test of psychiatric judgment. The pseudopatients did say that they had auditory hallucinations at the time of their admission and psychiatrists, as do physicians diagnosing physical diseases, have to assume that patients are telling the truth. Furthermore, within a month or two all of the pseudopatients were discharged, albeit with a diagnosis of schizophrenia, in remission, in most cases.

icity or what they call the *social breakdown syndrome.*

1. Precondition: deficiency in self-concept. The social breakdown syndrome will occur only in persons with deficient inner standards regarding rules of behavior and social roles. Because they are lacking in self-confidence, their picture of who they are in relation to others and how it is proper to act is easily disturbed.
2. Dependence on current cues. When experiencing some acute disturbance (the incident that lands them initially in a mental hospital), they become unusually dependent on others for determining what is right and wrong, true and false, to be acted upon and to be inhibited.
3. Social labeling as incompetent and dangerous. The social environment defines the person as incompetent, dangerous, and incapable of self-control. This is done variously by calling the person "crazy," by ridicule, by legal proceedings, and by sending the person to a mental hospital.
4. Induction into the sick role. The person is now defined as a "patient," passive, helpless, and sick—with little prospect of change.
5. Learning the chronic sick role. Institutions offer roles of chronic withdrawal, chronic or intermittent aggression, or chronic dependency without ex-

treme withdrawal (the good working patient). The patient shifts from an identity based on acute disturbance to one of these more chronic roles.
6. Atrophy of work and social skills. In the hospital the patient has little opportunity to use previously acquired skills of everyday living such as cooking, sewing, driving, and specific work skills.
7. Identification with the sick. At some point the patient accepts this chronic state of sick functioning as like that of the other sick people in the hospital. The patient has become a member of the community.

The views expressed by Gruenberg and Zusman may underrate the severity of the psychological disorder prior to admission, but they do clearly point out the dangers of long-term institutionalization.

THE CASE FOR

The Therapeutic Community. Instead of trying to avoid hospitalization altogether, some mental health professionals have advocated drastic changes in the hospital setting so as to provide a more therapeutic environment. The basic idea is not new. The York

Scene from the film *One Flew over the Cuckoo's Nest.* Most modern mental hospitals may not be as bad as the one portrayed in this film, but the impersonal and dehumanizing treatment of patients continues to be a problem that is difficult to solve in any large institution.

Retreat, founded by William Tuke in 1792, was designed to be a place of refuge where patients would be treated with kindness and respected as persons.

Maxwell Jones (1953) was one of the first problem clinicians to implement such an approach. He developed the "social rehabilitation unit" at Belmont Hospital near London, and called his approach the *therapeutic community*. Patients were urged to be active participants in their own therapy as well as others' and in other aspects of the overall hospital routine—in sharp contrast to their usually more passive roles. Patients were also permitted to wear their own clothes instead of the usual hospital uniforms and allowed to have a reasonable degree of privacy and freedom to come and go within the ward or hospital. Staff roles were likewise changed. At community meetings physicians, nurses, social workers, attendants, and other staff were expected to abandon their usual status roles and interact with each other and with patients as persons. The overall aim of this *milieu therapy* was to provide an atmosphere of acceptance and respect that would help restore the patients' frequently shattered self-esteem and convey to them that they were expected to take an active part in the process of their own rehabilitation.

In the 1950s and 1960s many hospitals introduced programs that were called therapeutic communities. Research on the effectiveness of this approach has yielded mixed results (Ellsworth, 1964; Kasius, 1966). Although these programs may have helped in some cases to reduce the antitherapeutic aspects of the institution, clearly they have not emptied hospitals of the mentally ill. The problem, perhaps, is in implementation. The program is deceptively simple in conception, but few mental hospital staffs have the talent or wherewithal to sustain it on a 24-hour-a-day basis.

It is difficult to draw any firm conclusion about the effectiveness of the therapeutic community since there has been so much variation in its implementation. Treating patients like human beings rather than "patients," and conveying an expectancy that they can successfully assume increasing responsibility for their own lives is not only more humane but may constitute *one* active ingredient in any treatment program.

The Token Economy. The *token economy,* an extension of the operant learning model from one patient to an entire group of patients, has been applied within hospitals as well as in programs designed to help patients make the transition from the hospital to the community. The key feature in this approach is the use of tokens, usually plastic chips or cards, as *generalized conditioned reinforcers.* The term simply means that because the tokens can be used to obtain backup reinforcers of various kinds, they acquire some conditioned reinforcement value of their own. Money, of course, is an example of tokens that have considerable conditioned reinforcement value for most of us.

Tokens have many advantages as reinforcers for

At Walter Reed Army Medical Center a token economy program was devised initially for soldiers with severe personality disorders and later was extended to the treatment of schizophrenics and drug addicts. On the left is shown a general planning meeting where soldiers earn points for attendance and additional points for a brief, relevant speech. The soldier on the right is "spending" some of the points he has earned to play pool.

a large group: (1) They permit the reinforcement of a response at any time, whether or not backup reinforcers are immediately available, and thus bridge the delay between response and reinforcement; (2) sequences of responses can be reinforced with minimal interruption; (3) they maintain their reinforcing properties because of their relative independence of deprivation states such as hunger; and (4) they provide similar degrees of reinforcement for individuals who have different preferences for backup reinforcers (Kazdin & Bootzin, 1972).

Research has clearly confirmed the value of token economies in improving within-hospital adjustment (for example, Atthowe & Krasner, 1968; Henderson & Scoles, 1970; Schaefer & Martin, 1966). Token economies seem to be effective, however, only *as long as the token system is in effect*. When token systems are abandoned, the behavior of the patients frequently reverts to what it had been before the token economy was begun. This reversion is simply an example of extinction, exactly what social learning theory would predict. The problem is how to "fade out" the token reinforcers in such a way that other, more natural reinforcers in the environment take over and, more important, how to use the token reinforcers to effect a gradual transition to responsible living outside the hospital. Paul and Lentz (1977) have conducted the most comprehensive study yet done of both the therapeutic community and a social learning approach. A token economy was a major component of the social learning treatment. In both approaches major attention was given to facilitating a transition from hospital to community. The social learning approach was clearly superior on most measures, including releases from the hospital, compared to the therapeutic community and to usual hospital treatment. See Research Report 17-2 for more details on this important study.

Levine and Fasnacht (1974) raise a basic question about token economies: Do token rewards lead to "token learning"? These authors review a number of studies that support the general conclusion that if persons perceive themselves as performing some activity because they *want* to (an internal attribution of motive) they will both enjoy and persist at the task more than if they perceive the reason for their behavior to be an external reward (such as money or tokens). Remember how Tom Sawyer got his friends to whitewash the fence!

In one study (Deci, 1971), for example, college students were asked to reproduce four configurations drawn on paper from a set of Soma blocks (a puzzle that students ordinarily enjoy). If the subject could not solve a puzzle in ten minutes, the experimenter explained how to do it. After completing the puzzles, the subject was left alone in the room for eight minutes, free to do anything, for example, read magazines or work on the puzzles. With respect to the initial set of four puzzles, half of the students were told that they would receive one dollar for each correct solution; the other half were not promised any rewards. Students who were paid spent significantly *less* time working the puzzles when left alone than did those who were not paid.

This paradoxical finding, confirmed by many studies with children, adults, and even monkeys, is difficult to explain by a narrow conception of operant learning; rewards should increase response tendencies, not decrease them. Whatever the best theoretical interpretation of this relationship turns out to be, there is an important warning here for those who hope that token economies will produce changes that last after the tokens have been removed. The implication is that treatment programs should allow patients to share in decision making as much as possible rather than rely solely on externally administered rewards for achieving externally set goals.

Combining the Therapeutic Community with the Token Economy. An especially interesting development is the combination of milieu therapy and the token system. Olson and Greenberg (1972) found the combined approach more effective than milieu therapy alone, and Greenberg et al. (1975) found the combined approach more effective than a token economy alone. In the Greenberg et al. study the contrast between the token economy and the combination conditions was that in the former the staff had the responsibility for initiating treatment goals and specific plans, whereas in the latter these decision-making responsibilities were turned over to the patients themselves. Thus, in the combined approach, patients were placed in groups of five to seven members that met twice a week. The purpose of the groups was to make recommendations for treatment programs for each member of the group. Tokens were given to the group for coming up with feasible proposals.

Social Learning and Milieu Approaches with Chronic Mental Patients

Paul and Lentz (1977) evaluated the relative effectiveness of a social learning approach, a milieu or therapeutic community approach, and regular hospital treatment. The patients were chronic, process schizophrenics who had been hospitalized for an average of over 14 years. Both the social learning and milieu programs attempted to create a nonmedical atmosphere by calling patients residents, using first names and wearing street clothes by both staff and residents, and generally creating an expectation that residents could gradually take charge of their lives and eventually live responsibly in the community. Both programs encouraged the acquisition of social skills, stressed clarity of communication, provided opportunity to practice vocational and housekeeping skills, reintroduced residents to the outside world, and discouraged "crazy" talk and action. In the milieu condition special emphasis was placed on individual and group decision making and problem solving and on cohesiveness within certain small living groups. A token economy was a central feature of the social learning approach. Residents were given tokens for performing desired behaviors such as grooming, housekeeping, participating in meetings, communicating clearly, and so on. These tokens could then be "spent" later on canteen items or the purchase of certain activities such as use of the telephone, an extra bath, and hiring laundry service.

An Inpatient Assessment Battery composed of behavioral items reflecting functioning in various areas was administered every six months over the four and one-half years of in-hospital treatment. Results for the three treatment approaches are shown in Figure 17-2, in which it can be seen that the social learning group had the greatest improvement, with the milieu and regular hospital groups showing relatively little change overall and not being significantly different from each other. At the end of this in-hospital period all

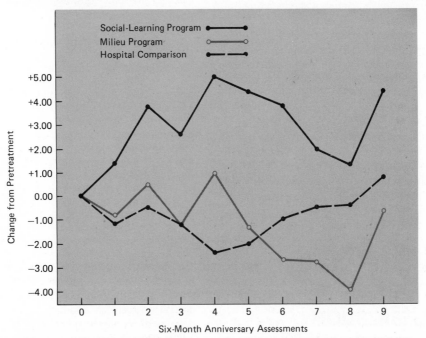

FIGURE 17-2. Changes in overall functioning from the Inpatient Assessment Battery during the treatment period for the social learning, milieu, and usual hospital treatment programs. From Paul and Lentz (1977), copyright Harvard University Press, 1977, and reproduced with permission.

residents were evaluated for possible discharge to supervised community living arrangements. The percentage of residents in each program that were able to achieve at least a minimum of a 90-day continuous stay out of the hospital are shown in Table 17-1. The social learning group was again most effective by this criterion, followed by the milieu group, which was in turn followed by the regular hospital group. Given that these severely disabled, chronic schizophrenic persons had spent about two-thirds of their adult lives in the confines of mental institutions, the effectiveness of the social learning program in helping them leave the hospital, even if it was only to live in supervised community placements, is impressive. Such an intensive program might be even more effective with less debilitated individuals, but this remains to be demonstrated.

TABLE 17-1
Percentage of Individuals Released for a Continuous Community Stay of at Least 90 Days

Treatment Program	Number of Individuals	Percent
Social learning	28	94.6
Milieu therapy	28	67.9
Regular hospital	28	46.4

Adapted from Paul and Lentz (1977).

The combined program represents an interesting approach to the question of whether token economies produce token learning: Patients are given tokens for making their own decisions. Will this condition lead to token learning in the sense that patients will stop making their own decisions as soon as the tokens are withdrawn? Or will the fact that they are making their own decisions lead to an internal attribution of responsibility that social psychological research suggests should be associated with more lasting effects? Although no long-term follow-up was reported, the moderately chronic patients in the combined condition spent more time outside the hospital during the one-year period of the study than did patients in the token-economy-only condition. This particular combination of the token economy with individual responsibility for planning and decision making would seem to be especially promising.

Deinstitutionalization: Alternatives to Hospitalization

Despite attempts to improve hospital treatment by such approaches as the therapeutic community and the token economy, many professionals have preferred to avoid hospitalization altogether or at least reduce it to a minimum. The community mental health movement has led a determined effort to get patients out of, or never let them into, the presumed antitherapeutic milieu of the mental hospital. Advocates of this view believe that many patients can be treated in the community with no hospitalization at all, or if the individual is experiencing an acute psychotic reaction, brief hospitalization, preferably in the psychiatric ward of a local general hospital, should be followed quickly by release and follow-up community treatment. The philosophy of the community mental health movement is well summarized in the report of the Joint Commission on Mental Illness and Health (1961):

The objective of modern treatment of persons with major mental illness is to enable the patient to maintain himself in the community in a normal manner. To do so, it is necessary (1) to save the patient from the debilitating effects of institutionalization as much as possible, (2) if the patient requires hospitalization, to return him to home and community life as soon as possible, and (3) thereafter to maintain him in the community as long as possible. Therefore, aftercare and rehabilitation are essential parts of all service to mental patients, and the various methods of achieving rehabilitation should be integrated in all forms of services, among them day hospitals, night hospitals, aftercare clinics, public health nursing services, foster family care, convalescent nursing homes, rehabilitation centers, work services, and ex-patient groups.

Implementation of the philosophy of the community mental health movement plus the advent of the tranquilizing drugs, especially the phenothiazines, did indeed result in a large drop in the number of patients in mental hospitals during the 1960s and 1970s (Bassuk & Gerson, 1978); see Figure 17-3. The trend toward deinstitutionalization has been further reinforced by legal and judicial pressures that

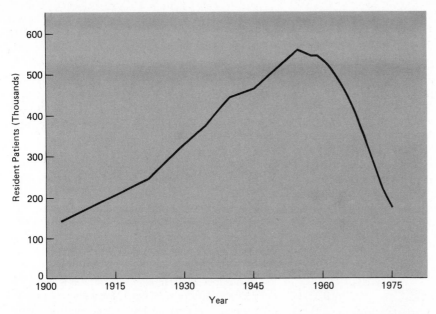

FIGURE 17-3. Inpatient population of state and county mental hospitals rose steadily from the turn of the century until 1955, after which it has decreased sharply. These data do not include private or Federal hospitals, whose population has held fairly constant at between 50,000 and 75,000. From Bassuk and Gerson (1978). Copyright 1978 by Scientific American and used with permission.

make involuntary commitments more difficult and that assert the right to treatment (*Rouse* v. *Cameron,* 1966) and the right of nondangerous persons to freedom (*O'Conner* v. *Donaldson,* 1975).

Let us consider, then, some of the specific ways that the deinstitutionalization movement has been implemented and the evidence for their effectiveness.

HALFWAY AND OTHER BOARD-AND-CARE HOMES

In the 1960s there was considerable interest in establishing halfway homes, where recently discharged patients could make a partially supervised transition to independent community living. Then in the 1970s a number of states made a massive investment in more long-term board-and-care facilities, and great numbers of chronic mental patients were moved from hospitals to these community-based settings. Typically, such a facility might consist of an old apartment building in which 50–200 ex–mental

patients are provided regular meals, an occasional visit by a psychiatrist to regulate phenothiazine drug levels, possibly some available social activities, and freedom to come and go in the community. Although on the surface the large-scale movement of patients from hospitals to community placements seemed like a successful accomplishment of a major goal of the community mental health movement, it has become clear that, *as usually implemented,* this strategy has not solved the problem of what to do for the chronic mental patient. Two shortcomings of this approach have become apparent. First, there is the marked increase in the "revolving door" phenomenon. Although discharge rates increased sharply, readmission rates also went up. In one review of studies, Anthony et al. (1972) found that 40 to 50 percent of patients were readmitted to mental hospitals within one year of discharge. Thus the policy of brief hospitalization and quick return to the community was not particularly effective in keeping individuals functioning outside of the hospital. Second, many chronic patients who were not rehospitalized have shown very little change in their symptoms and competencies (Lamb & Goertzel, 1972). Findings of this kind led many to conclude that the chronic mental patient had simply been moved (some would say "dumped") from one custodial situation to another (Kohen & Paul, 1976). There remains a hard core of chronic, process schizophrenic individuals who, despite continual medication on phenothiazine drugs, either remain in traditional mental hospitals or live very marginal existences in extended-care facilities.

Perhaps this rather negative conclusion should be qualified slightly. A certain proportion of patients in extended-care facilities definitely prefer to be there than confined in hospitals, and although their lives may seem restricted and empty by normal comparisons, some of these individuals do seem to enjoy a

Recent changes in commitment laws have resulted in the discharge of many patients from mental hospitals. Some of these individuals can manage a marginal adjustment at best, and communities frequently do not have facilities, such as half-way houses, that would smooth their return to society.

measure of contentment and appreciate the freedom of nonconfinement. For example, one 44-year-old schizophrenic man had experienced a lifetime of economic hardship, vocational failure, petty crime, and being in and out of jail and occasionally hospitals before coming to a board-and-care home two years previously. His periods of acute disturbances had disappeared, and he expressed relief and contentment with the living situation (Lamb, 1979).

SPECIAL COMMUNITY PROGRAMS

Despite the overall ineffectiveness to date of community-based treatment for the chronic patient, there are several specific programs, usually involving rather intensive efforts, that are promising. Test and Stein (1978) reviewed research in this area and concluded that a number of these intensive programs were indeed effective in preventing rehospitalization and in maintaining a reasonable level of adequate functioning *as long as they were in effect.* There was a general tendency in most programs for relapse rates to rise within a year or two after termination of the program. These relatively successful programs vary in their focus but in general tend to emphasize the development and maintenance of psychosocial skills. Thus hospitalization was reduced by Langsley and Kaplan (1968) with family crisis therapy; by Stein and Test (1978) with the teaching of skills necessary to live in the community such as how to shop, budget, do laundry, obtain and keep jobs, and participate in leisure time activities; by Fairweather et al. (1969) with a group living arrangement centered around the running of a janitorial business; by Budson et al. (1977) with the building and maintaining of an extended social support network; and by Mosher and Menn (1978) with a non-drug-oriented, small-group, therapeutic community-type living arrangement.

Let us look at the last approach in a bit more detail. The group home established by Mosher and Menn (1978), called Soteria (Greek for salvation or deliverance), is a house in a "transitional" neighborhood in the San Francisco Bay area. The schizophrenic persons at Soteria are called residents, not patients, and are limited to six in number at any one time. Decision making and responsibilities are shared between staff and residents. Drug treatment is infrequently used, and no formal psychotherapy is provided. The primary staff is made up of young non-professionals selected for their potential to accept and understand the residents. The staff tends to view the schizophrenic reaction (this label is never used) as involving an altered state of consciousness and fragmented and occasionally terrifying experiences, and as having unique potential for reintegration and growth. The schizophrenic experience, in other words, is not "disqualified" but accepted as real for the person undergoing it. The staff members attempt to accompany the persons on their schizophrenic journey, guiding them through to a more integrated existence—an orientation very similar to that of Laing.

The effectiveness of the Soteria program was compared with a well-staffed, small community mental health center where all of the schizophrenic patients in the comparison group had received high doses of phenothiazine drugs. Most of the Soteria residents received no drugs at all. Overall their results indicated that the Soteria residents did just as well as the comparison group, with some trends suggesting more improvement in the Soteria group; for example, two years after admission more Soteria individuals were living alone or with peers and showed less decline in general occupational level from their prepsychotic status.

Based on the results of these relatively effective programs the National Institute of Mental Health has begun to support a number of programs in which a continuing effort is directed toward the development and maintenance of social support systems and skills related to work, community living, and leisure time activities (Turner & Ten Hoor, 1978). Time will tell whether these psychosocially oriented programs will live up to their promise. To the extent that schizophrenia involves a biological defect, these programs can be seen as raising the person's level of functioning to as near his or her potential as can be achieved, which may still be below normal in some respects yet a great improvement over the almost total incapacitation seen in severe, chronic schizophrenia. To the extent that schizophrenia is the result of psychosocial factors, either in interaction with biological defects or by themselves, the goals of rehabilitation may still be limited for some individuals by the severe dysfunctions produced by the early social learning experiences. The most effective approaches to promoting full and satisfying lives for severely schizophrenic persons may not be devised until we more fully understand the biological and psychosocial factors that produce this disorder or disorders.

COMMUNITY REACTION TO DEINSTITUTIONALIZATION

People are not always overjoyed at the prospect of having former mental patients as neighbors. In Long Beach, New York, for example, the reaction was particularly strong after some 500 to 1000 ex–mental patients moved into poorly supervised group homes or lived on their own in old hotels and rooming houses. Such ex-patients are rarely dangerous, but they can become neighborhood nuisances as well as objects of irrational fear since some of them do occasionally behave in strange ways. Officials of New York State's Department of Mental Hygiene conceded that problems had been created for some communities, but contended that their department was in a bind: On the one hand, they were accused of dumping patients into neighborhoods; on the other hand, state law made it difficult to commit or hold patients against their will without good medical or social reasons.

Until well-supervised halfway houses, group homes, or intensive after-discharge training in coping skills are available, there is a real question as to how humane it is to send mental patients into hostile communities. As Robert Reich (1974), director of psychiatry for New York City's Department of Social Services, said: "Freedom to be sick, helpless, and isolated is not freedom. It is a return to the Middle Ages, when the mentally ill roamed the streets and little boys threw rocks at them."

There is no easy solution to the problem of where to treat the mentally ill—in the hospital, which may lead to institutionalism—or in the community, which is often hostile. It can be solved in part by educating and accustoming communities to the nature and basic safety of well-supervised group homes. Sandall et al. (1975), for example, found that after three years of operation their St. Louis program was well accepted by the community. Neighbors of community homes frequently approached staff members, either to offer new apartments or to request help with their own problems. The authors felt that their program had promoted neighborhood stability in an area marginal both economically and in terms of social services.

Summary

1. Phenothiazine drugs have been shown effective in reducing the symptoms of schizophrenia in many patients. However, some patients on the drugs show only limited improvement and still cannot get along outside the hospital, and other patients develop troublesome side effects such as tradive dyskenesia.

2. Psychodynamic therapy with schizophrenic patients emphasizes a relationship of trust between the therapist and the patient. The patient, learning by deeds, not words, that another person can be trusted, is presumably enabled to overcome the anxiety about close interpersonal relationships produced by early childhood hurts.

3. Studies with adequate controls have shown, at best, mixed results for the effectiveness of insight therapy with schizophrenic persons.

4. Many specific psychotic behaviors can be modified by operant learning procedures, but there is some question whether the broader schizophrenic disorder is "cured" by this approach. Interpersonal skill training conducted in a broader social learning framework may be more promising.

5. The traditional mental hospital has been condemned by many as an antitherapeutic setting that causes patients to regress further into states of apathy and loss of identity.

6. The therapeutic community approach is an attempt to break institutions into smaller living units, make them more humane, and give patients more responsibility for running their own lives. Community homes and halfway houses frequently attempt to follow the therapeutic community concept to serve as a bridge from the isolated institution to the community.

7. The token economy is a logical extension of the operant learning model from one patient to an entire group of patients. This approach has been found to result in decreases in psychotic behaviors and increases in social interaction and various self-help activities. These benefits, however, are usually lost when the token economy is stopped. Investigators continue to work on the problem of how to get these positive effects to generalize beyond the immediate token economy. One promising approach has been to combine the token approach with the milieu approach and reward (with tokens) individual responsibility for making decisions about treatment.

8. The community mental health movement, the effectiveness of the phenothiazine drugs, and, more recently, attacks on the legality of involuntary commitments have led to a sharp reduction in the number of patients in mental hospitals. Although attempts to avoid hospitalization by quick discharges and follow-up community contacts have met with some success, this has not proved to be a lasting solution. Many patients are readmitted, and even those that remain in the community frequently lead a marginal existence.

9. Especially promising are ongoing community-based programs that provide fairly intensive skills training and the development of social support networks.

10. The strong push to return mental patients to the community has created a backlash. Citizens' groups have complained, and there is certain to be some continuing conflict between these opposing points of view.

Suggested Readings

A good discussion of various approaches to the treatment of schizophrenia can be found in W. M. Mendel, *Schizophrenia: The experience and its treatment* (Jossey-Bass, 1976), and in J. M. Neale and T. Oltmanns's *Schizophrenia* (Wiley, 1980). E. L. Bassuk and S. Gerson discuss the trend in deinstitutionalization of mental patients in the *Scientific American* (Vol. 238, February, 1978).

18

Affective Disorders and Suicide

- Can a person feel too good, be too self-confident, be too energetic? What is mania?

- How does the normal enjoyment of life get twisted into self-blame and despair? What is depression?

- Are the extreme disturbances in mood seen in affective disorders determined by genes, chemical imbalances in the brain, psychosocial experiences, or what?

- "Sometimes I'm up, sometimes I'm down." What kind of biological and psychological changes occur when a person switches from a depressed to a manic state?

- Peter Pan advised, "Think lovely thoughts, and up you'll go!" Does that work? What if you always do the opposite?

- Is it true that people who talk about suicide rarely commit suicide?

- What causes an adolescent to attempt suicide?

- Do suicide prevention centers actually prevent suicides?

Joe A.: Great Plans in the Making

Joe A. had recently embarked on a grandiose business venture. By virtue of fast talk and unshakable optimism he had persuaded conservative businessmen to invest in his enterprise. When disaster struck and his scheme was in shambles, Joe A. became more frantic and hyperactive. Swearing, babbling, and shouting, he was finally escorted by policemen to the local mental hospital. There he continued his "pitch":

. . . You look like a couple of bright, alert, hard working, clean-cut, energetic, go-getters and I could use you in my organization! I need guys that are loyal and enthusiastic about the great opportunities life offers on this planet! It's yours for the taking! Too many people pass opportunity by without hearing it knock because they don't know how to grasp the moment and strike while the iron is hot! . . . Be there firstest with the mostest! my guts and your blood! That's the system! I know, you know, he, she, or it knows it's the only way to travel! Get 'em off balance, baby, and the rest is leverage! Use your head and save your heels! What's this deal? Who are these guys? Have you got a telephone and a secretary I can have instanter if not sooner? What I need is office space and the old LDO [long-distance operator] . . . (McNeil, 1967, p. 147)

Van Wyck Brooks: A Season in Hell

Van Wyck Brooks (1957), once known to many as the dean of American letters, gave the following description of some of his experiences during a four-year period of depression:

There came a time in the middle twenties when my own bubble burst, when the dome under which I have lived crumbled into ruin, when I was consumed with a sense of failure, a feeling that my work had all gone wrong and that I was mistaken in all I had said or thought. What had I been doing? I had only ploughed the sea, as a certain great man once remarked, and I thought of my writing "with rage and shame," E. M. Forster's phrase for his own feeling about his early work. I was pursued especially with nightmares in which Henry James turned great luminous menacing eyes upon me . . . and I was possessed now with a fantasy of suicide that filled my mind as the full moon fills the sky. It was a fixed idea. I could not expel this fantasy that shimmered in my brain and I saw every knife as something with which to cut one's throat and every high building as something to jump from. . . .
     I was to find myself presently in an English sanitarium where I spent eight months at Harrow-on-the-Hill in a long low Queen Anne manor-house that was later to become the infirmary of the neighbouring Harrow school. There I conceived the delusion that I was about to be buried alive, not in the earth but walled in a small chamber; and I believed that "they" were coming for me. For many mornings, waking early from an artificial sleep, I heard them putting together a large box for me below, a box that, in my fantasy, had arrived in sections to be hammered together in the house with nails or pegs. (pp. 187, 188, 190)

Angela: A Less Severe Depression

Angela, age 22, contacted a counseling center because she had been troubled by continuing despondency and frequent crying spells since she had broken up with her boyfriend two months before. She had begun to feel as if it were a huge effort just to walk around, and going to work was especially difficult; she found it almost impossible to concentrate on her job. Initiating a conversation with other people was hard, and on some occasions her lips felt "stiff" so that an extra effort was required to make them move. She had a difficult time getting to sleep at night, and when she did fall asleep, she was frequently troubled by upsetting dreams. She was constantly tired and bothered by loud noises; she preferred to be by herself, often lying on her bed and crying. (Adapted from Leon, 1974)

Affective Disorders

Affective disorders consist of a prolonged disturbance in mood that colors the whole psychic life. They generally involve either depression or elation. In DSM-III these disorders are divided into the following categories:

Major Affective Disorders
    Bipolar disorder
    Major depression
Other Specific Affective Disorders
    Cyclothymic disorder (milder less incapacitating
      mood swings of a manic and depressive type)
    Dysthymic disorder (neurotic depression)

BIPOLAR DISORDER

All persons who have experienced a *manic episode* are diagnosed as having a *bipolar disorder.* The vast majority of these individuals will at some time in their lives also have an episode of severe depression, thus the term bipolar, referring to the two poles of mania and depression. In some instances the person may switch almost immediately from one kind of episode to the other with no intervening period of normality. In other cases a period of normal mental health may occur between episodes. In the past these disorders have been considered part of a somewhat broader category called manic-depressive psychosis. Let us consider the features of a manic episode in more detail.

A manic episode is characterized by excessive elation, irritability, talkativeness, flight of ideas, and accelerated speech and motor behavior. Joe A. showed most of these features. The elevated mood is usually cheerful and euphoric, and tends to involve an unceasing and unselective enthusiasm for relating to people. The individual, as was true for Joe A., is likely to make all kinds of unrealistic plans—occupational, political, or religious—and sometimes embark on poorly thought-out projects. In some cases the euphoric mood is accompanied by irritability, especially if the person is thwarted in some activity. Manic speech is typically loud, rapid, and often full

Van Wyck Brooks (1886–1963), American critic and author. In *Days of the Phoenix* he describes his own experience with a severe depression.

of jokes, puns, and plays on words. The individual may burst into song or other theatrical displays. Hallucinations and delusions may occur and, when they do, are usually related to the euphoric, overconfident mood.

MAJOR DEPRESSION

Depressive symptoms are so widespread among clients at mental health facilities that these symptoms have sometimes been called the common cold of psychopathology, an appropriate comparison in terms of pervasiveness but perhaps inaccurate in terms of the implication of mildness. Individuals with depressive disorders, such as Van Wyck Brooks and Angela, show many of the following symptoms: All zest for living is lost. Feelings of pleasure and joy give way to sadness or to a nonfeeling state of emotional numbness. Spontaneous initiative in activities, whether in work or play, yield to passivity and apathy. Interest in food or sex is lost or turns into a revulsion against these biological needs. Attitudes of self-acceptance and hopefulness are twisted into attitudes of self-blame and despair. The person thinks, "What's the use?", "It's all my fault," "Things will never get better." Sleep does not come at night, and bodily concerns can grow into preoccupation with fears of disease. And ultimately even the desire to live may be replaced with a wish to die. How can it happen that the normal enjoyment of life can become so distorted into this chronic pattern of unhappiness that we call depression? We will address this question in detail later in the chapter.

The diagnosis of *major depression* is reserved for individuals showing severe depressive symptoms but no manic symptoms, such as Van Wyck Brooks. The less severe but more common depressions, such as shown by Angela, have been called *neurotic depressions* and more recently *dysthymic disorders* in DSM-III.

THE BIPOLAR-UNIPOLAR DISTINCTION

When major depressions recur, they are sometimes called unipolar depressions. There is growing evidence that bipolar depressions and unipolar depressions of this kind are distinctive disorders with differences in symptoms, age of onset, and genetic determinants. Beigel and Murphy (1971), for example, matched 25 bipolar patients who were experiencing a depressive episode with 25 unipolar patients on age, sex, and severity of depression. The unipolar patients were significantly more anxious, agitated (based on a rating of "pacing" behavior), likely to express anger overtly, and likely to have somatic complaints. These differences are illustrated by written observations of nurses on the unit. A patient with bipolar affective disorder was described like this:

Depressed, frequently dozing, non-involved . . . appears depressed and preoccupied . . . sitting in dayroom most of evening . . . answers only direct questions . . . little or no interaction with peers . . . spent day reading in dayroom . . . asked if she wished to talk and replied, "No, it doesn't do any good" . . . speaks only when spoken to. (p. 218)

A unipolar depressed patient, on the other hand, behaved like this:

Looking depressed and anxious; has a painful look about her and continues to pace and wring hands . . . presents angry appearance; making angry side remarks . . . continues to pace in corridor . . . pacing much of morning . . . pacing in the halls this afternoon . . . complaining of a headache during husband's visit . . . patient retching frequently. (p. 21)

The median age of onset of bipolar depressions is in the early thirties compared with a later onset in the early forties for unipolar depressions (Angst et al., 1973), and there is a much higher likelihood of a history of manic or hypomanic (mild manic) disorders in the close relatives of bipolar patients but not for unipolar patients (Depue & Monroe, 1978). Thus the distinction between bipolar disorders and recurring major depressions appears to be an important one, and I will return to it when discussing etiology.

RECOVERY AND RECURRENCE

There is a strong tendency toward "spontaneous" recovery and recurrence in the Affective Disorders, as illustrated by the following statistics obtained by Rennie (1942) on 208 patients with manic-depressive psychosis admitted to a mental hospital between 1913 and 1916. The treatment these patients received was limited almost entirely to custodial care, so the study provides an estimate of recovery rates without benefit of more recent forms of treatment. Rennie found that over a 20-year period, 93 percent of the patients recovered from the first episode, but 79 percent had a second episode, 64 percent a third, and 45 percent a fourth. In a similar study, Morrison et al. (1973) reported follow-up ratings on 87 patients with *bipolar affective disorders*, 202 with *unipolar depressive reactions* and 183 poor-premorbid schizophrenics. The results are striking. After five years approximately 80 percent of the patients with affective disorders had recovered, compared to 14 percent of those with poor-premorbid or process schizophrenia (Figure 18-1). As in Rennie's study, all these patients were hospitalized before either electroshock or tranquilizer drugs were used at their hospital; thus these data tend to show the "natural" or untreated course of the disorders.

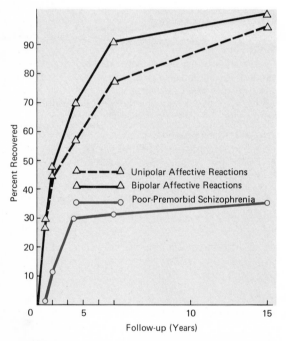

FIGURE 18-1. Percent recovery in patients over time. Follow-up information was obtained at different times for different groups of patients, so each point on the curves represents a different group of patients. (Adapted from Morrison, Winokur, Crowe, & Clancy, 1973. Copyright 1973 by the American Medical Association and used with permission.)

PREVALENCE

DSM-III, based on studies in Europe and the United States, estimates that about 18–23 percent of the females and 8–11 percent of the males have at some time had a depressive episode and that the episode had been severe enough to require hospitalization in 6 percent of the females and 3 percent of the males. From 0.4 to 1.2 percent of the adult population are estimated to have had a bipolar affective disorder.

Development of Affective Disorders

HEREDITY

As with schizophrenia a consistently higher prevalence of affective disorders is found among close relatives (parents, siblings, and children) of individuals with affective disorders than for the population at large (Rosenthal, 1971). More clearly implicating genetic influence are a number of twin studies in which much higher concordance rates are found for identical than fraternal twins. Concordances range from 30 to 93 percent for identical twins and from 0 to 38.5 percent for fraternal twins (Table 18-1). The index twins in these studies had the more severe forms of affective disorders, frequently carrying the old diagnosis of manic-depressive psychosis. Twin studies of the milder or remote forms of depression have not shown a clear genetic contribution (Slater & Shields, 1969).

The Bertelsen et al. (1977) study may be the least biased in terms of sampling since it is based on the total population of twins obtained from the Danish birth registry. These authors also divided their index twins into those whose affective disorder took the bipolar form and those that took the unipolar form (recurring major depressions) and found that concordance rates for identical twins were higher in the bipolar type (74 percent) than in the unipolar type (43 percent), suggesting that the bipolar type is more strongly influenced by heredity than the unipolar type. Perris (1966) also had found evidence favoring a greater genetic contribution to bipolar disorders in studying the close relatives of persons with these two

TABLE 18-1 **Concordance for Affective Disorders in Identical and Fraternal Twins**

	Number of Twin Pairs		Percent Concordance[a]	
Investigator	*Identical*	*Fraternal*	*Identical*	*Fraternal*
Rosanoff (1934), U.S.A.	23	67	70	16
Kallmann (1953), U.S.A.	27	55	93	24
Slater (1953), England	7	17	57	23.5
Da Fonseca (1959), England	21	39	71	38.5
Kringlen (1967), Norway	6	20	33	0
Bertelsen, Harvald, and Hauge (1977), Denmark	55	52	58	17

[a]Rounded to nearest whole number.

types of affective disorders. Furthermore, when twins were concordant, they were much more likely to both be bipolar or both be unipolar than would occur by chance. This finding is also consistent with the possibility that relatively different genotypes are involved in these two disorders. These findings are a good example of how genetic research can help validate a diagnostic distinction and indicate that the distinction is not just an arbitrary or superficial one that has no implication for etiology.

Biological Correlates. Before specific biological theories are described a word is in order about the terms *endogenous* and *exogenous* depressions. The former were thought to result primarily from genetic and biological causes and the latter from life stresses and past psychosocial learning experiences. The exogenous type has also been called neurotic or reactive depression. Note the similarity to the concepts of process and reactive schizophrenia. The endogenous-exogenous distinction has lost popularity in recent years, in part because even the so-called endogenous depressions are frequently associated with precipitating life stresses and also because it has been difficult to clearly define the criteria for exogenous depressions. In fact, in one study 18 percent of a group of patients who had originally been diagnosed as having neurotic (exogenous) depressions subsequently developed bipolar affective disorders, considered a form of endogenous depression, within three to four years (Akiskal et al., 1978).

Biological Bases for Subtypes. One of the important tasks in understanding the causes of affective disorders is identifying subcategories that have different patterns of causative factors. This is especially important if there are several depressive disorders mediated by distinctive biological mechanisms, because radically different kinds of treatment may be effective in the various types. An important start in this area is the separation of the bipolar disorders from the rest of the affective disorders on the basis of the evidence reviewed above. Criteria for subdividing the remaining depressive disorders are not so clear at this time, although there are some interesting possibilities. The more severe and recurring major depressive disorders, the unipolar type, probably have some genetic basis. However, it has not been possible to develop entirely satisfactory criteria for separating these depressive disorders from those largely determined by psychosocial factors. Perhaps no such sharp distinction can be made. See Research Report 18-1 for a description of research on the relationship of brain neurotransmitters, such as norepinephrine and serotonin, to affective disorders and the possibility of identifying subcategories of affective disorders on the basis of biochemical differences.

Switching from Depression to Mania. Additional evidence for the role of brain norepinephrine in bipolar disorders is provided by Bunney et al. (1972), who carefully followed the transition from depression to mania, and from mania to depression, for ten patients.

During depression the patients conformed more to the retarded than the agitated depressive pattern, tending to be seclusive, unresponsive, and dozing during much of the day. For all patients the transition to the manic state was preceded by a normal phase,

**RESEARCH
REPORT
18-1**

Neurotransmitters and the Affective Disorders

When one neuron fires, the signal is transported across the synaptic space to another neuron by means of organic chemicals called biogenic amines. We have seen that one biogenic amine, dopamine, is thought to play a role in schizophrenia. Other biogenic amines involved in the synaptic transmission of nerve impulses are norepinephrine, serotonin, and tryptamine. See Figure 18-2 for an outline of the steps in the synthesis (production) and metabolism of these biogenic amines. Two of these biogenic amines have been implicated in affective disorders. It has been proposed that (1) depression results from a depletion of serotonin, or (2) depression results from a deficiency of norepinephrine and mania from an excess of norepinephrine, or (3) affective disorders result from some combination of abnormal levels of these two amines. It is easy to imagine how the depletion of a neurotransmitter could produce symptoms of depression. If the number of neurons being activated is greatly reduced, then one might well see the mental and behavioral slowing down, the reduction in energy, and the unresponsiveness seen in depression. Or if the number of neurons being activated is greatly increased, the overactivity associated with mania might well result.

What is the evidence for these theories? In the early 1950s a chemical called iproniazid was synthesized for the treatment of tuberculosis. Physicians noticed that this drug seemed to make some patients mildly euphoric. Animal research indicated that iproniazid increased both norepinephrine and serotonin concentration in the brain. It was subsequently discovered that it had this effect by inhibiting an enzyme, monoamine oxidase,

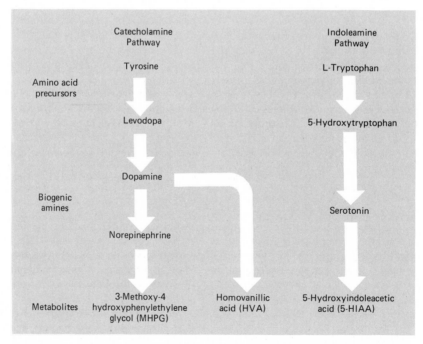

FIGURE 18-2. Precursors and metabolic products of two groups of biogenic amines. (Adapted from Akiskal & McKinney, 1975. Copyright 1975 by the American Medical Association and used with permission.)

that breaks down norepinephrine and serotonin. Iproniazid apparently increased these amines by preventing their breakdown. When iproniazid was given to depressed patients it was indeed found to be moderately successful in relieving their symptoms. Other drugs that inhibited monoamine oxidase were also found to be useful in reducing depression in some patients.

At about the same time it was noticed that a new drug being used to treat high blood pressure, reserpine, occasionally induced depressive reactions. Animal studies showed reserpine depleted norepinephrine and serotonin in the brain. Thus we find that a drug, iproniazid, that increases norepinephrine and serotonin alleviates depression, and a drug, reserpine, that decreases norepinephrine and serotonin produces depression. Later, more effective antidepressant drugs, the tricyclics, were developed and were found to increase the available amounts of norepinephrine. After a neurotransmitter crosses the synapse and acts on the second neuron, some of it is taken back up into the first neuron, a process called reuptake. Research has shown that the tricyclic drugs block the reuptake process and thereby produce an increase in synaptic norepinephrine.

Although this mechanism of action of the tricyclic drugs has been accepted by many as explaining the drug's effectiveness, there has been one puzzling problem with this theory. The inhibition of reuptake should take place within minutes of drug ingestion, yet clinical improvement in depressed patients does not occur sooner than eight days and frequently takes longer. Montigny and Aghajanian (1978) report results that may resolve this enigma. They found that tricyclic drugs increased the responsivity of rat forebrain neurons to serotonin and that this increased sensitivity took from one to two weeks, a time course closely paralleling improvement in depressed humans. These results, then, point to a defect in mechanisms affecting the sensitivity of serotonin receptors. In other words, depression may result from factors that decrease the sensitivity of serotonin receptors in certain areas of the brain.

Other research has indicated that only one subgroup of depressions is associated with low levels of serotonin (Asberg, Thoren, et al., 1976). These authors measured one of the metabolic products of serotonin (5-HIAA) in the cerebrospinal fluid, a measure that is assumed to reflect levels of available serotonin in the brain. They obtained such measures of 5-HIAA in 43 patients with severe depression and found two rather distinct subgroups, one showing lower than normal levels of 5-HIAA and the other showing relatively normal levels. They repeated the study on another sample of patients and found the same bimodal distribution (Figure 18-3). Within the groups with low levels of 5-HIAA they found large and significant negative correlations between levels of 5-HIAA and ratings of severity of depression; the lower the 5-HIAA levels the more severe the depression. Goodwin & Athanasios (1979) repeated these findings and also looked to see if there was any tendency for bipolar or unipolar depressions to be associated with either of the subgroups defined by low or normal serotonin levels. There was not. The picture, then, remains a bit unclear as to how biochemically defined subgroups of depressive disorders will contribute to our ultimate understanding of the varieties of depressive disorders, but results to date suggest that these biochemical distinctions will be important in separating out depressions that may have important differences in their biological correlates.

With respect to mania, lithium carbonate has been found to be effective in treating this disorder, and animal experiments have shown that this drug decreases levels of brain norepinephrine—findings that support an association between high levels of norepinephrine and manic behavior. One theory, supported by indirect evidence, is that lithium carbonate reduces abnormally high levels of intraneuronal sodium, which has been preventing the reuptake of norepinephrine and thus causing excessive amounts of this neurotransmitter to accumulate (Goodwin & Athanasios, 1979). Urinary levels of norepinephrine have also been found to increase as individual patients change from depressed to manic states.

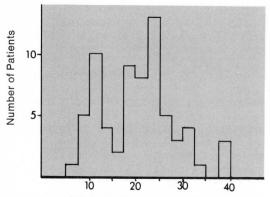

FIGURE 18-3. Distribution of depressed patients as a function of amount of 5-HIAA in the cerebrospinal fluid (an indirect indicator of serotonin levels in the brain). Deviation from a normal curve is significant (chi square = 19.8, p = .02). Results suggest that one type of severe depression may be related to serotonin depletion. (Adapted from Asberg, Thoren, Traskman, Bertilsson, & Ringberger, 1976. Copyright 1976 by the American Association for the Advancement of Science and used with permission.)

lasting from one to four days, in which they began to initiate conversation, became more physically active, and showed more thoughtfulness in their relationships with others. The patients' moods improved and they joined in group activities. The manic period frequently showed a progressive development. On the first day there was sudden and marked increase in the amount of talking and physical activity over the previous normal period. Within several days the activity level of the person increased further until the behavior was characterized by incessant talking, shouting, and movement, poor judgment, sexual preoccupation, anger, and aggression. Finally most patients reached a state of grandiose and psychotic beliefs, flights of ideas including rhyming and punning, and physical combativeness when restrained. (Notes on one patient before, during, and after the switch to mania are shown in Table 18-2.) On the average, the patients slept little the night before their mania began, and still less during the manic period, averaging around three to five hours of sleep per night.

Urinary levels of various neurotransmitters were measured on a daily basis. Only norepinephrine showed a clear and significant increase on "day mi-

nus-one," the day before the behavioral symptoms of mania appeared. The level of norepinephrine remained high during the manic phase and returned somewhat more gradually to its previous low level when mania switched to depression. Each of nine patients for whom this measure was obtained showed an increase in norepinephrine levels on the day preceding the onset of mania. This study, then, clearly illustrates the dramatic shift from depression to mania that can occur in some patients. The fact that the norepinephrine levels had begun to increase somewhat before the more obvious behavioral changes suggests that this biochemical change may play a causative role in the switch rather than be a secondary result of increased activity level.

PSYCHOSOCIAL CORRELATES

As is the case for schizophrenia, the fact that identical twins are not 100 percent concordant for affective disorders is conclusive evidence that environmental events must play some part in their causation. Since one event that frequently precipitates a depressive reaction is a loss of some kind and since some features of the depressive disorder resemble the sadness associated with normal grief, let us begin our consideration of psychosocial correlates with a discussion of the normal grief reaction.

The Normal Grieving Process. Humans as well as other primates show a typical grieving reaction to an important psychological loss, such as the death of a loved one: First there is protest, with crying, agitation, or denial of the loss; next comes the depression-withdrawal phase, in which the person becomes apathetic and unresponsive, giving up on finding any enjoyment in life; and finally the person shows a slow recovery to a normal responsiveness and interest in life.

Freud (Anna) and Burlingham (1943) describe grief reactions that occurred in normal children one to three years of age when they were separated from their parents during wartime evacuation of London and during extended periods of hospitalization. First, during the period of protest, the children cried a great deal, asked for their parents if they could talk, and were restless, hyperactive, and easily angered. After about a week some children decreased these overt

TABLE 18-2 Notes on a Patient during Depressed, Normal, and Manic Periods

Depressed (Days −12 to −4)	Normal (Days −3 to −1)	Manic (Days 0 to +26)
Day −10: Continued to seclude herself in room. Day −9 to −6: Continued to avoid others; often looked sad and deep in thought. Day −5: Remains alone. Stated "I guess I'm in one of my low periods." Day −4: Looked depressed. Secluded herself in room, but pleasant at times.	Day −3: In morning suddenly appeared to be functioning at good level. Voiced pleasure about her pass home on the next day. Expressed concern for new female patient. No depression. Day −2: Out on pass with mother. Day −1: Returned from pass in excellent spirits. Recounted all she did while at home. "I washed my windows, gave my dog a bath, took care of other odds and ends, and got my hair cut and styled." No depression.	Day 0: Up entire night. Mania started around midnight. "They better get another seclusion room ready." Very angry, somewhat euphoric at times; sarcastic and continuous talking during the day. Was loud, threatening, seductive, provoking fights. In afternoon shouting, dressing gaudily, bizarre makeup. Day +1: Very loud and threatening. Day +2: Dressed very gaudily and bizarrely. Shouted virtually continually. Day +3 to +26: Loud, obnoxious, provocative; mood frequently vacillating from tears to forced laughter; extreme anger.

Adapted from Bunney, Murphy, Goodwin, and Borge (1972). Copyright 1972 by the American Medical Association and used with permission.

protests and manifested despair, depression, or withdrawal. They became unresponsive and lost interest in the environment. Their facial muscles sagged in an expression of sadness and dejection. Loud wailing and crying were sometimes replaced by a low-intensity whimpering or sobbing. After several weeks most children of this age were likely to recover from this depression-withdrawal phase and return to a normal interest in and responsiveness to their environment.

Adult grief is complicated by cultural influences and various learned inhibitions about its expression. It nevertheless seems to follow in broad outline the same sequence as for the young child. Lindeman (1944) interviewed people who had lost close relatives in the Boston Coconut Grove fire, and Marris (1958) interviewed widows who had recently lost husbands. They found that the initial reaction is frequently shock, disbelief, and an inability to accept the fact that the loss has occurred. The bereaved person may obsessively recall memories of incidents with the dead person, have a "sense" of the dead person's presence, or act as if the person still lived. Agitation, insomnia, lack of appetite, and irritation at reminders of the loss are common. Many features of this response are consistent with the notion that the person is "protesting" the loss. As is true for the young child, the period of protest is usually followed by a period of despair and depression-withdrawal, in which the adult becomes apathetic and unresponsive. In time, however, the person begins to find new interests, to return to old ones, and to come back to a more normal life. Two other studies showing how separa-

Anna Freud, daughter of Sigmund Freud, became well known for her own psychoanalytic writings.

tion from the mother can precipitate a grieving sequence in both human and monkey infants are described in Research Report 18-2.

How does the normal grieving process relate to the more severe and longer-lasting depressive disorder? The kind of precipitating environmental events usually associated with depressive disorders can almost always be seen as similar to the losses that produce normal grieving or disappointment: the death of a parent, spouse, close friend, or child; the severance of a relationship by a boyfriend, girlfriend, or spouse; or a failure in school or at work. Individuals with depressive disorders, however, seem to become "stuck" in the depression-withdrawal phase of the grieving sequence. Just what might predispose a person to become stuck in this way we will consider in the following sections.

Operant Learning. Operant learning theorists have emphasized two conditions in the development and maintenance of depression:

1. *Reinforcement for depressed behavior.* The depressed person is thought to elicit positive social reinforcement in the form of attention and sympathy by behaving in a despondent, dejected, "poor little

me" way. This, however, may be a two-edged sword; the depressed person's whining bid for attention may in some cases drive people away and result in diminished sources of reinforcement. Some behavior of depressed persons may also be learned by negative reinforcement as a way of avoiding aversive consequences. Forrest and Hokanson (1975), for example, suggest that depressed individuals may have learned to make self-punitive responses in order to avoid aggressive responses from others. In summary, they found that depressed college students gave *themselves* more electric shocks than did nondepressed students when given the opportunity to either reward their partner, shock their partner, or shock themselves. This result occurred both during a baseline period in which there were no learning contingencies and during a learning phase in which self-shock resulted in a reduction in shock from the partner. The authors propose that in a more general way some depressed people have learned to make self-punishing, self-critical responses because they reduce criticisms from others. How can you find fault with a person's performance after they have beaten you to the punch by severely criticizing their own performance?

2. *Low rates of positive reinforcement for nondepressed behavior.* Ferster (1973) and Lewinsohn, et al. (1974) have suggested that the apathy and lack

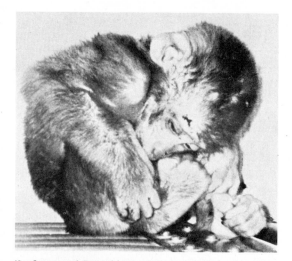

Kaufman and Rosenblum (1967) found that after separation from their mothers some infant-monkeys showed many features of human depression.

RESEARCH
REPORT
18-2

Separation from Mother Produces Depression-Withdrawal in Human and Monkey Infants

Spitz (1946) observed infants of unwed mothers in an institutional nursery. Although the mothers were encouraged to spend considerable time with their babies, some had to be away from their infants for long periods of time. From a sample of 123 infants observed during the first year of life, 19 were reported to have developed a clear-cut syndrome of depression. This reaction occurred only in infants whose mothers had to be away from them for about three months when the infants were between six and ten months of age, but not in all such infants.

Initially the children were described as showing a facial expression of sadness but occasionally making some feeble attempt to respond to an observer and participate in play. They clung to the observer and reacted with "sorrowful disappointment" when the observer left. As the reaction progressed further, the observer's approach provoked crying or screaming and little disappointment was shown at the observer's leaving. In the final stages of the depressive reaction the outward appearance of the child was one of complete dejection. There was lack of responsiveness to environmental events, slowness of movement, loss of muscle tone, refusal to eat, and insomnia. The active weeping behavior of the second stage had given way to almost complete withdrawal and apathy.

The depressive reaction began four to six weeks after the mother left. The availability of a substitute mother did not help much in most cases. There was no difference in general psychological and physical development prior to the mothers' leaving between the infants who became depressed and the infants whose mothers did not leave and who did not become depressed. The depressive reaction appeared to be reversible; when their mothers came back, the children eventually returned to normalcy. Possible long-term effects of the separation, however, were not studied.

In a more controlled experimental study, Kaufman and Rosenblum (1967) separated four infant monkeys from their mothers. Before separation the monkeys were reared in a group composed of the mother, the father, and another adult female. During separation, which lasted for four weeks, the infants remained with the father and the other adult female. This procedure avoided confounding separation from mother with being put in a strange environment.

The immediate response to separation was vigorous protest, involving loud screams, agitated pacing and searching, and a plaintive distress call referred to as cooing. This behavior lasted for 24 to 36 hours, during which the infant did not sleep.

Afterward, there was a marked change in three of the four monkeys. These monkeys became inactive, stopped responding to or making social gestures, and ceased play behavior. They frequently sat hunched over, almost in a ball, with their heads between their legs. Their facial muscles sagged and they presented the classical facial configuration of human dejection. They occasionally emitted the plaintive cooing sound. Two of the monkeys developed autoerotic activity in the form of penis sucking—a reaction not seen in this monkey colony before except in one case of unplanned separation from the mother.

This depression-withdrawal phase lasted about five or six days, after which the monkeys gradually began to recover. Their posture became more upright, exploration of the inanimate environment began, and a gradual increase in contacts with other monkeys occurred. For a while periods of depression alternated with periods of exploration and play. By the end of the month of separation the infants had almost returned to normal.

In both of these studies, separation from the mother produced a definite depressive reaction. The infant monkeys seemed to go through a "normal" grieving process of protest, depression-withdrawal, and recovery in about a month's time. Spitz did not report whether any of his infants recovered before the return of their mother, so we cannot conclude from his study that the parallel is perfect. Other investigators, however, such as Freud and Burlingham (1943), have found similar recovery patterns in somewhat older children.

of responsiveness associated with depression result from a lack of positive reinforcement for nondepressed behavior. The contingent nature of the reinforcement is emphasized, that is, the person must be reinforced for behaving in an active, outgoing, nondepressed manner. The notion of low rate of reinforcement is perhaps just another way of referring to the concept of "loss" emphasized in almost all theories of depression. Low rates of reinforcement might come about in several ways:

(a) Few events may be reinforcing. Some depressed persons may simply experience attention or social responsiveness as less reinforcing than do other people.

(b) Fewer reinforcing events are available. Depressed persons may have fewer friends and others to whom they can turn for reinforcing interaction. The death of a loved one or the breakup of a relationship, for example, might be especially devastating to a person who has few alternative sources for interpersonal satisfactions.

(c) Social reinforcements may be available and, in fact, reinforcing, but the depressed person may lack the social skills necessary to obtain these reinforcements. They do not know how to initiate new friendships or develop a mutually enjoyable social interaction. For example, in ordinary conversation most people look at the other person, nod or smile, and make verbal responses that indicate an interest

Depression is frequently accompanied by feelings of grief, self-depreciation, and sometimes thoughts of suicide.

and enjoyment in the interaction. These are effective reinforcers; they can sustain social interaction for some time and increase the probability that the two people will converse on future occasions. A person who does not reinforce others for social interchange is putting them on an extinction schedule, and other people will eventually cease to interact with the person.

(d) Persons may not only lack skill in initiating and maintaining enjoyable social interaction, they may have developed response styles that are aversive and that actually drive people away. This effect was shown in an experiment conducted by Coyne (1976). Female college students were asked to talk for 20 minutes on the telephone to either a depressed female outpatient, a nondepressed female outpatient, or a normal control female. Afterward, subjects who had talked to the depressed patients reported themselves to be significantly more depressed, anxious, and hostile than subjects who had talked to either of the other two types. They also were more rejecting of the depressed patients, expressing less willingness to interact with them in the future. It is not clear how the depressed patients induced a depressed feeling in the subjects, but the author speculates that one factor may have been a tendency to disclose personal problems inappropriately. For example, the depressed patients seemed to talk more about such matters as death, marital infidelities, hysterectomies, and family strife than did other individuals. If depressed persons manage to make talking to them an aversive experience, it would not be surprising if people began to avoid them, reducing even further their sources of social reinforcement. But why would a person so desperately in need of attention and support do the very thing that frustrates this need? Perhaps as a child the person had been given much attention and sympathy from parents or others contingent on feeling bad and complaining about life's misfortunes, so that a strong tendency to respond in this way was learned. As an adult the person may receive only occasional reinforcement for this behavior but this may be enough to maintain the response. If a cognitive component accompanies this behavior, it could take the form: "If I feel bad enough, long enough, somebody will feel sorry for me and comfort me." Unfortunately, in the present time, the mournful expressions and chronic complaining more often lead to the exact opposite.

(e) A final circumstance associated with low rates of positive social reinforcement is one in which an unusually high proportion of a person's behavior is controlled by negative reinforcement—that is, is aimed at avoiding aversive consequences. A student, for example, spends long hours studying because she is afraid of the disapproval and criticism that accompany low grades, or not completing college, or not getting into graduate school. Most of her social behavior is oriented toward pleasing others so that she will not be rejected by classmates or boyfriends. A life that is dominated by *aversive control* and has relatively little positive reinforcement might in time lead to depression and perhaps also to suppressed anger and resentment at having to put so much energy into avoidance behavior.

Cognitive Processes. Advocates of an operant learning analysis of depression such as Lewinsohn (1974) tend to view depressive cognitions as secondary elaborations of the dejected mood state, which is thought to result primarily from a low rate of positive reinforcement. In other words, persons first feel depressed and then have thoughts of futility, failure, and self-blame. Cognitive theorists, however, argue that it is the other way around, that persons feel depressed because they first tell themselves that they are a failure, that nobody likes them, and so on.

Beck (1976) especially has emphasized the role of cognitions in producing and maintaining depression. According to Beck these inner statements take three forms: (1) The person may *exaggerate the magnitude of obstacles,* responding to any minor frustration with thoughts such as "I'm licked," or "I might as well give up." (2) Or the person may *interpret relatively trivial events as important losses.* A wealthy businesswoman regards herself as poor whenever she hears of someone making more money than she does. A man who has to wait 30 seconds for an elevator thinks, "I'm losing valuable time"; later, in the waiting room, when he has to put down a magazine to start his appointment he feels deprived of the opportunity to finish the magazine. (3) The person may *be continually self-disparaging, magnifying criticisms and insults.* An outstanding student thinks whenever a teacher calls on another student, "She doesn't really think I'm smart or she would have called on me." A student who has difficulty getting a date on a single occasion thinks, "I must be re-

pulsive to girls." Beck believes that persistent thoughts of this kind cause the person to feel and act in a depressed manner.

Seligman (1975) has also proposed a cognitive theory of depression that centers on the person's belief that he or she has little control over the important events in his life. Seligman uses the term *learned helplessness* to refer to this learned belief or expectation that there is nothing one can do to improve a bad situation. The idea of learned helplessness originated in animal experiments in which Seligman and his colleagues were studying the relationship of fear conditioning to instrumental learning. They had been presenting tones followed by inescapable painful electric shocks to dogs that were restrained in a Pavlovian harness. Nothing the animal could do—tail wagging, struggling, barking—could influence the shocks. After this experience the dogs were placed in a shuttle box in which they could learn to avoid shock by jumping over a barrier from one side of the box to another at a given signal. Seligman describes what happened:

We intended to teach the dogs to become expert shock avoiders so that we could test the effects of the classically conditioned tones on their avoidance behavior. But what we saw was bizarre, and can best be appreciated if I first describe the behavior of a typical dog that has not been given uncontrollable shock.

When placed in a shuttle box, an experimentally naive dog, at the onset of the first electric shock, runs frantically about until it accidentally scrambles over the barrier and escapes the shock. On the next trial, the dog, running frantically, crosses the barrier more quickly than on the preceding trial; within a few trials it becomes very efficient at escaping, and soon learns to avoid shock altogether. After about fifty trials the dog becomes nonchalant and stands in front of the barrier; at the onset of the signal for shock it leaps gracefully across and never gets shocked again.

A dog that had first been given inescapable shock showed a strikingly different pattern. This dog's first reactions to shock in the shuttle box were much the same as those of a naive dog: It ran around frantically for about thirty seconds. But then it stopped moving; to our surprise, it lay down and quietly whined. After one minute of this we turned the shock off; the dog had failed to cross the barrier and had not escaped from shock. On the next trial, the dog did it again; at first it struggled a bit, and then, after a few seconds, it seemed to give up and to accept the shock passively.

On all succeeding trials, the dog failed to escape. (p. 22)

Seligman is hardly the first person to emphasize the importance of control over environmental events, but he has helped to focus our attention on this variable with respect to depression and to generate much research on the topic. For example, Seligman (1975) has shown that dogs with learned helplessness training show other similarities to human depression: loss of appetite, loss of weight, and on a physiological level, a decrease in norepinephrine. Evidence was described in Research Report 18-1 which suggests that a low level of this neurotransmitter accompanies human depression.

Learned helplessness as an explanation of depression has received considerable criticism (for example, Wortman & Dintzer, 1978). Basically the problem with the learned helplessness theory is that it takes one factor that probably does contribute to *some* features of *some* depressions and states it as the crucial causative factor for all aspects of most depressions. This tendency to overgeneralize the importance of a particular causative influence seems to be temptation to which theorists in the area of abnormal psychology are particularly prone—an example being Freud's belief that *all* neurotic symptoms had their origins in unresolved Oedipal conflicts. Seligman has recognized some of the limitations of his original learned helplessness theory (Abrahamson, Seligman, & Teasdale, 1978) and now suggests that only a subclass of depressions—the helplessness depression—is produced by learned helplessness.

The Psychoanalytic View. In one major respect psychoanalytic theory and social learning theory agree on the etiology of depression: Psychological losses play an important role. However, the psychoanalytic view stresses the significance of intrapsychic processes that originate early in life. Events that happen in the oral stage of psychosexual development are considered important in creating a susceptibility to later depressive reactions.

According to this theory, young infants' early interactions with their mothers inevitably involve both satisfactions and frustrations. Although mothers feed and hold infants, providing warmth, stimulation, and

relief from painful stimuli, they cannot always provide satisfaction immediately or with total success. Infants, then, begin to perceive mothers as both good and bad. In this early stage of development, infants do not make a clear distinction between the external world (mother, in this case) and their own selves. One way the infants learn to deal with the world is by taking it inside; the process is called *introjection* or the early beginnings of *identification.* Thus they introject the image of the good-bad mother into their own self-image.

Introjection need not lead to serious psychological problems later unless the infant has experienced an unusually intense love for the "good" mother and hate for the "bad" mother. Psychoanalytic theory states, however, that when such an intensely ambivalent image of the good-bad mother has been introjected, then later in life when the child or adult experiences a loss, this intense love-hate conflict from early infancy is reactivated. The anger and hatred become directed inward against that part of the individual that is the introjected bad mother. This inward turning of aggression, then, presumably explains the depressed person's self-derogatory attitude

Sometimes a surface calm belies feelings of rage underneath.

Margaret P.: Grieving Stopped Cold

Margaret P.'s depressive reaction began shortly after her husband's death. At the time of the death, Margaret's mother-in-law called to tell her that her husband had died of a heart attack. Margaret began a normal grief reaction accompanied by much crying. The next day her mother-in-law told her that her husband had actually hanged himself. Margaret P.'s normal grief reaction ceased abruptly when she heard this, and the more pathological depressive reaction began.

In the course of psychotherapy more facts were revealed about Margaret's relationship with her husband. Four years prior to his death, her husband had begun staying out late and associating with friends of whom Margaret disapproved. For six months she said nothing to him about it. She was hurt by his behavior, yet at the same time she blamed herself for, in some way, causing it. She apparently had always tended to blame herself when things went wrong, and much of her behavior was aimed at pleasing other people so that she would continue to be liked and appreciated.

When Margaret finally raised the subject of late hours with her husband, he merely laughed and said that any "trouble" was a figment of her imagination. To her own surprise, she lost her temper and screamed at him to get out of the house. He left immediately and remained away all night. She felt bad then and began to be overcome by a great longing for his return. When he did return the next morning, she begged him to stay. He agreed, providing that she would allow him to do just as he pleased without objection or comment from her. She needed him so desperately that she accepted these conditions without reservation.

As therapy progressed, Margaret's strong anger at her husband began to emerge. She first began to express resentment toward him for having, by his suicide, deserted her and the children. Then she began to express all the pent-up anger about the conditions that he imposed on their marriage, and she recalled times prior to his death when she had had fleeting wishes that he would die.

As she became able to express some of her anger, she also began to return to a normal grieving process. She could remember and talk about happy times they had shared, and with those memories came tears and a feeling of sadness over her loss. Eventually the pathological features of her depressive reaction decreased, and she began to have a renewed interest in people and various outside activities.

that finds its ultimate expression in suicidal impulses. Some combination of the mother's actual behavior (severe deprivation, perhaps, or overindulgence mixed with occasional frustrations) and the infant's fantasies would determine whether such a depression-producing introjection occurs.

It is difficult, of course, to test a theory that rests on the mental imagery of infants. However, many clinical reports indicate that persons who react to another person's death with a neurotic depression have had strongly ambivalent feelings toward the deceased—that they have been dependent upon the person for the satisfaction of affection and approval needs, but have also harbored intense anger, that is, neither expressed nor acknowledged. Clinical evidence of this kind suggests that an intense love-hate relationship may indeed play a role in the development of some depressions. Nemiah (1961) describes such an example, the case of Margaret P.

How might the strong ambivalent reactions of anger and need for affection have contributed to Margaret P.'s depressive reaction? First, let us consider what is involved in the normal grieving process. Grief is an unpleasant emotion, and the process whereby persons master their grief may be likened to the process that children and others use in coping with fear. Bereaved persons permit themselves to think about the loved person and recall memories of enjoyable occasions in small doses. Each time they experience the pain of grief and in time, with many approaches to and retreats from the grief-inducing memories, the emotion of grief will diminish (extinguish). Freed

The normal grieving process usually follows a sequence of protest, depression-withdrawal, and recovery. If the person had a severely conflicted relationship with the deceased then he or she might become "stuck" in the depression-withdrawal phase.

from their handicapping emotion, persons can begin to renew their interest in life. Freud (1917/1957) referred to this process as the work of mourning, an apt phrase for an active, self-administered treatment procedure.

If memories of the deceased tend to arouse not only grief but also intense reactions of anger, resentment, guilt, and self-blame, then the experience may be just too unbearable; the person avoids all emotional experiencing, with the resulting "deadness" and apathy characteristic of depression. The grieving process is stopped cold, or as I suggested earlier, the person becomes "stuck" in the depression-withdrawal phase of the normal grieving sequence. This may well have been what happened with Margaret P. Whether it is necessary to invoke an introjected good-bad mother, as psychoanalytic theory might suggest, to account for her depression is an open question. In social learning terms one might simply emphasize the learned avoidance response (avoidance of unbearable emotions) in a person who

had acquired a personality disposition to be self-blaming.

To summarize our discussion of the development of depression and affective disorders, a genetic contribution seems likely for the more severe bipolar and major depression disorders. For the less severe neurotic depressions (dysthymic disorders), in which genetic factors may be less strong, research and clinical experience clearly stress the role of loss whether seen as a deficit in social reinforcements or in some other terms. The precipitating loss usually involves some interpersonal separation, rejection or failure. Some but not all people react to such losses with depression, presumably because of past experiences that have resulted in a vulnerability to this reaction. According to one's theoretical bent the kind of past experiences producing such a vulnerability might be lack of skill in obtaining social reinforcements, driving people away with "depressive" talk, aversive control of one's behavior, learned depression-inducing cognitive self-statements, an introjected loved-hated mother, or a conflicted relationship with a loved one. Probably some combination of these factors contribute to most depressions.

CULTURE AND AFFECTIVE DISORDERS

Although affective disorders exist in almost all cultures, their relative frequency varies considerably. Eaton and Weil (1955) studied prevalence rates among the Hutterites, who have maintained a relatively homogeneous culture based on strict religious customs in isolated farming communities in the Dakotas and Canada. They found about four times as many manic-depressive reactions, primarily of a depressed type, as schizophrenic reactions among these people—almost the reverse of the relative prevalence of these disorders in the United States as a whole. The authors suggest that the combination of religious teachings of sin and guilt, the submission of the individual to the communal social structure, and the prohibition of any overt aggressiveness or competitiveness disposes a person to react to stresses with self-blame and depression. It is, of course, possible that this relatively small, self-contained population (about 8000 at the time of the study) carries with it a genetic disposition to depressive reactions.

The incidence of manic as opposed to depressive

reactions also varies considerably from culture to culture. Manic reactions are infrequent in Europe and the United States. In some African societies, on the other hand, mania is much more prevalent than depression. In fact, some early investigators reported almost no cases of depression among the African peoples they studied (for example, Carothers, 1953). Carothers ascribed the lack of depressive reactions to cultural and religious beliefs that deemphasize personal guilt for transgressions. Instead, personal misfortunes are automatically blamed on outside forces—usually deities that can be propitiated by well-defined rituals. Put another way, these African cultures are *externally* oriented to explain both successes and failures, whereas cultures in Europe and the United States (and especially the Hutterites) are more *internally* oriented.

However, the findings of low incidence of depression in African societies were frequently based on hospital populations, and direct studies of the larger culture have suggested some qualifications. For example, A. H. Leighton et al. (1963) found depressive symptoms common among the Yoruba in West Nigeria in spite of the fact that the Yoruba language has no word for depression, and Binitie (1975) found depressive symptoms among patients seen at a clinic in Uselu, Benin. In both of these studies the depressive symptoms consisted primarily of depressed mood, somatic symptoms, and motor retardation. Rarely were there feelings of guilt and personal sinfulness or suicidal ideas or action as seen in many Western cultures.

It seems likely that cultural influences do affect the relative prevalence as well as the form of affective disorders. So far, however, the data are subject to multiple interpretations. They are too imprecise to conclude whether cultural effects are more pronounced for the less severe neurotic depressions, or whether they differentially affect other categories such as the bipolar and the major depression (unipolar) types.

AN INTERACTIVE VIEW

There is growing evidence that affective disorders may be separated into subgroups that have different patterns of causation and that the relative weighting of genetic and psychosocial influences will vary among these subtypes. The bipolar affective disorders are the best example of a group that would seem to be distinctively different from the other affective disorders. This subgroup has a strong genetic component, and the role of precipitating environmental events or of learned personality dispositions seems to be less important. For the major depression (unipolar) types of depression genetic and psychosocial experiences probably interact to produce the eventual symptoms of depression; and for the neurotic depressions (dysthymic disorders) environmental stresses and learned personality styles (for example, to be self-blaming or to make oneself feel depressed) may be entirely responsible with no help from genetic dispositions.

There is considerable animal research showing that the unavoidable stress that produces learned helplessness also produces lowered levels of brain norepinephrine. Although different investigators disagree as to whether the helplessness is first learned and then produces the lowered levels of norepinephrine or the lowered levels of norepinephrine come first and cause the observed helplessness (Seligman, 1975; J. M. Weiss et al., 1974), there is agreement that environmental stresses have caused the reduction in norepinephrine. These findings should serve as a caution against too readily assuming that the lower levels of neurotransmitters such as norepinephrine and serotonin inferred to be present in some depressions reflect some primary, possibly inherited, biological defect. Perhaps these lowered levels have derived in part from the kind of unavoidable losses or learned personality dispositions thought to be associated with depression. On the other hand, genetic dispositions in some individuals could make these persons more likely to react to losses or inescapable stresses with greater than average decreases in levels of norepinephrine or serotonin. At this time we cannot afford to ignore either psychological or biological determinants.

TREATMENT OF AFFECTIVE DISORDERS

Drugs. The tricyclic compounds, of which imipramine (trade name Tofranil) is the most commonly used, have been found more effective than placebos in treating severe depressions of the unipolar type

(Akiskal & McKinney, 1975; Morris & Beck, 1974). Lithium carbonate has been shown to be more effective than placebos with bipolar patients, especially in treating the manic phase of the reaction (for example, Goodwin & Athanasios, 1979). This drug is not only an effective treatment for the acute symptoms of bipolar affective disorders but also with maintenance doses can reduce or prevent recurrences (Prien, 1979). As mentioned earlier, one theory to account for the effectiveness of lithium carbonate in the treatment of mania is that it reduces abnormally high levels of intraneuronal sodium, which had been preventing the reuptake of norepinephrine and thus causing an excessive amount of this neurotransmitter to accumulate.

Electroconvulsive Therapy.   Electroconvulsive therapy (ECT) was first introduced by two Italian psychiatrists, Cerletti and Bini, in 1933. In this treatment two electrodes are placed on either side of the head at the temples, and a voltage of about 100 volts AC is applied briefly (from 0.1 to 0.5 second). The electric current produces a convulsive seizure (similar to *grand mal epilepsy* described in Chapter 25) that lasts for 40 to 60 seconds. Patients lose consciousness immediately and do not regain it for several minutes. They are likely to be somewhat confused and dazed for an hour or so afterward. The procedure has been refined so that it is no longer as unpleasant or as likely to cause physical injury to the patient as it was initially. A short-acting sedative drug and a muscle relaxant are frequently administered intravenously before treatment, putting the person to sleep so that the strong muscle contractions will not fracture any bones. Ordinarily electroconvulsive treatments are given two to five times a week for a total of two to ten treatments, depending on how quickly improvement occurs.

Although ECT is condemned by many professionals as a modern-day version of torture (usually by those inclined to psychosocial interpretations of psychopathology), the plain fact is that it seems to work (Avery & Winokur, 1977)—in many, if not all, cases. In fact, it seems to work more quickly and possibly with a higher percentage of patients than do the antidepressant drugs (Avery & Winokur, 1977). At one time, in the 1940s and 1950s, ECT enjoyed widespread use with almost all forms of psychotic disorders, including schizophrenia. It seemed a boon

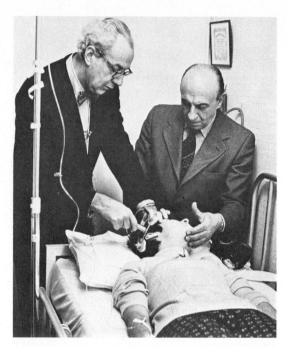

Dr. Leonard Cammer, a New York City psychiatrist, administers electroshock treatment to a patient suffering from severe depression. The use of this form of treatment is controversial, but it does seem to speed recovery from severe depression in many cases.

to harried professionals in understaffed mental hospitals; it was inexpensive and could efficiently be given to large numbers of patients. Research, however, consistently showed that its effectiveness was limited to severe depressive symptoms, and clinicians, for the most part, have come to restrict its use to these patients. ECT is not effective with the less severe depressions in which psychosocial factors seem important, a fact that bolsters the view that the more severe bipolar and unipolar depressions are different in some fundamental way from the less severe depressions (Mendels, 1967).

Another qualification is that although ECT definitely seems to speed up the process of recovery from depression (untreated severe depressions are likely to persist for about six months), there remains a high probability of recurrence. The basic factors leading to the depression obviously are not "cured" by ECT. Nor do we know why ECT works. There are many theories, some biological and some psychological, but none has been clearly borne out by research.

Furthermore, there is some question as to how much long-term memory loss occurs with electroconvulsive treatment. That the person forgets many of the preoccupations that were troublesome immediately preceding ECT is generally accepted, but anecdotal evidence suggests that some people lose many other memories from their past life—a loss that persists and can be extremely handicapping. Ernest Hemingway received two series of electroconvulsive treatments and complained bitterly to his friend and biographer, A. E. Hotchner, about how his memory was wrecked and how he was ruined as a writer. "What is the sense of ruining my head and erasing my memory, which is my capital, and putting me out of business?" (Hotchner, 1966, p. 280). Despite these reservations clinicians on occasion decide that ECT is preferable to antidepressant drugs because the drugs take considerably longer to work, and the risk of suicide in the meantime may be high.

Psychological Approaches. Even the most sanguine psychodynamic therapist admits to a feeling of hopelessness when faced with a profoundly depressed or manic patient. In one case the patient may be so unresponsive as to need tube feeding to be kept alive and may show almost no response to a therapist's verbal overtures. Likewise, the excited manic has little time or patience for the sedate verbal interchange of ordinary therapy. These impressions are backed up by some controlled research; Hollister (1972), for example, found that antidepressant drugs were more effective than traditional psychotherapy in treating severe depressions. With depressive reactions that are less severe, psychotherapy may, however, be helpful. Beck et al. (1980) have developed a "cognitive therapy" approach based on Beck's cognitive theory of depression in which they attempt to modify the various self-derogatory and despair-inducing self-statements presumed to be causing the depression. They report outcome research in support of the effectiveness of the approach, including some evidence that it is more effective than antidepressant drug treatment.

A good illustration of how self-reinforcement may be used in the treatment of depression is a study by Fuchs and Rehm (1977). Noting that depressed persons tend to give themselves low rates of self-rewards

The opportunity to fully experience grief with an accepting, supporting other person may prevent the development of depression following bereavement.

(for example, self-approvals) and high rates of self-punishments (for example, self-criticisms) relative to nondepressed people, these investigators devised a training procedure to reverse these self-reinforcing tendencies. First they taught their depressed women to attend more to positive or successful events, to set realistic, step-by-step goals for behavioral change, and to provide themselves with generous self-administered rewards *contingent* on successfully completing each small step toward their goals. This six-week program resulted in significant decreases in both self-report and behavioral measures of depression.

Raphael (1977) describes a study whose results suggest that many depressions precipitated by the death of loved ones might be prevented with certain crisis intervention procedures. He selected recently bereaved widows who were predicted to be at risk for developing depressive symptoms and randomly assigned them to a preventive intervention condition and a control condition. The widows were considered to be at risk if they reported low levels of support among friends and relatives or reported a highly ambivalent marital relationship with their deceased husband (recall our discussion of factors leading to depression). The intervention consisted of sessions of two or more hours (average of about four sessions) in which the women were encouraged to fully experience grieving-related emotions such as sadness, anger, despair, or guilt. They were urged to review both positive and negative aspects of the lost relationship. Raphael found that women in the control group made significantly more visits to doctors for general symptoms, had more feelings of panic and feelings of excessive tiredness, showed more weight loss, increased smoking and increase in use of alcohol, and decrease in work capacity than did women in the preventive intervention group. Four control women were hospitalized for depression compared with none in the preventive intervention group. The criteria for selecting women as being at risk were shown to have some validity. A third group of women who did not meet these criteria (lack of social support system or an ambivalent relationship to the deceased) showed significantly less development of symptoms than did the at-risk women in the control condition. In summary these results suggest two important conclusions: (1) A preventive intervention emphasizing the experience of a normal grieving reaction can prevent the development of more disabling symptoms, and (2) a person's social support system may be important in preventing the development of symptoms in the absence of any professional help.

Schizoaffective Disorders

Historically, the term *schizoaffective disorders* has been used in somewhat different ways. The category arose from the fact that some patients show symptoms of both schizophrenia and affective disorders— the perennial problem of patients complicating the diagnostician's task by not conforming to the prevailing labeling system. Until recently, at least in the United States, consistent with the tendency to use a broad definition of schizophrenia, this category was considered to be a subcategory of schizophrenia. Evidence, however, now suggests that patients with this combination of symptoms may have more in common with the affective disorders than with schizophrenia. Thus these patients have a tendency toward acute onset and recovery, absence of unusual

prevalence of schizophrenia in close relatives, and a higher than usual prevalence of affective disorders among close relatives. Since the relation of this symptom pattern to the major categories of schizophrenia and affective disorders is still unresolved, it is given the status of a separate category in DSM-III.

Suicide

According to government statistics, every year about one person out of 10,000 (0.01 percent) in the United States commits suicide. This figure is likely to be an underestimate since many deaths resulting from such causes as drug overdoses, automobile wrecks, alcoholism, acts of violence, and activities engaged in against medical advice may well derive from suicidal intent. Wexler et al. (1978) surveyed studies of suicide attempts, as opposed to completed suicides, in eight Western countries, and found annual rates for most countries to be 20–40 per 10,000. The highest rates tended to exist among young women, and pill ingestion was the most common method used in the attempt. Suicide ranks among the top ten causes of death in the Western world. For adolescents in the 15- to 19-year-old age group it ranks fifth—exceeded only by accidents, cancer, cardiovascular-renal disease, and homicide. Furthermore, the incidence of suicide among adolescents has shown a steady increase over the last 20 years. College students are especially vulnerable to depression and the suicide rate among college students tends to be 50 percent higher than among nonstudents of the same age (Beck & Young, 1978). Table 18-3 compares additional facts to myths about suicide.

Suicide is by no means always associated with severe depressions, but it is clear that a much higher proportion of individuals with diagnosed depressions commit suicide than in the population at large or in other diagnostic categories. In a survey of 17 studies, Guze and Robins (1970) found that approximately 30 times as many suicides occurred in individuals with affective disorders than in the general population. A number of these depressed patients had killed themselves within months after leaving the hospital. A potentially significant finding is that of Asberg, Traskman, & Thoren (1976). These investigators, you may recall, found that severely depressed patients fell into

TABLE 18-3   Some Myths and Facts About Suicide

Myth	Fact
People who talk about suicide do not commit suicide.	Evidence suggests that nearly 80 percent of persons who kill themselves have given some kind of warning beforehand.
Suicidal people seriously intend to die.	Most suicidal people are not sure that they want to die; they "gamble with death," hoping, perhaps, that others will save them.
Suicidal people remain suicidal forever.	The urge to kill oneself usually lasts for only a limited period of time.
Improvement following a period of depression means reduced risk of suicide.	Most suicides occur within about three months after the beginning of "improvement."
Suicide is more frequent among the rich, or among the poor.	Neither. Suicide occurs with equal frequency among the rich and the poor.
Suicide is inherited.	There is no evidence for an inherited disposition to commit suicide.
All suicidal individuals are mentally ill.	Although suicidal persons are extremely unhappy, they are not necessarily mentally ill.

Adapted from Shneidman and Farberow (1961).

two groups, one with an abnormally low level of a metabolite of serotonin in the cerebrospinal fluid and another with a more normal level. Patients in the low-serotonin group attempted suicide significantly more often than those in the normal-serotonin group, and they used more violent means. Two patients actually died from suicide and they were both in the low-serotonin group. Just how suicidal behavior is mediated by the presumed low levels of serotonin is not clear at this time.

Many suicides, then, appear to arise from the despair, hopelessness, and self-hate associated with severe depression. Other suicides, however, are likely to be in response to such stresses as severe or chronic physical illnesses and are not necessarily accompanied by a depressive disorder.

PSYCHOLOGICAL CORRELATES

Many investigators have tried to determine the type of personality traits or life experiences that are associated with individuals who attempt suicide. For example, Paykel et al. (1975) compared reports of stressful life events during the six-month period preceding a suicide attempt for 53 individuals who attempted suicide with 53 depressive control patients who had not attempted suicide, matched individually for age, sex, marital status, and race. Data were also obtained on a matched sample from the general population. Those who had attempted suicide reported four times as many stressful life events as did individuals in the general population sample, and one and one-half times as many as in the depressed sample. Some of the specific life events that were significantly different in frequency are shown in Table 18-4. These results suggest that two general types of events were present more often in the lives of the suicide attempters: interpersonal conflicts (as suggested by "arguments with spouse" and "new person in the home") and serious illness in a close family member or themselves.

Baechler (1979) studied 127 cases of suicide and proposed that suicidal acts could be grouped into four categories according to their meaning to the person: (1) For many, perhaps most, suicide represents an *escape* from an intolerable situation. The person may be experiencing intense shame, guilt, fear, or physical pain and sees suicide as the only way out. (2) For some individuals the main motive

TABLE 18-4   Frequency of Stressful Events Preceding Suicide Attempts

Event	Suicide Attempters (N = 53)	Depressives (N = 53)	General Population (N = 53)
Serious argument with spouse	19	8	0
New person in home	11	4	0
Engagement	7	0	4
Serious illness of close family member	17	7	4
Serious personal physical illness	15	5	1

Adapted from Paykel, Prusoff, and Myers (1975). Copyright 1975 by the American Medical Association and used with permission.

for suicide is aggression, to seek vengeance on others, to make them feel remorse. (3) Yet others commit suicide as an act of sacrifice, or in relation to some higher values. The immolations of Buddhist monks would be an example. (4) And finally there are suicides performed in the context of games or undergoing an ordeal in order to prove oneself. Russian roulette is an example of the former. These cat-

Marilyn Monroe, sex goddess of the 1950s and 1960s, ended her life with suicide. Loneliness and depression may sometimes lie behind a gay facade.

egories may not capture all the variations in suicidal motivation but they do serve to remind us that people commit suicide for a variety of reasons.

Social and economic circumstances may also contribute to the incidence of suicide. For example, there are data that suggest economic depressions are associated with increases in the suicide rate and, interestingly, that wars are associated with decreases (Sainsbury, 1968). Perhaps service in the armed forces provides a temporary protection from personal failures, either in love or work, or mobilizes some people's sense of importance as participants in a noble cause; or perhaps war provides an honorable way to throw away one's life, so that some war deaths are suicides in disguise.

How suicide rates in black persons compare with those of white persons has been difficult to assess. If official reports of suicide are used, then black persons commit suicide either less often or about the same as white persons, depending on the part of the country studied (Kramer et al., 1972). However, suicide in blacks may be underreported, and Warshauer and Monk (1978) provide evidence that such has been the case in New York City. Seiden (1970) has suggested that some deaths, especially of black males, not reported as suicides reflect what he calls "victim-precipitated" murder. The suicidally inclined person provokes others into killing him by wielding guns or taunting others with threats of violence. Thus a young man who looks on suicide as weak and unmanly might create violence around him, hurting others and at the same time getting himself killed.

Suicide notes have been studied for the light they shed on suicidal motivation. Tuckman et al. (1959) analyzed notes from 165 suicides and informally grouped them into several categories on the basis of the type and direction of feelings expressed. Here are some examples.

Hostility directed outward:

I hate you and all of your family and I hope you never have a piece of mind. I hope I haunt this house as long as you live here and I wish you all the bad luck in the world.

Hostility directed inward:

I know at last what I have to do, I pray to God to forgive me for all the many sins I have committed and for all the many people I have wronged, I no longer have the strength to go on, what I am about to do might seem wrong to a lot of people, but I don't think so, I have given it plenty of sober consideration.

Positive affect:

Please forgive me and please forget me, I'll always love you. All I have was yours. No one ever did more for me than you, oh please pray for me please. (p. 60)

ADOLESCENT SUICIDE

Jacobs (1971) reports an intensive study of 50 adolescents who attempted suicide. Thirty-one of them were matched with a like number of control subjects on age, race, sex, and family income. Parents rated a higher proportion of suicide attempters as gloomy, silent, withdrawn, and having run away from home. Suicide attempters were not found to differ significantly from control subjects on parent-reported disobedience, sassiness, or defiance.

The adolescents' reports of styles of parental discipline are also of interest. Although the differences were not great with respect to spanking and withholding of privileges, more than twice as many parents of the suicide attempters were perceived as criticizing, nagging, yelling, and withholding approval or affection. Seventy-one percent of the suicide attempters and 53 percent of the control subjects had experienced broken homes—not a striking difference. However, if only the five years prior to the suicide attempt are considered, the magnitude of the difference jumps sharply. Fifty-eight percent of the suicide attempters' parents and only 10 percent of the control adolescents' parents were divorced, separated, and/or remarried during this time. Thus dur-

ing the period of adolescence the control group had experienced a relatively stable home environment, whereas over half the suicide attempters had not.

The alienation from parents experienced by the teenage suicide attempters is illustrated in the following interview excerpts, the first with a 16-year-old boy and the second with a 15-year-old girl.

Doctor: What happened?

Boy: When? (Laughs.)

Doctor: Well, why you're here.

Boy: Well, because I tried to commit suicide.

Doctor: Why?

Boy: Well things weren't going too good at home. Uh, my—uh mother was always yelling at me, and my f-father was always yellin at me and criticizing me all the time. And the kids just wouldn't leave me alone.

Doctor: Criticizing you?

Boy: Yes.

Doctor: Why?

Boy: Well, he said I never did anything right, and that—uh I never had any respect for him and I was just stupid—and everytime I tried to do sumthin I always did it wrong, and so—so what's the use?

Doctor: —that's why I'm talking to you. So what happened?—what didya do?

Girl: It sounds stupid! My mother, she started arguing with me. Cause my father and my—and my mother had gone out. So—uh, they probably went and—I think they—they drank a couple of beers. So when my mother came, she was mad at me. And I didn't know why she was mad at me, cause I was just watchin television. And then—and then she started yellin at me. And then I was wonderin why she was mad at me. So then—uh, I was sposed to have sewn my sister's skirt. And then—and then she told me—I was sewin the—the hem. And so I didn't sew it right. So then my mother started yelling at me, and she said: "You mean that you—uh—you learn sewing at school and you don't even know how to sew!" And then, you know—but she was yellin and everything. And—and then I got mad at her, and then I told her, "At least I'm trying!" And then—my dad, he said, [to mother] "You don't have to yell at her. Why don't you talk nice to her instead of yellin and everything." And then my mother said, "Why don't you shut up?" And then she told him, "I'm the one that's teaching her." . . .

Doctor: Mm-hm—

Girl: And then—and then they got mad at one another. And so I—so I went to my room. Then my father said—said—uh, "You stay there and don't—come on out," cause she's yelling at me and everything. And so then—uh, my mother said, "Come back here! You'd better not go anywhere. Cause I'll slap you down so hard you won't know what hit you." And then—and then, so then—then my mother told me a bad word, and I told her back. And. . . . (Jacobs, 1971, pp. 75, 77–78)

From Jacobs's interviews, a picture emerges of the adolescent suicide attempter as a person who has had a long history of troubled relationships with parents, relationships in which the adolescent finds it especially difficult to communicate, confide, or obtain emotional support. Jacobs suggests that against this background there is an escalation of problems, usually in excess of those normally associated with adolescence—a progressive failure in the person's available adaptive techniques, an increasing isolation from meaningful social relationships, and frequently certain specific failures or rejections in the weeks or days before the suicide attempt. By this time the person has given up hope that there is anywhere to turn for help in resolving an emotionally intolerable situation.

Stanley and Barter (1970) compared adolescent suicide attempters who were hospitalized with a control group of emotionally disturbed adolescents who were also hospitalized. This comparison should provide a clearer delineation of factors specifically related to suicide attempts as opposed to factors generally related to emotional disturbances in adolescents. The authors found no significant differences between these two groups on the incidence of parental loss, amount of family conflict, degree of social isolation, or frequency of clear crises: All of these characteristics were present in both groups to a greater degree than in the general population. There were significantly more threats and talk about divorce or separation by the parents of the suicide attempters, and a strong, though nonsignificant, trend for more arguments with a boyfriend or girlfriend shortly before hospitalization for the suicide attempters. Posthospitalization attempts at suicide among the suicide at-

tempters were greatest for those who had poor relationships with their peers. This study, then, should make us cautious about accepting the characteristics of suicide attempters found in Jacobs's study as specifically related to suicidal tendencies. Some of these characteristics appear to be related to severe emotional disturbances in adolescence but not specifically to suicide attempts. On the other hand, the Stanley and Barter study does indicate that the theme of interpersonal loss is especially strong among adolescent suicide attempters.

CULTURE AND SUICIDE

A number of investigators have proposed an inverse relationship between the general tolerance and approval of aggression found in different cultures and the incidence of suicide: The less tolerant the society is of externally directed aggression, the greater should be the frequency of suicides. Durkheim (1952), for example, provided considerable evidence favoring

Yukio Mishima, defender of traditional Japanese customs. He closed his final speech with the old Japanese war cry "Tenno Banzai" (Long live the emperor), and then disappeared into a building and committed "hara-kiri," traditional Japanese suicide. Suicide rates are clearly affected by cultural attitudes.

such a relationship, showing that in France between 1826 and 1880 the suicide rate had risen steadily while indictments for unpremeditated murder had fallen, while similar changes had also occurred in Prussia, England, Italy, and Austria. Even within certain countries such as Italy, France, and Austria, there was a strong inverse relationship between the suicide and homicide rates of different provinces. Also during this time period, the three countries in Europe with the lowest suicide rates—Spain, Ireland, and Italy—were also those with the highest murder rates.

Do these relationships still hold in more recent times? Analysis of the mortality tables published by the United Nations (1968) showed that, for the 48 nations and other territories for which there were reliable statistics, there was a slight trend in this direction. Homicide and suicide rates correlated negatively ($r = -.27, p < .10$). Mexico and Guatemala ranked first and third in homicide and were the lowest two countries in suicide. The lowest homicide and highest suicide rates tended to be found primarily in western Europe (Kendell, 1970).

An inverse relationship between suicide and homicide is related to tendencies described earlier for depressive reactions to be more common in cultures that discourage outwardly directed aggression. But we should not forget that a negative correlation between suicide and homicide might be explained in a number of ways. For example, people who see aggression as a drive (whether instinctual, learned, or frustration-produced) that must be expressed one way or another would predict that if externally oriented expressions were culturally prohibited, then other outlets for the drive would have to be found, such as self-directed aggression. On the other hand, a social learning view might suggest that cultures that tend to suppress outwardly directed aggression also tend to teach internalizing, self-blaming tendencies. Suicide and homicide, in that case, would tend to be negatively correlated, but not because either one is directly inhibiting or replacing the other; they would be influenced in opposite ways by other variables in the culture, and no assumption need be made about a given amount of aggressive energy that has to be discharged.

The observed relationship is, at best, quite low, leaving room for many other factors to affect suicide in addition to prevailing cultural sanctions. For example, countries with a high proportion of Roman Catholics might be expected to have relatively low suicide rates because of the strong prohibition against suicide in this religion.

SUICIDE PREVENTION

Suicide prevention is one important goal of the crisis intervention approach to community mental health. The aim is to assist a person contemplating suicide to consider other alternatives and to direct the person to resources for psychotherapeutic or other forms of help. Some facilities, known as suicide prevention centers, are devoted entirely to the problem of suicide. These centers usually have widely publicized telephone numbers that individuals are encouraged to call when they begin to feel depressed or suicidal. The people who answer the telephones do not necessarily have advanced degrees in the mental health professions; often they are selected because of their ability to relate to others in a sensitive and understanding manner and are given some special training in the nature of suicidal tendencies and how best to talk to potential suicides on the telephone.

Speed of intervention, the reversal of despair, and the awakening of hope are important goals in suicide prevention. It is important to maintain contact with the suicidal persons and to help them see that there are other ways of dealing with their problems. Frequently it may be necessary to take a highly directive as well as supportive role, telling the person what to do and what not to do.

On the following page Atkinson (1970), a volunteer at a suicide prevention center, describes part of an afternoon's work.

There is little doubt that the callers to suicide prevention centers are a high-risk group. Wold and Litman (1973) reinterviewed a random sample of 417 people who had called a suicide prevention center two years earlier and found that nine were dead from suicide—a rate almost 100 times greater than in the general population. It is difficult, however, to evaluate the effectiveness of preventive efforts. Most comparisons of suicide rates before and after the introduction of a center have shown no decrease. For example, Nielsen and Videbech (1973) report that after a community psychiatric service was introduced to a small Danish island (population 6823) the fre-

I settle down at my desk and just then comes the soft chime of the suicide line. As always, I feel the familiar tightening in my throat and a sinking sensation in my stomach.

I answer: "Suicide and Crisis. Can I help you?" I hear a click and then a dial tone.

Entry in Log Book: 4:12—Anon. Hung up.

Stephanie hands me a file and says: "Here's one you ought to call back. She gave us permission. Marilyn was pretty worried about her and Marilyn's judgment is sharp."

I skim the file. Evelyn J. is 50 years old, has a husband and two grown sons. Deeply depressed and threatening suicide. Husband harsh and unsympathetic. She calls him "Daddy." She says her poodle is the only one that cares about her anymore and that's all that is keeping her alive. I call the number.

"Mrs. J.? I'm calling from the Suicide and Crisis office. I was just reading your file and I'm a little worried about you. How are you feeling now?"

Her voice is light and airy, in fact unnaturally so. "Oh, really? Isn't that nice!"

I answer, "Is it difficult for you to talk right now? Is there someone there?"

Her response comes in the same light tone. "That's right."

"Okay, Mrs. J. I'd really appreciate it if you would call back when you can. We want to know how you're doing."

"Fine, I'll do that. Goodbye."

Log Book Entry: 4:15—Called Evelyn J. She'll call back.

Betsy has come in by now and we chatter awhile about her date last weekend. Again come the chimes of the suicide phone.

"I'll get it," say Betsy as she settles down at the other desk. It is a student requesting information about our service for a paper he is writing. I do some more filing and chat with Stephanie. Again the phone rings on the second suicide line.

I answer and it is Evelyn J. calling me back. This time there is no airy quality in her voice. She is crying softly while she talks to me. She is at the end of her rope. She has tried so hard to please Daddy but nothing she does is right in his eyes. He makes $2000 a month and won't even buy her a car after all their years of work and struggle for financial independence. The one son at home has turned against her, too, because she has started drinking a little to ease her depression. Only her poodle cares. I find out that Evelyn has a bottle of sleeping pills she is saving for the big step to oblivion, and I urge her to go to a psychiatrist. It seems Daddy doesn't believe in psychiatrists and would never approve. I ask her about menopause symptoms and learn that she is beginning to have them. When I tell her she should go to a gynecologist for hormones, she seems surprised. Daddy doesn't believe in doctors for all that nonsense either. I tell her I'm 48 years old and know what I'm talking about; she gets interested and asks about me. I urge her to go to a doctor or therapist or both, regardless of what Daddy thinks. I point out that she has been a door mat long enough.

I tell her: "If he objects, tell him to go to hell!"

This brings a giggle from her and she stops crying.

"Oh, that's so funny! I think I'll do just that." She giggles off and on throughout the rest of our conversation whenever she thinks of the prospect of telling her husband off. She says she will call for an appointment and promises she will do nothing drastic until I call her again next week. She tells me I'm a darling girl and she's very grateful.

Entry: 4:55—Evelyn J. called back on follow-up. OK for now. (Atkinson, 1970 pp. 38–39)

quency of suicides was 0.17 per 1000 people per year over a ten-year period, compared with a rate of 0.14 for the ten-year period preceding the initiation of the service—a nonsignificant change. In this service all psychiatric help was free, there was practically no waiting time, and the general practitioners were cooperative in referring people in need of assistance. In England Jennings et al. (1978) carefully matched 15 towns in which suicide prevention centers existed (The Samaritans) with 15 towns in which they did not exist, and found that suicide rates had declined somewhat in both sets of towns and by almost exactly the same amount. There was, in other words, no indication that the suicide prevention centers had contributed to the decrease in suicides.

Another possible reason for the fact that studies have not shown suicide prevention centers to be especially effective is that most people who commit suicide do not call these centers. Wilkins (1970), for example, estimates that 98 percent of people who commit suicide do not make such calls. In general, results of evaluative attempts suggest that suicide prevention centers as presently operated are not the final answer.

Summary

1. Major affective disorders are subdivided, according to DSM-III, into bipolar disorders and major depressions. If persons have experienced a manic disorder, they will be diagnosed bipolar disorder, whether or not they have had a depressive episode. Milder depressions are called dysthymic disorders or neurotic depressions.

2. Manic disorders are characterized by excessive elation, irritability, talkativeness, flight of ideas, and increased activity level.

3. Depressive disorders involve loss of pleasure in living, lack of initiative in work and play, attitudes of self-blame and despair, bodily concerns, and sometimes suicidal tendencies. When experienced, hallucinations and delusions refer to feelings of guilt.

4. Episodic affective disorders are characterized by a tendency toward spontaneous recovery and recurrences.

5. The distinction between bipolar and unipolar (recurring major depressions) affective disorders is an important one, apparently involving differences in symptoms, age of onset, and different genetic determinants. Both types are influenced by genetic makeup, but the bipolar type seems to be more strongly determined in this way.

6. Biogenic amines may play a role in affective disorders. There is indirect evidence that the neurotransmitters norepinephrine and serotonin may be depleted in some depressions and that norepinephrine, but not serotonin, levels may be higher than usual in mania.

7. Psychological events are likely to be associated with some affective disorders: reinforcement for depressive behavior, lack of reinforcement for nondepressed behavior, a conflict with a person recently lost, and learned cognitive reactions of self-blame and futility.

8. Cross-cultural evidence indicates that both the prevalence and form of affective disorders vary from one culture to another.

9. In general, the causation of affective disorders probably reflects an interaction of biological and psychosocial influences.

10. Tricyclic compounds such as imipramine have been found effective in treating affective disorders, especially the major depression type.

11. Lithium carbonate is effective in treating bipolar affective disorders.

12. Electroconvulsive treatment, in which an electric current is used to induce a convulsive seizure, speeds up the recovery process with psychotic depressions but does not prevent future occurrences. Many clinicians argue against its use, citing especially the possibility of long-term memory loss.

13. Various forms of psychological treatment can be effective with the less severe forms of depression. Cognitive therapy and an approach emphasizing self-reinforcement were given as examples.

14. Suicide is a major cause of death in the Western world. Although by no means associated only with depressions, a much higher proportion of people with diagnosed depressions commit suicide than in the population at large or in other diagnostic categories.

15. Suicide attempters are more likely to have experienced stressful life events than other people, for example, breakup of an important relationship, failure, or health problems.

16. Adolescent suicide attempters are likely to have had a long history of troubled relationships with parents, with whom the adolescent finds it especially difficult to communicate, confide, or obtain emotional support.

17. There is some evidence indicating a low correlation between suicide rates and the lack of tolerance for or approval of aggression in different cultures, especially in the past when cultural patterns were more distinctive. Even if such a relationship exists, many other factors are likely to contribute to the decision of any one person to commit suicide.

18. Suicide prevention or crisis intervention centers have attempted to prevent suicides by providing telephone contact and, where feasible, more direct personal intervention. However, research does not indicate that these centers have actually decreased suicide rates.

Suggested Readings

Psychodynamic, behavioral, and biological approaches to understanding affective disorders are discussed in J. Becker's *Affective disorders* (General Learning Press, 1977) and in G. Usdin (Ed.), *Depression: Clinical, biological and psychological perspectives* (Brunner/Mazel, 1977). A. T. Beck, A. J. Rush, B. F. Shaw, and G. Emery describe their approach to treatment in *Cognitive therapy of depression* (Guilford Press, 1980). The phenomenon of suicide is covered in E. S. Shneidman, N. L. Faberow, and R. E. Litman (Eds.), *The logic of suicide* (Science House, 1970).

19

Involuntary Incarceration and Criminal Responsibility: Legal and Ethical Issues

- Have individuals been held for years in mental hospitals because they were judged incompetent to stand trial for some minor crime?

- How easy is it to escape punishment for a crime by pleading insanity?

- How dangerous are ex–mental patients?

- Should persons ever be involuntarily committed to a mental hospital? Given treatments that they do not want?

Louis Perroni: Incompetent to Stand Trial

For ten years until May 5, 1955, Louis Perroni operated a filling station in Syracuse, New York. On that day his world fell apart. He had been informed earlier that year that the lease on his service station was not going to be renewed, as a new shopping center was going to be constructed on this property. Although offered compensation, Perroni refused to vacate the premises. After the real estate developer allegedly threatened him with court action, he became more resolved than ever not to be "pushed around." On May 2 representatives of the real estate developer put up a sign on the gas station property. He argued with them and removed the sign. On May 5 two men appeared and proceeded to erect another sign. Mr. Perroni fired a warning shot into the air from a rifle, and the men left. Shortly thereafter he was arrested by the police.

Thus began 40-year-old Perroni's first contact with both the law and psychiatry. He had served for nearly five years in World War II, had been given an honorable discharge, and had lived thereafter as a responsible, self-supporting citizen.

At the request of the district attorney, the Onondaga County Court judge ordered him to undergo a pretrial psychiatric examination to determine his fitness to stand trial. He was seen by two court-appointed psychiatrists, found incapable of standing trial, and committed to the Matteawan State Hospital.

With help from his brothers he tried by every means possible, including an appeal to the United States Supreme Court, to go on trial. Finally, six years later in June 1961, a writ of habeas corpus was heard and sustained by a State Supreme Court Judge. Perroni was ordered to be tried or discharged. In spite of this order, the officials of Matteawan State Hospital sent him back to Onondaga County Jail only after they were faced with contempt-of-court charges. He was held incommunicado for several days and then instead of being indicted or released, he was ordered to undergo another pretrial psychiatric examination. A month later he was committed to Oakville State Hospital near Syracuse to determine once more whether he was competent to stand trial. The hearing was not held until April 12, 1962. The following is one brief excerpt from the hearing. A psychiatrist who is testifying that Perroni is still incompetent to stand trial is being examined by a defense lawyer.

Q: Let me ask you, Doctor, can Mr. Perroni handle his everyday affairs?

A: I would say no.

Q: All right. Now, as I understand it, you based your answer on the supposition that his judgment is not good?

A: That's correct.

Q: Will you please tell us, Doctor, in what realm his judgment is not good?

A: His judgment in—may I refer to my notes, please?

Q: Yes.

A: I feel that his judgment is affected by his illogical thinking processes.

Q: Doctor, can you give me a single example from the records, from your interview with Mr. Perroni—a single example of any illogical thinking processes?

A: When it was explained to Mr. Perroni the desirability of his cooperating fully for the examinations that we asked him to cooperate in taking, his comment was "What good is that—how is that going to help me?"

Q: Is that the only remark, Doctor, in the entire proceedings?

A: This is one that I clearly recall. There were others.

Q: I see. And can you think of one other, Doctor—just a single one?

A: I cannot recall another one that I am sure of.

Q: Well, Doctor, it is a fact, is it not, that there is such a thing as despair?

A: Yes.

Q: And wouldn't you say, Doctor, that after a man has been incarcerated for seven years, attempting to get out for the purpose of standing trial, that he may feel "What is the use of answering questions"? (From Szasz, 1965, pp. 106–107; postscript, 1973)

Despite the fact that for the first time a psychiatrist (Thomas Szasz) retained by the defense testified that Perroni was competent to stand trial, the judge found him incompetent to stand trial and he was sent back to Matteawan State Hospital. Louis Perroni was finally released from Matteawan State Hospital in 1968. He returned to Onondaga County for trial on the original charges, at which times the charges were dismissed. He had been incarcerated for 13 years.

Competency to Stand Trial

Although sometimes abused, as in the case of Louis Perroni, the concept of incompetency to stand trial arose from a concern for defendants, namely, that accused persons shall understand the nature of the charges against them and be able to participate rationally in their own defense. Certainly some individuals are so disordered in their thinking and general competency that they would not comprehend a trial procedure. What is one to do? The hope is that after a period of confinement and treatment for their mental disorder, such persons will regain their mental capacities and can then be given a fair trial. As the example of Louis Perroni demonstrates, this legal procedure has at times led to long-term confinement without the safeguards of a trial.

Szasz aptly characterized the tragic story of Louis Perroni as a case of psychiatric injustice. He points out the bind that the accused person is in when forced to submit to a pretrial psychiatric examination. He is under strong pressure to "cooperate" with the examining psychiatrists, but he may be damned if he does cooperate and damned if he does not. Perroni, for example, cooperated with the psychiatrists at his first examination, explaining his reasons for acting as he did. The psychiatrists regarded his reasons as evidence of mental illness and declared him unfit to stand trial. (He had no legal counsel at this time.) When his competence for standing trial was reconsidered seven years later, now assisted by a defense counsel, he was less cooperative. However, his refusal

David Berkowitz claimed that demons speaking with the voices of barking dogs had ordered him to kill six persons. The Court decided that he was competent to stand trial.

to answer questions was interpreted not as good judgment but as "negativism" and contributed to the second diagnosis of mental illness.

Fortunately the rights of individuals to be protected from unreasonable detentions based on incompetency to stand trial have been bolstered since the time of Perroni's difficulties. Thus the Supreme Court (*Jackson* v. *Indiana,* 1972) has ruled that the length of pretrial confinement should be limited and that after some reasonable period of time if it appears that the individual is not likely ever to become competent, then either the usual civil commitment procedures should be initiated or the person should be released.

David Berkowitz, self-styled "Son of Sam," is a good example of the difficulty involved in determining competency to stand trial. Charged with killing six persons and wounding seven others, Berkowitz said that demons, speaking with the voices of barking dogs, had ordered him out on his late-night hunts for victims. Two court-appointed psychiatrists concluded that he was psychotic and therefore incompetent to stand trial. A third psychiatrist, however, maintained that Berkowitz made up the story about the demons and that he was competent to stand trial. The Court agreed with the third psychiatrist, Abrahamsen, and Berkowitz was tried and found guilty. Abrahamsen (1979) based his conclusion on a number of things—the general impression of sanity that Berkowitz made on fellow employees, his capacity for careful planning and eventually eluding the police for a long period of time, indications that Berkowitz could decide whether or not to obey the demons, and the report of one attempted murder that happened a year before Berkowitz said that the demons began to talk to him. Abrahamsen was apparently correct in his conclusion. At least Berkowitz himself, after his conviction, wrote a letter to Abrahamsen in which he said, "Yes, it was all a hoax, a silly hoax, well planned and thought out."

Not Guilty by Reason of Insanity

Mental health professionals (psychiatrists and sometimes clinical psychologists) not only make recommendations about competency to stand trial; they also give testimony that can affect the outcome of the trial. This is especially true for the so-called insanity defense. There is a long tradition in English law that if persons are so mentally deranged that they have no comprehension of the meaning of their criminal act, then they are not legally responsible for the act.

One famous case that affected the interpretations of the insanity plea was that of Daniel McNaghten, who in 1893 was tried for the murder of a man whom he had believed to be the home secretary of the British government. In fact, McNaghten had mistakenly killed the wrong man, a government clerk. He explained his action by saying that he had been "instructed by the voice of God." The verdict was not guilty, on the ground of insanity. Subsequently, a committee of judges described the criteria that should be applied to such cases in the future: In order for a defendant to be ruled innocent by reason of insanity, it must be shown that "the accused was la-

boring under such defect of reason from disease of the mind, as not to know the nature and quality of the act he was doing, or as not to know that what he was doing was wrong." The McNaghten rule, as it came to be known, with its emphasis on knowing right from wrong, dominated the legal interpretation of mental disorders until recent times.

In the present century the psychiatric profession became more and more critical of this approach. The McNaghten rule, they believed, was based on a conception of people as rational beings who made free choices informed by conscious considerations. Modern psychiatry, influenced by Freud and other adherents of the psychodynamic movement, however, preferred a model that included irrational and unconscious as well as conscious determinants of behavior. The psychiatrists argued that it was difficult for them to testify as to whether a defendant knew right from wrong, but that they could bring their expertise to bear on whether the accused was suffering from a mental illness. In 1959 Judge Bazelon of the United States Court of Appeals wrote an opinion in the *Durham* case that formulated a new test of criminal responsibility, giving the psychiatrists what they asked for. The opinion held that an accused person is not criminally responsible if it is shown that the unlawful act was the product of a mental disease or defect.

In Judge Bazelon's view, however, the Durham rule never accomplished its intended goal, and 18 years later in 1972 he favored its abandonment (Bazelon, 1974). The basic problem, according to Bazelon, is that when psychiatrists testify, they limit themselves to conclusions (for example, that the defendant is mentally ill) without providing the jury with understandable evidence to support their conclusion or, for that matter, illuminating what the term *mentally ill* means in a given case. Psychiatric testimony, according to Bazelon, should be submitted to the same scrutiny and examination as any other kind of opinion presented at trials. Bazelon reports that a well-known psychiatrist told him that evidence of the sort he was asking for would require from 50 to 100 man-hours of interviewing and investigation to obtain; few hospitals could afford such an expenditure of effort. Bazelon replied that if that were the case, then psychiatrists should explain on the witness stand that their opinions are based on an inadequate study of the case and not pretend that they had learned all that would be helpful.

What did the jury mean by saying he was not guilty! I will never believe that anyone could be "not guilty" who wanted to murder a conservative Prime Minister!

Victoria R

Queen Victoria's comment on the attempted assassination of Sir Robert Peel on January 20, 1843, reflected the attitude of many Englishmen. When Daniel McNaughton shot Peel's secretary in the mistaken belief that he had killed the Prime Minister, and was absolved of the crime on the grounds of insanity, the public was outraged. The controversy continues as to whether a person should or should not be held responsible for a crime because of a mental disorder.

The insanity defense frequently evokes skeptical reactions in people who wonder if it is not a strategy that clever lawyers use to get guilty clients acquitted. This skepticism is not helped much by the fact that one psychiatric "expert" may testify that a defendant was insane at the time of a crime and another psychiatric expert testify that the defendant was sane. As one psychiatrist, experienced in legal testimony, put it, ". . . attorneys for the prosecution and defense will consult privately with as many potential psychiatric witnesses as necessary (when they can afford it) until they find one or two whose opinion they deem useful to their side" (Lunde, 1975).

Actually, the insanity defense is rarely used in the United States and is even more rarely successful; most such defendants are found sane by juries. In the past the end result has been little different for defendants whether they were found sane or insane. In the former case they spent many years in prison; in the latter case they spent, on the average, about the same number of years confined to a mental hospital (Lunde, 1975). Daniel McNaghten, though found "not guilty," spent the last 22 years of his life in an institution for the criminally insane, where he received essentially no treatment.

Recently, however, because of judicial rulings that make it more difficult to keep individuals involuntarily confined in mental hospitals, there is an increased likelihood that the "criminally insane" will be discharged. For example, in 1974, 200 criminally insane persons were released from Michigan state hospitals because the Michigan Supreme Court ruled that individuals could not be confined if they were not currently mentally ill (Herbert, 1979). In response to the public outcry that followed, the Michigan legislature changed the law so that a person can be found "guilty but mentally ill." If so convicted, treatment for the mental disorder is provided; when treatment is completed, the person is returned to prison to serve out the remainder of the sentence. Release becomes a decision for the justice system, not the mental health system. Illinois and other states are currently considering versions of this approach, which implies responsibility for criminal behavior but at the same time attempts to treat whatever mental disorder may be related to the criminal behavior.

Civil Commitment

We have until now been considering the application of the legal concepts of competency and insanity to those accused of crimes. A much larger group of mentally disturbed individuals (who are accused of no crime) are faced with a different legal procedure—involuntary commitment to mental hospitals. State laws generally emphasize the following criteria for legal commitment: Persons must be judged mentally ill and (1) likely to injure themselves or others, or (2) lacking in sufficient insight or capacity to take care of themselves and to make responsible decisions concerning their need for hospitalization.

Commitment proceedings vary from state to state. Typically, one or more persons must file an affidavit containing "evidence" that the subject is mentally ill. A court order is then issued requiring the person named to enter a hospital or other facility for observation and a psychiatric examination; this usually takes around 72 hours but in some cases may take considerably longer. A hearing is then conducted at which testimony is taken from interested parties and from one or more psychiatrists (sometimes from general practitioners without psychiatric training). The judge makes one of several decisions: (1) to dismiss the defendant, (2) to hold the defendant for further observation until the next hearing, or (3) to commit the defendant to a mental hospital.

Scheff (1964) conducted observations of both psychiatric examinations and commitment hearings and concluded that there was a strong *presumption* of mental illness on the part of the psychiatrists; that is, the very fact that the person was being seen at a commitment hearing produced an expectancy that the individual was indeed mentally ill. The fact that in 196 consecutive cases not a single person was recommended for release was enough to raise some suspicion. Twenty-six psychiatric examinations were directly observed and were found to be conducted in a hurried fashion, averaging about ten minutes per patient. Four characteristics indicated a presumption of mental illness:

First, the evidence for the decision often seemed arbitrary. For example, in a typical interview the examiner asked a series of 15 or 20 questions: the date, time, place, names of the current president and governor, the product of 11 times 10, and so on. Many

examiners seemed to feel that one wrong answer established lack of orientation even when preceded by a series of correct answers. There were no data on a normal group of the same age, education, and social background obtained under similar stress and time pressure to provide a comparison.

Second, in some cases the decision to recommend commitment was made even when no evidence was found. Some of the psychiatrists' remarks were a third ground for suspecting prejudgment. For example, examiners sometimes intimated mental illness by their use of language. One psychiatrist stated that there was "no gross evidence of delusions or hallucinations." This was misleading since there was *no* evidence, gross or otherwise. Another psychiatrist commented about those cases in which the patient's family or acquaintances had petitioned for commitment, "If the family wants to get rid of him, you know there is something wrong." Finally, Scheff found that many of the examinations were conducted in a careless and hasty manner.

Wenger and Fletcher (1969) found that a person who had legal counsel was significantly less likely to be committed than a person who did not have counsel, no matter what the degree of the patient's dangerousness or incapacitation. Thus, for patients who showed no evidence of dangerousness and no extreme degree of incapacitation, 10 of the 15 without legal counsel were committed while none of the 8 with legal counsel were committed.

The basic conflict associated with involuntary commitment is between the civil liberties of the individual on the one hand and two concerns of the larger society: protecting itself from dangerous people and providing sustenance and help for those too mentally incapacitated to understand their own plight. Despite the abuses that I have emphasized so far, few people would advocate a policy of no involuntary commitment. Because of publicity about some of these abuses and the determined work of such groups as the American Civil Liberties Union, many states have shifted the balance considerably toward the rights of the individual, making involuntary commitments more difficult to obtain and making it easier for the patient to get out of the hospital after commitment. This tendency has recently been reinforced by a decision of the U.S. Supreme Court, which ruled unanimously that people may not be civilly committed to mental institutions unless the state has presented "clear and convincing" evidence that they require involuntary hospitalization (*Addington* v. *Texas,* April 30, 1979). Perhaps partly as a result of the greater difficulty in making involuntary commitments, there has been a steady increase in the number of persons who voluntarily admit themselves to mental hospitals. At this time more than half of the admissions at most mental hospitals are voluntary. Of course, it is hard to know how many of these individuals are threatened with legal commitment proceedings if they do not go voluntarily.

Some would argue that the pendulum has swung too far and that many patients are being discharged prematurely. James (1979) describes the following case in point:

Wendy was severely depressed. She was having problems at work; her mother was ill. She was overweight, and her marriage life was, at best, less than exciting.

One day last spring, she decided to do something about it. Her husband was out and in the medicine cabinet was a bottle of sleeping pills. She took all of them.

Her husband came in and found her and called an ambulance. After three days in N.C. Memorial Hospital, Wendy was escorted to Dorothea Dix Mental Hospital.

Before she could be committed to the hospital against her will, Wendy had to have a hearing. She appeared before a judge with her counsel, and the judge decided that according to law, Wendy was not an "imminent danger to herself or others" and released her from the hospital.

Wendy (not her real name) made some frantic phone calls after she was released from the hospital, complaining about the way she was treated and that she was kept in an institution against her will.

"I don't know why they would want to put me away," she said. "I wasn't going to hurt anybody, and there's no hope for me anyway. Nobody can do anything to help me."

Two weeks after her release, Wendy tried suicide again. She succeeded. (p. 1)

Because of incidents of this kind, the state of North Carolina modified its commitment statutes so that a person could be committed if there is a "reasonable probability" of serious physical harm to the person within the "near future" unless the individual receives adequate treatment. State legislatures will no doubt continue to wrestle with the ethical and legal issues surrounding involuntary commitments.

How Dangerous Is the Ex–mental Patient?

As states move toward policies of fewer involuntary commitments and easier releases, the question of the potential dangerousness of ex–mental patients becomes a more troubling one to the public. You have all read headlines in the newspaper of the type, "Ex–mental patient shoots three." The natural reaction is, "They should have kept him locked up." The problem here is to keep some perspective on the issue. How many people who are not ex–mental patients also shoot other people? In general, are ex–mental patients more dangerous than a representative sample with the same socioeconomic background?

Although some early studies found that mental patients released in the 1930s and 1940s had lower arrest rates than the general population (for example, Brill & Malzberg, 1962), more recent research has not found this to be the case. Rabkin (1979) reviewed eight more recent studies of mental patients released during the 1950s through the 1970s. Overall, released mental patients, relative to the general population, were found to have been arrested more often for crimes of violence. This finding, however, needs to be qualified in important ways. First, in the four studies in which arrest records were obtained for a period of time before as well as after hospitalization it turns out that the small subset of patients with prior criminal records accounts for a large majority of postdischarge arrests. The arrest rates for ex–mental patients who had not been arrested before hospitalization were, for the most part, similar to arrest rates for the population at large. Second, no studies used an appropriately matched control group. Since released mental patients who commit crimes of violence tend to be males who are young, unmarried, unskilled, poor, and frequently members of minority groups, the question is whether arrest rates would be higher for released patients if they were compared to a similar group. Rabkin concludes that they probably would not be.

Finally, with respect to diagnostic category, arrest rates were higher for ex-patients who had been diagnosed primarily as being alcohol or drug abusers, or as having personality disorders. Again, Rabkin concludes that released patients without prior arrests who did not receive a primary diagnosis of substance abuse or personality disorder probably have *lower* arrest records than do members of the general population who have not been hospitalized for mental disorder. In the one study in which the sample was limited to former male patients who carried the diagnosis of schizophrenia, 99 percent of the ex-patients were *not* arrested for a crime of violence during the four-year follow-up period (Giovannoni & Gurel, 1967). Arrests prior to hospitalization were not assessed in this study. Arrests for violent crimes would probably have been decreased even further if patients with previous arrest records had been removed from the sample.

An important implication of these findings is that former mental patients *as a group* should not be stigmatized with respect to dangerousness. The vast majority of *all* former mental patients, probably over 90 percent, do not engage in crimes of violence. The factor that best predicts violent behavior in mental patients is the same factor that predicts it in non–mental patients—previous acts of violence.

The problem of protecting both society and individual rights would be a lot simpler, of course, if we could predict with high probability which mental patients are going to commit serious crimes, especially violent and injurious acts. Although a previous history of violence is probably our best predictor at this time, even in that case the prediction of a relatively rare event such as homicide cannot be made with much certainty. Another factor that makes prediction difficult is that violent behaviors (as well as most other behaviors) are determined as much by external circumstances as by personality dispositions. One must foresee environmental events as well as detect personality dispositions in order to predict behavior accurately. Inevitably, in order to predict the one person who will engage in the prescribed act, the investigator must make positive predictions that are not realized for another 50 to 100 persons, the so-called false positives. We are left then with a problem for which there is no easy answer. To keep 500 patients hospitalized because one might commit murder is hardly fair to the 499 who will not. The problem of assessing potential dangerousness is illustrated by the following sources of disagreements among a panel of mental health professionals who were asked to evaluate dangerousness in a group of chronic mental patients.

Is an individual who committed a violent act many years ago while suffering from a severe mental condition, which persists to the present, "dangerous," even though there have been no violent episodes in the intervening period? Is a patient to be considered dangerous by the panels if it is clear that he was not dangerous at the time of admission but has later engaged in assaultive acts while hospitalized? What should be made of the patient with a long history of threats but no actual harmful conduct? Finally, should a patient's delusions of persecution and the potential for a defensive response be an adequate base for a determination of dangerousness? (Kress, 1979, p. 213)

For the time being, the individuals responsible for commitment and discharge can only do the best they can in evaluating potential dangerousness, striving to maintain some reasonable balance between real threat to society and the individual patient's civil liberties.

The Right to Treatment

In 1962 Charles Rouse, aged 17, was walking after dark in Washington, D.C. Stopped by a policeman, he was found to be carrying a loaded pistol and some ammunition. Rouse, who already had a modest juvenile arrest record, was acquitted by reason of insanity, declared a "sociopath" (see Chapter 22), and given an indeterminate sentence to St. Elizabeth's Hospital, the capital's main facility for the mentally ill. He remained there for four and one-half years before an appeal reached, by luck, the court of Judge Bazelon. Bazelon sent the case back to the lower court with the injunction that it look into the question of whether Rouse had not in fact been deprived of his "right to treatment." The issue was taken up in the lower court, although Rouse was freed on other grounds before this particular issue was resolved (Goodman, 1974).

The stage was set, however, for the question of "right to treatment" to be pursued. In 1970 just such a case developed in Alabama. A class action suit was brought against the state of Alabama for not providing either mental patients or institutionalized mentally retarded individuals with a minimum degree of treatment. Treatment was extremely limited at both kinds of institutions; patients received primarily custodial care and were lucky if they were not abused by the hospital staff. District Judge Frank M. Johnson ruled in the class action suit: "To deprive any citizen of his or her liberty upon the altruistic theory that the confinement is for humane therapeutic reasons and then fail to provide adequate treatment violates the very fundamentals of due process" (Goodman, 1974, p. 22).

George Wallace, then governor of Alabama, appealed the decision, arguing that no federal court has the power to tell a state how to allocate its resources. The Fifth Circuit Court of Appeals, however, supported the original ruling, reaffirming the concept of right to treatment as a matter of constitutional law. (Even before the appeal decision was reached, Alabama had reduced by 50 percent the number of patients in mental hospitals and had doubled the state's mental health budget.) In 1975 the Supreme Court ruled unanimously in the case of Kenneth Donaldson that persons who are labeled mentally ill cannot be confined against their will without treatment if they are not dangerous to themselves or others and are capable of surviving on the outside. Donaldson was confined involuntarily in a Florida mental hospital for nearly 15 years, during which time he maintained that he received no treatment and his petitions for release were repeatedly refused by the courts. They dismissed as "unpersuasive" the psychiatrist's contention that the courts have no authority to pass on the adequacy of treatment, ruling that this was not the special province of the mental health professional.

This ruling adds further importance to the assessment of dangerousness which as we have seen is extremely difficult. Kress (1979) describes an attempt to apply the Donaldson ruling to three samples of chronic hospitalized mental patients, each sample being evaluated by a different panel of judges. Continued commitment was thought to be justified in less than half of the patients. More disquieting, Kress concluded that evaluations of dangerousness were more influenced by the models of mental disorder held by clinicians than by actual rates of previous aggressive behavior. For example, a strong adherent to the disease metaphor rated many more patients as potentially dangerous than did a strong adherent of a sociological model.

The establishment of the right to treatment, however, may produce its own set of problems. As in Alabama, one response to the law, if appropriate treatment cannot be provided, is to discharge a large number of mental patients. Communities may be ill-prepared to cope with the ex-patients, with few treatment facilities such as community homes or outpatient services. Underlying all legal, psychological, and social solutions to the right to treatment issue is the economic issue. How much are citizens willing to pay to change custodial institutions into treatment facilities? Perhaps they would be willing to pay more if there was evidence that a given approach, such as community homes or a preventive strategy, really worked. Continuing research is necessary to provide that evidence.

The Right Not To Be Treated

Patients who have been involuntarily committed are presumed in many cases not to fully understand the need for hospitalization or certain forms of treatment. Electroconvulsive shock treatment is the treatment most often objected to by patients, although some occasionally object to taking drugs. To what extent are hospital staff justified in forcing patients to receive a treatment that they do not want? The following example illustrates the ethical dilemma that can arise.

D. Y. is a 23-year-old unmarried white female who has been psychotic almost continuously since age 16. She has been hospitalized in numerous state and private hospitals with only a brief period of remission. Frequent periods of assaultiveness, pacing, confusion, auditory hallucinations, and disheveled dress have occurred. About the sixth year of her hospitalization it was noted that she began to develop periorbital mouth movements and smacking movements of the lips, generally considered early signs of tardive dyskinesia. Her medications were discontinued and her psychotic behavior became more florid. The staff was caught in a dilemma. During the period when medication was withdrawn, the patient became very psychotic and attacked a nurse on the night shift, attempting to strangle her. Only the fortunate intervention of another patient saved the nurse from death by strangulation. The decision was therefore made to reinstitute medication. Was the patient capable of participating in this decision? Was the decision made in the patient's best interests or to control her aggressive behavior? Was this done for the patient's benefit or to improve staff morale? (Klerman, 1977, p. 626)

In this case the patient was probably too psychotic to make such a decision. Consent of a third party is required in some states before certain treatments such as ECT can be given. The woman described above, however, had no family that could give such permission. At this time there is no generally accepted solution to this problem. Some mental hospitals have patients' rights committees or, in the case of Massachusetts, mental health legal advisors who could be consulted in instances such as the one just described. Stone (1975) proposes that patients should have the right to refuse treatment with certain hazardous or very unpleasant procedures such as ECT,

aversion conditioning, or highly addictive drugs (for example, methadone) but not with less dangerous or less unpleasant treatments.

Few, if any, of the legal and ethical issues dealt with in this chapter can be resolved by some absolute standard. In most cases we are faced with a conflict between the rights and liberties of the individual and the responsibility of the society to protect itself or take care of those incompetent to do so for themselves. No doubt there will be continuing tensions between those who differ in terms of where the optimum balance is between these two opposing concerns. In the long run the best solution may be to sidestep the ethical dilemmas by increasing the effectiveness of preventive efforts and nonhazardous treatments.

Summary

1. The legal concept of competency to stand trial has been abused in the past, but recently more safeguards for the patient's civil rights have been used.

2. The legal criteria for the insanity defense are still not clearly defined or generally agreed upon. Recently some states are including options such as "guilty but mentally ill" in which the person must serve out a sentence while receiving whatever treatment seems appropriate.

3. The process of involuntary commitment involves a conflict between two social concerns: the right of society to protect itself from dangerous persons (and the desire to provide treatment for those who lack sufficient understanding to take care of themselves) versus the civil liberties of the individual. There have clearly been past abuses of individual's civil liberties, and recent court rulings have gone far to restore some balance between society's and the individual's rights.

4. Ex–mental patients are probably no more dangerous than comparison populations matched on age, socioeconomic, and minority status. The evidence on this point remains incomplete, however.

5. The Supreme Court has ruled that persons who are labeled mentally ill cannot be confined against their will without treatment if they are not dangerous to themselves or others and are capable of surviving on the outside.

6. There is a growing concern about forcing involuntarily committed mental patients to submit to treatments they do not want. Patients' rights committees may be helpful in representing the patients' point of view in this regard.

Suggested Readings

R. H. Price and B. Denner bring together in one volume a stimulating selection of articles relating to societal reactions to mental illness and the commitment process in *The making of a mental patient* (Holt, Rinehart and Winston, 1973). Judge D. Bazelon provides an excellent discussion of the legal concept of insanity and psychiatric testimony in the *Scientific American* (1974, *270,* 18–23).

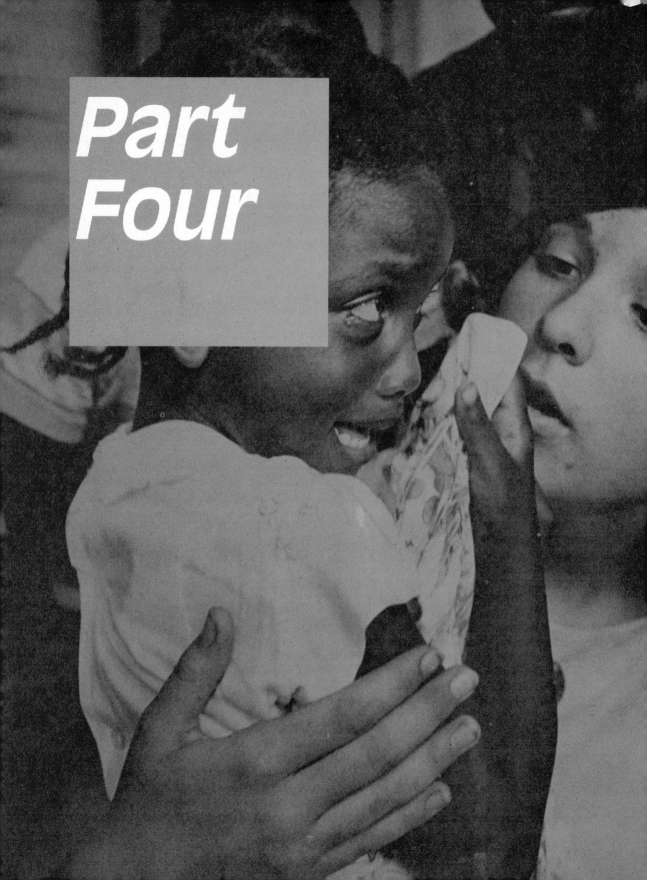

Part
Four

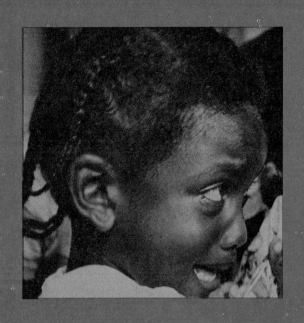

Developmental Disorders in Children

20

Some Specific Developmental Disorders of Childhood

- Do parents and teachers overestimate or underestimate the occurrence of problem behaviors in children?

- How important is the early mother-infant relationship for the later development of abnormal behavior?

- Did you know that very young infants get a kick out of controlling their environment?

- Can early separation from parents or placement in impersonal institutions produce lasting effects on individuals' personality?

- "Sit down, you're rocking the boat!" How do you handle a hyperactive child?

- If an older child wets the bed, is it a "message" to parents, or a matter of improper learning?

- Do we know what causes stuttering? Can we help the stutterer to speak in a normal way?

- Can dieting be carried too far? What is anorexia nervosa?

Billy: A Case of School Phobia

Billy, age 13, had been absent from school for seven weeks when he was referred for treatment. His intense fear began on the day that he was to return to school after a three-week illness. He was unable to eat breakfast and complained of chest pains. He nevertheless went to school, but there his trembling, crying, and increased chest pains induced the principal to call his parents and suggest that he be taken to a physician immediately. The physician found no organic basis for the symptoms and prescribed a tranquilizer which provided some immediate relief from the anxiety. The following morning, however, the symptoms reappeared in even more severe form and neither force, punishment, nor bribes could get Billy to return to school. (Smith & Sharpe, 1970)

Children display most of the psychological disorders shown in adults, though usually with some differences resulting from the fact that they are not so far advanced in their development. In this chapter we will not consider all disorders of childhood; several kinds of childhood symptoms such as anxiety and conversion disorders were covered in Chapters 8 and 9, and future chapters discuss childhood psychoses, aggressive behaviors, and mental retardation. Here we will concentrate on disturbances related to the early mother-infant relationship and on five other disorders that occur among children but rarely in adults (with the exception of stuttering): school phobia, hyperactivity, stuttering, persistent bedwetting, and anorexia nervosa (eating reduction and severe weight loss).

Varieties and Prevalence of Childhood "Symptoms"

A more complete listing of developmental disorders of childhood as they appear in DSM-III, excluding mental retardation and certain severe and pervasive disorders, is shown in Table 20-1. Most children seen in outpatient clinics fall along two broad dimensions of psychological disturbance: *conduct disorders,* involving disobedience, fighting, temper tantrums, and the like; and *anxious-withdrawn reactions,* involving feelings of inferiority, self-consciousness, social withdrawal, and anxiety (Quay, 1979). A study by Borgatta and Fanshel (1965), in which ratings were obtained

on 607 children at 30 outpatient clinics across the United States, provides more specific examples of the kinds of behavior that tend to cluster in these patterns. Not all of the behaviors listed under each category necessarily occur in the same child, although the general trend is for these characteristics to go together.

Conduct Disorders	Anxious-Withdrawn Disorders
Defiant	Overly nervous
Rebellious	Very tense
Shouts at parents	Fearful, anxious
Negativistic	Overreacts to minor
Takes revenge	illness and pains
Risks self-harm without	Has nightmares
apparent concern	Clings to adults
Reckless	dependently
Commits vandalism,	Acts babyish
destroys property	
Has temper tantrums	
Sullen or surly	

The personnel of mental health clinics see a biased sample of children—only children someone complains about. Because they rarely have a clear idea of how frequent a given kind of behavior is in the general population, clinicians are in danger of attributing more pathological significance to a symptom than it deserves. Leo Kanner (1957), one of the first child psychiatrists in this country, stated the problem clearly:

This selectiveness in the absence of normal controls has often resulted in a tendency to attribute to single behavior items an exaggerated "seriousness" with regard to their intrinsic psychopathologic signifi-

TABLE 20-1
Some Developmental Disorders of Childhood as Listed in DSM-III

Attention Deficit Disorders
  With hyperactivity
  Without hyperactivity
Conduct Disorders (more detail in Chapter 22)
Anxiety Disorders of Childhood or Adolescence
  Separation anxiety disorder
  Avoidant disorder: extreme shyness
  Overanxious disorder: similar to generalized
    anxiety disorder in adults
Other Disorders of Childhood and Adolescence
  Reactive attachment disorder of infancy:
    "failure to thrive" as a result of gross neglect
  Elective mutism: refusal to speak in certain
    situations
  Identity disorder: Severe distress resulting
    from uncertainty about "who one is" with
    respect to career goals, religious beliefs and
    moral values, political orientation, group
    loyalties, etc.
Eating Disorders
  Anorexia nervosa: drastic reduction in food
    intake with accompanying loss of weight
  Bulimia: an episodic pattern of binge eating
  Pica: persistent eating of nonnutritional
    substances such as hair, cloth, bugs, or
    leaves
Stereotyped Movement Disorders
  Transient or chronic motor tic disorder:
    recurring, involuntary, repetitive, rapid,
    purposeless muscular movements (such as
    eye blinks or facial muscular contractions)
  Tourette's disorder: motor tics, as well as
    involuntary vocal utterances such as grunts,
    yelps, barks, and the expression of
    obscenities
Other Disorders with Physical Manifestations
  Stuttering
  Functional enuresis: bedwetting
  Functional encopresis: soiling, inappropriate
    passage of feces

Temper tantrums are not uncommon in young children but tend to decrease markedly from age five to age eight.

Werry and Quay (1971) asked teachers and mothers of children in kindergarten through the third grade to check the presence or absence of a long list of symptoms. Teachers, as well as mothers, reported a high incidence of various problem behaviors. Many problems, however, such as social withdrawal, lack of self-confidence, temper tantrums, disruptiveness, and excessive activity showed rather marked decreases from age five to age eight for both sexes. Clearly the age of the child must be taken into account in interpreting the significance of a given symptom.

The data from this study support Kanner's (1957) contention that many children with behavioral symptoms do not come to the attention of professional mental health workers. It is a reasonable guess that a number of these symptoms are transitory and do not pose serious threats of future psychopathology. In other cases the child's symptoms reflect a persisting problem of some severity but do not bother the parents, or others, sufficiently to cause them to seek help.

A more accurate estimate of the true prevalence of psychological disturbance in children is provided by Rutter et al. (1975). They assessed "psychiatric disorder" in *all* ten-year-old children on the Isle of Wight and in a low socioeconomic borough of London with a screening questionnaire given to teachers and by interviews with parents. For the Isle of Wight 12.0 percent of the children were considered to have a definite psychiatric disorder compared with 25.9 percent of the children in the inner-city borough of London. These findings suggest that the prevalence of psychological disturbances in children may vary considerably from one locale to another.

cance. . . . The high annoyance threshold of many fond and fondly resourceful parents keeps away from clinics and out of the reach of statistics a multitude of early breath holders, nail biters, nose pickers, and casual masturbators who, largely because of this kind of parental attitude, develop into reasonably happy and well-adjusted adults. (p. 180)

Disturbances in Attachment and Exploratory Behavior

Many writers (for example, Erikson, 1963) have argued that what happens to infants in their early years lays a groundwork of personality characteristics that may endure for the rest of their lives, coloring their behavior and self-image. Especially important at this period of life are the development of attachments to other people and the assertion of autonomy in the exploration of the environment. There is evidence that severe disruptions in the development of attachment and exploratory behavior can have long-lasting effects.

Infants of many animal species manifest attachment to a specific adult, usually the mother, by tendencies to seek physical contact or proximity, maintain visual and auditory contact, and express distress at forced separation. The human infant during the first five months of life shows many of these reactions (smiling, vocalization, and visual-motor orientation) rather indiscriminately to people and for that matter to inanimate objects. Some time between 5 and 14 months of age, most human infants begin to make a clear discrimination between mother and other people and begin to reserve these kinds of attachment behaviors for her.

Once some degree of attachment has developed, much of the young infant's behavior, aside from satisfying basic needs for nourishment and sleep, reflects somewhat incompatible tendencies to seek proximity and contact with the mother (or primary caretaker) and to explore, by looking, listening, locomotion, and manipulation, the surrounding environment. The evolutionary significance of both attachment and exploratory behavior is obvious: The mother-infant attachment system ensures a degree of protection and care that is essential for survival in species whose young are relatively helpless, and exploratory behavior ensures that the infant will progressively learn more about how to live without the mother's aid.

There is a continuing interplay between attachment and exploratory behavior in the normal 8- to 15-month-old child. As soon as babies can crawl they are eager to move away from mother, to look at, feel,

Human infants have a strong tendency to explore the world around them.

taste, or listen to the world around them. But all the while they keep track of mother by occasional glances or by returning for some temporary physical contact before resuming worldly exploration. Mother seems to provide a secure base from which they can venture forth and, should some new experience become too frightening, they beat a hasty retreat to this haven.

EFFECTS OF THE MOTHER-INFANT RELATIONSHIP

Psychoanalytic writers have long stressed the importance of the infant's relationship with the mother for personality development, attributing special importance to the infant's experiences that center around feeding activities because of their relationship to the oral stage of development. According to this view, infants that experience severe deprivation of oral satisfactions or are overly indulged with oral satisfactions (by long delay of weaning, for example) may develop an *oral fixation* that has lasting effects on the personality. An orally deprived child might be expected as an adult to show *oral character traits:* general distrust of people, a pessimistic view and perhaps a number of oral mannerisms such as a tendency to suck or chew on pipes, cigars, or gum. The research evidence, however, is weak at best for a tie between early oral experience (at least as measured by such variables as breast versus bottle feeding, demand versus scheduled feeding, early versus late weaning, or abrupt versus gradual weaning) and later childhood or adult oral character traits (Caldwell, 1964). The behavior of most adults is affected by so many factors, current influences as well as a multitude of past experiences, that the effects of feeding variables may be overshadowed.

The general style of mother-infant interaction may be more important than specific feeding procedures. For instance, a substantial body of research suggests that when maternal stimulation falls below some minimal level, intellectual and social retardation are likely to occur (Beckwith, 1971; Yarrow, 1963). Findings point to the special importance of *contingent stimulation*. A mother, for example, might talk or sing to her baby, hold and rock the baby, and generally provide a lot of auditory and visual stimulation. However, this stimulation is *noncontingent* if it is not controlled by the infant, that is, if it happens no matter what the infant does. But if the infant smiles and the mother responds by shaking her head and nuzzling the infant, mother's response is contingent on the smile. If the infant further responds to the nuzzling with laughter, the mother may draw back and repeat the nuzzling response all over again, to which the infant laughs more uproariously than before. We have here another example of an interacting system. Each response the infant makes affects the mother's subsequent response, and each response the mother makes affects the next response of the infant; each person can be said to be controlling the other's behavior in this limited interaction. The relationship of maternal sensitivity to signals of the infant and the later development of an appropriate balance between attachment and exploration is described in Research Report 20-1.

RESEARCH REPORT 20-1

Maternal Sensitivity Is Associated with Infant Attachment and Exploration

Ainsworth and Bell (1969) directly observed 23 white, middle-class mothers interacting with their infants for four-hour periods every three weeks from birth until the infants were 54 weeks old. The researchers developed a system for categorizing different patterns of mother-child interaction associated with feeding. In one pattern the mothers were sensitive to the demands and rhythms of their infants, permitting them to play an active part in determining the timing, pacing, and termination of feeding. Another group of mothers were relatively insensitive and unresponsive to their babies during the feeding process.

When the babies were approximately one year old, Ainsworth and Bell measured the strength of their attachment and exploratory behavior in a series of standardized situations involving various combinations of the presence and absence of the mother and a stranger with the infant. All nine infants who responded to these situations with strong indications of attachment but who could also use the presence of their mother as a secure base for exploration fell in the feeding interaction pattern in which the mothers had been most sensitive to their signals. Of the 14 infants who either lacked interest in regaining or maintaining contact with their mothers when reunited or who intermingled contact-seeking behavior with rejection of the mother (for example, with anger or pushing away), 12 were in the group whose mothers had been least sensitive to them in the early feeding situation.

The measure of sensitivity in the feeding situation that Ainsworth and Bell used is not the same as demand versus scheduled feeding—a variable that has been frequently studied in the past. For example, a mother rated sensitive in their classification system might be moving the infant toward a regularly scheduled feeding time but doing so with flexibility and responsiveness to the infant's signals. Perhaps this characteristic of the feeding interaction will prove to be more predictive of future mother-child relations and child behaviors than the demand versus scheduled feeding variable, which has yielded generally inconclusive results.

Subsequently, Ainsworth et al. (1978) added more infants to the sample and studied the relationship of more general features of mother-child interaction at three months of age to behavior in situations involving a stranger at 12 months. Strongly attached infants who could use mother as a secure base for exploration had mothers who had responded sensitively to their three-month-old's signals in all areas, not just while feeding. Mothers of infants who were weakly attached and showed little interest in maintaining proximity, on the other hand, had been rejecting, ignoring, and unresponsive in most areas. Their babies had apparently found them aversive or at least not sufficiently rewarding to maintain approach behavior.

Infants who showed signs of excessive attachment—crying through separation periods, difficult to console when reunited with mother, and showing low levels of exploratory behavior—had mothers who displayed a mixture of positive and negative reactions. They interacted playfully and affectionately on occasion, but at many other times either highly interfered with the baby's exploration or grossly ignored it. These infants at 12 months were ambivalent toward their mothers: Although they showed signs of overattachment, their actual interaction with their mothers was frequently accompanied by angry, contact-resisting behavior. There is some recent evidence from another study that babies showing this ambivalent pattern may have had more "difficult" temperaments from birth on (Waters et al., 1980). The resulting disturbance in attachment, then, may reflect an interaction between infant temperament and maternal behaviors. Recall Michael's slow-to-warm-up temperament and the general findings on individual differences in children's temperament by Thomas et al. (1968).

The young infant seems to enjoy contingent stimulation even if the stimulus is inanimate. Watson and Ramey (1972) report intriguing results of a study in which mothers gave their eight-week-old infants the opportunity to make a colored mobile rotate by moving their heads in their cribs at home. Infants in the contingency mobile group clearly learned to make the head-moving response; whereas infants in a noncontingency mobile control group did not. The mothers in the contingency group reported that their infants showed obvious signs of enjoyment and interest in the task, manifesting a marked increase in smiling and cooing during the ten minutes per day in which they were exposed to the mobile. In other words, the experience of making the environment change is more rewarding to the infant then passively experiencing such changes. The mother's face is especially likely to become the focus of such interest because it is a stimulus capable of much variation in appearance that can to a large degree be brought under control of the infant's responses.

Sometimes infants who have been severely deprived of maternal stimulation even though the mother is physically present in the home show such marked apathy, withdrawal, and even physical retardation that they are referred to as showing a failure-to-thrive syndrome, similar in many respects to the reaction shown by some infants removed from their mothers and placed in impersonal institutions (Spitz, 1945). Ramey et al. (1972) used a form of contingent stimulation which they called *synchronous reinforce-*

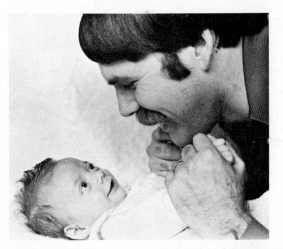

Infants show delight when they can produce changes in the environment. Interactive games between parent and infant may be important in providing the infant with stimulation that is contingent on the infant's behavior.

ment to modify vocal responses in two infants of this kind. Any vocalization by the infant would simultaneously produce a brightly colored geometric figure. As this procedure increased the amount of vocalizing, these generally withdrawn and apathetic infants began to show more normal responsiveness to the environment outside of the experimental situation. One infant showed a 21-point increase on the Cattell Infant Intelligence Scale.[1] These results are consistent with the hypothesis that a lack of contingent maternal stimulation produces the failure-to-thrive syndrome and that any contingent reinforcement experience, even using inanimate stimuli, can begin to reverse this process.

Lack of contingent responses from the environment, you may recall, is responsible for producing learned helplessness according to Seligman (1975). The findings of Watson and Ramey (1972) and Ramey et al. (1972) provide additional support for the idea that learned helplessness is important in the development of psychopathology.

Research has by no means clarified all the circumstances under which things may go wrong in the developing attachment-exploratory system in the first year or two of life. It seems safe to conclude, however, that some minimal level of stimulation is necessary and that some reasonable proportion of this stimulation should be contingent so that the infant learns to manipulate the environment and experience the joy of doing so. These may be the conditions that permit the infant to develop a "basic trust," as Erik Erikson (1963) would say, in the dependability and general benevolence of other people. Mothers, or primary caretakers, who respond positively to the infant's signals, play a crucial role in this aspect of infant development. This characteristic is probably an important component of what is usually called maternal warmth.

EFFECTS OF FORCED SEPARATION

So far we have seen how attachment and exploration develop in the intact mother-child relationship. Forced separations of children from their mothers or families can have drastic effects on the children's

[1]Measures of infant intelligence obtained before the age of 15 months show relatively little relationship to measures of intelligence obtained at older ages.

development, depending upon how long the separation lasts, the age at separation, and the circumstances in which the children find themselves.

Spitz (1945) reported extensive and long-lasting effects for infants placed in foundling homes at birth. Observing the children during the first year of life and after an interval of two years, he noted severe retardation in both physical and mental development as well as the apathy and unresponsiveness characteristic of depression in older persons. Not only was the development of normal attachment-exploratory behavior interfered with, but there was a generalized impairment in almost all aspects of the infant's behavior. This foundling home made few, if any, provisions for social or nonsocial stimulation, contingent or otherwise; the sides of the babies' cribs were frequently covered with blankets, no toys were provided, there was little auditory stimulation, and the children were rarely handled. They spent most of their time staring at a blank ceiling.

Goldfarb (1943, 1945) compared the later development of children reared in an institution for the first three years of their lives with children who had been brought up in foster homes since infancy. He selected children from four age groups, averaging about 3½, 6½, 8½, and 12 years. At all age levels, institution-reared children had lower scores on intelligence tests, were more aggressive (as evidenced by tantrums, lying, stealing, hitting other children, and destroying property), more demanding of attention from adults, and more distractible and hyperactive. These children also seemed generally incapable of forming strong, affectionate relationships with other people. Goldfarb concluded that the impersonal care and isolation of the institution had produced permanent psychological handicaps in the children.

Although the research studies conducted by Spitz and Goldfarb have methodological shortcomings, no subsequent evidence has cast doubt on the conclusion that severe deprivation during the first years of life can have devastating and possibly irreversible effects on the psychological development of children. One question that arises with respect to these studies involves sampling: To what population of infants or children can the results be generalized? Perhaps healthier children and children from middle- and upper-class backgrounds are more likely to be adopted or placed in foster homes than institutionalized. If that were the case, the infants left at the institution might

There is evidence that infants placed in impersonal institutions lacking in stimulation of any kind show severe psychological deficits (Spitz, 1945; Goldfarb, 1943).

from the outset have had more genetic or constitutional handicaps than the population at large. Subsequent deficits, then, could not be entirely attributed to institutionalization. Also, we should not be too quick to condemn all such child-care institutions. Modern foundling homes and orphanages are rarely so totally lacking in stimulation (in part because of the work of investigators like Spitz and Goldfarb), and thus the severe effects observed by these authors are not often seen.

The findings of Spitz and Goldfarb are similar to results obtained in carefully controlled laboratory studies of our primate cousin, the rhesus monkey. Harlow and Harlow (1969) separated infant monkeys from their mothers at birth and raised them in physical but not visual or auditory isolation. Several behaviors were characteristic of these monkeys during isolation: sucking of thumbs, fingers, toes, or penis; self-clutching; social indifference, that is, staring vacantly without response to ordinary stimulation such as calls or movements of other animals or activity of caretakers; stereotyped repetitive movements such as pacing back and forth; and self-directed aggression, such as biting their own hands, feet, or legs.

In a second study Harlow and Harlow (1969) found more and more severe impairments as they increased the duration of total social isolation from 3 to 6 to 12 months. At age three the monkeys who had been isolated for 12 months avoided all social contacts when placed with other monkeys, showed essentially no play or sex behavior and engaged in no acts of aggression. Although generalizations from monkey to man should be made with caution, these results are strongly supportive of the less rigorous observations on human infants.

SEPARATION ANXIETY

Complementary tendencies toward attachment and exploration are not limited to infancy; conceived more broadly as the balance between strivings for dependence and independence, they endure throughout life. Most of us have known adults who are handicapped by strong dependency needs; they seemingly cannot get along in life without continuing reassurance and support from others, they seek help on the most trivial matters, and frequently cannot assert their own interests for fear of alienating those they depend on. One of the disorders listed in DSM-III is Dependent Personality Disorder. We have already seen that some infants in the first year of life show signs of strong dependency in the form of overattachment to their mothers, and Ainsworth's research (see Research Report 20-1) suggested that one contributing factor to overattachment was a

 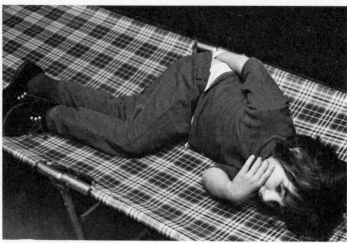

(Left) Monkey reared in isolation shows severe impairments in social, sex, and play behavior (Harlow & Harlow, 1969). **(Right)** The human child rarely experiences the degree of social isolation given to this rhesus monkey, but it seems likely that lesser degrees of deprivation would also produce some adverse effects.

mother-infant interaction in which the mother inconsistently rewarded and punished the infant's dependency behavior. Sears, Maccoby, and Levin (1957) found the same relationship for five-year-old children; mothers who were both rewarding and highly punishing of dependent behavior were more likely to have overly dependent children.

Even when punishment for dependency is low, excessive rewarding of this behavior in the form of overprotectiveness seems to promote it. In one study, Kagan and Moss (1962) found an index of maternal overprotectiveness (based on rewarding of dependent overtures, active encouragement of the child to be dependent on her, and overconcern about illness and dangers) was associated with dependency and passivity in children aged three to six.

When young children become strongly dependent upon an adult, they are likely to show great distress when forced to separate from this adult. An acute form of this distress is called *separation anxiety.* Eisenberg's (1958) study of 11 children attending a nursery school for emotionally disturbed children illustrates the unusual intensity of the parent-child bond when separation anxiety is strong. Mothers and children were directly observed during the early phases of nursery school attendance. At first the children remained close to their mothers; then they began to oscillate toward and away from the attraction

of the play area. As the children began to look less at their mothers and move away, the mothers would take a seat closer to their children and occasionally use a pretext of wiping the nose or checking toilet needs for intruding into the children's activity; separation was as difficult for the mothers as for the children. Resistance to separation was also shown by mothers required to move to an adjacent room as part of the program for reducing the mutual separation anxiety.

Interviews with the mothers indicated that in most cases they had treated their children with apprehensive oversolicitude during infancy. The babies were not entrusted to sitters outside the immediate family; later they were constantly warned of hazards if they ventured away from the home. The circumstances in the mothers' lives that led to this behavior were varied. For some the child was a late arrival after many sterile years. Some saw the child in terms of their own unhappy childhood and wished to protect the child from similar experiences. Others were frustrated in their marriage relationship and turned to their children for a secure relationship. Many mothers experienced angry feelings toward the child, displaced perhaps from an unhappy marriage or, paradoxically, from being tied down so much by the child. When the mothers occasionally became aware of this anger or impulsively expressed it toward the child, they would compensate by being protective, tightening the bond even further. Note the similarity of these findings to those of Ainsworth who found that mothers of overly attached infants have inconsistently rewarded and punished the infants' dependency behaviors. Another feature of the behavior of Ainsworth's overattached infants that is similar to clinical descriptions of older children with separation anxiety is that their interactions with the mothers were frequently accompanied by angry, contact-resisting behaviors despite the fact that they were strongly inclined to be near their mothers. Several investigators have reported that a substantial number of children with separation anxiety express fears of harm befalling their mother when separated from her (for example, Garvey & Hegrenes, 1966; Hersov, 1960). A psychodynamic interpretation might be that the child's anger at the mother stimulates fantasies of maternal harm, which in turn arouse fear that the fantasies might come true.

The observed relationship between parental overprotection and separation anxiety still leaves unanswered the question of how the fear response becomes associated with separation. One way that both human children and animals master fear in new situations is by repeatedly approaching and withdrawing from the feared object. The repeated arousal of the fear response in small, controlled doses leads eventually to the mastery, or extinction, of the fear. Rather than learning to master fear actively in this way, the overprotected child may learn instead to turn too quickly to mother for safety in the face of new situations, bodily hurts, and teasing by other children. The child eventually learns to coerce the mother into providing "mothering" at the onset of any disturbing situation by emitting the first signs of distress—a whimper, a few tears, or a yell. The result is a tightly interlocked system in which the mother reinforces the child for staying near her by providing comfort, while the child reinforces the mother for providing this comfort by ceasing to emit signs of distress. When children in such a system experience a major separation involving a new situation with many unknowns, such as entry into nursery school, they may be overwhelmed with fear.

Research has not followed all the details of this hypothetical process longitudinally from infancy to nursery school. Traits of temperament, such as the slow-to-warm-up personality shown by Michael

Some children experience intense separation anxiety when they first go to school.

(Chapter 5), also may contribute to a close parent-child bond and possible separation anxieties even when the parent is not particularly overprotective.

School Phobia

DEVELOPMENT

Sometimes children, usually in elementary or junior high school, develop intense anxiety about going to school and resist all efforts to get them to attend. In many cases this may reflect a continuing problem of overattachment to a parent with accompanying separation anxiety. For example, Waldron et al. (1975) compared ratings of family characteristics made from case history files of 35 school phobic children with families of 35 children showing other neurotic symptoms. Mothers of school phobic children were rated more often as having difficulty separating from their child (74 percent vs. 32 percent); both fathers and mothers of school phobic children were rated more often as resenting their child's demands (73 percent vs. 47 percent); and the mothers of school phobic children were more often rated as saying that the relationship with their child was more important than their relationship with their husband. Once again we see maternal ambivalence, the overprotective behavior combined with resentment against the child. Waldron et al. also found that unusual stress (for example, serious physical illness or injury to another family member; absence of a parent or depression in a parent) occurred more often in the year before referral in the families of the school phobic children (46 percent vs. 17 percent).

Other authors, however (for example, Ross, 1980), suggest that in some instances the school phobic reaction results primarily from traumatic experiences at school. The child may be ridiculed by classmates, receive a low grade on a test, be threatened or beaten by other pupils, or have a scolding, uncongenial teacher.

Although the onset of the school phobia reaction may seem abrupt to teachers and parents, usually the child has been unhappy at school for some time, and some new stress precipitates the more acute reaction. Children are generally aware that their parents, and for that matter the whole world, expect them to go to school, so they are reluctant to raise the question of not going to school until their discomfort reaches overwhelming proportions. Children frequently develop physical symptoms that provide a more acceptable reason for not going to school than unreasonable fears. They get headaches, vomit, or generally feel ill. As the reaction becomes more acute, they begin to resist all efforts to get them to go to school; they may become violently ill, cry, kick, scream, or even faint. School phobia, then, can be an extremely disrupting reaction that immediately brings children into a head-on conflict not only with their immediate family but (from a child's view) with most of the outside world.

Billy: Possible Causes of School Phobia

When Billy was subsequently seen at a clinic, he was described by his parents as having been a submissive, somewhat tense, and perfectionistic child, who had a history of physical illnesses and allergies. The mother felt that these illnesses might have caused her to be especially nurturant and perhaps overprotective with Billy. He had recently transferred to a large, new junior high school and his grades had begun to drop from As and Bs to Cs and Ds. And although his relationships with peers had always been good in his former schools, in the new school some of the students apparently taunted him because of his academic difficulties and sickly physical appearance. (Smith & Sharpe, 1970)

TREATMENT

Psychodynamic approaches to treatment emphasize working through the unresolved dependency relationship between mother and child, and firmly but gradually insisting on the return of the child to school. More behaviorally oriented therapists sometimes use a real-life approach in which the therapist accompanies the child through a gradual series of steps that progressively approach full participation at school.

Kennedy (1965) reported 100 percent success in treating 50 school phobic children with a procedure that might best be described as *in vivo* flooding. Parents and school personnel were asked to see to it firmly that the child did attend school no matter how upset the child became. The therapist created a strong expectation in the parents and the child that this would work and that the child would get over the fear. At the end of each day the child was praised for any progress. After only three days all children were back in school and follow-up telephone calls to parents several years later revealed no relapses. Kennedy emphasizes that the children seen in this study were limited to those in whom school phobia was the only psychological symptom. Children whose refusal to go to school was part of a larger pattern of relatively severe disturbance were not included, and Kennedy's approach might well be less effective for such children.

Hyperactivity

> Tom was constantly in trouble as a young boy. He disappeared one day and was finally discovered, after a lengthy search, in the barn sitting on a collection of goose eggs that he seemed to be hopeful of hatching. On another occasion in a warehouse he tumbled into a great pile of wheat and was almost smothered before he could be got out. Once he held a skate-strap for another boy, who was trying to shorten it by means of an axe; the chief result was that Tom lost the tip of his finger. One of his more sensational adventures was the time he built a fire in a neighbor's barn, with the result that the barn burned up in a spectacular blaze and Tom subsequently received a public whipping from his father. Tom's behavior in the first grade was so obstreperous that his teacher called him "addled" and his mother withdrew him from school and tutored him herself. (Bryan, 1926)
>
> Winston's continual overactivity so infuriated his first governess that she resigned, angrily denouncing him as an incorrigible child. His first school was chosen by his mother for its good reputation and social prestige; but Winston resisted the sadistic headmaster's behavior stoutly, kicked the man's hat to pieces, and was withdrawn by his mother and sent to a school in Brighton run by two kindly old ladies. In this benign atmosphere, Winston was called the naughtiest small boy in England by his dancing teacher. He was frequently permitted to leave the classroom and run about in the schoolyard to release his exuberant energies. He did not want to study Latin or Greek there, or mathematics, and he was not coerced. (Goertzel & Goertzel, 1962, pp. 264–265)

Tom, as you may have recognized, was Thomas Alva Edison and Winston was Winston Churchill. These two difficult boys might well have been labeled *hyperactive* and possibly considered by some as suffering from *minimal brain dysfunction* had they encountered the teachers, psychologists, and psychiatrists of today. Their family pediatrician might even have prescribed drugs to calm these energetic boys down and help them profit from their respective school systems.

Central to the *hyperactivity syndrome* (sometimes called *hyperkinetic disorder*) is a high level of bodily activity. The hyperactive child cannot sit still, fidgets, wriggles, and is constantly on the move from one place of interest to another. Other characteristics frequently associated with this syndrome are short attention span, distractibility, poor muscular coordination, and low frustration tolerance. In DSM-III (see Table 20-1) the label hyperactivity has been replaced by the term *attention deficit disorder with hyperactivity*, thus giving more emphasis to the features of short attention span and distractibility. These behavioral features are illustrated in the findings of Stewart et al. (1966) who compared a sample of 37 hyperactive children with a sample of 37 control children; see Table 20-2. The ratings were based on interviews with parents, medical histories, and school records. Interestingly enough, in another study when hyperactive preschool children were observed in a free-play situation they were indistinguishable from normal children in activity level (Schleifer et al., 1975). However, when the children were required to remain seated

TABLE 20-2 Percentage of Occurrence of Behavioral Symptoms in Hyperactive and Control Children

Behavior	Hyperactive (n = 37)	Control (n = 37)
Overactive	100	37
Can't sit still	81	8
Fidgets	84	30
Leaves class without permission	35	0
Can't accept correction	35	0
Temper tantrums	51	0
Fights	59	3
Defiant	49	0
Doesn't complete project	84	0
Doesn't stay with games	78	3
Doesn't listen to whole story	49	0
Moves from one activity to another in class	46	6
Doesn't follow directions	62	3
Hard to get to bed	49	3
Unpopular with peers	46	0
Talks too much	68	20
Wears out toys, furniture, etc.	68	8
Gets into things	54	11
Unpredictable	59	3
Destructive	41	0
Unresponsive to discipline	57	0
Lies	43	3

NOTE: There are 32 boys and 5 girls in each group.
These data were taken from M. A. Stewart, F. N. Pitts, A. G. Craig, & W. Dieruf, The hyperactive child syndrome. *American Journal of Orthopsychiatry*, 1966, *36*, 861–867. Copyright 1966, The American Orthopsychiatric Association, Inc. Reproduced by permission.

and participate in activities structured by the teacher, the hyperactive children were out of their chairs more, left the table more, and were more aggressive than the control children. It would appear that so-called hyperactive behavior is most noticeable in situations, such as a school classroom, requiring the inhibition of irrelevant behavior.

PREVALENCE

In the surveys of problem behavior reported at the beginning of the chapter, mothers of nearly half of the children described their youngsters as overactive, and kindergarten teachers reported that about 38 percent of their boys were hyperactive. It is unlikely that many of these children would be considered abnormal by usual clinical standards, but apparently parents and teachers view high levels of activity as a

problem, making their job of caring for or teaching children more difficult. Results of studies in which *both* teachers and psychiatrists have collaborated in evaluating activity level have indicated that from 4 to 10 percent of the children are rated as overactive (for example, Gorin & Kramer, 1973; Miller et al., 1973). Three to four times as many boys as girls are labeled hyperactive.

ONE SYNDROME OR SEVERAL?

There are many examples in the field of abnormal psychology of particular diagnostic labels that become faddish. Hyperactivity is one of these. For example, journal articles on the topic of hyperactivity increased dramatically as shown in Figure 20-1 from the early 1950s to the early 1970s. Did more children actually become hyperactive over this time period or

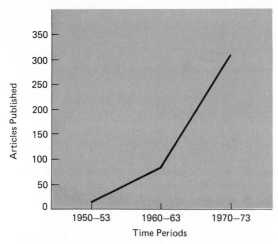

FIGURE 20-1. Number of articles published on the topic of hyperactivity during three time periods. Drawn from data given by Winchell (1975).

did professionals simply begin to apply the term to a broader and broader range of children? We cannot say for sure. The answer may well be some of both.

Despite the widespread popularity of the hyperactivity diagnosis there is a growing body of evidence suggesting that this term has been used in an overly loose fashion to refer to several patterns of child behavior that may have quite different causes. For example, Werry (1968) intercorrelated measures derived from a psychiatric examination, neurological examination, brain wave records, medical records, and psychological tests on 103 children diagnosed as hyperactive. There was little relationship between measures obtained from these different sources. In a similar study, Routh and Roberts (1972) also found little relationship between teacher ratings of hyperactivity and measures obtained from diagnostic procedures in the clinic. More recently, however, Loney et al. (1978), using ratings based only on materials in clinical records, found that a dimension of hyperactivity seems to exist independently of a dimension of aggressiveness and that these two dimensions did show some appropriate correlations with teacher and parent ratings. More on this study later. A handy label such as hyperactivity can lead us to believe that it is one disorder with one kind of cause. The results of these and other studies suggest caution in accepting this conclusion.

DEVELOPMENT

Heredity. Evidence from twin studies suggests that variation over the normal range of activity levels is affected by genetic makeup (Torgersen, 1973; Willerman, 1973). For those cases in which the hyperactivity represents an extreme position on the distribution of activity levels in the general population then heredity would seem to play an important role. It would be premature, however, to assume that all instances of diagnosed hyperactivity simply represent an extreme of a normal trait of temperament. Perhaps more relevant to the clinical syndrome of hyperactivity are studies by Morrison and Stewart (1971) and Cantwell (1972) in which a higher percentage of the biological parents of adopted children diagnosed as hyperactive reported being hyperactive themselves as children than was true for adoptive parents of hyperactive children. The adopted hyperactive children had had no contact with their biological parents since birth. These studies indicate that genetic predispositions may contribute to some cases of hyperactivity.

Minimal Brain Dysfunction. Early investigators of hyperactivity thought it resulted from damage to the

Hyperactive children are constantly on the go.

developing brain, especially from encephalitis (an infection of the central nervous system) or injuries associated with birth, including anoxia (deprivation of oxygen) (Rosenfeld & Bradley, 1948; Strecker & Ebaugh, 1924). Subsequent research has failed to demonstrate so clear-cut an etiology but does continue to show a weak, if somewhat elusive relationship to possible brain malfunctioning. Children with known brain damage are not generally found to be more hyperactive than control children (Werry & Sprague, 1970). On the other hand, when samples of hyperactive children are examined, they are frequently found to have experienced a somewhat higher number of events that might have caused brain damage and to show a higher frequency of "soft" neurological signs: brain wave abnormalities, poor fine-motor coordination, impaired visual-motor coordination, poor balance, clumsiness, and incoordination of the eyeballs (Werry, 1979). "Soft" refers to the fact that signs of this kind occur fairly often with no other "hard" evidence of brain damage; they do not necessarily reflect a clear-cut brain disorder. Moreover, much overlap exists between hyperactive and normal children on these measures, with many hyperactive children not even showing these "soft" indications of brain disorder. Also possibly suggestive of a biological etiology are the findings in two studies of a greater than normal incidence of minor physical anomalies (for example, widely spaced eyes, curved fifth finger, or furrowed tongue) present at birth in hyperactive children (Rapoport et al., 1974; Waldrop et al., 1968).

The possible relationship of brain damage to hyperactivity and associated perceptual-motor abnormalities has given rise to the concept of *minimal brain dysfunction*. This term has been criticized for being so loosely defined that almost any child who has a high activity level and associated academic difficulties can be given this label, which implies some kind of brain dysfunction when in fact the criteria for diagnosis are usually behavioral (hyperactivity, perceptual-motor impairment, and so on). *Learning disability* is another term sometimes used interchangeably with minimal brain dysfunction. This label is applied to children who experience difficulty in mastering one or more academic subjects such as reading or arithmetic, and for whom the disability cannot be explained in terms of low intelligence, obvious brain damage, or emotional maladjustment. This

concept has also been criticized for being overly loose in definition and implying brain dysfunction on the basis of behavioral data. Despite problems and abuses associated with these concepts, it would be a mistake to ignore the possibility that some behavioral and learning problems of childhood are caused, in part, by brain dysfunctions too subtle to be measured by current techniques.

There is evidence that some cases of hyperactivity may result from the ingestion of lead in amounts too low to produce obvious symptoms of lead poisoning, usually caused by the eating of lead-pigment paints in deteriorating urban housing areas (David et al., 1972). Pihl and Parkes (1977) analyzed hair samples from 31 learning disabled children (not all of whom were necessarily hyperactive) and 22 normal children matched for socioeconomic status, and found significantly greater amounts of lead and cadmium in the hair of the learning disabled-children. Other biologically oriented theories have attributed hyperactivity to such diverse causes as food additives (Feingold, 1975), radiation from fluorescent lighting (Ott, 1974), and maternal smoking (Denson et al., 1975). More research is needed to see to what extent any of these factors might be related to some instances of hyperactivity.

Psychosocial Influences. There is little direct evidence for the role of social learning in the development of hyperactivity. However, as we will see in the next section, the fact that hyperactive behavior can be decreased through psychological intervention suggests that, at least in part, it may have been learned in the first place. Hyperactive behaviors, in other words, may have been unwittingly reinforced by parents or others and perhaps modeled by parents since there is some indication that parents of hyperactive children were themselves often hyperactive as children. McNamara (1972) has suggested that environmental restraints frequently associated with inner city living may contribute to the prevalence of hyperactivity. The child who lives in an overcrowded home in a high-density slum, attends an overcrowded school, and has no green space or recreational outlet experiences a major restriction on physical activity. According to McNamara, the lack of an outlet for normal childhood activity results in the restlessness, distractibility, and academic indifference seen in so-called hyperactive children.

More likely, however, many cases of hyperactivity may reflect an interaction between biological dispositions and social learning experiences in much the same way that Michael's adjustment difficulties (Chapter 5) resulted from an interplay of a slow-to-warm-up temperament and environmental events. The young child may have a strong disposition toward a high activity level, either genetically determined or resulting from subtle brain dysfunction; parents may respond with impatience, unreasonable demands to be less active, arbitrary punishments, and in other ways that might further increase the activity level and associated aggressive or emotional outbursts. Finding difficulty in sitting still and paying attention, the child is likely to have trouble in school. In time, poor school performance and increasing friction with teachers makes the whole academic scene unpleasant; the child turns even more to disruptive classroom behavior in order to avoid the frustrating exercises in reading, writing, and arithmetic, and also perhaps to gain reinforcement in the form of attention from peers and even "negative" attention from teachers.

Consistent with this view are the results of a study by Loney et al. (1978), referred to briefly at the beginning of this section, in which a procedure called factor analysis was applied to ratings based on the clinical records of 135 boys who had been referred with a possible diagnosis of minimal brain damage or hyperkinesis. Two independent dimensions were found to account for the relationship among these ratings. The dimension called *Aggression* was the strongest, and ratings on delinquent acts, negative emotions, and aggressive interpersonal behavior were most highly related to this dimension. The second dimension, called *Hyperactivity*, was most closely associated with such ratings as excessive demand for teacher's attention, restless/overactive, and inattentive. Since the dimensions are independent, a high or low score on Hyperactivity was not necessarily associated with a high or low score on Aggression, at least within this select sample. Lahey et al. (1978) found similar results and also some indication that a dimension of learning disability might be distinguished from both Aggression and Hyperactivity.

Loney and his associates suggest that their results provide a basis for separating behavioral characteristics into primary and secondary symptoms of the hyperkinetic syndrome. The primary or core symptoms would be those associated with the Hyperactivity dimension, such as being restless, overactive, and inattentive. The symptoms of aggressiveness are thought to develop secondarily, frequently as a result of interactions with parents, teachers, and peers. Consistent with this interpretation the authors found that parental attitudes of hostility toward the child and lax discipline correlated with the Aggression dimension but not with the Hyperactivity dimension. And, perhaps of special significance, positive response to medication was associated with high scores on the Hyperactivity dimension but not with high scores on the Aggression dimension.

In conclusion, it seems unlikely that all children labeled hyperactive show exactly the same pattern of behavior or symptoms and even more unlikely that there is *one* underlying cause for this behavioral pattern. As so often happens with a vaguely defined symptom pattern with uncertain etiology becomes a popular label, theories of causation multiply and new discoveries of the "true" cause abound, usually associated with new forms of treatment promising to "cure" the hitherto difficult-to-treat disorder.

TREATMENT

Some early reports suggested that hyperactivity tends to decrease with age with or without treatment (Cromwell et al., 1961; Schulman et al., 1965). However, more recent research has not yielded such an optimistic view. Huessy et al. (1974) studied 84 hyperactive children who had been placed on medication eight to ten years earlier, and found these children to be seriously at risk for academic, emotional, and social problems in later life. The dropout rate from school was five times higher than expected. One-third of those who had jobs had a poor work record, and many were in trouble with the law. These more pessimistic findings about the long-term outcome of childhood hyperactivity add importance to the search for an effective treatment.

Stimulant Drugs. Curiously enough, central nervous system stimulants (methylphenidate, which goes by the trade name of Ritalin, and dextroamphetamine are the most commonly used) have been found to be useful in treating hyperactivity. Based on a survey of 31 studies Barkley (1977) found that on the av-

Sometimes hyperactive children engage in an excessive amount of attention-seeking behavior.

erage 75 percent of hyperactive children given stimulant drugs showed improvement. The remaining 25 percent were either unchanged or worse. The average response to placebos in eight studies was 39 percent improvement. Improvement is reflected primarily in less classroom restlessness and increased attention span. Stimulant medication apparently has little effect on a child's activity level in an unstructured, free-field situation (for example, Ellis et al., 1974). Recall the previously mentioned study in which observers found hyperactive children (who were not medicated) to be indistinguishable from nonhyperactive children in a free-play situation (Schleifer et al., 1975). Fears that stimulant drugs will turn children into zombies would seem to be unfounded. There is substantial support, however, for the proposition that stimulant drugs decrease restlessness and task-irrelevant behavior in the classroom or other situations that make high demands for attention to a specific task (for example, Sprague et al., 1970).

Sprague and Sleator (1977) showed that different target behaviors are affected differently by variations in dose levels. They found that children's learning on a laboratory task showed optimal improvement at a moderate dose level, whereas teacher ratings of social behavior showed most improvement at a higher level (see Figure 20-2). Physicians frequently recommend doses higher than the highest level used in this study, which according to these data would be much higher than is optimal for learning. Children who respond least favorably to medication are more likely to have problems with peers and negative attitudes to school and authority figures (Hoffman et al., 1974; Loney et al., 1978), a finding that suggests, as previously mentioned, that aggressive behavior may be separate from or secondary to the basic hyperactive syndrome.

Despite research that rather strongly supports the short-term improvement in attentional capacities, it is still not clear what the benefits may be for long-term academic achievement. Weiss et al. (1974) found that children who were given Ritalin over a three- to five-year period were more manageable at school and at home *while on drugs*. However, five years later, when no longer on drugs, they did no

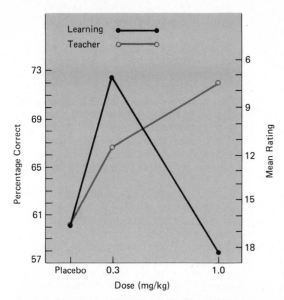

FIGURE 20-2. The effects on learning (left-hand ordinate) and on teacher ratings of undesirable social behavior (right-hand ordinate) as a function of placebo and two levels of Ritalin dosage. Smaller numbers on the teacher's ratings represent improved social behavior. From Sprague and Sleator (1977) Copyright by American Association for the Advancement of Science and used with permission.

better than a matched hyperactive group that had not been given medication on measures of emotional adjustment and number of grades failed. Nor did Rie et al. (1976) find greater scholastic improvement in children with learning disabilities who were given Ritalin than in similar children given a placebo, despite the fact that children on Ritalin showed greater reduction in activity level and increased attentional capacities.

And what about side effects? Apparently, few children show serious, immediate side effects. If the drug is taken in the afternoon, though, they may have trouble sleeping at night. Some children show decreased appetite and irritability. There is some indication that physical growth may be temporarily retarded in children maintained on methylphenidate (Satterfield et al., 1979). The adverse effect on growth was relatively small and occurred only in the first year. This first-year deficit was offset by greater than expected growth in the second year.

Despite the proven effectiveness of drugs in reducing some forms of hyperactivity, they should be used with caution. Drugs are sometimes prescribed too readily for controlling behaviors that are only loosely related to the hyperactivity syndrome. Aggressive, rebellious behavior in itself is not a necessary part of hyperactivity; in all likelihood it derives from a somewhat different set of social learning experiences (see Chapter 22). Likewise, restlessness and inattention may result from hunger, an overcrowded classroom, or an intelligence level too low to benefit from academic instruction. The uncritical use of drugs to make children behave the way we want them to is a prospect that appeals to few of us. On the other hand, the judicious use of drugs in carefully followed cases may be beneficial. Many clinicians prefer not to rely on drugs alone for treatment under any circumstances. They would rather combine drugs with psychological intervention in the hope that in time the drugs can be withdrawn.

Psychological Approaches. Little research has been done on the effectiveness of psychotherapy alone in treating hyperactivity. In one study Eisenberg et al. (1961) found short-term psychotherapy to be of little value. A variety of behavioral approaches have been found to show immediate effectiveness in reducing hyperactivity, but long-term follow-ups are still lacking (Ross & Ross, 1976). These behavioral programs usually provide positive reinforcement for on-task behavior and either ignore or use Time-Out (usually involves about 5 minutes in a room without other people, toys or interesting activities) for off-task or disruptive behavior. The inclusion of parents in these programs would seem to be especially important as a way of maintaining long-term gains. See Research Report 20-2 for a description of two behavioral programs.

Stuttering

Stuttering is a disturbance in speech typically characterized by blocks, numerous repetitions of words or syllables, and prolongations of speech sounds. Approximately 1 percent of all children are persistent stutterers, and another 4 to 5 percent show transitory stuttering when young but outgrow it in time. Stut-

Behavioral Intervention Decreases Hyperactivity

Behavioral interventions in the classroom have been found to be effective in reducing hyperactivity and improving academic performance in hyperactive children. Rosenbaum et al. (1975), for example, trained teachers to give reward cards (a colored card with a smiling face on it) to hyperactive children after each hour in which the child worked appropriately on academic assignments. Half the children were able to trade in their reward cards at the end of the day for individual payoffs in the form of candy; the other half of the hyperactive children received the same individual payoff and in addition the rest of the class also received the same number of pieces of candy. Both conditions resulted in a significant decrease in hyperactive behavior that was maintained at a one-month follow up, with the whole classroom reward condition showing the most improvement.

In another study O'Leary et al. (1976) included the parents in a program that had five components: (1) specification of each child's daily classroom goals, (2) praising the child for efforts to achieve those goals, (3) end-of-day evaluation of the child's behavior relevant to the specified goals, (4) sending the parents a daily report card on their child's progress, and (5) rewarding of the child by the parent for progress toward the specified goals. Selection of appropriate rewards for the individual child is a key feature in programs of this kind. Some examples of rewards provided by the parents were: an extra 30 minutes of television, a special dessert, spending time with either parent playing a game such as checkers, and money to spend. In addition to the daily rewards they were given weekly rewards when four out of five daily report cards showed improvement. These rewards consisted of such things as a fishing trip with father, a dinner at a favorite aunt's, and a family meal at a "fast-food" restaurant.

None of the hyperactive children in the study was currently on drugs. As can be seen in Figure 20-3, there was a sharp drop in problem behaviors for children receiving this program in contrast to a control group of similar children who did not receive the treatment.

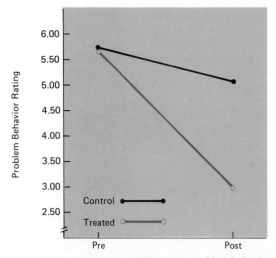

FIGURE 20-3. Comparison of the mean problem behavior ratings of nine hyperkinetic children treated with behavior therapy, and of eight similar controls. From O'Leary, Pelham, Rosenbaum and Price (1976). Copyright by J. B. Lippincott and used with permission.

tering almost always starts before the age of eight and, for reasons as yet unclear, occurs at least three times more frequently in boys than girls.

Although we may take normal speech for granted, it is an exceedingly complicated skill involving the delicate coordination of voluntary and involuntary neuromuscular systems. It is hardly surprising that things can go wrong in the complex developmental sequences involved in the mastery of this task, and indeed almost all young children show some signs of speech disturbance in the course of learning to talk.

DEVELOPMENT

As was the case for hyperactivity, theories of stuttering abound, and as yet there is no generally accepted explanation for this disorder. Biologically oriented theories hold that physical malfunction of the speech system plays a primary role in causing stuttering. The fact that stuttering is more common in the relatives of stutterers is consistent with the possibility of some genetic predisposition. It is equally consistent, however, with the possibility that the stutterer learns by imitation or otherwise from other stutterers in the environment. The fact that stuttering is so much more common in boys also suggests that a sex-linked genetic difference may exist in some aspect of the muscular or neurological systems involved in speech.

Another biologically oriented theory of stuttering is that weak *cerebral dominance* plays a role. Most people have strong dominance in the left hemisphere, associated with being right-handed. The evidence for an association between stuttering and right hemisphere dominance (usually involving left-handedness) is conflicting (Beech & Fransella, 1968); weak dominance, that is, not clear dominance of either hemisphere, appears to be somewhat more consistently related to stuttering (Wada & Rasmussen, 1960). The notion that forcing left-handed children to become right-handed will cause stuttering has not been clearly borne out by research (Jones, 1970).

Psychologically oriented theories have tended to emphasize factors that create anxiety or concern about speaking properly (Bloodstein, 1975; Johnson, 1959; Sheehan, 1975). Johnson, for example, proposed that almost all children show some disturbances in the course of learning to talk and that the critical factor is how parents react to these normal stammers. If parents, alarmed that their child's speech is not developing correctly, criticize or exert excessive pressure, then the child is likely to become anxious about speaking, be hesitant and unsure in vocalizations, and eventually show the more extreme and persistent symptoms of stuttering. It is difficult to separate cause from effect, but there is considerable evidence that parents of stutterers do show overconcern about speech at a relatively early age (Beech & Fransella, 1968; Bloodstein, 1975). Somewhat inconsistent with Johnson's emphasis on normal disfluencies is evidence that difficulties in articulation or delayed speech development are present to a greater than usual degree in young stutterers before they develop the stuttering symptom (Bloodstein, 1975). Thus the combination of some difficulty or slowness in speech development with excessive parental concerns and pressures might be especially conducive to the de-

velopment of tensions and fears about proper speech. These fears could produce disturbances in speech, which in turn could eventually lead to stuttering.

Consistent with an anxiety or tension theory Lanyon (1978) suggests that the stuttering act is preceded and accompanied by a physical struggle to speak—involving excessive muscle tension, especially in speech-related areas—plus breathing irregularities and a variety of extraneous body movements. According to Lanyon, the stuttered word appears to be the end point of a chain of events, of which the initial event appears to be the perception that a disruption in fluency is about to occur. This perception has become conditioned to elicit the physical struggle that eventuates in the stuttered response. More on this theory when we consider treatment.

Psychodynamic theories tend to emphasize the symbolic meaning of stuttering—as, for example, in the view of one psychoanalytic scholar, Fenichel (1945), who suggests that stuttering stems from conflict around the expression of anal-sadistic impulses. Speaking has come to be associated with the utterance of obscene, especially anal, words and the expression of verbal aggression.

The same motives which in childhood were directed against pleasurable playing with feces make their appearance again in the form of inhibitions or prohibitions of the pleasure of playing with words. The expulsion and retention of feces, and actually the retention of words, just as previously the retention of feces, may either be the reassurance against possible loss or a pleasurable auto-erotic activity. One may speak in stuttering, of a displacement upwards of the functions of the anal sphincters . . . (pp. 311–312)

There is little convincing evidence for this theory as a general explanation of stuttering, nor is there any clear evidence that young stutterers as a group show a higher incidence of neurotic disturbance. Several studies, however, report higher levels of anxiety and hostility in older stutterers, findings that could reflect secondary reactions to the social consequences of stuttering just as well as primary causes (Beech & Fransella, 1968). Stuttering occasionally does occur in the context of more general psychopathology, and in these instances the likelihood that broader personality problems contribute to the disorder may be greater.

TREATMENT

My Friend, I now visit you for Nothing, but only to talk with you about the *Infirmity* in your *Speech,* and offer you my Advice about it; because I suppose tis a Thing that greatly troubles you. What I advise you do, is, to seek a Cure for it, in the Method of *Deliberation.* Did you ever know any one *stammer* in singing of the *Psalms?*

While you go to *snatch* at Words, and are too *quick* at bringing of them out, you'll be *stop'd* a thousand Times in a Day. But first use yourself to a very *deliberate* Way of *Speaking;* a *Drawling* that shall be little short of *Singing.* Even this *Drawling* will be better than *Stammering;* especially if what you speak, be well worth out waiting for. (Bormann, 1969, pp. 459–460)

The above advice was given to Cotton Mather, the prominent Puritan minister, who stuttered so severely that he began studying medicine rather than preparing for the ministry, which was his primary aim. This advice, at least according to Mather, was most helpful to him in overcoming this handicap.

Half or more of the individuals who begin to stutter will recover with little or no professional help (Wingate, 1976). This is especially true for the younger child. For stutterers who have sought treatment, psychotherapy alone has not been found to be particularly effective. Many speech therapists use a combination of psychotherapy or counseling and more specific techniques that focus on the stuttering response itself. The personal counseling part of the treatment program is aimed at helping the person overcome anxiety and improve self-esteem. Whether primary or secondary from a causative standpoint, stutterers are likely to be apprehensive in situations requiring speech and to have developed feelings of inadequacy by the time they seek help.

Stutterers themselves are usually aware of circumstances in which their disfluency disappears or is greatly diminished. Bloodstein (1949), for example, found that at least 90 percent of the stutterers sampled reported substantial reduction in stuttering when:

Reading in chorus (that is, group reading)
Speaking to an animal or to an infant
Singing
Swearing
Speaking to a rhythmic swing of the arm or foot tapping

Stuttering is frequently eliminated if a person's speech is played back through earphones with about a one-tenth of a second delay. The improvement, however, is not maintained after leaving the delayed feedback situation.

Imitating a regional or foreign dialect
Feeling calm and relaxed

A number of techniques, some similar to those reported above by stutterers, have been shown in more systematic research to have an immediate and sometimes dramatic effect in reducing stuttering. The problem has been in getting the improved speech to generalize to more normal ways of speaking outside of the clinic.

One example of a technique that has been found consistently to produce an immediate reduction in stuttering is *delayed auditory feedback.* When nonstutterers talk while hearing their own speech played back through earphones with about a one-tenth-second delay, they tend to show marked disruptions in speech similar to stuttering. Paradoxically, when a stutterer's speech is delayed in this fashion, the stuttering is almost completely suppressed. Another example is *rhythmic cuing,* in which the person is asked to speak in a rhythmical, singsong fashion, usually with the aid of a metronome. Wingate (1976) has suggested that the important common factor in these and other procedures found to reduce stuttering is a slowing down of speech that permits a deliberate substitution of a nonstuttered utterance.

Researchers have recently begun to focus on the

problem of the transfer of fluent speech to normal speaking situations and the withdrawal of "gimmicks" such as delayed feedback and rhythmic cuing. The basic idea is that with sufficient practice the person can learn to substitute the nonstuttered response without the aid of some external slowing-down procedure. Ryan and Van Kirk (1974), for example, used delay of auditory feedback as the initial step to reduce stuttering and then phased out the delayed feedback procedure while giving intensive practice in speaking in a variety of situations (classroom, home, telephone, to strangers, and so on). This was followed by a maintenance program in which regular checks were made to see how well the person was maintaining fluent speech. Although there was no control group in this study, almost all individuals showed a marked decrease in stuttering that transferred to other situations and was being successfully maintained at the time of the report. Lanyon (1978) devised a treatment for stuttering based on his theory that muscle tension and struggle responses play a key role in this disorder. Four stutterers were taught to relax muscle tension associated with speaking and were given practice in a variety of situations. At an 18-month follow-up they continued to show a substantial reduction in disfluent speech. It is hoped that the effectiveness of this procedure will be assessed on a larger sample of stutterers.

Functional Enuresis

Functional enuresis is chronic bedwetting in children beyond the age by which bladder control would ordinarily have been acquired and for which no organic cause can be found. Estimates suggest that over 85 percent of children have stopped wetting their beds by 4½ years of age, 90 percent by 7½ years of age, and 99 percent by adulthood (Pierce, 1967). Enuretic boys outnumber enuretic girls by two to one.

Although few consider enuresis in itself to represent a serious disorder, from the perspective of the young child it can be a source of intense psychological discomfort—the jeers and taunts of unsympathetic peers and the obvious irritation of parents and others who have to cope with soiled bedding. The older child begins to avoid certain activities, such as sleeping at a friend's house, because of the potential embarrassment.

DEVELOPMENT

Since a specific physical basis for enuresis is found in no more than 10 percent of the cases, most investigators have turned to psychological theories in their attempt to understand this disorder. Psychodynamic theorists look for the meaning of the symptom in terms of intrapsychic conflicts that have their origins in disturbed family relationships. Wetting the bed may be seen, for example, as an unconscious expression of hostility toward a parent, a stubborn refusal to accommodate the parent's demand for more age-appropriate behavior, or a wish to remain infantile.

From a behavioral or social learning point of view enuresis reflects faulty learning. For the young infant urination is an automatic reflex response to a distended bladder. Most children as they grow older, usually with some formal or informal tutelage from their parents, learn to inhibit this reflexive response, even while sleeping, and learn to make the response at the right time and place. The enuretic child, for some reason, has difficulty in achieving this control. Perhaps, for as yet undetermined physiological reasons, it is simply more difficult for some children to delay urination, so that learning is less easy, or perhaps conditions are sometimes not favorable for learning the requisite responses.

The data seem to support the behavioral view more than the psychodynamic view. If enuresis were a symptom of more pervasive underlying psychological disturbance, we would expect enuretic children (relative to children as a whole) to show a greater incidence of other signs of emotional disorder as well as to come from more disturbed family backgrounds. Neither of these associations was found in a study of 3440 children (Cullen, 1966). In adult enuretics, on the other hand, there is evidence for more general psychological disturbance (Blackman & Goldstein, 1965). Also lending support to a behavioral interpretation is the fact that a conditioning procedure that totally ignores psychodynamic processes is relatively effective in the treatment of enuresis, whereas psychotherapy is relatively ineffective. Nor do other symptoms tend to replace the enuresis (symptom substitution) following the conditioning treatment as psychodynamically oriented clinicians suggested they might. In fact, other changes associated with successful symptom removal are positive in almost all cases (Baller & Schalock, 1956; Lovibond & Coote, 1970). The child is rid of an embarrassing habit likely to have evoked considerable ridicule and teasing, so self-esteem and general happiness may increase.

TREATMENT

Let us look closely at the conditioning procedure used to treat enuresis and at some of the research on its effectiveness. The procedure itself is quite simple. The child sleeps on a pad that, when moistened by urine, completes an electric circuit, causing a bell to sound, awakening the child. Although the treatment was originally based on the classical conditioning model, an operant interpretation is probably just as reasonable. The child upon awakening has a chance to practice urinary control in the presence of stimuli associated with bladder distension so that in time these stimuli become conditioned to the bladder control responses or the bladder control responses become operantly learned. A number of studies have shown this approach to be effective when administered by parents or older children themselves *under careful professional monitoring* (Lovibond & Coote, 1970). However, relapse rates have been found to be fairly high with about 35 percent of the children returning to bedwetting. Azrin and Thienes (1978) have developed a procedure that omits the conditioning apparatus and includes training in rapid awakening, practice in and reinforcement for withholding urine, practice in correct toileting, and increased social motivation to be nonenuretic. They found an intensive one-day training session to be more effective and show fewer relapses than the conditioning procedure. Bollard and Woodroffe (1977) found similar positive results when using parents to conduct the procedure rather than trained professionals.

Anorexia Nervosa

In *anorexia nervosa* eating is reduced to a point where severe weight loss occurs. This disorder may be as much as ten times more frequent in females than males and develops usually between the ages of 12 and 18 years. In severe cases death by starvation may occur.

Some adolescent girls with this disorder seem obsessed by fear of gaining weight and begin the process of starting diets of one kind or another. They may also engage in prolonged exercise—extensive cycling or jogging, for example—despite increasing fatigue and weakness, and may deny that they are underweight. Social and sexual development is frequently retarded.

DEVELOPMENT

With respect to development psychoanalytic writers have proposed that anorectic individuals when faced with the anxiety-arousing prospect of genital sexuality at adolescence regress to already existing oral fixations. Denial of eating is thought to reflect denial of sexuality or, even more specifically, in some cases guilt over the unconscious wish to be impregnated through the mouth.

Family systems therapists have emphasized conflicts around issues of independence and changing from childhood to adult ways. Anorectic children are likely to appear in families that are excessively enmeshed, emotionally speaking, have overprotective parents, and lack effective ways of directly resolving conflicts. Thus the anorectic girl may be seen as asserting her independence in the only way she can, by refusing to eat. Recall the case of Laura in Chapter 12.

Crisp et al. (1974), in a study of 15 females, provide some evidence that is consistent with a family systems view of this disorder. First, they found that parents of daughters who showed the least improvement with therapy had significantly higher levels of psychopathology measured by questionnaire. Even more relevant is their finding that successful treatment of the daughters was associated with an *increase* in parental disturbance. This increase in parental disturbance was especially marked when the marital relationship was poor; mothers tended to show an increase in anxiety and fathers an increase in depression. The authors concluded that the daughter's illness sometimes serves a protective function for one or both parents when the parents are threatened by the prospect of the daughter's independence.

TREATMENT

Results of behavioral approaches, primarily operant, to anorexia nervosa have been mixed. A number of reports based on small samples have shown immediate successes in terms of weight gains, but follow-up studies have either not been done or have shown that weight gains have not been maintained in a number of cases (Bemis, 1978). Minuchin et al. (1978) report a success rate for family therapy of 86 percent after follow-up periods ranging from three months to four years. This is an impressive result, although no information is provided on interobserver reliability or "blindness" of the individuals making the judgment of recovery. The return to normal weight, however, should be a relatively objective measure, and the results probably reflect a substantial degree of effectiveness of Minuchin's family therapy approach to this disorder.

Summary

1. Many psychological disturbances of childhood fall along two broad dimensions: conduct disorders, involving disobedience and aggressive behavior; and anxious-withdrawn reactions, involving feelings of inferiority, social withdrawal, and anxiety.

2. Both mothers and teachers report relatively high levels of various "symptoms" in young children. Many of these problem behaviors are transitory and are not likely to develop into more serious disorders.

3. Attachment and exploration are important features of the early mother-child relationship. Disturbances in this system may have long-lasting consequences for the child's psychological development.

4. Positive maternal stimulation that is contingent upon the infant's behavior may be especially important in the psychological development of the infant, representing an important component of what is usually called warmth.

5. Extended forced separations from the mother (or mother surrogate) tend to produce depression-withdrawal reactions in the young child. Usually these reactions are reversible, but under extreme conditions of deprivation long-lasting psychological impairment may occur.

6. Attachment that becomes extreme and persists into the childhood years may produce separation anxiety. An interacting system characterized by parental overprotectiveness may play an especially important role in the development of this reaction.

7. School phobias in older children may involve some separation anxiety but are also likely to be associated with poor academic performance or incidents such as teasing by classmates.

8. Hyperactivity may result from different patterns of causative factors in different children. Brain dysfunction or a temperamental disposition toward high activity levels may play a role in some cases; in others, social learning experiences may be the most important determinant.

9. Stimulant drugs, such as the amphetamines, and behavior modification programs are effective in reducing hyperactivity in many children.

10. Stuttering is also a symptom that occurs in most instances without indications of other signs of psychological disorder (in young children but not in adults). The biological and/or learning bases of the disorder have yet to be clearly understood.

11. No single treatment has been found to be completely effective for stuttering. At this time, approaches that use techniques such as delayed auditory feedback or muscular relaxation of speech-related muscles and provide practice in a variety of situations appear promising. Psychotherapy may be useful as an adjunct when the person has developed low self-confidence and generalized concerns about speaking in public.

12. Enuresis or bedwetting is a symptom that occurs in most instances without other signs of psychological disorder. It responds favorably to a multifactor behavioral treatment procedure.

13. No organic basis for enuresis can be identified in most cases, and it is assumed that faulty learning is involved.

14. In anorexia nervosa, eating is reduced to a point where severe weight loss occurs. It is most frequent in adolescent girls, and clinicians have frequently interpreted the symptoms as a manifestation of resistance on the part of both child and parents against increasing independence and developing sexual interests.

Suggested Readings

J. Bowlby's two volumes continue to be important references on attachment and separation anxiety, *Attachment* (Basic Books, 1969) and *Attachment and Loss, Vol. 2: Separation anxiety and anger* (Basic Books, 1973). A. O. Ross discusses the nature and treatment of a variety of childhood disorders in *Psychological disorders of children* (McGraw-Hill, 1980).

21

Pervasive Developmental Disorders

- Did you know that some children are almost totally unresponsive to people?

- What is early infantile autism?

- What do we know about the causes of autism and childhood psychoses?

- Can children with these disorders be helped?

- Can warmth and reassurance make a child's behavior worse?

- What happens to autistic and psychotic children when they grow up?

Peter: An Autistic Child

More troubling was the fact that Peter didn't look at us, or smile, and wouldn't play the games that seemed as much a part of babyhood as diapers. While he didn't cry, he rarely laughed, and when he did, it was at things that didn't seem funny to us. He didn't cuddle, but sat upright in my lap, even when I rocked him. But children differ and we were content to let Peter be himself. We thought it hilarious when my brother, visiting us when Peter was 8 months old, observed that "That kid has no social instincts, whatsoever." Although Peter was a first child, he was not isolated. I frequently put him in his playpen in front of the house, where the school children stopped to play with him as they passed. He ignored them too.

It was Kitty, a personality kid, born two years later, whose responsiveness emphasized the degree of Peter's difference. When I went into her room for the late feeding, her little head bobbed up and she greeted me with a smile that reached from her head to her toes. And the realization of that difference chilled me more than the wintry bedroom.

Peter's babbling had not turned into speech by the time he was three. His play was solitary and repetitious. He tore paper into long thin strips, bushel baskets of it every day. He spun the lids from my canning jars and became upset if we tried to divert him. Only rarely could I catch his eye, and then saw his focus change from me to the reflection in my glasses.

His adventures into our suburban neighbourhood had been unhappy. He had disregarded the universal rule that sand is to be kept in sandboxes, and the children themselves had punished him. He walked around a sad and solitary figure, always carrying a toy aeroplane, a toy he never played with. At that time, I had not heard the word that was to dominate our lives, to hover over every conversation, to sit through every meal beside us. That word was autism. (Eberhardy, 1967, p. 258)

Some autistic children seem to want to shut out external stimulation.

The pattern of symptoms shown by Peter is characteristic of *early infantile autism* (or simply *autism*), one of the two forms of childhood disorder listed under Pervasive Developmental Disorders in DSM-III. The other form of severe childhood disorder is called *childhood psychosis.* In the past many of these latter disorders were diagnosed as *childhood schizophrenia.*

Early Infantile Autism

SYMPTOMS

Kanner (1943), a child psychiatrist, first formulated the concept of early infantile autism on the basis of a careful study of 11 children. As was true for Peter, all of these children showed a strange indifference to people. Kanner (1943) describes this lack of interest in people:

Every one of the children, upon entering the office, immediately went after blocks, toys, or other objects, without paying the least attention to the persons present. It would be wrong to say that they were not aware of the presence of persons. But the people, as long as they left the child alone, figured in about the same manner as did the desk, the bookshelf, or the filing cabinet. When the child was addressed, he was not bothered. He had the choice between not responding at all or, if a question was repeated too insistently, "getting it over with" and continuing with whatever he had been doing. Comings and goings, even of the mother, did not seem to register. Conversation going on in the room elicited no interest. If the adults did not try to enter the child's domain, he would at times, while moving between them, gently touch a hand or a knee as on other occasions he patted the desk or the couch. But he never looked into anyone's face. (pp. 246–247)

Kanner's description of the core features of autism has held up well over the years, and the more current description of symptoms described below (based on Rutter, 1978, and DSM-III) follow Kanner in the essential characteristics.

1. Early Onset. The symptoms of autism are almost always apparent before the age of 30 months. For some children certain features of the disorder may be present within the first six months of life. However, when severe symptoms develop after age three, they are likely to have a nature and course different from that of autism.

2. Inability to Relate to People. Many autistic children's inability to relate to people becomes apparent early in life, as was the case for Peter. They do not develop a normal attachment to their mothers; for example, when picked up or cuddled, they arch their bodies away and do not mold themselves against the mother as a normal infant would. They tend to be generally unresponsive and fail to smile or maintain eye contact when parents or others attempt to engage them in play.

The autistic child's tendency to avoid looking at the human face is illustrated in a study by Hutt and Ounsted (1970). Autistic and severely emotionally disturbed, nonautistic children were individually placed in a room in which five models representing human and animal faces were mounted on stands. The autistic children spent less than 5 percent of the time

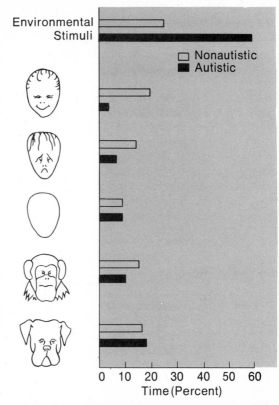

FIGURE 21-1. Percentage of time spent by autistic and nonautistic children inspecting face models and environmental stimuli such as room fixtures. (Adapted from Hutt & Ounsted, 1970; © 1970 by Pergamon Press and reprinted by permission.)

looking at the normal human face and more than 60 percent of the time looking at environmental stimuli such as lights, windows, and faucets. The nonautistic children spread their attention more evenly across the various stimuli (Figure 21-1).

After age five the impaired social relationships are most evident in a lack of cooperative play with other children, a failure to make personal friendships, and a failure to perceive other people's feelings and responses.

3. Lack of Speech for Communication. A high proportion, about 50 percent, of autistic children do not speak at all; those who do speak use speech not to convey meaning but rather primarily to name objects and to repeat phrases, rhymes, or songs. In fact, the child may have an excellent memory for names, pictures, or tunes. Some children simply repeat words or phrases that others say (*echolalia*) or reverse personal pronouns so as to refer to themselves as "you" or "he" and to others as "I." The combination of general unresponsiveness and lack of speech found in some autistic children has led their parents and family doctors to mistakenly suspect deafness. The degree of impairment in speaking is an important predictor of the child's later adjustment. Eisenberg and Kanner (1956) followed up a sample of 80 autistic children and found that 50 percent of the children who had some ability to speak at age five were rated as showing fair or good adjustment, but only 3 percent of the nonspeaking children had achieved this degree of adjustment.

4. Insistence on Sameness and Stereotypic Behaviors. Young autistic children frequently engage in rigid and limited play patterns that lack variety and imagination. They might, for example, endlessly line up toys or collect curious objects such as stones of a special shape. In some cases they develop such intense attachments to these objects that they have to have them available or always carry them around. For long periods of time they can be engrossed in repetitive activity: spinning objects, making noises, or rhythmic bodily movements. Some children hold their hands in front of their eyes and writhe or twist the fingers and palms, or engage in "hand flapping," involving rapid alternating flexion and extension of the fingers or hand. As they get older they are likely to develop obsessive preoccupations with things such as train timetables, colors, numbers, and patterns. The tendency to persist in repetitive, monotonous behaviors is perhaps related to the autistic child's insistence on sameness. Many of these children become extremely upset if their familiar environment is changed: a rearrangement of furniture, or new eating utensils, toys, or clothing.

5. Associated Features. Other features may be

Not interested in interaction with people, autistic children can become engrossed in the tactile–visual exploration of inanimate objects.

present but not as consistently as the ones described above. These can include extreme fear of certain loud noises and moving objects such as vacuum cleaners, egg beaters, and elevators. Moods may be unpredictable: These children may cry inconsolably or laugh without discernible cause. They may not appreciate real dangers such as moving vehicles or heights, and they may engage in self-injurious behavior such as biting or hitting parts of the body. During the first year of life they may have eating difficulties, including vomiting and food refusal. Their physical appearance, however, is almost always normal.

A 31-year-old man who had been autistic since early childhood was able to describe his memories of what his early years had been like. Bemporad (1979) summarizes these recollections as follows:

> According to Jerry, his childhood experience could be summarized as consisting of two predominant experiential states: confusion and terror. The recurrent theme that ran through all of Jerry's recollections was that of living in a frightening world presenting painful stimuli that could not be mastered. Noises were unbearably loud, smells overpowering. Nothing seemed constant; everything was unpredictable and strange. Animate beings were a particular problem. Dogs were remembered as eerie

> and terrifying. As a child, he believed they were somehow humanoid (since they moved of their own volition, etc.), yet they were not really human, a puzzle that mystified him. They were especially unpredictable; they could move quickly without provocation. To this day, Jerry is phobic of dogs.
>
> He was also frightened of other children, fearing that they might hurt him in some way. He could never predict or understand their behavior. Elementary school was remembered as a horrifying experience. The classroom was total confusion, and he always felt he "would go to pieces."
>
> There were also enjoyable experiences. He liked going to grocery stores with his mother so he could look at the labels of canned goods as well as the prices of objects. . . . His life seemed to have markedly changed when he discovered multiplication tables at around age 8. . . . He said he simply liked working with numbers. . . . It is significant that he did not mention any relationship to family members when reconstructing his childhood; they seemed of little importance. (pp. 192–193)

When infantile autism is defined rather narrowly in terms of the first four criteria listed above, it is found to be a rare disorder, with a prevalence of about two to four cases per 10,000 people and occurs three times as often in boys as in girls (Wing et al., 1976).

RESEARCH REPORT 21-1

What Is the Basic Defect in Autism?

Kanner (1943) emphasized a social behavior deficit, an inability to form normal emotional contacts with other people, as the basic problem in autism. Richer (1976, 1978) provides evidence in line with Kanner's view—namely, that autistic children have a deeply ingrained tendency to avoid social interaction. In one study observers coded the behavior of autistic and a matched sample of nonautistic children in a school playground. The occurrence of avoidance behavior was tabulated following two types of preceding behavior by other children, threatening and nonthreatening. Autistic children much more often responded to nonthreatening approaches by others with avoidance. There was, however, no difference between the groups in avoidance behavior following threatening behavior, although the nonsignificant trend favored the nonautistic children (see Figure 21-2). Thus under nonthreatening circumstances in which there was no reason to avoid, the autistic children nevertheless did so to a far greater extent than nonautistic children. In a second study Richer videotaped autistic and nonautistic children interacting with their class teachers. When the teacher approached the autistic children, they oriented away from the teacher much more often than the nonautistic children. Richer argues that these tendencies to avoid social interaction are deeply ingrained, almost reflexive, reactions and that at least some of the deficit in language development may result as a consequence of not engaging in the kind of social interactive sequences in which words and gestures acquire meaning.

Other investigators have emphasized other deficits as being fundamental to the autistic disorder. Lovaas et al. (1979) suggest that many of the autistic child's difficulties may result from "stimulus overselectivity," by which they mean a tendency to selectively respond to only part of the relevant cues in the environment. In some instances the autistic child responds to some minor or even irrelevant aspect of the stimulus situation. Lovaas and his associates report a number of studies demonstrating the autistic child's difficulty in responding to multiple cues. For example, autistic and normal children were reinforced for responding to a complex stimulus that included a visual, auditory, and tactile component presented simultaneously. Subsequently, when these components

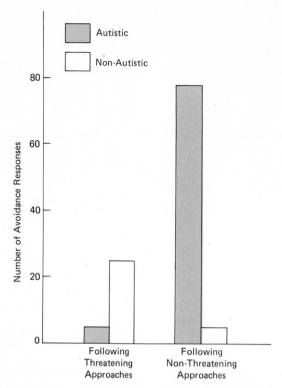

**FIGURE 21-2. Total number of avoidance responses fol-
lowing either threatening or nonthreatening approaches
by other children for autistic and nonautistic children.
Adapted from Richer (1978).**

were presented separately, the autistic children tended to respond to only one component and ignore the other two. The normal children responded to each component
equally. Lovaas et al. go on to suggest how an extreme tendency to ignore many aspects
of relevant environmental information could result in many of the symptoms seen in
autism and in the difficulty in teaching such children the use of language and other skills.

Along somewhat different lines Rutter (1978) marshals evidence to support the centrality of a cognitive deficit in autism, especially a defect in the ability to form abstractions
and to develop meanings to words or events. The autistic child's intellectual impairment
does not ordinarily extend to all areas of functioning. Thus on certain visual-spatial problems such as making a design with blocks or putting a puzzle together (the Block Design
and Object Assembly subtests of the Wechsler Intelligence Test) autistic children perform
about as well as normal children (Lockyer & Rutter, 1969). However, on tasks that require
forming abstractions, based on verbal meanings, even though no speech is required,
such as arranging a series of pictures in a correct order to tell a brief story, the autistic
children do very poorly. Likewise, Hermelin and O'Connor (1970) showed that, in marked
contrast to normal children, autistic children made relatively little use of meaning in
remembering words or sentences. The autistic child's recall for words depended more
on the sound of the word than on the word's meaning or grammatical usage.

TABLE 21-1   Total Number of Correctly Recalled Three-Letter Sequences

Subjects	Temporal	Spatial	Random	Total
Normal	118	26	16	160
Autistic	16	132	12	160
Deaf	43	103	14	160

From Hermelin (1978). Copyright 1978, Plenum Press; reproduced with permission.

O'Connor and Hermelin (1973) performed another study that ingeniously demonstrates the autistic child's dependence on a visual-spatial mode of thinking. When we use visual imagery to solve a problem, we organize our experience in a spatial mode. Imagine coming into a familiar room in the dark and trying to get to the light switch across the room. Most of us would form a spatial image of the room in our "mind's eye" and use that image to guide ourselves across the room. On the other hand, imagine that you are asked to remember a series of numbers orally presented. Most of us will approach this task by remembering in our "mind's ear" the temporal sequence of the spoken numbers. Or some of us might choose to visualize the numbers in a spatial arrangement from left to right. O'Connor and Hermelin reasoned that autistic children, because they have a specific deficit in cognitively replaying the temporal sequence of auditory inputs, would use a visual-spatial mode of thinking whenever possible.

The task they gave to the subjects permitted this kind of choice. Three letters were displayed successively at one of three windows placed horizontally from left to right on a screen. They were, however, never presented in a straight left-to-right sequence. For example, if the sequence of presentation was A E M, then A would appear first, but in the right-hand window, E was shown second in the left-hand window, and M last, in the middle. The children were asked to recall each set of three letters after they had been briefly presented. It was predetermined that the difficulty level of the task was such that all the children could remember the letters, one way or another.

If children were using the auditory-temporal mode of performing this task, it would be expected that they would repeat the letters in the temporal sequence in which they were presented—A E M. If children were using the visual-spatial mode, then they would most likely recall the letters as they would appear in the "mind's eye" from left to right—E M A. The autistic children did indeed report the letters in a sequence suggesting the use of the visual-spatial mode more often than normal children (see Table 21-1). The authors had also included a group of deaf children, predicting that they would also prefer the visual-spatial mode since they would have little or no experience with the auditory-temporal mode. And, indeed, they showed the greatest relative use of the visual-spatial mode.

After considering the various research findings, it is difficult to conclude whether social avoidance, stimulus overselectivity, or a cognitive deficit in the auditory-temporal mode is the most basic impairment. They may all reflect rather direct effects of some even more fundamental defect, whatever that may turn out to be. Of course, each of these impairments can contribute to and worsen the other. For example, the inability to communicate resulting from a cognitive deficit would likely further strengthen the child's tendency to avoid social relations.

DEVELOPMENT

Despite its rarity, autism has been the object of intense investigation, which unfortunately has not yet yielded a clear understanding of this disorder's etiology. Heredity, central nervous system dysfunction, and psychological experiences have all been offered as explanations.

Heredity.   The fact that autism does not usually occur with more than normal frequency in the close relatives of autistic individuals would, at first glance, seem to suggest that genetic factors are not important. Autistic persons, however, rarely marry, and there is only one published report of one having given birth to a child (Kanner & Eisenberg, 1955). One should, therefore, not be surprised that few autistic children have autistic parents. Also, the extreme rarity of the disorder reduces the likelihood of a positive family history.

The best twin study to date (Folstein & Rutter, 1977) does, in fact, suggest that heredity contributes to the development of this disorder, at least in some cases. These authors found a 36 percent concordance for autism in 11 identical twins and a 0 percent concordance for 10 fraternal twins. An assessment of cognitive/linguistic impairment was also made for each twin. A twin was considered cognitively/linguistically impaired if he or she showed at least one of the following features: lack of phrase speech by 30 months, a verbal IQ below 70, grossly abnormal articulation persisting to age five or older, or scholastic difficulties of such severity as to require special schooling. The evidence for a genetic contribution was even stronger when comparisons were made on this variable. Identical twins yielded an 83 percent concordance rate compared with a 10 percent concordance rate for fraternal twins. Folstein and Rutter concluded that a cognitive deficit associated with the acquisition of spoken language was genetically transmitted and that this deficit increased the likelihood that the full autistic syndrome would develop.

They also found that when twins were discordant for autism, the autistic twin was more likely to have experienced a "biological hazard" (for example, birth complications or multiple congenital anomalies). There were six discordant twin pairs in which only one twin had experienced a biological hazard, and in *all* six cases it was the autistic twin who was affected. The authors further concluded that the central nervous system defect associated with autism is transmitted genetically in some proportion of the cases, and is produced by environmental events such as birth complications or physical illnesses in other cases.

Biological Correlates. The profound disturbance in the autistic child's behavior and ability to relate to the world of people is present at such an early age that it strongly suggests some kind of biological impairment. Kanner (1943) thought that was the case: "We must . . . assume that these children have come into the world with innate inability to form the usual, biologically provided affective contact with people, just as other children come into the world with innate physical or intellectual handicaps" (p. 250).

Many studies have pointed to impaired brain functioning in at least a subset of autistic children. Folstein and Rutter (1977), as just indicated, concluded that biological hazards contributed to some cases of autism. Other researchers have found similar evidence. For example, DeLong (1978) found indications of anatomical deviations in the brains of some autistic children as measured by pneumoencephalograms. The deviation consisted of a dilation of the temporal horn of the left lateral ventricle. For autism that was apparent soon after birth, Harper and Williams (1975) found higher than normal frequencies of neurological signs, birth difficulties, and maternal rubella (measles) during pregnancy. Piggott (1979), after reviewing a number of studies that indicated a physiological disturbance in autism, concluded that the autistic syndrome can probably result from a number of different physiological disorders, injuries, and diseases.

Psychological Correlates. When he first identified early infantile autism, Kanner noted that the parents of the 11 children in his original sample appeared to be rather cool and distant in their interpersonal relationships. "In the whole group there are few really warmhearted fathers and mothers. For the most part the antecedents and collaterals are persons strongly preoccupied with abstraction of a scientific, literary, or artistic nature and limited in genuine contact with people" (1957, p. 742). Other writers, sharing this impression, developed psychological theories of autism in which the parents' aloofness was thought to produce the lack of responsivity in the child (for example, Despert, 1951). Kanner himself, as the earlier quote indicates, did not see this as the basic cause of autism.

Subsequent research has, for the most part, not supported the notion of lack of warmth in parents of autistic children. When DeMyer et al. (1972) compared the child-rearing behaviors of parents of matched samples of autistic, brain-injured, and normal children, they found that all three groups of parents provided at least average amounts of warmth, attention, and stimulation to their children during infancy. Cantwell et al. (1978), after reviewing numerous studies conducted over a 20-year period, concluded that the personality characteristics and child-rearing approaches of parents of autistic children were not especially deviant. It seems most unlikely, then, that these profound symptoms that appear so early in life are caused by the parents' style of interacting with this particular child.

Although autistic children occur in all social classes, a number of investigators have found parents of autistic children on the average to have higher IQs and to have higher socioeconomic status than the general population (see Cantwell et al., 1978, for a review). Schopler et al. (1979), however, suggest that the somewhat higher socioeconomic levels of these parents might result in part from middle- and upper-class parents' seeking and being more willing to travel long distances to obtain expert (and expensive) diagnostic appraisals for their children. Autistic children of more affluent parents would as a result have more often come to the attention of the early clinical investigators such as Kanner.

THE AUTISTIC CHILD GROWS UP

What happens when the autistic child grows up? How favorable is the prognosis, with or without treatment? Kanner et al. (1972) have reported follow-up information on 96 autistic children. Most of these children as adults continued to require varying degrees of custodial care, but 11 had achieved an adequate social adjustment. Three of the 11 had graduated from college, three from junior college, one was still in college, and the other four did not go beyond high school or special education. Their occupations included bank teller, lab technician, duplicating machine operator, accountant, and several types of unskilled work. None of the 11 (10 were males) had shown spontaneous interest in the opposite sex or marriage. The outcomes for these 96 children were not affected by whether they had received psychiatric treatment. The best single predictor of successful later adjustment was the development of useful speech by age five. Lotter (1978) summarized the results of eight follow-up studies and reported that 5–17 percent of the autistic children had "good" outcomes and 61–74 percent had "poor" or "very poor" outcomes. Around half were in institutions. Donald is an example of a successful outcome.

We cannot know for sure what factors accounted for Donald's adequate development, but the farm experience suggests that a firm yet accepting social environment in which his special talents were encouraged and frustrations over his handicap were minimized were probably important. Nor should we forget that this success story represents a distinct minority of the total sample of autistic children.

Donald: Thirty Years Later

In 1942 [when he was nine], his parents placed him on a tenant farm. . . . I was amazed at the wisdom of the couple who took care of him. . . . They made him use his preoccupation with measurements by having him dig a well and report on its depth. When he kept collecting dead birds and bugs, they gave him a spot for a "graveyard" and had him put up markers; on each he wrote a first name, the type of animal as a middle name, and the farmer's last name, for example, "John Snail Lewis." . . . When he kept counting rows of corn over and over, they had him count the rows while plowing them. . . . It was obvious that Mr. and Mrs. Lewis [the farm couple] were very fond of him and just as obvious that they were gently firm. He attended a country school where his peculiarities were accepted and where he made good scholastic progress.

The rest of the story is contained in a letter from Donald's mother, dated April 6, 1970:

"Don is now 36 years old, a bachelor living at home with us. . . . Since receiving his A.B. degree in 1958, he has worked in the local bank as a teller. He is satisfied to remain a teller, having no real desire for promotion. . . . His chief hobby is golf, playing four or five times a week at the local country club. . . . Other interests are Kiwanis Club (served as president one term), Jaycees, Investment Club, Secretary of Presbyterian Sunday School. He is dependable, accurate, shows originality in editing the Jaycee program information, is even-tempered but has a mind of his own. . . . In college his major was French and he showed a particular aptitude for languages. Lack of initiative seems to be his most serious drawback. He takes very little part in social conversation and shows no interest in the opposite sex.

"While Don is not completely normal, he has taken his place in society very well, so much better than we ever hoped for." (Kanner, 1971, pp. 121–122)

Childhood Psychoses

Mary: A Psychotic Child

Mary was eight and a half years old when she entered the Orthogenic School of the University of Chicago run by Bruno Bettelheim. Mary had shown increasingly troublesome behavior, stealing from stores in the neighborhood and fighting constantly with other children, including an attempted attack on another child with a knife. But long before these recent episodes she had been of serious concern to various social agencies in the city. When Mary was three she had been sent off to nursery school alone by bus, causing comment from other people about the tiny child who sat on the bus and talked and sang to herself. At nursery school she remained aloof from the other children, frequently lying in the middle of the play yard and openly masturbating. Also as a young child she had been preoccupied with animals and had shown great cruelty toward them. Once, for example, she tried to kill a cat by burning it. At other times she would pretend to love a certain animal but would almost squeeze it to death; in some instances she actually did so.

When Mary first arrived at the school she was very withdrawn. Although she talked with some fluency, she used speech as a means of avoiding contact, of getting rid of the person she was talking to. She showed almost no emotion. After about ten days, however, she began to display violent outbursts of hostility in which she would emit ear-piercing screams, sometimes punctuated by shouts of "I'm going to kill you." Almost any minor frustration could set off these screaming episodes. The tiniest scratch, for example, that even the most anxious children of the school could more or less ignore would set her screaming for hours on end.

Her progress at the school was erratic. At one point she regressed into a schizophrenic episode in which she completely lost contact with her counselors and the other children. She could not speak of what troubled her, developed a blinking tic, and avoided looking at people, as though she wished to shut the world from her sight. Intense night terrors reappeared. For long periods of time she showed no signs of emotional response whatsoever, and when feelings did occur, they were inappropriate. One time, for example, she suddenly came up to another girl and bit her on the nipple. Delusional thinking was suggested by certain comments, such as saying that she was the only person present in a room occupied by a counselor and several other children. (Bettelheim, 1955)

DSM-III uses the extremely awkward term *Childhood Onset Pervasive Developmental Disorder* to refer to these severe disorders that have often been called childhood psychoses by previous investigators. For the sake of readability and ease of remembering, I will continue to use the term *childhood psychoses* as a label for these disturbances.

SYMPTOMS

Children such as Mary who show continuing severe disturbances in their relations with people and who exhibit various kinds of bizarre behaviors have also in the past been given the diagnosis of *childhood schizophrenia*. The relationship of these psychotic symptoms in children to adult schizophrenia is not entirely clear, although findings indicate that a substantial proportion of these children do not develop the classical picture of schizophrenia as adults. When children do show the more central symptoms of schizophrenia such as delusions, hallucinations, and severe thought disorder, they would simply be diagnosed as schizophrenic. These symptoms, however, are extremely rare in preadolescent children. The DSM-III criteria for these disorders are:

1. Onset of the full symptom pattern after 30 months of age and before 12 years of age. This criterion, of course, provides a clear, if somewhat arbitrary, distinction from autism.
2. Severe impairments in social relationships such as inappropriate emotional reactions (wild outbursts of aggression, for example), unusual clinging behavior, and lack of peer friendships.
3. Bizarre behaviors such as acute, irrational anxiety and catastrophic reactions to minor frustrations; ritualistic and repetitive behaviors: speech peculiarities such as questionlike melody and monotonous tone of voice; and self-mutilation in the form of biting, hitting, or head banging.
4. Absence of delusions, hallucinations, or marked loosening of associations.

Because of variations in definition of these psychotic reactions in childhood there are no good prevalence statistics at this time (Werry, 1979). They are undoubtedly rare in an absolute sense, but they are probably somewhat more common than autism and tend to occur more often in boys than girls.

Some of the symptoms are similar to those seen in autism. However, in addition to the rather arbitrary age-of-onset distinction, there are other characteristics that tend to distinguish autistic children from psychotic children or those previously called childhood schizophrenics:

1. *Physical responsiveness.* Whereas autistic children are stiff, unresponsive, and do not adapt their bodies to their mothers, "schizophrenic" children have a strong tendency to "mold" to adults like plastic or dough.
2. *Motor performance.* Autistic children often display extraordinary motor dexterity with regard to both gross body movements and finger dexterity. "Schizophrenic" children are more often characterized by awkward, poorly coordinated movements.

3. *Special talents.* The unusual memory, musical, and mechanical performances found in some autistic children are rarely seen in "schizophrenic" children.
4. *Family background.* There is less history of schizophrenic disorders in the family backgrounds of autistic children.

DEVELOPMENT

Most past research on the etiology of childhood psychoses is not clearly relevant to this DSM-III category since samples have frequently contained varying mixtures of children with autism, organically based psychoses, and disorders called childhood schizophrenia. With this qualification in mind let us consider the possible role of biological and psychological factors in these severe disorders.

Biological Correlates. Studies uniformly find a higher than normal incidence of neurological and EEG (electroencephalogram) abnormalities and complications of pregnancy in samples of psychotic children (see Werry, 1979, for a review). Although some subset of children in some of these studies may be autistic, the prevalence of these abnormalities is too high to be explained by the inclusion of a few autistic children. Research to date, however, provides little support for any particular theory of just what kind of brain impairment, possibly in interaction with environmental factors, might lead to these psychotic disorders.

Psychological Correlates. In contrast to the family environments of the autistic child, which seem to be essentially normal, the family environments of children called psychotic or "schizophrenic" show more evidence of psychopathology. Bender (1974), for example, found that three-fourths of 100 families with a "schizophrenic" child were severely pathological. Mothers, fathers, and sometimes both were either psychotic, disturbed, or inadequate. Meyers and Goldfarb (1962) also found that a high percentage of parents of a sample of psychotic children were diagnosed schizophrenic—30.6 percent of the mothers and 20.4 percent of the fathers. Taft and Goldfarb (1963) had observers make ratings of family interaction on the basis of a three-hour home visit and families with psychotic children were rated less "adequate" than families with normal children. One aspect of "inadequate" family interaction was called *maternal perplexity* and consisted of a lack of spontaneity of maternal interaction, indecisiveness, inconsistency of emotional relatedness, inappropriate control of the child, inappropriate anticipation of physical needs, and inappropriate meeting of the child's demands. Mrs. A., for example, rated high on maternal perplexity:

When asked about her maternal feelings Mrs. A responded, "My maternal feelings were of responsibility, not of joy, because I was so overanxious. I remember once I was so strict to my schedule that I gave Betty (schizophrenic child) a bath when she was sleeping." . . .

In response to a question about how her husband cooperated in the feeding of the children when they were infants, she said, "We were both afraid to touch her. We thought that she would break. Both of us got up in the night and one gave her the bottle and one held the baby. I put a handkerchief in his hand to hold the baby's head because I was afraid that if he would touch her with his bare hand her head would dilapidate." . . .

When asked how she handled temper tantrums, Mrs. A. said, "Then I get a temper tantrum, too. I don't want to hit Sam because you can sometimes hit him harder than you want. Betty I hit a lot. Now I lock Sam up in a room, but only in the daytime; if it is in the evening I put on the light, naturally, and I try to make it as short as possible." (pp. 561–562)

Massie (1978a, 1978b) reports an interesting study in which he was able to find a sample of families who had taken home movies of early mother-infant interaction *before* the child became psychotic. The mothers of the prepsychotic infants initiated less eye gaze and touching contact than the mothers of a control group of normal infants. The mothers of the prepsychotic infants also responded less when their infants initiated eye gaze contact or touching. Overall ratings of maternal responsiveness to the infants showed mothers of prepsychotic infants to be significantly less responsive ($p < .01$) than mothers of normal infants. The prepsychotic infants, as a group, were not significantly different from the normal infants in their initiations of eye gaze and touching contact. These group averages, however, obscure some interesting differences in individual mother-infant pairs. There were several pairs in which infant nonresponsiveness preceded or occurred simulta-

neously with maternal nonresponsiveness. In one pair of twins, for example, one eventually was diagnosed as autistic and the other remained normal. The home movies showed that the mother behaved similarly to both infants, being physically brusque and insensitive to the infants' moods or actions. Yet only one became autistic. Massie concludes that this infant probably had an organic disposition to psychosis (or autism) that the other did not have.

In another case the infant (later diagnosed as autistic) seemed to have less-than-normal activity in the first three months but showed normal "attachment" behaviors—smiling, eye gaze, sucking, clinging, and touching—until the sixth month. The mother, however, prior to six months avoided eye contact with the infant. Massie gives an example of an episode that happened at four months:

In this episode, Mrs. L. is holding Joan and both appear relaxed. Smiling, Joan turns her head and eyes toward her mother's face. Mrs. L's expression becomes tense; and as Mrs. L. tenses instead of smiling and turning to her child, Joan loses her smile. Mrs. L. then inclines her head backwards and to the side of Joan's face so that the child's head is blocked from turning. Joan cannot turn her head further to bring herself face to face with her mother; her eyes are as far to the right as she can look, but she cannot see her mother's face or eyes. Joan's affect in quick succession becomes tense, then desperate, then dejected. Finally, she gives up trying to turn to her mother; the mother herself is more relaxed, the evasive actions having been successful. Mrs. L. and Joan then resume the same postures as in the beginning of the sequence, although Joan's affect is depressed. Mrs. L. then begins to caress her daughter's head; Joan smiles and drools. Then the whole interactional sequence repeats itself as Joan again attempts unsuccessfully to look at her mother. (p. 31)

We must be a little cautious in interpreting the group comparisons in this study since the control group was matched with the prepsychotic infant group only on number of first- and second-born infants. Socioeconomic level, for example, was not equated. Also, the psychoses when they later developed were given various diagnoses (autism, childhood psychosis, childhood schizophrenia), so we cannot draw conclusions about current DSM-III diagnosis of autism or childhood psychosis. Nevertheless, the glimpses one gets of the disturbances in normal mother-infant interaction are provocative and suggest that very early in life interactive sequences are occurring that may be importantly related to the later development of severe disorders. In some cases the mother's lack of responsiveness may have been, in part, a reaction to the child's nonresponsiveness but in others the mother's lack of responsiveness would seem to have been present first. Whether maternal nonresponsiveness is sufficient in itself to produce these severe disorders is by no means clear. Perhaps the maternal nonresponsiveness facilitates the development of psychosis only in children with some biological predisposition.

Mary, the psychotic girl described earlier, experienced much stress and disturbed family relations (Bettelheim, 1955).

She was a full-term baby, weighed five pounds at birth, and seemed to be in generally good physical health. She spoke simple words at nine months and walked at the age of 13 months. Her father died when she was three and a half months old, leaving her mother without financial resources. According to various reports, her mother became depressed after her husband's death and after a while physically ill. She withdrew from the world, and never left the two small rooms in which they lived. An older sister, Frances, age ten, became more or less wholly responsible for Mary. In this kind of environment it seems unlikely that Mary could have experienced anything like a normal development of attachment and exploratory behaviors (Chapter 20), and some of her tendencies toward alternate emotional withdrawal and aggressive striking out may have originated in this period.

After the mother's death the two children were eventually placed in the home of a maternal aunt who did not want them but whose husband convinced her that it was her duty to take them in. She was an unfortunate choice, as the aunt was in no mood to accept Mary's already developing difficulties. The aunt was appalled by Mary's masturbation, thumb-sucking, wetting, and other asocial behaviors. The "good" behavior of the aunt's own children was held up to Mary and Frances for comparison. This rejecting home situation was so bad that a social agency first tried to secure psychiatric help for Mary and then to remove her from the home, but the aunt refused to cooperate in any way—apparently feeling that such actions would reflect upon her social status. The living circumstances were so unhappy that the older sister, Frances, tried at least twice to commit suicide by taking aspirin in quantity. There was reason to believe that Mary underwent a number of sexual experiences during this period. At age seven she was accosted by a man who offered her money, which she accepted, to go with him to a nearby building, where he exposed himself to her. All in all the first eight years of Mary's life were filled with more than enough psychological trauma to account for many of her symptoms. There were no indications of the autistic syndrome and, in terms of available information, no neurological abnormalities. We cannot, of course, rule out the possibility of some genetic predisposition.

THE PSYCHOTIC CHILD GROWS UP

Bender (1973) reported follow-up information on 100 psychotic children seen at the Bellevue Children's Service in New York between the years 1935 and 1952. These individuals ranged from 22 to 46 years of age at the time of the follow-up. About two-thirds were found to have been placed in institutions for the mentally ill or mentally retarded. The remaining one-third were living in the community with varying degrees of assistance. Those individuals with an unfavorable outcome were more likely to have had an associated organic disorder or a predominant picture of infantile autism. Various treatment programs at different age levels were available to most of these children so that these outcomes do not necessarily reflect the "natural" courses of the disorders without treatment.

Eggers (1978) provided follow-up data on 57 children diagnosed as childhood schizophrenic (at ages 7 to 13 years) in which great care was taken to exclude children who were autistic, whose psychoses were associated with organic brain disease, or who were mentally deficient. Most of these children, especially those 7 to 10 years old at the time of original diagnosis, would probably qualify for the current diagnosis of childhood psychosis. After an average follow-up period of 15 years about half of the individuals had shown satisfactory improvement and half continued to show fair to very poor adjustment. Twenty percent had fully recovered and showed no signs of their previous disorder. Of special interest is the finding that all of the children with good outcomes had an onset of their psychoses when 10 years of age or older. *All* children who became psychotic before age 10 had a poor outcome. Also of interest is that ratings of disturbed family atmosphere showed no relationship to outcome, whereas ratings of prepsychotic personality did. Children who were strongly introverted, shy, and inhibited before the onset of their psychotic symptoms were more likely to have a poor outcome. As the children with poor outcome got older, their symptoms in many cases became similar to those seen in adult schizophrenia, with delusions and hallucinations becoming common. This study, with its "purified" sample, suggests that childhood schizophrenia may well be an appropriate label for some subset of children diagnosed as childhood psychosis (or as "childhood onset pervasive developmental disorder" in DSM-III).

Treatment

PSYCHODYNAMIC APPROACHES

There is little reason to believe that the isolated application of an insight-oriented psychodynamic approach such as play therapy would be of much help in the treatment of either autism or childhood psychoses. Frequently, these children's handicaps are so massive that ordinarily they must be placed in a social environment totally geared toward encouraging the development of adaptive behavior. Bettelheim's Orthogenic School at the University of Chicago is one such place in which a basically psychodynamic view is translated into a full-scale and full-time social environment. Although Bettelheim does not deny the

possible role of constitutional and organic factors, his emphasis is clearly on the view that psychological experiences have produced the child's disturbed behavior.

The basic strategy of the Orthogenic School is to provide a benign setting in which children have another opportunity to relax their defenses, fully express their troubled emotions, and put together a more adaptive personality pattern. For example, when Mary was brought to the school at age 8½, she was permitted to scream and express hostile impulses without reprisal (as long as she did not physically injure other children or adults); she was permitted to masturbate as much as she wished and reassured that it was not harmful and that no one disapproved. Trained counselors provided generous amounts of affection and support. The structure of the program involved schooling (with competition deemphasized), play and recreational activities, and special play or talk therapy sessions. The psychodynamic framework in which Mary's treatment occurred is illustrated by the following interpretive comments of Bettelheim (1955).

Mary remained at the Orthogenic School for about four years. At age 15, three years after leaving, she was doing relatively well in a foster home that she liked, performing adequately at school, and although she had some fairly normal adolescent conflicts about sex and relations with other boys and girls, she was making a good social adjustment.

Bettelheim (1973) claims that more than 85 percent of the children at his school have returned to full participation in life. These data are perhaps somewhat "soft"; for example, assessment procedures are informal and there is no control group of equally disturbed untreated children, but considering the severity of the disturbances and the poor prognosis for these children (for example, Bender, 1973), the results are remarkable.

Bettelheim's reports shed little light on theoretical issues, such as psychodynamic versus behavioral approaches. His program is so complex, involving so many influences over such a long period, that ascribing effectiveness to any one technique or theory would be unjustified. Also Bettelheim did not make a distinction between infantile autism and childhood psychosis. Most of the children probably would not fit the current DSM-III criteria for autism.

What we did not realize at this time (because we learned about her early life only later) was that in her disorganized and aimless screaming she might have been reexperiencing the earliest trauma of her life, when her crying went unnoticed by a melancholic mother. We did not fathom that her angry insistence that everyone else be quiet as she screamed might have been a recreation of the earliest setting she had known, when everyone around her (her depressive mother) had been silent, and she alone had cried in the wilderness. Neither did we know that her insistence on not being awakened ("I'll kill you if you wake me up") was an effort to protect the only satisfying experience she had known: that of escaping it all by sleeping. (p. 169)

Worst of all, she was convinced that she, herself, had brought about her misery by killing her mother through her uncontrolled hostility (kicking her mother in the gallbladder). This burden of guilt she felt she had to carry for the rest of her life. In retaliation, she expected to be equally destroyed. She should suffer as she had made her mother suffer—hence her terrific fear that one of her little real or imagined ailments would utterly destroy her. This was also a clue to her melancholic withdrawal from the world and retirement to her bed. She deserved nothing but to be sick in bed and uncared for, as she, through her imaginary kicking, had caused her mother to be sick and uncared for. Moreover, only by staying quietly in bed, or remaining inactive, could Mary make sure that she would not add further to her guilt by destroying other persons through her hostile actions. Such stern repression of her hostility was necessary to prevent her from being put up for sale, kicked, or otherwise hurt, in retaliation for her having kicked her mother. After all, it had been her own act of hostility, so Mary imagined, that had led to her mother's dying and therefore to Mary's being put out of the home. (p. 233)

THE SOCIAL LEARNING APPROACH

In the 1960s a number of individual case studies appeared in which substantial improvements in an autistic child's symptomatic behavior was accomplished by rearranging environmental contingencies (for example, Wolf et al., 1964). Some psychologists began to focus specifically on the problem of teaching speech to autistic children. In an early study Hewett (1965) used a shaping or successive approximation procedure to increase the child's attending behavior, then systematically rewarded the child for vocalizations that became increasingly similar to those modeled by a therapist. Despite some success with this approach it was apparent that the direct shaping approach was limited in its effectiveness.

Normal children acquire much of their speech on an imitative basis, but careful observations of autistic children indicated that they seemed to learn very little this way. Perhaps if autistic children could learn a generalized tendency to imitate, this would open many possibilities for learning speech as well as other adaptive behaviors. Metz (1966) demonstrated that nonimitating autistic children could learn to imitate a model's nonverbal behavior if the child's imitative response was reinforced. Lovaas et al. (1966) went on to show that it was possible to build imitative verbal behavior in previously mute autistic children. More recently they have defined their procedures for teaching speech (Lovaas et al., 1974):

Step 1. The therapist increases the child's vocalizations of any kind by reinforcing such behavior (usually with food).

Step 2. The child's vocalizations are reinforced only if they occur in response to (within five seconds of) the therapist's speech.

Step 3. By successive approximations the child's speech sound is shaped until it matches the particular sound made by the therapist; that is, reinforcement is given only for those sounds that more and more resemble the therapist's sound.

Step 4. Step 3 is repeated for another sound.

Following this general sequence, the child is taught to imitate an increasingly large range of sounds, words, and eventually sentences. Once mute children learn to imitate in this fashion, they become essentially like echolalic children; they can parrot back the

(*Top left*) Therapist aids autistic child to articulate correct speech sounds by helping to form mouth in proper way. (*Top right*) Therapist rewards imitation of her speech sounds with food on fork, and (*left*) with smile and occasional food from plate on the table. These pictures show some of the Lovaas program techniques in speech therapy with austic children.

speech of others but have no comprehension of the meaning of the words they utter.

After the imitative tendency has been established, the therapist begins to work toward the meaningful use of speech in two ways: by teaching *expressive* speech, which in the beginning consists primarily of labeling objects in the environment; and by teaching language *comprehension,* in which the child learns to make some response, usually nonverbal in the beginning, to another person's verbalization, for example, by following instructions. These learnings are made functional, that is, a meaningful part of the children's lives, as soon as possible. For example, as soon as children have learned the label for a food, they are fed when they ask for that food. In time the therapist proceeds to more abstract uses of language, such as the use of pronouns, some grammar,

and story telling. Results have shown this approach to be moderately effective in teaching speech to autistic children (Lovaas et al., 1973; 1974). However, the totally mute child does not tend to achieve the higher levels of speech proficiency.

Lovaas and his colleagues have been particularly successful in using behavioral techniques to reduce self-injurious behavior in autistic children. The children may sometimes bite off parts of their shoulders or arms, chew off part of a finger, or hit their heads so violently against the wall that they detach their retinas. Some autistic children spend most of their lives in restraints because of the severe and potentially lethal nature of their self-injurious behavior.

Psychodynamic clinicians have speculated that the autistic child's self-destructive behavior reflects underlying feelings of worthlessness and self-hate (for example, Bettelheim, 1967). In one study Lovaas et al. (1974) treated such behaviors with an approach based on this psychodynamic assumption: Affection, understanding, and sympathetic comments were provided to reassure children of their worth whenever they behaved in a self-injurious way. For one child, Gregory, baseline frequencies of self-hitting behavior were obtained in two sessions; they were found to be quite low. In session three, concern and affection were given every time he hit himself, and the rate of hitting jumped dramatically. In session four no response was made to the self-hitting, and frequencies of this response decreased. The contingent affection was reinstated in session five, and the self-hitting jumped to the almost unbelievable rate of 200 times in ten minutes. Again when the contingencies were withdrawn, the rates became low. The *reversal design* used in this study of one child provides convincing evidence that it was the giving of affection (reinforcement) contingent upon self-hitting that caused this symptom to increase. In other words, the case of Gregory is one more demonstration of operant learning. The lesson to be derived from this demonstration is obvious—good intentions must go hand in hand with good theory. A compassionate adult (or therapist) who attempts to alleviate a child's self-injurious behavior with contingent warmth and affection produces the opposite result. In this case that result could be serious indeed.

If self-injurious behavior can be reinforced by affection from others, then it should extinguish if all social consequences are withheld. This is exactly what Lovaas and his associates have shown for many children. When a sample of self-injurious children were left free to injure themselves without parents or nursing staff intervening, the self-destructive behavior decreased as predicted, from a high of some 4000 self-injurious acts in the first hour, to 3500 in the second hour, later to 300, and finally by the tenth hour to zero (sessions were spaced out over several days). The children clearly discriminated the situation in which reinforcement would not occur. Thus in the room where they had been "run to extinction" they would not hurt themselves, but if they had been comforted for self-injurious behavior in another room they would resume self-injurious behavior at full strength there.

Some children's self-injurious behavior is so damaging that they might hurt themselves severely during an extinction procedure. Self-injurious behaviors in these children have been dramatically stopped in a number of cases by the contingent application of an aversive stimulus, such as a painful electric shock (Lovaas & Simmons, 1969). Few people feel comfortable about inflicting pain on children, but in making an ethical evaluation of this procedure one has to keep in mind the alternative—keeping children's arms and legs tied down permanently so that they will not damage themselves irreparably. Investigators continue to seek ways of modifying self-injurious behavior that minimize any discomforts involved.

Perhaps the most important development in the treatment of autistic children has been the enlistment of parents as cotherapists (Hemsley et al., 1978; Lovaas, 1978; Schopler & Reichler, 1971). Taking, for the most part, a social learning orientation, these programs are implemented in various ways. Parents may come to a clinic for training (Schopler & Reichler) or the training may be done at the home (Hemsley et al.). Generally, parents are taught to respond to the child in such a way as to increase the child's social and communication skills and decrease the child's inappropriate behavior. Hemsley et al. (1978), in the only study to use a control group, were effective in improving the quality of parent-child interaction and the use of communicative language in the child. However, only autistic children with IQs greater than 60 (about two-thirds of all autistic children have IQs less than 60) were included, so these results cannot be generalized to all autistic children. Short (1980) evaluated the effects of Schopler and Reichler's approach, using families as their own control by requiring them to wait at least two months before beginning treatment. He found significant improvement in home-based measures of social interaction and use of communicative language. In none of these approaches is a claim made that autism has been "cured." What has been accomplished is a relative improvement in social and language skills, a result that hopefully will increase the child's chances of avoiding institutionalization and attaining the kind of independent adult adjustment that Donald (previous section) achieved.

MAKING PARENTS FEEL GUILTY

Because lack of warmth in parents was at one time viewed as the cause of autism, parents have sometimes been made to suffer guilt unnecessarily.

The mother of Peter, the autistic boy described at the beginning of the chapter, eloquently describes the frustrations and pain that the parents of autistic children sometimes endure. Peter was taken to pediatricians, speech and hearing clinics, neurologists, and psychiatrists for a number of years until, by good fortune, his mother had a chance to consult with Kanner. The following quotation describes her experience at a child guidance clinic:

I told my [clinician] about Peter, but her questions were directed to me.

How did I get along with my parents, siblings, the people at work? As well as most people, I thought.

Had I wanted the baby? Yes, I had gone through sterility studies to get pregnant.

Why had I wanted a baby? Why? I had never reasoned it out. They are part of life, just like food, sunshine, friends, and marriage.

How did I get along with my husband? Very well. She snapped to attention. "Why?" she asked. "Are you afraid to quarrel with him?" Well—we were both in our thirties. We had no serious problems and could laugh at our small differences. Years of separation by the war had made us treasure the ordinary joys of life.

How could I expect Peter to be warm when I was so cold to him? How could I be anything but cold after years of trying to warm up this icy child of mine? Even with your own son, friendship is a two-way street. We hadn't rejected Peter, he had rejected us. Even rejection was too strong a word. Peter accepted us as he did the furniture, as tools to get what he wanted. He simply didn't recognize us as people. Proving this was as difficult as proving which came first, the chicken or the egg.

I asked the [clinician] for suggestions, but she had none to offer. What I did was not so important as how I felt about it. What could I read that would help me understand Peter? She could suggest no reading nor would she advise it. I sounded like a schoolteacher already. My use of the Tracy course was held up as an example of my intellectual approach to motherhood. My questions as to the cause of Peter's trouble, she evaded—an eloquent answer, indeed! (Eberhardy, 1967, pp. 259–260)

Throughout this book I have emphasized the importance of the family environment as a possible influence on psychopathological development. Does it necessarily follow that mental health professionals need communicate a message of blame to parents who are unfortunate enough to have psychologically disturbed children? Two points are relevant here. First, for some childhood disorders, especially autism, the evidence suggests that parent-child relations are not a primary cause. For these disorders to place a burden of guilt on the parents is hardly justified. Second, even for those childhood disorders in which parent-child interactions contribute in a primary way, there is no therapeutic or ethical justification for adopting an accusatory attitude toward the parents. Most parents are doing the best they can and may be desperately trying to keep their own head above water, psychologically speaking. The initial message from the mental health professional might best be formulated this way: "No matter how things got to be the way they are, we believe we can help you and your child cope with this problem more effectively." Later in the course of treatment, parental responses as well as child responses that seem to be maintaining symptomatic behavior in either person can be identified in a nonaccusatory way.

Summary

1. Early infantile autism is characterized by early onset (before 30 months of age), inability to relate to people, lack of speech for communication, and insistence on sameness and stereotyped behaviors.

2. The cause or causes of autism remain unknown, but the weight of the evidence strongly suggests that an impairment in brain functioning plays a more important role than social learning experiences. Heredity as well as biological injuries and illnesses may contribute to the organic malfunctioning.

3. A small proportion of autistic children are able to achieve an adequate social adjustment when they grow up even without special treatment. Social learning approaches have shown considerable promise in assisting speech and social development of autistic children but are still a long way from helping the child achieve a completely normal adjustment.

4. Childhood psychosis is characterized by later onset (after 30 months of age), severe impairment in social relationships, and bizarre behaviors.

5. Childhood psychoses may reflect a more heterogeneous collection of disorders than autism and therefore may have more varied causative influences. The presence of neurological abnormalities in many of these children suggests an organic etiology in some cases, but destructive psychological environments (without neurological abnormalities) suggest social learning determinants in other cases.

6. The prognosis for children diagnosed as childhood psychosis is only fair, but intensive long-term treatment efforts, such as those used by Bettelheim, have shown promising results.

7. It is unnecessary to make parents feel guilty about their severely disturbed youngsters, whether or not parent-child interaction played some role in the development of the disorder.

Suggested Readings

A number of experts discuss various aspects of autism in M. Rutter and E. Schopler (Eds.), *Autism: A reappraisal of concepts and treatment* (Plenum, 1978). J. S. Werry considers the childhood psychoses in H. C. Quay and J. S. Werry (Eds.), *Psychopathological disorders of childhood* (Wiley, 1979). B. Bettelheim provides psychodynamically oriented clinical studies of psychotic children in *The empty fortress* (Free Press, 1967).

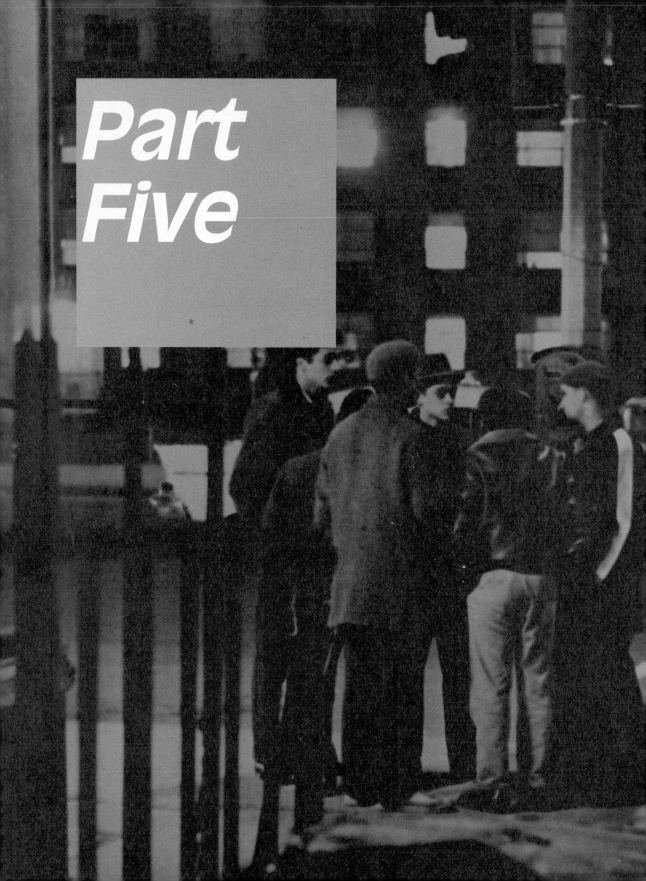

Part
Five

Social Deviations

22

Antisocial Behavior, Violence, and Crime

- Did you know that some people can repeatedly cheat, lie, steal, and murder, and yet feel no remorse? Can people of this kind be helped?

- Were antisocial adults antisocial children?

- What could make an ordinarily gentle person explode into violence?

- Your little boy won't stop raiding the cookie jar. Should you yell and hit him? Tell him he is making you cry? Tell him you are saving one apiece for supper? Look the other way? Stop stealing cookies yourself? Or what?

- "You can only get out of jail after you successfully complete our treatment program." Is it right to *make* criminals undergo therapy?

Two Antisocial Personalities

Charles Manson

When Charles Manson was 12, his mother tried to put him in a foster home; but none was available, so he was sent to the Gibault School for Boys, a caretaking institution in Indiana. He remained there ten months, then ran away and returned to his mother. She did not want him; he ran away again and burglarized a grocery store. Later he broke into several other stores and was finally caught. Placed in the juvenile center in Indianapolis, he escaped the next day. When caught again, the court, erroneously thinking he was Catholic, made arrangements to send him to Father Flanagan's Boys Town.

Four days after his arrival, he and another boy stole a car and drove to the home of the other boy's uncle in Peoria, Illinois. On the way they robbed a grocery store and a gambling casino. Thus Manson committed his first "violent" crime, armed robbery, at the age of 13. The uncle, a criminal in his own right, was glad to see them since they were small enough to slip through skylights. He put them to work immediately, and they broke into a grocery store and stole $1500, for which the uncle permitted them to keep $150. Two weeks later they were caught attempting a similar job. Manson was sent to the Indiana School for Boys at Plainfield.

He stayed there three years, running away a total of 18 times. According to his teachers, "He professed no trust in anyone" and "did good work only for those from whom he figured he could obtain something." In early 1951 he and two other 16-year-olds escaped and headed for California, stealing cars along the way for transportation, and burglarizing gas stations for needed cash. Near Beaver, Utah, a roadblock set up for a robbery suspect netted them instead. Taking stolen vehicles across a state line is a federal offense, so in March 1951 Manson was sent to the National Training School for Boys in Washington, D.C. During his stay there a psychiatrist wrote "that because of his small stature, illegitimacy, and lack of parental love, he is constantly striving for status with the other boys. . . . He developed certain facile techniques for dealing with people. These for the most part consist of a good sense of humor, an ability to ingratiate himself. . . . This could add up to a fairly 'slick' institutionalized youth, but one is left with the feeling that behind all this lies an extremely sensitive boy who has not yet given up in terms of securing some kind of love and affection from the world."

Manson was due for a parole hearing in February 1952, and with an offer from his aunt to provide a home and employment for him the chances looked good. Less than a month before the hearing, however, he took a razor blade and held it against another boy's throat while he sodomized him. As a result he was transferred to the federal reformatory at Petersburg, Virginia. By August he had committed eight serious offenses, including three homosexual acts, in his new placement, and as a result he was transferred to an even more secure institution, the federal reformatory at Chillicothe, Ohio. There was a marked improvement in his behavior and attitude during the nearly two years he spent at Chillicothe, and he raised his educational level from the fourth- to seventh-grade level. In May 1954 he was granted parole.

Manson, however, continued his life of stealing autos, using stolen credit cards, and violating various federal laws such as forging a United States Treasury check and transporting women for the purpose of prostitution across state lines. In July 1961 he found himself back in a federal penitentiary, where he stayed until March 1967.

When released, he was given permission to go to San Francisco—a fateful decision. During this time Manson discovered Haight-Ashbury. Here were young people, naive and eager to believe and to belong. Possibilities were unlimited for any self-styled guru in the making, and Manson quickly sensed that he had stumbled on a unique opportunity. Being an ex-con gave him some automatic status as antiestablishment, and rapping a line of metaphysical jargon that borrowed as much from the drug culture as from Scientology and Buddhism, he had no trouble attracting followers. This meeting of the individual psychological influences that produced a psychopathic person with a set of historical and sociological conditions, the drug and counterculture movement of the late 1960s, resulted ultimately in the tragic Tate-LaBianca murders.

The Duke of Deception

"My father could, however, be coaxed to reveal his bona fides. He had been schooled at Groton and passed along to Yale. . . . After Yale—class of late nineteen-twenty something, or early nineteen-thirty something—my father batted around the country, living a high life in New York among school and college chums, flying as a test pilot, marrying my mother, the daughter of a rear admiral. I was born a year after the marriage, in 1937, and three years after that my father went to England as a fighter pilot with Eagle Squadron, a group of American volunteers in the Royal Air Force. Later he transferred to the OSS, and was in Yugoslavia with the partisans; just before the Invasion he was parachuted into Normandy. . . .

A pretty history for an American clubman. Its fault is that it was not true. My father was a bullshit artist. True, there were many boarding schools, each less pleased with the little Duke than the last, but none of them was Groton. There was no Yale. . ." (Wolff, 1979, pp. 8–9).

So does Geoffrey Wolff describe his father, Duke Wolff. Geoffrey grew up believing it was perfectly natural to move from a small tract house (in southern California) to a mansion (in Birmingham, Alabama) to a boarding house (in Atlanta) to a honeymoon suite (in Niagara Falls) to a cold-water walk-up (in Manhattan) following the rise and fall of his father's fortunes. His father, Duke, led a life of lies, debt, drinking, and irresponsibility—clever enough at times to get high paying jobs as an aeronautical engineer (with false credentials) before piling up debts so high that he was forced to flee his creditors. Eventually, after his third release from prison, and estranged from his sons and two ex-wives, he died alone in a small, barren apartment in a seedy California town.

According to the FBI Uniform Crime Reports a violent crime was committed in the United States on the average once every 30 seconds during 1978. Violent crimes include murder, forcible rape, robbery, and aggravated assault. During the four-year period between 1974 and 1978 forcible rape (per 100,000 population) had increased 66.5 percent and aggravated assaults (per 100,000 population) had increased 65.6 percent. Clearly violence is a problem of major proportion for our society. In the first part of this chapter we will focus on certain types of individuals who lead antisocial or violent lives, the *antisocial personality* and the *explosive personality*, rather than on violence and crime in general. In the latter part of the chapter we will consider factors that contribute to broader categories of crime as exemplified by the juvenile delinquent and the adult criminal.

The Antisocial Personality Disorder

The term *antisocial personality disorder* applies to individuals who have a long history of continuous conflict with society, seem incapable of loyalty to individuals or groups, are impulsive, and do not learn from experience or punishment. Their behavior does not fall into any of the diagnostic categories so far considered; nor is there any indication of mental retardation or brain injury. It is not their criminality that is puzzling. Much as we deplore bank robbing, burglarizing, and embezzlement, most of us can understand the motives behind such behavior. But the repeated, poorly planned antisocial acts, the occasional senseless violence, and the almost total lack of lasting emotional attachments to other people are less

[portions of text obscured by an inserted sheet bearing the handwritten note "Conditioned Response (CR)"]

...ral in-
...d but
..." the
...ished,
...imself
...f life."
...sycho-
...havior,
...editary
...pathic
...e most
...ial per-
...-III for
..., how-

...gths to
...athic or
...acteris-
...various
...ord and

... When
...andard,
...hysically
...e regret,

remorse, or "twinge of conscience." The psychopath does not. One psychopath describes how he murdered three people: "The two little kids started crying, wanting water. I gave them some and she [their mother] drove a while—and I turned around and started shooting in the back seat and then turned back and shot her. She fell over against me and onto the floor" (Symkal & Thorne, 1951, p. 311). After giving the children a drink of water, he shot them, and later related the story without compassion or remorse. In psychoanalytic terminology, the psychopath has little or no superego and no guilt feelings about wrongdoing.

2. *Impulsivity; inability to delay gratification.* Psychopaths tend to act upon the impulse of the moment. They seem unable or unwilling to delay gratification for more long-term rewards. Therefore they are likely to commit impulsive, poorly planned criminal acts, flit from one mate to another (with or without marriage), quit or be fired from job after job because they cannot stand the restrictions or demands of ordinary work, and in general lead erratic and unstable lives. When frustrated in seeking immediate gratification they are likely to respond with aggression or violence against their perceived frustrators.

3. *Inability to profit from mistakes.* Most people, caught in some criminal or antisocial act and given some appropriate punishment, either develop their criminal expertise so that they are less likely to get caught the next time or give up criminal activities. Not so with psychopaths; although they may be caught in many crimes and receive varying kinds of punishment, they do not seem to learn from these experiences and frequently repeat the same antisocial behavior in the future.

4. *Lack of emotional ties to other people.* Psychopaths are loners; they seem incapable of binding ties or loyalties to other people. Although they may form fleeting attachments, these lack emotional depth and tenderness, and not uncommonly end abruptly in aggressive explosions. They can behave as callously toward their own wives, children, or parents as toward anyone else. Other people are treated as objects to be manipulated for the psychopath's own pleasure.

5. *Stimulus seeking.* Most psychopaths become bored quickly with the humdrum of everyday life. They search constantly for new thrills and experiences—daring robberies, impersonations, confidence games, new varieties of drugs, and deviant sexual behavior.

6. *Ability to make a good impression on others.* There is no reason to believe that psychopaths, on

the average, are any more or less intelligent than the rest of us. Many of them have learned as part of their manipulative strategies to appear intelligent, likable, charming, and witty. Frequently they talk their way out of tight spots, "con" people into dubious investments, or convince judges, juries, probation officers, or therapists of their good intentions for the future.

In DSM-III antisocial personality is listed as one kind of personality disorder (see Chapter 7 for a description of other kinds of personality disorders such as the histrionic, the dependent, and the compulsive personality). To qualify for the DSM-III diagnosis the person must be at least 18 years of age, have shown antisocial behavior (lying, stealing, truancy, fighting, or other manifestations) before the age of 15, and persisted in these and other antisocial behaviors (for example, poor occupational performance) into adult life.

Hare and Cox (1978) have found that ratings of psychopathy based on Cleckley's (1976) criteria (similar to the six characteristics listed above) can be made with high reliability if extensive case history data are available. Different raters correlate well over .80. These authors are concerned that the DSM-III criteria are structured in such a way that individuals might be given the diagnosis who do not show some of the central features of Cleckley's description. As of this time no research has been reported on the DSM-III criteria and I have given more weight to Cleckley's classical description in characterizing the symptoms of psychopathy.

EXPERIMENTAL STUDIES OF PSYCHOPATHY

Is Punishment Effective with Psychopaths? Experimental research has helped to confirm and define more precisely some of the characteristics of psychopathy derived from clinical observation. For example, studies have suggested that the psychopath's inability to profit from mistakes derives from a lack of anxiety about future punishment and a relatively poor ability to learn responses motivated by avoidance of pain or other forms of punishment. Punishment is effective in deterring most people from repeating undesired behavior because the person learns to respond with anxiety in anticipation of

being caught. In a study by Hare (1965a), subjects watched consecutive numbers 1 to 12 appear on a display. They were told that each time the number 8 appeared they would receive an electric shock equal in intensity to one earlier determined to be the strongest they could tolerate. Both normals and nonpsychopathic criminals showed anticipatory rises in palmar sweat gland activity (referred to as electrodermal activity or skin conductance), but psychopathic criminals did not. Using various forms of anticipated stress, this basic finding has been repeated in four additional studies (see Hare, 1978, for a review). "Resting" level measures of palmar skin conductance obtained before the start of experimental procedures were found to be significantly lower for psychopathic criminals than nonpsychopathic criminals when averaged over eight different studies (Hare, 1978). These "resting" level measures of palmar sweat gland activity might also be seen as reflecting the degree of anticipatory anxiety a subject might feel before an experiment begins. Given a relative lack of anticipatory anxiety one would expect psychopaths to learn conditioned electrodermal responses less well than nonpsychopaths. This has indeed been shown to be the case (Hare, 1965b; Lykken, 1957); see Figure 22-1. In these studies the electrodermal response was conditioned to auditory stimuli and electric shock was used as the unconditioned stimulus. Not only should psychopaths learn less well in the classical conditioning procedure, they should show poorer avoidance learning when an anxiety-arousing stimulus, such as electric shock, is used to motivate the avoidance learning. Again, this has been found to be so (Lykken, 1957; Schmauk, 1970). Overall, then, there is considerable support for the conclusion that psychopaths, defined according to Cleckley's criteria, show less anxiety than nonpsychopaths in stressful situations. This characteristic may play a role in psychopaths' willingness to indulge in risky behavior and their difficulty in learning to inhibit antisocial behavior.

Many of the above studies imply that psychopaths have a primary biological deficit, such as a low level of physiological responsiveness. The lack of fear (or physiological arousal more generally) may, however, result secondarily from certain cognitive styles. Psychopaths, for example, may cognitively label many laboratory experiences as boring and not care about making a good impression on the experimenter.

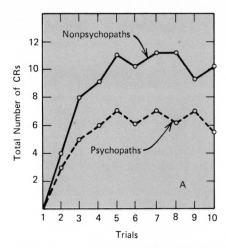

FIGURE 22-1. Conditioning of the galvanic skin response (GSR) in psychopathic and nonpsychopathic criminals. (Adapted from Hare, 1965a. Copyright 1965 by The Journal Press and redrawn with permission.)

Such attitudes should reduce physiological manifestations of fear or anxiety.

Also suggestive of cognitive factors are findings that show psychopaths to not always be unresponsive to certain kinds of punishments. For example, Schmauk (1970) found that although psychopaths learned avoidance responses less well than nonpsychopaths when electric shock was the aversive stimulus, they learned the same avoidance response just as well as nonpsychopaths when the punishment involved taking away money (quarters from a pile given to them at the beginning of the task). Thus we should be cautious in concluding how general the psychopath's relative indifference to punishment is.

Siegel (1978), however, found that depriving psychopaths of money is also relatively ineffective as a punishment under certain conditions. He suggested that some psychopaths delude themselves about the likelihood of being caught, and thereby punished, when committing crimes, and are thus more likely to be affected by threats of future punishment when punishment is a virtual certainty but fail to be affected when there is some degree of uncertainty. This is indeed what Siegel found when he had subjects play a series of 10 probability card games in which the probability of punishment (taking back money) varied from 0 to 100 percent in the different games. Psychopaths did not suppress their rate of respond-

ing as much as nonpsychopathic criminals or noncriminals when there was a fair degree of uncertainty. When certainty for either punishment or no punishment was high, there was no difference in response suppression between the psychopaths and the other two groups. The psychopaths may have unrealistically believed that the chances of punishment were low when there was some degree of uncertainty—a characteristic referred to by Cleckley as superstitious logic or magical thinking.

Whether the lack of effectiveness of punishment on psychopaths is explained best in terms of physiological underresponsiveness, cognitive styles, magical thinking, or some combination of these factors is not clear at this time. The studies do provide support for the clinical impression that psychopaths worry less about the future than most of us.

Do Psychopaths Seek Stimulation? Quay (1977) theorized that a primary characteristic of psychopaths that might explain much of their behavior is an inordinate need for increases or changes in stimulation. There is some empirical support for this view. Emmons and Webb (1974), for example, found psychopathic criminals to score higher than nonpsychopathic criminals on self-report scales measuring interests in travel, mind-affecting drugs, unconventional people, boredom susceptibility, a variety of sexual partners, wild parties, and gambling. Of course, some of these very characteristics probably contributed to the diagnosis of psychopathy in the first place. More precisely focused on stimulation seeking was Skrzypek's (1969) study. He found that psychopathic delinquents showed a greater preference for complex stimuli (random shapes varying in complexity) and for novel pictures (familiar versus unusual or incongruous pictures) than did neurotic delinquents. After a brief period of perceptual isolation (lying on a bed with reduced visual and auditory input) the psychopathic subjects showed an even greater preference for both complexity and novelty than did the comparison group.

It has been more difficult to provide supportive evidence for neurophysiological theories that might account for the psychopath's stimulus-seeking behavior. The most common theory of this kind is that psychopaths are physiologically underaroused and thus seek stimulation to bring themselves up to an optimal state of pleasurable arousal. This theory has

RESEARCH
REPORT
22-1

Psychopathy, Intelligence, and Violent Crime

Past attempts to predict future crimes of violence among criminal or delinquent populations using personality measures such as the MMPI have not been particularly successful. Recall the discussion of the general difficulty in predicting violence in ex–mental patients (Chapter 19). Heilbrun (1979) has shed further light on this problem by demonstrating the role that intelligence may play in the commission of violent and impulsive crimes.

In this study 76 white male prisoners in Georgia's penal system were divided into four groups: high psychopathic–high intelligence, high psychopathic–low intelligence, low psychopathic–high intelligence, and low psychopathic–low intelligence. Psychopathy was assessed by two scales, the Psychopathic Deviant scale of the MMPI and the Socialization scale of the California Psychological Inventory. Intelligence was measured by a nonverbal test (IPAT Culture Free Intelligence Test) in an effort to reduce the effects of cultural and educational backgrounds. The four groups were formed by dividing the total sample into high and low psychopathic groups (above and below the median score) and then dividing each of those groups into high and low intelligence groups (above and below the median score). The crimes that the individuals were imprisoned for were then divided into violent crimes (for example, murder, rape, assault) and nonviolent crimes (for example, car theft, forgery, manufacturing liquor).

Results were striking. Among the psychopathic criminals only those in the low-intelligence group showed a preference for violent crimes—a very strong preference indeed, with over eight times as many violent as nonviolent crimes being committed. See Table 22-1. For the nonpsychopaths there was a tendency for the more intelligent to commit violent crimes but this trend was not statistically significant. Ratings of impulsiveness of criminal act were also higher for the low-intelligence psychopaths than for any other group.

This study did not *predict* violent crime. It was *postdictive* in the sense that the crimes had already been committed. Nevertheless, the results are strongly suggestive that the prediction of violent crime among psychopathic individuals would be greatly enhanced if intelligence were included as a predictor variable. Perhaps the inconsistency of past findings may be explained in part by the neglect of this variable.

How does low intelligence act to raise the probability of violence in psychopaths? Remember, low intelligence in nonpsychopathic criminals was not associated with higher rates of violent crime so that low intelligence by itself is not the complete answer. Perhaps what is important is the inability to think of alternative modes of action when faced with some frustration or temptation, combined with the other qualities of psychopathy. More research is needed to clarify the specific ways in which low intelligence interacts with psychopathy to produce the high levels of violent crime.

TABLE 22-1   Frequencies of Violent and Nonviolent Crime as a Function of Psychopathy and Intelligence

Level of Psychopathy	Level of Intelligence			
	Higher		Lower	
	Violent	Nonviolent	Violent	Nonviolent
Psychopathic	10	9	17	2
Nonpsychopathic	15	7	8	8

Adapted from Heilbrun (1979). Copyright 1979 by American Psychological Association and used with permission.

some overlap with the theories of low anxiety response to stress or punishment just discussed. Blackburn (1978), however, after reviewing the literature and reporting results of his own research concludes that the evidence is not at all convincing that psychopaths have generally lower levels of physiological arousal.

DEVELOPMENT

Antisocial Behavior Starts in Childhood. Robins (1978a) describes two studies in which measures of childhood antisocial behavior are related to antisocial behavior in adults. In the first study, children who had attended a child guidance clinic in St. Louis in the 1920s were followed up some 30 years later in 1955–56. In the second study a nonclinic sample of young black males was selected from public elementary school records and followed up some 20 years later in 1966. A striking finding in both studies is the high percentage of antisocial adults who had shown high degrees of antisocial behavior as children: 82 percent in the first study and 67 percent in the second study. If children with moderate degrees of antisocial behavior are included, these percentages rise to 95 and 88 respectively. Almost all antisocial adults, then, had shown either moderate or high rates of antisocial behavior as children. Persistent antisocial or psychopathic behavior rarely seems to start in adulthood and has frequently been present *before* adolescence. No specific kind of childhood antisocial behavior was better than the others in predicting adult antisocial behavior—arrests, truancy, use of alcohol at an early age, fighting, and dropping out of school were all predictive. The best overall predictor of adult antisocial behavior was simply the total number of different antisocial behaviors shown by the child.

Does this mean that all antisocial children become antisocial adults? No, most antisocial children do not go on to become antisocial adults. In the first study, 36 percent of children with high levels of antisocial behavior showed high levels of antisocial behavior as adults. The corresponding figure in study two was 41 percent. For a sizable proportion of antisocial children, factors in the environment (treatment in some cases) or within themselves deflect the course away from a life of persistent crime or other form of psychopathy.

Heredity. A few years back evidence for a genetic contribution to behavior disorders could only be marshaled for schizophrenia and certain affective disorders, and this evidence was largely limited to twin studies, which were not entirely convincing. Now a genetic contribution to schizophrenia and certain affective disorders is no longer in dispute; moreover, evidence is mounting for a genetic contribution to anxiety reactions, certain psychophysiological disorders, and autism. It will come as no surprise, then, to learn that recent evidence suggests a genetic contribution to psychopathy and possibly to criminality more broadly conceived.

In the two best twin studies an attempt was made to obtain information about all twins born in a given geographical region. Dalgaard and Kringlen (1976) searched the Norwegian Twin Register for all twins born in Norway between 1921 and 1930 where one or both twins were found to have been convicted of a crime. Christianson (1977) examined a similar population of twins born in the eastern half of Denmark between 1881 and 1910. The results in Table 22-2 show higher concordance rates for identical than fraternal twins, although the difference in rates in the Dalgaard and Kringlen study was not statistically significant. Also, the fact that the absolute levels of concordances for identical twins (25.8 and 35) are relatively low suggests that genetic factors are weak relative to environmental influences. Christianson further divided his large twin population into various subgroups and found greater differences between identical and fraternal twins when the twins were female, lived in rural areas, and came from higher social classes. These results are interesting because they suggest that when individuals live in circumstances where relatively higher crime rates prevail—are poor and reside in cities—environmental factors overshadow genetic factors. When, however, environmental influences are diminished, such as for a middle- or upper-class person living in a more rural area, then the effects of different genetic makeups are more likely to make themselves known.

As mentioned before, adoption studies are more convincing than twin studies because they are not subject to the criticism that identical twins are treated more alike than fraternal twins. Schulsinger (1977) conducted an adoption study in which psychopathy, rather than the more general concept of criminality, was used as the behavior of interest. Again the Danish records were used as a basis for subject identification, and psychiatrists identified 57 adoptees as meeting the criteria for psychopathy. A control group of 57 adoptees, judged not to be psychopathic or have other forms of mental illness, were matched with the psychopathic group. All psychiatric institutions in Denmark were searched for the records of any parent who had been institutionalized, and these records were used to make a diagnosis of psychopathy. The results are shown in Table 22-3, where it can be seen that psychopathy was more than four times as great for the biological parents as for the adoptive parents of the psychopathic adoptees. Rates of psychopathy were also lower in the biological and adoptive parents of the nonpsychopathic control group. In considering the low absolute levels of psychopathy in these groups, it must be remembered that only parents who had been admitted to psychiatric institutions would be picked up in this study. Many psychopaths, perhaps most, are not admitted to psychiatric hospitals. Other adoption studies have found evidence for genetic factors in criminality (Cadoret, 1978; Crowe, 1974; Hutchings & Mednick, 1977), but a study by Bohmen (1978) did not.

What should we make of this evidence for possible genetic factors in psychopathy or criminality? First, the evidence is not quite as clear-cut or indicative of as strong a genetic influence as in bipolar affective disorders or severe, chronic schizophrenia. Certainly criminality per se is not inherited. Perhaps the most reasonable view at this time is that some subset of psychopaths have a genetically determined biological characteristic (toward impulsivity or difficulty in learning responses based on punishment, for example) that increases their likelihood of developing antisocial behaviors. Under environmental conditions that do not favor the development of antisocial behavior—a rural, upper-middle-class background, for example—a genetic factor of this kind might assume more importance. Individuals with the full pattern of psychopathic traits probably make up a minority of

TABLE 22-3
Percentage of Biological and Adoptive Parents Diagnosed as Psychopaths

Children	Parents	
	Biological	*Adoptive*
Psychopathic	4.5	0.9
Nonpsychopathic	0.9	0.0

From Schulsinger (1977). Copyright Gardner Press, 1977, and used with permission.

the criminal population, and those psychopaths with a genetic predisposition would represent an ever smaller proportion of the total criminal population, which may account for the somewhat less consistent findings of a genetic factor in the general criminal population.

Biological Correlates. I have already mentioned evidence for one kind of biological correlate, lack of electrodermal responsivity when anticipating punishment. Another biological measure that has attracted a lot of interest in this area is the EEG. The cortex of the human brain continuously generates electric potentials that can be measured by attaching electrodes to the scalp. These potentials, usually rhythmical, reflect degrees of physiological and psychological arousal as well as organic impairments in brain functioning. Recordings of the electric potentials are called an *electroencephalogram* or EEG.

In the average person who is resting awake quietly with eyes closed the dominant rhythm obtained from the back of the head is of relatively high amplitude (voltage) with a frequency of from 8 to 13 hertz (cycles per second). This relatively low-frequency wave is called the *alpha rhythm*. Mental activity of almost any kind—paying attention to novel or changing stimuli, solving a problem "mentally," experiencing anxiety—tends to disrupt the alpha rhythm, which is then replaced by a high-frequency, low-voltage rhythm, the *beta rhythm*. Figure 22-2 shows examples of these and other brain wave patterns.

TABLE 22-2 Percentage Concordance in Criminality in Two Twin Studies

Study	Total Pairs		Percent Concordance	
	Identical	*Fraternal*	*Identical*	*Fraternal*
Dalgaard and Kringlen	31	54	25.8	14.9
Christianson	325	611	35	13

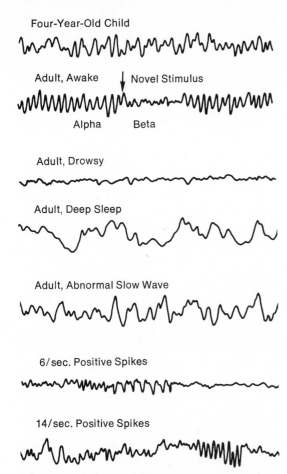

Four-Year-Old Child

Adult, Awake ↓ Novel Stimulus

Alpha   Beta

Adult, Drowsy

Adult, Deep Sleep

Adult, Abnormal Slow Wave

6/sec. Positive Spikes

14/sec. Positive Spikes

FIGURE 22-2. Examples of different kinds of brain waves, as recorded by electroencephalogram. (Adapted from Hare, 1970. Copyright 1970 by John Wiley & Sons and reproduced with permission.)

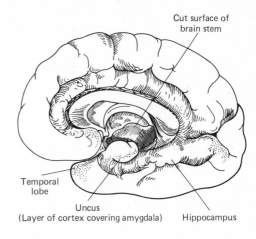

Cut surface of brain stem

Temporal lobe

Uncus
(Layer of cortex covering amygdala)   Hippocampus

FIGURE 22-3.   A cross-section of the human brain.

Syndulko (1978), after considering some 40 years of EEG research on individuals labeled psychopaths, concluded that a subset of these persons do show an excessive incidence of EEG abnormalities. Whether the subset of psychopaths with abnormal EEGs is the same as those thought to have a genetic predisposition has not been determined, although this would clearly be important information to have. The EEG abnormalities usually found in psychopaths tend to be of two kinds: very slow waves ordinarily characteristic of normal infants and young children, and positive spikes involving bursts of waves at 6–8 and 14–16 hertz, usually occurring near the temporal lobes of the brain (Figure 22-3). The finding that the brain wave pattern in some psychopaths resembles that found in young children has led to the speculation that psychopathy represents a form of central nervous system immaturity. This hypothesis has a certain appeal since it fits nicely with the fact that several key features of the psychopathic personality resemble characteristics frequently seen in young children—impulsivity, inability to delay gratification, and egocentricity.

In general, the presence of some kind of EEG abnormality in a substantial proportion of psychopathic individuals suggests that a malfunctioning in the brain may contribute to the development of this disorder. This kind of evidence, however, is indirect, and we should not lose sight of the fact that at least half of the people diagnosed psychopathic do not have abnormal brain waves and 15 percent of the normal population do have them.

Psychosocial Correlates.   If all psychopathy cannot be explained in terms of brain malfunctioning, then what aspect of the social development of these individuals leads to such an antisocial life-style? Somewhere in the socialization process society has failed to inculcate the ability to delay gratification, to experience remorse, and to acquire a sense of loyalty to close friends, relatives, or groups. Where did we go wrong with the psychopath? For some time psychologists have been interested in how children *in-*

ternalize the values, prohibitions, and proscriptions of the social community. Their theories and findings may be relevant to an understanding of how psychopathy develops.

Young infants are hedonists, adherents of what Freud called the *pleasure principle.* They seek what they want when they want it and have little inclination to delay, regulate, or otherwise show the niceties of civilized restraint. Yet sooner or later young children do begin to exercise control over their own behavior, go to the bathroom at the proper place, desist from physical attacks on others, share toys and food, and eventually endure long stretches of effort to achieve some ultimate goal such as a college degree. In short, they become *socialized.*

When we say that a child has internalized or acquired self-control over certain responses, we usually mean the child will make (or not make) certain responses *in the absence of immediate external re-*

wards or punishments. A young child who resists the temptation to eat a forbidden piece of candy between meals only when likely to be caught is showing restraint but has not internalized the control of behavior. One who refrains from eating the candy when no one is around has internalized the parents' prohibition.

Experimental research has shown that *cognitive structuring* (such as giving reasons for the prohibition), *modeling of self-control by others,* and *conditioned emotional reactions* all contribute to internalization. An example of a conditioned emotional reaction would be a situation in which a child considers committing some wrongdoing, imagines parental disapproval, and experiences some anticipatory shame or other negative emotion. Research Report 22-2 offers a survey of experimental research on internalization.

**RESEARCH
REPORT
22-2**

Learning Self-Control

Experimental research has shown that *cognitive structuring, modeling,* and *conditioned emotional reactions* may all contribute to internalization. A usual experimental paradigm is to ask young children not to play with some especially desirable toys and then leave the children alone in the room with the toys. By various means, it is possible to tell whether the children have complied with the request. Before telling the child not to play with the toys, children in different groups undergo different experiences reflecting, in miniature, certain features of parental socialization techniques. Studies of this kind have strongly indicated that when the experimenter provides cognitive structuring in the form of reasons and justifications for the prohibition, the children are more likely to abide by the experimenter's request. (for example, Parke, 1969)

Speaking more broadly, what these and similar researches suggest is that children learn to give themselves instructions when nobody else is present, and these self-administered instructions give an added degree of control over their behavior. These self-instructions can also include information about consequences that are likely to follow a given action: approval, disapproval, painful injury, and so on.

Experimental studies with children also indicate that a child who has observed other people model self-controlling behavior will show more self-control (Mischel & Liebert, 1966). The more the model is seen as powerful (controlling resources important to the child) and the more the model is rewarded for self-denying behavior, the stronger is the child's tendency to imitate the model. (Bandura et al., 1967b)

Aronfreed (1968) has proposed that learned empathic emotional responses play an important role in internalization processes. According to this view, positive and negative emotional reactions in the child become conditioned to expressive cues associated with emotional reactions in other people. Thus it is presumed that generally positive emotional states on the part of a parent are more likely to be paired with generally positive emotional states in the infant; and generally negative emotional states in the parent are more likely to be paired with generally negative emotions in the child. Such a rough pairing of emotional experiences provides the basis for conditioning in which the overt expressive cues of the parent (smiling, frowning, tone of voice) become conditioned stimuli, eliciting empathic reactions. Eventually cognitive mediators (thoughts such as "Mom is angry") supplement the observed expressive cues as elicitors of emotional reactions in the child.

Aronfreed and Paskal (1965) reported an ingenious study with six- to eight-year-old children in which a positive empathic response was conditioned to expressive cues from the experimenter. These results showed that the explicit pairing of the child's positive emotional reaction with the experimenter's expressive cues resulted in greater "altruism," foregoing candy in order to elicit the experimenter's expressive cues of pleasure, than various control conditions. This study and others (for example, Aronfreed & Paskal, 1966) generally support the notion that conditioned emotional reactions to expressive cues (or internal thoughts) associated with other people's emotional responses play a role in the internalization of altruistic, sympathetic, and other self-denying behaviors. Of course, within this context the behavior is not entirely self-denying since it results in a positive emotional reaction or the avoidance of a negative emotional reaction.

Whether a conditioned emotion is literally empathic—similar to that of the other persons—is not particularly relevant to the basic issue here. Children, for example, may well learn conditioned emotional reactions of shame, fear, and unspecifiable blends of negative emotion to expressive cues associated with parental anger, disapproval, or withdrawal. Eventually these emotional reactions may be elicited by just anticipating parental approval or disapproval. Then these conditioned emotions and associated cognitions could provide a powerful mechanism for controlling behavior in the absence of external agents—conscience. Similar emotional reactions could also become conditioned to actual transgressions and might motivate behavior aimed at reparation, confession, and punishment seeking.

Much more research on the role of conditioned emotional reactions on the development of internalization must be done in order to confirm these speculations.

For older children a *love-oriented* approach to discipline has been found in a number of studies to be related to internalized reactions to transgression (Martin, 1975). A love-oriented approach is characterized by many of the factors that experimental research indicates are related to internalization. Thus the parent makes use of cognitive structuring or reasoning by clearly describing what is expected, explaining why a rule should be obeyed (usually with an emphasis on abstract principles of right and wrong), and describing long-term consequences. Rather than using physical or materialistic punishment, the love-oriented parent is more likely to emphasize how hurt or disappointed the child's misbehavior makes the parent or others feel. To the extent that the child has developed empathic emotional reactions, this strategy is likely to produce guilt.

Hoffman and Saltzstein (1967) studied the way children completed unfinished stories in which a child has committed some forbidden act. The authors found that some children were more concerned about the external consequences of getting caught than with internal reactions of guilt or remorse. A *power-assertive* approach to discipline was related to this external orientation to transgression. In many ways this kind of discipline is the opposite of *love-oriented*. It is likely to be harsh and arbitrary, involving a crude display of parental power. Physical punishments like hitting or slapping, verbal abuse, parental anger, and unreasonable deprivations of privileges are frequent accompaniments.

How well do Charles Manson's and Duke Wolff's childhood experiences fit the pattern expected to be associated with low internalization of societal values? Keep this question in mind while reading the following account.

Development of Two Antisocial Personalities

Charles Manson

Charles Manson was born "no name Maddox" on November 12, 1934, in Cincinnati, Ohio, the illegitimate son of a 16-year-old girl named Kathleen Maddox. Relatives said that "Kathleen ran around a lot, drank, and got into trouble." She lived with a succession of men; William Manson, to whom she was married briefly, provided a last name for young Charles. Kathleen provided little mothering or stability. She would leave the child with obliging neighbors for an hour, then disappear for days or weeks. After a while he would be picked up by his grandmother or maternal aunt. Most of his early years were spent with one of these two in West Virginia, Kentucky, or Ohio.

Charles Manson, convicted of the Tate-LaBianca murders, typifies many features of the antisocial or psychopathic personality.

In 1939 Kathleen and her brother Luther robbed a service station, knocking out the attendant with Coke bottles. They were caught and sentenced to five years in the state penitentiary. While his mother was in prison Charles lived with his aunt, a person who thought all pleasures were sinful but who did give him some love. When his mother was paroled in 1942, she reclaimed him. He was eight then, and the next several years were spent in a succession of rundown hotel rooms with a variety of newly introduced "uncles."

Duke Wolff

Duke Wolff grew up in an atmosphere of financial affluence as the son of a respected surgeon. A cousin remembers him as a spoiled child, given an incredible quantity of toys. "... you couldn't walk across it (his room) without breaking a toy because there was no room on the floor for them all." A young friend recalls him as a "toy-breaker." A day or two after Christmas most of the toys were broken. Duke's father, either unable or unwilling to spend time with his son, lavished toys and other material things on him. His father also had a violent temper, which was occasionally unleashed against him. Duke's cousin remembers the father chasing the boy, trying to hit him with a chair, threatening to kill him with it, but doesn't remember why. The cousin believed Duke's predominant feeling toward his father was fear, which accounted for a developing stammer.

Duke, his wife, and son, Geoffrey, at a Los Angeles country club, 1940.

Duke's mother doted on her little boy, dressed him like a doll, and showered praise on him. He no doubt reciprocated this love, but he was also capable of tantrums of his own (imitation of his father?) when not allowed to get his way. His mother did not tell his father about these outbursts of temper, wanting to keep the peace. Duke was apparently able to get his way with his friends and mother by being bright, talented, and charming—or occasionally by a display of temper. None of this apparently worked with his father, who seemed to require attainments that his son was unable to meet, so that according to Geoffrey Wolff, "my father must very early have become a student of evasion, plotting ways around the judgment and daunting standards of someone sixty-five when he was thirteen." (Wolff, 1979, p. 24)

As Duke grew into later childhood and early adolescence he acquired the reputation among the neighbors as a "wild boy"—breaking windows, charging small items at the drug store to his mother's account without her permission, and borrowing small amounts of money from his classmates. At age 13 he was sent off to what was to be a series of failing experiences at various prestige eastern boarding schools. All in all he was kicked out, flunked out, or eased out of five of these schools. The pattern was pretty much the same at each. He would become progressively less willing to make the academic effort to do passing work and more and more involved in various violations of school regulations. Relations with his father, and finally with his mother, became strained and finally disrupted. His father's reaction alternated between punishments (arbitrarily extreme at times) and a pained "how can you do this to me" stance.

In thinking back over the experimental and correlational literature on the internalization of social values, we can see several factors that might have contributed to Manson's psychopathic personality. His mother modeled a life of prostitution, irresponsibility, and crime. She probably provided little in the way of cognitive structuring about rules, consequences, or values. It seems unlikely that she gave enough consistent love to provide an approach to child rearing that could even remotely be called love-oriented. In fact, Manson as a child was moved around so much that he probably experienced little consistent parenting by anyone. What he did learn was to take what he wanted without concern for others' reactions, and when necessary to exploit and manipulate others by charm, fast talk, religious-philosophical jargon, promises of repentance, and fear.

In many ways Duke Wolff and Charles Manson are very different people. Duke was much more of a "gentleman," he didn't burglarize stores in the dark of night or even come close to the kind of violence, finally including murder, shown by Manson. With the manners and know-how derived from an upper-class background, he could pull off deceits and impersonations (as a Yale alumnus, for example) that were beyond Manson's capabilities. Yet there are common

threads. Neither seemed to experience any shame or guilt for his transgressions against the social establishment or even those close to him. They had both learned manipulative techniques to get what they wanted with little concern about the consequences to others, and both seemed doomed to repeat endlessly certain stratagems that frequently worked in the short term but in the long run kept them impoverished and in and out of prison.

The features in Duke's childhood that seem relevant to the development of these personality traits are the father who seemed to irrationally find that his son never measured up to some expectations that were probably not clearly specified and who gave lavishly of material things but little in the realm of interpersonal relating that might be called love. At some point Duke must have given up on getting support and appreciation from his father and decided that a strategy of deception and evasion would at least get him the material goods. And Duke's mother probably unwittingly reinforced this line of development by rewarding his charming and clever tactics while at the same time covering up for early antisocial behaviors. It should be mentioned that Duke did spend time with his own son, Geoffrey, and did seem on occasion to genuinely experience love for Geoffrey. To this extent he falls short (fortunately for Geoffrey) of the pure psychopathic pattern. But then few individuals score perfectly on any psychiatric category. Manson too may not be the perfect psychopath. Some of his rather queer and messianic ideas suggest a departure from reality that has a schizophrenic quality.

The way in which early antisocial tendencies in young children can interact with environmental events to produce a snowballing effect toward a lifelong pattern is nicely illustrated by Robins (1978a):

The typical psychopath's childhood behaviour problems begin when he enters school, detests it, fails to learn to read, "acts up" in class, fights on the playground, begins missing school, and apparently does not try very hard while he is there. This set of behaviours very rapidly gets him disliked both by his teachers and his schoolmates. The whole sad picture is frequently in place before the end of his very first year of school. . . . Psychopaths have been described as hostile and paranoid people. If one considers that in response to their early antisocial behaviour, parents beat them, schools expel them, and police chase them, their subjective experience of the world as unfriendly and dangerous may not be wholly irrational. Once they perceive the world in these terms, the chances that they will continue deviant behaviour may be greatly increased. . . . Early truancy leads to leaving school before graduation, which in turn creates job problems, which then encourages theft, which leads to jail, which alienates spouse and relatives. (p. 269)

And so it goes.

Explosive Disorders

Jennie: An Explosive Disorder

Jennie's troubles began on New Year's Eve of the year that she was 13. When her aunt told her to turn down the volume on her record player, Jennie reacted by going berserk. She smashed the furniture in her room, broke windows, and created such a disturbance that the police had to be called. Shortly after this, while she was babysitting with her stepsisters, she was very disturbed by one youngster's constant crying, so she put a plastic bag over the child's head and suffocated her. Jennie was frightened by what she'd done and ran to a girlfriend's house, where the police found her. Because her action was so senseless, and because she was so young, she was sent to a mental institution for observation. While she was being questioned by a psychiatrist there, she confessed that she had also killed another younger stepsister, who was thought to have died of pneumonia. (Mark & Ervin, 1970, p. 112)

BEHAVIORAL CHARACTERISTICS

Jennie would be diagnosed an *intermittent explosive disorder,* described in DSM-III as consisting of recurrent episodes of loss of control of aggressive impulses that result in serious assault or destruction of property. The intensity of the aggressive attack is grossly out of proportion to any circumstances that may have played a role in eliciting the reaction. The episode comes on quickly and, regardless of duration, ceases almost as quickly. Following an episode there is genuine regret or self-reproach about the consequences. Between episodes the person behaves normally with no signs of unusual impulsivity or aggressiveness. Individuals who show this pattern of behavior only once are diagnosed as *isolated explosive disorder.*

Individuals showing this kind of episodic violence are quite different from the psychopathic personality in that most of the time they behave normally, have incorporated the values of their community, and ordinarily are capable of having loyalties and ties to family and friends. Nor is there any evidence of a schizophrenic disorder that might explain their violence in terms of paranoid counterattacks or the homicidal outbursts of the catatonic.

After studying the histories of violent individuals (somewhat more broadly defined than the DSM-III definition just given), Mark and Ervin (1970) concluded that these individuals usually have four characteristics: (1) a history of physical assault, especially wife and child beating; (2) an association between drinking even a small amount of alcohol and violent behavior; (3) a history of impulsive sexual behavior, at times including sexual assault; and (4) a history (in those who drove cars) of many traffic violations and serious automobile accidents. These authors refer to this pattern of violent behavior as the *dyscontrol syndrome* and suggest that some degree of brain dysfunction may be partly responsible for it.

DEVELOPMENT

There is no clear evidence that tendencies toward episodic violence are transmitted from one generation to the next by genetic mechanisms. Considerable controversy, however, has centered around the possibility that a chromosomal anomaly known as the XYY genotype may be related to acts of violence in males.

The XYY Genotype. Among the 46 chromosomes in the normal human body are two chromosomes that determine the sex of the individual, the X and Y chromosomes. Females have two X chromosomes and males have one X and one Y chromosome. Occcasionally males are born with an extra 47th chromosome of the Y type, the XYY genotype. A chromosomal anomaly of this kind probably is not inherited but results from some accident of development. In 1965 Jacobs et al. reported that seven individuals from a population of 197 mentally retarded criminals had the XYY genotype. In addition to being mentally retarded and prone to aggressive violence, all these individuals were unusually tall. The investigators hypothesized that the extra Y chromosome was responsible for a syndrome of borderline intelligence, unusual height, and episodic aggressive outbursts.

Since the original publication of Jacobs et al., a number of investigations have looked into the relationship of the XYY genotype to violent crime (for example, Jarvik et al., 1973). The incidence of this genotype in the normal population is rare. Hook (1973) estimated an incidence rate ranging from about one in every 1000 males to one in every 1500 males. It has generally been found to occur more frequently among inmates of penal institutions (for example, Hook, 1973) and consistently higher (2 to 20 times) among individuals who have shown both criminal and mentally disordered behavior (Borgaonkar & Shah, 1975). These findings provide some support for the hypothesized relationship of the XYY genotype to crime. What is not shown in these studies is a clear relationship to *violent* crime. In fact, several studies have not found XYY males in penal institutions to behave more aggressively than various comparison groups (Borgaonkar & Shah, 1975). The most comprehensive study was performed by Witkin et al. (1977) in which they attempted to study all tall males born in Copenhagen, Denmark, between 1944 and 1947. Out of the 4139 tall males studied only 12 were XYYs, but they had indeed been convicted of crimes more often than the comparison group of 4096 XYs, 41.7 percent (5 out of 12) compared with 9.3 percent, respectively. However, only one of the XYY men had committed an aggressive crime, and that crime was not particularly violent; the other four XYYs had committed property crimes. XYYs tend, on the average, to have lower intelligence, and the authors suggest that this may account for the greater rate of crime, or at least of getting caught. The overall evidence then does not support a relationship between the XYY genotype and violent crime.

Specific Lesions and Localized Electrical Activity. Occasionally it can be shown that violent behavior is associated with specific brain abnormalities such as tumors or localized disturbances in electrical activity.

Cases like that of Jennie suggest that certain regions of the brain are especially involved in the expression and control of primitive emotions and motivations. Research with animals has indeed shown that in a part of the inner brain known as the *limbic system* are structures that are related to aggressive, attacking behaviors and fleeing or fearful behavior. Klüver and Bucy (1939) showed, for example, that when both temporal lobes (which include many important limbic structures) are removed, monkeys become placid and do not respond aggressively even to attacks by other monkeys. Likewise they do not

> When Jennie (the 13-year-old girl who suffocated a young child) was given a thorough psychiatric and neurological examination including an EEG, no abnormalities were discovered. A neurologist, however, continued to be suspicious of the possibility of *temporal lobe epilepsy*, a condition known to be associated with violence in some cases. In a surgical operation, electrodes were implanted on the surface of Jennie's temporal lobe and also deep within it in the hippocampus (Figure 22-3). Brain wave recordings from the surface of the temporal lobe were normal, but those from the hippocampus were strikingly abnormal, indicating the presence of localized epileptic discharges (in Chapter 25 brain wave patterns associated with epileptic seizures will be described). The authors knew that a baby's cry was able to provoke an extreme behavioral change in Jennie, frequently including vicious assaults. When a recording of a baby crying was played to Jennie, it not only elicited a behavioral response of discomfort and anxiety but also a burst of abnormal seizure-related electrical activity in several parts of the interior of her temporal lobes. The investigators concluded that some dysfunction in these deep structures of Jennie's brain was the cause of her occasional violence and gave her a drug known to control seizures in most epileptic patients. Unfortunately, she was soon sent to a state mental institution where the authors had no authority to continue their treatment program. (Mark & Ervin, 1970)

show their normal fear response to such stimuli as snakes. More recent research has shown that the portion of the limbic system known as the *amygdala* is especially related to aggressive behavior. Downer (1962), for example, surgically separated the two halves of a rhesus monkey's brain so that its right eye projected visual images only to the right hemisphere. He then removed the right amygdala but not the left, after which the monkey showed a truly split personality. When approached from the right, it was a docile animal; when approached from the left, it reacted with the combination of fearful and aggressive behavior that is normal for rhesus monkeys.

We must, of course, be cautious in generalizing from animal experiments to human behavior; we might expect in humans that the more fully developed cerebral cortex and the associated capacities for thought, language, and cultural development would exert a more controlling influence on the primitive parts of the brain. But the primitive parts of the brain are still there and in certain forms of brain pathology may find relatively uninhibited expression. That, at least, is the view of neuropsychiatrists such as Mark and Ervin (1970). In addition to the case of Jennie, these authors cite several other examples of human violence that they believe to be directly caused by diseased brains. For example, Donald, a 43-year-old man, had to be restrained in heavy fish netting when first admitted to the hospital. He snarled,

showed his teeth, and lashed out with either arm or leg whenever anyone approached him. His wife and daughter reported that for no apparent reason he had taken a butcher knife and tried his best to kill them. They said that six months previously Donald had undergone a striking change in personality and had also begun to complain of severe headaches and blurred vision. X rays indicated that he had a tumor underneath the right frontal lobe that was pressing directly on the limbic system. When the tumor was removed, Donald's symptoms disappeared and he peaceably went back to work as a night watchman.

Having made the case for the relationship of *some* violent behavior to brain dysfunction, I should now caution against carrying this viewpoint too far. Probably only a small percentage of violent crimes are committed by persons with measurable brain dysfunction, and we should guard against assuming the presence of brain disorders in instances of violence in which no clear evidence for such disorder is present. It may well turn out that most violent behavior is not effected by specific brain malfunctioning but by past social learning experiences and events in the current social environment. And since some violence is related in part to political, economic, and racial factors, it would be a particularly insidious viewpoint to imply that this kind of violence is caused by brain disease. Although the possibility of the "establishment" using brain surgery to "cure" dissidents of their aggressive and rebellious actions seems a little unlikely, it is an outcome toward which we would not want to take even small steps.

Psychosocial Determinants. Most forms of sudden, unexplained violence probably are not associated with brain pathology. Usually the individual is described by such adjectives as shy, gentle, nice, polite, soft-spoken, and he or she may have sung in the church choir. Fred Cowan was characterized by his sister-in-law as "a very gentle man who loved children," by his parochial school principal as a boy with an "extremely exemplary character," and by a co-worker as "a nice, quiet guy who seldom, if ever, talked. He was someone you could push around." But this large man, six feet tall, weighing 250 pounds, would not be pushed around forever. Two weeks after he had been suspended from his job as a furniture mover for refusing to move a refrigerator, he killed four co-workers and a policeman, and wounded five others before taking his own life (Zimbardo, 1977).

Zimbardo (1977) suggests that these individuals as children developed personality styles (called neurotic traits in Chapter 7) in which they submitted and conformed to their more assertive peers and to the demands of parents and teachers—but at a cost of growing resentment and anger. These resentments build but are held in check by anxiety over the expression of all strong emotions and lack of skill in appropriate assertion. Then one day the rage and resentment become too strong; some minor frustration or insult sends them over the threshold, and one or more people die.

Zimbardo (1977) provides some evidence for the relationship between this shy personality style and unpredictable violence. He compared three groups of prison inmates: 10 sudden murderers whose homicide was their first criminal offense; 9 murderers who were habitual criminals with prior arrests for violent acts; and 16 inmates convicted of nonviolent crimes. On several personality tests the sudden murderers were found to be shy, overcontrolled, and feminine compared with the other two groups. We might conclude, then, that circumstances (biological and psychosocial) that tend to produce unusually intense conflict between submissive conformity and resentful anger may contribute to the likelihood of one form of explosive violence.

Conduct Disorders, Delinquency, and Adult Criminality

In DSM-III *undersocialized conduct disorder* and *socialized conduct disorder* appear as subcategories under Conduct Disorders (limited to childhood and adolescence). I mentioned conduct disorders briefly in Chapter 20 (Some Specific Developmental Disorders of Childhood), but have waited to discuss these disorders in more detail in the general context of aggressive and violent behavior. Studies of children and adolescents based on questionnaires and ratings from case history data have repeatedly isolated two clusters of personality patterns associated with the two subtypes just mentioned plus a third category, neurotic-antisocial behavior, which is not included as a separate category in DSM-III (Quay, 1979).

BEHAVIORAL CHARACTERISTICS

Characteristics associated with these three categories are as follows:

1. *Undersocialized conduct disorder.* Assaultive, impulsive, cruel, steals, defies authority, malicious, truant from school, shows little if any guilt, and does not show a normal degree of attachment and loyalty to friends, family, or others. DSM-III divides this category into children who do or do not show overt aggression as part of their antisocial pattern.
2. *Socialized conduct disorder.* Aggressive and antisocial but has attachments and loyalties to others, usually with companions (or gangs) involved in similar antisocial acts. Sometimes called subcultural conduct disorder, or subcultural delinquency or criminality.
3. *Neurotic antisocial disorder.* Impulsive and aggressive but also experiences anxiety, guilt, remorse, or depression.

The undersocialized conduct disorder is the type that most closely resembles the antisocial or psychopathic personality, and it is likely that from this population the adult psychopath emerges, although, as

do not constitute an organized gang (Griffin & Griffin, 1978). These small, loosely organized friendship groups are not formed for the express purpose of pursuing delinquent activities, and most of their activities are probably nondelinquent in nature. The individuals "hang around" together and occasionally become involved in delinquent-type behavior—ranging from excessive drinking in inappropriate places, reckless driving, and some pill popping to burglary and assaultive behavior.

Sometimes, of course, violence may become almost an end in itself for a given clique or gang, a pattern of values and actions that Cloward and Ohlin (1960) referred to as existing in the *conflict subculture*. Aggression, physical courage, and the ability to create fear and intimidation are the valued characteristics in members of this subculture. Prestige and status go to the individual with the greatest skill and daring in promoting exploits of violence.

Whenever we attempt to categorize people into types such as the undersocialized, socialized, or neurotic conduct disorders we find that few individuals are pure types. For example, a given person may show some of the characteristics of the undersocial-

previously mentioned, only a minority of children with this diagnosis will go on to become adult psychopaths. The children with neurotic conduct disorders are more likely to remain caught up in the emotional dynamics of the family. Their antisocial acts tend to reflect rebellion against their parents, and these delinquents are not entirely free of the anxiety and guilt that such rebellion produces. Neurotically motivated acts of delinquency frequently have a compulsive quality; for example, a compulsion to steal, set fires, or be sexually promiscuous. In some cases neurotic delinquents behave in ways that ensure their getting caught, as though they unconsciously sought punishment.

The socialized or subcultural conduct disorders comprise the largest category. Although a popular conception portrays the subcultural delinquent as a member of a big-city gang, as shown in *West Side Story* and more contemporary movies, more commonly adolescent delinquents commit their antisocial acts (theft, use or sale of illicit drugs, truancy, and so on) in the company of several companions who

Adolescents who hang around together and become involved in delinquent activities would ordinarily be considered to fall in the class of socialized or subcultural conduct disorders.

ized conduct disorder but not others and at the same time show some characteristics of the socialized and neurotic conduct disorders. How do we decide in such cases whether a person is or is not to be labeled undersocialized conduct disorder? (The same problem holds for adults given the label psychopath or antisocial personality.) One solution to this problem is to think in terms of dimensions rather than typologies. Thus each person who is showing some continuing antisocial behavior may reflect a particular combination of neurotic, undersocialized, or socialized features and related causative influences. In this view, we may occasionally encounter a person who is consistently high on dimensions related to one type, say socialized delinquency, and low on dimensions related to the neurotic and the undersocialized personality types—the relatively pure type; however, most individuals will show some mixture of these characteristics. The relative usefulness of a typological versus a dimensional approach may in time become further clarified as we gain greater understanding of the nature and etiology of different forms of antisocial behavior.

DEVELOPMENT

In this section we will be concerned primarily with the subcultural type of delinquent and, to a lesser extent, with the unsocialized-aggressive type, although, as we have just indicated, a sharp distinction between the two categories cannot be made.

Biological Correlates. There are no twin studies and only one adoption study of juvenile delinquency. The adoption study (Bohmen, 1973) did not show any evidence for a genetic factor in the sample of children, who were all 15 or less years of age. The twin and adoption studies of older psychopaths and criminals would suggest that some subgroup of the antisocial adolescent population might have a genetic vulnerablity for antisocial development. This will probably turn out to be a relatively small subgroup, but for the present there is too little research to reach any conclusion.

Like adults diagnosed psychopathic personality, adolescents diagnosed as undersocialized conduct disorders have been found more often to have abnormal brain waves than normal control children

(Arthurs & Cahoon, 1964). This finding suggests that brain dysfunction might play some role in a subgroup of this kind of delinquent. However, most undersocialized conduct disordered adolescents have normal brain wave patterns.

Psychosocial Correlates. Both the community and the family may encourage the development of delinquency. Sociologists have emphasized social disorganization as a factor contributing to antisocial behavior (for example, McKay, 1967). Socially disorganized neighborhoods are likely to be characterized by poverty, unemployment, minimal family controls over children, and reduced effectiveness of other agencies of social control such as the schools or police because of lack of parental support or cooperation. The apparent success of older criminals—their money, free time, and prestige—does not go unnoticed by adolescents. Communities with already existing high crime rates provide both multiple models for the child to imitate and reinforcement in the form of acclaim for early accomplishments in crime. Cloward and Ohlin (1960) emphasize the discrepancy for lower-class youth between culturally induced aspirations and the likelihood of achieving these goals by legitimate means. Such a frustrating gap between hopes and realities may produce anger, alienation, and a readiness to join a delinquent subculture.

Even within the generally crime-producing context of such communities, the particular peer group with whom a person associates is important in determining whether a person will actually adopt a career in crime. For example, McCord, McCord, and Zola (1959) found that 75 percent of individuals who had associated with delinquent peers had subsequent criminal records, whereas only 30 percent of those who had not associated with delinquent peers became criminals. All the children in this study came from high-delinquency areas.

In the family setting, broader sociological and more individualized determinants intersect; thus family interaction probably contributes to both socialized and unsocialized conduct disorders. The same factors probably contribute to the development of antisocial behavior within the family setting as in the larger social environment: (1) modeling, (2) aggression-inducing frustrations, (3) reinforcement for antisocial behavior, and (4) lack of teaching cognitive controls. Recall that these same conditions were re-

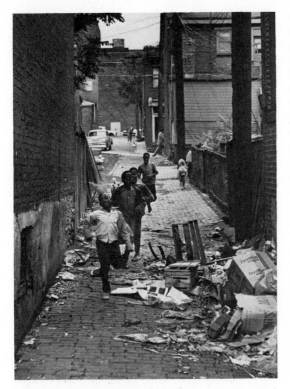

Neighborhoods characterized by poverty, unemployment, and minimal family controls over children tend to have high rates of antisocial behavior.

lated to the lack of internalization in psychopaths. This should not be surprising, since the distinctions between these categories are not sharp and since many adult psychopaths would probably have been characterized as unsocialized-aggressive delinquents in their youth.

After reviewing the extensive literature in this area, Hetherington and Martin (1979) concluded that there was considerable evidence that these conditions are related to aggressive behavior in children. Parents of aggressive children or adolescent delinquents model aggressive, impulsive, and antisocial behavior to a greater extent than parents of nondeviant children. One area in which aggressive, undercontrolled behavior can be effectively modeled is the marriage relationship. Rutter (1971), for example, studied a sample of London families in which one or both parents had been under psychiatric care. When families were divided into three groups according to the quality of the marriage (in terms of affection, communication, mutual enjoyment of each other's company, and so on), the percentage of boys showing antisocial behavior was strongly related to these groupings (Figure 22-4). There were no antisocial boys in homes where the marriage was "good," compared with 22 percent when the marriage was "fair," and 39 percent when the marriage was "very poor." Rutter's data are further broken down in Figure 22-5 to show the association of the sons' antisocial behavior to both the quality of their relationship with their parents and the quality of the marriage. When the marriage was "very poor" and the boy had a poor relationship with both parents, 90 percent of these boys showed antisocial behavior.

Similar findings have been reported by Johnson and Lobitz (1974) in this country for a sample of families referred for treatment because of active behavior problems with one or more children. Within this group of families, marital maladjustment correlated .45 ($p < .05$) with child deviant behavior as observed in the home and .50 with parental negativeness toward the child. The data from both these studies strongly confirm the importance of the marital relationship in the development of antisocial behavior.

Parents of antisocial children are more likely than other parents to use harsh discipline, often in the form of physical beatings accompanied by yelling and abusive language that arouse angry and aggressive responses in the child. These parents are frequently lax in enforcing rules and inconsistent in applying discipline. Thus they administer harsh discipline in an erratic and unpredictable manner. The atmosphere in a home that is conducive to antisocial behavior is frequently negligent and somewhat chaotic. Parents do not attend closely to the child's behavior, reward desirable behaviors with any consistency, or discipline antisocial responses. Only after the child's disruptiveness has reached a high level of intensity are the parents likely finally to pay attention, and then they may well respond with an aggressive outburst of their own. These are the family conditions that are associated with at least some forms of child abuse (Burgess & Conger, 1978).

These parental behaviors not only serve as anger-inducing frustrations to the child but also provide an additional model of aggression. Although punish-

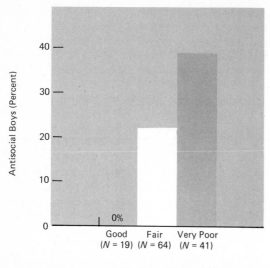

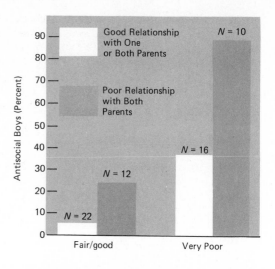

FIGURE 22-4. Parents' marital relationship and antisocial behavior in boys (left). **FIGURE 22-5.** Antisocial behavior in boys as a function of both the parent-child relationship and the marriage relationship. (Both adapted from Rutter, 1971. Copyright 1971 by Pergamon Press and redrawn with permission.)

ment generally might be expected to have a suppressing effect on the behavior that is punished, in these families the facilitating effects of anger-inducing frustration and modeling may outweigh the suppressing effects. Even if this kind of punishment of child aggression has an immediate suppressing effect, the long-term effect is likely to be an increase in aggression, especially aggression toward objects and people other than the original punisher. Three studies, in fact, have shown that parental punishment seems to have lost its effectiveness on children with conduct disorders (Kopfstein, 1972; Patterson, 1976; Snyder, 1977). Children with conduct disorders actually were more likely to persist in certain disobedient behavior when the behavior was followed by punishment than when it was not! Normal children, on the other hand, showed the expected suppression effect.

Patterson (1979) has developed a theory of *coercive* control to explain this kind of finding. Essentially the theory states that in families that produce aggressive children, various family members develop aggressive, coercive styles of interaction because of reinforcement contingencies. Thus if Alex wants to play with Johnny's toys, he escalates his coercive demands to whatever level is needed, overt aggression

if necessary, to get his way. When Johnny eventually gives in, he (Johnny) is negatively reinforced (he makes a response, letting his brother play with his toys, which terminates an aversive stimulus, his brother's attack), and Alex is reinforced for using his coercive tactics by obtaining the desired toys. Reinforcement for coercive tactics may not pay off all the time for all family members, but a partial reinforcement schedule would strongly maintain the behavior.

Patterson (1977) provides data indicating that mothers, especially, may be victims of coercive tactics by aggressive children, becoming trapped in the kind of coercive cycles just described. This may lead to feelings of helplessness in the mother that further contribute to her ineptness as a parent. This picture of mutual, or alternating, coercion underscores the interactive character of the parent-child relationships—that children "train" parents as well as vice versa. Thus a disobedient, exasperating child is likely to evoke more parental anger and harsher punishments than a quiet, obedient child. What we finally see in such families are well-established interactive patterns in which all members are contributing to the initiation and maintenance of the aggressive interchanges.

Individuals with criminal or delinquent records are more likely than the general population to come from homes disrupted by desertion, divorce, death, or absence of the father. Nevertheless, not all broken homes produce antisocial behavior. It is important to consider the cause of the broken home and the kind of conflict that preceded parental separation. Thus, death of a parent seems to contribute less to the development of antisocial behavior than separation by divorce (Hetherington & Martin, 1979). In fact, Rutter (1971) concludes after reviewing his data as well as others' that the rate of antisocial behavior is likely to be higher for children from unbroken homes in which there is great parental discord than for children who live in harmonious but broken homes.

Treatment

DRUGS AND PSYCHOSURGERY

Most clinicians consider drugs and psychosurgical procedures appropriate treatments only for individuals whose explosive episodes of violence seem clearly related to brain dysfunction. Thus Jennie was given seizure-controlling drugs, and brain surgery was performed on Donald to remove a tumor. Even when neurological examinations indicate that brain malfunctioning is likely to be at the root of the violent behavior, authors such as Mark and Ervin suggest

Malcolm X was a member of the criminal subculture before he became converted to the Black Muslim religion and became a leader in the fight for racial equality.

Malcolm X: From Criminal to Dynamic Leader

Malcolm X is a good example of subcultural criminality. His earliest memories of life in a poor black family were of violent arguments between his father and mother. His father was impatient with Malcolm's brothers and sisters and occasionally beat the older ones "almost savagely if they broke any of his rules." Malcolm thought that it was because he was the lightest skinned that his father never hit him.

The childhood memory that left the deepest scar was the death of his father when Malcolm was six. His body was discovered one evening lying across the streetcar tracks. Malcolm's father had been an active organizer for Marcus Garvey's Universal Negro Improvement Association, and many people thought that he had been killed by white vigilantes.

Later, after being discouraged by a high school teacher from aspiring to become a lawyer because it was "unrealistic for a black," Malcolm went to Boston and later to New York. He became actively involved in the criminal subculture as small-time hustler, drug addict, pimp, alcoholic, numbers runner, and robber. Caught and put

> in prison, he was converted to the Black Muslim religion, and after release he became a world-famous dynamic leader.
>
> Although individual psychological influences undoubtedly played some role in Malcolm X's criminal development, sociological circumstances seem to be the most important. If Malcolm X had not been born black, if his father had not presumably been killed by white racists, if he had not been discouraged from seeking an establishment career as a lawyer, and had not lived in the ghetto areas of Boston and New York, would he have become an habitual criminal? It seems unlikely. (Malcolm X, 1966)

that drug therapy and possibly certain forms of behavioral therapy be tried first. If these fail, brain surgery might be used when there is reason to believe it will be helpful. Modern technology involving implanted electrodes has made it possible to destroy in a fairly precise and limited way only those areas of the brain thought to be producing the uncontrollable violence.

PSYCHOLOGICAL APPROACHES

Experienced clinicians have been pessimistic about the effectiveness of any kind of psychological approach—psychodynamic, behavioral, or any other—to the treatment of individuals, such as Charles Manson, who have long-standing psychopathic characteristics. This clinical lore should probably be respected until research has demonstrated otherwise. On the other hand, there is evidence that juvenile delinquents can be helped by traditional psychotherapy as well as by certain behaviorally oriented programs. Although a small proportion of these adolescent delinquents would probably be characterized as psychopathic personalities, it would be a mistake to conclude from the research summarized below that the more extreme forms of psychopathy can be successfully modified by these procedures.

Persons (1966, 1967) found a combination of group and individual therapy to be effective relative to a no-therapy control group. Nine and one-half months after discharge from the institution the treatment group had fewer parole violations, fewer readmissions to penal institutions, and more boys gainfully employed than the control group. However, psychotherapy is a rather vaguely defined process, and it is not always easy to duplicate the procedure at another institution.

Alexander and Parsons (1973) provided families with delinquent adolescents a short-term family systems intervention in which skills in clear communication and the negotiation of conflicts were taught. The adolescents showed a significant reduction in *recidivism* (future arrests or convictions after being discharged)—only 26 percent, compared to adolescents in a no-treatment control group (50 percent) and a group in which the families received client-centered group discussion (47 percent). The recidivism rate for 2800 cases seen in the whole county for a given year was 51 percent. Equally important, Klein et al. (1977) followed up siblings of these same identified delinquents and found that 2½ to 3½ years after termination of treatment only 20 percent of the families given the family systems intervention had had court contacts for siblings, compared with 40 percent for the no-treatment control group and 59 percent for the client-centered discussion groups. These findings provide support for the assumption that the larger family system has been successfully modified rather than just the behavior of the individual delinquent. This study also provides one of the few demonstrations of the *prevention* of antisocial behavior as opposed to the modification of this behavior after it has developed.

Patterson and Fleischman (1979) report success in several studies using a social learning approach to modifying antisocial behavior in preadolescent boys who seemed destined for delinquent careers. The treatment techniques have been evolved to decrease the use of the kind of coercive tactics previously described. Thus parents are taught some fundamental concepts of child management:

1. The realization that the effects of negative reinforcement as applied by the child (e.g., that acceding to a child's whining or crying), though providing a short-term respite, will have disastrous consequences in the long run.
2. What the norms are for appropriate child behavior.
3. How to negotiate compromises.
4. The dual skills of applying mild punishment (such

as time out or boring work) on the one hand, and giving social and tangible reinforcers contingent on socially approved behaviors on the other.

Based on direct observations in the home Patterson and Fleischman report significant decreases following treatment in coercive behaviors not only for the identified antisocial child but for siblings and mothers as well. Changes for the fathers on this variable were not significant. There were also changes indicating that parental punishment began to be more effective in controlling coercive behaviors in children than it had been prior to treatment.

Although each of the approaches reviewed in this section has shown some success in reducing delinquency or aggressive behavior, none has succeeded with all families, follow-ups have not been lengthy in some cases, and many of the adolescent delinquents treated probably should not be considered "hard core." Since broader sociological and economic factors contribute in an important way to crime and delinquency, it seems unrealistic to expect such individually oriented approaches to be entirely successful. Any long-term solution must include the elimination of poverty and discrimination and the attainment of equal opportunities for all.

BEHAVIOR MODIFICATION IN PRISON: LEGAL AND ETHICAL ISSUES

Critics in many instances have tended to lump brain surgery, drug treatment, and electroconvulsive shock treatment, together with psychological interventions such as token economies, under the general heading of "behavior modification." We have already discussed the ethics of brain surgery as a means of altering behavior: Such an approach should be considered only in those few cases in which there is strong evidence for a relationship between specific brain malfunctioning and violent behavior. In this section we will limit our concern to the kind of psychological interventions that most investigators mean when they use the term *behavior modification*—the arrangement of environmental contingencies so as to increase desired behavior and decrease undesired behavior.

The central ethical issue in the use of any rehabilitative procedure with prisoners is the question of voluntary consent. The person who asks a therapist to help him get rid of a fear of flying in airplanes voluntarily consents to participate in certain procedures in order to accomplish this goal. When prison authorities offer inmates the opportunity to "volun-

Patuxent prison. Should release from prison be made contingent on proper performance in rehabilitation programs? This has been the policy of Patuxent. Prisoners cannot, however, be confined longer than their original sentence.

tarily" participate in a given rehabilitation program, to what extent is it actually voluntary?

Let us consider a fairly extreme example. When Patuxent Institution in Jessup, Maryland, opened its gates in 1955, it was considered to be one of the most progressive and enlightened penal institutions. Mental health professionals rather than prison guards were in charge, and the inmates were the more incorrigible delinquents, described by Maryland statutes as showing "persistent, aggravated antisocial or criminal behavior." Individuals were committed to Patuxent for an *indeterminate* period of time, and

were to be released only after treatment (including group therapy and a programmed system of earning privileges) had yielded significant improvement in their behavior. Patuxent boasted of an unusually low recidivism rate of about 7 percent, but critics argued that this figure might have been misleading since the individuals most likely to be recidivists were kept in the institution indefinitely. Although participation in the therapeutic programs was "voluntary," the inmates were acutely aware that it was the only way out of the institution.

Edward McNeil: Unjust Imprisonment

Edward McNeil at age 19 was convicted of assault with intent to rape and of assault of a police officer, charges he repeatedly denied. He was sentenced to imprisonment for not more than five years and sent to Patuxent for evaluation. Because he was appealing his original conviction he refused to cooperate with the precommitment evaluation procedures. As a result, the institution declined to diagnose him, kept him on the receiving section without benefit of treatment, and asserted the right to hold him, without court commitment, indefinitely. Note certain similarities to the case of Louis Perroni (Chapter 19), who was kept locked up in a mental institution because he had been judged incompetent to stand trial. Eventually the United States Supreme Court ordered McNeil's immediate release, saying that Patuxent could not hold noncommitted patients whose original sentences had expired. Upon his release McNeil had been imprisoned for almost six years. If he had been sent to a regular prison, he would have been eligible for parole after 15 months. (*American Psychological Association Monitor*, May 1975)

As a result of criticisms of the indeterminate sentencing policy, Maryland law was changed in 1977 so that now all prisoners must have freely chosen to come to Patuxent and must have at least three years of their sentence left to serve. Otherwise, the program is essentially the same, with prisoners being able to work up through four levels of increasing privileges

by their active participation in various educational and vocational programs. Although they may earn parole at an earlier time, they cannot be kept past the end of their original sentence. It will be interesting to see how effective this approach will be in reducing recidivism in released prisoners.

Summary

1. The antisocial or psychopathic personality is characterized by lack of conscience, impulsivity, inability to profit from mistakes, lack of emotional ties to other people, stimulus seeking, and ability to make a good impression on others.

2. There is some evidence that a proportion of individuals with antisocial personalities may have genetically determined tendencies that increase the likelihood of antisocial behavior.

3. Research bears out the clinical impression that psychopaths do not learn as well under punishment as nonpsychopaths and that they seek out stimulation.

4. Abnormal brain waves are found more frequently in psychopathic personalities than in normals, suggesting the possibility of some brain malfunctioning. This evidence is indirect, however, and at least half the individuals diagnosed as psychopaths do not have these abnormalities.

5. Important contributors to psychopathic behavior are social learning experiences that result in a lack of internalization of the values and restraints of the community. Experimental research suggests that cognitive structuring, modeling of self-control by others, and conditioned emotional reactions are important for the learning of internalization. Naturalistic studies of parent-child interaction indicate that a power-assertive approach to child discipline is likely to be correlated with low internalization and antisocial behavior on the part of the child.

6. The explosive personality is characterized by gross outbursts of rage that are inconsistent with the person's usual behavior and seem beyond the person's ability to control.

7. A small proportion of individuals showing episodes of explosive violence may have specific brain abnormalities such as temporal lobe epilepsy.

8. Three personality patterns have been associated with conduct disorders in children and adolescents: undersocialized, socialized (or subcultural), and neurotic.

9. Pure types of antisocial behavior are rare. It probably makes more sense to consider the characteristics associated with this behavior to vary along dimensions so that a specific antisocial individual can be seen as reflecting a particular combination of neurotic, psychopathic, and subcultural features.

10. Subcultural crime and delinquency are associated with poverty, unemployment, and antagonism toward stable, middle-class society. Association with delinquent peers further enhances the likelihood of delinquency.

11. The psychopathic personality and both the undersocialized and socialized conduct disorders are strongly influenced by the family setting. Modeling, aggression-inducing frustrations, and reinforcement contingencies for aggression in the family context contribute to the development of antisocial behavior.

12. Punitive, inconsistent discipline in the context of a poor marital relationship appears to be an especially potent combination for producing antisocial children. In families with an antisocial child many family members are likely to use coercive tactics in getting their way.

13. Drugs and psychosurgery may have a limited place in the treatment of violence. Psychosurgery especially should be limited to those relatively few individuals for whom a relationship between uncontrollable, explosive episodes of violence and specific brain malfunction has been demonstrated.

14. Psychological treatment of the individual with extreme, long-standing psychopathic characteristics remains difficult and uncertain. There is evidence that adolescent delinquents can be helped to change their antisocial behavior by traditional psychotherapy and by behaviorally oriented family intervention. The eventual elimination of crime and other forms of antisocial behavior, however, will depend also on changes in economic, political, and social injustices.

15. The use of rehabilitative programs in prisons raises ethical and legal questions of whether it is possible to obtain "voluntary" participation. Prisoners' rights in this respect have probably been abused in some institutions.

Suggested Readings

Research on the antisocial personality, or psychopath, is discussed by a variety of authors in R. D. Hare and D. Schalling (Eds.), (Wiley, 1978). *Psychopathic behavior: Approaches to research.* Psychodynamic, sociological, and biological approaches to understanding psychopathy can be found in a book edited by W. H. Reid, *The psychopath* (Brunner/Mazel, 1978). *The mask of sanity* by H. Cleckley (C. V. Mosby, 1976) continues to be a classic clinical description of psychopathic behavior. *The Duke of Deception* by G. Wolff (Random House, 1979) is an interesting account of a psychopathic personality by his son. V. H. Mark and F. R. Irvin's *Violence and the brain* (Harper & Row, 1970) makes a strong case for brain dysfunctions as a cause of some forms of unpredictable violence. E. M. Hetherington and B. Martin discuss family interaction correlates of aggressive behavior in children and adolescents in H. C. Quay and J. S. Werry (Eds.) *Psychopathological disorders of childhood* (Wiley, 1979).

23

Drug Abuse

- What is psychological dependency? Physical dependency?

- Who is an alcoholic?

- One drink and you lose control. True, if you are an alcoholic?

- Why do some heavy drinkers become alcoholic and others do not?

- What is the withdrawal syndrome? What is tolerance?

- Does drinking relax you—or make you more tense?

- "Like father, like son"? If parents use drugs, will their children follow suit?

- If you had become addicted to heroin in Vietnam, what would have been your chances of breaking the addiction?

Sam: A Downhill Course

Sam started drinking when he was 18 but didn't begin to drink seriously until his mid-twenties, when his work as a salesman involved considerable "entertaining" of clients.

"About this time, I passed from controlled to uncontrolled drinking. Now it gradually crept in. There were times I was drinking more than the function called for. I began not being able to function the next day. But it didn't stand out in the crowd I was with. I just began arranging so that Monday would be an easy day."

Sam married a wife who drank along with him. "Over the next five or six years, we lived in nine different towns, and I held 27 different jobs. I was in jail 17 times."

"I sold everything—from shady deals to what-have-you. Crooked or honest, I did it. As money became more of a problem, my ethics on how I got it became less."

"I had learned how to get by with being an alcoholic. You had to be good one day a week to get by. You develop skills for survival. I used to sell enough in one day to get by the whole week."

Sam's life continued on a downhill course. He separated from his wife and moved into a three-dollar-a-week room. One Sunday morning, broke and thirsty, "I went to the office where I worked. I took a check out of the back of the book, and forged the owner's name. I had to send my wife money, so I sent her some and bought liquor with the rest."

Sam spent two weeks in jail before the forgery charge was dropped. Someone gave him the name of a Methodist minister, whom he went to see. "I started to cry. I sobbed like a little boy. . . . He asked me if I drank, and I said yes. He asked me if I had a problem with it, and I said, 'I reckon I do—I have problems with every other damned thing in my life.' "

The minister sent Sam to Alcoholics Anonymous. (Martin, 1974)

Drug Use throughout History

A Guatemalan Indian, asked why he drank so much of the local beverage, aguardiente, replied: "A man must sometimes take a rest from his memory" (Taylor, 1963). The need to forget our cares seems to be universal, and in almost all cultures throughout recorded history one way of achieving this has been by using drugs.

The Greek historian Herodotus writes of the Scythians reaching certain pleasurable states by casting hemp seeds over open fires and inhaling the vapors. The Aztecs described, in great detail, their ritual drugs: teonanacatl (psilocybin), peyotl (peyote), ololiuqui (morning glory seeds), piecetl, and toloatzin. In many a South American country, away from the cities, individuals prepare a potent hallucinogenic drink from the plant *Banisteriopsis caapi,* which they call ayahuasca or caapi. Inhabitants of the South Pacific

Islands use a drug called kava; people in the East Indian archipelago ingest nutmeg; people of the West Indies turn on to cohoba snuff; while both the Siberians and the Norsemen swallowed small amounts of the potentially deadly *Amanita muscaria* or fly agaric mushroom, which reportedly passes through the kidneys unchanged so that one could drink one's own urine (or a friend's) and regain the effect. Finally, fruits or vegetables fermented into some variant of alcohol are probably among what we know to be the earliest known intoxicants.

The drug that has been used most effectively as an analgesic (pain reducer) throughout the centuries is opium. Both the Egyptians and the Persians used it medicinally, and the Greek physician Theophrastus mentions its effectiveness as a sleep inducer and pain reliever. In addition, opium became the standard therapeutic agent for cough and hysteria. Despite its wide medicinal use, its potential for producing psychological and physiological dependency was unnoticed by the medical profession. In fact, addiction to opium did not become widespread until the British East India Company imported the drug on a large scale into Europe during the nineteenth century (Maurer & Vogel, 1954).

There are, then, an impressive number of substances that have been used by human beings to alter thinking, mood, and perception. Some of these have been used in religion or medical treatment, and others, with less official sanction, in an attempt to attain a degree of euphoria. Almost every society appears to allow, if not directly employ, one or more mind-altering substances for certain segments of the population. These substances are not considered dangerous by their particular cultural group in terms of short- or even long-range effects, nor is there much concern over their potential for producing physiological or psychological dependency. Social conventions or rituals control the ingestion of these chemicals by defining the user population, the time, the place, and often the amount of acceptable use, as well as the effects that such use should produce. Negative sanctions, either social or legal, are applied when an individual uses these substances in excess of the prescribed limits, at nonprescribed times, or with unacceptable effects.

Drug Dependence

Drug use ranges from occasional intake with no abuse to a complete dependency on and compulsive use of drugs that literally destroy the person's life. There is no objective line that divides abuse from nonabuse. I will define abuse as the use of one or more drugs so heavily that physical health or psychological functioning is impaired. When the psychological handicap is extreme, the person may be unable to work, unable to maintain normal interpersonal relationships as a friend, parent, or spouse, and unable to find satisfactions in life other than the drug. By this definition it would be inappropriate to say that a person is abusing a drug if, in fact, there is little physical or psychological impairment, regardless of whether we happen to approve of the drug or whether it is legal.

Most people abusing drugs show some evidence of drug dependence, a compulsive tendency to continue drug usage accompanied by strong discomfort when use is discontinued for any period of time. Two kinds of drug dependency are recognized: *psychological dependence* and *physical dependence*. Persons with psychological dependence require periodic or continuous administration of a drug to produce pleasure or avoid discomfort. They experience intense cravings for the drug when deprived of it and are likely to persist compulsively in their drug habit. Indications of physical dependence may or may not accompany psychological dependence.

Physical dependence is an adaptive state that manifests itself by intense physical disturbance when the continuous administration of the drug is suspended. The physical disturbance, called the *withdrawal syndrome,* shows specific symptom patterns characteristic of each drug type. For example, the withdrawal syndrome that follows the abrupt cessation of morphine or heroin use is different from the one that occurs when the barbiturate drugs are discontinued. These physical conditions are relieved by the readministration of the same drug or by using another, similar agent within the same family of drugs. If an adequate dose level of a particular drug is maintained, no signs of physical dependence will appear. Physical dependence on a particular drug is considered a powerful factor in the reinforcement of psychological dependence as well as a major factor in the tendency towards relapse once the individual has been withdrawn from the agent.

Psychological dependence can occur without physical dependence, but physical dependence is usually accompanied by psychological dependence. Physical dependence is an *inevitable* consequence of the pharmacologic action of some classes of drugs, given the repeated use of a sufficient amount of the agent. Psychological dependence, though also related to pharmacologic action, is a manifestation of the individual's psychological reaction to the effects of a particular agent and tends to vary from person to person as well as from drug to drug. The term *addiction* has been used rather loosely, sometimes to refer to physical dependence and sometimes to both physical and psychological independence. For the sake of clarity I will limit our terminology to the two kinds of drug dependencies.

The prolonged use of most of the abused drugs can produce *tolerance,* a condition in which increasing amounts of the drug are required to produce the same effect or there is a diminished response to the same quantity of drug. Tolerance occurs not only in

TABLE 23-1. Drugs with Abuse Potential and Their Characteristics

Official Name of Drug or Chemical	Method of Taking	Medical Use
Alcohol whiskey gin beer wine	Swallowing liquid.	Rare; sometimes used as a sedative (for tension).

Sedatives
 Barbiturates
  Nembutal
  Seconal
  Phenobarbital
 Doriden
 Chloral hydrate
 Meprobamate
 Miltown, Equinil
 Valium, Librium
 Quaalude (Sopors)
	Swallowing pills or capsules.	Treatment of insomnia and tension. Induction of anesthesia.

Stimulants
 Caffeine
  coffee, tea
  Coca Cola
  No-Doz
	Swallowing liquid.	Mild stimulant; treatment of some forms of coma.

Nicotine cigarettes cigars	Smoking (inhalation).	None.
Amphetamines Benzedrine Methedrine Dexedrine	Swallowing pills or capsules, or injecting in veins.	Treatment of obesity, narcolepsy, fatigue, depression.
Cocaine	Sniffing or injecting in veins.	Anesthesia of eye and throat.

almost all drugs that produce physical dependence but also in drugs that are not associated with physical dependency. In the case of the amphetamines, for example, many times the apparent lethal standard dose can be taken by the chronic user without any obvious serious consequences.

Many substances, drugs and nondrugs, have potential for abuse—alcohol, caffeine (coffee, tea), nicotine (cigarettes), marijuana, sugar and other foods, as well as the so-called hard drugs such as heroin and barbiturates. I will not attempt to discuss all the substances to which addictive behavior can occur;

Potential for Dependence		Overall Potential for Abuse	Usual Short-Term Effects	Usual Long-Term Effects
Psycho-logical	Physio-logical			
High	Yes	High	Depression of central nervous system. Relaxation (sedation). Drowsiness. Impairment in judgment, reaction time, coordination, and emotional control. Frequent aggressive behavior and driving accidents.	Tolerance. Irreversible damage to brain and liver. Severe withdrawal illness (DTs) after development of physical dependence. Diversion of energy and money.
High	Yes	High	Depression of central nervous system. Sleep, relaxation (sedation), or drowsiness. Sometimes euphoria. Impaired judgment, reaction time, coordination, and emotional control. Relief of anxiety tension. Muscle relaxation.	Irritability, weight loss. Physical dependence with severe withdrawal illness. Diversion of energy and money. Tolerance.
High	Yes	High	Stimulation of central nervous system. Increased alertness. Reduction of fatigue.	Sometimes insomnia and restlessness. Tolerance.
High	No	Moderate	Stimulation of central nervous system. Relaxation or distraction due to the process of smoking.	Lung cancer and other cancer. Heart and blood vessel disease. Smoker's cough. Tolerance.
High	No	High	Stimulation of central nervous system. Increased alertness, reduction of fatigue, loss of appetite, insomnia. Often euphoria.	Irritability, weight loss. Restlessness. Toxic psychosis (mainly paranoid). Diversion of energy and money. Tolerance.
				Extreme irritability. Toxic psychosis.

Continued on next page

the psychological aspects of abuse and dependency may well be the same for most of these substances. In the remainder of the chapter we will consider the nature, development, and treatment of the abuse of alcohol, barbiturates, opiates, stimulants, and hallucinogens. Most attention will be given to alcohol abuse since this may well be the nation's number one mental health problem, outdistancing even schizophrenia in the costs to society. The effects, potential for dependency, and other characteristics of drugs with abuse possibilities are compared in Table 23-1.

TABLE 23-1. Drugs with Abuse Potential and Their Characteristics (*Continued*)

Official Name of Drug or Chemical	Method of Taking	Medical Use
Cannabis sativa (marijuana)	Smoking (inhalation) or swallowing.	Potentially may be used for hypertension and other disorders.
Opiates (narcotics, analgesics) opium, heroin methadone morphine codeine Percodan Demerol cough syrup	Smoking (inhalation). Injecting in muscle or vein.	Treatment of severe pain, diarrhea, and cough.
Hallucinogens LSD psilocybin mescaline STP, MDA	Swallowing liquid, capsules, or pill (or sugar cube). Chewing plant.	Experimental study of mind and brain function.
Miscellaneous volatile solvents (glue, gasoline) nutmeg	Variable; usually inhalation (sniffing or "huffing").	None.
PCP	Swallowing.	None.

DSM-III Categories for Substance Use Disorders

For purposes of diagnostic categorization DSM-III lists two categories under the heading of Substance Use Disorders.

Substance Abuse
The abuse must have occurred for at least one month. There must be a pattern of pathological use: for example, intoxication throughout the day, inability to cut down or stop use, or need for daily use for adequate functioning. Social functioning must have been impaired (for example, failure to meet important obligations to friends and family, inappropriate expression of aggressive feelings, or missing work or school).

Potential for Dependence		Overall Potential for Abuse		
Psycho-logical	Physio-logical		*Usual Short-Term Effects*	*Usual Long-Term Effects*
Moderate	No	Moderate	Relaxation, euphoria, increased appetite. Some alteration of time perception, possible impairment of judgment and coordination. Probable depression of central nervous system.	Usually none. Possible diversion of energy and money.
High	Yes	High	Depression of central nervous system. Sedation, euphoria, relief of pain. Impaired intellectual functioning and coordination.	Constipation, loss of appetite, weight loss, temporary impotency and sterility. Tolerance and physical dependence, with unpleasant and painful withdrawal illness.
Minimal	No	Moderate	Production of visual imagery, increased sensory awareness. Anxiety, nausea, impaired coordination. Sometimes consciousness expansion.	Usually none. Sometimes precipitates or intensifies an already existing psychosis. More commonly produces a panic reaction when the user is improperly prepared.
Minimal to moderate	No	Moderate	A "high" (euphoria) with impaired coordination and judgment.	Sometimes serious damage to liver or kidney. Reports of brain damage.
Moderate	No	Moderate	A "high" (euphoria). Can produce delirium and delusional reaction.	Unknown.

Substance Dependence

A more severe form of Substance Use Disorder in which, in addition to the criteria for substance abuse, there is either tolerance or withdrawal symptoms.

Alcohol Abuse

PROBLEM DRINKING AND ALCOHOLISM

There is no clear agreement on precise definitions for either problem drinking or alcoholism. A problem drinker is commonly considered to be a person who shows one or more of these characteristics:

1. Must drink in order to function or "cope with life."
2. By a personal definition, or that of family and friends, frequently drinks to a state of intoxication.

3. Goes to work intoxicated.
4. Drives a car while intoxicated.
5. Sustains bodily injury requiring medical attention as a consequence of an intoxicated state.
6. Does something out of character under the influence of alcohol.

Alcoholism is usually considered to involve a more severe and long-term preoccupation with alcohol, and might be defined most simply as chronic, excessive drinking of alcohol that leads to significant impairments in physical and psychosocial functioning. Psychological and/or physical dependence is almost always present. Signs considered indicative of the development of alcoholism are early morning drinking "to get started," solitary drinking, and blackouts. A blackout is not passing out, but a period of activity that a person cannot remember.

Other definitions of alcoholism have frequently included concepts that have been difficult to tie

It is estimated that skid-row derelicts compose less than 5 percent of problem and alcoholic drinkers.

down, such as "loss of control" or "irresistible craving," or have assumed a physiological basis that has not as yet been demonstrated. We will consider some of these ideas later, but they will not be included as part of the general definition of alcoholism.

THE COSTS

However we define the terms, there is general agreement that the problem is widespread: It is estimated that ten million people in the United States have drinking problems. Perhaps the term *alcoholic* evokes the mental picture of a skid-row derelict, but, in fact, "skid row" contains less than 5 percent of the nation's problem drinkers and alcoholics. More than 70 percent live in respectable neighborhoods with their husbands or wives, send their children to school, belong to clubs, attend church, and pay taxes. Approximately 80 percent of alcoholic persons are estimated to be men and 20 percent women; however, the proportion of women has been increasing in recent years.

The personal price of alcoholism is high. The life expectancy of alcoholic drinkers is shorter by 10 to 12 years than that of the average person. Effects are not limited to the drinker: The drinker's family, employer, and society at large are all harmed. Unhappy marriages, broken homes, desertion, divorce, impoverished families, and victims of alcohol-related car accidents are all part of the toll.

The National Institute of Alcohol Abuse and Alcoholism (1978) reports the following statistics on the human and economic costs of problem drinking and alcoholism:

Alcohol is involved in half of all highway fatalities, and drivers with chronic drinking problems are responsible for about two-thirds of the alcohol-related deaths (see Figure 23-1). It is estimated that up to 40 percent of fatal industrial accidents, 69 percent of drownings, 83 percent of fire fatalities, and 70 percent of fatal falls are alcohol-related. Alcohol can release violent behavior in some individuals that is unlikely or even unthinkable when they are sober. Half of all homicides and one-third of all suicides may be alcohol-related. Excessive drinking has been implicated in child abuse, child molesting, and marital violence. Employees with drinking problems are absent from work about two and one-half times as fre-

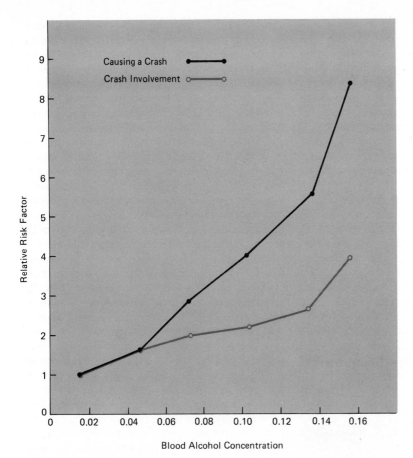

FIGURE 23-1. Relative probability that a driver causes and is involved in a crash as a function of blood alcohol level. For example, a risk of 5 means that a driver has a five times greater risk of causing a crash than a driver whose blood alcohol level is less than .03 percent. From Aarens, Cameron, Roizen, Roizen, Room, Schneberk and Wingard, 1977. Reproduced with permission of National Institute on Alcohol Abuse and Alcoholism.)

quently as the general work force. Their drinking may result in friction with co-workers, lowered morale, bad executive decisions, and poor customer and public relations for their employers. Berry et al. (1977) estimated the economic costs of alcohol-related problems to the United States in 1975 to have been almost 42 billion dollars.

EFFECTS OF ALCOHOL

Generally speaking, alcohol tends to depress activity in all living cells, and in that sense it is a de-

pressant. The casual observer of a cocktail party or a college beer party might wonder about just how "depressing" alcohol is as he or she notices the increasing talkativeness, laughter, and general expansiveness. The standard explanation for this paradoxical effect is that alcohol, initially at least, selectively depresses those more recently evolved parts of the cerebral cortex that are concerned with self-evaluation and control—thus serving to release the emotional-motivational centers from cortical control. There is, however, evidence that some metabolic products of alcohol may more directly produce stimulating effects, possibly by increasing levels of certain neurotransmitters such as norepinephrine (Lahti & Majchrowicz, 1974). In addition, some of the uninhibited behavior associated with alcohol probably results from learned expectations about how to behave when "high." After a certain level of alcohol accumulates in the blood, the well-known syndrome of drunkenness occurs, with increasing impairment of cognitive functioning and physical coordination. If consumption continues, the result is a state of total incoordination and incapacitation, leading to a loss of consciousness.

Continued use of alcohol in large quantities has a variety of physical consequences, the least serious of which is the chronic irritation of the stomach lining, resulting in indigestion or ulceration. Extensive use also results in the accumulation of fat in the liver, reducing its functioning, and eventuating, if continued, in a marked impairment of this organ called hepatic cirrhosis. X-ray scanning procedures have shown that cerebral atrophy is associated with extensive and chronic alcoholic abuse (Fox et al., 1976). In some cases this cerebral atrophy can be reversed, as indicated by brain X rays taken before and after periods of one to four months of abstinence (Carlen

et al., 1978). The reversible atrophy occurred only in individuals who showed improvement in psychological functioning during the abstinent period. The authors speculate that many brain neurons had been only partially damaged and that new dendrites had "sprouted" on the still viable axons. A variety of other debilitating and potentially lethal consequences can also follow chronic and extensive use, including damage to the cardiovascular system and the development of a life-style that renders the chronic abuser vulnerable to a variety of serious diseases. How much these effects are due to the direct pharmacologic effect of alcohol and how much to the life-style that accompanies chronic and protracted use is not always clear. Recently, however, it has been shown that alcohol has a direct effect upon cells taken from rat embryos, retarding both their growth and rate of differentiation (Brown et al., 1979). There is also mounting evidence that women who drink heavily during pregnancy are more likely to have babies with physical and behavioral deviations (Landesman-Dwyer et al., 1978; Rosett et al, 1978).

Three specific syndromes that may follow heavy and prolonged use of alcohol are *delirium tremens, alcohol hallucinosis,* and *Korsakoff's psychosis.*

Delirium Tremens. *Delirium tremens,* or the DTs, occurs in about five percent of individuals who have developed a strong dependence on alcohol. Usually it begins after a period of nondrinking when the alcohol level in the blood drops suddenly. Initially the person is restless, cannot sleep, and is made nervous by slight noises. This trouble develops into a psychological disturbance of psychotic proportions in which the person becomes disoriented in place and time, has visual hallucinations (frequently of fast-moving animals—rats, cockroaches, snakes, spiders, and the like—that seem to swarm over the wall, bed, or the person's body), develops gross tremors of the arms and legs, sweats profusely, and has a fast but weak heartbeat. The person may react with terror to the hallucinated animals, hiding under the bedcovers or desperately fighting them off. The acute phase of the DTs, which usually lasts from three to six days, is viewed as a serious medical problem. In the past, approximately 10 percent of individuals with this disorder died as a result of convulsions, heart failure, and other complications. Recent drugs, however, have reduced the death rate.

Blood alcohol levels can be estimated by breathing into this apparatus.

Alcohol Hallucinosis. The essential feature of this disorder is the persistence of hallucinations *after* the person has recovered from alcohol withdrawal and is no longer drinking. The hallucinations are usually auditory, and the person does not have the physical symptoms and disorientation associated with delirium tremens. This disorder is rare, and there is no general agreement as to whether the hallucinations represent the precipitation of a psychosis in an already prone person or result more directly from the excessive use of alcohol.

Korsakoff's Psychosis. Another reaction, first described by the Russian psychiatrist Korsakoff in 1887, afflicts about 1 percent of chronic alcoholics. Called Korsakoff's psychosis, it involves a defect in remembering recent events. The person, however, fills in the gaps in memory with imaginary happenings, a process usually referred to as *confabulation.* These patients are also likely to show *polyneuritis,* the inflammation of a large number of peripheral nerves. Korsakoff's psychosis is thought to result from a deficiency of vitamin B associated with the alcoholic's poor dietary habits over a long period of time. Massive doses of this vitamin are frequently helpful in treatment, although in some cases if the vitamin supplements are not given in time, the intellectual impairment becomes irreversible.

Delirium tremens

DEVELOPMENT OF ALCOHOLISM

Biological Correlates. Nowhere, with the possible exception of schizophrenia, has the clash between the biological disease model of psychopathology and the psychosocial model been so intense as with alcoholism. The disease conception is well conveyed by Mann (1968):

Alcoholism is a disease which manifests itself chiefly by the uncontrollable drinking of the victim, who is known as an alcoholic. It is a progressive disease, which, if left untreated, grows more virulent year by year, driving its victims further and further from the normal world and deeper and deeper into an abyss which has only two outlets: insanity or death. (p. 3)

A congenital biological disposition to be an alcoholic is clearly stated by Kessel (1962):

Since some people apparently blessed with everything that should save them from alcoholism . . . take to drink uncontrollably, whereas others much less well endowed by fate can drink without crossing the fatal frontier, a certain conclusion is inevitable: One does not *become* an alcoholic. One is *born* an alcoholic. (p. 128)

Attempts in the 1930s through the 1950s to label alcoholism as a disease were not, in fact, based on any convincing evidence that alcoholics had some specific physiological defect that nonalcoholics did not have. On the other hand, whether right or wrong scientifically, the widespread advocacy of the disease concept served to remove some of the moralistic stigma associated with this problem and to focus attention on what could be done to help alcoholics rather than simply condemn them for their sinful ways.

Current research indicates, rather indirectly, that there may indeed be some biological factors that contribute to the development of alcoholism. Genetic influences, for example, may exist. There is little doubt that alcoholism tends to run in families. Winokur et al. (1970) found that about 40 percent of 259 hospitalized alcoholics had a parent, usually the father, who was an alcoholic. Although twin research has been only partially supportive of genetic factors, adoption studies have more clearly suggested a role for heredity (Goodwin, 1979). Goodwin et al. (1973) found that sons of alcoholics placed in foster homes early in life were nearly four times more likely to develop alcoholism than were adoptees without known alcoholism in their biological parents. The adoptive parents of the two groups (all living in Denmark) did not differ in socioeconomic backgrounds, rates of alcoholism, or other psychological disorders. In a subsequent study using a subset of the same sample, Goodwin et al. (1974) compared rates of alcoholism for sons of alcoholic parents, adopted in infancy, with their brothers who remained with their alcoholic parents. If social learning factors were important, we would expect higher rates of later alcoholism for those sons who lived with the alcoholic parents. On the contrary, both groups had high rates of alcoholism that were not significantly different, 25 percent for adopted sons and 17 percent for nonadopted sons.

Of some interest was the finding that the sons of alcoholics and sons of nonalcoholics did not differ on a wide range of other variables: depression, personality disorders, criminality or "heavy drinking" (defined as drinking daily and occasionally large amounts but without adverse consequences). This would suggest that any genetic factor is rather specific for alcoholism and is not a general tendency toward psychopathology or deviant behavior. The fact that heavy drinking showed no genetic influence is especially interesting, implying that heavy drinking proceeds to alcoholism only if certain genetically determined biological factors are present. Goodwin et al. (1977) in a similar adoption study found inconclusive results for a genetic factor in the daughters of alcoholics.

What might the biological mechanisms be that would mediate the effects of a possible genetic factor? One speculation has been that some individuals are protected from alcoholism because they inherit a tendency to respond to even small amounts of alcohol with very unpleasant reactions—a reaction that would tend to inhibit extensive drinking or perhaps any drinking at all. Research has shown that about three-fourths of Oriental people respond to alcohol in this negative fashion, a fact that may account for the low rate of alcoholism among Orientals (Wolff, 1972). The lack of this negative reaction to alcohol, however, seems unlikely to be the general mechanism for alcoholic vulnerability, since many individuals drink moderately or even heavily without going on to become alcoholics.

When alcohol is metabolized in the body, one of the first breakdown products is acetaldehyde. There is some evidence that this metabolite may play a role in alcoholism. Korsten et al. (1975) found that when a controlled dose of alcohol was given intravenously, blood levels of acetaldehyde were higher in alcoholics than in matched nonalcoholics. There is evidence that acetaldehyde is a potent releaser of biogenic amines, including norepinephrine (for example, Lahti & Majchrowicz, 1974), and evidence that high levels of brain norepinephrine lead to increased alcohol consumption in rats (Amit et al., 1977) and to a greater euphoria associated with drinking alcohol in humans (Ahlenius et al., 1973). These findings, then, suggest the possibility that a person vulnerable to alcoholic dependency may be one who responds to alcohol with greater than normal levels of acetaldehyde, which increase levels of norepinephrine in certain portions of the brain, and this increase in turn creates a more positive response to alcohol. The latter may contribute to the reported craving for alcohol. This line of speculation is further reinforced by the finding that the sons of alcoholics showed significantly greater increases in blood levels of acetaldehyde after a controlled dose of alcohol than did a matched comparison group (Schuckit & Rayses, 1979). The average age in both groups was 23. No sons of alcoholics who were already alcoholic (3 percent) were included in the sample. That this biological difference was present in the sons of alcoholics *before* they had developed alcoholism themselves suggests that this difference might be inherited from an alcoholic parent and increase their vulnerability to becoming alcoholic themselves.

Psychosocial Determinants. Psychoanalytic theorists have suggested variously that fixation at the oral stage of psychosexual development, self-destructive impulses, and latent homosexuality (or some combination of these) underlie the alcoholic's compulsive drinking. Fenichel (1945), for example, argued that passive, dependent, oral urges in which intake through the mouth is a major source of gratification, motivate the alcoholic. McCord et al. (1960), however, found no difference in the oral behavior of children who later became alcoholics and those who did not. This one study does not necessarily disprove the theory of oral fixation since one could argue that degree of oral fixation had not been validly measured. That self-destructive impulses, latent homosexuality, or oral behaviors may be present in some alcoholics would not be surprising. It is another matter to demonstrate that these specific characteristics play a primary role in the development of all, or most, alcoholics. That has not been done.

Social learning theorists have objected strongly to the disease model of alcoholism, suggesting instead that the excessive drinking can be explained as a learned response. Eventually, when physiological dependency has developed, the learned response can be further maintained by avoidance of the withdrawal syndrome.

Some years ago Conger (1951) performed experiments with rats that have served as a model for a tension reduction theory of how alcoholism is learned. Rats learned to approach the end of a runway where they were fed. On later trials they were shocked at the end of the runway, producing an approach-avoidance conflict. Experimental rats given an injection of alcohol were less affected than control rats (given a placebo injection) by this conflict and made more approach responses to the goal area. In a second experiment Conger demonstrated that it was the avoidance response that was reduced by alcohol; the approach tendency was unaffected. Conger suggested that alcoholism in humans was learned because alcohol reduces the anxiety associated with many life circumstances. Social learning principles suggest that the immediate reinforcing effects of tension reduction exert more control over behavior than do the long-term negative consequences of excessive drinking.

Other studies have shown that animals choose to drink alcoholic rather than nonalcoholic beverages when under stress. For example, Clark and Polish (1960) showed that alcohol consumption by monkeys increased during a period of shock-avoidance learning and decreased following the learning sessions. These animal studies suggest a rather simple model for the development of alcoholism: Life stresses increase discomfort and tension; alcohol provides quick relief from stress-induced states of discomfort; if alcohol is available, the individual learns to make the stress-reducing drinking response and persists with it because the immediate reinforcement outweighs long-term negative consequences. Furthermore, once physical dependency has developed, another powerful source of reinforcement is present—avoidance of the extremely unpleasant withdrawal symptoms by continued drinking.

We are still left, however, with the problem of explaining why most drinkers do not go on to become alcoholics. The answer to this question may lie either in a biological vulnerability, as we have already discussed, or in the social learning histories of the individuals (or both). With respect to social learning, one person may have learned to respond to frustrating, tension-producing life situations with active and successful coping strategies, another with handicapping defensive mechanisms, and a third by drinking alcohol. Marlatt and his colleagues have examined circumstances under which alcoholics relapsed after treatment (Marlatt, 1973; Marlatt & Gordon, 1979). Most commonly they had taken their first drink in one of three situations: interpersonal conflicts in which they had had to cope with frustration and anger; negative emotional states such as anxiety, depression, loneliness, and boredom; or social pressures by friends or others to have a drink.

Marlatt and his associates have further demonstrated the importance of environmental circumstances in drinking behavior by a series of experiments with heavy social, but nonalcoholic, drinkers. In all studies subjects made "taste ratings" of wine under conditions that disguised the fact that the amount of wine drunk was of interest to the experimenter. In one study subjects who were angered (frustrated and insulted by a confederate during a problem-solving task) but who did not have an opportunity to express anger toward the provoking confederate, drank significantly more wine in the subsequent wine-tasting situation than did subjects who did have a chance to express their anger (Marlatt et al., 1975). In a second study (Higgins & Marlatt, 1975) male subjects described as heavy drinkers were told that following the taste test they were to talk to a group of girls about interpersonal attractiveness and be rated by the girls on a number of qualities. These subjects drank significantly more wine than did subjects in nonevaluational control conditions (see Figure 23-2). The results of these studies are clearly consistent with the possibility that some people learn to drink excessively as a way of coping with social frustrations and anxieties.

Research is less definitive on the question of whether alcoholics have particular childhood social learning experiences that predispose them to this problem. Several studies have found childhood personality differences between adult alcoholics and nonalcoholics (Goodwin et al., 1975; Jones, 1968; Tarter et al., 1977). The prealcoholic's childhood personality is more often characterized in a way reminiscent of the hyperactivity syndrome: impulsive, restless, short attention span, rebellious, aggressive, and disobedient. Characteristics of this sort might well be associated with a later lack of restraint in the use of alcohol. Both genetic and psychosocial influences could contribute to the development of these traits.

Psychosocial factors that are likely to promote a tendency to use alcohol as a way of coping with frustrations and anxieties are the availability of alcohol

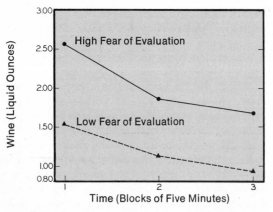

FIGURE 23-2. Amount of wine consumed in the high and low fear of evaluation conditions during the taste-testing task, based on estimates of ounces consumed per sip by each subject in five-minute blocks. (Adapted from Higgins & Marlatt, 1975. Copyright 1975 by the American Psychological Association and used with permission.)

and the modeling and reinforcement of drinking by peers or parents. The importance of parental modeling is suggested in results reported by McCord et al. (1960). Young boys and their families were studied intensively as part of an attempt to prevent juvenile delinquency (Teuber & Powers, 1953). Years later when most of the subjects were in their thirties it was determined that about 10 percent had become alcoholics. This group was compared with a "normal" group that had shown neither alcoholism nor criminality. Mothers who had responded to crises in escapist ways—by retiring to their rooms, becoming sexually promiscuous, drinking, or just ignoring the crisis—had a much higher percentage of sons who became alcoholic (38 percent) than did mothers who responded realistically (15 percent) or who responded aggressively but not necessarily realistically (14 percent).

There is some evidence, then, consistent with the view that alcoholism is a learned response that is continually reinforced by reducing tensions arising from social frustrations and anxieties. However, at this point we must introduce a slight note of discord. Some research raises a question as to just how tension-reducing alcohol really is for the chronic alcoholic. Findings with heavy social drinkers or problem drinkers are generally consistent with the idea that alcohol is tension-reducing, especially the first few drinks. Eddy (1979), for example, found women problem drinkers to show significantly less self-reported anxiety under stress after drinking approximately 1½ ounces of 100-proof liquor than under a nonalcohol condition. Williams (1966) obtained self-reports on college students' reactions to drinking at stag cocktail parties. For both problem and non-problem drinkers, anxiety and depression decreased significantly after the first two drinks (four to six ounces); at eight ounces and above these trends reversed and anxiety and depression increased, rising to the preparty levels. Such a finding is still partially consistent with a tension reduction model, at least as an explanation of initial drinking behavior.

Studies with alcoholics, rather than social drinkers, have shown less evidence for tension reduction, at least as measured by self-report. Mayfield and Allen (1967) compared self-reports of mood among groups of alcoholics, depressed patients, and normals after intravenous administration of alcohol. Depressed patients reported an improvement in mood, but alcoholics showed no change. Several other studies have found *increases* in feelings of anxiety and depression after prolonged drinking. Mendelson et al. (1964) obtained measures of affective state from ten alcoholics during several experimental phases: a nondrinking baseline; a 5-day period during which the subjects drank from 6 to 30 ounces of whiskey per day; a 14-day period during which all subjects drank 30 ounces per day; and a 5-day period during which subjects drank 40 ounces per day. During the first 5-day drinking period there was no change in emotional state; during the last two periods the alcoholics reported feeling more anxious, more depressed, and more aggressive. Previous to the study these individuals had reported that alcohol usually made them feel less tense, an expectation not borne out by their actual reactions. Also, despite the fact that they reported increasingly negative emotional reactions, these alcoholics continued to be *strongly motivated to drink*. These results have been verified in several other studies (for example, McNamee et al., 1968; Nathan & O'Brien, 1971).

If alcohol is not experienced as tension-reducing, at least in chronic alcoholics, how can we explain the persistence of the drinking response? One possibility is that self-reports of mood change in terms of tension, anxiety, or depression are an incomplete picture of all the subjective changes experienced by the alcoholic who takes a drink. It is possible that even more immediate physical sensations associated with taking a drink continue to reinforce the drinking response more powerfully than the somewhat less specifically associated mood states. Also there is evidence that schedules of reinforcement involving mixtures of rewards and punishments may, somewhat paradoxically, lead to more persistent behavior than rewards alone (Martin, 1963). Or, to put it a little differently, the past history of rewards and punishments have brought the drinking under stimulus control (the barroom scene, the smell and taste of favorite beverages, the presence of drinking companions, and so on) and less under the control of consequent mood states. And one final possibility. If feelings of depression and anxiety increase after a period of drinking, these too can eventually be escaped by further drinking to oblivion. Thus a final reinforcement for prolonged drinking would be provided. Related to this last point is the suggestion of Nathan et al. (1972) that most chronic alcoholics tend not to remember many of the unpleasant events that happen in the later phases of a binge and therefore will be relatively unaffected by such memories when they anticipate drinking again.

Alcoholism has also been viewed from a family systems point of view, usually with special emphasis on the spouse relationship. Steiner (1969), for example, suggests that alcoholics and their spouses frequently play certain "games" that maintain the drinking behavior. In one such game the alcoholic plays "victim." By drinking excessively he evokes disappointment from his wife (or other family members), who in turn can play the role of virtuous blamers. The game from the alcoholic's point of view is "You're good, I'm bad, try and stop me." Presumably, both participants experience satisfaction in the payoffs of the game: The alcoholic has defeated the virtuous blamer's attempts to stop his drinking, and the virtuous blamer can continue to feel virtuous and justified in his or her disapproval. A variation on this game is one in which the spouse has great difficulty in providing emotional or sexual support. The spouse may then reinforce in devious ways the alcoholic's drinking so that the spouse's own deficiencies are not exposed. These proposals have not been verified by systematic research, and there is the problem of to what extent an observed marital interaction pattern is a secondary result of an alcoholic spouse rather than a primary cause of the alcoholism.

Cultural Influences. The values and customs of the community influence individual drinking behavior. Rates of alcoholism, for example, vary widely in different cultures. Countries that have high incidence include northern France, the United States, Sweden, Switzerland, Poland, and northern Russia. In the past relatively low incidence has characterized Greece, Italy, and Spain. Rates of alcoholism, however, may be changing in some countries. In 1954 Italy ranked near the bottom of European countries in deaths caused by cirrhosis of the liver (usually attributed to alcoholism), but in figures published in 1966 Italy ranked near the top, below France and Austria. Differences between subcultures have been found within the United States. When the total population of New York City was 10 percent Irish and 15 percent Italian, 40 percent of the alcoholic persons were Irish and only 1 percent were Italian. These percentages would not necessarily hold for today's population.

Low rates cannot be attributed in all cases to abstinence. Moslems do not drink because of religious beliefs and their alcoholism rates are low; a large percentage of Jews do drink, yet their alcoholism rates are low too. The usual explanation for low rates of alcoholism in cultures that condone drinking is that customs, values, and sanctions with respect to drinking are well established, known and agreed upon by all, and consistent with the rest of the culture. In general, it has been found that among groups who use alcohol freely, the lowest incidence of alcoholism is associated with eight characteristics:

1. Children are exposed to alcohol early in life, within a strong family or religious group. Whatever the beverage, it is served in diluted and small quantities, with consequent low blood alcohol levels.
2. The beverages commonly, though not invariably, used contain relatively large amounts of nonalcoholic components (wines and beers), which also give low blood alcohol levels.
3. The beverage is considered mainly as a food and is usually consumed with meals, again with consequent low blood alcohol levels.
4. Parents present a constant example of moderate drinking.
5. No moral importance is attached to drinking. It is considered neither a virtue nor a sin.
6. Drinking is not viewed as proof of adulthood or virility.
7. Abstinence is socially acceptable. It is no more rude or ungracious to decline a drink than to decline a piece of cake.
8. Excessive drinking or intoxication is not socially acceptable. It is not considered stylish, comic, or tolerable.

TREATMENT OF ALCOHOLISM

Psychodynamic Therapies. Most psychodynamically oriented therapists consider the chronic alcoholic extremely difficult to help, in part because they view alcoholism as stemming from a defect in character rather than a neurotic conflict. Although some psychoanalytically oriented therapists have claimed success with alcoholics (for example, Silber, 1970), an extensive review of the research and clinical literature led Hill and Blane (1967) to conclude that the value of psychotherapy for alcoholics had not been clearly demonstrated.

At Alcoholics Anonymous meetings, testimonials and confessions are made, and members develop friendships and attitudes of mutual support.

Alcoholics Anonymous. In the early 1930s Bill W. overcame his alcoholism through a basic spiritual change. He immediately sought out his friend Dr. Bob and was able to help him achieve recovery also. Both began to help other alcoholics, partly as a self-help program to keep themselves from relapsing, and in 1935 they formed Alcoholics Anonymous (AA). Since then AA has grown to over 10,000 groups located around the world, with more than a million members.

The AA approach may be likened to a combination of religious belief and group therapy. Several tenets are fundamental to AA: Persons must admit that they are powerless over alcohol, must turn the direction of their lives over to God as they understand Him, must recognize that they can never drink again, must concern themselves with going for one day at a time without alcohol rather than with the long-term problem of alcoholism, and must seek to help other alcoholics. At weekly meetings, which have an inspirational quality, close bonds are developed among members, and testimonials and confessions are made. When members feel on the verge of succumbing to the temptation to drink, they learn to contact another member for emotional support. Helping other members in this way probably bolsters their own "will power." In general, AA not only attempts to stop members from drinking but also, and perhaps most important, provides social relationships and responsibilities to replace the frustrations and emptiness that usually have come to characterize the alcoholic's life. Put somewhat differently, AA provides other responses that can be substituted for drinking.

Does AA work? It is hard to say, since AA is not a research-oriented organization. A review of attempts to evaluate AA led Leach (1973) to conclude that it was effective for many alcoholics. A crucial factor to consider in evaluating the effectiveness of AA is that many alcoholics are not "ready" for AA; that is, either they have not recognized that their drinking is out of control or they have other reasons for refusing to participate in the AA program. Thus AA members probably represent a subsample of alcoholics, those who have developed some definite motivation for change.

Sam, described in the introductory case example to this chapter, was successfully helped by AA and at the time the article was written had been abstinent for many years. He continued to believe, consistent with the AA viewpoint, that once an alcoholic, always an alcoholic. "I still believe I'm an alcoholic. I still believe I have to arrange every morning when I get up not to drink that day. I'll die an alcoholic, but I hope to die sober."

Aversion Conditioning. Early attempts to treat alcoholism from a behavioral perspective used a simple aversion conditioning model. Lemere and Voegtlin (1950), for example, paired a nausea-inducing drug with the sight, taste, and smell of alcohol in four to seven brief sessions distributed over a period of about ten days. At follow-ups ranging from one to ten years these authors found that 51 percent of the 4096 alcoholics treated were completely abstinent. In general, the percentage of individuals showing complete abstinence decreased as the follow-up period increased. Abstinence rates were also higher among those who had stable employment histories,

were from upper-class backgrounds, and who joined "abstinence clubs" after treatment. Other investigators using similar aversion conditioning procedures have reported similar results (for example, Thinman, 1949).

More recently, aversion conditioning based on painful electric shocks (Vogler et al., 1970) and covert sensitization, in which nauseous experiences are *imagined* (Cautela, 1970), have also been tried. Wilson (1978) after reviewing the rather extensive literature concludes that electrical aversion conditioning does not work and should be discontinued. He concluded that research on the effectiveness of covert desensitization was mixed, with no clear support for its effectiveness. Although not strictly a form of aversion conditioning, the drug Antabuse has also been used to control alcoholism. The presence of this drug in the bloodstream even in small amounts produces extremely unpleasant effects (such as nausea, and cold sweats) when alcohol is drunk. The problem with Antabuse is that the person must be motivated to take the drug every two to three days.

Although chemical aversion therapy using drug-induced nausea has some degree of effectiveness, it is not the complete answer to the treatment of alcoholism. Most writers, including those who conducted the above studies, agree that stopping the alcoholic's drinking response is only half the battle. An alcoholic's life is likely to have deteriorated so far that a substantial proportion of energy and time have become centered around drinking. Simply to take away the drinking response is to leave no alternative ways of coping with those life stresses that may have driven the person to drink in the first place. The person must therefore be helped to develop competencies, ways of coping with frustrations, and new interests that can replace the old alcoholic life-style.

Multidimensional Approaches. A number of treatment facilities specializing in the alcoholic patient have emerged in recent decades. Individuals are encouraged to remain in the facility for periods ranging from two weeks to six months (four weeks being fairly typical), during which they may receive some combination of AA, group therapy, educational lectures and films, vocational training, medication, or aversion therapy. Surveys of the effectiveness of many of these programs have shown them to be fairly effective, with around two-thirds of the patients being either "improved" or abstinent at follow-ups of around one year after discharge (Bromet et al., 1977; Emrick, 1975). Bromet et al. found, not surprisingly, that patients who participated most actively in whatever the program content tended to have the best outcomes. On the other hand, patients given more medications (usually sedatives and antianxiety drugs) showed relatively poor outcomes.

Approaches that seem especially promising are those—usually deriving from a social learning orientation—that explictly focus on first identifying those circumstances that tend to elicit heavy drinking or relapses and to teach the person alternative ways of coping with these circumstances. (Chaney, 1976; Sobell & Sobell, 1973). Chaney and his colleagues developed a social skill training program based on coping with the kind of life events that Marlatt had found to be associated with relapses. Training was tailored to the individual so that one person might focus on learning to resist social pressure and another on coping with feelings of loneliness. This procedure was found to be more effective than various comparison groups in reducing relapse rates.

One Drink and Loss of Control? It has been dogma among many of the workers in the field of alcoholism, including those in AA, that total abstinence is the only alternative for the alcoholic, that an alcoholic cannot learn to drink in moderation. This view has been based on the belief that one drink will lead to uncontrolled drinking, an outcome thought to be inevitable within the disease model framework. Actually, there is little research support for this idea. Pattison et al. (1977) refer to numerous studies in which alcoholics are able to control their drinking under appropriate circumstances. For example, Oki (reported in Pattison et al., 1977) observed 80 consecutive male admissions to an alcoholic treatment center who were all skid-row chronic drunkenness offenders suffering severe social and economic impairment. These individuals could choose either abstinence or controlled drinking as their treatment objective and were free to switch their objective at a later time if they wished. Daily drinking data were obtained for all subjects throughout their stay. Overall the men were able to demonstrate good control over their drinking. When persons set a goal of controlled drinking, in only 9 percent of the times did this lead

to uncontrolled drinking. When the individuals set abstinence as their goal, uncontrolled drinking occurred in 12 percent of the times. The high level of control shown by these chronic alcoholics occurred in the treatment center environment, and there is little reason to believe that they would control their drinking to that degree when back on the streets again. But that is the whole point. Whether or not alcoholics can control their drinking would seem to depend more upon external circumstances than upon some internally produced biological craving.

Further supporting this conclusion are studies that show that it is alcoholics' *beliefs* about whether they are drinking alcohol that are more highly associated with desire for additional drinks than whether, in fact, they are drinking alcohol. Thus Marlatt et al. (1973) used a taste preference task similar to the one previously described and found that whether alcoholics were given an initial drink of actual alcohol or plain tonic did not affect their subsequent drinking. But alcoholics who *believed* that they were drinking alcohol, whether they were or not, drank more than those who *believed* they were not. The results of this and similar studies are difficult to explain on the basis of some biological craving inevitably produced by the ingestion of alcohol.

Sobell and Sobell (1973) report evidence that suggests that some alcoholics can become controlled drinkers. In their study, alcoholics who indicated a desire to become controlled drinkers and who had available significant outside social support to help maintain controlled drinking were candidates for the controlled drinking condition. The other alcoholics were assigned to a nondrinking condition. For our present purposes we are only interested in the controlled drinking condition. Individuals considered appropriate for controlled drinking training were then randomly assigned to either the controlled drinking condition or to the usual hospital treatment, which consisted of a combination of AA, vocational training, medication, and group therapy—all of which emphasized abstinence. During the six-month period at the end of a two-year follow-up, individuals in the controlled drinking group had been functioning well (either abstinent or drinking moderately) on 87 percent of the days compared with 44 percent of the days for the control group. These results clearly imply that *some* alcoholics can learn to drink in moderation. Vogler et al. (1977) also were successful in training alcoholics to become controlled drinkers and in addition obtained information on which alcoholics were the best candidates for such training. Not surprisingly, perhaps, they found that younger alcoholics who had been drinking excessively for fewer years, drank relatively lower amounts of alcohol per month, had a more stable vocational history, and had less physical deterioration from drinking were most able to become controlled drinkers. At this time then, it would appear that an absolutist position on abstinence is not justified. Nevertheless, there may well be a population of older, chronic alcoholics for whom controlled drinking is an extremely difficult goal to achieve.

To summarize the discussion of treatment, all approaches require some initial motivation on the part of alcoholics to change their drinking behavior. Given that motivation, AA and other multidimensional approaches have shown some effectiveness. An especially significant development is the identification of those social and emotional circumstances associated with relapse and the teaching of new ways of coping with these life situations.

Barbiturate Abuse

Barbiturates, like alcohol, are sedative drugs, and have been widely prescribed for relief of anxiety and insomnia. Next to alcohol, barbiturates are the most abused type of drug. A person who has ingested enough barbiturates to become intoxicated shows clouding of consciousness, impairment in intellectual functioning, disequilibrium, poor judgment, confusion, and loss of emotional control. In other words, it is difficult to distinguish between barbiturate-induced intoxication and that resulting from drinking too much alcohol, except for the fact that the barbiturate users have no alcohol odor on their breath.

Abrupt withdrawal of barbiturates from a heavily dependent individual produces a withdrawal syndrome that is severe and potentially lethal. Thus it is standard medical practice that withdrawal always take place in a hospital, under close observation, with stringent treatment procedures. Without such pro-

cedures, which require a slow and cautious decrease in the amount of barbiturates administered daily (approximately a ten percent decrease in the daily dosage the individual has been used to taking), the classic barbiturate abstinence syndrome occurs.

Although barbiturate abusers usually stay with one kind of drug, in some cases they mix barbiturates with other drugs. Thus some individuals use barbiturates to counteract the effect of various stimulant drugs, such as the amphetamines. A cyclical pattern then emerges, in which the individual is alternately stimulated and sedated. Each drug effect is used to counteract the pharmacologic effect of the other. The agents are frequently referred to as "uppers" (amphetamines) and "downers" (barbiturates), and the syndrome is referred to as the amphetamine-barbiturate abuse cycle. A dependency on both stimulants and sedatives can result in a variety of medical complications, some with fatal outcomes. One of the difficulties encountered by the abuser of both substances is that while tolerance occurs in both cases, the tolerance levels associated with the barbiturates are limited, whereas very high doses of amphetamines can be ingested by the chronic user without serious effects. An equivalent increase in barbiturate intake levels will result in death due to respiratory failure.

Another pattern involves the abuse of barbiturates in individuals who have had chronic dependency problems with other drugs, such as alcohol and the opiate compounds. Some alcoholics attempt to counteract the alcohol withdrawal syndrome by "tapering off" with barbiturates. In the past barbiturates were used to "treat" alcoholism, on the assumption that it was somehow better to be intoxicated on barbiturates than alcohol. The dangers associated with barbiturate dependency made this practice extremely hazardous. An even more dangerous practice involves the combining of alcohol and barbiturates in order to "boost" their effects and produce a better "high." The effects of both drugs are cumulative, due to their almost identical pharmacologic properties, and the result can be, at best, serious and severe intoxication; moreover, death from inhibition of the respiratory centers is always a risk with this combination. Other individuals have used sedatives in a medically approved manner but have used alcohol at the same time with lethal consequences.

The Opiates: Opium, Morphine, and Heroin

A BRIEF HISTORY

Opiates— or *narcotics,* to use the common term—are depressants that have their major effect on the central nervous system and respiration. They are most commonly used as analgesics, or pain killers, although they are also frequently prescribed for use in cough suppressants and for diarrhea. For centuries the most frequently used medications throughout the civilized world contained high concentrations of opium. The concern over its dependency-producing characteristics is of recent origin; until lately, dependency and withdrawal tended to be seen as characteristics of the illness treated rather than the drug, and effects were milder since the drug was administered orally and usually in combination with other substances until the latter half of the nineteenth century.

The abuse of opiates in the United States has been attributed to a number of factors. First was the isolation of a more potent alkaloid form of opium, morphine, in Germany in 1804. This compound, like heroin almost a century later, was originally hailed as a cure for the opium habit, since morphine could be substituted for opium without any signs of withdrawal. Second, the effect of this more potent compound was found to be enhanced by intravenous infusion with a hypodermic needle in the mid-nineteenth century. Interestingly, it was long felt by physicians that the administration of morphine hypodermically was a means of avoiding addiction.

The extensive casualties of the Civil War provided the first opportunity for the widespread use of hypodermically administered morphine. The drug was used both for its pain-relieving properties and as a treatment of dysentery and other intestinal disorders. So frequent were the addictive states caused by military physicians' injudicious use of morphine that well into the twentieth century the Pension Bureau was handling large numbers of cases of Civil War veterans suffering from what was euphemistically called the "army disease" or the "soldier's disease."

Also during the nineteenth century the importation of Chinese laborers to assist in building the trans-

continental railroad brought the practice of smoking opium into this country. The opium smoker tended to be older and more settled than the current "junkie," and was usually well established in a profession, whether criminal or law-abiding. By the last decade of the nineteenth century, the United States had become one of the largest consumers of smoking opium in the world (Isbell, 1959).

During this period the medical profession had also shifted its orientation regarding narcotic dependency. While initially viewing dependence as a "morbid appetite," that is, a habit or a vice, doctors later saw it as a disease. Thus opiate-dependent individuals were either withdrawn from the drug as part of regular office practice or were maintained on the drug by regular prescriptions. No one was quite sure how to treat this problem, and to many physicians the most humane policy seemed to be to continue administering the drug so as to avoid the discomfort and complications associated with withdrawal. One highly touted miracle cure, which was reported to have all the therapeutic properties of morphine but none of its dangers, was a compound isolated in Germany in 1898 known as diacetyl-morphine, more commonly called *heroin.*

The past 75 years have seen major shifts in drug use patterns, types of drugs abused, and race and age of users. In the 1930s the typical user (as indicated by rates of admission to the Public Health Service Hospital at Lexington, Kentucky) was white, southern, and in his or her late thirties. Further, the drug used was typically not heroin but morphine, paregoric, or codeine. By 1962 the typical user was young, lived in a northern metropolitan center, and was taking heroin. The proportion of black and Puerto Rican users had risen substantially (Ball & Chambers, 1970).

OPIATE ABUSE

Under a clinically effective dose of morphine, the individual is somnolent, lacking any observable anxiety or discomfort. The skin flushes, body temperature decreases, pulse and respiration are decreased, blood pressure drops, and pupils become constricted. With chronic use the individual becomes constipated and lacks sexual drive; in women, menstruation ceases. In effect, many of the bodily func-

Edgar Allan Poe, American poet and author, was reported to be addicted to opium.

after, begins to diminish and eventually vanishes, even the initial rush. In order to obtain the desired effects, larger and larger doses are required. Most chronic users report that after a period of use they cease even attempting to obtain the high and use the drug just to "feel right" or avoid withdrawal symptoms. It is at this time that some individuals turn themselves in for a "cure," while others quit use altogether.

Because of the heavy demand for drugs and the profit involved, most illegal narcotics available today are highly diluted, and the typical street user cannot count on obtaining any more than 2 to 5 percent heroin in any "bag," equivalent to about 10 percent active drug. Thus the development of a classic withdrawal syndrome has become less common. Members of Synanon report that despite their demand that all entering the program "kick" without any chemical mediation, they rarely encounter any major difficulty. At worst they say the modern abstinence syndrome is like having "a bad case of the flu" (Yablonsky, 1967).

Some relatively affluent individuals are able to pay for their drugs while continuing to lead a more or less normal life. For many people, however, being "hooked" on drugs means a life-style almost totally devoted to ensuring the next "fix." Males resort to burglary or mugging; females turn to prostitution; and both sexes may become pushers. As social life, family relations, and occupational adjustment tend to deteriorate, the person may become part of a local drug culture.

tions are slowed down. Until tolerance reaches a high level, the heroin-dependent individual also experiences a sense of euphoria following each infusion. Interestingly enough, morphine administered experimentally to so-called normal individuals rarely produces euphoria. Instead, frequently there is dysphoria, including restlessness, agitation, anxiety, nausea, and general discomfort.

The initial stages of morphine or heroin usage are sometimes referred to as the "honeymoon" period, when the drug works just as it "should" for the person. That is, individuals tend to experience increasing euphoria as they increase the dose and the frequency of administration. The subjective state is described as a feeling of ease with the world, less bothered and distressed. Troubles seem to lose their impact and significance, although one is still aware of them. This experience seems analogous to the subjective reports of individuals who have been administered morphine for intense pain; they are still aware of the pain, but it no longer bothers them. As the person gets more into the habit and begins to experience signs of tolerance, the honeymoon comes to an end. The feeling of pleasure, so highly sought

Abuse of Stimulant Drugs: The Amphetamines

First synthesized in the 1920s, the amphetamines initially found their way into approved medical use as the active ingredients in nasal decongestant inhalers. Soon doctors noted their effectiveness as a central nervous system stimulant: They produce increased alertness, wakefulness, euphoria, and an increased ability to concentrate. Users often talk and behave at a faster rate than is usual for them. For this stimulation, amphetamines are abused by truck drivers attempting to make up time on long hauls, students cramming for examinations, and executives facing a strenuous work week.

Other effects of the amphetamines include suppression of appetite and an increase in both systolic and diastolic blood pressure. Most often the drug is prescribed to inhibit appetite. Many middle-aged homemakers who initially utilized amphetamines for weight reduction and control have begun to abuse them for their euphoria-producing properties.

The amphetamines, of course, do not provide a magical source of extra physical or mental energy. They serve rather as a means of expending a greater amount of energy reserves, which eventually are depleted. The depletion of energy reserves can be potentially hazardous, especially when the individual using the drug must peform complex tasks, such as driving long distances. Truckers have frequently reported a sudden onset of fatigue following extensive use. In addition, with chronic heavy use of amphetamines, perceptual distortions and even hallucinations can occur. Sometimes long-distance truckers who have ingested large amounts of amphetamines over an extended period of time report suddenly seeming to see headlights coming toward them on their side of the road, causing them to swerve to avoid a head-on collision, and to overturn. Other unwanted side effects may interfere when students are cramming for exams. Although the drugs do enhance talkativeness and facilitate the learning of rote material, they seem to cause a parallel decrease in accuracy and some problem in abstract reasoning.

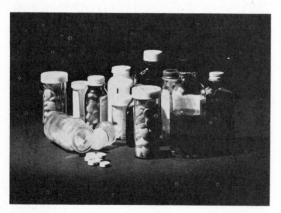

In addition, the sense of increased well-being and confidence can lead to serious errors in judgment or encourage overly simple solutions for complex problems.

Most complications reported in regard to amphetamine abuse result from chronic consumption. When amphetamine dosage is kept within the therapeutic range (5–15 mg), tolerance to the drugs develops slowly. However, progressive increments in dose levels accelerate the development of tolerance to amounts hundreds of times greater than the therapeutic dose, often without apparent serious physiological effects (Carey & Mandel, 1968). There are reports of individuals who were able routinely to ingest several thousand milligrams, and most chronic abusers can develop a tolerance to amounts far greater than standard minimal lethal doses. An unusual feature of amphetamine tolerance is that the cardiovascular system becomes tolerant to large doses rather rapidly, so that heartbeat and blood pressure may not be significantly increased in chronic abusers. Similarly, with extensive use the pupils may no longer show dilation, and the individual's overall physical examination is often within normal limits, despite active abuse (Carey & Mandel, 1968). The absence of significant physical changes may account for the difficulty in identifying the amphetamine abuser, particularly when there is a tendency to deny such use. The most effective means of identification involves the use of urine samples, which require the person's cooperation and are not routinely tested in most situations.

Many heavy and chronic users of amphetamines become irritable, impulsive, and unstable in their personal adjustment. Unlike the experience with hallucinogens such as LSD or mescaline or with marijuana, quiet and contemplation are impossible, as is any connected, goal-directed problem solving. Things seem to be happening much too quickly within one's head to allow for any long-term activities. The user is distractible, unable to keep to any subject for any protracted period of time, and wanders, both physically and psychologically. At the same time, compulsive, repetitive, and apparently aimless actions are common, such as stringing beads endlessly, doodling for hours, or carving or whittling on a piece of wood, all without any observable purpose.

When a toxic reaction occurs as a result of prolonged consumption, a high percentage of the individuals exhibit a schizophrenic-like psychotic episode (Ellinwood, 1967). We discussed this reaction in Chapter 16 when considering possible physiological mechanisms in schizophrenia. The "amphetamine psychosis" can be almost indistinguishable from paranoid schizophrenia, except that the reaction disappears some three to six days after discontinuation of the drug.

Heavy abusers of amphetamines may also commit acts of violence, which may or may not be associated with a psychotic reaction. Ellinwood (1971) hypothesizes that three fairly distinct phases lead to the violent act: (1) chronic amphetamine abuse, (2) an acute change in emotional arousal (due to a sudden increase in the dosage level, chronic loss of sleep, or the use of other drugs), and (3) a situation, often minor or trivial, that triggers the specific events leading to the act of violence. The drug-related conditions of hyperactivity, suspiciousness, and labile (rapidly changing) mood make the abuser sensitive to otherwise minor frustrations and thus increase the potential for aggressive, impulsive acts.

No one is capable of continuing on a speed "run" for more than three days or so. Just as users "get off" with a bang, so they "come down" with a "crash," a period of almost total exhaustion marked by a deep sleep lasting for one or two days. This period is followed by a period of intense and excessive irritability.

The Hallucinogens

The hallucinogens are a class of drugs that produce marked changes in mood and sensory perception. They form a class only because of their effects, since they include a wide variety of substances with very different chemical and pharmacologic properties as well as sources. These drugs range from the naturally occurring variants such as peyote, psilocybin, and amanita muscaria to laboratory synthesized substances such as lysergic acid diethylamide (LSD), mescaline, and the "letter" or "alphabet" drugs such as STP (DOM), MDA, MMDA, DMT, and PCP. The hallucinogens generally tend to be effective in rather small dosages, produce some tolerance but not physical dependence, and primarily effect changes in mood and distortions in visual and auditory perceptions.

EFFECTS OF LSD

LSD, first synthesized by Hoffman, a Swiss chemist, was introduced into this country in the early 1950s. It was initially used in research because it was thought to produce a model of the schizophrenic reaction. Subsequently, researchers have concluded that the LSD experience is quite different from schizophrenia. LSD has also been used as an adjunct in the treatment of neuroses, psychoses, and alcoholism, but it has not been shown to be uniformly helpful in this respect.

The LSD experience typically lasts about eight hours. Perhaps the most striking effects of the drug are sensory and perceptual. Chairs, rugs, trees, and other objects become sharper and brighter; details not ordinarily noticed become clear. Ordinary things become endowed with an almost mystical meaning. Thus Alan Watts (1962) describes how a rotten log looked to him under the influence of LSD:

A rotten log bearing rows of fungus and patches of moss became as precious as any work of Cellini—an inwardly luminous construct of jet, amber, jade, and ivory, all porous and spongy disintegrations of the wood seeming to have been carved out with infinite patience and skill. (p. 52)

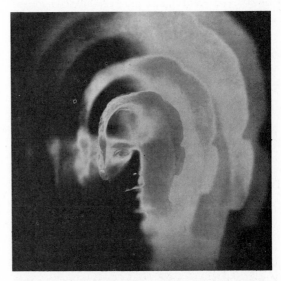

LSD has especially striking sensory and perceptual effects as well as producing strong and sometimes contradictory emotional reactions.

POSSIBLE ADVERSE REACTIONS

Occasionally individuals have adverse reactions to LSD, so-called bad trips involving dramatic episodes of panic and massive anxiety. In rare instances persons become suicidal or unthinkingly jump from high places, run into heavy traffic, or set themselves aflame. These disturbing reactions are unpredictable, and even the most veteran "trippers" report having experienced varying degrees of panic. The risk of a bad reaction has been estimated to be as high as 10 percent of the times that the drug is taken, a probability estimate that increases with higher dosages, uncertain circumstances (such as taking the drug in unfamiliar environments or among strangers), instability of the user, and the lack of quality control of bootlegged and black market preparations (Brecher, 1972). Such panic states have been most frequent among younger and inexperienced drug users, although there is a fairly widespread belief that almost anyone who "drops acid" will undergo a "bummer" at some time. For the most part these states are transient, rarely lasting longer than 24 to 48 hours. However, because the drug tends to distort the experience of time, the user may feel that this period is an eternity, causing an escalation of panic. While support or reassurance from friends or "guides" is often sufficient to reduce the panic, too frequently it is not and the individual is brought to the emergency room of a local hospital. Sometimes there are long-lasting or recurring aftereffects of LSD use, including feelings of confusion, perplexity, sudden mood changes, and "flashbacks," the reexperiencing of some aspect of the LSD episode such as a visual hallucination.

Development of Drug Dependence

BIOLOGICAL CORRELATES

There is no clear evidence at this time of physiological differences that predispose one person more than another to drug dependency. However, researchers have begun to identify specific areas in the brain where certain drugs may be having their effects. Pert and Snyder (1973), for example, have shown that specific nerve cells in the brains of rats

serve as *receptor sites* for opiate drugs; that is, the drug molecules "fit" into these sites like a key in a lock. Nonopiate drugs do not become bound to the same sites. These findings may open the way for a more exact knowledge of how drugs produce their effects at a neurophysiological level. Perhaps in time they will provide a basis for physiological approaches to treatment of physical dependency.

PSYCHOSOCIAL CORRELATES

The same factors associated with alcohol dependency are likely to be associated with dependency on other drugs: immediate reinforcement in the form of escape from the tensions and frustrations of life, induction of a pleasurable mood state, and, if physical dependency develops, the avoidance of withdrawal symptoms. In addition, few authorities disagree that characteristics of the immediate social community have a powerful influence on the initiation and maintenance of drug behavior. Potential teenage drug abusers are likely to be strongly affected by the availability of certain drugs and modeling and social reinforcement by peers for drug usage. Several longitudinal studies have shown that variables such as perceived drug use in the peer group and perceived peer tolerance for drug use predict future drug use in adolescents *before* they have begun using drugs (Kandel et al., 1978). In other words, the relationship of drug use to peer group acceptance of drug use cannot be explained entirely in terms of already drug-using adolescents seeking out drug-using peers. The effect of drug availability, setting, and peer group behavior is powerfully shown in a study that compared Vietnam soldiers with a matched control group (Robins, 1978b). The initiation of narcotic drug use (for example, heroin) increased dramatically during the soldiers' stay in Vietnam and returned to a level somewhat lower than their pre-Vietnam level after they were discharged. The control group showed no comparable change (see Figure 23-3).

Nevertheless, most individuals who live in communities in which drug abuse is high do not become drug abusers, and we must once again supplement immediate environmental determinants with influences derived from past social learning histories. Harbin and Maziar (1975) and Stanton, et al. (1978) have reviewed research on the family background of drug abusers. Parents of drug abusers tended to have higher rates of separation (for reasons other than death), more indications of psychological disturbance, and higher rates of drug use. The modeling effect is suggested in results reported by Smart and Fejer (1972). A positive relationship was found between the parents' use of tranquilizing drugs, alcohol, and tobacco (as reported by the students) and the students' use of drugs of all kinds. Cause and effect is not too much of a problem with variables such as the above since it seems implausible that adolescent drug usage was a primary cause of parental separation, psychological disorders in parents, or drug use by parents—although the child's drug use may have contributed in a secondary way. Relationships with parents, however, might well be severely strained as a result of the child's drug use, so it is especially interesting that Kandel et al. (1978) found that adolescents' perceived lack of closeness to their father predicted their *subsequent* initiation of hard-drug usage—heroin, amphetamines, and barbiturates. Consistent with the idea that drugs may represent a way of dealing with personal problems is the finding that self-reported depression in adolescents predicted future initiation of hard-drug usage but not future initiation of marijuana usage (Kandel et al., 1978).

Stanton et al. (1978) conclude that a common pattern in families of male drug abusers is one in which the mother is indulgent, overprotective, and overly permissive, and frequently puts the son in the position of favored child. The father is detached, uninvolved, weak, or absent. On the basis of extensive clinical experience with families of heroin addicts Stanton and his colleagues suggested that these families foster a dependency and fear of separation in the addicted son. The family seems to be saying, "We will suffer almost anything, but please don't leave us." The son's involvement in the drug scene provides him with a kind of pseudoindependence. He "hustles" to make money to support his habit and develops friendships with fellow addicts. The successful, grown-up image is illusory, however; for in fact he is being competent only within the framework of an unsuccessful, incompetent subculture. The heroin blunts the anxiety associated with separation from family, and the son may become aggressive and assertive toward the family while under the drug's influ-

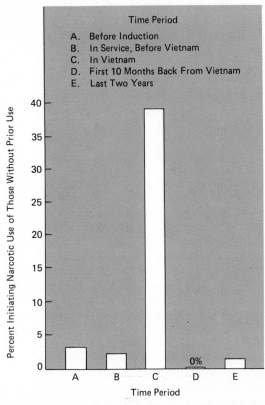

FIGURE 23-3. Percentage of veterans initiating narcotic use (usually heroin) during five time periods before, during, and after tours in Vietnam. The percentages are based on the number of veterans without prior narcotic use who initiated use in that time period. The number of veterans without prior use would, of course, decrease across the different time periods. (Adapted from Robins, 1978.)

ence. This autonomy is also superficial—and is discounted by the family, who blames it on the drug. "He isn't really this way. He doesn't hate us—he is just high." The authors maintain that young heroin addicts remain emotionally involved with their families to a surprising degree, even when living some distance off. From a systems point of view it is proposed that the drug serves a purpose in keeping the family together, that when the addicted son begins to behave in a more mature, responsible fashion, other crises develop in the family—the parents have a fight or other family members develop symptoms.

As with family correlates of schizophrenia and

other disorders it appears unlikely that any one pattern of family interaction will be found to be uniquely related to drug abuse. It is a reasonable hypothesis, however, that the social learning experiences in the family, even though the pattern may vary from family to family, do contribute to the probability of later drug abuse.

ARE SOFT DRUGS STEPPING-STONES TO HARD DRUGS?

It is sometimes argued that individuals who begin to use soft drugs such as marijuana are taking a step along the road to hard-drug usage. Kandel and Faust (1975) have given us some empirical data on this question that partially remove it from the realm of opinion. These authors followed a group of 5468 students, representing a random sampling among New York State high schools. The students responded to questionnaires about their drug usage in the fall and again in the spring (1971–1972). The authors found that drug use starts with legal drugs (tobacco, alcohol) and that legal drug use is a necessary stage between nonuse and illegal use of drugs. Only 1 percent of the nonusers went directly to illicit drugs without prior experience with a legal drug. Changes in the other direction were similar: Illegal drug users do not return directly to nonuse. About 20 percent of the students using marijuana, 11 percent using pills (amphetamines, barbiturates, or tranquilizers), and 7 percent using hallucinogens returned to legal drug use exclusively from the fall to the spring.

The probablities of moving from one status of drug use to another during the five-month interval are shown in Figure 23-4. Thus if students had been nonusers in the fall the probability was .28 (28 out of 100 nonusing students) that they would begin drinking beer or wine before spring. If they were drinking beer or wine in the fall the probability was .32 that they would be drinking hard liquor by the spring. If they were smoking cigarettes and drinking hard liquor in the fall the probability was .27 that they would be using marijuana in the spring, and so on. During this period 26 percent of the students who initially reported using marijuana did progress to harder drugs, most often to pills. From these data, then, we might conclude that marijuana is a stepping-stone to harder drug use in the sense that the majority of users of hard drugs begin with marijuana. However, most users of marijuana did not go on to use harder drugs. This study, of course, covered only a five-month period; we do not know what happened after that.

Treatment of Drug Abuse

Addiction to heroin has long been considered extremely difficult to break, and relapse is thought to be highly probable. Efforts to treat narcotic dependency at institutions such as the U.S. Public Health Service treatment centers at Lexington, Kentucky or Fort Worth, Texas have tended to confirm this pes-

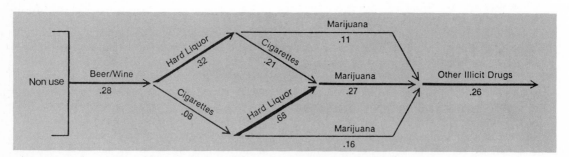

FIGURE 23-4. Probabilities of moving from each type of drug use to a more serious type, based on changes between fall 1971 and spring 1972 for a sample of New York State high school students. (From Kandel & Faust, 1975. Copyright 1975 by the American Medical Association and used with permission.)

simistic view. Vaillant (1966, 1973), for example, found that 96 percent of Lexington patients had relapsed within a year after discharge, although at 20 years following discharge 35 percent had achieved stable abstinence. Treatment at these government centers was compulsory, and in many cases the addicted person had been given the choice between compulsory treatment and a prison sentence, the latter usually for crimes associated with their addiction. These patients in all likelihood were not a representative sample of narcotic addicts. There is evidence that suggests that a substantial number of heroin-addicted individuals can break their habit. Robins (1973) found a high rate of recovery from heroin addiction in Vietnam veterans and also found that many men who reported addiction in Vietnam had used narcotics occasionally afterward without becoming readdicted.

An encounter group session at Daytop Village. Groups such as this one help a person confront the rationalizations used in justifying drug abuse and provide support for a drug-free lifestyle.

GROUP APPROACHES

The treatment of individuals dependent on hard drugs, especially opiates, presents the same basic problems as the treatment of chronic alcoholics. Helping the person to take the initial step of stopping drug use and go through the withdrawal process is only the beginning, and if left at that the odds are high that the person will return to drug abuse. Various group-living approaches have been developed in an attempt to provide these broader alternatives to the drug habit.

One such approach, called Synanon, was founded by a member of AA who had developed a problem with hard drugs (Casriel, 1963). Synanon members live together, and new members are not allowed to leave the residence for the first several months. Members are expected to renounce their former way of life, including all their drug-abusing friends. In addition to assuming household responsibilities, members are expected to participate in a form of group encounter in which the group (no professional leaders are involved) focuses on the self-deceptions by which drug abusers justify their drug use. Direct verbal attacks and ridicule are frequently used to strip persons of their psychological defenses and set the stage for a reexamination of their life goals. Despite

the confronting, attacking quality of these sessions, the overall atmosphere in a Synanon house is one of strong group cohesiveness and support. Psychologically, one might say that the group-living experience becomes a substitute for the drug scene. Similar approaches have been incorporated by groups such as Daytop Village on Staten Island and Phoenix House in New York City.

Are Synanon and Other Group-Living Approaches Effective? There is not much hard evidence on this question. First, as with AA and methadone treatment, individuals must have some motivation to give up their drug life-style or they simply will not join the organization. For those who do join it appears to have some value. Volkmann and Cressey (1963) followed up former members of a Synanon group and found that 8 percent had returned to the community and were free of drugs, 44 percent had remained in the Synanon residence, and 48 percent had left and were unaccounted for. It might be assumed that many of the latter had returned to drugs. Thus Synanon and similar organizations probably succeed with some proportion of their members but do not provide a comprehensive solution to the problems of drug abuse.

METHADONE

Methadone, a synthetic narcotic related to heroin, has been used with some success in the treatment of heroin dependency. Methadone does not produce the same euphoric reaction as heroin and also prevents heroin from producing a euphoric reaction. In addition, it reduces the craving for heroin. In essence, dependency on one drug, methadone, is substituted for dependency on another, heroin. When methadone treatment is combined with vocational and personal counseling, it is relatively effective (Dole et al., 1968). It has enabled many former heroin addicts to become productive and responsible members of their communities. There is also evidence that urban crime rates have decreased in areas where methadone has been used (Dupont & Katon, 1971).

The idea of society keeping people dependent on a narcotic, methadone, does not appeal to everyone.

The proponents of the methadone approach point out that other approaches have not been successful and that in methadone treatment the quality of the drug is controlled, tolerance does not develop (the dose does not have to be increased), individuals are freed of the necessity of hustling for their fixes in the drug scene, and they can resume productive lives. However, methadone treatment requires cooperation and motivation on the part of the person involved, and a number of heroin abusers either do not seek methadone treatment in the first place or decide to abandon it once started. Forcing individuals to take methadone raises serious questions about civil liberties and, practically speaking, would not stop people from illegally abusing drugs anyway. Voluntary methadone treatment plus counseling, then, seems useful for those heroin abusers motivated to break away from the heroin-abuse life-style.

Summary

1. Mind-altering drugs have been used throughout recorded history as an escape or relief from the strains and frustrations of life.

2. Drug abuse can be said to occur when a person's physical health or psychological functioning are seriously impaired.

3. There are two kinds of drug dependency: psychological and physical. In the former the person experiences intense craving for the drug and compulsively persists in the drug habit. Signs of physical dependency may or may not be present. Physical dependency is associated with a withdrawal syndrome in which the person experiences physical symptoms and discomfort when drug use is suspended.

4. Tolerance is said to occur when a larger dose of a drug is required to produce the same effect. Tolerance is usually associated with drugs that produce physical dependency, such as alcohol, opiates, and barbiturates, but it may also develop with drugs that do not produce physical dependency, such as the amphetamines.

5. Alcohol, a sedative type of drug, slows down many brain activities. The abuse of alcohol is more costly to our society than the abuse of any other drug. The continued use of alcohol in large quantities can produce physical damage such as cirrhosis of the liver or destruction of brain cells, general deterioration of the person's social and occupational status, and occasionally severe physical-psychological disorders such as delirium tremens, alcohol hallucinosis, or Korsakoff's syndrome.

6. There is some evidence for a genetic factor in alcoholism. No definite biological basis for alcoholism has yet been discovered, although there are some suggestive leads as in the greater production of acetaldehyde in response to alcohol in the sons of alcoholics.

7. From a social learning viewpoint alcoholism might develop as follows: Life stresses increase discomfort and tension; alcohol provides quick relief from stress-induced states of discomfort; if alcohol is available, the individual will learn to make the stress-reducing drinking response and persist with it because the immediate rewards outweigh long-term negative consequences. Prior social learning experiences in the family and surrounding culture, such as the modeling of drug use by parents, will help determine whether a person follows the sequence. A tension-reduction view of alcoholism, however, must accommodate findings that heavy drinking in alcoholics is accompanied by self-reports of increased anxiety and depression.

8. Alcoholics Anonymous has been partially successful in helping alcoholics who are motivated to stop drinking. A social learning approach to treatment, in which alcoholics in addition to being helped to stop drinking are also taught to substitute alternative ways of coping with life stresses, appears promising at this time.

9. There is considerable evidence that *some* alcoholics can become controlled drinkers, that one drink does not necessarily lead to loss of control.

10. The barbiturates are sedatives like alcohol and induce an intoxication similar to that of alcohol. The withdrawal syndrome for barbiturates is especially dangerous physically and can lead to death if not properly supervised.

11. The opiates (narcotics) are a class of drugs that includes opium and its derivatives, morphine and heroin. Originally used as pain killers, these drugs produce a state of euphoria when injected intravenously, and can produce physiological dependence.

12. The amphetamine drugs have a stimulating effect on the central nervous system. These drugs can produce an initial rush of pleasure, an extended run of physical and mental hyperactivity, and a crash period of exhaustion and sleep. While on a run or crashing, the user is prone to sudden acts of violence.

13. The hallucinogen class of drugs produce marked changes in mood and sensory perception. Occasionally a person may experience long-lasting or recurring aftereffects of LSD use.

14. The same basic psychological principles are probably involved in the development of the abuse of other drugs—barbiturates, opiates, stimulants, and hallucinogens—as in the abuse of alcohol.

15. Hard-drug use is usually preceded by the use of soft drugs, the use of illegal drugs by legal drugs. However, most people who use a soft drug such as marijuana probably do not go on to use harder drugs.

16. Methadone treatment of heroin dependency, though controversial, has succeeded with some individuals motivated to change. The same can be said for organizations such as Synanon. However, no approach has yet been shown to be effective on a wide scale. Most approaches to treatment are likely to be ineffective with individuals not motivated to change.

Suggested Readings

Alcoholism from a behavioral perspective can be found in P. E. Nathan, G. A. Marlatt, and T. Loberg (Eds.), *Alcoholism: New directions in behavioral research and treatment* (Plenum, 1978). Factors involved in drug abuse are considered in R. Pickens and L. Heston (Eds.), *Psychiatric factors in drug abuse* (Grune and Stratton, 1979).

Part
Six

Impaired Brain
Functioning

24

Mental Retardation

- What is intelligence? Can we validly measure it?

- Is there more to intelligence than good grades?

- Did you know that most people called "mentally retarded" can achieve a fully independent adjustment as adults?

- How is an elephant like a mouse? Why do retarded persons have difficulty answering?

- Is there a fundamental difference in the way retarded individuals think? Or do they progress through the same stages of intellectual development as normal individuals but at a slower pace and to a lower ceiling?

- What are the causes of mental retardation?

- Can retardation be prevented?

- Can a mother's apathy affect a child's intelligence?

A Retarded Family

Edith, age 19, IQ 60, was admitted to an institution for the retarded at age seven. She had twice been excluded from first grade because of extremely aggressive behavior toward other children. She was described as overactive, noisy, destructive, having a short attention span, and tending to wander from home. After 11 years in the institution Edith was moved six months ago to a halfway house, a transitional sheltered group living situation from which she is expectd to move eventually into independent community living. She is now employed.

When Edith became pregnant, she was encouraged to have an abortion, to which she consented provided that she was not also sterilized. One of her concerns regarding the abortion was its cost. Seemingly illustrating the reasoning impairment of a retarded individual was her comment that if the operation was expensive, she would just as soon skip it and have the baby.

Edith's brother, John, age 17, IQ 65, is employed as a plumber's helper. Always the favorite child, he was reportedly pampered by his parents, who were unable to maintain any control over his behavior. John had a poor school adjustment; he repeated first grade and was absent a lot. Although recognized as eligible for special-class placement by the third grade, John remained in the regular classroom.

His chronic truancy led to court referral at age ten. At that time his mother was in a psychiatric hospital, and the court saw him as a "neglected" rather than "delinquent" child. At ages 12 and 14 he was again referred to the court, but the charge of "malicious mischief" was now added to the truancy. Seen as beyond parental control, John was sent to a juvenile correction institution for one year. On returning home he was placed in a junior high school special class, but he again left school and is now working as a "helper." No significant problems were noted by the probation officer in the year following his return home and entry into employment.

Doris, age 16, IQ 54, is in the same institution as was her sister Edith. Doris and the third sister, Susan, were both institutionalized about one year ago when the foster family with whom they were living had other problems and was no longer able to care for them. Until puberty Doris had made an adequate adjustment in the foster home and in a special-education class, but thereafter she presented problems in both settings and in the vehicle which carried her to school. Doris is said to have exposed herself in the vehicle, especially during her menstrual periods. In the classroom she was usually cooperative though excessively demanding of the teacher's attention. At present Doris is described as a friendly girl, somewhat quieter than her sister Edith, and operating at the third-grade level. (Baroff, 1974, pp. 86–87)

Mental retardation has been defined as "significantly *subaverage general intellectual functioning* existing concurrently with *deficits in adaptive behavior,* and manifested during the *developmental period*" (Grossman, 1973). This definition emphasizes that mental retardation is more than just poor performance on an intelligence test, that such persons are likely to experience adjustment difficulties in many aspects of their lives, and that these adjustive problems become apparent at an early age. Edith, John, and Doris showed all of these characteristics.

The Nature of Intellectual Deficit

Retardation refers to subaverage general intelligence. But what is intelligence? *Intelligence* usually refers to behaviors that reflect learning ability, knowledge, and coping with new situations. Learning ability itself has at least two dimensions, rate and depth; retarded individuals generally learn more slowly and to a lesser degree. Their knowledge, too, is more limited, presumably because of the learning difficulty. Of the three kinds of behaviors, coping with new situations is probably the most common way in which intelligence is shown; retarded persons are notoriously uneasy in new or unfamiliar situations.

SUBAVERAGE INTELLIGENCE AND LEVELS OF RETARDATION

Intelligence is formally measured by intelligence tests, scored in terms of an intelligence quotient (IQ). Tests are so calibrated that an IQ of 100 is average (see Figure 24-1). Somewhat arbitrarily, individuals with IQs less than 70 (two standard deviations below the mean) are considered mentally retarded. Because 2 to 3 percent of the total population fall in this IQ range, this number of people is commonly cited in prevalence figures for mental retardation.

Below 70 IQ, four levels of retardation are distinguished: mild, moderate, severe, and profound. These levels, their associated Wechsler Intelligence Test IQ ranges, and the proportion of retarded persons in each level are shown in Table 24-1. A similar system for categorizing mental retardation, frequently used by educators, distinguishes three levels: educable (50–75 IQ), trainable (25–49 IQ), and profound (below 25 IQ).

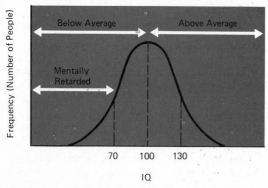

FIGURE 24-1. The normal or bell-shaped distribution of IQ scores in the general population. An IQ of 70 arbitrarily divides the range of normal intelligence from that of mental retardation.

Mild Retardation. Mildly retarded individuals make up the vast majority of those with this disorder—89 percent in terms of Wechsler intelligence scores. During the preschool years these individuals develop social and communication skills and show little or no impairment in motor activities. They are often not distinguished from normal children until a later age. Their subnormal intelligence becomes apparent during the school years, and they tend to fall behind their age group. With persistence they can learn academic skills roughly comparable to a sixth-grade level by their late teens. As adults they can usually acquire vocational skills necessary for economic independence.

Moderate Retardation. These individuals usually learn to talk during the preschool years but later and more slowly than normal children. They are likely to show impairments in sensorimotor development such as poor coordination, and their social skills are likely to be below average. They gain little at all from the usual academic instruction at school but can, in special classes, profit from training in social and occupational skills. As adults they are unlikely to achieve complete independence but can contribute to their own support in the protective environment of sheltered work conditions.

Severe Mental Retardation. Impaired development is apparent in infancy or early childhood in the form of poor motor development, minimal speech, and fairly often the presence of physical deformities. They do not profit as much from training as the moderately retarded, although as they get older many can learn to talk in simple words and phrases and learn elementary health and grooming habits. As adults they may learn to perform certain routine tasks but generally require complete supervision and economic support.

Profound Retardation. Retardation is extreme in both intellectual and sensorimotor functions, and is apparent early in life. Some limited goals of habit training may be achieved in the older child, but usually these people will require total care for the rest of their lives. Many have severe physical deformities that further restrict their capacity to walk or otherwise cope with environmental demands.

TABLE 24-1 Levels of Retardation by IQ and Percent of Retarded Persons at Each Level

Level of Retardation	IQ Ranges on Wechsler Intelligence Test	Percent of All Retarded Persons
Mild	55–69	89.0
Moderate	40–54	6.0
Severe	25–39	3.5
Profound	0–24	1.5

This classification system was proposed by the American Association on Mental Deficiency (Grossman, 1973).

IQ AND MENTAL AGE

To understand the nature of the intellectual deficit in mental retardation it is necessary to consider another important measure obtained from intelligence tests, *mental age.* The meaning of mental age and IQ is illustrated in the analysis of the following hypothetical case. A six-year-old first-grade boy is functioning far below his classmates, although he seems well motivated, is free of visual or hearing problems, and the language of his teacher is his native tongue. In addition to his academic deficiencies he is also operating at a different level in other areas as well. He needs more assistance in dressing, his general motor coordination is poorer, his speech is less complex in structure and also less well articulated, and his social interactions appear immature. In seeking a better understanding of the child's academic difficulties the teacher might request an educational assessment, which would be expected to include intelligence testing.

The intelligence testing of such a child might be done with either the Stanford-Binet or the Wechsler Intelligence Scale for Children (WISC). For our example we will use the Binet because it provides a direct measure of mental age. The Binet test consists of a series of tasks, grouped by the chronological age at which the majority of children succeed. At the six-year level, for example, the tasks consist of defining words like *orange,* giving differences (such as the difference between a bird and a dog), finding missing parts in pictures of common objects (such as a dog with only one ear), understanding number concepts up to ten (for instance, selecting nine blocks), and solving mazes. Most of the test items have a mental age value of two months, and the child's mental age

is simply the sum, in years and months, of the individual items succeeded on.

A six-year-old of average intelligence would attain a total mental age (MA) of about six years, but the six-year-old child just described might attain a mental age of four years, which is normal for children who are two years his junior. He may have missed every item at the six-year level and most at the five-year level. Given this and other assessment data, the teacher may quickly recognize that the immaturity of this six-year-old child in all aspects of development, and particularly in the academic sphere, can be at least partially attributed to a degree of mental development that is two years behind that expected for his chronological age.

I do not mean to imply that a retarded child with a mental age of four years is identical in cognitive functioning to a normal four-year-old. The retarded child is likely to be less curious, less creative in problem solving, and more dependent on external cues than a normal mental-age counterpart. Whether these differences are inherent in retardation or are the results of the kinds of experiences encountered by the retarded child has been the subject of a lively theoretical debate. In any case, our six-year-old may be more advanced than the average four-year-old in self-help skills (feeding, dressing, and toileting) but may lag behind in reading and number skills. His mental age of four years does mean, however, that the "average" of his intellectual abilities more closely approximates that of a four-year-old than that of any other age child.

The learning difficulties our six-year-old experiences in first grade are now much more comprehensible. He is expected to cope successfully with tasks at a six-year or first-grade level of complexity when his mental development is still only at that of a prekindergarten-age child! We do not expect the average four-year-old child to function, academically or otherwise, like a six-year-old; yet this is precisely the situation in which the retarded child finds himself.

Intellectual assessment produces not only a mental age but also an IQ, which tells us how the child's present level of mental development compares with that of other children of the same age. The IQ used to be computed from the Stanford-Binet Test by dividing mental age by chronological age and multiplying by 100. In our example the six-year-old would have an IQ of 4/6 × 100 = 67. Since the 1960 revision of the Stanford-Binet, the IQ is defined in terms of relative variation from the mean score (arbitrarily set at 100) for each age group. More specifically, a score that is one standard deviation above or below the mean for a child's age group is given an IQ equal to 100 plus or minus 16 points. If the score was 1.5 standard deviations below the mean, the IQ would be 76. The Wechsler Intelligence Tests have always used this way of computing IQ, except that the standard deviation for these tests is 15 rather than 16.

Our retarded six-year-old is already two years behind his classmate of average intelligence, and if his mental development continues at the rate suggested by his present IQ, the difference between their mental ages *will grow greater with time.* We can also think of the IQ as an indicator of the *rate* of mental development, with an IQ of 67 reflecting a rate which is two-thirds of normal. Thus while the child with IQ 100 gains 12 months of mental age over one year, the child with IQ 67 gains only two-thirds as much, or eight months of mental age. Assuming a relative constancy in rate of mental growth, there will be a cumulative deficit which increases by four months each year during the mental age growth period (see Figure 24-2). At age six there is a two-year mental age difference; it increases to four years at age 12 and to five years at age 18.

THE MENTAL AGE GROWTH PERIOD

We now come to a very important aspect of intelligence that can be confused by the ordinary meaning of the term *retarded.* In its usual sense *retarded* suggests delay rather than arrest and it might be imagined that mental retardation is merely a con-

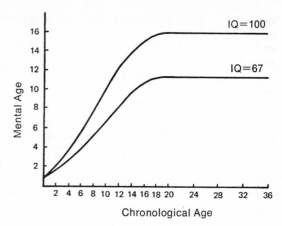

FIGURE 24-2. Mental age growth curves corresponding to IQs of 100 and 67. Based on 1960 Binet IQs from Terman & Merrill, 1960.

dition of slower-than-average mental growth, which, given a sufficient period of time, is eventually overcome. On the contrary, mental growth is like physical growth in the sense that it occurs only during a specific time period. It is recognized that growth in height, for example, occurs from infancy to adolescence and that by late adolescence we have ordinarily attained our maximum height. The same principle seems to apply to mental growth; we grow in mental age from infancy to young adulthood, with a virtual completion of the process by age 18 (Terman & Merrill, 1960). Our mental powers grow continuously during this period at a rate indicated by IQ. At age six we can solve problems that were beyond us at three, at nine we can solve problems that were too difficult for us at six, and so on. After 18, however, mental age scores on the Binet do not increase, although it is clear that this cessation of mental age growth is to some degree related to the content of the Binet test itself. For example, a somewhat different pattern emerges on the Wechsler Adult Intelligence Scale (Wechsler, 1955). On this test "raw" scores increase up to age 26 (Bayley, 1970) and remain fairly constant to old age; even then, there is very little decline in persons who are still in good health (Bayley, 1970; Birren, 1968).

The existence of a specific period during which mental growth occurs applies to all people, retarded as well as normal. The retarded individual does not "catch up" to the normal one in mental age because his or her mental growth is limited by the same time frame. The effect is a permanent disparity in mental age between the retarded and normal child (see Figure 24-2).

It is important that we distinguish between a limited growth period and our capacity to learn. To suggest that our mental powers have fully flowered by 18 or 26 is not to say that we stop learning after these ages. We can and do learn throughout our lives, retarded as well as normal; it is only that the basic mental equipment with which we learn is fully developed by late adolescence or young adulthood. Research Report 24-1 compares that basic equipment for normal and retarded persons.

SAME SEQUENCE OR QUALITATIVE DIFFERENCE?

Some investigators propose that retarded individuals follow the same sequence of intellectual development as nonretarded individuals but pass through the stages more slowly and attain a lower upper limit (Zigler, 1969). Others suggest that there are differences that go beyond mere rate and ceiling of development (Milgram, 1973). Weisz and Zigler (1979)

reviewed 28 cross-sectional and three longitudinal studies and concluded that the evidence strongly favored, with a few exceptions, the *same-sequence* hypothesis. In one of the most comprehensive studies Stephens and her colleagues (Stephens, 1974; Stephens et al., 1972) obtained measures before and after a two-year interval from retarded and nonretarded persons on a great variety of reasoning tasks—largely based on Piaget's (1970) theories of cognitive development. Changes in mastery of the various tasks tended to follow the same sequence for both groups of children and was generally consistent with previous findings. Thus with respect to the development of the concept of conservation of various properties, they found that the concept of conservation of substance precedes conservation of weight and that conservation of weight precedes conservation of volume. The concept of conservation can be illustrated by the conservation of volume: If a given volume of liquid (colored for clear visibility) is poured from one container to a differently shaped container, children below a certain mental age may think that the actual volume has changed, which, of course, it has not. The same-sequence hypothesis held best for those retarded persons who did not show signs of organic brain defects such as abnormal EEGs.

RESEARCH REPORT 24–1

The Quality of Thinking in Retarded Persons

The intellectual deficit in mental retardation has been defined according to such dimensions as IQ and mental age. We now consider it in terms of the quality of thought processes. The research that illuminates this topic has been done largely with mildly retarded individuals, but it is assumed that the characteristics described would be merely intensified at more severe levels of deficit.

SUGGESTIBILITY AND LEARNED HELPLESSNESS

Retarded persons have long been seen as particularly suggestible or, in Zigler's (1966) terms, more dependent on external cues than nonretarded individuals. They are perceived as more easily influenced and, therefore, more likely to have difficulty if external cues are misleading. Their thinking has a quality of passivity and dependence. Zigler does not regard this greater vulnerability to outside influences as inherent in mental retardation but attributes it to a learned distrust of their own judgment growing out of frequent failure experiences. Weisz (1979) obtained several measures of helplessness when confronted with certain problem-solving tasks as well as teacher ratings of helplessness. He found no difference in helplessness between relatively young retarded individuals and nonretarded individuals of the same mental age (who, of course, would be even younger chronologically). Older retarded individuals did show greater helplessness than nonretarded individuals of the same mental age. These results are consistent with the idea that as retarded individuals are continually confronted with tasks on which they fail, they come increasingly to believe that there is little point in making the effort to cope with intellectual challenges. This increasing degree of learned helplessness may cause them to avoid problems that they could solve if they tried.

MEMORY

The recall of material that one seeks to remember is aided by its repetition or rehearsal. It has been suggested that memory deficiencies in retarded persons are at least partly attributable to failure to engage spontaneously in such rehearsal (Anders, 1971; Ellis, 1968). Recall is also facilitated by a reorganization or restructuring of the material so as to create links between the items to be remembered. In so-called paired-associate learning tasks, the learner seeks links between unrelated items (dog and shoe, for example) and then remembers the link. Thus one may combine the items in an image (Segal, 1971), a sentence, or a category (concept). When the memory task entails the recall of a series of numbers, the grouping or "chunking" of the original series into smaller groups aids recall (Dember, 1974). Thus the last four digits of a telephone number ending 1-9-2-4 are more easily remembered as two numbers, 19-24.

In each of these tasks the normal learner *actively* engages the material to be memorized. Retarded persons are thought to be less prone to spontaneously generate or *innovate* the kinds of "mediators" that aid retention (for example, MacMillan, 1972). Although the innovation of problem-solving strategies occurs less frequently in retarded persons, there is considerable evidence that such strategies can be taught to them. There is yet no evidence whether they retain the strategies for a long time (Gerjuoy & Alvarez, 1969) or that they transfer or generalize them to other situations.

More recently Saccuzzo et al. (1979) have found evidence suggesting even more fundamental deficits in memory functioning in retarded persons. Memory researchers have suggested that there are several stages involved in the processing of stimuli that are to be stored as memories. The first stage has been called the iconic storage, in which for a very brief period, less than a second, the stimulus is directly represented on some neural structure. In succeeding stages the information from this representation is taken and processed by other parts of the brain and among other things put into short-term memory storage. Saccuzzo et al. (1979) found that retarded persons needed to have a visual stimulus, a letter, presented for a longer duration than did nonretarded persons of the same mental age in order to get the stimulus into iconic storage. Furthermore, once the visual stimulus was in iconic storage, it took the retarded individuals longer to transfer the information into the more central memory systems. To show the latter finding, they used a procedure based on the well-demonstrated fact that if a briefly presented visual stimulus is followed after a brief interval by a superimposed noninformational pattern stimulus, generally known as the mask, a subject will be less able to remember the initial stimulus whenever the mask has been presented before the informational content of the initial stimulus has been transferred to more central stages of information processing. Once the stimulus has been transferred to the more central stages of information processing, the masking stimulus will have no effect. The retarded persons in this study, as I have indicated, required longer presentations of the initial stimulus as well as a longer interval before the masking stimulus was presented to reach the same criterion of accuracy of memory as the nonretarded individuals. Such limitations in the time taken to both take in and process new information would obviously restrict new learning and could have a cumulative effect on the course of development. These results suggest a possible integration of the same-sequence hypothesis and the qualitative difference hypothesis referred to earlier; namely, that the qualitative difference in memory functioning might retard intellectual development in such a way that the individuals pass through similar stages at a slower rate. The retarded subjects used in this research were mild or moderately retarded and did not include persons with known organic bases for the retardation.

ABSTRACT THINKING

A good example of abstract thinking is the processes involved in solving similarity problems, such as "In what way are an elephant and a mouse alike?" The task entails discovering a likeness between nonidentical entities and the deliberate ignoring of the perceptual or associational differences that determine its difficulty. The most common solution for an older child is that they are both animals, a reply that incorporates the use of a category or concept. The ability to solve similarity problems is another dimension of intelligence on which retarded people have more difficulty.

In solving similarity problems one of the major difficulties lies not in the absence of the concept necessary to solution but rather in the application of concepts already possessed (for example, Zigler & Balla, 1971). Thus while a retarded youth or a normal child of the same mental age might both know that an elephant and a mouse are both animals, they might fail to solve the item because the size disparity throws them off. As the difference between things to be grouped by similarity increases and solution becomes more difficult, retarded persons seem likelier to reject the very possibility of similarity and to assert only the palpable difference ("A mouse and an elephant cannot be the same because a mouse is small and an elephant is big"). Retarded persons have more difficulty in recognizing that differences and similarities can exist simultaneously. It is the more blatant aspect that captures their attention and gives their thinking a quality of concreteness and rigidity.

Their learning also tends to be specific to the context in which it has occurred rather than generalizing to others that share a basic similarity. The consequence is that there is need for greater repetition of experiences and more frequent explanations before a principle is grasped. For example, the retarded child who has learned to wait his turn in a classroom game will need to have that same experience repeated numerous times in other settings before he comes to understand the adaptive significance of "waiting one's turn."

Another aspect of concreteness in retardation is a relatively weak ability for imaginative and creative activities. To imagine or to create is to go beyond whatever is given to our senses, beyond what "is," and to generate something new. It requires an active reorganizing of existing reality or its use as a stimulus for creating a new one. But the situation-specific quality of thought in retarded persons seems to bind them to what is and to make more difficult the creation of what might be.

ISSUES IN INTELLIGENCE TESTING

Although the definition of retardation includes impairment in adaptive behavior as one component, people tend to equate retardation with IQ alone. Since disproportionately large numbers of disadvantaged minority youth show IQs in the subaverage range, resulting in individual and group stigma, it is understandable that questions about the IQ have been raised. What is the relationship between IQ and general adjustment and how valid are intelligence tests?

IQ and General Adjustment. One of the major difficulties in equating mental retardation with IQ alone relates to the distinction between scores on an intelligence test and general adjustment. Although subaverage intelligence undoubtedly affects school achievement, it does not necessarily preclude adequate functioning in other behavioral realms. Even very limited reading and number skills (indeed, illiteracy itself) need not prevent one from achieving independence in adulthood.

The distinction between IQ and adjustment also has a cultural dimension. The impact of limited intelligence is determined by the behavioral demands that a particular culture makes of us. In technologically underdeveloped societies persons with some degree of intellectual inadequacy can still meet their culture's criteria for a grossly normal adjustment. In technologically more advanced societies, however, the same individuals would be at a serious disadvantage. This distinction between IQ and adaptive potential is particularly relevant to persons with mild retardation since at more severe levels of impairment adaptive difficulties can be expected in any culture.

The Validity of Intelligence Tests. Perhaps the most important criticism of intelligence tests pertains to their *validity* or appropriateness as measures of general intelligence. Tests have been criticized as too narrow in the abilities sampled (Dingman & Meyers, 1966; Sarason & Doris, 1969), as evaluating only answers to questions without regard for the way in which answers are derived (Haeussermann, 1958; Sigel, 1963), as penalizing unconventional answers (Sigel, 1963), and as presenting problems that are irrelevant to the life experiences of some children (Anastasi, 1961; Sarason & Doris, 1969). Finally, the question has been raised as to whether the verbal skill deficits shown by disadvantaged youth are "true" deficits or merely artifacts of the conditions under which they are tested. What has been called cultural *deprivation* may only be cultural *difference* (Cole & Bruner, 1971; Labov, 1970).

In one sense the question about the validity of intelligence tests as measures of general intelligence is unresolvable. Intelligence has no tangible reality; it is merely a term that we apply to certain behaviors. But developers of intelligence tests do not have unlimited freedom to represent their tests as measures of intelligence, since the tests' acceptance depends on meeting some agreed-upon criteria. The main criterion has been school achievement, and a test that is a good predictor of a child's ability to master those linguistic, numerical, and problem-solving skills associated with academic success is accepted by most people as having at least some degree of validity.

Criticisms of standard intelligence tests such as the Stanford-Binet (Terman & Merrill, 1960) and the Wechsler Scales (Wechsler, 1949, 1955, 1963) have led to efforts to develop "culture-free" or "culture-fair" tests. Two of these are the Davis-Eells Games (Davis & Eells, 1953) and the Culture Fair Intelligence Test (Cattell, 1959). The former, entirely pictorial in content, consists solely of problem situations drawn from the life experiences of inner-city children. Neither test has proved to be uninfluenced by socioeconomic differences, which has led to the assertion (Wesman, 1968) that culture-free intelligence tests are unattainable since intelligence is, in part at least, a product of one's learning experiences.

Biological and Psychological Determinants of Intelligence. From the first, intelligence tests have been involved in the controversy around the relative contribution of biological (usually conceived as genetic) and environmental factors to intelligence. The debate has intensified again in recent years. The arguments can become complex, involving careful evaluations of various methodological pitfalls. In general, however, the evidence favors *some* genetic contribution to intelligence. Samples of identical twins are uniformly more alike on intelligence test scores than fraternal twins; and identical twins reared apart are more alike than fraternal twins reared together (Scarr, 1975). In the latter case, if environment were the *only* determiner of intelligence, same-sex fraternal twins reared in the same home should be more similar than separated identical pairs since they experience a more similar environment. However, the opposite is found, suggesting that identical twins carry some degree of genetically endowed intelligence with them to their separate environments.

Another source of evidence for some genetic determination of intelligence comes from studies of adopted children. If heredity accounts for most of the individual differences in intelligence, then the IQs of children adopted shortly after birth should correlate more highly with measures reflecting the intellectual competence of their biological parents than of their adoptive parents. If environment is more important, then the IQs of adopted children should correlate most highly with their adoptive parents' IQs. Munzinger (1975) critically evaluated all studies of adopted children to that time and retained findings from five studies (involving 351 families) in which, in his opinion, adequate methodology was used. The average correlation between the mean of the biological parents' mental ages and the IQs of the adopted children was .48. The same correlation between the adoptive parents and the children was .19. Munzinger concluded that heredity was more important than environment in determining IQ. Two more recent studies are consistent with this conclusion (Horn et al., 1979; Scarr & Weinberg, 1978).

RESEARCH REPORT 24-2

A New Way to Study the Genetics of Intelligence

Rose et al. (1979) have recently applied a different design to a study of the genetics of intelligence that incorporates features of both the twin and adoption studies. They studied the children of identical twins who have married and are now raising separate families. The children in each of these two families have one parent who is an identical twin and from whom they derive half of their genes. These children all have an uncle or aunt who has exactly the same genetic makeup as one of their parents. Since the children and the aunt or uncle (identical twin of their parent) do not live in the same households, their relationship is somewhat comparable to that between adopted children and their biological mother or father. The advantages of studying children of identical twins over the study of adopted children are: The children are reared by their biological parents in their own homes so that there is no disruption of the family environment; there is no problem of selective placement in which the degree of intellectual stimulation provided by the adoptive parents might be correlated with the levels of intelligence of the biological parents; and biological fathers are available for study, which is usually not the case in adoption studies.

The authors used one measure of nonverbal intelligence, the block design subtest of the Wechsler Intelligence Test, and for comparison purposes a nonintellectual measure known to be almost completely determined by heredity, fingerprint ridge counts. They found on this estimate of intelligence that children correlated about the same with their parents as with their aunt or uncle who was the identical twin of one of their parents, and did not correlate above chance with the spouse of the twin aunt or uncle. These results were parallel to but of lesser magnitude than those for the fingerprint ridge counts (see Table 24-2). The correlation between the identical twins was .68 for the intelligence measure and .96 for the fingerprint measure. These results, then, provide yet another source of evidence that genetic factors make a significant contribution to differences in intellectual ability.

TABLE 24-2 **Regression Coefficients[a] for the Block Design Test and Fingerprint Ridge Counts**

Relationship	Block Design Regression	N	Ridge Count Regression	N
Child with parent	.28	572	.42	564
Nephew or niece with twin uncle or aunt	.23	318	.37	310
Nephew or niece with spouse of twin uncle or aunt	−.01	241	−.06	247

[a]Regression coefficients may be viewed as roughly similar to correlation coefficients. All are significantly different from zero except those of −.01 and −.06. Adapted from Rose, Harris, Christian, and Nance (1979). Copyright 1979, American Association for the Advancement of Science, and used with permission.

But environment also affects intellectual abilities. Identical twins reared apart are less alike than those reared together (Erlenmeyer-Kimling & Jarvik, 1963), and in a later section we will review research which suggests that special enrichment programs can increase the IQs of lower-class children. As with so many other behavioral characteristics considered in this book, we must conclude that individual differences in intelligence result from the interactive influences of both genes and environment.

In summary, criticisms of intelligence testing and of the IQ focus on abuses in testing and from misunderstanding of test information. Although present tests may not measure all aspects of what is construed as intelligence, there is no doubt that they do measure some aspects of it, and it is intelligence that is the core problem in mental retardation.

The Social Adjustment of Retarded Persons

So far we have focused on the intellectual development of retarded persons, but the fact of retardation also has enormous implications for all other aspects of their lives. Let us consider some of the adjustive difficulties that most retarded people experience.

SOCIAL SKILLS

The quality of interpersonal relationships of retarded children reflects both the degree of retardation and the extent of their emotional acceptance by parents and sibs. Retardation will cause children to appear immature in the way they relate to others because at any given age their behavior will be more like that of younger children. At age five, for example, retarded children may still need much help in dressing and eating, and still may not be fully toilet-trained. Their speech is likely to be primitive in structure (oneword or two-word phrases rather than sentences) and of limited intelligibility, their coordination poor, their "understanding" not that of a five-year-old. Their emotional behavior is likely to reveal an easier emotionality, greater impulsivity, and expressions of emotion more appropriate to a younger child. Without the intervention of adults or exposure to preschool nursery or day-care experiences, the child's immaturity is likely to evoke rejection by age-mates and to maintain intense dependency on parents long after other children have developed relationships outside the family.

SELF-ESTEEM

The extent to which retarded persons develop a positive attitude about themselves will be affected by family and peer relations. For the mild and moderately retarded it is the school years when repeated failures and the sometimes cruel teasing of peers exert their most damaging effects on self-esteem.

Parents have a tendency to see their children as extensions of themselves, so children of whom parents can feel proud tend to increase parental self-esteem. Conversely, when children have negatively valued characteristics, parents are prone to view them as an unfavorable reflection of themselves and react with feelings of shame, hostility, and often guilt—all contributing to a lowered sense of self-regard in the children.

For some parents the psychological pain associated with having a retarded child is so unbearable that they erect defenses to mitigate it. These may include such inappropriate behaviors as overprotection, denial, or rejection. When parental attitudes reflect either covert rejection as in denial or, more rarely, overt rejection, the child feels unloved and, later, unlovable. Such children may be driven to seek approval and are very sensitive to criticism. Overprotection, too, can reflect covert rejection; in such cases the children are likely to be exposed to parents who vacillate in attitudes toward them. Unfavorable parental attitudes are more often encountered in parents who place a high value on the very abilities that the child lacks. Such achievement-oriented parents have greater difficulty in accepting the child and add personality problems to a child already burdened with extensive coping problems. Since these personality problems interfere with the child's ability to relate appropriately to other adults, their prevention through early family counseling is an important and still largely unmet need (Baroff, 1974).

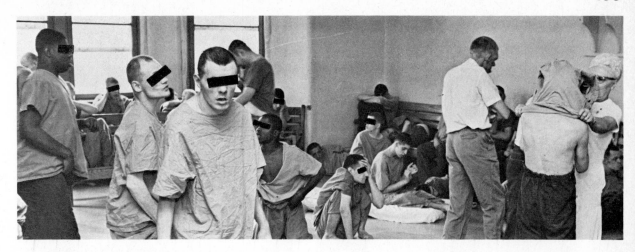

Institutions for the mentally retarded are sometimes overcrowded and provide little opportunity for personal, social, or occupational development.

SELF-MANAGEMENT AND EMPLOYMENT IN ADULTHOOD

Among retarded adults are found all degrees of self-management from full independence to total dependence. A fully independent adjustment is common in mildly retarded adults, although its quality may be somewhat marginal. Access to nonretarded persons who can serve as "advisors" seems to be particularly helpful. At greater levels of retardation full independence is not usually achieved; throughout life there will be dependency on others, the degree relating to the extent of the retardation. For most of the dependent retarded adult's life, as during the preadult years, the family is the primary source of support and supervision, but when access to parents or to sibs is no longer possible, extrafamily resources become necessary. Until recently the large state residential institutions have typically provided this care but, increasingly, community-based alternatives are being developed. These consist of group homes, family foster care, and supervised apartments (Baroff, 1974).

All levels of employability are seen in retarded persons. Mildly retarded persons are usually found in competitive employment, albeit of an unskilled nature, though some with good manual ability can aspire to semiskilled employment as "helpers" in the trades. Their academic limitations, however, preclude attainment of full journeyman status. Moderately retarded persons are usually employed in sheltered workshops where they typically engage in a variety of unskilled light assembly tasks. The workshop provides regular employment, although the level of individual worker productivity is ordinarily less than that found in competitive employment. Employees are paid in accordance with the extent to which their rate of production reaches the expected level for nonhandicapped workers. Sheltered workshops also are much used to train retarded and other handicapped workers for regular employment. Severely and profoundly retarded persons usually lack economically productive work skills; their rate of work may be very slow, and without training they may have little ability to persist at a task. Some of these severely impaired individuals can nevertheless acquire simple work skills in day activity centers, where work is combined with activities of an instructional and recreational nature.

Baller et al. (1967) conducted a long-term follow-up of 119 educable (IQs between 50 and 70) retarded individuals when their average age was 56. Only eight had been institutionalized, primarily for physical handicaps; 48 percent were married and living with their spouses, compared with 84 percent in

Many retarded persons can be trained for useful employment such as routine production jobs (left) or horticultural work (right).

More progressive institutions do offer programs such as this sheltered workshop. In some cases participants in such a workshop live in the community rather than in an institution.

a comparison group of borderline persons (IQs between 75 and 85). Sixty-five percent of the retarded persons were entirely self-supporting, compared with 94 percent of the borderline group; and 72 percent of the retarded individuals, compared with 50 percent of the borderline, worked in semiskilled or unskilled jobs. These statistics should remind us that many mild and some moderately retarded persons can get along reasonably well in society.

In concluding this section I would caution against slipping into a labeling frame of mind in which we refer to "retardates" (or for that matter, schizophrenics, neurotics, and so on) as though they are a species apart from the rest of us. It is well to keep in mind that most of these persons have more in common with us than they have differences. Shylock's statement about what it meant to be a Jew in a Christian world could equally be spoken for retarded persons:

I am retarded. Hath not a retarded person eyes? Hath not a retarded person hands, organs, dimensions, senses, affections, passions; fed with the same food, hurt with the same weapons, subject to the same diseases, healed by the same means, warmed and cooled by the same winter and summer . . . ? If you prick us do we not bleed? If you tickle us do we not laugh? If you poison us do we not die? (Adapted from Shakespeare, *The Merchant of Venice*)

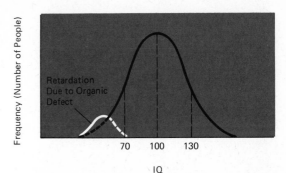

FIGURE 24-3. The distribution of IQ scores, showing the bump that would appear if individuals in institutions were sampled as well as those outside institutions. The bump is thought to reflect individuals whose retardation results from specific organic defect.

The Etiology of Mental Retardation

In addition to classifying mentally retarded individuals by severity of intellectual impairment, psychologists have also classified them in terms of etiology. Mentally retarded people are divided into two broad categories, those whose retardation results from *cultural-familial* influences and those in whom organic factors have produced retardation. In the cultural-familial type no specific physical causes can be identified, and some combination of environmental and genetic influences is probably involved.

DISORDERS WITH SPECIFIC ORGANIC CAUSES

The organic group consists of a number of different kinds of physiologically caused retardation. Persons whose IQs fall into the severe and profound categories (Wechsler IQs below 39) are almost always in this category. Zigler (1967) points out that if the distribution of IQ scores from a sample of the total population, including those in institutions for the mentally retarded, is plotted, it forms the usual bell-shaped normal curve except at the very low end, where there tends to be a bump (Figure 24-3). He suggests that this "bump" represents individuals who would have fallen in the regular IQ distribution if they had not been the victim of an organic defect that seriously impaired their intelligence.

Chromosomal and Genetic Abnormalities. The best-known chromosomal abnormality is *Down's syndrome* (*mongolism*), a common form of mental retardation caused by the presence of an extra chro-

mosome. In most cases, the extra chromosome results from the failure of the twenty-first pair of the mother's chromosomes to separate during meiosis (cell division). These two chromosomes then join with the single twenty-first chromosome of the father to give three number twenty-one chromosomes, sometimes referred to as *trisomy 21*. The extra chromosome produces intellectual impairment as well as a wide variety of physical anomalies: a large fissured tongue that tends to protrude from the mouth, almond shaped eyes, flat nasal bridge, a short crooked fifth finger, and broad hands with a crease running across the palm. Down's syndrome occurs once in about 700 births. The incidence increases from one in 2000 births for 20-year-old mothers to one in 25 for mothers 45 or over. The frequency of occurrence of Down's syndrome in older mothers has decreased somewhat in recent years as a result of procedures for identifying such fetuses early in pregnancy and more liberal abortion laws (for example, Zarfas & Wolf, 1979). About 15 to 20 percent of individuals in institutions for the mentally retarded have this disorder. The condition was given the name *mongolism* more than a century ago because of the facial resemblance of affected persons to Asians of Mongolian extraction. In fact, the similarity is superficial, inasmuch as the condition is easily recognizable in Oriental as well as Caucasian children (Kramm, 1963). IQs of these individuals tend to range from the 30s to the 70s.

Down's syndrome is one of a number of condi-

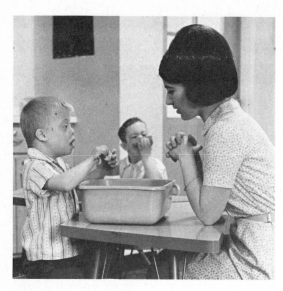

A child with Down's syndrome is being given an individualized learning experience.

tions that can now be detected prenatally through *amniocentesis.* This procedure involves removing cells shed by the fetus into the amniotic fluid and studying them for chromosomal or genetic abnormalities. Amniocentesis is especially appropriate when there has been a previous Down's syndrome pregnancy, since the second child is more apt to be affected. Such a prenatal diagnosis allows parents to decide whether they want to terminate the pregnancy.

At the gene level there are numerous *recessive* inherited forms of retardation, a lesser number of *dominant* inherited ones, and the possibility of a *polygenic* mechanism of inheritance. One of the best known of the recessive syndromes is *phenylketonuria* (PKU), a mental-retardation-producing metabolic error in protein metabolism. The individual lacks liver enzymes necessary to convert the amino acid phenylalanine, which is found in many foods, into another amino acid, tyronine. As a result phenylalanine accumulates and is converted into phenylpyruvic acid and other abnormal metabolites that cause brain damage, hyperactivity, and seizures. The metabolic error is detectable at birth, and a special low-phenylalanine diet that can prevent retardation is available.

Other recessive forms of retardation are *galactosemia* and *Tay-Sach's disease* (also identifiable prenatally through amniocentesis). Among the dom-

inantly inherited forms, *tuberous sclerosis* (epiloia) is probably the most widely known. This condition, caused by tuberous calcifications in the brain, produces retardation and commonly epilepsy. The disease is quite variable in its manifestations, a characteristic of dominantly inherited disorders, and evidence is often lacking of affected persons in successive generations.

The third gene mechanism, *polygenic inheritance,* refers to conditions attributed to the cumulative action of one or more pairs of genes. This modality is thought by some to play a significant role in cultural-familial retardation (for example, Jensen, 1970). We will consider the etiology of this form of retardation later.

Damage in the Prenatal Environment. During pregnancy the embryo and fetus may be exposed to a variety of harmful biological influences. Those that have been either directly or indirectly associated with retardation are poor maternal health, including acute and chronic maternal infections, maternal-fetal blood incompatibility, anoxia, radiation, drugs, and prematurity.

The most common prenatal infections associated with retardation are rubella, toxoplasmosis, syphilis, and cytomegalovirus. Rubella produces retardation by infection of the fetus through the mother during the first three months of pregnancy. Immunization is now available against this dreadful disease. Rh disease, the best known of the blood incompatibilities, occurs only when the mother's blood lacks a certain chemical factor that is in the fetus's blood—the mother is Rh negative and the fetus is Rh positive. Typically in later-born pregnancies, the mother's body mobilizes against the Rh factor, causing destruction of red blood cells, lack of oxygen, and a toxic state that can result in both mental and motor handicap. Rh disease has been treated by blood transfusions at birth and during the pregnancy itself, as well as by a new drug which is purported actually to block the mother's sensitization to her baby's "foreign" blood.

Prematurity refers to birth weights of less than five pounds. Premature infants have greater health risks, and one obstetric goal is to reduce the incidence of prematurity. Prematurity is clearly related to socioeconomic status and to the pregnant woman's general state of health, particularly her diet (Kagan,

1969). In the past decade there have been major efforts to improve prenatal health care to economically disadvantaged groups.

During the process of birth the newborn may be subject to physical trauma to the head and brain, which can produce the motor symptoms called *cerebral palsy*. Persons with cerebral palsy commonly show paralysis, involuntary movements, and disorders of balance and gait. Speech difficulties are also common. Although about one-quarter of affected persons have perfectly normal mental functioning, the remainder show some degree of intellectual impairment, with about one-half of these being mentally retarded (Taylor, 1959).

Cretinism is a form of mental retardation caused by impaired functioning of the thyroid gland. Intellectual deficit, usually severe, is accompanied by certain characteristic physical features—stunted growth, dry skin, coarse hair, and a large head. Preventive efforts have led to the virtual elimination of this kind of retardation in the Western world. Even when cretinism occurs, most of the impairment can be avoided if a thyroid supplement is added to the infant's diet early enough.

Postnatal Hazards. Adverse biological events occur postnatally as well as during pregnancy and at birth. Infectious diseases that involve the brain, such as encephalitis and meningitis, are probably the most important retardation-producing conditions; other postnatal causes are head trauma, lead poisoning, brain tumors, and epilepsy. There is also the very important question of whether infant diets deficient in protein may impair mental development if not actually cause retardation.

Of these conditions, public attention has recently been focused on lead encephalitis, a complication of lead poisoning. This is a disease of the child of poverty because it results from prolonged ingestion of the kind of flaking peels of leaded paint found in dilapidated housing (Lin-Fu, 1972). About 6 percent of children treated for lead poisoning are found to have suffered severe retardation. Recent efforts to prevent lead poisoning include removing leaded paints and boarding up wall space within reach of young children.

With reference to dietary protein intake, there is some indication that children in underdeveloped countries where diets are rich in carbohydrates but low in protein may suffer retardation in both mental and physical growth (Birch & Cravioto, 1966). The latter third of the prenatal period and the years of infancy and early childhood appear to be the time when inadequate protein can impair mental development (Winick, 1970). This is the time of the most rapid brain growth; by age three the brain has already reached 80 percent of its adult weight. In contrast, body weight at three years is only 20 percent of its adult weight.

CULTURAL-FAMILIAL RETARDATION

Cultural-familial retardation involves no specific physical causes. Many psychologists view it as simply reflecting those 2 or 3 percent of the general population that fall at the lower end of the distribution of intelligence. Consistent with this view is the fact that there is a much higher probability that other family members will also be retarded than is the case for mental retardation caused by specific organic disorders. The cultural-familial category includes by far the largest number, about 75 percent, of individuals labeled retarded.

Heredity and Environment. If cultural-familial retardation is seen as reflecting the lower end of the distribution of intelligence, then the question of causation becomes identical with the question of the relative contribution of heredity and environment to intelligence generally. The evidence, as we saw, indicates that both contribute to intellectual development. The data on which this conclusion is based, however, are largely limited to white families and do not involve extremes of poverty and deprivation.

Edith, John, and Doris, the mildly retarded siblings described at the beginning of the chapter, come from the kind of family background frequently associated with cultural-familial retardation. Consistent with some genetic contribution is the presence of retardation in more than one sibling as well as the mother. Consistent with environmental determinants are the impoverished living conditions of this family. The children frequently lacked the basic necessities, often going without adequate clothing or food. The mother, in addition to having subnormal intellectual ability herself, experienced a series of depressions requiring hospitalizations and was easily upset and unable to tolerate stress; the father quit school in the third grade and as an adult became a chronic alcoholic. These circumstances were hardly conducive to even minimal intellectual stimulation.

Lack of Cognitive Stimulation. In Chapter 20 it was proposed that the experience of contingent stimulation was an important, perhaps essential, requirement for normal development in infancy. Contingent stimulation, you may recall, refers to the situation in which infants can learn to make the environment give it pleasures or satisfactions, and to stop unpleasant stimulation from occurring. I especially emphasized the importance of "interactive games" between infants and other people. Research reviewed in that chapter indicated that profoundly destructive effects can occur in many aspects of development, not just intellectual, when infants are severely deprived of this kind of stimulation, as happens in impersonal institutions. It is a reasonable hypothesis that lesser degrees of stimulus deprivation may result in less severe but nonetheless important deficits in mental functioning.

Intelligence test scores are generally found to be correlated with social class, with individuals at the lowest socioeconomic levels tending to perform most poorly. A rather large body of literature has accumulated that also shows an association between certain features of mother-child interaction and social class (e.g., Bee et al., 1969; Hess & Shipman, 1965). For example, when mothers are asked to teach their child how to solve a standard problem, middle-class mothers tend to give more verbal explanations with their instructions, more positive feedback in the form of praise, more specific feedback, and more suggestions in the form of questions. Lower-class mothers make more nonverbal intrusions (such as placing a block herself) and give more negative responses in the form of criticism.

A more extreme example of the relationship of mother-child interaction to intellectual competence in the child is provided by Polansky et al. (1972). The authors studied impoverished families in rural Appalachia and identified a particular constellation of maternal characteristics called "apathy-futility" that seemed to be especially related to retarded development in the children. Apathy-futility is characterized by a feeling that nothing is worth doing, absence of meaningful personal relationships (including the

marital relationship), generalized incompetence, a lack of motivation to acquire competence, and an uncanny ability to infect those who try to help them with the same feelings of futility. Within the sample of 65 mother-child pairs studied (all living at or below the poverty level) they found a negative correlation between ratings of maternal apathy-futility and child IQ—the more apathetic the mother, the lower the child's IQ. This relationship held even when the mothers' own IQs were held constant by partial correlation. In addition, maternal apathy-futility was correlated positively with lethargic, withdrawn, dependent, and clinging children. This study suggests that although being raised in poverty by mothers of low intelligence may have some adverse effects on the child's intellectual development, even more serious impairment can be expected if the mother's behavior is characterized by apathy-futility.

However, definite conclusions about cause and effect cannot be drawn from correlational studies. It is possible, for example, that a mentally slow child tends to elicit a lack of responses in some lower-class mothers rather than vice versa. More convincing are experimental studies to be reviewed shortly that show that when lower-class mothers are taught to provide their children more cognitive stimulation and to interact with them in a more responsive, positive way that the children's IQs increase relative to control groups that have not received such stimulation. If we take these experimental studies into account, it seems reasonable to conclude that deprived social environments lacking in cognitive stimulation do contribute to the occurrence of cultural-familial retardation.

The Prevention of Mental Retardation

In light of our review of the causes of retardation, its prevention obviously involves both biological and psychological measures. The biological ones primarily pertain to the provision of adequate prenatal care for economically disadvantaged pregnant women and, later, basic health care for their infants and young children. The psychological ones refer to opportunities for mental growth-enhancing experiences in the home and in preschool programs.

PRENATAL PREVENTION

The incidence of mental retardation can be reduced by *family planning* prior to pregnancy and by securing health services during pregnancy itself. Family planning considerations will have the greatest impact of reducing retardation for prospective parents who are themselves retarded. For the most part these will be mildly retarded individuals with the cultural-familial form of retardation, for whom it can be expected that about one-half of their children will also be retarded (Baroff, 1974). Family planning for them should include a careful consideration of the needs of prospective children and the parents' perceived capacities to meet them. A more specialized facet of family planning that touches all socioeconomic levels is *genetic counseling*. The concern here is with assisting couples for whom there is a high probability of having a retarded child because of specific genetic defects. These families are often not identified until an affected child has been born, but once this has occurred the risk for future pregnancies is often very clear. In the case of recessively inherited forms of retardation such as phenylketonuria (PKU) and Tay-Sach's disease, the risk at each pregnancy is as high as one in four. In dominantly inherited ones, for example, tuberous sclerosis, it can be as high as one in two. Given this kind of information, prospective parents are in a position to make reasonably informed decisions regarding future pregnancies. Where risks are taken, either knowingly or unknowingly, amniocentesis permits the identification of some children who would ultimately be retarded.

Another very important prenatal measure is for the pregnant woman to avail herself of periodic medical evaluation. As we have seen, her health status during pregnancy influences the likelihood of bearing a low-birth-weight (premature) child, and it is these newborns who are particularly vulnerable to health problems. Not only is there greater prematurity in economically disadvantaged populations, but there is also higher infant mortality and, according to Payne (1971), increased numbers of retarded children with organic brain damage.

POSTNATAL PREVENTION

The focus of postnatal prevention is the child of poverty who is born free of signs of organic abnor-mality. At the biological level, prevention involves the provision of basic health care, usually through the local health department, a diet adequate in protein, and the avoidance of lead poisoning. At the psychological level it involves providing the kind of early childhood environment that will help the child develop cognitive resources more fully and to emulate desirable peer and adult models. This goal is most likely to be achieved through special home intervention programs and participation in preschool day nurseries (child development centers), especially those in which cognitive training is a conscious concern (Baroff, 1974). McKay et al. (1978) found such a multidimensional program to be effective in improving intellectual competencies in children of low socioeconomic Colombian families who would otherwise have been chronically undernourished. By school age the gap in cognitive ability between the treated children and a group of privileged children in the same city had been significantly narrowed.

Raising IQ by Home Intervention. Several investigators have attempted to increase the intellectual competencies of lower-class children by providing them and their mothers with special training in cognitive and interactional skills. In one such study aides made home visits to lower-class black families with two-year-old children. At each visit the aide gave the child a new toy and spent about 30 minutes interacting with the mother and the child about the use of the toy—describing what she was doing, using the toy to elicit verbal responses from the mother and child, encouraging their interactions, and giving lots of positive reinforcement to both. When this interaction was conducted over a two-year period it was found to be effective in raising IQ scores. The increased IQ scores were retained into the first grade of school (Levenstein, 1970; Madden et al., 1976).

The Milwaukee Project. Heber and his associates have attempted to raise intelligence levels in children likely to become mentally retarded (Garber & Heber, 1978; Heber & Garber, 1980). First they conducted a survey of the prevalence of mental retardation in the most impoverished section of a black ghetto in Milwaukee, Wisconsin. They found that although mothers with IQs of less than 80 constituted less than half of all mothers tested, they accounted for almost 80 percent of children with IQs below 80. Thus slum

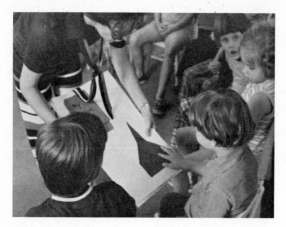

Cognitive training in a preschool for retarded or potentially retarded children. Generous reinforcement is given
for acquiring new cognitive skills. (Top left) "Touch
church"; (top right) "atta boy!"; (right) "That's right!"

residence in itself did not account for retardation in
these children; it was the combination of living in a
slum area *and* having a retarded mother that seemed
to be important.

Children of mothers whose Wechsler IQs were
less than 75 were randomly assigned to an experimental and control condition (20 in each group). At
three months of age children in the experimental
group began attending a special enrichment program at a nearby school facility. This program continued all day, 5 days a week, 12 months a year until
the children entered school at age six. The children
were provided with perceptual-motor, cognitive-lan-
guage, and social-emotional experiences appropriate
to their age level. In addition mothers were given
some remedial academics, homemaking and child-
rearing instructions, and a long period of vocational
training.

Various measures of intelligence were obtained
at six-month intervals for both groups. Experimental
children averaged over 20 IQ points higher between
two and ten years of age. At age six the average IQ
for the experimental children was 121 and for the
control children was 87, over 30 points difference. At
age ten, four years after all intervention had stopped,
the average IQs were 105 and 85, respectively—still

a large and significant difference between the groups,
although the experimental group's average IQ had
dropped to a slightly-above-average level. Further research is clearly needed to confirm, or not confirm,
these findings, which have such far-reaching implications for the prevention of cultural-familial retardation.

Summary

1. Mental retardation has been defined as "significantly subaverage general intellectual functioning existing concurrently with deficits in adaptive behavior and manifested during the developmental period."

2. Intelligence is usually measured by IQ tests. Individuals with IQs less than 70 are considered mentally retarded. Two to three percent of the population fall within this category. Four levels of retardation are distinguished on the basis of IQ scores: mild, moderate, severe, and profound.

3. Intelligence tests have been criticized on a number of grounds, for example, as being too narrow in the abilities sampled and as presenting problems that are irrelevant to the life experiences of many individuals. But even if present tests do not measure all aspects of intelligence, it is reasonable to conclude that what they do measure includes a part of intelligence and that they have some validity in measuring at least part of the deficit involved in mental retardation.

4. Although controversy continues as to the relative contribution of heredity and environment to intellectual ability, it is likely that both contribute to a substantial degree.

5. When intelligence is conceived in terms of mental age, it is found that during the developmental period retarded persons fall further and further behind their normal age-mates rather than maintaining a constant difference or catching up.

6. Most mentally retarded persons differ from normals in being more suggestible, having a poorer memory, and less capacity for abstract thinking.

7. Because of their frequent failures and perhaps unrealistic expectations on the part of parents, retarded persons are likely to experience low self-esteem.

8. Some degree of self-management and employment in unskilled jobs or sheltered workshops can be achieved by less severely retarded persons.

9. Two basic categories of causation are usually distinguished: organic and cultural-familial.

10. Some of the more common forms of mental retardation with known organic causes are Down's syndrome (an extra chromosome), phenylketonuria (recessively inherited metabolic defect), retardation associated with damage in the prenatal environment (for example, rubella), and retardation associated with birth injury as is sometimes the cause in cerebral palsy.

11. Evidence suggests that cultural-familial retardation may result from *both* inherited low intelligence and environmental deprivation, although some writers argue strongly for one as opposed to the other.

12. Certain forms of organically caused retardation may be prevented by adequate prenatal and postnatal care, early detection and treatment (as for phenylketonuria or cretinism), or genetic counseling. Cultural-familial retardation may also be prevented, or at least reduced in severity, by environmental enrichment programs. The evidence in this regard, however, is still preliminary.

Suggested Readings

Two comprehensive textbooks on the subject of mental retardation are N. M. Robinson and H. Robinson's *The mentally retarded child* (McGraw-Hill, 1976) and G. S. Baroff's *Mental retardation: Nature, cause and management* (Hemisphere Press, 1974). An excellent chapter on intellectual development and mental retardation is in T. M. Achenbach's *Developmental psychopathology* (Ronald, 1974—a new edition is forthcoming).

25
Organic Brain Syndromes

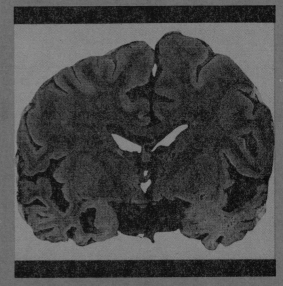

- Do persons sometimes develop symptoms of senility before old age?

- In *Through the Looking-Glass,* Alice walked through a wood where things had no name. Do people really have that kind of experience?

- Does brain damage in the right hemisphere produce the same effects as in the left hemisphere?

- What is Huntington's disease (the disorder that folksinger Woody Guthrie had)?

- If you notice symptoms that might be of syphilis, and then they seem to go away, should you go to the doctor anyway?

- What are the different forms of epilepsy? Did you know that particular brain wave patterns (EEGs) are associated with each type?

Martha: Symptoms of a Brain Disorder

Martha was 56 years old when she was admitted to a neurological institute for a neuropsychiatric examination. For most of her life she had shown no signs of psychological disturbance. About a year and a half before, however, her husband noticed that she frequently began to burn food when cooking because she apparently forgot that it was on the stove. Her behavior became increasingly strange. She lost interest in her work as a dressmaker and began to sit at home and read weekly magazines, perusing the same stories over and over again without realizing that she had read them before. About this time her brother died, which seemed to precipitate even more bizarre behavior. On several occasions she imagined that she saw him and ran into the street to greet him, once when she was not fully dressed. She recognized her husband, her sister, and her dog but was confused about the identity of other people. She talked about seeing the "funniest cat" across the street; it had legs all over its body, with one claw on each leg.

At the neurological institute she cried occasionally when she thought she saw her brother on the street and felt that he was going away hungry. She would frequently sit and sing as she read, and gradually her prevailing mood became one of mild euphoria. She seemed not in the least self-conscious about her rather unusual behaviors. Neurological examination led to the diagnosis of Pick's disease, a rare form of degenerative brain disorder that strikes people in middle or late middle age. (Goldstein & Katz, 1937)

Throughout this book I have emphasized the interplay between biological and psychological contributions to abnormal behaviors. The contribution of inherited traits of temperament to childhood behavior problems, of allergies and other biological vulnerabilities to psychophysiological disorders, of possible biochemical determinants to schizophrenia and affective psychoses, and of brain disease to certain forms of violent behavior have all been considered. Clearly I have not waited until this last chapter to consider biological determinants of abnormal behavior. The difference, and it is only a relative difference, is that for the disorders considered in this chapter the *primary causative event* is some identifiable disease, injury, or malfunction of the brain. Secondarily, psychological factors also affect the symptoms and the course of the organic brain syndrome.

In 1975 patients diagnosed with organic brain syndromes accounted for about 22.5 percent of all residents (excluding the mentally retarded) in state and county mental hospitals. The absolute number of this group of patients, however, had declined 58 percent over the seven-year period from 1969 to 1975. A major contributing factor in this trend has been the tendency to transfer many elderly patients with organic brain disorders from mental hospitals to nursing homes. Nevertheless, in 1975, 57 percent of the patients hospitalized for organic brain syndromes were over 64 years of age.

Categories of Organic Brain Syndromes

In DSM-III the different categories of organic brain syndromes are based on symptoms rather than types of causation. Thus *delirium* is one kind of organic brain syndrome but may result from a number of different organic causes. The categories of organic syndromes are listed below.

DELIRIUM AND DEMENTIA

The mental impairment in these conditions is relatively global. Delirious states can vary in intensity. In the more severe cases the persons are confused, disoriented, and incoherent. They have great difficulty maintaining attention to environmental events or engaging in goal-directed thinking or behavior. In some cases there is reduced wakefulness, sometimes called a "clouded consciousness." More often the person is restless, over-alert, and cannot sleep. Perceptual distortions are common and may become hallucinatory, with visual hallucinations predominating.

Toxic conditions of various kinds can produce delirium: high fever accompanying diseases such as malaria or pneumonia; carbon monoxide, lead or other metallic poisoning; excessive use of alcohol, barbiturates, or other drugs; withdrawal reactions after excessive drug use; liver or kidney disease; or certain kinds of brain injuries. The onset of delirium is usually rapid and the duration is usually brief, an average of about a week. In previous DSMs, a delirious reaction to toxic substances was considered a form of *acute* brain syndrome in contrast to more *chronic* syndromes that resulted from long-lasting and usually irreversible brain damage. The acute-chronic distinction is no longer given as much importance since there are a number of disorders where that distinction becomes blurred.

Dementia refers to a deterioration from one's previous level of intellectual capacity. Impairments are especially prominent in memory, abstract thinking, and judgment. In addition, the person is likely to show poor impulse control. With respect to memory, persons may begin to forget names, telephone numbers, directions, and recent events. They may leave tasks undone because they forget to return to them if interrupted. The gas may be left on, the water running, or the iron connected. Martha burned food because she forgot it was on the stove. She could not give her home address and said that she lived with her four children, Alvin, Margaret, Bernard, and Rita. In fact, these were the names of her brothers and sisters. Because of their poor memory these individuals may be disoriented as to time and place. Martha, for example, was not sure how old she was or when she was born. She did not know where she had been one week before and said that she was "going home tonight." Some individuals may be unable to find their way home if they should wander a few blocks away. Martha was quite capable of going without help from her ward to a workroom in another part of the hospital over a well-practiced route, but when taken off this route she would become confused and unable to find her way.

For patients suffering from damage to the frontal lobes, Goldstein (1939) especially emphasized the loss of the *abstract attitude* and their reliance on the *concrete attitude.* By concrete attitude Goldstein meant that the person's responses are controlled by specific external stimuli rather than more abstract, cognitive processes. As long as Martha could respond "unthinkingly" to external stimuli she performed well, but when circumstances changed to require some understanding or judgment she became confused and perplexed. For example, when she was knitting (which she could do quite well) and was asked, "Show us your work," she failed to understand the request. It was as if the presence of the knitting needles in her hands so controlled her behavior that she could do nothing other than continue to knit. In another instance Martha was asked to draw a series of oblong figures such as arrows in horizontal positions after being shown the figures for a short period of time. She did so satisfactorily. Then the same figures were presented in a vertical position and she was again asked to draw them. She persisted in drawing the figures in a horizontal direction and no amount of instruction could induce her to do otherwise. On other occasions she persisted with vertical drawings when these were presented first. It is as though she became "stuck" on responding in a certain way and could not change when the situation required it.

A final example illustrates Martha's inability to use imagination. Given a key, she was readily able to demonstrate how it was used; she looked around, went to the door, put the key in the keyhole, and correctly executed the locking movement. However, if a key were not physically present, she could not demonstrate with an imaginary key how it was used. A general corollary of this concrete way of thinking is that the person is unable to plan ahead and remains at the mercy of the immediate stimuli.

Impairment in both judgment and impulse control may be reflected in the use of coarse language, neglect of personal appearance and hygiene, and disregard for conventional rules of social conduct. The individual, for example, might attempt sexual contact with a stranger. Before Martha came to the institute she had become sloppy in her appearance, though previously she had been neat. On the ward she took no initiative with respect to personal hygiene or everyday habits of dress. If guided to the bathroom, she would wash herself; if told to, she undressed in the evening. Emotional loss of control is also common. Persons may overreact emotionally, laughing or crying inappropriately. Martha's moods varied unpredictably. She cried when she thought she saw her brother in the street, or she would sit and sing. Generally, though, she seemed in a cheerful, euphoric mood and did not display the degree of shallow, labile emotionality that some brain-injured patients show.

Dementias may result from many causes. The senile and presenile dementias, which we will return to shortly, involve degenerative processes of unknown cause that affect most of the brain. Martha suffered from a rare form of presenile dementia called Pick's disease. Other dementias result from infectious diseases of the brain (such as neurosyphilis), tumors, brain injuries, and strokes.

AMNESTIC SYNDROME AND ORGANIC HALLUCINOSIS

In these conditions relatively selective areas of cognition are impaired. The essential feature in the amnestic syndrome is an impairment in both short- and long-term memory that does not occur in the context of delirium or a more general dementia. These individuals are able to remember new information for only a short period of time; for example, they can repeat back digits correctly within a few seconds, but are unable to remember anything that happened more than 25 minutes ago. They seem to be unable to transfer new memories into long-term storage. They are also unable to recall material that was known in the past, are likely to show some degree of disorientation, and may fill in memory gaps with invented stories (confabulation). This syndrome can be caused by damage to certain limbic structures located in the temporal lobe such as the hippocampus. The most common form of this disorder is that associated with Korsakoff's syndrome, produced by a deficiency of the vitamin thiamine and by chronic alcohol abuse.

In organic hallucinosis the primary characteristic is the presence of hallucinations directly associated with some organic agent. Hallucinations produced by hallucinogenic drugs or the excessive use of alcohol are examples of this condition.

ORGANIC DELUSIONAL SYNDROME AND ORGANIC AFFECTIVE SYNDROME

In the organic delusional syndrome, the essential feature is the presence of delusional beliefs clearly associated with some organic factor. These delusions, which can vary in degree of organization, may be associated with brain tumor, amphetamine intoxication, or other organic conditions. In the organic affective syndrome, the basic feature is a disturbance of mood that may resemble either a depressive or manic episode.

ORGANIC PERSONALITY SYNDROME

The organic personality syndrome involves a marked change in personality. A common pattern is for the person to become more emotionally labile and to show poor impulse control and social judgment.

INTOXICATION AND WITHDRAWAL

Intoxication, as used here, refers to more than "usual" maladaptive behavior associated with ingesting toxic substances. Belligerence and severely impaired judgment associated with drinking alcohol would be an example. Withdrawal refers to the symptom patterns described in Chapter 23 that are associated with stopping the intake of a substance that has been regularly used.

Primary and Secondary Symptoms

Some symptoms of organic brain disorder, such as delirium and various cognitive impairments, result directly from the organic damage. Other symptoms, such as delusional beliefs, feelings of depression, and certain personality changes, might best be seen as secondary responses to the stress and frustration of not being able to function normally. One such reaction, originally called the *catastrophic reaction* by Goldstein (1939), is described by Kolb (1973):

Confronted with a problem he cannot solve, the brain-injured individual becomes suddenly anxious and agitated and may appear dazed. A change in his color may appear, he fumbles at the task, and he may present other evidence of autonomic disturbances, such as irregular pulse and changes in respiratory rate. If he was initially in good spirits, he now becomes evasive, sullen, irritable, and even aggressive. (p. 68)

Aphasia

Thus far we have not concerned ourselves to any extent with the relationship between type and location of brain damage to the kind of psychological impairments shown. A good example of a disorder that has a clear relationship to certain brain areas is *aphasia.* This term refers to various difficulties in the expression and comprehension of language. *Expressive aphasias* involve disturbances in speaking and writing, and *comprehension aphasias* include defects in understanding other people's speech and in reading. For right-handed persons aphasia is almost always related to damage in the dominant left hemisphere. For left-handed individuals aphasia seems to occur about as often with left- or with right-hemisphere lesions, suggesting hemispheric dominance may be less pronounced in left-handed people.

C. Scott Moss, a clinical psychologist, suffered a rather severe stroke that left him almost totally aphasic and also paralyzed on the right side. He made an excellent recovery and subsequently wrote an account of his experience with aphasia. His description conveys better than an "objective" clinical account what aphasia means to the person.

I recollect trying to read the headlines of the *Chicago Tribune* but they didn't make any sense to me at all. I didn't have any difficulty focusing; it was simply that the words, individually or in combination, didn't have meaning, and even more amazing, I was only a trifle bothered by that fact. . . .

The second week I ran into a colleague who happened to mention that it must be very frustrating for me to be aphasic since prior to that I had been so verbally facile. I assured him that it was not upsetting and then later found myself wondering why it was not. I think part of the explanation was relatively simple. If I had lost the ability to converse with others, I had also lost the ability even to engage in self-talk. In other words, I did not have the ability to think about the future—to worry, to anticipate or perceive it—at least not with words. Thus, for the first five or six weeks after hospitalization I simply existed. So the fact that I could not use words even internally was, in fact, a safeguard. I imagine it was somewhat similar to undergoing a lobotomy or lobectomy in the dissociation from the future. It was as if without words I could not be concerned about tomorrow.

It took a great deal of effort for me to keep an abstraction in mind. For example, in talking with the speech therapist I would begin to give a definition of an abstract concern, but as I held it in mind it would sort of fade, and chances were that I'd end up giving a simplified version rather than one at the original level of conception. It was as though giving an abstraction required so much of my addled intelligence that halfway through the definition I would run out of the energy available to me and regress to a more concrete answer. (Moss, 1972, pp. 4–5, 10)

Studies of aphasic individuals have increased our understanding of those parts of the brain involved in the use of language. Although many aphasics have rather widespread brain damage that impairs both expressive and comprehending functions (Schuell, 1974), occasionally there are individuals in whom the damage has been restricted to a single location. Research with these individuals has shown that aphasic defects do vary in a meaningful way as a function of the part of the brain that has been damaged (Goodglass & Geschwind, 1976). Figure 25-1 shows three areas of the brain that lead to different kinds of aphasic symptoms when lesions are limited to these areas.

The area labeled B (for Broca's area) is located in the anterior (front) part of the brain near the lower part of the motor association area, where control of the mouth and other muscles involved in speech are located. Anterior aphasics, as they are sometimes called, have a great deal of difficulty in articulating speech sounds and in putting words together to form meaningful sentences. The latter is sometimes referred to as agrammatic speech because it seems to involve a loss of the ability to express grammatical relationships. Anterior aphasics have not lost the meaning of specific words, especially nouns, and when asked to point to a book or a pair of scissors they can do so readily. The following is an example

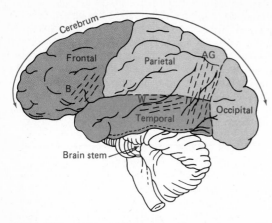

FIGURE 25-1.   Lobes of the cerebral hemispheres with shaded areas representing Broca's area (B), Wernicke's area (W), and the angular gyrus (AG). Adapted from McConnell (1974). Copyright 1974 Holt, Rinehart and Winston and used with permission.

of agrammatic speech in which the patient is attempting to explain that he came into the hospital for dental surgery:

Yes . . . ah . . . Monday . . . er . . . Dad and Peter H . . . (his own name), and Dad . . . er . . . hospital . . . and ah . . . Wednesday. . . . Wednesday, nine o'clock . . . and oh . . . Thursday . . . ten o'clock, ah doctors . . . two . . . an' doctors. . . . and er . . . teeth . . . yah. (Goodglass & Geschwind, 1976, p. 408)

The anterior aphasic's difficulties would seem to be largely expressive in nature. The close relationship to the motor association area is consistent with the difficulty in transmitting commands to the muscles involved in speech, and the close relationship to the frontal lobes may explain the difficulty in putting words together in grammatical relationships, since the frontal lobes are thought to be especially involved in planning ahead and understanding relationships among objects or ideas. Impairment is not entirely limited to expressive functions, however; anterior aphasics may also have difficulty in comprehending certain grammatical or relational constructions. Writing is usually impaired to the same degree as speech, but reading is less severely impaired—or the impairment may be more subtle in terms of comprehending relational concepts and thus not be so obvious (Caramazza & Berndt, 1978).

The area in Figure 25-1 labeled W (for Wernicke's area) is next to the auditory center and appears to be essential for the comprehension of the meaning of language. The nearness to the auditory center indicates the close tie between the auditory or acoustic representation of words in the brain and their meanings. When this area has been damaged, individuals have trouble associating meanings to the sounds of speech. Asked to point to a book, which is mixed in with other objects, posterior (back part of the brain) aphasics cannot do so. They hear the word book but cannot attribute meaning to the sound of the word. Their vocabulary, especially nouns, is severely depleted. Nevertheless, in contrast to anterior aphasics, they are quite fluent in articulating words and have not lost the ability to construct grammatical sentences (Caramazza & Berndt, 1978). Their speech is sometimes characterized as "empty" because of the lack of appropriate nouns and the substitution of indefinite words like "things." Both reading and writing tend also to be impaired in posterior aphasics.

The following excerpt illustrates how a posterior aphasic can be relatively fluent and use grammatical constructions but at the same time have great difficulty in thinking of the right words. Note how the person repeats the same word or phrase over and over, and relies heavily on the indefinite word "something."

Patient: Good. All right. And . . . the boys went . . . out there Saturday morning and over there, and over there in the corner there. Saturday morning I gave someone cigarettes, I suppose, over there, corner.

Doctor Could you speak a little louder, Mr. Wilson?

Patient: All right.

Doctor: So I can hear you?

Patient: And I gave him something over there.

Doctor: Who, who are you talking about?

Patient: Over there, there, over there . . . too, I guess, I gave him something too. God Almighty, and then I gave him something over there. I gave him cheese and everything else, I guess. I gave him something over there. I gave him something over there.

Doctor: What did you give him?

Patient: Yes, I know. And I gave him something.

Doctor: What did you give him?

Patient: Cookies, chocolate, something else, over

there. God Almighty, I gave him something over there in the corner, over there, I gave him something, I . . . over there in the corner over there, once. Once I gave him something, that, I gave him something, God damn it, I gave him something, something. I gave him something. And I gave him something. God Almighty, I gave him something too. I gave him something, also. Also I gave him something. (Laffal, 1965, p. 169)

The third area of the brain shown in Figure 25-1, labeled AG (for angular gyrus), is located immediately in front of the primary visual zone and is involved in giving meaning to visual input. Lesions limited to this area do not impair auditory comprehension or oral expression of language, but they do impair the recognition of letters and other visual stimuli. Thus a lesion in this area can severely damage the capacity to both read and write without significantly affecting speech or auditory comprehension.

Some Specific Causes of Organic Brain Syndromes

The syndromes described thus far might result from a variety of different kinds of brain tumors, injuries, and diseases. In this section we will consider some specific disease processes that result in symptoms of a particular nature and course.

SENILE AND PRESENILE DEMENTIA[1]

Although the general symptoms of *senile* and *presenile dementia* are similar, the age of onset is different. Somewhat arbitrarily, dementia is labeled senile dementia if it begins after age 65 and presenile dementia if it begins before age 65.

Upon postmortem examination the brain of the senile person shows considerable destruction of nervous tissues: The brain has decreased in size, the cortical convolutions have narrowed, and the fissures between them have widened. Nevertheless, the cause of senile dementia is uncertain. The fact that the de-

gree of dementia and behavioral disturbance is not always highly correlated with degree of brain degeneration suggests that the person's prior personality and current social situation interact significantly with the brain impairment to produce the observed symptoms. Secondary reactions occur in about half the individuals. Some have acute neurotic reactions, frequently depression; others have psychotic reactions. About 15 to 25 percent develop paranoid ideas.

Alzheimer's disease is the most common degenerative disorder of the brain. Until recently this disorder was considered a form of presenile dementia, but investigations have shown that it can begin well past age 65 (Liston, 1979). The degeneration develops slowly and spreads throughout the brain, with death usually occurring after about five years. Under the microscope the brains of victims of Alzheimer's disease show two characteristics of deterioration: senile plaques and neurofibrillary tangles. Senile plaques consist of clusters of abnormal dendrites, which probably interfere with the transmission of nerve impulses. The neurofibrillary tangles consist of an accumulation of tiny nerve fibers wrapped around each other. These tangles may prevent an adequate supply of nutrients from reaching the brain's nerve cells. Alzheimer's disease cannot be definitely diagnosed from behavioral deficits alone, and it is usually only after death that the disease is confirmed by brain examinations. This disease tends to run in families, with close relatives being much more likely to get the disorder than the general population (Heston & Mastri, 1977). A genetic contribution is thus suggested.

Pick's disease is rarer than Alzheimer's disease, frequently produces a presenile (before 65) dementia, and degeneration is more localized, limited primarily to the frontal lobes. Martha's symptoms are typical of this disorder.

Cerebral arteriosclerosis, hardening and thickening of the cerebral blood vessels, has also been considered a cause of senile dementia. However, recent opinion is that relatively few cases of senile dementia result from this factor (Wells, 1978). When arteriosclerosis results in a complete blocking of a cerebral artery, then symptoms of dementia may appear. The onset of the cognitive deficit is usually abrupt in this case rather than slow as for the degenerative disorders. Initial symptoms of such a blocked artery, usually called a stroke, are likely to include headache, faintness, confusion, memory lapses, aphasia, and in

---

[1]In DSM-III senile and presenile dementia are subsumed under the heading of *progressive idiopathic dementia.*

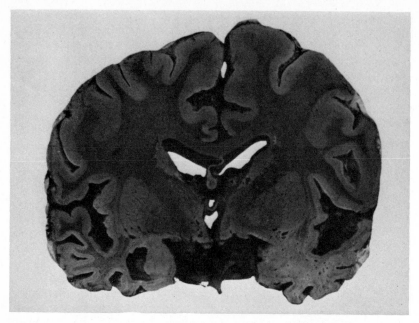

Alzheimer's disease. There is generalized cortical atrophy and the spaces (sulci) between the lobes and in the interior cavities (ventricles) have widened considerably.

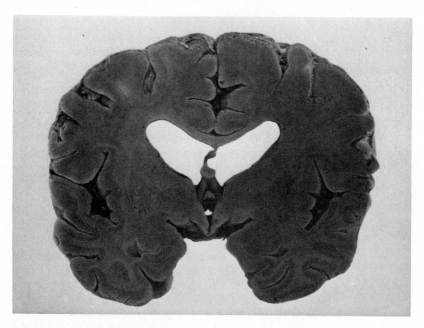

Huntington's disease. The interior cavities are especially enlarged, indicating extensive atrophy in the caudate nucleus.

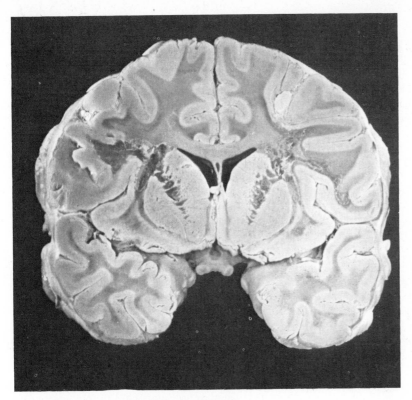

Cross section of the cerebrum of a normal brain.

many cases, temporary paralysis in various body parts. Frequently the person makes a rather good physical and mental recovery from the first stroke, but succeeding strokes are likely to produce increasing impairments from which the person may recover only partially. In DSM-III dementia resulting from multiple blockings of arteries is called *multi-infarct dementia.* In one series of autopsies of 50 successive cases of senile dementia patients, arteriosclerosis and associated arterial blocking accounted definitely for the symptoms in only 12 percent of the cases. Alzheimer's disease accounted for 50 percent of the cases (Tomlinson et al., 1970).

HUNTINGTON'S DISEASE

George Huntington, his father, and his grandfather practiced medicine on Long Island for a period covering 78 years. They were able to trace through several generations the occurrence of an incurable disorder involving uncontrollable tremors and various mental symptoms. They observed that no person ever developed the disease without having a parent who also had the disorder.

Now known as *Huntington's disease,* this disorder is inherited through a single dominant gene, which means that the children of a person with this disorder have a 50 percent chance of being afflicted. Postmortem analyses show widespread cerebral atrophy and the presence of scar cells. There is evidence that a genetically determined deficiency in an inhibitory neurotransmitter, GABA (gamma-aminobutyric acid), in a part of the brain known as the basal ganglia plays an important role in this disorder (Wells, 1978). The symptoms, which do not ordinarily appear until persons are in their thirties or early forties, include progressive dementia, apathy, depression, involuntary tremors in the arms or legs, difficulty in maintaining balance while walking, smacking of the lips and tongue, and explosive speech. Sometimes the physical and intellectual changes occur without accompanying personality changes, but in many cases the person shows neurotic or psychotic responses. Woody Guthrie, the American folksinger, was a victim of Huntington's disease. On several occasions his peculiar lopsided walk and poorly articulated speech led others to believe that he was drunk.

GENERAL PARESIS

Brain tissues can be damaged by such infectious diseases as syphilis, encephalitis, or brain abscesses. I will describe only the first. The discovery that the syndrome known as *general paresis* is caused by a syphilitic infection was a landmark in the development of the organic view of psychopathology. Only a small proportion of individuals (less than 5 percent) who contract syphilis and fail to get treatment ultimately develop the symptoms of general paresis. It is not known why.

Untreated syphilis progresses through several stages. The first sign of the disease is a sore (chancre) that usually appears on the penis or vagina in 10 to 40 days after infection. If ignored, the sore goes away within a month or six weeks, and persons mistakenly think they are cured. The second stage may not be so obvious. About three to six weeks after the sore has gone away a rather mild copper-colored skin rash may break out, sometimes accompanied by headaches and a mild fever. These symptoms disappear, and a lengthy period follows in which outward signs of disease disappear. During this stage the spirochetes may invade the heart, spinal cord, brain, or other organs. Ten to 30 years after this latency period, overt symptoms may again appear, this time in the form of the symptoms of general paresis. If the spirochetes have attacked the brain, widespread destruction occurs, accompanied by progressive dementia and paralysis.

Symptoms that tend to be associated specifically with general paresis are: failure of the pupil of the eye to contract to light, failure of other reflexes such as the knee jerk reflex, slurred speech, and shaky handwriting. For example, a person asked to repeat the words "Methodist Episcopal Church" might say, "Mesdus Episfal Chursh," sounding like a drunken person. Behavioral changes also occur, frequently so slowly that family and friends are not aware that changes are taking place. Such individuals are likely to become more irritable and have periods of depression or confusion. As the disease progresses they may become neglectful of dress, forgetful of social amenities, and lose ordinary inhibitions in the expression of aggressive or sexual impulses. In some cases grandiose delusions of great power or wealth develop; in other cases there is simply a progressive dementia. An example of the latter course is shown in the following example:

A woman of 26 was brought to the hospital because she had become lost when she attempted to return home from a neighboring grocery store. About seven months before the patient's admission, her husband noticed that she was becoming careless of her personal appearance and neglectful of her household duties. She often forgot to prepare the family meals, or, in an apparent preoccupation, would burn the food. She seemed to have little appreciation of time

Woody Guthrie, a popular folksinger in the 1940s, was a victim of Huntington's disease.

and would not realize when to get up or go to bed. The patient would sit idly about the house, staring uncomprehendingly into space.

At the hospital the patient entered the admission office with an unsteady gait. There, by way of greeting, the physician inquired, "How are you today?" to which she replied in a monotonous, tremulous tone, "N-yes-s, I was op-er-a-ted on for 'pen-pendici-ci-tis." She never made any spontaneous remarks and when, a few days after her admission, she was asked if she were sad or happy, she stared vacantly at the physician and, with a fatuous smile, answered, "Yeah." The patient sat about the ward for hours, taking no interest in its activities. Sometimes she would hold a book in her lap, aimlessly turning the pages, never reading but often pointing out pictures like a small child and showing satisfaction when she found a new one to demonstrate. Neurological examination showed dilated pupils that reacted only slightly to light and on convergence. There was a tremor of lips and facial muscles on attempting to speak. The protruded tongue showed a coarse tremor. All deep tendon reflexes were hyperactive. The Wasserman reaction was strongly positive in both blood serum and cerebrospinal fluid. (Kolb, 1973, pp. 228–229)

The Wasserman test of the cerebrospinal fluid is almost 100 percent effective in detecting the presence of a syphilitic infection (not necessarily in the brain) at almost any stage of the disease. Penicillin is an effective treatment for syphilis and can prevent the development of general paresis if begun early enough. Once damage has been done to the central nervous system it cannot be undone, although further destruction can be prevented. After the widespread use of penicillin, the number of syphilis cases dropped spectacularly in the 1950s. However, starting around 1960 the incidence of syphilis began to increase again, doubling between 1960 and 1970. It was estimated that in 1970 there were one million persons who had untreated syphilis (Strage, 1971). These statistics suggest that sometime in the 1980s we can expect a resurgence of cases of general paresis.

EPILEPSY

Epilepsy should not be viewed as a single disorder with a specific cause, but rather as a symptom that can result from a variety of causes. Epileptic symptoms consist of recurrent episodes of altered

Julius Caesar is reported to have suffered from epileptic seizures.

consciousness accompanied by changes in the electrical activity of the brain. Some persons have involuntary movements or seizures during the attack; others do not. In many cases there is no measurable indication of brain impairment other than certain abnormalities in brain wave patterns; in others a recognizable brain disorder appears to be related to the epileptic symptoms. The incidence of epilepsy in the United States is about one case per 200 people (Kolb, 1973). A number of historically prominent individuals have been afflicted with this symptom, including Julius Caesar, Alfred the Great, Lord Byron, and Dostoevsky. There are three major types of epilepsy:

1. *Grand mal.* Grand mal is the most dramatic and most common form of epilepsy. In most cases the seizure is preceded by a premonitory signal or warning called the *aura* in which the person may

consciously experience sensory or motor symptoms—a feeling of numbness or tingling, or an hallucinatory experience such as flashes of light or certain odors. Following the aura the person falls to the ground unconscious, often with a cry, and has a convulsive seizure. The convulsions begin with a short period of 10 to 20 seconds during which the muscles of the entire body become rigid, the jaws are clenched, and breathing stops. This is followed by spasmodic contractions of various muscle groups. During this second phase the person may foam at the mouth, bite the tongue, and lose sphincter control. The muscular contractions soon subside and the person goes into a coma or deep sleep that might last from a few minutes to an hour or more. On waking, the person has no memory of the episode. The frequency of untreated grand mal seizures varies from once a day to once or twice in a lifetime.

2. *Petit mal.* In the petit mal seizure there is a brief loss or diminution of consciousness lasting only a few seconds. There are no convulsions as in the grand mal type, and within a few seconds the person can resume normal activity, in some cases without even knowing that the attack occurred. The person may simply "freeze" and stare blankly for a moment, remain standing, or slip and fall. This form of epilepsy is most common in children.

3. *Psychomotor epilepsy.* In psychomotor epilepsy, the person does not lose consciousness entirely. There is, however, a psychological disturbance during which the person may engage in "automatic" behavior which may appear either purposeful or confused: for example, mumbling, grinding the teeth, or wandering aimlessly. In rare instances the person may become violently assaultive. (Recall the discussion of temporal lobe epilepsy in Chapter 22.)

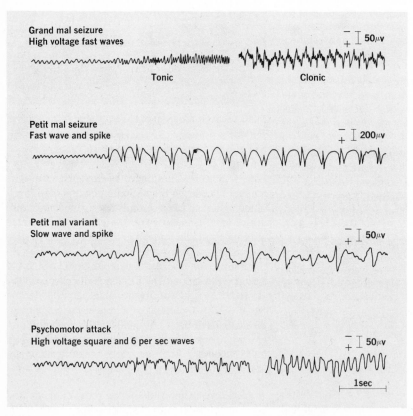

FIGURE 25-2. EEG patterns in persons with grand mal epilepsy, petit mal epilepsy, and psychomotor attack. (Adapted from Gibbs, Gibbs, & Lennox, 1935, p. 1112.)

Epilepsy and the EEG. Most epileptic seizures are accompanied by rather intense electrical discharges in the brain that can be measured by the EEG (electroencephalogram). The type of abnormality present in the EEG tends to be specific for each form of epilepsy (Figure 25-2). Similar abnormalities may exist when the person is not having a seizure; thus the EEG can be used as an aid in the diagnosis of epilepsy in doubtful cases, for example, in distinguishing epilepsy from hysterical seizures. An abnormal EEG is not a foolproof sign of epilepsy, however, since approximately 10 percent of the population show some irregularity in brain wave patterns, yet only 0.5 percent of the population have epileptic seizures.

Etiology and Treatment of Epilepsy. Epilepsy can have many origins: known organic damage such as brain tumors, cerebral arteriosclerosis, head injuries, and so on, or unknown causes in cases in which brain functioning appears otherwise normal. Heredity may contribute to a tendency toward abnormal brain wave patterns, but as yet we know little about the specific mechanisms in epilepsy.

Except in cases in which epilepsy is associated with marked brain damage there is no evidence for any intellectual impairment. Nor is there any convincing evidence that epileptics have personality traits any different from the rest of us, unless the epilepsy and other people's reaction to it has produced some sensitivity to their disorder. Many forms of epileptic seizures have been controlled successfully with drugs: Dilantin for grand mal seizures, Tridione for petit mal seizures, and Phenurone for psychomotor seizures.

Summary

1. The primary causative events for organic brain syndromes are some identifiable disease, injury, or malfunctioning of the brain.

2. In DSM-III the categories of organic brain syndromes are based on symptoms rather than types of causation. These syndromes are:

a. Delirium, which can result from high fever, metallic poisoning, drugs, and certain kinds of brain injuries. In this condition the person is confused, disoriented, and often incoherent.

b. Dementia, involving a deterioration from one's previous level of intellectual capacity, especially in memory, abstract thinking, and judgment. This syndrome can result from degenerative processes, infectious diseases, tumors, strokes, and brain injuries.

c. Other syndromes include the amnestic, the delusional, the hallucinatory, the affective, the personality change, the intoxication, and the withdrawal syndromes.

3. Aphasia is an impairment in either the comprehension or the expressive aspects of language and speech, related to damage in specific areas of the brain.

4. When progressive dementia occurs before age 65 it is called presenile dementia; when it develops after age 65 it is called senile dementia.

5. Alzheimer's disease and Pick's disease are examples of presenile dementia, although Alzheimer's disease can also develop after age 65.

6. Cerebral arteriosclerosis probably does not account for as many cases of senile dementia as was previously thought. For the small proportion of persons who have experienced multiple strokes (blocking of cerebral arteries) some dementia is likely to occur.

7. An inherited disorder that produces organic brain syndromes is Huntington's disease. The symptoms include progressive dementia, apathy, depression, involuntary tremors in the limbs, and difficulty in maintaining balance.

8. Syphilis is one infectious disease that leads to a specific organic brain syndrome, general paresis. Treating syphilis with penicillin can prevent the development of general paresis.

9. Three major forms of epilepsy are grand mal, petit mal, and psychomotor seizures. Brain wave patterns tend to be specific for each form of epilepsy.

Suggested Readings

More details can be found on organic brain syndromes in D. Benson and D. Blumer (Eds.), *Psychiatric aspects of neurologic disease* (Grune & Stratton, 1975). C. Scott Moss, a clinical psychologist, describes his own experience and recovery from a stroke that left him aphasic in *Recovery with aphasia* (University of Illinois Press, 1972).

Glossary

Abnormal behavior. Behavior that is socially disturbing to others, subjectively distressing, or *psychologically handicapping.**

Abreaction. Expression of pent-up emotion.

Abstinence syndrome. *See Withdrawal syndrome.*

Acute-chronic dimension. Usually refers to the extent to which a psychotic reaction has been either of recent onset with acute, florid symptomatology or has been chronically present for a long time.

Addiction to drugs. Term used with various meanings; in this book is similar to *drug dependency.*

Adjustment disorder. Psychological symptoms or maladaptive behavior related to some immediate life circumstance. The symptoms ordinarily disappear when the life circumstance changes.

Adult genital stage. In Freudian theory a stage in which libidinal instincts find adequate outlet through adult heterosexual intercourse.

Affective disorders. Class of *psychotic* disorders in which the primary symptoms are disturbances in mood, as manic or depressive episodes.

Alcohol hallucinosis. Persistent *hallucinations* after the person has recovered from alcohol withdrawal.

Alcoholism. Excessive use of alcohol, usually associated with *psychological* and *physical dependency,* which impairs ability to function in several areas of life.

Alpha rhythm. A relatively low-frequency, high-voltage wave obtained from *EEG* measurement; usually occurs during periods of relaxation when there is little external or internal stimulation.

Alzheimer's disease. Degenerative disorder of the brain that may begin during the 40–60 age period.

Amnesia. A *dissociative reaction* in which the person

*Words or phrases in italics are defined in another part of the glossary.

cannot remember events during the dissociated state.

Amphetamine drugs. A class of stimulant drugs.

Amygdala. Part of the *limbic system* of the brain; associated with emotional-motivational functioning.

Anal stage. In Freudian theory a stage in which the satisfactions of the *libido* center around the expulsion or retention of feces.

Anesthesias. Phenomenon in which parts of the body surface lose the sense of touch or feel numb.

Anorexia nervosa. Disorder, most common in adolescent females, in which eating is drastically reduced and extreme weight loss occurs.

Antabuse. Drug used to control alcoholism; produces nausea if combined with alcohol. Generic name disulfiram.

Antisocial personality. Long-standing personality disorder characterized by chronic antisocial behavior, impulsivity, and lack of interpersonal ties or loyalties.

Anxiety. Strong fear response; usually unrealistic or irrational.

Anxiety disorders. A class of disorders in which anxiety plays a prominent role.

Aphasia. Difficulty in expression or understanding of words; usually associated with brain damage in specific parts of the brain.

Assertive training. A therapeutic technique, usually involving *behavior rehearsal,* in which persons learn to assert themselves appropriately.

Attachment behavior. Behavior reflecting tendency of infants of most species to remain close to an adult, usually the mother.

Autism. *See Early infantile autism.*

Autistic. Refers to self-centered preoccupation with one's thoughts or inner world.

Autonomic nervous system. Portion of the nervous system that controls the functioning of many internal bodily processes such as heartrate, digestive processes, and so on.

Aversion conditioning. A procedure in which a painful or distressing stimulus is paired with some thought or behavior as a way of preventing the thought or behavior from occurring in the future.

Avoidance learning. Phenomenon in which an organism learns to avoid some distressing experience by making a response under the right circumstances.

Barbiturate. A class of sedative drugs that can lead to physical and psychological dependency; withdrawal syndrome is especially severe and can be fatal.

Behavior disorder. *See Abnormal behavior.*

Behavior modification. Procedures based on learning principles used by behaviorally oriented clinicians to modify behavior; usually a form of treatment for abnormal behavior.

Behavior rehearsal. A therapeutic technique in which persons practice behavior that they ordinarily have difficulty performing.

Behavior therapy/modification. Therapeutic techniques based on learning principles.

Behaviorism. An approach to understanding behavior that emphasizes the relation between observable behavior and specifiable environmental events (or stimuli).

Biofeedback training. Procedure in which some biological response such as heartbeat or muscle tension is displayed back to persons as an aid in learning to control these responses.

Biogenic amines. Organic chemical compounds that play a role in the transmission of neural impulses.

Bipolar affective disorders. Disorder in which person has shown at least one manic episode. At some time the person is also likely to have experienced a depressive episode. The term manic-depressive psychosis has been used in the past to refer to these disorders.

Case study. The study of an individual person.

Catatonic schizophrenia. Subtype of *schizophrenia;* characterized by rigid, unresponsive immobility and in some instances by violent excitement.

Catharsis. Similar to *abreaction;* refers to expression of pent-up emotion.

Cerebral arteriosclerosis. Condition in which reduced blood supply to parts of the brain becomes reduced as a result of thickening or complete blocking of arteries.

Childhood schizophrenia. Severe psychological disorder of childhood that resembles adult *schizophrenia* in some but not all ways.

Chromosomes. Elongated bodies in cells that carry genetic information; there are 23 pairs of chromosomes in human cells.

Classical conditioning. Sometimes called Pavlovian conditioning; results when a *conditioned stimulus* is repeatedly paired with an *unconditioned stimulus* so that eventually the conditioned stimulus comes to elicit a *conditioned response.*

Client-centered therapy. A type of experiential therapy developed by Carl Rogers that emphasizes letting clients make their own decisions in an accepting atmosphere.

Clinical psychologist. Person who obtains a Ph.D. degree in clinical psychology, including training in assessment, treatment, and research.

Clitoris. Small, heavily innervated, erectile structure located above vaginal opening; site of primary sexual responsiveness in the female.

Cognitions or cognitive mediators. Intervening thoughts or expectations considered to affect overt behavior.

Cognitive-change therapy. Therapeutic procedure that emphasizes changing beliefs, thoughts, and self-statements.

Combat fatigue. Psychological and physical symptoms resulting from the stresses of combat.

Commitment (to mental hospital). Procedure whereby persons can be legally declared mentally ill and hospitalized, even against their wills.

Community psychology. Approach to mental health and disorder that emphasizes the changing of social systems so as to prevent psychological disorders, and the seeking out of potential difficulties, rather than waiting for already disturbed people to come for help.

Compulsion. Action that the person feels irrationally compelled to perform.

Concordance. Term used in twin studies to refer to percentage of co-twins that have the same disorder or trait as the *index twins.*

Conditioned response. A response that has been learned to a *conditioned stimulus* after repeated pairing of an *unconditioned stimulus* with a *conditioned stimulus.*

Conditioned stimulus. An originally neutral stimulus that becomes capable of eliciting a *conditioned response* after repeated pairing with an *unconditioned stimulus.*

Conditioning. A learning process. *See Classical conditioning* and *Operant conditioning.*

Conduct disorders. Usually refers to children who are behaving in a defiant, aggressive, out-of-control fashion.

Conflict-free sphere of the ego. Later development in psychoanalytic theory in which the ego is said to have some capacities and functions independent of the *id;* id-produced conflicts are not necessarily present.

Construct validity. The extent to which a theoretical concept is supported by empirical research.

Control group. Compared with *experimental groups* in *experimental research,* control groups are treated exactly like the experimental group except for the one manipulation being studied.

Conversion disorder. A type of disorder involving bodily symptoms, usually of the skeletal musculature and sensory functions, caused by psychological factors.

Correlation coefficient. A statistical measure of the degree of relationship between two sets of measures that varies between -1.00 and $+1.00$ (e.g., the correlation between height and weight in a sample of people).

Correlational research. Research in which the relationships between two or more *variables* are studied but no experimental manipulations are used.

Counterconditioning. A conditioning process in which a previously learned *conditioned response* is replaced by an incompatible conditioned response through appropriate pairing of stimuli and responses.

Covert sensitization. Form of behavior therapy in which the person is asked to imagine an upsetting scene in order to produce a form of *aversion conditioning.*

Crisis intervention. Psychological intervention at a time of crisis, aimed at preventing the development of more disabling and chronic disorders.

Cultural-familial retardation. Mental retardation thought to represent the lower end of the IQ distribution; believed to be caused by both genetic and environmental factors.

Defense mechanism. General term derived originally from psychoanalytic theory that refers to strategies (e.g., *repression*) whereby a person avoids anxiety-arousing experiences.

Delirium tremens. A severe psychoticlike reaction that occurs in some chronic alcoholics; usually begins in a period of abstinence following a bout of heavy drinking.

Delusion. Belief that is contrary to the consensus of other people.

Dementia. Deterioration and incapacitation in intellectual functioning.

Dementia praecox. Term used by Kraepelin to refer to a form of *psychosis* now called *schizophrenia.*

Demonology. A theory that some forms of abnormal behavior are caused by demon possession.

Denial. A defense mechanism in which the person denies some aspect of internal or external reality.

Depression. A psychological disorder involving dejection, sadness, apathy, and self-blaming attitudes.

Desensitization. *See Systematic desensitization.*

Discriminative stimulus. A stimulus that serves as a signal that a certain response will lead to a *reinforcement.*

Displacement. Defense mechanism in which the person shifts a reaction from some original target person or situation to some other person or situation (e.g., anger displaced from boss to family).

Dissociation or dissociative disorder. An altered state of consciousness in which persons usually cannot remember who they are or any other aspects of their ordinary mental state; nor can they remember the dissociated state when they return to their usual state.

Dopamine. A chemical neurotransmitter (*bigenic amine*) found in the brain, and believed by some to be present in excessive amounts in *schizophrenia.*

Double bind. Situation in which the person receives contradictory messages from an emotionally important person but cannot escape.

Double-blind. Research strategy, used mostly in drug research, in which both patients and drug administrators are "blind" with respect to the nature of the drug being given.

Down's syndrome. A form of mental retardation associated with an extra (47th) *chromosome.*

Drug dependence. State in which the person experiences a compulsive need to use drugs because of either a *psychological* or *physical dependency* or both; in this book used synonymously with *drug addiction.*

Dysthymic disorder. Mild to moderately severe depressions in which environmental events and personality characteristics are thought to play major roles. Also called *neurotic depressions.*

Early infantile autism. Severe social-emotional disorder that begins in early childhood; especially characterized by lack of social responsiveness.

Ego. In Freudian theory that part of the mind that mediates between *id* impulses and external reality.

Ejaculation. The expulsion of semen in male orgasm.

Electroencephalogram or electroencephalograph (EEG). Tracings obtained from an apparatus that measures brainwave patterns from electrodes attached to the outer surface of the scalp.

Electromyogram or electromyograph. Apparatus for measuring muscle tension as indicated by electrical activity in the muscles.

Electroshock treatment (EST) or electroconvulsive treatment (ECT). Therapeutic induction of convulsive seizures by applying electrical current to the head; found to have some effectiveness with severe depressions.

Encounter group. Group including features of the *T-group* and the *sensitivity group,* emphasizes personal growth.

Endogenous depression. Depressions thought to arise primarily from biological and genetic factors.

Enuresis. Chronic bedwetting beyond the age at which bladder control would ordinarily have been acquired.

Enzyme. Complex protein molecule that acts as a catalyst in facilitating metabolic activities such as digestion.

Epilepsy. A disorder involving convulsive seizures and/or altered states of consciousness.

Epileptic seizures. Seizures taking various forms, some of which involve convulsions and others transitory loss or alterations in consciousness. *See Grand mal, Petit mal, and Psychomotor epilepsy.*

Epinephrine (adrenalin). A hormone released from the adrenal medulla during activation of the *sympathetic division* of the *autonomic nervous system;* produces a continuation of many autonomic responses.

Essential hypertension. High blood pressure without known organic cause. Emotional factors are thought to play a role.

Etiology. Refers to the causative factors that determine the development of abnormal behaviors; also used with respect to physical diseases.

Exhibitionist. Person who gains sexual satisfaction from exposing genitalia to others, usually strangers.

Existential approach. Emphasis on making free, "authentic" decisions in the immediate moment.

Exogenous depressions. Depressions thought to be caused to a great degree by external stresses.

Exorcism. Process by which people thought to be possessed by demons are freed of them, usually by prayer and physical abuse.

Expectancy effects. Effects of treatments of abnormal behaviors that result from the person's belief or expectation that the treatment will be effective.

Experiential approach. Usually considered part of

humanistic approach. Emphasis is on here and now subjective experiencing of person.

Experimental group. Group on which the manipulation of interest is performed in an *experimental research* design.

Experimental research. Research in which conditions are manipulated in order to test the effects of manipulations on various measures.

Explosive disorder. Person ordinarily behaves more or less normally but is given to unpredictable outbursts of violence.

Extinction. Repeated presentation of the *conditioned stimulus* without the *unconditioned stimulus;* the frequency and strength of *conditioned responses* tend to decrease, eventually to zero.

Factor analysis. Statistical procedure for estimating how many independent dimensions are necessary to account for the observed relationships among a number of *variables.*

Fetishism. Exclusive use of an object or body part (other than genitals) for sexual arousal and satisfaction.

Fixation. In Freudian theory refers to an unusual investment of *libidinal* energy at a certain *psychosexual stage.*

Flooding. Therapeutic technique in which the person is made to confront the stimuli that arouse anxiety until the anxiety extinguishes.

Fraternal twins. Twins that result from the simultaneous fertilization of two separate ova; such a pair has the same degree of genetic similarity as any two nontwin siblings born to the same parents.

Free association. Basic procedure in psychoanalysis in which the patient is asked to say whatever comes to mind without censorship.

Fugue reaction. A *dissociative reaction* in which the primary characteristic is flight from a distressing situation.

Functional analysis. Term used by behaviorally oriented psychologists to refer to a study of the relationship between an organism's responses and the *reinforcing* contingencies and *discriminative stimuli* in the environment.

Functional psychoses. *Psychoses* without known organic causes.

Gene. Unit of hereditary information carried in a chromosome by DNA.

General paresis. Severe disorder characterized by various mental symptoms as well as bodily paralyses; caused by a syphilitic infection in the brain.

Generalization. Extent to which an observation or research finding can be applied to other settings or to other populations. See also *stimulus generalization.*

Genotype. Total set of inherited characteristics determined by a person's genetic makeup.

Gestalt therapy. Therapeutic approach developed by Frederick Perls that focuses on experiencing in the here and now.

Glove anesthesia. Lack of feeling or numbness in an area of the hand and wrist that would be covered by a glove.

Grand mal epilepsy. Type of *epilepsy* involving a convulsive seizure and loss of consciousness.

Habituation. Lessening of a response (usually a physiological response) as a function of repeated presentations of the same eliciting stimulus.

Halfway house. A group living situation in which former mental patients or drug addicts have a chance to adjust to the outside world in a supervised environment before becoming completely independent.

Hallucination. Experience of sensations or perceptions from an external source when in fact there is no external source.

Hallucinogens. A class of drugs, including LSD, that produce dramatic changes in sensory and perceptual experiences.

Hebephrenic schizophrenia. Subtype of *schizophrenia* characterized by severe personality disorganization and inappropriate mannerisms.

Heroin. Opiate drug derived from morphine; can produce strong physical and psychological dependency.

Hippocampus. Part of *limbic system* of the brain; involved in emotional and motivational functions.

Homeostatic mechanism. Process whereby equilibrium or balance is maintained in a dynamic system.

Humanistic approach. Emphasis on viewing people as whole human beings rather than on analyzing them in an impersonal fashion.

Huntington's disease. A rare and fatal form of mental and physical disorder inherited as a dominant trait; symptoms include psychotic behavior and spasmodic jerking of the limbs.

Hyperactivity. Label rather loosely applied to children who are unusually active, restless, distractable, and lacking in a normal attention span.

Hypnosis. A trancelike state induced through suggestion in cooperative subjects.

Hysteria. *Neurosis* involving bodily symptoms or altered states of consciousness.

Hysterical personality. Pattern of personality characteristics that includes self-centeredness, exhibitionism, emotional lability and strong dependency.

Id. In Freudian theory that part of the mind from which instinctual impulses originate.

Idea of reference. False interpretation of events in terms of special meaning for the self.

Identical twins. Twins resulting from the splitting of a single fertilized ovum who have exactly the same genetic makeup.

Identification. In Freudian theory a *defense mechanism* in which the person takes in or incorporates aspects of the behavior of another person.

Imipramine. Antidepressant drug in the *tricyclic compounds* group; most effect with *unipolar depressions*.

Implosive therapy. Form of *flooding* therapy.

Impotence. Inability by a male to maintain erection for purposes of sexual intercourse.

Index twin. Term used in twin studies to refer to the one twin that was originally diagnosed as having a certain characteristic, such as schizophrenia.

Infantile autism. See *Early infantile autism.*

Insanity. Legal term implying severe mental incapacitation as in psychoses.

Insight-therapy. Term used to refer to approaches to psychotherapy that emphasize self-understanding and the relationship between therapist and patient.

Instrumental conditioning or learning. See *Operant learning.*

Intellectualization. Defense mechanism in which the person *isolates* or otherwise suppresses emotional reactions ordinarily associated with what the person is thinking about or doing.

Internalization. Process whereby individuals incorporate the do's and don't's of parents and society; similar to the concepts of conscience and *superego.*

Interobserver reliability. Extent to which independent observers can agree on a rating or other score.

Intrapsychic. Refers to unobservable mental events such as ideas, wishes, and unconscious conflicts.

IQ or intelligence quotient. Estimate of relative intellectual ability; IQ = *mental age* divided by chronological age, multiplied by 100.

Isolation. *Defense mechanism* in which person separates emotions from intellectual content, or otherwise separates experiences that would be anxiety arousing if permitted to occur together.

Korsakoff's psychosis. *Psychosis* produced by vitamin B deficiency, usually occurring in chronic alcoholics; loss of memory and confabulation (filling in memory gaps with falsehoods) are prominent symptoms.

La belle indifference. Unconcern frequently shown by *hysterical* patients about their symptoms.

Latency period. In Freudian theory a stage that follows the *phallic stage* and repression of the *oedipal conflict.*

Learned helplessness. Reaction that results from experiencing inescapable aversive stimuli or other situations in which there is nothing that the person can do to effect desired changes in the environment.

Libido. Psychoanalytic concept referring to the sexual instincts.

Limbic system. That part of the primitive, lower part of the cortex associated with emotional and motivational functions.

Lobotomy. *See Prefrontal lobotomy.*

Major depression. Severe depression, sometimes with psychotic features such as delusions. Recurring major depressions without manic episodes are called *unipolar depressions.*

Malingering. The intentional faking of an abnormal behavior symptom.

Mania. A disorder involving extreme euphoria, hyperactivity, and grandiose thinking.

Manic-depressive reaction or psychosis. Severe *psychosis* characterized by extreme swings in mood toward either *depression* or *mania* or both. Term no longer used in DSM-III.

Masochism. Preference for obtaining sexual gratification by experiencing pain inflicted on oneself.

McNaghten rule. Decree by the British courts in 1843 that a person could be found not guilty by reason of insanity if the person could not tell right from wrong.

Mediating processes. Unobservable thoughts, emotions, drive states, or other processes that affect a person's behavior.

Medical model. Views of abnormal behavior as analogous to physical disease; seeks underlying causes for symptoms.

Mental age (MA). Scale unit, independent of chronological age, corresponding to the age at which intelligence test performance represents the average for that age; a four-year-old child, for example, might have a mental age of 6 years.

Mental illness. *See Abnormal behavior.*

Mentalistic. Refers to psychological theories based on subjective and unobservable mental events.

Mesmerism. Closely related to the phenomenon of *hypnosis;* term derived from the techniques of Anton Mesmer.

Migraine headache. Headache associated with spasms of the cranial arteries and dilation of blood vessels in the brain.

Milieu therapy. *See Therapeutic community.*

Minimal brain dysfunction. Label sometimes rather loosely applied to children who are hyperactive and show possible signs of neurological dysfunction.

Minnesota Multiphasic Personality Inventory (MMPI). Personality questionnaire developed as an aid in diagnosing various forms of abnormal behavior.

Monoamine oxidase (MAO) inhibitors. Class of antidepressant drugs found to be effective with some depressions.

Multiple personality. Rare *dissociative reaction* in which relatively separate and distinctive personalities develop within the same person.

Narcotics. Drugs that can result in physiological dependence and increased tolerance. *See Opiates.*

Neurosis. Non*psychotic* psychological disorder involving a variety of symptoms such as *anxiety, depression, hysteria,* or *obsessions* and *compulsions.* No longer used in DSM-III.

Neurotic depression. *Depression* of moderate severity but without the extreme symptoms or delusions associated with more severe depressions. Called *dysthymic disorder* in DSM-III.

Neurotic traits. Styles of behavior, usually originating in early childhood, that serve a protective or avoidance function in the personality.

Neurosyphilis. Same as *general paresis.*

Nonspecific effects. All effects in psychological treatment that do not result from the specific treatment technique, such as *placebo* or *expectancy effects.*

Norepinephrine (noradrenalin). Hormone or *biogenic amine* that plays a chemical role in the transmission of neural impulses in many parts of the body, including the brain.

Normal curve. Bell-shaped distribution usually found when a large sample of individuals is measured on most psychological characteristics or traits.

Normative research. Research that provides descriptive information about some sample of persons.

Observational learning. Responses learned on the basis of observing other organisms make (model) the response.

Obsession. Thoughts and impulses (usually unacceptable) that intrude into awareness; the person experiences these intrusions as alien and uncontrollable.

Obsessive-compulsive disorder. Type of disorder characterized by *obsessions* and *compulsions.* A form of *anxiety disorder* in DSM-III.

Oedipal conflict or complex. In Freudian theory the erotic attachment to opposite-sex parent, involving feelings of competition and hostility toward the same-sex parent, and fears of retaliation (castration anxiety in boys) from the same-sex parent.

Operant conditioning or learning. Learning process in which the organism learns to make a response in certain situations because the response brings *reinforcement.*

Opiates. Form of drug on which a person can become *physiologically dependent;* has analgesic and pain reducing properties and can induce euphoric mood.

Oral stage. In Freudian theory an early stage in which *libidinal* satisfactions center around such oral activities as eating, sucking, and chewing.

Organic brain syndrome. Psychological and physical disturbances caused by some known physical disease or injury to the brain.

Organic psychoses. *Psychoses* with known and identifiable organic causes.

Organic view. Belief that *abnormal behavior* is caused primarily by biological factors.

Orgasmic reconditioning. Conditioning procedure, usually involving masturbation, designed to change object of sexual arousal, for example, from *fetishistic* object to heterosexual contact.

Paranoia. Type of *psychosis* characterized primarily by a well-organized delusional belief.

Paranoid schizophrenia. A subtype of *schizophrenia* characterized by *delusions, hallucinations,* and some personality disorganization.

Paraphilias. Sexual deviations in which the person obtains sexual satisfaction primarily with nonhuman objects or through sexual activity with humans involving pain or humiliation.

Paraprofessional. Individual who has not had formal training or obtained a degree in one of the mental health professions, but who is given brief training and on-the-job experience as a mental health worker.

Parasympathetic nervous system. Division of the *autonomic nervous system* primarily involved in conservation of energy, such as increasing digestive processes.

Partial or intermittent reinforcement. Schedule of *reinforcement* in which reward is not given every time the organism makes the response; tends to produce learning that is more resistant to extinction.

Pedophiliac. Person who seeks sexual satisfaction with young children.

Personality disorders. Includes a variety of life-long personality characteristics such as neurotic traits, milder forms of psychotic reactions and antisocial

behaviors; acute symptoms are usually not present.

Petit mal epilepsy. Form of epileptic seizure in which there is a momentary loss of consciousness but no convulsive seizure.

Phallic stage. In Freudian theory a stage in which the young child's *libidinal* instincts begin to center in the genital area.

Phenomenological approach. Approach that emphasizes understanding the person's world as the person experiences it.

Phenothiazine drugs. Class of drugs that have been found effective in reducing symptoms of *schizophrenia;* sometimes called major tranquilizers.

Phenotype. Observed characteristics that result from the interaction between *genotype* and environmental influences.

Phenylketonuria. Rare form of mental retardation caused by error in protein metabolism, recessively inherited.

Phobia. Strong, irrational fear of some specific object, animal, or situation.

Physical dependency on drugs. Condition necessitating continuing use of drugs because an intense physical disturbance occurs when drug use is suspended (the *withdrawal* or *abstinence syndrome*).

Placebo. Usually an inert pill or liquid; the experimental subject, however, may be told that it will have important effects.

Placebo effect. Any effect caused by creating a belief or expectancy that a change will occur.

Post-traumatic stress disorder. Psychological symptoms, usually anxiety in some form, resulting from intense stress such as wartime combat or a natural disaster.

Prefrontal lobotomy. Operation that severs the nerve tracts from the frontal lobes to the lower centers of the brain; in the past used as a treatment for severe and chronic schizophrenia.

Premorbid adjustment. Usually refers to adjustment of schizophrenic persons before they become schizophrenic; often categorized as good or poor premorbid adjustment.

Presenile dementias. Relatively rare disorders that begin in late middle-age, involve progressive degeneration of brain tissues, and produce symptoms similar to *senile dementia.*

Primary process thinking. Freudian concept of the illogical and emotionally determined thought processes associated with the *id* or the unconscious.

Primary reinforcers. Events, usually biological in nature, that almost always provide *reinforcement,* such as eating when hungry; primary reinforcers do not acquire their reinforcing properties through learning.

Process schizophrenia. Type or endpoint on a continuum representing *schizophrenia* with gradual onset, poor premorbid history, and low likelihood of recovery.

Projection. *Defense mechanism* in which the person disowns some impulse and attributes it to another person.

Projective tests. Tests on which the person is presented with ambiguous stimulus materials and asked to respond in some way; based on assumption that persons project characteristics of their own *intrapsychic* processes into their responses.

Psychiatric social worker. Person who has obtained Master of Social Work degree with specialization for work with patients and families in psychiatric settings.

Psychiatrist. Physician who specializes in the treatment of psychological disorders.

Psychoanalysis. Form of treatment of abnormal behavior developed by Freud.

Psychoanalyst. Person, usually an MD, who has received specialized training at a psychoanalytic institute.

Psychological dependence on drugs. Condition in which person requires continuing use of drugs to produce pleasure or avoid psychological discomfort.

Psychological handicap. Condition in which person experiences a restriction in alternative behaviors.

Psychomotor epilepsy. Type of *epileptic seizure* in which there is a disturbance in consciousness during which the person may engage in "automatic" behavior or wander aimlessly.

Psychopathic personality. Same as *antisocial personality.*

Psychopathology. *See Abnormal behavior.*

Psychosexual development. In Freud's theory a series of certain biologically determined stages through which individuals pass: the five stages are *oral, anal, phallic, latency,* and *adult genital.*

Psychosis. Severe psychological disturbance involving personality disorganization and loss of contact with reality.

Psychosomatic or psychophysiological disorder. Physical symptoms, usually involving the *autonomic nervous system,* caused in part by psychological factors.

Racial or collective unconscious. Jung's idea that all humanity shares certain racial memories in an unconscious part of the mind.

Radical behaviorism. Model of human behavior that focuses on the relation between observable behavior and environmental stimuli.

Random sample. Individuals (or other entities) selected by chance from some larger population.

Rational-emotive therapy. Therapeutic approach developed by Albert Ellis that emphasizes *cognitive-change techniques.*

Reaction formation. *Defense mechanism* in which person behaves in a way directly opposite from some underlying impulse.

Reactive depression. Sometimes used synonomously with *neurotic depression;* emphasizes importance of precipitating environmental events.

Reactive schizophrenia. Type or endpoint on a continuum representing a schizophrenic disorder with abrupt onset, good premorbid history, and good likelihood of recovery.

Recidivism. Repetition of previous acts, as in tendency of some criminals to relapse into illegal activities for which they are convicted.

Regression. In Freudian theory refers to a return to some earlier stage of *psychosexual development* in the face of some current frustration.

Reinforcement. Consequence following a response that increases the likelihood that, in the same situation, the response will be repeated in the future.

Reliability. Extent to which a scale consistently measures the same thing.

Repression. *Defense mechanism* in which an anxiety-arousing memory or impulse is prevented from becoming conscious.

Resistance. In psychoanalysis the phenomenon in which patients unconsciously resist gaining insight into unconscious motives and conflicts.

Resistance to extinction. Extent to which the organism continues to make a learned response after all reinforcements have been withdrawn.

Reticular formation. Location in brain stem, contributes to arousal of the cortex and to processing of incoming stimulation.

Reversal design. Experimental design in which new reinforcement contingencies are instated for a period of time, followed by reinstatement of the old reinforcement contingencies, and finally the installment of the original, new contingencies; sometimes a fourth reversal is included. Purpose is to show that the new contingencies are causing any observed changes in behavior.

Ritalin. A stimulant drug (methylphenidate) used to treat *hyperactive* children.

Rorschach test. Test composed of ambiguous ink blots to which the person reacts; responses are thought to indicate important aspects of the individual's personality.

Sadism. Preference for obtaining sexual gratification by inflicting pain on partner.

Sample. In psychological research, sample refers to the selection, usually random, of a group of individuals (or other entities) representative of some larger population.

Schizoaffective disorder. A disorder that includes symptoms of *mania* as well as symptoms of *schizophrenia*.

Schizophrenia. A severe *psychosis* involving disturbed thought processes and various emotional and behavioral symptoms.

Secondary reinforcers. Events or stimuli that are not innately sources of reinforcement can acquire secondary reinforcing properties as a result of being paired with *primary reinforcers.*

Self-reinforcement. *Reinforcement* given by the individual to him- or herself.

Senile dementia. Psychological disturbance resulting from progressive degeneration of brain tissues; characterized by loss of immediate memory, poor judgment, and everyday habits of hygiene.

Sensitivity group. Group similar to the *T-group* but with more emphasis on acquiring understanding of how one affects other people.

Separation anxiety. Anxiety that some young children show on being separated from a parent or other caretaker.

Serotonin. A hormone or *biogenic amine* that plays a role in the transmission of neural impulses in the brain.

Sheltered workshop. A supervised job or occupational training situation for mentally retarded or other handicapped people.

Significant difference. Statistical concept that the probability of an occurrence is greater than through chance alone. For example, a difference between two means is considered significant if a difference of this magnitude would occur by chance less than 1 out of 20 occasions.

Social learning approach. Behaviorally oriented approach to the study of human behavior that applies principles derived from the scientific study of learning, and includes some mediating processes in its theoretical formulations.

Socialized conduct disorder. Aggressive or antisocial behavior performed as part of a subculture or gang.

Societal-reaction theory. Theory that many symptoms of abnormal behavior are secondary responses to society's reaction to some initial deviance.

Sodomy. Anal intercourse.

Somnambulism. *Dissociative reaction* that occurs in a sleeplike state; sometimes called sleep walking. In DSM-III listed under disorders first evident in childhood and simply called sleep walking.

Stimulus generalization. Tendency to respond to similar stimuli other than the original stimuli to which one learned to respond.

Stress. Situation or stimulus that strains the psychological or physiological capacities of the organism.

Sublimation. Nonpathological *defense mechanism* in which *libidinal* (sexual) energy is redirected into more socially acceptable modes of expression.

Superego. In Freudian theory the internalized representative of parental or cultural values.

Sympathetic nervous system. Division of the *autonomic nervous system* primarily involved in stress or emergency reactions. For example, produces an increase in heartrate and blood pressure.

Symptom substitution. Concept derived primarily from the psychodynamic approach, in which it is proposed that if a symptom is removed without attention to underlying processes another symptom will take its place.

Syndrome. Pattern of symptoms that tends to occur together in a particular disease.

Systematic desensitization. Therapeutic technique based on counterconditioning principles, used primarily with *phobias* and *anxiety disorders*.

Systems approach. In this view abnormal behavior is seen as residing in the system of interaction among several individuals, as in a family system.

T-group. Training group in which participants learn about the dynamics of effective group functioning.

Tardive dyskinesia. Occasional long term side-effect of phenothiazine treatment of schizophrenia. Involves rhythmical, stereotyped movements and lip smacking.

Temperament. Behavioral characteristics present at an early age and considered to have some basis in biological processes partly determined by heredity.

Temporal lobe epilepsy. Form of *epileptic seizure* associated with lesions or *EEG* abnormalities in the temporal lobe of the brain; sometimes associated with violent behavior.

Thematic Apperception Test (TAT). Test consisting

of a series of pictures about which the subject tells stories; thought to indicate important aspects of the individual's personality.

Therapeutic community. Attempt to create a therapeutic environment on an entire ward or section of a hospital by emphasizing humane attitudes and encouraging responsible participation in decision making by patients. Also called milieu therapy.

Tic. Involuntary muscular twitching, usually in the facial muscles.

Token economy. A group approach to treatment based on the *operant learning model;* makes uses of tokens as reinforcers for desired behaviors.

Tolerance to drugs. Condition in which the continued use of some drugs results in the need for larger and larger doses to produce the same effect.

Transactional Analysis. Form of group therapy developed by Eric Berne.

Transference. Irrational emotional reaction of a patient to the therapist (usually in psychoanalysis) in which early attitudes toward parents are "transferred" to the therapist.

Transsexual. Person whose sense of sexual identity is contrary to his or her biological makeup.

Transvestite. Person who gets sexual pleasure from dressing in clothes of the opposite sex.

Traumatic neuroses. Neurotic symptoms resulting from an acute stress situation. *See Post-traumatic stress disorders.*

Tricyclic compound. Kind of antidepressant drug found to be most effective with *unipolar depressions.*

Unconditioned response. Response which occurs naturally or innately to an *unconditioned stimulus.*

Unconditioned stimulus. Stimulus that is naturally capable of eliciting a certain response (*the unconditioned response*).

Unconscious motivation. Important concept in psychoanalytic theory that states that people are not aware of many impulses and conflicts that determine their behavior.

Undersocialized conduct disorder. Individual engages in various forms of antisocial behavior and does not show a normal degree of attachment or loyalty to friends or family.

Undoing. *Defense mechanism* in which the person engages in some action or thought process designed to "undo" imagined harm resulting from an unacceptable impulse.

Unipolar affective disorder. Disorder in which the person experiences recurring *major depressions.*

Validity. The extent to which a scale measures what it is supposed to.

Variable. Characteristic on which people, objects, or situations vary.

Voyeur. Person who gains sexual gratification by looking (peeping) at nude persons or at sexual activity between other people.

Withdrawal syndrome. Consequence of physical dependency on drugs; involves intense physical reaction when drug is discontinued.

Working through. In psychoanalysis the time consuming process whereby the patient gains insight into all aspects of a particular conflict.

References

Aarens, M., Cameron, T., Roizen, J., Roizen, R., Room, R., Schneberk, D., & Wingard, D. *Alcohol casualties and crime.* Special report prepared for National Institute on Alcohol Abuse and Alcoholism under contract no. ADM 281-76-0027, 1977.

Abrahamsen, D. Unmasking 'Son of Sam's' demons. *New York Times Magazine,* July, 1979.

Abrahamson, L. Y., Seligman, M. E. P., & Teasdale, J. D. Learned helplessness in humans: Critique and reformulation. *Journal of Abnormal Psychology,* 1978, *87,* 49–74.

Achenbach, T. M. *Developmental psychopathology.* New York: Ronald, 1974.

Ackerman, P. T., Dykman, R. A., & Peters, J. E. Teenage status of hyperactive and nonhyperactive learning disabled boys. *American Journal of Orthopsychiatry,* 1977, *47,* 577–597.

Adams, H. E., Feuerstein, M., & Fowler, J. L. Migraine headache: Review of parameters, etiology, and intervention. *Psychological Bulletin,* 1980, *82,* 217–237.

Adams, H. E., & Sturgis, E. T. Status of behavioral reorientation techniques in the modification of homosexuality: A review. *Psychological Bulletin,* 1977, *84,* 1171–1188.

Adams, P. L. *Obsessive children.* New York: Brunner/Mazel, 1973.

Ahlenius, S., Carlsson, A., Engel, J., Svensson, H., & Sodersten, P. Antagonism by alphamethylthyrosine of the ethanol-induced stimulation and euphoria in man. *Clinical Pharmacology and Therapeutics,* 1973, *14,* 586–591.

Ainsworth, M. D. S., & Bell, S. M. Some contemporary patterns of mother-infant interaction in the feeding situation. In J. A. Ambrose (Ed.), *Stimulation in early infancy.* London: Academic Press, 1969.

Ainsworth, M. D. S., Bell, S. M., & Stayton, D. J. Individual differences in strange-situation behavior of one-year-olds. In H. R. Schaffer (Ed.), *The origins of human social relations.* London: Academic Press, 1971.

Ainsworth, M. D. S., Blehar, M. C., Waters, E., & Wall, S. *Patterns of attachment: A psychological study of the strange situation.* Hillsdale, N. J.: Erlbaum, 1978.

Akinkugbe, O. O. *High blood pressure in the African.* London: Churchill Livingstone, 1972.

Akiskal, H. S., Bitar, A. H., Puzantin, V. R., Rosenthal, T. L., & Parks, W. W. The nosological status of the neurotic depression. *Archives of General Psychiatry,* 1978, *35,* 756–766.

Akiskal, H. S., & McKinney, W. T. Overview of recent research on depression. *Archives of General Psychiatry,* 1975, *32,* 285–304.

Albee, G. W. Myths, models, and manpower. *Mental Hygiene,* 1968, *52,* 2–10.

Alexander, F., & French, T. M. *Psychoanalytic therapy.* New York: Ronald, 1946.

Alexander, J. F., & Parsons, B. V. Short-term behavioral intervention with delinquent families: Impact on family process and recidivism. *Journal of Abnormal Psychology,* 1973, *81,* 199–218.

Allen, K. E., & Harris, F. R. Elimination of a child's excessive scratching by training the mother in reinforcement procedures. *Behaviour Research and Therapy,* 1966, *4,* 79–84.

Allen, K. E., Hart, B. Buell, J. S., Harris, F. R., & Wolf, M. M. Effects of social reinforcement on isolate behavior of a nursery school child. *Child Development,* 1964, *35,* 511–518.

American Psychological Association Monitor. Washington, D.C., March 1974.

American Psychological Association Monitor. Washington, D.C., May 1975.

Amit, Z., Brown, Z. W., Levitan, D. E., & Ogren, S. O. Noradrenergic medication of the positive reinforcing properties of ethanol. *Archives Interna-*

tionales de Pharmacodynamie et de Therapie, 1977, *230,* 65–75.

Anastasi, A. Psychological testing. New York: Macmillan, 1961.

Anders, T. Short-term memory for presented supraspan information in nonretarded and mentally retarded individuals. *American Journal of Mental Deficiency,* 1971, *75,* 571–578.

Angrist, B. M., & Gershon, S. The phenomenology of experimentally induced amphetamine psychosis: Preliminary observations. *Biological Psychiatry,* 1970, *2,* 97–107.

Angrist, B. M., Sathananthan, G., Wilk, S., & Gershon, S. In E. Usdin & S. H. Snyder (Eds.), *Frontiers in catecholamine research.* New York: Pergamon, 1974.

Angst, J. The etiology and nosology of endogenous depressive psychoses. *Foreign Psychiatry,* 1973, *2,* 1–108.

Anonymous. On being diagnosed schizophrenic. *Schizophrenia Bulletin,* 1977, *3,* 4.

Anthony, W. A., Buell, G. J., Sharratt, S., & Althoff, M. E. Efficacy of psychiatric rehabilitation. *Psychological Bulletin,* 1972, *78,* 447–456.

Aponte, H., & Hoffman, L. The open door: A structural approach to a family with an anorectic child. *Family Process,* 1973, *12,* 1–44.

Archibald, H. C., & Tuddenham, R. D. Persistent stress reaction after combat. *Archives of General Psychiatry,* 1965, *12,* 475–481.

Aronfreed, J. *Conduct and conscience.* New York: Academic Press, 1968.

Aronfreed, J., & Paskal, V. Altruism, empathy, and the conditioning of positive affect. Unpublished manuscript, University of Pennsylvania, 1965. (Also described in Aronfreed, 1968.)

Aronson, E. *The social animal.* San Francisco: W. H. Freeman, 1972.

Arthurs, R. G. S., & Cahoon, E. B. A clinical and electroencephalographic survey of psychopathic personality. *American Journal of Psychiatry,* 1964, *120,* 875–882.

Asarnow, R. F., & MacCrimmon, D. J. Residual performance deficit in clinically remitted schizophrenics: A marker of schizophrenia. *Journal of Abnormal Psychology,* 1978, *87,* 597–608.

Asarnow, R. F., Steffy, R. A., & MacCrimmon, D. J. An attentional assessment of foster children at risk for schizophrenia. *Journal of Abnormal Psychology,* 1977, *86,* 267–275.

Asberg, M., Thoren, P., Traskman, L., Bertilsson, L., & Ringberger, V. "Serotonin depression"—A biochemical subgroup within the affective disorders. *Science,* 1976, *191,* 478–480.

Asberg, M., Traskman, L., & Thoren, P. 5-HIAA in the cerebrospinal fluid: A biochemical suicide predictor? *Archives of General Psychiatry,* 1976, *33,* 1193–1197.

Atkinson, E. Four hours on the suicide phones. *Bulletin of Suicidology.* Chevy Chase, Md.: National Institute of Mental Health, 1970, No. 7.

Atthowe, J. M., & Krasner, L. Preliminary report on the application of contingent reinforcement procedures (token economy) on a "chronic" psychiatric ward. *Journal of Abnormal Psychology,* 1968, *73,* 37–43.

Auerback, A. H., & Luborsky, L. Accuracy of judgments and the nature of the "good hour." In J. M. Shlien (Ed.), *Research in psychotherapy,* Vol. III. Washington, D.C.: American Psychological Association, 1968.

Avery, D., & Winokur, G. The efficacy of electroconvulsive therapy and antidepressants in depression. *Biological Psychiatry,* 1977, *12,* 507–523.

Ayllon, T., & Haughton, E. Modification of symptomatic verbal behavior of mental patients. *Behaviour Research and Therapy,* 1964, *2,* 87–97.

Ax, A. F., Beckett, P. G. S., Cohen, B. D., Frohman, C. E., Tourney, G., & Gottlieb, J. S. Psychophysiological patterns in chronic schizophrenia. In J. Wortis (Ed.), *Recent advances in biological psychiatry,* Vol. 4. New York: Plenum, 1962.

Azrin, N. H., Sneed, T. J., & Foxx, R. M. Drybed training: Rapid elimination of childhood enuresis. *Behaviour Research and Therapy,* 1974, *12,* 147–156.

Azrin, N. H., & Thienes, P. M. Rapid elimination of enuresis by intensive learning without a conditioning apparatus. *Behavior Therapy,* 1978, *9,* 342–354.

Bacopoulos, N. C., Spokes, E. G., Bird, E. D., & Roth, R. H. Antipsychotic drug action in schizophrenic patients: Effect on cortical dopamine metabolism after long-term treatment. *Science,* 1979, *205,* 1405–1407.

Baechler, J. *Suicides.* New York: Basic Books, 1979.

Baer, L., Durell, J., & Bunney, W. E. Sodium balance and distribution in lithium carbonate therapy. *Archives of General Psychiatry,* 1970, *22,* 40–44.

Ball, J. C., & Chambers, C. D. *The epidemiology of opiate addiction in the United States.* Springfield, Ill.: Charles C Thomas, 1970.

Ballar, W. R., Charles, D. C., & Miller, E. L. Midlife attainment of the mentally retarded: A longitudinal study. *Genetic Psychology Monographs,* 1967, *74,* 235–329.

Baller, W., & Schalock, H. Conditioned response treatment of enuresis. *Exceptional Child,* 1956, *22,* 233–236.

Bandura, A. *Principles of behavior modification.* New York: Holt, Rinehart and Winston, 1969.

Bandura, A. *Social learning theory.* Englewood Cliffs, N.J.: Prentice-Hall, 1977.

Bandura, A., Adams, N. E., & Beyer, J. Cognitive processes mediating behavioral change. *Journal of Personality and Social Psychology,* 1977, *35,* 125–139.

Bandura, A., Blanchard, E. B., & Ritter, B. Relative efficacy of desensitization and modeling approaches for inducing behavioral, affective, and attitudinal changes. *Journal of Personality and Social Psychology,* 1969, *13,* 173–199.

Bandura, A., Grusec, J. E., & Menlove, F. L. Vicarious extinction of avoidance behavior. *Journal of Personality and Social Psychology,* 1967, *5,* 16–23. (a)

Bandura, A., Grusec, J. E., & Menlove, F. L. Some social determinants of self-monitoring reinforcement systems. *Journal of Personality and Social Psychology,* 1967, *5,* 449–455. (b)

Barkley, R. A. A review of stimulant drug research with hyperactive children. *Journal of Child Psychology and Psychiatry,* 1977, *18,* 137–165.

Barlow, D. H. Behavioral assessment in clinical settings: Developing issues. In J. D. Cove and R. P. Hawkins (Eds.), *Behavioral assessment: New directions in clinical psychology.* New York: Brunner/Mazel, 1977.

Barlow, D. H., Leitenberg, H., & Agras, W. S. Experimental control of sexual deviation through manipulation of the noxious scene in covert sensitization. *Journal of Abnormal Psychology,* 1969, *74,* 596–601.

Barlow, D. H., Reynolds, J., & Agras, S. Gender identity change in a transsexual. *Archives of General Psychiatry,* 1973, *28,* 569–576.

Baroff, G. S. *Mental retardation: Nature, cause and management.* Washington, D.C.: Hemisphere, 1974.

Bassuk, E. L., & Gerson, S. Deinstitutionalization and mental health services. *Scientific American,* 1978, *238,* 46–53.

Bateson, G., Jackson, D. D., Haley, J., & Weakland, J. Toward a theory of schizophrenia. *Behavioral Science,* 1956, *1,* 251–264.

Baum, M. Extinction of avoidance responding through response prevention (flooding). *Psychological Bulletin,* 1970, *74,* 274–284.

Bayley, N. Development of mental abilities. In P. H. Mussen (Ed.), *Carmichael's manual of child psychology,* 3d ed., Vol. I. New York: Wiley, 1970, 1175–1176.

Bazelon, D. Psychiatrists and the adversary process. *Scientific American,* 1974, *230,* 18–23.

Beck, A. T. *Cognitive therapy and emotional disorders.* New York: International Universities Press, 1976.

Beck, A. T., Rush, A. J., Shaw, B. F., & Emery, G. *Cognitive therapy of depression.* New York: Guilford Press, 1979.

Beck, A. T., Ward, C. H., Mendelson, M., Mock, J. E., & Erbaugh, J. K. Reliability of psychiatric diagnoses II: A study of consistency of clinical judgments and ratings. *American Journal of Psychiatry,* 1962, *119,* 351–357.

Beck, A. T., & Young, J. E. College blues. *Psychology Today,* September 1978.

Beckwith, L. Relationships between attributes of mothers and their infants' IQ scores. *Child Development,* 1971, *42,* 1083–1097.

Bee, H. L., Van Egeren, L. F., Streissguth, A. P., Nyman, B. A., & Leckie, M. S. Social class differences in maternal teaching strategies and speech patterns. *Developmental Psychology,* 1969, *1,* 726–734.

Beech, H. R., & Fransella, F. *Research and experiment in stuttering.* Oxford: Pergamon, 1968.

Beigel, A., & Murphy, D. L. Unipolar and bipolar affective illness. *Archives of General Psychiatry,* 1971, *24,* 215–220.

Bell, A. P., & Weinberg, M. S. *Homosexualities: A study of diversity among men and women.* New York: Simon and Schuster, 1978.

Bemis, K. M. Current approaches to the etiology and treatment of anorexia nervosa. *Psychological Bulletin,* 1978, *85,* 593–617.

Bemporad, J. R. Adult recollections of a formerly autistic child. *Journal of Autism and Developmental Disorders,* 1979, *9,* 179–197.

Bender, L. Twenty years of research on schizophrenic children with special reference to those under twenty years of age. In G. Kaplan (Ed.), *Emotional problems of early childhood.* New York: Basic Books, 1955.

Bender, L. The life course of children with schizophrenia. *American Journal of Psychiatry,* 1973, *130,* 783–786.

Bender, L. The family patterns of 100 schizophrenic

children observed at Bellevue, 1935–1952. *Journal of Autism and Childhood Schizophrenia,* 1974, *4,* 279–292.

Benedict, R. Anthropology and the abnormal. *Journal of General Psychology,* 1934, *10,* 59–82.

Benson, H. *The relaxation response.* New York: Morrow, 1975.

Benson, H., & Wallace, R. K. Decreased blood pressure in hypertensive subjects who practiced meditation. *Circulation,* Supplement II, 1972, Vols. 45 & 46.

Bergin, A. E. The effects of psychotherapy: Negative results revisited. *Journal of Counseling Psychology,* 1963, *10,* 244–250.

Bergin, A. E., & Lambert, M. J. The evaluation of therapeutic outcomes. In S. L. Garfield & A. E. Bergin (Eds.), *Handbook of psychotherapy and behavior change.* New York: Wiley, 1978.

Berkman, L. F., & Syme, S. L. Social networks, host resistance, and mortality: A nine-year follow-up study of Alameda County residents. *American Journal of Epidemiology,* 1979, *109,* 186–204.

Berle, B. B., Pinsky, R. H., Wolf, S., & Wolff, H. G. Appraisal of the results of treatment in stress disorders. *Research Publication of the Association for Nervous and Mental Diseases,* 1953, *31,* 167–177.

Berne, E. Games people play. New York: Grove Press, 1964.

Berry, R., Boland, J., Smart, C., & Kanak, J. *The economic costs of alcohol abuse and alcoholism—1975.* Report prepared for National Institute on Alcohol Abuse and Alcoholism, 1977.

Bertelsen, A., Harvald, A., & Hauge, M. A Danish twin study of manic-depressive disorders. *British Journal of Psychiatry,* 1977, *130,* 330–351.

Bettelheim, B. *Truants from life.* Glencoe, Ill.: The Free Press, 1955.

Bettelheim, B. *The empty fortress.* New York: Free Press, 1967.

Bettelheim, B. *A home for the heart.* New York: Knopf, 1973.

Bieber, I. A discussion of "homosexuality: The ethical challenge." *Journal of Consulting and Clinical Psychology,* 1976, *44,* 163–166.

Bieber, I., Dain, H. J., Dince, P. R., Drelich, M. G., Grand, H. C., Gundlach, R. H., Kremer, M. W., Rifkin, A. H., Wilbur, C. B., & Bieber, T. B. *Homosexuality: A psychoanalytical study.* New York: Random House, 1962.

Billings, A. Conflict resolution in distressed and nondistressed married couples. *Journal of Consulting and Clinical Psychology,* 1979, *47,* 368–376.

Binitie, A. A factor-analytical study of depression across cultures (African and European). *British Journal of Psychiatry,* 1975, *127,* 559–563.

Binswanger, L. *Being in the world.* New York: Harper & Row, 1967.

Birch, H. G., & Cravioto, J. Infection, nutrition, and environment in mental development. In H. V. Eichenwald (Ed.), *The prevention of mental retardation through the control of infectious disease* (Public Health Service Publication No. 1692). Washington, D.C.; Government Printing Office, 1966.

Birchler, G. R., Weiss, R. L., & Wampler, L. D. Differential patterns of social reinforcement as a function of degree of marital distress and level of intimacy. Paper presented at the Western Psychological Association meeting in Portland, Oregon, April 1972.

Birren, J. E. Psychological aspects of aging: Intellectual functioning. *Gerontologist,* 1968, *8,* 16–19.

Blackburn, R. Psychopathy arousal, and the need for stimulation. In R. D. Hare & D. Schalling (Eds.), *Psychopathic behavior: Approaches to research.* New York: Wiley, 1978.

Blackman, S., & Goldstein, K. M. A comparison of MMPIs of enuretic with nonenuretic adults. *Journal of Clinical Psychology,* 1965, *21,* 282–283.

Blanchard, E. B., Theobald, D. E., Williamson, D. A., Silver, B. V., & Brown, D. A. Temperature biofeedback in the treatment of migraine headaches. *Archives of General Psychiatry,* 1978, *35,* 581–588.

Blanchard, E. B., & Young, L. B. Self-control of cardiac functioning: A promise as yet unfulfilled. *Psychological Bulletin,* 1973, *79,* 145–163.

Blatty, W. P. *I'll tell them I remember you.* New York: Signet, 1974.

Bleuler, E. The basic symptoms of schizophrenia. In D. Rapaport (Ed.), *Organization and pathology of thought.* New York: Columbia University Press, 1951.

Bleuler, E. *Dementia praecox or the group of schizophrenias.* New York: International Universities Press, 1950.

Bloch, H. S. Army clinical psychiatry in the combat zone, 1967–1968. *American Journal of Psychiatry,* 1969, *126,* 289–298.

Block, J., Jennings, P. H., Harvey, E., & Simpson, E. Interaction between allergic potential and psychopathology in childhood asthma. *Psychosomatic Medicine,* 1964, *26,* 307–320.

Bloodstein, O. Conditions under which stuttering is reduced or absent: A review of the literature. *Journal of Speech and Hearing Disorders,* 1949, *14,* 295–302.

Bloodstein, O. Stuttering as tension and fragmentation. In J. Eisenson (Ed.), *Stuttering: A second symposium.* New York: Harper & Row, 1975.

Bohmen, M. Unwanted children—a prognostic study: Child adoption. *Journal of Association of British Adoption Agencies,* 1973, *2,* 13–25.

Bohmen, M. Some genetic aspects of alcoholism and criminality. *Archives of General Psychiatry,* 1978, *35,* 269–276.

Bollard, R. J., & Woodroffe, P. The effect of parent-administered dry-bed training on nocturnal enuresis in children. *Behavior Research and Therapy,* 1977, *15,* 159–165.

Bond, D. D. *The love and fear of flying.* New York: International Universities Press, 1952.

Borgaonkar, D. S., & Shah, S. A. The XYY chromosome male—or syndrome? In A. A. Steinberg & A. G. Bearn (Eds.), *Progress in medical genetics,* Vol. 10. New York: Grune & Stratton, 1975.

Borgatta, E. F., & Fanshel, D. *Behavioral characteristics of children known to psychiatric outpatient clinics.* New York: Child Welfare League of America, 1965.

Bormann, E. G. Ephphata, or some advice to stammerers. *Journal of Speech and Hearing Research,* 1969, *12,* 453–461.

Bowen, M. *Family therapy in clinical practice.* New York: Jason Aronson, 1978.

Bowlby, J. *Attachment and loss.* Vol. 2: *Separation, anxiety and anger.* New York: Basic Books, 1973.

Brecher, J. and the Editors of *Consumer Reports.* *Licit and illicit drugs.* Mount Vernon, N.Y.: Consumers Union, 1972.

Bregman, E. An attempt to modify the emotional attitudes of infants by the conditioned response technique. *Journal of Genetic Psychology,* 1934, *45,* 169–196.

Brenner, M. H. *Mental illness and the economy.* Cambridge, Mass.: Harvard University Press, 1973.

Brill, N., Koegler, R., Epstein, L., & Forgy, E. Controlled study of psychiatric outpatient treatment. *Archives of General Psychiatry,* 1964, *10,* 581–595.

Brill, H., & Malzberg, B. Statistical report on the arrest record of male ex-patients, age 16 or over, released from New York State mental hospitals, during the period 1946–48. *Mental Hospital Service Supplemental Report 153.* Washington, D.C.: American Psychiatric Association, 1962.

Brodie, H. K. H., Gartrell, N., & Doerring, C. Plasma testosterone levels in heterosexual and homosexual men. *American Journal of Psychiatry,* 1974, *131,* 82–83.

Broen, W. E. *Schizophrenia: Research and theory.* New York: Academic Press, 1968.

Bromet, E., Moos, R., Bliss, F., & Wuthmann, C. Posttreatment functioning of alcoholic patients: Its relation to program participation. *Journal of Consulting and Clinical Psychology,* 1977, *45,* 829–842.

Brooks, V. W. *Days of the phoenix.* New York: Dutton, 1957.

Brown, N., Goulding, E. H., & Fabro, S. Ethanol embryotoxicity: Direct effects on mammalian embryos in vitro. *Science,* 1979, *206,* 573–575.

Brownell, K. D., Hayes, S. C., & Barlow, D. H. Patterns of appropriate and deviant sexual arousal: The behavioral treatment of multiple sexual deviations. *Journal of Consulting and Clinical Psychology,* 1977, *45,* 1144–1155.

Bryan, G. S. *Edison: The man and his work.* New York: Knopf, 1926.

Buchsbaum, M. S. Psychophysiology and schizophrenia. *Schizophrenia Bulletin,* 1977, *3,* 7–14.

Budson, R. D., Grob, M. C., & Singer, J. E. A follow-up study of Berkeley House—A psychiatric halfway house. *International Journal of Social Psychiatry,* 1977, *23,* 120–131.

Bugliosi, V., with Gentry, C. *Helter skelter.* New York: Bantam, 1975.

Bunney, W. E., Murphy, D. L., Goodwin, F. K., & Borge, G. F. The "switch process" in manic-depressive illness. *Archives of General Psychiatry,* 1972, *27,* 295–303.

Bunney, W. E., Pert, A., Rosenblatt, J., Pert, C. B., & Gallaper, D. Mode of lithium. *Archives of General Psychiatry,* 1979, *36,* 898–901.

Burgess, R. L., & Conger, R. D. Family interaction in abusive, neglectful and normal families. *Child Development,* 1978, *49,* 1163–1173.

Burks, H. F. Effects of amphetamine therapy on hyperkinetic children. *Archives of General Psychiatry,* 1964, *11,* 604–609.

Butcher, J. N. *Objective personality assessment.* New York: General Learning Press, 1971.

Cadoret, R. J. Psychopathology in adopted-away offspring of biologic parents with antisocial behavior. *Archives of General Psychiatry,* 1978, *35,* 176–184.

Caldwell, B. M. The effects of infant care. In M. L. Hoffman & L. W. Hoffman (Eds.), *Review of child development research,* Vol. I. New York: Russell Sage, 1964.

Cameron, N. *The psychology of behavior disorders.* Boston: Houghton Mifflin, 1947.

Cameron, N. *Personality development and psychopathology: A dynamic approach.* Boston: Houghton Mifflin, 1963.

Campbell, D., Sanderson, R. E., & Laverty, S. G. Characteristics of a conditioned response in human subjects during extinction trials following a single traumatic conditioning trial. *Journal of Abnormal and Social Psychology,* 1964, *68,* 627–639.

Cantwell, D. P. Psychiatric illness in the families of hyperactive children. *Archives of General Psychiatry,* 1972, *27,* 414–417.

Cantwell, D. P., Baker, L., & Rutter, M. Family factors. In M. Rutter and E. Schopler (Eds.), *Autism: A reappraisal of concepts and treatment.* New York: Plenum Press, 1978.

Caramazza, A., & Berndt, R. S. Semantic and syntactic processes in aphasia: A review of the literature. *Psychological Bulletin,* 1978, *85,* 898–918.

Carey, J. T., & Mandel, J. A San Francisco "speed" scene. *Journal of Health and Social Behavior,* 1968, *9,* 164–174.

Carlen, P. L., Wortzman, G., Holgate, R. C., Wilkinson, D. A., & Rankin, J. G. Reversible cerebral atrophy in recently abstinent chronic alcoholics measured by computed tomography scans. *Science,* 1978, *200,* 1076–1078.

Carlsson, A. Antipsychotic drugs, neurotransmitters and schizophrenia. *American Journal of Psychiatry,* 1978, *135,* 164–173.

Carlsson, A., & Lindquist, M. Effect of chlorpromazine or haloperidol on the formation of 3-methoxyramine and normetanephrine in mouse brains. *Acta Pharmacologica et Toxicologica,* 1963, *20,* 140–144.

Carothers, J. C. *The African mind in health and disease.* Geneva: World Health Organization, 1953.

Casey, J. F., Bennett, I. F., Lindley, C. J., Hollister, L. E., Gordon, M. H., & Springer, N. N. Drug therapy and schizophrenia: A controlled study of the effectiveness of chlorpromazine, promazine, phenobarbital and placebo. *Archives of General Psychiatry,* 1960, *2,* 210–220.

Casriel, D. *So fair a house: The story of Synanon.* Englewood Ciffs, N.J.: Prentice-Hall, 1963.

Castiglioni, A. *Adventures of the mind.* New York: Knopf, 1946.

Cattell, R. B. *Handbook for the Culture-Fair Intelligence Test: A measure of "G".* Champaign, Ill.: Institute for Personality and Ability Testing, 1959.

Cautela, J. R. Treatment of compulsive behavior by covert sensitization. *Psychological Record,* 1966, *16,* 33–41.

Cautela, J. R. The treatment of alcoholism by covert sensitization. *Psychotherapy: Theory, research and practice,* 1970, *7,* 86–90.

Chaney, E. F. *Skill training with alcoholics.* Unpublished doctoral dissertation, University of Washington, 1976.

Chang, J., & Block, J. A study of identification in

male homosexuals. *Journal of Consulting Psychology,* 1960, *24,* 307–310.

Chapman, L. J., & Chapman, J. P. *Disordered thought in schizophrenia.* Englewood Cliffs, N.J.; Prentice-Hall, 1973. (a)

Chapman, L. J., & Chapman, J. P. Problems in the measurement of cognitive deficit. *Psychological Bulletin,* 1973, *79,* 380–385. (b)

Chapman, L. J., Chapman, J. P., & Miller, G. A. A theory of verbal behavior in schizophrenia. In B. A. Maher (Ed.), *Progress in experimental personality research.* New York: Academic Press, 1964.

Charcot, J.-M., & Marie, P. Hysteria. In D. H. Tuke (Ed.), *Dictionary of psychological medicine.* London: Churchill, 1892.

Chaves, J. F., & Barber, T. X. Cognitive strategies, experimenter modeling, and expectation in the attenuation of pain. *Journal of Abnormal Psychology,* 1974, *83,* 356–363.

Chesler, P. *Women and madness.* New York: Doubleday, 1972.

Chodoff, P. Late effects of the concentration camp syndrome. *Archives of General Psychiatry,* 1963, *8,* 323–333.

Christianson, K. O. A preliminary study of criminality among twins. In S. A. Mednick & K. O. Christianson (Eds.), *Biosocial bases of criminal behavior.* New York: Gardner Press, 1977.

Clark, R., & Polish, E. Avoidance conditioning and alcohol consumption in rhesus monkeys. *Science,* 1960, *132,* 223–224.

Cleckley, H. *The mask of sanity,* 5th ed. St. Louis: Mosby, 1976.

Clement, P. W., & Milne, D. C. Group play therapy and tangible reinforcers used to modify the behavior of eight-year-old boys. *Behaviour Research and Therapy,* 1967, *5,* 301–312.

Cline, D. W., & Chosy, J. J. A prospective study of life changes and subsequent health changes. *Archives of General Psychiatry,* 1972, *27,* 51–53.

Cloward, R. A., & Ohlin, L. E. *Delinquency and opportunity.* New York: Free Press, 1960.

Cobb, S. Physiologic changes in men whose jobs were abolished. *Journal of Psychosomatic Research,* 1974, *18,* 245–258.

Cobb, S. Social support as a moderator of life stress. *Psychosomatic Medicine,* 1976, *38,* 300–314.

Cobb, S., & Rose, R. M. Hypertension, peptic ulcer, and diabetes in air traffic controllers. *Journal of the American Medical Association,* 1973, *224,* 489–492.

Colby, K. M. *The skeptical psychoanalyst.* New York: Ronald, 1958.

Colby, K. M. Appraisal of four psychological theories of paranoid phenomena. *Journal of Abnormal Psychology,* 1977, *86,* 54–59.

Cole, M., & Bruner, J. S. Cultural differences and inferences about psychological processes. *American Psychologist,* 1971, *26,* 867–875.

Colson, C. An objective-analytic approach to the classification of suicidal motivation. *Acta Psychiatrica Scandinavica,* 1973, *49,* 105–113.

Conger, J. J. The effects of alcohol on conflict behavior in the albino rat. *Quarterly Journal of Studies on Alcohol,* 1951, *12,* 1–29.

Conners, C. K., Eisenberg, L., & Barcai, A. The effect of dextroamphetamine on children with learning disabilities and school behavior problems. *Archives of General Psychiatry,* 1967, *17,* 478–485.

Cooper, J. E., Kendell, R. E., Gurland, B. J., Sharpe, L., Copeland, J. R. M., & Simon, R. *Psychiatric diagnosis in New York and London.* London: Oxford University Press, 1972.

Corrodi, H., Fuxe, K., & Johnsson, G. Effects of caffeine on central monoamine neurons. *Journal of Pharmacy and Pharmacology,* 1972, *24,* 155–158.

Cowen, E. L. The effectiveness of secondary prevention programs using nonprofessionals in the school setting. *Proceedings of the 76th Annual Convention of the American Psychological Association,* 1968, *2,* 705–706.

Cowen, E. L., Carlisle, R. L., & Kaufman, G. Evaluation of a college student volunteer program with primary graders experiencing school adjustment problems. *Psychology in the Schools,* 1969, *6,* 371–375.

Cowen, E. L., Gesten, E. L., & Wilson, A. B. The primary mental health project (PMHP): Evaluation of current program effectiveness. *American Journal of Community Psychology,* 1979, *7,* 293–303.

Cowen, E. L., Leibowitz, E., & Leibowitz, G. The utilization of retired people as mental health aides in the schools. *American Journal of Orthopsychiatry,* 1968, *38,* 900–909.

Cowen, E. L., Lorion, R. P., Dorr, D., Clarfield, S. P., & Wilson, A. B. Evaluation of a preventively oriented, school-based mental health program. *Psychology in the Schools,* 1975, *12,* 161–166.

Cowen, E. L., & Zax, M. Early detection and prevention of emotional disorder: Conceptualizations and programming. In J. W. Carter (Ed.), *Research contributions from psychology to community mental health.* New York: Behavioral Publications, 1969.

Coyne, J. C. Depression and the response of others. *Journal of Abnormal Psychology,* 1976, *85,* 186–193.

Crisp, A. H., Harding, B., & McGuinness, B. Anorexia nervosa: Psychoneurotic characteristics of parents: Relationship to progress. *Journal of Psychosomatic Research,* 1974, *18,* 167–173.

Cromwell, R. L., Palk, B. E., & Foshee, J. G. Studies in activity level. V: The relationships among eyelid conditioning, intelligence, activity level and age. *American Journal of Mental Deficiency,* 1961, *65,* 744–748.

Crowder, D., & Thornton, D. Effects of systematic desensitization, programmed fantasy, and bibliotherapy on a specific fear. *Behavior Research and Therapy,* 1970, *8,* 35–42.

Crowe, R. R. An adoption study of antisocial personality. *Archives of General Psychiatry,* 1974, *31,* 785–791.

Cullen, K. J. Clinical observations concerning behavior disorders in children. *Medical Journal of Australia,* 1966, *1,* 712–715.

Cummings, S. T., Bayley, H. C., & Rie, H. E. The effects of the child's deficiency on the mother: A study of mothers of mentally retarded, chronically ill and neurotic children. *American Journal of Orthopsychiatry,* 1966, *36,* 595–608.

Da Fonseca (1959), as reported by Zerbin-Rudin, E. Endogene psychosen. In P. E. Becker (Ed.), *Humangenetic,* section 2. Stuttgart: Georg Thieme Verlag, 1967.

Dahlstrom, W. G., Welsh, G. S., & Dahlstrom, L. E. *An MMPI handbook, Vol. II: Research applications.* Minneapolis: University of Minnesota Press, 1975.

Dalgaard, O. S., & Kringlen, E. A Norwegian twin study of criminality. *British Journal of Criminology,* 1976, *16,* 213–232.

Darwin, C. *The expression of emotions in man and animals.* New York: Philosophical Library, 1955. (Originally published, 1873).

David, O., Clark, J., & Voeller, K. Lead and hyperactivity. *Lancet,* 1972, *2,* 900–903.

Davis, A., & Eells, K. *Davis-Eells games: Davis-Eells test of general intelligence of problem-solving ability.* Tarrytown-on-Hudson, N.Y.: World Book Company, 1953.

Davison, G. C. Systematic desensitization as a counterconditioning process. *Journal of Abnormal Psychology,* 1968, *73,* 91–99.

Davison, G. C., & Neale, J. M. *Abnormal psychology.* New York: Wiley, 1978.

de Araujo, G., van Arsdel, P. P., Holmes, T. H., & Dudley, D. L. Life change, coping ability and chronic intrinsic asthma. *Journal of Psychosomatic Research,* 1973, *17,* 359–363.

Deci, E. L. Effects of externally mediated rewards on intrinsic motivation. *Journal of Personality and Social Psychology,* 1971, *18,* 105–115.

Dekker, E., & Groen, J. Reproducible psychogenic attacks of asthma. *Journal of Psychosomatic Research,* 1956, *1,* 58–67.

Dekker, E., Pelse, H. E., & Groen, J. Conditioning as a cause of asthmatic attacks. *Journal of Psychosomatic Research,* 1957, *2,* 97–108.

DeLong, G. R. A neuropsychologic interpretation of infantile autism. In M. Rutter and E. Schopler (Eds.), *Autism: A reappraisal of concepts and treatments.* New York: Plenum Press, 1978.

Dember, W. N. Motivation and the cognitive revolution. *American Psychologist,* 1974, *29,* 161–168.

DeMeyer, M. K., Pontius, W., Norton, J. A., Barton, S., Allen, J., & Steele, R. Parental practices and innate activity in normal, autistic, and brain-damaged infants. *Journal of Autism and Childhood Schizophrenia,* 1972, *2,* 49–66.

Denson, R., Nanson, J. L., & McWatters, N. A. Hyperkinesis and maternal smoking. *Canadian Psychiatric Association Journal,* 1975, *20,* 183–187.

Depue, R. A., & Monroe, S. M. The unipolar-bipolar distinction in the depressive disorders. *Psychological Bulletin,* 1978, *85,* 1001–1029.

Despert, J. L. Psychotherapy in childhood schizophrenia. *American Journal of Psychiatry,* 1947, *104,* 36–43.

Despert, J. L. Some considerations relating to the genesis of autistic behavior in children. *American Journal of Orthopsychiatry,* 1951, *21,* 335–350.

Devereux, G. "Normal and abnormal," the key problem of psychiatric anthropology. *Some uses of anthropology, theoretical and applied.* The Anthropological Society of Washington, D.C., 1956.

DeVoge, J. T., & Beck, S. The therapist-client relationship in behavior therapy. In M. Hersen, R. M. Eisler, and P. M. Miller (Eds.), *Progress in behavior modification.* New York: Academic Press, 1978.

Diagnostic and Statistical Manual of Mental Disorders, Third Edition. Washington, D.C.: American Psychiatric Association, 1980.

Dingman, H. F., & Meyers, C. E. Structure of intellect in the mental retardate. In N. R. Ellis (Ed.), *International review of research in mental retardation.* Vol. I. New York: Academic Press, 1966.

Dohrenwend, B. P. & Dohrenwend, B. S. Social and cultural influences on psychopathology. In M. R. Rosenzweig & L. W. Porter (Eds.), *Annual Review of Psychology.* Palo Alto, Calif.: Annual Reviews, 1974.

Dohrenwend, B. P., & Dohrenwend, B. S. Epidemiological and related research on the problem of schizophrenia: Findings and implications. In R. Littlestone, M. Katz, M. Roath, & M. Tuma (Eds.), *Schizophrenia: Implications of research findings for treatment and teaching.* New York: Basic Books, 1975.

Dole, V. P., Nyswander, M. E., & Warner, A. Successful treatment of 750 criminal addicts. *Journal of the American Medical Association,* 1968, *206,* 2708–2711.

Downer, J. L. de C. Interhemispheric integration in the visual system. In V. B. Mountcastle (Ed.), *Conference on interhemispheric relations and cerebral dominance.* Baltimore: Johns Hopkins Press, 1962.

Dunbar, F. *Emotions and bodily changes: A survey of literature on psychosomatic interrelationships.* New York: Columbia University Press, 1935.

Dupont, R. L., & Katon, R. N. Development of a heroin-addiction treatment program: Effect on urban crime. *Journal of the American Medical Association,* 1971, *216,* 1320–1324.

Durkheim, E. *Suicide* (J. A. Spaulding & G. Simpson, Trans.). London: Routledge & Kegan Paul, 1952.

Durlak, J. A. Comparative effectiveness of paraprofessional and professional helpers. *Psychological Bulletin,* 1979, *86,* 80–92.

Eaton, J. W., & Weil, R. J. *Culture and mental disorders.* New York: Free Press, 1955.

Eaves, L., & Eysenck, H. The nature of extraversion: A genetical analysis. *Journal of Personality and Social Psychology,* 1975, *32,* 102–112.

Eberhardy, F. The view from "the couch." *Journal of Child Psychology and Psychiatry,* 1967, *8,* 257–263.

Eddy, C. The effects of alcohol on anxiety in problem- and non-problem-drinking women. *Alcoholism: Clinical and Experimental Research,* 1979, *3,* 107–114.

Eggers, C. Course and prognosis of childhood schizophrenia. *Journal of Autism and Childhood Schizophrenia,* 1978, *8,* 21–36.

Eisenberg, L. School phobia: A study in the communication of anxiety. *American Journal of Psychiatry,* 1958, *114,* 712–718.

Eisenberg, L., Gilbert, A., Cytryn, L., & Molling, P. A. The effectiveness of psychotherapy alone and in conjunction with perphenazine or placebo in treatment of neurotic and hyperkinetic children. *American Journal of Psychiatry,* 1961, *117,* 1088–1093.

Eisenberg, L., & Kanner, L. Early infantile autism.

American Journal of Orthopsychiatry, 1956, *26,* 556–566.

Ellenberger, H. F. The story of "Anna O": A critical review with new data. *Journal of the History of the Behavioral Sciences,* 1972, *8,* 267–279.

Ellinwood, E. H. Amphetamine psychosis. I: Description of the individuals and process. *Journal of Nervous and Mental Disease,* 1967, *144,* 273–283.

Ellis, A. *Reason and emotion in psychotherapy.* New York: Lyle Stuart, 1962.

Ellis, A. *Humanistic psychotherapy: The rational-emotive approach.* New York: Julian Press, 1973.

Ellis, M. J., Witt, P. A., Reynolds, R., & Sprague, R. L. Methylphenidate and the activity of hyperactives in the informal setting. *Child Development,* 1974, *45,* 217–220.

Ellis, N. R. Memory processes in retardates and normals: Theoretical and empirical considerations. Paper presented at the Gatlinburg, Tenn., Conference on Mental Retardation, 1968.

Ellsworth, R. B. The psychiatric aide as rehabilitation therapist. *Rehabilitation Counseling Bulletin,* 1964, *7,* 81–86.

Emmons, T. D., & Webb, W. W. Subjective correlates of emotional responsivity and stimulation seeking in psychopaths, normals, and acting-out neurotics. *Journal of Consulting and Clinical Psychology,* 1974, *42,* 620.

Emrick, C. A. A review of psychologically oriented treatment of alcoholism. *Journal of Studies on Alcohol,* 1975, *36,* 88–108.

Erhardt, A. A. Maternalism in fetal hormonal and related syndromes. In J. Zubin & J. Money (Eds.), *Contemporary sexual behavior: Critical issues in the 1970s.* Baltimore: Johns Hopkins Press, 1973.

Erikson, E. H. *Childhood and society.* New York: Norton, 1963.

Erlenmeyer-Kimling, L. A prospective study of children at risk for schizophrenia. Methodological considerations and some preliminary findings. In R. Wirt, G. Winokur, & M. Roff (Eds.), *Life history research in psychopathology,* Vol. 4. Minneapolis: University of Minnesota Press, 1976.

Erlenmeyer-Kimling, L., & Jarvik, L. Genetics and intelligence: A review. *Science,* 1963, *142,* 1477–1479.

Ernhart, C. B., Graham, F. K., Eichman, P. L., Marshall, J. M., & Thurston, D. Brain injury in the preschool child: Some developmental considerations: II—Comparison of brain injured and normal children. *Psychological Monograph,* 1963, *77,* 17–33.

Esler, M., Julius, S., Zweifler, A., Randall, O., Harburg, E., Hermsworth, G., & DeQuattro, V. Mild high resin hypertension: Neurogenic human hypertension? *New England Journal of Medicine,* 1977, *296,* 405–411.

Essen-Möller, E. Psychiatrische Untersuchungen an einer Serie von Zwillingen, *Acta Psychiatrica et Neurologica Scandinavica,* 1941, Supplement 23.

Evans, R. B. Childhood parental relationships of homosexual men. *Journal of Consulting and Clinical Psychology,* 1969, *33,* 129–135.

Exner, J. E. *The Rorschach: A comprehensive system.* New York: Wiley, 1974.

Exner, J. E. *The Rorschach: A comprehensive system,* Vol. 2: *Current research and advanced interpretation.* New York: Wiley, 1978.

Eysenck, H. J. *The effects of psychotherapy.* New York: Science House, 1969.

Fairweather, G. W., Sanders, D. H., Crissler, D. L., & Maynard, H. *Community life for the mentally ill.* Chicago: Aldine, 1969.

Farberow, N. L., & McEvoy, T. L. Suicide among patients with diagnoses of anxiety reaction or depressive reaction in general medical and surgical hospitals. *Journal of Abnormal Psychology,* 1966, *71,* 287–299.

Faris, R. E. L., & Dunham, H. W. *Mental disorders in urban areas: An ecological study of schizophrenia and other psychoses.* Chicago: University of Chicago Press, 1939.

Federal Bureau of Investigation. *Uniform crime reports.* Washington, D.C.: Government Printing Office, 1979.

Feighner, J., Robins, E., Guze, S., Woodruff, R. A., Winokur, G., & Munoz, R. Diagnostic criteria for use in psychiatric research. *Archives of General Psychiatry,* 1972, *26,* 57–63.

Feinbloom, D. H. *Transvestites/transsexuals.* New York: Delacorte Press, 1963.

Feingold, B. F. Hyperkinesis and learning disabilities linked to artificial food flavors and colors. *American Journal of Nursing,* 1975, *75,* 797–803.

Fenichel, O. *The psychoanalytic theory of neurosis.* New York: Norton, 1945.

Ferster, C. B. A functional analysis of depression. *American Psychologist,* 1973, *28,* 857–870.

Ferster, C. B., & DeMeyer, M. K. The development of performances in autistic children in an automatically controlled environment. *Journal of Chronic Diseases,* 1961, *13,* 312–345.

Field, M. J. Mental disorder in rural Ghana. *Journal of Mental Science,* 1958, *104,* 1043–1051.

Finch, B. E., & Wallace, C. J. Successful interpersonal skills training with schizophrenic inpatients.

Journal of Consulting and Clinical Psychology, 1977, *45,* 885–890.

Fischer, M. Genetic and environmental factors in schizophrenia. *Acta Psychiatrica Scandinavica,* 1973, Supplement 238.

Foa, E. G., & Goldstein, A. Continuous exposure and complete response prevention in the treatment of obsessive-compulsive neurosis. *Behavior Therapy,* 1978, *9,* 821–829.

Folstein, S., & Rutter, M. Infantile autism: A genetic study of 21 twin pairs. *Journal of Child Psychology and Psychiatry,* 1977, *18,* 297–321.

Ford, C. S., & Beach, F. A. *Patterns of sexual behavior.* New York: Harper & Row, 1951.

Forrest, M. S., & Hokanson, J. E. Depression and autonomic arousal reduction accompanying self-punitive behavior. *Journal of Abnormal Psychology,* 1975, *84,* 346–357.

Fort, J. *Drugs and youth, the pleasure seekers: The drug crisis, youth and society.* New York: Grove Press, 1969.

Fowler, R. D. Automated interpretation of personality test data. In J. N. Butcher (Ed.), *MMPI: Research developments and clinical applications.* New York: McGraw-Hill, 1969.

Fox, J. H., Ramsey, R. G., Huckman, M. S., & Proske, A. E. *Journal of the American Medical Association,* 1976, *236,* 365.

Frank, J. D. *Persuasion and healing.* Baltimore: Johns Hopkins Press, 1961.

Frankenhaeuser, M., Jarpe, G., Svan, H., & Wrangsjo, B. Physiological reactions to two different placebo treatments. *Scandinavian Journal of Psychology,* 1963, *47,* 285–293.

Frankl, V. E. The will to meaning. Ontario, Canada: Don Mills, 1969.

Freedman, B., & Chapman, L. J. Early subjective experience in schizophrenic episodes. *Journal of Abnormal Psychology,* 1973, *82,* 46–54.

Freedman, D. G. An ethological approach to the genetical study of human behavior. In S. G. Vandenburg (Ed.), *Methods and goals in human behavior genetics.* New York: Academic Press, 1965.

French, T. M., & Alexander, F. Psychogenic factors in bronchial asthma. *Psychosomatic Medicine Monographs,* 1941, No. 4.

Freud, A., & Burlingham, D. T. *War and children.* New York: Willard, 1943.

Freud, S. Charcot. In *Collected papers,* Vol. 1. London: Hogarth Press, 1948.

Freud, S. *Standard edition of the complete psychological works of Sigmund Freud, Vol. 10.* London: Hogarth Press, 1948.

Freud, S. Mourning and melancholia. *Standard edition of the complete works of Sigmund Freud, Vol. 16.* London: Hogarth Press, 1957.

Freud, S. *Standard edition of the complete psychological works of Sigmund Freud, Vol. 3.* London: Hogarth Press, 1962.

Freud, S. *Standard edition of the complete psychological works of Sigmund Freud, Vols. 15–16.* London: Hogarth Press, 1963.

Freud, S. *The interpretation of dreams.* New York: Avon, 1965.

Freud, S., & Breuer, J. *Studies on hysteria.* New York: Avon Books, 1966. (Originally published as Breuer, J., & Freud, S. in 1895).

Friedman, M., & Rosenman, R. H. *Type A behavior and your heart.* Greenwich, Conn.: Fawcett, 1975.

Frumkin, K., Nathan, R. J., Prout, M. F., & Cohen, M. C. Nonpharmacologic control of essential hypertension in man: A critical review of the experimental literature. *Psychosomatic Medicine,* 1978, *40,* 294–320.

Fuchs, C. Z., & Rehm, L. P. A self-control behavior therapy program for depression. *Journal of Consulting and Clinical Psychology,* 1977, *45,* 206–215.

Garber, H., & Heber, R. The efficacy of early intervention with family rehabilitation. Paper presented at conference on prevention of retarded development in psychosocially disadvantaged children, University of Wisconsin, Madison, July 1978.

Garduk, E. L., & Haggard, E. A. Immediate effects on patients of psychoanalytic interpretations. *Psychological Issues,* 1972, *7,* Monograph 28.

Garfinkel, B. D., Webster, C. D., & Sloman, L. Methylphenidate and caffeine in the treatment of children with minimal brain dysfunction. *American Journal of Psychiatry,* 1975, *132,* 723–728.

Garner, A. M., & Wenar, C. *The mother-child interaction in psychosomatic disorders.* Urbana: University of Illinois Press, 1959.

Garvey, W. P., & Hegrenes, J. R. Desensitization techniques in the treatment of school phobia. *American Journal of Orthopsychiatry,* 1966, *36,* 147–152.

Gelder, M. G., Bancroft, J. H., Gath, D. H., Johnston, D. W., Matthews, A. M., & Shaw, P. M. Specific and non-specific factors in behaviour therapy. *British Journal of Psychiatry,* 1973, *123,* 445–462.

Gelder, M. G., Marks, I. M., & Wolff, H. H. Desensitization and psychotherapy in the treatment of phobic states: A controlled inquiry. *British Journal of Psychiatry,* 1967, *113,* 53–73.

Gelder, M. G., & Marks, I. M. Aversion treatment in transvestism and transsexualism. In R. Green &

J. Money (Eds.), *Transsexualism and sex reassignment.* Baltimore: Johns Hopkins Press, 1969.

Gerard, D. L., & Houston, L. G. Family setting and the social ecology of schizophrenia. *Psychiatric Quarterly,* 1953, *27,* 90–101.

Gerjouy, I. R., & Alvarez, J. M. Transfer of learning in associative clustering of retardates and normals. *American Journal of Mental Deficiency,* 1969, *73,* 733–738.

Gibbs, F. A., Gibbs, E. C., & Lennox, W. G. The electro-encephalogram in epilepsy and in conditions of impaired consciousness. *Archives of Neurology and Psychiatry,* 1935, *34,* 1133–1148.

Gill, M., Newman, R., & Redlich, F. C. *The initial interview in psychiatric practice.* New York: International Universities Press, 1954.

Giovannoni, J. F., & Gurel, L. Socially disruptive behavior of ex-mental patients. *Archives of General Psychiatry,* 1967, *17,* 146–153.

Glidewell, J. C., Gildea, M. C., & Kaufman, M. K. The preventive and therapeutic effects of two school mental health programs. *American Journal of Community Psychology,* 1973, *1,* 295–329.

Glidewell, J. C., & Swallow, C. *The prevalance of maladjustment in elementary schools.* Chicago: University of Chicago Press, 1969.

Gliedman, L. H., Nash, E. H., Imber, S. D., Stone, A. R., & Frank, J. D. Reduction of symptoms by pharmacologically inert substances and by short-term psychotherapy. *Archives of Neurology and Psychiatry,* 1958, *79,* 345–351.

Goertzel, W., & Goertzel, M. G. *Cradles of eminence.* Boston: Little, Brown, 1962.

Goldberg, E. M., & Morrison, S. L. Schizophrenia and social class. *British Journal of Psychiatry,* 1963, *109,* 785–802.

Goldfarb, W. The effects of early institutional care on adolescent personality. *Journal of Experimental Education,* 1943, *12,* 107–129.

Goldfarb, W. Infant rearing as a factor in foster home placement. *American Journal of Orthopsychiatry,* 1945, *102,* 18–33.

Goldfarb, W. *Childhood schizophrenia.* Cambridge, Mass.: Harvard University Press, 1961.

Goldfried, M. R., & Davison, G. C. *Clinical behavior therapy.* New York: Holt, Rinehart and Winston, 1976.

Goldsmith, J. B., & McFall, R. M. Development and evaluation of an interpersonal skill-training program for psychiatric patients. *Journal of Abnormal Psychology,* 1975, *84,* 51–58.

Goldstein, K. *The organism.* New York: American Book, 1939.

Goldstein, K., & Katz, S. E. The psychopathology of Pick's disease. *Archives of Neurology and Psychiatry,* 1937, *38,* 473–490.

Goldstein, M. J., & Palmer, J. O. *The experience of anxiety.* New York: Oxford University Press, 1975.

Goodglass, H., & Geschwind, N. Disorders of language and speech. In E. C. Carterette & M. P. Friedman (Eds.), *Handbook of perception.* New York: Academic Press, 1976.

Goodman, W. The constitution vs. the snakepit. *The New York Times Magazine,* March 17, 1974.

Goodwin, D. W. Alcoholism and heredity. *Archives of General Psychiatry,* 1979, *36,* 57–61.

Goodwin, D. W., Schulsinger, F., Hermansen, L., Guze, S. B., & Winokur, G. Alcohol problems in adoptees raised apart from alcoholic biological parents. *Archives of General Psychiatry,* 1973, *28,* 238–243.

Goodwin, D. W., Schulsinger, F., Hermansen, L., Guze, S. B., & Winokur, G. Alcoholism and the hyperactive child syndrome. *Journal of Nervous and Mental Disease,* 1975, *160,* 349–353.

Goodwin, D. W., Schulsinger, F., Knop, J., Mednick, S., & Guze, S. B. Alcoholism and depression in adopted-out daughters of alcoholics. *Archives of General Psychiatry,* 1977, *34,* 751–754.

Goodwin, D. W., Schulsinger, F., Moller, N., Hermansen, L. Winokur, G. & Guze, S. B. Drinking problems in adopted and nonadopted sons of alcoholics. *Archives of General Psychiatry,* 1974, *31,* 164–169.

Goodwin, F. K., & Athanasios, P. Z. Lithium in the treatment of mania. *Archives of General Psychiatry,* 1979, *36,* 840–844.

Goodwin, F. K., Cowdy, R., Jimmerson, D. Serotonin and norepinephrine "subgroups" in depression: Metabolite findings and clinical-pharmacological correlations. *Scientific Proceedings of American Psychiatric Association,* 1977, *130,* 108.

Gorin, T., & Kramer, R. A. The hyperkinetic behavior syndrome. *Connecticut Medicine,* 1973, *37,* 559–563.

Gottesman, I. Differential inheritance of the psychoneuroses. *Eugenics Quarterly,* 1962, *9,* 223–227.

Gottesman, I., & Shields, J. *Schizophrenia and genetics: A twin vantage point.* New York: Academic Press, 1972.

Gottman, J. M. *Marital interaction.* New York: Academic Press, 1979.

Gove, W., & Howell, P. Individual resources and mental hospitalization: A comparison and evaluation of the societal reaction and psychiatric perspectives. *American Sociological Review,* 1974, *39,* 86–100.

Gove, W. R., & Tudor, J. F. Adult sex roles and mental illness. *American Journal of Sociology*, 1973, *78*, 812–835.

Goy, R. W. Experimental control of psychosexuality. *Philosophical Transactions of the Royal Society of London Biological*, 1970.

Grace, W. J., Pinsky, R. H., & Wolff, H. G. Treatment of ulcerative colitis. *Gastroenterology*, 1954, *26*, 462–468.

Green, R. *Sexual identity conflict in children and adults*. New York: Basic Books, 1974.

Greenberg, D. J., Scott, S. B., Pisa, A., & Friesen, D. D. Beyond the token economy: A comparison of two contingency programs. *Journal of Consulting and Clinical Psychology*, 1975, *43*, 498–503.

Greer, S., & Morris, T. Psychological attributes of women who develop breast cancer: A controlled study. *Journal of Psychosomatic Research*, 1975, *19*, 147–153.

Grier, W. H., & Cobbs, P. M. *Black rage*. New York: Basic Books, 1968.

Griffin, B. S., & Griffin, C. T. *Juvenile delinquency in perspective*. New York: Harper & Row, 1978.

Griffith, J. D., Cavanaugh, J., Held, N. N., & Oates, J. A. Dextroamphetamine: Evaluation of psychotominetic properties in man. *Archives of General Psychiatry*, 1972, *26*, 97–100.

Grinspoon, L., Dwalt, J. R., & Shader, R. Psychotherapy and pharmacotherapy in chronic schizophrenia. *American Journal of Psychiatry*, 1968, *124*, 1645–1652.

Groen, J. J., & Pelser, H. E. Experiences with, and results of group psychotherapy in patients with bronchial asthma. *Journal of Psychosomatic Research*, 1960, *4*, 191–205.

Gross, H. S., Herbert, M. R., Knaterud, G. L., & Donner, L. The effect of race and sex on the variation of diagnosis and disposition in a psychiatric emergency room. *Journal of Nervous and Mental Disease*, 1969, *148*, 638–642.

Grossman, F. *Brothers and sisters of retarded children: An exploratory study*. Syracuse, N. Y.: Syracuse University Press, 1973.

Groth, A. N., Burgess, A. W., & Holmstrom, L. L. Rape: Power, anger, and sexuality. *American Journal of Psychiatry*, 1977, *134*, 1239–1243.

Gruenberg, E. M. & Zusman, J. The natural history of schizophrenia. *International Psychiatry Clinics*, 1964, *1*, 699–714.

Gurman, A. S., & Kniskern, D. P. Research on marital and family therapy. In S. L. Garfield & A. E. Bergin (Eds.), *Handbook of psychotherapy and behavior change*. New York: Wiley, 1978.

Guze, S., & Robins, E. Suicide and primary affective

disorders. *British Journal of Psychiatry*, 1970, *117*, 437–438.

Haas, H., Fink, H., & Hartfelder, G. The placebo problem. *Psychopharmacology Service Center Bulletin*, 1963, *2*, 1–65.

Haeussermann, E. *Developmental potential of preschool children*. New York: Grune & Stratton, 1958.

Hafner, R. J. The husbands of agoraphobic women and their influence on treatment outcome. *British Journal of Psychiatry*, 1977, *131*, 289–294.

Hain, J. D., Butcher, R. H. G., & Stevenson, I. Systematic desensitization therapy: An analysis of results in twenty-seven patients. *British Journal of Psychiatry*, 1966, *112*, 295–307.

Halleck, S. L. Another response to "Homosexuality: The ethical challenge." *Journal of Consulting and Clinical Psychology*, 1976, *44*, 167–170.

Halpern, J. Projection: A test of the psychoanalytic hypothesis. *Journal of Abnormal Psychology*, 1977, *86*, 536–542.

Hammen, C. L., & Peters, S. D. Differential responses to male and female depressive reactions. *Journal of Consulting and Clinical Psychology*, 1977, *45*, 994–1001.

Hanson, D. R., Gottesman, I. I., & Hester, L. L. Some possible childhood indicators of adult schizophrenia inferred from children of schizophrenics. *British Journal of Psychiatry*, 1976, *129*, 142–154.

Harbin, H. T., & Maziar, H. M. The families of drug abusers: A literature review. *Family Process*, 1975, *14*, 411–432.

Harburg, E., Erfurt, J. C., Hauenstein, L. S., Chape, C., Schull, W. J., & Schork, M. A. Socio-ecological stress, suppressed hostility, skin color and black-white male blood pressure: Detroit. *Psychosomatic Medicine*, 1973, *35*, 276–296.

Hare, E. H. Mental illness and social conditions in Bristol. *Journal of Mental Science*, 1956, *102*, 349–357.

Hare, R. D. Temporal gradient of fear arousal in psychopaths. *Journal of Abnormal Psychology*, 1965, *70*, 442–445. (a)

Hare, R. D. Acquisition and generalization of a conditioned-fear response in psychopathic and nonpsychopathic criminals. *Journal of Psychology*, 1965, *59*, 367–370. (b)

Hare, R. D. *Psychopathy: Theory and research*. New York: Wiley, 1970.

Hare, R. D. Electrodermal and cardiovascular correlates of psychopathy. In R. D. Hare & D. Schalling (Eds.), *Psychopathic behavior: Approaches to research*. New York: Wiley, 1978.

Hare, R. D., & Cox, D. N. Clinical and empirical conceptions of psychopathy, and the selection of subjects for research. In R. D. Hare and D. Schalling (Eds.), *Psychopathic behavior: Approaches to research.* New York: Wiley, 1978.

Harlow, H. F., & Harlow, M. K. Effects of various mother-infant relationships on rhesus monkey behaviors. In B. M. Foss (Ed.), *Determinants of infant behavior IV.* London: Methuen, 1969.

Harper, J., & Williams, S. Age and type of onset as critical variables in early infantile autism. *Journal of Autism and Childhood Schizophrenia,* 1975, *5,* 25–36.

Hartmann, H. *Ego psychology and the problem of adaptation.* New York: International Universities Press, 1958.

Harvald, B., & Hauge, M. Hereditary factors elucidated by twin studies. In J. V. Neel, M. W. Shaw, & W. J. Schull, (Eds.), *Genetics and the epidemiology of chronic diseases.* Public Health Service Publication 1163. U.S. Department of Health, Education, and Welfare, 1965.

Hastings, D. W. Follow-up results in psychiatric illness. *American Journal of Psychiatry,* 1958, *114,* 1057–1066.

Hastings, D., & Markland, C. Post-surgical adjustment of twenty-five transsexuals (male-to-female) in the University of Minnesota study. *Archives of Sexual Behavior,* 1978, *7,* 327–336.

Hathaway, S. R., & McKinley, J. C. *Manual for the Minnesota Multiphasic Personality Inventory.* New York: Psychological Corporation, 1943.

Hayward, M. L., & Taylor, J. E. A schizophrenic patient describes the action of intensive psychotherapy. *Psychiatric Quarterly,* 1956, *30,* 210–244.

Heber, R., & Garber, H. Prevention of cultural-familial retardation. In A. Jeger and R. Slotnick (Eds.), *Community mental health: A behavioral-ecological perspective.* New York: Plenum, 1980.

Heilbrun, A. B. Perceptual distortion and schizophrenia. *American Journal of Orthopsychiatry,* 1960, *30,* 412–418. (a)

Heilbrun, A. B. Perception of maternal childrearing attitudes in schizophrenia. *Journal of Consulting Psychology,* 1960, *24,* 169–173. (b)

Heilbrun, A. B. Psychopathy and violent crime. *Journal of Consulting and Clinical Psychology,* 1979, *47,* 509–516.

Helzer, J. E., Clayton, P. J., Pambakian, R., Reich, T., Woodruff, R. A., & Reveley, M. A. Reliability of psychiatric diagnosis: II. The test/retest reliability of diagnostic classification. *Archives of General Psychiatry,* 1977, *34,* 136–141.

Hemsley, R., Howlin, P., Berger, M., Hersov, L., Holbrook, D., Rutter, M., & Yule, W. Treating autistic children in a family context. In M. Rutter and E. Schopler (Eds.), *Autism: A reappraisal of concepts and treatment.* New York: Plenum, 1978.

Henderson, J. D., & Scoles, P. E. Conditioning techniques in a community-based operant environment for psychotic men. *Behavior Therapy,* 1970, *1,* 245–251.

Herbert, W. States ponder notion of criminal insanity. *APA Monitor,* April 1979, 8–9.

Hereford, C. F. *Changing parental attitudes through group discussion.* Austin: University of Texas Press, 1963.

Hermelin, B. Images and language. In M. Rutter and E. Schopler (Eds.), *Autism: A reappraisal of concepts and treatment.* New York: Plenum, 1978.

Hermelin, B., & O'Connor, N. *Psychological experiment with autistic children.* Oxford: Pergamon, 1970.

Hersov, L. A. Persistent non-attendance at school. *Journal of Child Psychology and Psychiatry,* 1960, *1,* 130–136.

Hess, R. D., & Shipman, V. C. Early experiences and the socialization of cognitive modes in children. *Child Development,* 1965, *36,* 869–886.

Heston, L. L. Psychiatric disorders in foster-home-reared children of schizophrenic mothers. *British Journal of Psychiatry,* 1966, *112,* 819–825.

Heston, L. L., & Mastri, A. R. The genetics of Alzheimer's disease: Associations with hematologic malignancy and Down's syndrome. *Archives of General Psychiatry,* 1977, *34,* 976–981.

Hetherington, E. M., & Martin, B. Family Interaction. In H. C. Quay & J. S. Werry (Eds.), *Psychopathological disorders of childhood.* New York: Wiley, 1979.

Hewett, F. M. Teaching speech to an autistic child through operant conditioning. *American Journal of Orthopsychiatry,* 1965, *35,* 927–936.

Higgins, J., & Peterson, J. Concept of process-reactive schizophrenia: A critique. *Psychological Bulletin,* 1966, *66,* 201–206.

Higgins, R. L., & Marlatt, G. A. Fear of interpersonal evaluation as a determinant of alcohol consumption in male social drinkers. *Journal of Abnormal Psychology,* 1975, *84,* 644–651.

Hilgard, E. R. Pain as puzzle for psychology and physiology. *American Psychologist,* 1969, *24,* 103–113.

Hilgard, E. R., Hilgard, J. R., MacDonald, H., Morgan, A. H., & Johnson, L. S. Covert pain in hypnotic analgesia: Its reality as tested by the real-simulator design. *Journal of Abnormal Psychology,* 1978, *87,* 655–663.

Hilgard, E. R., MacDonald, H., Morgan, A. H., & Johnson, L. S. The reality of hypnotic analgesia: A comparison of highly hypnotizables with simulators. *Journal of Abnormal Psychology,* 1978, *87,* 239–246.

Hill, M. J., & Blane, H. T. Evaluation of psychotherapy with alcoholics: A critical review. *Quarterly Journal of Studies on Alcohol,* 1967, *28,* 76–104.

Hirschfeld, M. *Sexual anomalies and perversions.* New York: Emerson Books, 1948.

Hodapp, V., Weyer, G., & Becker, J. Situational stereotypy in essential hypertension patients. *Journal of Psychosomatic Research,* 1975, *19,* 113–121.

Hoffman, M. L., & Saltzstein, H. D. Parent discipline and the child's moral development. *Journal of Personality and Social Psychology,* 1967, *5,* 45–57.

Hoffman, S. P., Engelhardt, D. M., Margolis, R. A., Polizos, P., Waizer, J., & Rosenfeld, R. Response to methylphenidate in low socioeconomic hyperactive children. *Archives of General Psychiatry,* 1974, *30,* 354–359.

Hogarty, G. E., Schooler, N., Ulrich, R., Mussare, F., Ferro, P., & Herron, E. Depot fluphenazine and social therapy in the aftercare of schizophrenic patients: Relapse analyses of a two-year controlled trial. *Archives of General Psychiatry,* in press.

Hogarty, G. E., & Ulrich, R. F. Temporal effects of drug and placebo in delaying relapse in schizophrenic outpatients. *Archives of General Psychiatry,* 1977, *34,* 297–301.

Hokanson, J. E., & Burgess, M. The effects of status, type of frustration, and aggression on vascular processes. *Journal of Abnormal and Social Psychology,* 1962, *65,* 232–237.

Holden, C. Cancer and the mind: How are they connected? *Science,* 1978, *200,* 1363–1369.

Hollingshead, A. B., & Redlich, F. C. *Social class and mental illness.* New York: Wiley, 1958.

Hollister, L. E. Drug therapy: Mental disorders—antipsychotic and antimanic drugs. *New England Journal of Medicine,* 1972, *286,* 984–987.

Holzman, P. S., & Levy, D. L. Smooth pursuit eye movements and functional psychoses: A review. *Schizophrenia Bulletin,* 1977, *3,* 15–27.

Honsberger, R., & Wilson, A. F. Transcendental meditation in treating asthma. *Respiratory Therapy: The Journal of Inhalation Technology,* 1973, *3,* 79–81.

Hook, E. B. Behavioral implications of the human XYY genotype. *Science,* 1973, *179,* 139–150.

Horn, A. S., & Snyder, S. H. Chloropromazine and dopamine: Conformational similarities that correlate with the antischizophrenic activity of phenothiazine drugs. *Proceedings of the National Academy of Sciences,* 1971, *68,* 2325–2328.

Horn, J. M., Loehlin, J. C., & Willerman, L. Intellectual resemblance among adoptive and biological relatives: The Texas Adoption Project. *Behavior Genetics,* 1979, *9,* 177–207.

Horn, J. M., Plomin, R., & Rosenman, R. Heritability of personality traits in adult male twins. *Behavior Genetics,* 1976, *6,* 17–30.

Horney, K. *The neurotic personality of our time.* New York: Norton, 1937.

Hotchner, A. E. *Papa Hemingway: A personal memoir.* New York: Random House, 1966.

House, J. S. Occupational stress and coronary heart disease: A review and theoretical integration. *Journal of Health and Science Behavior,* 1974, *15,* 12–27.

Huessy, H. R., Metoyer, M., & Townsend, M. Eight to ten year follow-up of 84 children treated for behavioral disorder in rural Vermont. *Acta Paedopsychiatrica,* 1974, *40,* 230–235.

Hume, W. I. Physiological measures in twins. In G. Claridge, S. Canter, & S. E. Hume (Eds.), *Personality differences and biological variations: A study of twins.* Oxford: Pergamon, 1973.

Hunt, W. A., & Arnhoff, F. N. Some standardized scales for disorganization in schizophrenic thinking. *Journal of Consulting Psychology,* 1955, *19,* 171–174.

Hutchings, B., & Mednick, S. A. Criminality in adoptees and their adoptive and biological parents: A pilot study. In S. A. Mednick & K. O. Christianson (Eds.), *Biosocial bases of criminal behavior.* New York: Garden Press, 1977.

Hutt, C., & Ounsted, C. The biological significance of gaze aversion with particular reference to the syndrome of infantile autism. *Behavioral Science,* 1966, *11,* 346–356.

Inouye, E. Similarity and dissimilarity of schizophrenia in twins. *Proceedings of the Third International Congress of Psychiatry,* 1961, *1,* 524–530. (Montreal: University of Toronto Press, 1963).

Isbell, H. Clinical research on addiction in the United States. In R. B. Livingston (Ed.), *Narcotic drug addiction problems.* Public Health Service Publication No. 1050, Washington, D.C.: Government Printing Office, 1959.

Itil, T. M. Qualitative and quantitative EEG findings in schizophrenia. *Schizophrenia Bulletin,* 1977, *3,* 61–79.

Jackson, D. The study of the family. *Family Process,* 1965, *4,* 1–19.

Jacob, T. Family interaction in disturbed and normal families: A methodological and substantive review. *Psychological Bulletin,* 1975, *82,* 33–65.

Jacobs, A., Brunton, M., & Mellville, M. M. Aggressive behavior, mental subnormality, and the XYY male. *Nature*, 1965, *208*, 1351–1352.

Jacobs, J. *Adolescent suicide.* New York: Wiley, 1971.

Jacobsen, E. *Progressive relaxation.* Chicago: University of Chicago Press, 1938.

Jacobson, N. S. Problem solving and contingency contracting in the treatment of marital discord. *Journal of Consulting and Clinical Psychology,* 1977, *45,* 92–100.

Jacobson, N. S. A review of the research on the effectiveness of marital therapy. In T. J. Paolino and B. S. McCrady (Eds.), *Marriage and marital therapy: Psychoanalytic, behavioral and systems theory perspectives.* New York: Brunner/Mazel, 1978. (a)

Jacobson, N. S. Specific and nonspecific factors in the effectiveness of a behavioral approach to the treatment of marital discord. *Journal of Consulting and Clinical Psychology,* 1978, *46,* 442–452. (b)

Jacobson, N. S., & Margolin, G. *Marital therapy.* New York: Brunner/Mazel, 1979.

James, D. New laws change criteria for involuntary commitment. (University of North Carolina) *Daily Tar Heel,* December 5, 1979.

James, S. A., & Kleinbaum, D. G. Socioecologic stress and hypertension related to mortality rates in North Carolina. *American Journal of Public Health,* 1976, *66,* 354–358.

Janis, I. L. *Psychological stress.* New York: Wiley, 1958.

Janowsky, D. S., El-Yousef, M. K., Davis, J. M., & Serkerke, H. J. Provocation of schizophrenic symptoms by intravenous methylphenidate. *Archives of General Psychiatry,* 1973, *28,* 185–191.

Jarvik, L. F., Klodin, V., & Matsuyama, S. S. Human aggression and the extra Y chromosome: Fact or fiction. *American Psychologist,* 1973, *28,* 674–676.

Jenkins, R. L. Psychiatric syndromes in children and their relation to family background. *American Journal of Orthopsychiatry,* 1966, *36,* 450–457.

Jennings, C., Barraclaugh, B. M., & Moss, J. R. Have the Samaritans lowered the suicide rate? A controlled study. *Psychological Medicine,* 1978, *8,* 413–422.

Jensen, A. R. A theory of primary and secondary familial mental retardation. In N. Ellis (Ed.), *International review of research in mental retardation, Vol. 4.* New York: Academic Press, 1970.

Jersild, A. T., & Holmes, F. B. Children's fears. *Child Development Monographs,* 1935, No. 20.

Jeste, D. V., & Wyatt, R. J. In search of treatment for tardive dyskinesia. *Schizophrenia Bulletin,* 1979, *5,* 251–293.

Johnson, F. N. *Lithium research and therapy.* London: Academic Press, 1975.

Johnson, S. M., & Lobitz, G. K. The personal and marital adjustment of parents as related to observed child deviance and parenting behaviors. *Journal of Abnormal Child Psychiatry,* 1974, *2,* 192–207.

Johnson, W. *The onset of stuttering.* Minneapolis: University of Minnesota Press, 1959.

Joint Commission on Mental Illness and Health. *Action for mental health.* New York: Basic Books, 1961.

Jones, H. G. Stuttering. In C. G. Costello (Ed.), *Symptoms of psychopathology.* New York: Wiley, 1970.

Jones, M. *The therapeutic community.* New York: Basic Books, 1953.

Jones, M. C. Personality correlates and antecedents of drinking patterns in males. *Journal of Consulting and Clinical Psychology,* 1968, *32,* 2–12.

Jones, M. C. The elimination of children's fears. *Journal of Experimental Psychology,* 1924, *7,* 382–390.

Kagan, B. M. The premature infant. In V. C. Kelley (Ed.), *Brennermann's practice of pediatrics,* Vol. 1. New York: Harper & Row, 1969.

Kagan, J., & Moss, H. A. *Birth to maturity: A study in psychological development.* New York: Wiley, 1962.

Kallmann, F. J. Comparative twin study in the genetic aspects of male homosexuality. *Journal of Nervous and Mental Disease,* 1952, *115,* 283–298.

Kallmann, F. J. *Heredity in health and mental disorder.* New York: Norton, 1953.

Kandel, D., & Faust, R. Sequence and stages in patterns of adolescent drug use. *Archives of General Psychiatry,* 1975, *32,* 923–932.

Kandel, D. B., Kessler, R. C., & Margulies, R. Z. Antecedents of adolescent initiation into stages of drug use: A developmental analysis. In D. B. Kandel (Ed.), *Longitudinal research on drug use.* Washington, D.C.: Hemisphere, 1978.

Kanfer, F. H., & Saslow, G. Behavioral diagnosis. In C. M. Franks (Ed.), *Behavior therapy: Appraisal and status.* New York: McGraw-Hill, 1969.

Kanner, L. Autistic disturbances of affective contact. *Nervous Child,* 1943, *2,* 217–250.

Kanner, L. *Child psychiatry,* 3d ed. Springfield, Ill.: Charles C Thomas, 1957.

Kanner, L. Follow-up study of eleven autistic children

originally reported in 1943. *Journal of Autism and Childhood Schizophrenia,* 1971, *1,* 119–145.

Kanner, L., & Eisenberg, L. Notes on the follow-up studies of autistic children. In P. H. Hoch and J. Zubin (Eds.). *Psychopathology of childhood.* New York: Grune & Stratton, 1955.

Kanner, L., Rodriguez, A., & Alexander, B. How far can autistic children go in matters of social adaptation? *Journal of Autism and Childhood Schizophrenia,* 1972, *2,* 9–33.

Kantor, R. E., Wallner, J. M., & Winder, C. L. Process and reactive schizophrenia. *Journal of Consulting and Clinical Psychology,* 1953, *17,* 157–162.

Kaplan, H. S. *The new sex therapy.* New York: Brunner/Mazel, 1974.

Kaplan, N. M. *Your blood pressure—the most deadly high: A physician's guide to controlling your hypertension.* New York: Medcom, 1974.

Karlsruher, A. E. The nonprofessional as a psychotherapeutic agent. *American Journal of Community Psychology,* 1974, *2,* 61–77.

Karon, B. P., & Vanden Bos, G. R. The consequences of psychotherapy for schizophrenic patients. *Psychotherapy: Theory, Research, and Practice,* 1972, *9,* 111–120.

Kasius, R. V. The social breakdown syndrome in a cohort of long-stay patients in the Dutchess County Unit, 1960–1963. In E. M. Gruenberg (Ed.), *Evaluating the effectiveness of community mental health services.* New York: Milbank, 1966.

Kasl, S. V., & Cobb, S. Blood pressure changes in men undergoing job loss: A preliminary report. *Psychosomatic Medicine,* 1970, *32,* 19–38.

Kaufman, I. C., & Rosenblum, L. A. The reaction to separation in infant monkeys: Anaclitic depression and conservation-withdrawal. *Psychosomatic Medicine,* 1967, *29,* 648–675.

Kazdin, A. E. Covert modeling, imagery assessment, and assertive behavior. *Journal of Consulting Psychology,* 1975, *43,* 716–724.

Kazdin, A. E., & Bootzin, R. R. The token economy: An evaluative review. *Journal of Applied Behavior Analysis,* 1972, *5,* 343–372.

Kazdin, A. E., & Wilcoxon, L. A. Systematic desensitization and nonspecific treatment effects: A methodological evaluation. *Psychological Bulletin,* 1976, *83,* 729–758.

Kendall, R. E. The classification of depressive illnesses. *Maudsley Monograph No. 18.* London: Oxford University Press, 1968.

Kendell, R. E. Relationship between aggression and depression. *Archives of General Psychiatry,* 1970, *22,* 308–318.

Kennedy, W. A. School phobia: Rapid treatment of

fifty cases. *Journal of Abnormal Psychology,* 1965, *70,* 285–289.

Kessel, J. *The road back, a report on Alcoholics Anonymous.* New York: Knopf, 1962.

Kety, S. S., Rosenthal, D., Wender, P. H., & Schulsinger, F. Studies based on a total sample of adopted individuals and their relatives: Why they were necessary, what they demonstrated and failed to demonstrate. *Schizophrenia Bulletin,* 1976, *2,* 413–428.

Kiev, A. Transcultural psychiatry: Research problems in perspectives. In C. S. Plog and R. B. Edgerton (Eds.), *Changing perspectives in mental illness.* New York: Holt, Rinehart and Winston, 1969.

Kiloh, L. G., & Garside, R. F. The independence of neurotic and endogenous depression. *British Journal of Psychiatry,* 1963, *109,* 451–463.

Kimmel, H. D. Instrumental conditioning of autonomically mediated responses in human beings. *American Psychologist,* 1974, *29,* 325–335.

Kinney, J. M., Madsen, B., & Fleming, T. Homebuilders: Keeping families together. *Journal of Consulting and Clinical Psychology,* 1977, *45,* 667–673.

Kinsey, A. C., Pomeroy, W. B., & Martin, C. E. *Sexual behavior in the human male.* Philadelphia: Saunders, 1948.

Kinsey, A. C., Pomeroy, W. B., Martin, C. E., & Gebhard, P. H. *Sexual behavior in the human female.* Philadelphia: Saunders, 1953.

Kissen, D. M. Personality characteristics in males conducive to lung cancer. *British Journal of Medical Psychology,* 1963, *36,* 27–36.

Kissen, D. M., Brown, R. I. F., & Kissen, M. A further report on personality and psychosocial factors in lung cancer. *Annals of the New York Academy of Sciences,* 1969, *164,* 535–545.

Klebanoff, L. D. A comparison of parental attitudes of mothers of schizophrenics, brain injured, and normal children. *American Journal of Orthopsychiatry,* 1959, *24,* 445–454.

Klein, N. C., Alexander, J. F., & Parson, B. V. Impact of family systems intervention on recidivism and sibling delinquency: A model of primary prevention and program evaluation. *Journal of Consulting and Clinical Psychology,* 1977, *45,* 469–474.

Klerman, G. L. Better but not well: Social and ethical issues in the deinstitutionalization of the mentally ill. *Schizophrenia Bulletin,* 1977, *3,* 617–631.

Klorman, R., Strauss, J., & Kokes, R. Some biological approaches to research on premorbid functioning in schizophrenia. *Schizophrenia Bulletin,* 1977, *3,* 226–239.

Klüver, H., & Bucy, P. C. Preliminary analysis functions of temporal lobes in monkeys. *Archives of General Psychiatry*, 1939, *42*, 979–1000.

Kohen, W., & Paul, G. L. Current trends and recommended changes in extended-care placement of mental patients: The Illinois system as a case in point. *Schizophrenia Bulletin*, 1976, *2*, 575–594.

Kohn, M. L. Social class and schizophrenia: A critical review. In D. Rosenthal & S. S. Kety (Eds.), *The transmission of schizophrenia*. New York: Pergamon, 1968.

Kokes, R., Strauss, J., & Klorman, R. Measuring premorbid adjustment: The instruments and their development. *Schizophrenia Bulletin*, 1977, *3*, 186–213.

Kolb, L. C. *Modern clinical psychiatry*. Philadelphia: Saunders, 1973.

Kolodny, R. C., Masters, W. H., Hendryx, J., & Toro, G. Plasma testosterone and the semen analysis in male homosexuals. *New England Journal of Medicine*, 1971, *285*, 1170–1174.

Kopfstein, D. The effects of accelerating and decelerating consequences on the social behavior of trainable retarded children. *Child Development*, 1972, *43*, 800–809.

Korsten, M. A., Shohei, M., Feinman, L., & Lieber, C. S. High blood acetaldehyde levels after ethanol administration. *New England Journal of Medicine*, 1975, *292*, 386–389.

Kramer, M., Pollock, E., & Redick, R. *Mental disorders/Suicide*. Cambridge, Mass.: Harvard University Press, 1972.

Kramm, E. R. *Families of mongoloid children*. Children's Bureau Publication No. 401. Washington, D.C.: U.S. Department of Health, Education and Welfare, 1963.

Krapfl, J. E., Nawas, M. M. Differential ordering of stimulus presentation in systematic desensitization. *Journal of Abnormal Psychology*, 1970, *75*, 333–337.

Kreitman, N., Sainsbury, P., Morrissey, J., Towers, J., & Scrivener, J. The reliability of psychiatric assessment: An analysis. *Journal of Mental Science*, 1961, *107*, 887–908.

Kress, F. Evaluations of dangerousness. *Schizophrenia Bulletin*, 1979, *5*, 211–217.

Kringlen, E. *Heredity and environment in the functional psychoses*. London: Heinemann, 1967.

Kuriansky, J. B., Deming, W. E., & Gurland, B. J. On trends in the diagnosis of schizophrenia. *American Journal of Psychiatry*, 1974, *131*, 402–408.

Kutchinsky, B. The effect of easy availability of pornography on the incidence of sex crimes: The Danish experience. *Journal of Social Issues*, 1973, *29*, 163–181.

Labov, W. The logical non-standard English. In F. Williams (Ed.), *Language and poverty*. Chicago: Markham Press, 1970.

Lader, M. H., & Wing, L. Physiological measures, sedative drugs, and morbid anxiety. *Maudsley Monograph No. 14*. New York: Oxford, 1966.

Laffal, J. *Pathological and normal language*. New York: Atherton, 1965.

Lahey, B. B., Stempniak, M., Robinson, E. J., & Tyroler, M. J. Hyperactivity and learning disabilities as independent dimensions of child behavior problems. *Journal of Abnormal Psychology*, 1978, *87*, 333–340.

Lahti, R. A., & Majchrowicz, E. Ethanol and acetaldehyde effects on metabolism and binding of biogenic amines. *Quarterly Journal of Studies of Alcohol*, 1974, *35*, 1–14.

Laing, R. D., & Esterson, A. *Sanity, madness, and the family*. New York: Basic Books, 1971.

Lamb, H. R. The new asylums in the community. *Archives of General Psychiatry*, 1979, *36*, 129–134.

Lamb, H. R., & Goertzel, V. The demise of the State hospital—A premature obituary. *Archives of General Psychiatry*, 1972, *26*, 489–495.

Lambert, M. J., DeJulio, S. S., & Stein, D. M. Therapist interpersonal skills: Process, outcome, methodological considerations, and recommendations for future research. *Psychological Bulletin*, 1978, *85*, 467–489.

Landesman-Dwyer, S., Keller, S., & Streissguth, A. P. Naturalistic observations of newborns: Effects of maternal alcohol intake. *Alcoholism: Clinical and Experimental Research*, 1978, *2*, 171–177.

Lang, P. J., Lazovik, A. D., & Reynolds, D. J. Desensitization, suggestibility, and pseudotherapy. *Journal of Abnormal and Social Psychology*, 1965, *70*, 395–402.

Lang, P. J., & Melamed, B. G. Avoidance conditioning therapy of an infant with chronic ruminative vomiting. *Journal of Abnormal Psychology*, 1969, *74*, 1–8.

Langer, E. J., & Abelson, R. P. A patient by any other name . . .: Clinician group difference in labeling bias. *Journal of Consulting and Clinical Psychology*, 1974, *42*, 4–9.

Langsley, D. G., & Kaplan, D. M. *The treatment of families in crisis*. New York: Grune & Stratton, 1968.

Langford, W. Anxiety attacks in children. *American Journal of Orthopsychiatry*, 1937, *7*, 210–219.

Lanyon, R. I. Behavioral approaches to stuttering. In M. Hersen, R. M. Eisler, & P. M. Miller (Eds.), *Prog-*

ress in behavior modification. New York: Academic Press, 1978.

Lapouse, R., & Monk, M. Fears and worries in a representative sample of children. *American Journal of Orthopsychiatry,* 1959, *29,* 803–818.

Laxer, R. M., & Walker, K. Counter conditioning versus relaxation in the desensitization of test anxiety. *Journal of Counseling Psychology,* 1970, *17,* 431–436.

Lazarus, A. A. Group therapy of phobic disorders by systematic desensitization. *Journal of Abnormal and Social Psychology,* 1961, *63,* 504–510.

Lazarus, A. A. The elimination of children's phobias by deconditioning. In H. J. Eysenck (Ed.), *Behavior therapy and the neuroses.* New York: Pergamon, 1960.

Lazarus, A. A. The results of behavior therapy in 126 cases of severe neurosis. *Behavior Research and Therapy,* 1963, *1,* 65–78.

Lazarus, R. S., Opton, E. M., Nomikos, M. S., & Rankin, N. O. The principle of short-circuiting of threat: Further evidence. *Journal of Personality,* 1965, *33,* 622–635.

Leach, B. Does Alcoholics Anonymous really work? In P. G. Bourne & R. Fox (Eds.), *Alcoholism: Progress in research and treatment.* New York: Academic Press, 1973.

Leff, J. P., Fischer, M., & Bertelsen, A. A cross-national epidemiological study of mania. *British Journal of Psychiatry,* 1976, *129,* 428–442.

Leighton, A. H., Lambo, T. H., & Hughes, C. C. *Psychiatric disorder among the Yoruba.* Ithaca, N. Y.: Cornell University Press, 1963.

Lemere, F., & Voegtlin, W. An evaluation of the aversion treatment of alcoholism. *Quarterly Journal of Studies on Alcohol,* 1950, *11,* 199–204.

Leon, G. R. *Case histories of deviant behavior: A social learning analysis.* Boston: Holbrook Press, 1974.

Leopold, R. L., & Dillon, H. Psychoanatomy of a disaster: A long-term study of post-traumatic neuroses in survivors of a marine explosion. *American Journal of Psychiatry,* 1963, *119,* 913–921.

Levenstein, P. Cognitive growth in preschoolers through verbal interaction with mothers. *American Journal of Orthopsychiatry,* 1970, *40,* 426–432.

Levenstein, P., & Sunley, R. Stimulation of verbal interaction between disadvantaged mothers and children. *American Journal of Orthopsychiatry,* 1968, *38,* 116–121.

Levine, F. N., & Fasnacht, G. Token rewards may lead to token learning. *American Psychologist,* 1974, *29,* 816–820.

Levis, D. J., & Boyd, T. L. Symptom maintenance: An infrahuman analysis and extension of the conservation of anxiety principle. *Journal of Abnormal Psychology,* 1979, *88,* 107–120.

Lewin, K. Dynamic theory of personality. New York: McGraw-Hill, 1935.

Lewinsohn, P. M. A behavioral approach to depression. In R. J. Friedman and M. M. Katz (Eds.), The psychology of depression. Washington, D.C.: V. H. Winston & Sons, 1974.

Lidz, T., Fleck, S., & Cornelison, A. *Schizophrenia and the family.* New York: International Universities Press, 1965.

Lieberman, M. A. Change induction in small groups. In M. R. Rosenzweig & L. W. Porter (Eds.), *Annual review of psychology.* Palo Alto, Calif.: Annual Reviews, 1976.

Lieberman, M. A., Yalom, I. E., & Miles, M. B. *Encounter groups: First facts.* New York: Basic Books, 1973.

Liljefors, I., & Rahe, R. H. An identical twin study of psychosocial factors in coronary heart disease in Sweden. *Psychosomatic Medicine,* 1970, *32,* 523–542.

Lindeman, E. Symptomatology and management of acute grief. *American Journal of Psychiatry,* 1944, *101,* 141–148.

Lin-Fu, J. S. Undue absorption of lead among children: A new look at an old problem. *New England Journal of Medicine,* 1972, *286,* 702–710.

Liston, E. H. The clinical phenomenology of presenile dementia: A critical review of the literature. *Journal of Nervous and Mental Disease,* 1979, *167,* 329–336.

Little, L. M. & Curran, J. P. Covert sensitization: A clinical procedure in need of some explanations. *Psychological Bulletin,* 1978, *85,* 513–531.

Lobitz, W. C., & LoPiccolo, J. New methods in the behavioral treatment of sexual dysfunction. *Journal of Behavior Therapy and Experimental Psychiatry,* 1972, *3,* 265–271.

Lockyer, L., & Rutter, M. A five- to fifteen-year follow-up study of infantile psychosis. *British Journal of Psychiatry,* 1969, *115,* 865–882.

Loney, J., Langhorne, J. E., & Paternite, C. E. An empirical basis for subgrouping the hyperkinetic/minimal brain dysfunction syndrome. *Journal of Abnormal Psychology,* 1978, *87,* 431–441.

Long, R. T., Lamont, J. H., Whipple, B., Bandler, L., Blom, G. E., Burgin, L., & Jessner, L. A psychosomatic study of allergic and emotional factors in children with asthma. *American Journal of Psychiatry,* 1958, *114,* 890–899.

Lorion, R. P., Cowen, E. L., & Caldwell, R. A. Problem types of children referred to a school-based mental health program: Identification and outcome. *Journal of Consulting and Clinical Psychology,* 1974, *42,* 491–496.

Lotter, V. Follow-up studies. In M. Rutter and E. Schopler (Eds.), *Autism: A reappraisal of concepts and treatment.* New York: Plenum Press, 1978.

Lovaas, O. I. Parents as therapists. In M. Rutter & E. Schopler (Eds.), *Autism: A reappraisal of concepts and treatment.* New York: Plenum, 1978.

Lovaas, O. I., Berberich, J. P., Perloff, B. F., & Schaeffer, B. Acquisition of imitative speech by schizophrenic children. *Science,* 1966, *151,* 705–707.

Lovaas, O. I., Koegel, R. L., & Schreibman, L. Stimulus overselectivity in autism: A review of research. *Psychological Bulletin,* 1979, *86,* 1236–1254.

Lovaas, O. I., Koegel, R. L., Simmons, J. Q., & Long, J. Some generalization and follow-up measures on autistic children in behavior therapy. *Journal of Applied Behavior Analysis,* 1973, *6,* 131–166.

Lovaas, O. I., Schreibman, L., & Koegel, R. L. A behavior modification approach to the treatment of autistic children. *Journal of Autism and Childhood Schizophrenia,* 1974, *4,* 111–129.

Lovaas, O. I., & Simmons, J. Q. Manipulation of self-destruction in three retarded children. *Journal of Applied Behavior Analysis,* 1969, *2,* 143–157.

Lovibond, S. H. Conditioning and enuresis. Oxford: Pergamon, 1964.

Lovibond, S. H., & Coote, M. A. Enuresis. In C. G. Costello (Ed.), *Symptoms of psychopathology.* New York: Wiley, 1970.

Luborsky, L., & Spence, D. P. Quantitative research on psychoanalytic therapy. In A. E. Bergin & S. L. Garfield (Eds.), *Handbook of psychotherapy and behavior change: An empirical analysis.* New York: Wiley, 1971.

Lucas, R. N. Migraine in twins. *Journal of Psychosomatic Research,* 1977, *20,* 147–156.

Lunde, D. T. *Murder and madness.* Stanford, Calif.: Stanford University Press, 1975.

Luxenburger, H. Vorläufiger bericht über psychiatrische serienuntersuchungen an zwillingen. *Zeitschrift für die gesamte Neurologic und Psychiatric,* 1928, *116,* 297–326.

Lykken, D. T. A study of anxiety in the sociopathic personality. *Journal of Abnormal and Social Psychology,* 1957, *55,* 6–10.

MacDonald, N. The other side: Living with schizophrenia. *Canadian Medical Association Journal,* 1960, *82,* 218–221.

MacMillan, D. L. Paired-associate learning as a function of explicitness of mediational set by EMR and non-retarded children. *American Journal of Mental Deficiency,* 1972, *76,* 686–691.

Madden, J., Levenstein, P., & Levenstein, S. Longitudinal IQ outcomes of the mother-child home program. *Child Development,* 1976, *47,* 1015–1025.

Madison, P. *Personality development in college.* Reading, Mass.: Addison-Wesley, 1969.

Maher, B. A., McKean, K., & McLaughlin, B. Studies in psychotic language. In P. Stone (Ed.), *The general inquirer: A computer approach to content analysis.* Cambridge, Mass.: Massachusetts Institute of Technology, 1966.

Mahrer, A. R. *Experiencing: A humanistic theory of psychology and psychiatry.* New York: Brunner/Mazel, 1978.

Mahoney, M. J. *Cognition and behavior modification.* Cambridge, Mass.: Ballinger, 1974.

Malan, D. H., Heath, E. S., Bacal, H. A., & Balfour, F. H. G. Psychodynamic changes in untreated neurotic patients—II. Apparently genuine improvements. *Archives of General Psychiatry,* 1975, *32,* 110–126.

Malcolm X, with assistance of Alex Haley. *The autobiography of Malcolm X.* New York: Grove Press, 1966.

Maletzky, B. M. "Assisted" covert sensitization in the treatment of exhibitionism. *Journal of Consulting and Clinical Psychology,* 1974, *42,* 34–40.

Malmo, R. B. Hysterical deafness in a young girl. In A. Burton & R. E. Harris (Eds.), *Clinical studies in personality.* New York: Harper & Row, 1955.

Malmo, R. B., Boag, T. J., & Raginsky, B. B. Electromyographic study of hypnotic deafness. *International Journal of Clinical and Experimental Hypnosis,* 1954, *2,* 305–317.

Mann, M. *New primer on alcoholism,* 2d ed. New York: Holt, Rinehart and Winston, 1968.

Mark, J. C. The attitudes of the mothers of male schizophrenics toward child behavior. *Journal of Abnormal and Social Psychology,* 1953, *48,* 185–189.

Mark, V. H., & Ervin, F. R. *Violence and the brain.* New York: Harper & Row, 1970.

Marks, I., Boulougouris, J., & Marset, P. Flooding versus desensitization in the treatment of phobic patients: A crossover study. *British Journal of Psychiatry,* 1971, *119,* 353–375.

Marlatt, G. A. A comparison of aversion conditioning procedures in the treatment of alcoholism. Paper presented at the meeting of the Western Psychological Association, Anaheim, California, April 1973.

Marlatt, G. A., Demming, B., & Reid, J. B. Loss-of-control drinking in alcoholics: An experimental analogue. *Journal of Abnormal Psychology,* 1973, *81,* 233–241.

Marlatt, G. A., & Gordon, J. R. Determinants of relapse: Implications for the maintenance of behavior change. In P. Davidson (Ed.), *Behavioral medicine: Changing health lifestyles.* New York: Brunner/Mazel, 1979.

Marlatt, G. A., Kosturn, C. F., & Lang, A. R. Provocation of anger and opportunity for retaliation as determinants of alcohol consumption in social drinkers. *Journal of Abnormal Psychology,* 1975, *84,* 652–659.

Marmor, J. New direction in psychoanalytic theory and therapy. In J. Marmor (Ed.), *Modern psychoanalysis.* New York: Basic Books, 1968.

Marris, P. *Widows and their families.* London: Routledge and Kegan Paul, 1958.

Martin, B. Reward and punishment associated with the same goal response: a factor in the learning of motives. *Psychological Bulletin,* 1963, *60,* 441–451.

Martin, B. *Anxiety and neurotic disorders.* New York: Wiley, 1971.

Martin, B. *Abnormal psychology.* Glenview, Ill.: Scott, Foresman, 1973.

Martin, B. Parent-child relations. Ir F. D. Horowtiz (Ed.), *Review of Child Development Research.* Chicago: University of Chicago Press, 1975.

Martin, B. Brief family intervention: Effectiveness and the importance of including the father. *Journal of Consulting and Clinical Psychology,* 1977, *45,* 1002–1010.

Martin, E. The life of a problem drinker. *Durham (N.C.) Morning Herald,* April 21, 1974, 1E.

Massie, H. N. Blind ratings of mother-infant interaction in home movies of prepsychotic and normal infants. *American Journal of Psychiatry,* 1978, *135,* 1371–1374. (a)

Massie, H. N. The early natural history of childhood psychosis. *Journal of the American Academy of Child Psychiatry,* 1978, *17,* 29–45. (b)

Masters, W. H., & Johnson, V. E. *Human sexual response.* Boston: Little, Brown, 1966.

Masters, W. H., & Johnson, V. E. *Human sexual inadequacy.* Boston: Little, Brown, 1970.

Maurer, D. W., & Vogel, V. H. *Narcotics and narcotics addiction.* Springfield, Ill.: Charles C Thomas, 1954.

May, P. R. A., Tuma, A. H., Yale, C., Potepan, P., & Dixon, N. J. Schizophrenia—A follow-up study of results of treatment. *Archives of General Psychiatry,* 1976, *33,* 481–486.

May, R. *Psychology and the human dilemma.* New York: Van Nostrand, 1967.

Mayfield, D., & Allen, D. Alcohol and affect: Psychopharmacological study. *American Journal of Psychiatry,* 1967, *123,* 1346–1351.

McClelland, D. C. *Power: The inner experience.* New York: Irvington-Halsted-Wiley, 1975.

McClelland, D. C. Inhibited power motivation and high blood pressure in men. *Journal of Abnormal Psychology,* 1979, *88,* 182–190.

McCord, W., & McCord, J. *The psychopath: An essay on the criminal mind.* New York: Van Nostrand Reinhold, 1964.

McCord, W., McCord, J., & Gudeman, J. *Origins of alcoholism.* Stanford, Calif.: Stanford University Press, 1960.

McCord, W., McCord, J., & Zola, I. K. *Origins of crime.* New York: Columbia University Press, 1959.

McCord, W., Porta, J., & McCord, J. The familial genesis of psychoses. *Psychiatry,* 1962, *25,* 60–71.

McGhie, A., & Chapman, J. S. Disorders of attention and perception in early schizophrenia. *British Journal of Medical Psychology,* 1961, *34,* 103–116.

McGinn, N. F., Harburg, E., Julius, S., & McLeod, J. Psychological correlates of blood pressure. *Psychological Bulletin,* 1964, *61,* 209–219.

McGuire, R. J., Carlisle, J. M., & Young, B. G. Sexual deviations as conditioned behavior: A hypothesis. *Behaviour Research and Therapy,* 1965, *2,* 185–190.

McKay, H. D. Report on the careers of male delinquents in Chicago. In U.S. Task Force on Juvenile Delinquency, *Juvenile delinquency and youth crime,* Washington, D.C.: U.S. Government Printing Office, 1967.

McKay, H., Sinisterra, L., McKay, A., Gomez, H., & Lloreda, P. Improving cognitive ability in chronically deprived children. *Science,* 1978, *200,* 270–278.

McKinley, R. A. Perceived parental attributes of schizophrenics as a function of premorbid adjustment. Unpublished doctoral dissertation, University of Iowa, 1963. Also described in A. B. Heilbrun, *Aversive maternal control.* New York: Wiley, 1973.

McNamara, J. J. Hyperactivity in the apartment bound child. *Clinical Pediatrics,* 1972, *11,* 371–372.

McNamee, H. B., Mello, N. K., & Mendelson, J. H. Experimental analysis of drinking patterns in alcoholics: Concurrent psychiatric observations. *American Journal of Psychiatry,* 1968, *124,* 1063–1071.

McNeil, E. B. *The quiet furies.* Englewood Cliffs, N. J.: Prentice-Hall, 1967.

Mednick, S. A., & Schulsinger, F. Some premorbid characteristics related to breakdown in children with schizophrenic mothers. In D. Rosenthal & S. S. Kety (Eds.), *The transmission of schizophrenia.* New York: Pergamon, 1968.

Mednick, S. A., & Schulsinger, F. A learning theory of schizophrenia: Thirteen years later. In M. Hammer, K. Salzinger, & S. Sutton (Eds.), *Psychopathology: Contributions from the social, behavioral, and biological sciences.* New York: Wiley, 1973.

Mednick, S. A., Schulsinger, H., & Schulsinger, F. Schizophrenia in children of schizophrenic mothers. In A. Davids (Ed.), *Child personality and psychopathology: Current topics.* Vol. 2. New York: Wiley, 1975.

Meehl, P. E. Schizotaxia, schizotypy, schizophrenia. *American Psychologist,* 1962, *17,* 827–838.

Meichenbaum, D. H. Cognitive modification of test anxious college students. *Journal of Consulting and Clinical Psychology,* 1972, *39,* 370–380.

Meichenbaum, D. *Cognitive-behavior modification.* New York: Plenum, 1977.

Meichenbaum, D., & Cameron, R. Stress inoculation: A skills training approach to anxiety management. Unpublished manuscript, University of Waterloo, 1972. Described in detail in D. Meichenbaum, *Cognitive behavior modification.* New York: Plenum, 1977.

Mendels, J. The prediction of response to electroconvulsive therapy. *American Journal of Psychiatry,* 1967, *124,* 153–159.

Mendelson, J. H., LaDou, L., & Solomon, P. Experimentally induced chronic intoxication and withdrawal in alcoholics. Part 3: Psychiatric findings. *Quarterly Journal of Studies of Alcohol,* 1964, *40,* Supplement 2.

Metz, J. R. Conditioning generalized imitation in autistic children. In J. Fisher & R. E. Harris (Eds.), *Reinforcement theory in psychological treatment—A symposium. California Mental Health Research Monograph,* 1966, *8,* 40–49.

Meyer, J. K., & Reter, D. J. Sex reassignment. *Archives of General Psychiatry,* 1979, *36,* 1010–1015.

Meyer-Bahlburg, H. F. L. Sex hormones and female homosexuality: A critical examination. *Archives of Sexual Behavior,* 1979, *8,* 101–118.

Meyers, E. I., & Goldfarb, W. Psychiatric appraisal of parents and siblings of schizophrenic children. *American Journal of Psychiatry,* 1962, *118,* 902–908.

Milgram, N. A. Cognition and language in mental retardation: Distinctions and implications. In D. K. Routh (Ed.), *The experimental psychology of mental retardation.* Chicago: Aldine, 1973.

Miller, N. E. Learnable drives and rewards. In S. Stevens (Ed.), *Handbook of experimental psychology.* New York: Wiley, 1951.

Miller, N. E. Learning of visceral and glandular responses. *Science,* 1969, *163,* 434–445.

Miller, N. E. Biofeedback and visceral learning. In M. R. Rosenzweig and L. W. Porter (Eds.). *Annual review of psychology, 1978.* Palo Alto, Calif.: Annual Reviews, Inc., 1978.

Miller, P. McC., & Ingham, J. G. Friends, confidants, and symptoms. *Social Psychiatry,* 1976, *11,* 51–58.

Miller, R. G., Palkes, H. S., & Stewart, M. A. Hyperactive children in suburban elementary schools. *Child Psychiatry and Human Development,* 1973, *4,* 121–127.

Millon, T., & Millon, R. *Abnormal behavior and personality.* Philadelphia: Saunders, 1974.

Mineka, S. The role of fear in theories of avoidance learning, flooding, and extinction. *Psychological Bulletin,* 1979, *86,* 985–1010.

Mintz, N. L., & Schwartz, D. T. Ecological factors in the incidence of schizophrenic and manic-depressive psychoses. In N. L. Corah & E. N. Gale (Eds.), *The origins of abnormal behavior.* Reading, Mass.: Addison-Wesley, 1971.

Minuchin, S. *Families and family therapy.* Cambridge, Mass.: Harvard University Press, 1974.

Minuchin, S., Rosman, B. L., & Baker, L. *Psychosomatic families: Anorexia nervosa in context.* Cambridge, Mass.: Harvard University Press, 1978.

Mischel, W., & Liebert, R. M. Effects of discrepancies between observed and imposed reward criteria on their acquisition and transmission. *Journal of Personality and Social Psychology,* 1966, *3,* 45–53.

Mishler, E., & Waxler, N. *Interaction in families: An experimental study of family processes and schizophrenia.* New York: Wiley, 1968.

Mitchell, K. M., Truax, C. B., Bozarth, J. D., Krauft, C. C. *Antecedents to psychotherapeutic outcome.* National Institute of Mental Health Final Report, 1973.

Mitchell, K. R., & White, R. G. Behavioral self-management: An application to the problem of migraine headaches. *Behavior Therapy,* 1977, *8,* 213–221.

Modlin, H. C. The postaccident anxiety syndrome: Psychosocial aspects. *American Journal of Psychiatry,* 1967, *123,* 1108–1121.

Mohr, G. J., Tausend, H., Selesnick, S., & Augenbraun, B. Studies of eczema and asthma in the preschool child. *Journal of American Academy of Child Psychiatry,* 1963, *2,* 271–291.

Montigny, C. D., & Aghajanian, G. K. Tricyclic antidepressants: Long-term treatment increases responsivity of rat forebrain neurons to serotonin. *Science,* 1978, *202,* 1303–1305.

Moore, N. Behaviour therapy in bronchial asthma: A controlled study. *Journal of Psychosomatic Research,* 1965, *9,* 257–276.

Morganstern, K. P. Implosive therapy and flooding procedures. *Psychological Bulletin,* 1973, *79,* 318–334.

Morris, J. *Conundrum.* New York: New American Library, 1974.

Morris, J. B., & Beck, A. T. The efficacy of antidepressant drugs. *Archives of General Psychiatry,* 1974, *30,* 667–671.

Morrison, J. R., & Stewart, M. A. A family study of the hyperactive child syndrome. *Biological Psychiatry,* 1971, *3,* 189–195.

Morrison, J., Winokur, G., Crowe, R., & Clancy, J. The Iowa 500: The first follow-up. *Archives of General Psychiatry,* 1973, *29,* 678–682.

Mosher, L. R., & Keith, S. J. Psychosocial treatment: Individual, group, family, and community support approaches. *Schizophrenia Bulletin.* 1980, *6,* 10–41.

Mosher, L. R., & Menn, A. Community residential treatment for schizophrenia: Two year follow-up data. *Hospital and Community Psychiatry,* 1978, *29,* 715–723.

Moss, C. S. Brief successful psychotherapy of a chronic phobic reaction. *Journal of Abnormal Psychology,* 1960, *60,* 266–270.

Moss, C. S. Recovery with aphasia. Chicago: University of Illinois Press, 1972.

Mowrer, O. H. *Learning theory and personality dynamics.* New York: Ronald, 1950.

Mucha, T. F., & Reinhardt, R. F. Conversion reactions in student aviators. *American Journal of Psychiatry,* 1970, *127,* 493–497.

Mueller, D. P., Edwards, D. W., & Yarvis, R. M. Stressful life events and psychiatric symptomatology: Change or undesirability? *Journal of Health and Social Behavior,* 1977, *18,* 307–317.

Munzinger, H. The adopted child's IQ: A critical review. *Psychological Bulletin,* 1975, *82,* 623–659.

Murphy, H. B. M. Cultural factors in the genesis of schizophrenia. In D. Rosenthal & S. S. Kety (Eds.), *The transmission of schizophrenia.* New York: Pergamon, 1968.

Murphy, H. B. M., Wittkower, E. D., Fried, J., & Ellenberger, H. A cross-cultural survey of schizophrenic symptomatology. *International Journal of Social Psychiatry,* 1963, *9,* 237–249.

Murphy, J. M. Psychotherapeutic aspect of Shamanism on St. Lawrence Island, Alaska. In A. Kiev (Ed.), *Magic, faith, and healing.* New York: Free Press, Macmillan, 1964.

Nathan, P. E., Goldman, M. S., Lisman, S. A., & Taylor, H. A. Alcohol and alcoholics: A behavioral approach. *Transactions of the New York Academy of Science,* 1972, *34,* 602–627.

Nathan, P. E., & O'Brien, J. S. An experimental analysis of the behavior of alcoholics and non-alcoholics during prolonged experimental drinking: A necessary precursor of behavior therapy? *Behavior Therapy,* 1971, *2,* 455–476.

Nathan, P. E., Simpson, H. F., Andberg, M. M., & Patch, V. D. A systems analytic model of diagnosis III: The diagnostic validity of abnormal cognitive behavior. *Journal of Clinical Psychology,* 1969, *25,* 120–130.

National Institute of Alcohol Abuse and Alcoholism. *Alcohol and health.* Rockville, Md., 1978.

National Institute of Mental Health. The cost of mental illness. Rockville, Md.: Statistical Note 125, 1976.

Neale, J. M. Perceptual span in schizophrenia. *Journal of Abnormal Psychology,* 1971, *77,* 196–204.

Neisser, V. *Cognitive psychology.* New York: Appleton, 1967.

Nemiah, J. C. *Foundations of psychopathology.* New York: Oxford University Press, 1961.

Nielsen, J. & Videbech, T. Suicide frequency before and after introduction of community psychiatry in a Danish island. *British Journal of Psychiatry,* 1973, *123,* 35–39.

Noyes, R., Clancy, J., Crowe, R., Hoenk, P. R., & Slymen, D. J. The familial prevalence of anxiety neurosis. *Archives of General Psychiatry,* 1978, *35,* 1057–1059.

Nunnally, J. C. Psychometric theory. New York: McGraw-Hill, 1967.

Nyback, H., Borzecki, Z., & Sedvall, G. Accumulation and disappearance of catecholamines formed from tyrosine-C in mouse brain; effect of some psychotropic drugs. *European Journal of Pharmacology,* 1968, *4,* 395–402.

Obler, M. Systematic desensitization in sexual disorders. *Journal of Behavior Therapy and Experimental Psychiatry,* 1973, *4,* 93–101.

O'Connor, N., & Hermelin, B. The spatial or temporal organization of short term memory. *Quarterly Journal of Experimental Psychology,* 1973, *25,* 335–343.

O'Connor, R. D. Modification of social withdrawal through symbolic modeling. *Journal of Applied Behavior Analysis,* 1969, *2,* 15–22.

O'Donnell, J. A. Lifetime patterns of narcotic addiction. In M. A. Roff, L. N. Robins, & M. Pollack (Eds.), *Life history research in psychopathology,* Vol. 2. Minneapolis: University of Minnesota Press, 1972.

O'Leary, K. D., Pelham, W. E., Rosenbaum, A., & Price, G. H. Behavioral treatment of hyperkinetic children. *Clinical Pediatrics,* 1976, *15,* 510–515.

Olson, R. P., & Greenberg, D. J. Effects of contingency-contracting and decision-making groups with chronic mental patients. *Journal of Consulting and Clinical Psychology,* 1972, *38,* 376–383.

Oltmanns, T. F., Broderick, J. E., & O'Leary, K. D. Marital adjustment and the efficacy of behavior therapy with children. *Journal of Consulting and Clinical Psychology,* 1977, *45,* 724–729.

Opler, M. K. Cultural differences in mental disorders: An Italian and Irish contrast in the schizophrenics—U.S.A. In M. K. Opler, (Ed.), *Culture and mental health.* New York: Macmillan, 1954.

Ott, J. The eyes' dual function. Part II. *Eye, Ear, Nose, and Throat Monthly,* 1974, *53,* 377–381.

Owen, A. R. G. *Hysteria, hypnosis, and healing: The work of J. M. Charcot.* London: Dobson, 1971.

Parke, R. D. Effectiveness of punishment as an interaction of intensity, timing, agent nurturance, and cognitive structuring. *Child Development,* 1969, *40,* 211–235.

Parry-Jones, W. L., Santer-Westrate, H. C., & Crawley, R. C. Behaviour therapy in a case of hysterical blindness. *Behaviour Research and Therapy,* 1970, *8,* 79–85.

Pasamanick, B. Some misconceptions concerning differences in the racial prevalance of mental disease. *American Journal of Orthopsychiatry,* 1963, *33,* 72–86.

Patterson, G. R. The aggressive child: Victim and architect of a coercive system. In E. Mash, L. Hamerlynck, & L. Handy (Eds.), *Behavior modification and families. I. Theory and research.* New York: Brunner/Mazel, 1976.

Patterson, G. R. Mothers, the unacknowledged victims. In J. H. Steven & M. Matthews (Eds.), *Mother-child, father-child relations.* Washington, D.C.: N.A.E.Y.C., 1977.

Patterson, G. R. A performance theory for coercive family interaction. In R. B. Cairns (Ed.), *Social interactional analysis: Methods and illustrations.* New York: Lawrence Erlbaum Associates, 1979.

Patterson, G. R., & Fleischman, M. J. Maintenance of treatment effects: Some considerations concerning family systems and follow-up data. *Behavior Therapy,* 1979, *10,* 168–185.

Pattison, E. M., Sobell, M. B., & Sobell, L. C. *Emerg-ing concepts of alcohol dependence.* New York: Springer, 1977.

Paul, G. L. *Insight vs. desensitization in psychotherapy.* Stanford, Calif.: Stanford University Press, 1966.

Paul, G. L. Insight versus desensitization in psychotherapy two years after termination. *Journal of Consulting Psychology,* 1967, *31,* 333–348.

Paul, G. L., & Lentz, R. J. *Psychosocial treatment of chronic mental patients: Milieu versus social-learning programs.* Cambridge, Mass.: Harvard University Press, 1977.

Paul, I. H. *Letters to Simon: On the conduct of psychotherapy.* New York: International Universities Press, 1973.

Pauly, I. Male psychosexual inversion: Transsexualism. *Archives of General Psychiatry,* 1965, *13,* 172–181.

Pavlov, I. P. *Lectures on conditioned reflexes* (W. H. Gannt, Trans.). New York: International Publishers, 1928.

Paykel, E. S., Prusoff, B. A., & Myers, J. K. Suicide attempts and recent life events. *Archives of General Psychiatry,* 1975, *32,* 327–331.

Payne, J. S. Prevalence survey of severely mentally retarded in Wyandotte County, Kansas. *Training School Bulletin,* 1971, *67,* 220–227.

Perls, F. S. *Gestalt therapy verbatim.* Lafayette, Calif.; Real People Press, 1969.

Perris, C. A study of bipolar (manic-depressive) and unipolar recurrent depressive psychoses. *Acta Psychiatrica Scandinavica,* 1966, Supplement 194.

Perrucci, R. *Circle of madness.* Englewood Cliffs, N. J.: Prentice-Hall, 1974.

Persons, R. W. Psychological and behavioral change in delinquents following psychotherapy. *Journal of Clinical Psychology,* 1966, *22,* 337–340.

Persons, R. W. Relationship between psychotherapy with institutionalized boys and subsequent community adjustment. *Journal of Consulting Psychology,* 1967, *31,* 137–141.

Pert, C. B., & Snyder, S. H. Opiate receptor: Demonstration in nervous tissue. *Science,* 1973, *179,* 1011–1014.

Phillips, L. Case history data and prognosis in schizophrenia. *Journal of Nervous and Mental Disease,* 1953, *117,* 515–525.

Piaget, J. Piaget's theory. In P. H. Mussen (Ed.), *Carmichael's manual of child psychology,* 3d ed. New York: Wiley, 1970.

Pierce, C. M. Enuresis. In A. M. Freedman & H. I. Kaplan (Eds.), *Comprehensive textbook of psychiatry.* Baltimore: Williams & Wilkins, 1967.

Piggott, L. R. Overview of selected basic research in autism. *Journal of Autism and Developmental Disorders,* 1979, *9,* 199–218.

Pihl, R. O., & Parkes, M. Hair element contents in learning disabled children. *Science,* 1977, *198,* 204–206.

Polansky, N. A., Borgman, R. D., & De Saix, C. *Roots of futility.* San Francisco: Jossey-Bass, 1972.

Pollin, W., & Stabenau, J. R. Biological, psychological, and historical differences in a series of monozygotic twins discordant for schizophrenia. In D. Rosenthal & S. S. Kety (Eds.), *The transmission of schizophrenia.* New York: Pergamon, 1968.

Post, R. M., Fink, E., Carpenter, W. T., & Goodwin, F. K. Cerebrospinal fluid amine metabolites in acute schizophrenia. *Archives of General Psychiatry,* 1975, *32,* 1063–1069.

Prichard, J. C. *Treatise on insanity.* London: Gilbert and Piper, 1835.

Prien, R. J. Lithium in the prophylactic treatment of affective disorders. *Archives of General Psychiatry,* 1979, *36,* 847–848.

Proctor, J. T. Hysteria in childhood. *American Journal of Orthopsychiatry,* 1958, *28,* 394–406.

Purcell, K. Distinctions between subgroups of asthmatic children: Children's perceptions of events associated with asthma. *Pediatrics,* 1963, *31,* 486–494.

Purcell, K. Childhood asthma: The role of family relationships, personality, and emotions. In A. Davids (Ed.), *Child personality and psychopathology: Current topics Vol. 2.* New York: Wiley, 1975.

Purcell, K., Brady, K., Chai, H., Muser, J., Molk, L., Gordon, N., & Means, J. The effect on asthma in children of experimental separation from the family. *Psychosomatic Medicine,* 1969, *31,* 144–164.

Quay, H. C. Psychopathic behavior: Reflections on its nature, origins, and treatment. In F. Weizmann & I. Uzgiris (Eds.), *The structuring of experience.* New York: Plenum, 1977.

Quay, H. C. Classification. In H. C. Quay & J. S. Werry (Eds.), *Psychopathological disorders of childhood.* New York: Wiley, 1979.

Rabkin, J. G. Criminal behavior of discharged mental patients: A critical appraisal of the research. *Psychological Bulletin,* 1979, *86,* 1–27.

Rachman, S. *The effects of psychotherapy.* New York: Pergamon, 1971.

Rachman, S. The conditioning theory of fear acquisition: A critical examination. *Behavior Research and Therapy,* 1977, *15,* 375–387.

Rahe, R. H. Life-change measurement as a predictor of illness. *Proceedings of the Royal Society of Medicine,* 1968, *61,* 1124–1126.

Ramey, C. T., Hieger, L., & Klisz, D. Synchronous reinforcement of vocal responses in failure-to-thrive infants. *Child Development,* 1972, *43,* 1449–1455.

Raphael, B. Preventive intervention with the recently bereaved. *Archives of General Psychiatry,* 1977, *34,* 1450–1454.

Rapoport, J. L., Quinn, P. O., & Lamprecht, F. Minor physical anomalies and plasma dopamine-beta-hydroxylose activity in hyperactive boys. *American Journal of Psychiatry,* 1974, *131,* 386–390.

Rattan, R. B., & Chapman, L. J. Associative intrusions in schizophrenic verbal behavior. *Journal of Abnormal Psychology,* 1973, *82,* 169–173.

Raymond, M. J. Case of fetishism treated by aversion therapy. *British Medical Journal,* 1956, *2,* 854–857.

Razran, G. The observable unconscious and the inferable conscious in current Soviet psychophysiology: Interoceptive conditioning, semantic conditioning, and the orienting reflex. *Psychological Review,* 1961, *68,* 81–147.

Redlich, F. C., & Freedman, D. X. *The theory and practice of psychiatry.* New York: Basic Books, 1966.

Rees, L. The importance of psychological, allergic, and infective factors in childhood asthma. *Journal of Psychosomatic Research,* 1964, *7,* 253–262.

Rehm, L. P., & Marston, A. R. Reduction in social anxiety through modification of self-reinforcement: An instigation therapy technique. *Journal of Consulting and Clinical Psychology,* 1968, *32,* 565–574.

Reich, R. *American Psychological Association Monitor.* Washington, D.C., March 1974.

Reiff, R., & Riessman, F. The indigenous nonprofessional. A strategy of change in community action and community mental health programs. *Community Mental Health Journal,* Monograph No. 1, 1965.

Reilly, F., Harrow, M., & Tucker, G. Language and thought content in acute psychoses. *American Journal of Psychiatry,* 1973, *130,* 411–417.

Rennie, T. A. C. Prognosis in manic-depressive psychoses. *American Journal of Psychiatry,* 1942, *98,* 801–814.

Rich, A. R., & Schroeder, H. E. Research issues in assertiveness training. *Psychological Bulletin,* 1976, *83,* 1081–1096.

Richer, J. The social-avoidance behavior of autistic children. *Animal Behavior,* 1976, *24,* 898–906.

Richer, J. The partial noncommunication of culture to autistic children—An application of human ethology. In M. Rutter and E. Schopler (Eds.), *Autism: A reappraisal of concepts and treatment.* New York: Plenum Press, 1978.

Richmond, J. B., Lipton, E. L., & Steinschneider, A. Autonomic function in the neonate. V. Individual homeostatic capacity in cardiac response. *Psychosomatic Medicine,* 1962, *24,* 66–74.

Rickels, K., Downing, R. W., & Howard, M. A. Chlordiazepoxide in the treatment of anxiety. *Clinical Pharmacology and Therapeutics,* 1971, *12,* 263–273.

Ricks, D., & Nameche, G. Symbiosis, sacrifice and schizophrenia. *Mental Hygiene,* 1966, *50,* 541–551.

Rie, E., Rie, E. D., Stewart, S., & Ambuel, J. P. Effects of Ritalin on underachieving children: A replication. *American Journal of Orthopsychiatry,* 1976, *46,* 313–321.

Rimm, D. C., Janda, L. H., Lancaster, D. W., Nahl, M., & Dittmar, K. An exploratory investigation of the origin and maintenance of phobias. *Behavior Research and Therapy,* 1977, *15,* 231–238.

Rioch, M. J. Pilot projects in training mental health counselors. In E. L. Cowen, E. A. Gardner, & M. Zax (Eds.), *Emergent approaches to mental health problems.* New York: Appleton, 1967.

Robins, L. N. *A follow-up of Vietnam drug users* (Interim Final Report, Special Action Office Monograph, Series A, No. 1.) Washington: Government Printing Office, 1973.

Robins, L. N. Aetiological implications in studies of childhood histories relating to antisocial personality. In R. D. Hare & D. Schalling (Eds.), *Psychopathic behavior: Approaches to research.* New York: Wiley, 1978. (a)

Robins, L. N. The interaction of setting and predisposition in explaining novel behavior: Drug initiations before, in, and after Vietnam. Washington, D.C.: Hemisphere, 1978. (b)

Rogers, C. R. *Counseling and psychotherapy: New concepts in practice.* Boston: Houghton Mifflin, 1942.

Rogers, C. R. *Client-centered therapy.* Boston: Houghton Mifflin, 1951.

Rogers, C. R. The necessary and sufficient conditions of therapeutic personality change. *Journal of Consulting Psychology,* 1957, *21,* 95–103.

Rogers, C. R. *On becoming a person.* Boston: Houghton Mifflin, 1961.

Rogers, C. R. Client-centered psychotherapy. In A. M. Freedman & H. I. Kaplan (Eds.), *Comprehensive textbook of psychiatry.* Baltimore: Williams & Wilkins, 1967.

Rogers, C. R., Gendlin, E. T., Kiesler, D. J., & Truax, C. B. (Eds.). *The therapeutic relationship and its impact: A study of psychotherapy with schizophrenics.* Madison: University of Wisconsin Press, 1967.

Romano, J. On the nature of schizophrenia: Changes in the observer as well as the observed. *Schizophrenia Bulletin,* 1977, *3,* 532–558.

Rosanoff, A. J., Handy, L. M., Plesset, I. R., & Brush, S. The etiology of so-called schizophrenic psychoses with special reference to their occurrence in twins. *American Journal of Psychiatry,* 1934, *91,* 247–286.

Rose, R. J., Harris, E. L., Christian, J. C., & Nance, W. E. Genetic variance in nonverbal intelligence: Data from the kinships of identical twins. *Science,* 1979, *205,* 1153–1155.

Rosen, G. *Madness in society.* Chicago: University of Chicago Press, 1968.

Rosenbaum, A., O'Leary, K. D., & Jacob, R. G. Behavioral intervention with hyperactive children: Group consequences as a supplement to individual contingencies. *Behavior Therapy,* 1975, *6,* 315–323.

Rosenfeld, G. B., & Bradley, C. Childhood behavior sequelae of asphyxia in infancy: With special reference to pertussis and asphyxia neonatorum. *Pediatrics,* 1948, *2,* 74–78.

Rosenhan, D. L. On being sane in insane places. *Science,* 1973, *179,* 250–258.

Rosenthal, D. Some factors associated with concordance and discordance with respect to schizophrenia in monozygotic twins. *Journal of Nervous and Mental Disease,* 1959, *129,* 1–10.

Rosenthal, D. *Genetics of psychopathology.* New York: McGraw-Hill, 1971.

Rosenthal, D., Wender, P. H., Kety, S. S., Schulsinger, F., Welner, J., & Rieder, R. Parent-child relationships and psychopathological disorder in the child. *Archives of General Psychiatry,* 1975, *32,* 466–476.

Rosenthal, D., Wender, P. H., Kety, S. S., Schulsinger, F., Welner, J., & Ostergaard, L. Schizophrenics' offspring reared in adoptive homes. In D. Rosenthal & S. S. Kety (Eds.), *The transmission of schizophrenia.* New York: Pergamon, 1968.

Rosett, H. L., Ouellette, E. M.; Weiner, L., & Owens, E. Therapy of heavy drinking during pregnancy. *Obstetrics-Gynecology,* 1978, *51,* 41–51.

Ross, A. O. *Psychological disorders of children.* New York: McGraw-Hill, 1980.

Ross, D. M., & Ross, S. A. *Hyperactivity: Research, theory, and action.* New York: Wiley, 1976.

Ro-Trock, G. K., Wellisch, D. K., & Schoolar, J. C. A family therapy outcome study in an inpatient setting. *American Journal of Orthopsychiatry,* 1977, *47,* 514–522.

Routh, D. K., & Roberts, R. D. Minimal brain dysfunction in children: Failure to find evidence for a behavioral syndrome. *Psychological Reports,* 1972, *31,* 307–314.

Rubens, R. L., & Lapidus, L. B. Schizophrenic patterns of arousal and stimulus barrier functioning. *Journal of Abnormal Psychology,* 1978, *87,* 199–211.

Runyon, R. P., & Haber, A. *Fundamentals of behavioral statistics,* 2d ed. Reading, Mass.: Addison-Wesley, 1971.

Russell, A., & Winkler, R. Evaluation of assertive training and homosexual guidance service groups designed to improve homosexual functioning. *Journal of Consulting and Clinical Psychology,* 1977, *45,* 1–13.

Rutter, M. Parent-child separation: Psychological effects on the children. *Journal of Child Psychology and Psychiatry,* 1971, *12,* 233–256.

Rutter, M. Diagnosis and definition. In M. Rutter and E. Schopler (Eds.), *Autism: A reappraisal of concepts and treatment.* New York: Plenum, 1978.

Rutter, M., Cox, A., Tupling, C., Berger, M., & Yule, W. Attainment and adjustment in two geographical areas. *British Journal of Psychiatry,* 1975, *126,* 493–509.

Ryan, B. P., & Van Kirk, B. The establishment, transfer, and maintenance of fluent speech in 50 stutterers using delayed auditory feedback and operant procedures. *Journal of Speech and Hearing Disorders,* 1974, *39,* 3–10.

Saccuzzo, D. P., Kerr, M., Marcus, A., & Brown, R. Input capability and speed of processing in mental retardation. *Journal of Abnormal Psychology,* 1979, *88,* 341–345.

Sackheim, H. A., Nordlie, J. W., & Gur, R. C. A model of hysterical and hypnotic blindness: Cognition, motivation, and awareness. *Journal of Abnormal Psychology,* 1979, *88,* 474–489.

Sacks, O. *Migraine: Evolution of a common disorder.* Berkeley: University of California Press, 1973.

Sainsbury, P. Suicide and depression. In A. Coppen & A. Walk (Eds.), *Recent developments in affective disorders.* Ashford, England: Headley, 1968.

Salzman, L. F., & Klein, R. H. Habituation and conditioning of electrodermal responses in high risk children. *Schizophrenia Bulletin,* 1978, *4,* 210–222.

Sandall, H., Hawley, T. T., & Gordon, G. C. The St. Louis Community homes program: Graduated support for long term care. *American Journal of Psychiatry,* 1975, *132,* 617–622.

Sarason, I. G., Johnson, J. H., & Siegel, J. M. Assessing the impact of life changes: Development of the life experiences survey. *Journal of Consulting and Clinical Psychology,* 1978, *46,* 932–946.

Sarason, S. B., & Doris, J. *Psychological problems in mental deficiency.* New York: Harper & Row, 1969.

Satir, V. *Conjoint family therapy.* Palo Alto, Calif.: Science & Behavior Books, 1964.

Satterfield, J. H., Cantwell, D. P., Schell, A., & Blashke, T. Growth of hyperactive children treated with methylphenidate. *Archives of General Psychiatry,* 1979, *36,* 212–217.

Saul, L. A. Hostility in cases of essential hypertension. *Psychosomatic Medicine,* 1939, *1,* 153–161.

Scarr, S. Social introversion-extroversion as a heritable response. *Child Development,* 1969, *40,* 823–832.

Scarr, S. Genetics and the development of intelligence. In F. D. Horowitz (Ed.), *Child development research, Vol. 4.* Chicago: University of Chicago Press, 1975.

Scarr, S., & Weinberg, R. A. The influence of "family background" on intellectual attainment. *American Sociological Review,* 1978, *43,* 674–692.

Schaefer, H. H., & Martin, P. L. Behavioral therapy for "apathy" of hospitalized schizophrenics. *Psychological Reports,* 1966, *19,* 1147–1158.

Schatzman, M. *Soul murder.* New York: Random House, 1973.

Scheff, T. J. The societal reaction to deviance: Ascriptive elements in the psychiatric screening of mental patients in a midwestern state. *Social Problems,* 1964, *11,* 401–413.

Scheff, T. J. (Ed.) *Labelling madness.* Englewood Cliffs, N. J.: Prentice-Hall, 1975.

Schildkraut, J. J., Orsulak, P. J., Schatzberg, A. F., Gudeman, J. E., Cole, J. O., Rohde, W. A., & LaBrie, R. A. Toward a biochemical classification of depressive disorders. *Archives of General Psychiatry,* 1978, *35,* 1427–1433.

Schleifer, M., Weiss, G., Cohen, N., Elman, M., Evejic, H., & Kruger, E. Hyperactivity in preschoolers and the effect of methylphenidate. *American Journal of Orthopsychiatry,* 1975, *45,* 38–50.

Schmauk, F. J. Punishment, arousal, and avoidance learning. *Journal of Abnormal Psychology,* 1970, *76,* 325–335.

Schopler, E., Andrews, C. E., & Strupp, K. Do autistic children come from upper-middle-class parents? *Journal of Autism and Developmental Disorders,* 1979, *9,* 139–152.

Schopler, E., & Reichler, R. J. Developmental therapy by parents with their own autistic child. In M. Rutter (Ed.), *Infantile autism: Concepts, characteristics and treatment.* London: Churchill-Livingstone, 1971.

Schopsin, B., Gershon, S., Thompson, H., & Collins, P. Psychoactive drugs in mania. *Archives of General Psychiatry,* 1975, *32,* 34–42.

Schreiber, F. R. *Sybil.* New York: Warner, 1973.

Schroeder, C. W. Mental disorders in cities. *American Journal of Sociology,* 1954, *60,* 140–151.

Schuckit, M. A., & Rayses, V. Ethanol ingestion: Differences in blood acetaldehyde concentrations in relatives of alcoholics and controls. *Science,* 1979, *203,* 54–55.

Schuell, H. *Aphasia theory and therapy: Selected lectures and papers of Hildred Schuell.* Baltimore: University Park Press, 1974.

Schuler, E. A., & Parenton, V. J. A recent epidemic of hysteria in a Louisiana high school. *Journal of Social Psychology,* 1943, *17,* 221–235.

Schulman, J. L., Kaspar, J. C., & Throne, F. M. *Brain damage and behavior: A clinical-experimental study.* Springfield, Ill.: Charles C Thomas, 1965.

Schulsinger, F. Psychopathy: Heredity and environment. In S. A. Mednick & K. O. Christianson (Eds.), *Biosocial bases of criminal behavior.* New York: Gardner Press, 1977.

Schwab, J. J., Fennell, E. B., & Warheit, G. J. The epidemiology of psychosomatic disorders. *Psychosomatics,* 1974, *15,* 88–93.

Schwartz, D. A. A re-view of the "paranoid" concept. *Archives of General Psychiatry,* 1963, *8,* 349–361.

Sears, R. R., Maccoby, E. E., & Levin, H. *Patterns of child rearing.* New York: Harper & Row, 1957.

Seer, P. Psychological control of essential hypertension: Review of the literature and methodological critique. *Psychological Bulletin,* 1979, *86,* 1015–1043.

Segal, J. J. *Imagery: Current cognitive approaches.* New York: Academic Press, 1971.

Seiden, R. H. We're driving young blacks to suicide. *Psychology Today,* 1970, *4,* 24–28.

Seligman, M., & Hager, J. (Eds.) *Biological boundaries of learning.* New York: Appleton, 1972.

Seligman, M. E. P. *Helplessness.* San Francisco: W. H. Freeman, 1975.

Seligman, M. E. P., & Maier, S. F. Failure to escape traumatic shock. *Journal of Experimental Psychology,* 1967, *74,* 1–9.

Selye, H. *The stress of life.* New York: McGraw-Hill, 1956.

Shakow, D. Segmental set: A theory of the formal psychological deficit in schizophrenia. *Archives of General Psychiatry,* 1961, *6,* 1–17.

Shakow, D. Psychological deficit in schizophrenia. *Behavioral Science,* 1963, *8,* 275–305.

Sheehan, J. G. Conflict theory and avoidance-reduction therapy. In J. Eisenson (Ed.), *Stuttering: A second symposium.* New York: Harper & Row, 1975.

Shaywitz, B. A., Yager, R. D., & Klopper, J. H. Selective brain dopamine depletion in developing rats: An experimental model of minimal brain dysfunction. *Science,* 1976, *191,* 305–307.

Shields, J. Monozygotic twins: Brought up apart and brought up together. New York: Oxford University Press, 1962.

Shields. J. The genetics of schizophrenia in historical context. In A. Coppen & A. Walk (Eds.), *Recent developments in schizophrenia.* British Journal of Psychiatry Special Publication No. 1. Ashford, England: Headley, 1967.

Shields, J., & Slater, E. Heredity and psychological abnormality. In H. J. Eysenck (Ed.), *Handbook of abnormal psychology.* New York: Basic Books, 1961.

Shipley, R. H., Butt, J. H., Horwitz, B., & Farbry, J. E. Preparation for a stressful medical procedure: Effect of amount of stimulus preexposure and coping style. *Journal of Consulting and Clinical Psychology,* 1978, *46,* 499–507.

Shlien, J. M., Mosak, H. H., & Dreikurs, R. Effect of time limits: A comparison of two psychotherapies. *Journal of Counseling Psychology,* 1963, *9,* 31–34.

Shneidman, E. S. Acute paranoid schizophrenia in a veteran. In A. Burton & R. E. Harris (Eds.), *Clinical studies of personality.* New York: Harper & Row, 1955.

Shneidman, E. S., & Farberow, N. L. *Some facts about suicide.* Rockville, Md.: National Institute of Mental Health, 1961.

Shopsin, B., Klein, H., Aaronsom, R. N., & Collora, M. Clozapine, chlorpromazine, and placebo in newly hospitalized, acutely schizophrenic patients. *Archives of General Psychiatry,* 1979, *36,* 657–664.

Short, A. Evaluation of short-term treatment outcome using parents as co-therapists for their own psychotic children. Unpublished doctoral dissertation, University of North Carolina, 1980.

Siegel, R. A. Probability of punishment and suppression of behavior in psychopathic and nonpsychopathic offenders. *Journal of Abnormal Psychology,* 1978, *87,* 514–522.

Siegelman, M. Adjustment of homosexual and heterosexual women. *British Journal of Psychiatry,* 1972, *120,* 477–481. (a)

Siegelman, M. Adjustment of male homosexuals and heterosexuals. *Archives of Sexual Behavior,* 1972, *2,* 9. (b)

Sigel, I. E. How intelligence tests limit understanding of intelligence. *Merrill-Palmer Quarterly,* 1963, *9,* 39–56.

Silber, A. An addendum to the technique of psychotherapy with alcoholics. *Journal of Nervous and Mental Disease,* 1970, *150,* 423–437.

Singer, M. T., & Wynne, L. C. Thought disorder and family relations of schizophrenics: IV. Results and implications. *Archives of General Psychiatry,* 1965, *12,* 201–206.

Skinner, B. F. The behavior of organisms. New York: Appleton, 1938.

Skrzypek, G. J. Effect of perceptual isolation and arousal on anxiety, complexity preference, and novelty preference in psychopathic and neurotic delinquents. *Journal of Abnormal Psychology,* 1969, *74,* 321–329.

Slater, E. *Psychotic and neurotic illnesses in twins.* London: Her Majesty's Stationery Office, 1953.

Slater, E. The thirty-fifth Maudsley lecture: "Hysteria 311." *Journal of Mental Science,* 1961, *107,* 359–381.

Slater, E., & Glithero, E. A follow-up of patients diagnosed as suffering from hysteria. *Journal of Psychosomatic Research,* 1965, *9,* 9–13.

Slater, E., & Shields, J. Genetical aspects of anxiety. In M. H. Lader (Ed.), *Studies of anxiety.* Ashford, England: Headley, 1969.

Sloane, R. B., Staples, F. R., Yorkston, W., Cristol, A., & Whipple, K. Behavior therapy versus psychotherapy. Cambridge, Mass.: Commonwealth Publication of the Harvard University Press, 1975.

Smart, R. G., & Fejer, D. Drug use among adolescents and their parents: Closing the generation gap in mood modification. *Journal of Abnormal Psychology,* 1972, *79,* 153–160.

Smith, R. E., & Sharpe, T. M. Treatment of a school phobia with implosive therapy. *Journal of Consulting and Clinical Psychology,* 1970, *35,* 239–243.

Snyder, J. J. A reinforcement analysis of interaction in problem and non-problem families. *Journal of Abnormal Psychology,* 1977, *86,* 528–535.

Snyder, S. H. Madness and the brain. New York: McGraw-Hill, 1974.

Sobell, M. B., & Sobell, L. C. Individualized behavior therapy for alcoholics. *Behavior Therapy,* 1973, *4,* 49–72.

Solomon, R. L., Kamin, L. J., & Wynne, L. C. Trau-

matic avoidance learning: The outcomes of several extinction procedures with dogs. *Journal of Abnormal and Social Psychology,* 1953, *48,* 291–302.

Sotile, W. M., & Kilmann, P. R. Treatments of psychogenic female sexual dysfunctions. *Psychological Bulletin,* 1977, *84,* 619–633.

Speer, F. Allergic factors in migraine. *Modern Medicine,* 1971, 100–106.

Speisman, J. C., Lazarus, R. S., Mordkoff, A. M., & Davison, L. A. Experimental reduction of stress based on ego-defense theory. *Journal of Abnormal and Social Psychology,* 1964, *68,* 367–380.

Spielberger, C. D. (Ed.), *Anxiety: Current trends in theory and research,* Vol. 1. New York: Academic Press, 1972.

Spitz, R. A. Hospitalism. *The Psychoanalytic Study of the Child,* 1945, *1,* 53–74.

Spitz, R. A. Anaclitic depression. *The Psychoanalytic Study of the Child,* 1946, *2,* 313–342.

Spohn, H. E., Lacoursiere, R. B., Thompson, K., & Coyne, L. Phenothiazine effects on psychological and psychophysiological dysfunction in chronic schizophrenics. *Archives of General Psychiatry,* 1977, *34,* 633–644.

Sprague, R. L., Barnes, K. R., & Werry, J. S. Methylphenidate and thioridazine: Learning, reaction time, activity, and classroom behavior in disturbed children. *American Journal of Orthopsychiatry,* 1970, *40,* 615–628.

Sprague, R. L., & Sleator, E. K. Methylphenidate in hyperkinetic children: Differences in dose effects on learning and social behavior. *Science,* 1977, *198,* 1274–1276.

Srole, L., Langner, T. S., Michael, S. T., Opler, M. K., & Rennie, T. A. C. *Mental health in the metropolis: Midtown Manhattan study,* Vol. 1. New York: McGraw-Hill, 1962.

Stampfl, T. G., & Levis, D. J. Essentials of implosive therapy. A learning theory based psychodynamic behavioral therapy. *Journal of Abnormal Psychology,* 1967, *72,* 496–503.

Stanley, E. J., & Barter, J. T. Adolescent suicidal behavior. *American Journal of Orthopsychiatry,* 1970, *40,* 87–96.

Stanton, M. D., Todd, T. C., Heard, D. B., Kirschner, S., Kleiman, J. T., Mowatt, D. T., Riley, P., Scott, S. M., & Vandeusen, J. M. Heroin addiction as a family phenomenon. A new conceptual model. *American Journal of Drug and Alcohol Abuse,* 1978, *5,* 125–150.

Starkey, M. L. *The devil in Massachusetts.* New York, N. Y.: Doubleday, 1961.

Steele, R. S. The physiological concomitants of psychogenic motive arousal in college males. Unpublished doctoral dissertation, Harvard University, 1973.

Stein, L. I., & Test, M. A. An alternative to mental hospital treatment. In L. I. Stein and M. A. Test (Eds.), *Alternatives to mental hospital treatment.* New York: Plenum, 1978.

Steiner, C. M. The alcoholic game. *Quarterly Journal of Studies on Alcohol,* 1969, *30,* 920–938.

Steiner, C. M. *Scripts people live.* New York: Grove Press, 1974.

Stephens, B. Symposium: Developmental gains in the reasoning, moral judgments, and moral conduct of retarded and nonretarded persons. *American Journal of Mental Deficiency,* 1974, *79,* 113–115.

Stephens, B., Mahaney, D. J., & McLaughlin, J. A. Mental ages for achievement of Piagetian reasoning assessment. *Education and Training of the Mentally Retarded,* 1972, *7,* 124–128.

Stephens, J. H. Long-term prognosis and follow-up in schizophrenia. *Schizophrenia Bulletin,* 1978, *4,* 25–47.

Stephens, J. H., & Kamp, M. On some aspects of hysteria: A clinical study. *Journal of Nervous and Mental Disease,* 1962, *134,* 305–315.

Stephens, J. H., O'Connor, G. O., & Wiener, G. Long-term prognosis in schizophrenia using the Becker-Wittman Scale and the Phillips Scale. Paper presented at the 124th Annual Meeting of the American Psychiatric Association, 1968.

Stewart, M. A., Pitts, F. N., Craig, A. G., & Dieruf, W. The hyperactive child syndrome. *American Journal of Orthopsychiatry,* 1966, *36,* 861–867.

Stone, A. A. *Mental health and law: A system in transition.* Rockville, Md.: National Institute of Mental Health, 1975.

Strage, M. VD: The clock is ticking. *Today's Health,* 1971, *49,* 16–18, 69–71.

Strecker, E. A., & Ebaugh, F. G. Neuropsychiatric sequelae of cerebral trauma in children. *Archives of Neurology and Psychiatry,* 1924, *12,* 443–453.

Strupp, H. H. *Psychotherapy and the modification of abnormal behavior.* New York: McGraw-Hill, 1971.

Strupp, H., & Hadley, S. W. Specific versus nonspecific factors in psychotherapy: A controlled study of outcome. *Archives of General Psychiatry,* 1979, *36,* 1125–1136.

Sullivan, H. S. The interpersonal theory of psychiatry. New York: Norton, 1953.

Sundby, P., & Nyhus, P. Major and minor psychiatric disorders in males in Oslo: An epidemiological study. *Acta Psychiatrica Scandinavica,* 1963, *39,* 519–547.

Symkal, A., & Thorne, F. C. Etiological studies of psychopathic personality. *Journal of Clinical Psychology,* 1951, *7,* 299–316.

Syndulko, K. Electrocortical investigation of sociopathy. In R. D. Hare & D. Schalling (Eds.), *Psychopathy behavior: Approaches to research.* New York: Wiley, 1978.

Szasz, T. S. The myth of mental illness. *American Psychologist,* 1960, *15,* 113–118.

Szasz, T. S. *Psychiatric justice.* New York: Macmillan, 1965.

Szasz, T. S. *The manufacture of madness.* New York: Harper & Row, 1970.

Szasz, T. S. Postscript to "Psychiatric justice: The case of Mr. Louis Perroni." In O. Milton & R. G. Wahler, (Eds.), *Behavior disorders: Perspectives and trends.* Philadelphia: Lippincott, 1973.

Taft, L. T., & Goldfarb, W. Prenatal and perinatal factors in childhood schizophrenia. *Developmental Medicine and Child Neurology,* 1963, *6,* 32–43.

Tarler-Benlolo, L. The role of relaxation in biofeedback training: A critical review of the literature. *Psychological Bulletin,* 1978, *85,* 727–755.

Tarter, R. E., McBride, H., Buonpane, N., & Schneider, D. U. Differentiation of alcoholics: Childhood history of minimal brain dysfunction, family history and drinking pattern. *Archives of General Psychiatry,* 1977, *34,* 761–768.

Taylor, E. M. *Psychological appraisal of children with cerebral defects.* Cambridge, Mass.: Harvard University Press, 1959.

Taylor, N. *Narcotics: Nature's dangerous gift.* New York: Delta Books, 1963.

Temerlin, M. K. Diagnostic bias in community mental health. *Community Mental Health Journal,* 1970, *6,* 110–117.

Terman, L. M., & Merrill, M. A. *Stanford-Binet Intelligence Scale.* Boston: Houghton Mifflin, 1960.

Test, M. A., & Stein, L. I. Community treatment of the chronic patient: Research overview. *Schizophrenia Bulletin,* 1978, *4,* 350–364.

Teuber, H. L., & Powers, E. Evaluating therapy in a delinquency prevention program. *Psychiatric Treatment,* 1953, *21,* 138–147.

Thigpen, C. H., & Cleckley, H. M. *Three faces of Eve.* Kingsport, Tenn.: Kingsport Press, 1957.

Thinman, J. Conditioned reflex treatment of alcoholism. II: The risks of its application, its indications, contraindications, and psychotherapeutic aspects. *New England Journal of Medicine,* 1949, *241,* 406–410.

Thomas, A., & Chess, S. *Temperament and development.* New York: Brunner/Mazel, 1977.

Thomas, A., Chess, S., & Birch, H. G. *Temperament and behavior disorders in children.* New York: New York University Press, 1968.

Thomson, K., & Hendrie, H. Environmental stress in primary depressive illness. *Archives of General Psychiatry,* 1972, *26,* 130–132.

Thompson, N. L., Jr., McCandless, B. R., & Strickland, B. R. Personal adjustment of male and female homosexuals and heterosexuals. *Journal of Abnormal Psychology,* 1971, *78,* 237–240.

Thorndike, E. L. *Animal intelligence.* New York: Macmillan, 1911.

Thorndike, E. L. The psychology of wants, interests and attitudes. New York: Appleton, 1935.

Tienari, P. Schizophrenia in monozygotic male twins. In D. Rosenthal & S. S. Kety (Eds.), *The transmission of schizophrenia.* New York: Pergamon, 1968.

Tienari, P. Schizophrenia and monozygotic twins. *Psychiatria Fennica,* 1971, 97–104.

Titchener, J. L., Sheldon, M. B., & Ross, W. D. Changes in blood pressure of hypertensive patients with and without group psychotherapy. *Journal of Psychosomatic Research,* 1959, *4,* 10–12.

Tomlinson, B. E., Blessed, G., & Roth, M. Observations on the brains of demented old people. *Journal of Neurological Science,* 1970, *11,* 205–242.

Torgersen, A. M. Temperamental differences in infants: Their cause as shown through twin studies. Unpublished doctoral dissertation. University of Oslo, Norway, 1973. Also summarized in A. Thomas, & C. Chess, *Temperament and development.* New York: Brunner/Mazel, 1977.

Torgersen, S. The nature and origin of common phobic fears. *British Journal of Psychiatry,* 1979, *134,* 343–351.

Tourney, G., Petrilli, A. J., & Hatfield, L. M. Hormonal relationships in homosexual men. *American Journal of Psychiatry,* 1975, *132,* 288–290.

Truax, C. B. Reinforcement and nonreinforcement in Rogerian therapy. *Journal of Abnormal Psychology,* 1966, *71,* 1–9.

Truax, C. B., & Carkhuff, R. C. *Toward effective counseling and psychotherapy.* Chicago: Aldine 1967.

Tuckman, J., Kleiner, R., & Lavell, M. Emotional content of suicide notes. *American Journal of Psychiatry,* 1959, *116,* 59–63.

Turner, J. C. & Ten Hoor, W. J. The NIMH community support program: Pilot approach to a needed social reform. *Schizophrenia Bulletin,* 1978, *4,* 319–349.

Turner, R. J., & Wagonfeld, M. O. Occupational mobility and schizophrenia. *American Sociological Review,* 1967, *32,* 104–113.

Ullmann, L. P., & Krasner, L. *A psychological approach to abnormal behavior,* 2d ed. Englewood Cliffs, N.J.: Prentice-Hall, 1975.

United Nations. *Demographic yearbook, 1967.* New York: United Nations, 1968.

United States Department of Health, Education, and Welfare, National Center for Health Statistics. Public Health Service Publications Series 10, No. 83, and Series 11, No. 37. Washington, D.C., 1968, 1970.

United States Department of Health, Education, and Welfare. *Alcohol and health.* Rockville, Md.: NIAAA, 1978.

Vaillant, G. E. A twelve year follow-up of New York narcotic addicts. I. The relation of treatment to outcome. *American Journal of Psychiatry,* 1966, *122,* 727–737.

Vaillant, G. E. 20-year follow-up of New York narcotic addicts. *Archives of General Psychiatry,* 1973, *29,* 237–241.

Van Dyke, J. L., Rosenthal, D., & Rasmussen, P. V, Electrodermal functioning in adopted-away offspring of schizophrenics. *Journal of Psychiatric Research,* 1974, *10,* 199–215.

van Praag, H. M., & Korf, J. Neuroleptics, catecholamines, and psychoses: A study of their interrelations. *American Journal of Psychiatry,* 1975, *132,* 593–597.

Van Putten, T., Crumpton, E., & Yale, C. Drug refusal in schizophrenia and the wish to be crazy. *Archives of General Psychiatry,* 1976, *33,* 1443–1446.

Venables, P. H. The electrodermal psychophysiology of schizophrenics and children at risk for schizophrenia: Controversies and developments. *Schizophrenia Bulletin,* 1977, *3,* 28–48.

Veroff, J., Atkinson, J. W., Feld, S. C., & Gurin, G. The use of thematic apperception to assess motivation in a nationwide interview study. *Psychological Monographs,* 1960, *74,* (2, Whole no. 499).

Vogler, R. E., Lunde, S. E., Johnson, G. R., & Martin, P. L. Electrical aversion conditioning with chronic alcoholics. *Journal of Consulting and Clinical Psychology,* 1970, *34,* 302–307.

Vogler, R. E., Weissbach, T. A., & Compton, J. V. Learning techniques for alcohol abuse. *Behavior Research and Therapy,* 1977, *15,* 31–38.

Volavka, J., Davis, L. G., & Ehrlich, Y. H. Endorphins, Dopamine, and schizophrenia. *Schizophrenia Bulletin,* 1979, *5,* 227–239.

Volkmann, R., & Cressey, D. R., Differential association and the rehabilitation of drug addicts. *American Journal of Sociology,* 1963, *64,* 129–142.

Wada, J., & Rasmussen, T. Intra-carotid injection of sodium amytal for the lateralization of cerebral speech dominance: Experimental and clinical observations. *Journal of Neurosurgery,* 1960, *17,* 266–282.

Wahl, O. F. Monozygotic twins discordant for schizophrenia: A review. *Psychological Bulletin,* 1976, *83,* 91–106.

Waldron, S., Shrier, D. K., Stone, B., & Tobin, F. School phobia and other childhood neuroses: A systematic study of the children and their families. *American Journal of Psychiatry,* 1975, *132,* 802–808.

Waldrop, M. F., Pedersen, F. A., & Bell, R. Q. Minor physical anomalies and behavior in preschool children. *Child Development,* 1968, *39,* 391–400.

Warheit, G. J., Holzer, C. E., & Arey, S. A. Race and mental illness: An epidemiologic update. *Journal of Health and Social Behavior,* 1975, *16,* 243–256.

Waring, M., & Ricks, D. Family patterns of children who become adult schizophrenics. *Journal of Nervous and Mental Disease,* 1965, *140,* 351–364.

Warshauer, M. E., & Monk, M. Problems in suicide statistics for Whites and Blacks. *American Journal of Public Health,* 1978, *68,* 383–388.

Waters, E., Vaugh, B. E., & Egeland, B. R. Individual differences in infant-mother attachment relationships at age one: Antecedents in neonatal behavior in an urban economically disadvantaged sample. *Child Development,* 1980, *51,* 208–216.

Waters, W. E. Migraine: Intelligence, social class and familial prevalence. *British Medical Journal,* 1971, *2,* 77–78.

Watkins, B. A., Cowan, M. A., & Davis, W. E. Differential diagnosis imbalance as a race related phenomenon. *Journal of Clinical Psychology,* 1975, *31,* 267–268.

Watson, J. B., & Rayner, R. Conditioned emotional reactions. *Journal of Experimental Psychology,* 1920, *3,* 1–14.

Watson, J. S., & Ramey, C. T. Reactions to response-contingent stimulation in early infancy. *Merrill-Palmer Quarterly,* 1972, *18,* 219–227.

Watts, A. *The joyous cosmology.* New York: Random House, 1962.

Watts, F. N. Habituation model of systematic desensitization. *Psychological Bulletin,* 1979, *86,* 627–637.

Wechsler, D. *Wechsler Intelligence Scale for Children.* New York: Psychological Corporation, 1949.

Wechsler, D. *Wechsler Adult Intelligence Scale.* New York: Psychological Corporation, 1955.

Wechsler, D. *Wechsler Preschool and Primary Scale of Intelligence.* New York: Psychological Corporation, 1963, 1967.

Weil, A. T., Zinburg, N. E., & Nelsen, J. M. Clinical and psychological effects of marijuana in man. *Science,* 1968, *162,* 1234–1242.

Weinberg, M. S., & Williams, C. J. *Male homosexuals: Their problems and adaptations.* New York: Oxford University Press, 1974.

Weinberger, D. A., Schwartz, G. E., & Davidson, R. J. *Journal of Abnormal Psychology,* 1979, *88,* 369–380.

Weiss, G., Kruger, E., Danielson, V., & Elman, M. Long-term methylphenidate treatment of hyperkinetic children. *Psychopharmacology Bulletin,* 1974, *10,* 34–35.

Weiss, J. M., Glazer, H. I., & Pohorecky, L. A. Neurotransmitters and helplessness: A chemical bridge to depression. *Psychology Today,* 1974, *8* (7), 58–65.

Weissman, M., & Klerman, G. Sex differences and the epidemiology of depression. *Archives of General Psychiatry,* 1977, *34,* 98–111

Weissman, M. M., & Myers, J. K. Rates and risks of depressive symptoms in a United States urban community. *Acta Psychiatrica Scandinavica,* 1978, *57,* 219–231.

Weissman, M. M., Myers, J. K., & Harding, P. S. Psychiatric disorders in a U.S. urban community: 1975–1976. *American Journal of Psychiatry,* 1978, *135,* 459–462.

Weisz, J. R. Perceived control and learned helplessness among mentally retarded and nonretarded children: A developmental analysis. *Developmental Psychology,* 1979, *15,* 311–319.

Weisz, J. R., & Zigler, E. Cognitive development in retarded and nonretarded persons: Piagetian tests of the similar sequence hypothesis. *Psychological Bulletin,* 1979, *86,* 831–851.

Wells, C. E. Chronic brain disease: An overview. *American Journal of Psychiatry,* 1978, *135,* 1–12.

Wender, P. H. Dementia praecox: The development of the concept. *American Journal of Psychiatry,* 1963, *119,* 1143–1151.

Wender, P. H. Minimal brain dysfunction in children. New York: Wiley, 1971.

Wender, P. H., Rosenthal, D., Kety, S. S., Schulsinger, F., & Welner, J. Crossfostering: A research strategy for clarifying the role of genetic and experimental factors in the etiology of schizophrenia. *Archives of General Psychiatry,* 1974, *30,* 121–128.

Wender, P. H., Rosenthal, D., Rainer, J. D., Green-

hill, L., & Sarlin, B. Schizophrenics' adopting parents. *Archives of General Psychiatry*, 1977, *34*, 777–785.

Wenger, D. L., & Fletcher, C. R. The effect of legal counsel on admissions to a state mental hospital: A confrontation of professions. *Journal of Health and Human Behavior*, 1969, *10*, 66–72.

Werry, J. S. Studies on the hyperactive child. IV: An empirical analysis of the minimal brain dysfunction syndrome. *Archives of General Psychiatry*, 1968, *19*, 9–16.

Werry, J. S. The childhood psychoses. In H. C. Quay and J. S. Werry (Eds.), *Psychopathological disorders of childhood.* New York: Wiley, 1979.

Werry, J. S., & Quay, H. C. The prevalence of behavior symptoms in younger elementary school children. *American Journal of Orthopsychiatry*, 1971, *41*, 136–143.

Werry, J. S., & Sprague, R. L. Hyperactivity. In C. G. Costello (Ed.), *Symptoms of psychopathology.* New York: Wiley, 1970.

Wesman, A. G. Intelligent testing. *American Psychologist*, 1968, *23*, 267–274.

Wexler, L., Weissman, M. M., & Kasl, S. V. Suicide attempts 1970–75: Updating a United States study and comparisons with international trends. *British Journal of Psychiatry*, 1978, *132*, 180–185.

White, R. W. Criminal complaints: A true account by L. Percy King. In B. Kaplan (Ed.), *The inner world of mental illness.* New York: Harper & Row, 1964.

White, R. W. *Lives in progress.* New York: Holt, Rinehart and Winston, 1975.

White, R. W. *The enterprise of living.* New York: Holt, Rinehart and Winston, 1976.

Whitlock, F. A. The aetiology of hysteria. *Acta Psychiatrica Scandinavica*, 1967, *43*, 144–162.

Wilkins, J. A follow-up study of those who called a suicide prevention center. *American Journal of Psychiatry*, 1970, *127*, 155–161.

Willerman, L. Activity level and hyperactivity in twins. *Child Development*, 1973, *44*, 288–293.

Williams, A. F. Social drinking, anxiety, and depression. *Journal of Personality and Social Psychology*, 1966, *3*, 689–794.

Wilson, G. T. Alcoholism and aversion therapy: Issues, ethics and evidence. In G. A. Marlatt & P. E. Nathan (Eds.), *Behavioral approaches to alcoholism.* New Brunswick, N.J.; Rutgers Center of Alcohol Studies, 1978.

Winchell, C. A. *The hyperkinetic child.* Westport, Conn.: Greenwood Press, 1975.

Winer, D. Anger and dissociation: A case study of multiple personality. *Journal of Abnormal Psychology*, 1978, *87*, 368–372.

Wing, L., Yeates, S. R., Brierley, L. M., & Gould, J. The prevalence of early childhood autism: A comparison administrative and epidemiological studies. *Psychological Medicine*, 1976, *6*, 89–100.

Wingate, M. E. *Stuttering: Theory and treatment.* New York: Wiley, 1976.

Winick, M. Nutrition and mental development. *Mental Clinics of North America*, 1970, *54*, 1413–1428.

Winokur, G., Clayton, P., & Reich, T. *Manic-depressive illness.* St. Louis: C. V. Mosley, 1969.

Winokur, G., Reich, T., Rimmer, J., & Pitts, F. N., Alcoholism III: Diagnosis and familial psychiatric illness in 259 alcoholic probands. *Archives of General Psychiatry*, 1970, *23*, 104–11.

Witkin, H. A., Mednick, S. A., Schulsinger, F., Bakkestrom, E., Christianson, K. O., Goodenough, D. R., Hirschhorn, K., Lundsteen, C., Owen, D. R., Philip, J., Rubin, D. B., & Stocking, M. Criminality, aggression and intelligence among XYY and XXY men. In S. A. Mednick & K. O. Christianson (Eds.), *Biosocial bases of criminal behavior.* New York: Gardner Press, 1977.

Wolberg, L. R. *The technique of psychotherapy.* New York: Grune & Stratton, 1977.

Wold, C. I., & Litman, R. E. Suicide after contact with a suicide prevention center. *Archives of General Psychiatry*, 1973, *28*, 735–739.

Wolf, M. M., Risley, T., & Mees, H. Application of operant conditioning procedures to the behavior problems of an autistic child. *Behavior Research and Therapy*, 1964, *1*, 305–312.

Wolff, G. *The duke of deception.* New York: Random House, 1979.

Wolff, P. Ethnic differences in alcohol sensitivity. *Science*, 1972, *125*, 449–451.

Wolpe, J. Psychotherapy by reciprocal inhibition. Stanford, Calif.: Stanford University Press, 1958.

Wolpe, J. Isolation of a conditioning procedure as the crucial psychotherapeutic factor. *Journal of Nervous and Mental Diseases*, 1962, *134*, 316–324.

Wolpe, J. *The practice of behavior therapy.* New York: Pergamon, 1973.

Wolpe, J., & Rachman, S. Psychoanalytic "evidence" a critique based on Freud's case of Little Hans. *Journal of Nervous and Mental Disease*, 1960, *131*, 135–147.

World Health Organization. *The international pilot study of schizophrenia*, Vol. 1. Geneva: World Health Organization Press, 1973.

Wortman, C. B., & Dintzer, L. Is an attributional analysis of the learned helplessness phenomenon viable? A critique of the Abramson-Seligman-Teasdale reformulation. *Journal of Abnormal Psychology*, 1978, *87*, 75–90.

Wynne, L. C., Singer, M. T., & Toohey, M. L. Communication of the adoptive parents of schizophrenics. In J. Jorstad and J. Ugelstad (Eds.), *Schizophrenia 75: Psychotherapy, family studies research: Proceedings of the fifth international symposium on the psychotherapy of schizophrenia.* Oslo: Lie & Co., 1976.

Yablonsky, L. *Synanon: The tunnel back.* Baltimore: Penguin Books, 1967.

Yalom, I. D., Green, R., & Fisk, N. Prenatal exposure to female hormones. *Archives of General Psychiatry,* 1973, *28,* 554–560.

Yarrow, L. J. Research in dimensions of maternal care. *Merrill-Palmer Quarterly,* 1963, *9,* 101–114.

Yates, A. J. *Theory and practice in behavior therapy.* New York: Wiley, 1975.

Yolles, S. F., & Kramer, M. Vital statistics of schizophrenia. In L. Bellak & L. Loeb (Eds.), *The schizophrenic syndrome.* New York: Grune & Stratton, 1969.

Yorkston, N. J., McHugh, R. B., Brady, R., Serber, M., & Sergeant, H. G. S. Verbal desensitization in bronchial asthma. *Journal of Psychosomatic Research,* 1974, *18,* 371–376.

Zahn, T. P. On the bimodality of the distribution of electrodermal orienting responses in schizophrenic patients. *Journal of Nervous and Mental Disease,* 1976, *162,* 195–199.

Zahn, T. P. Autonomic nervous system characteristics possibly related to a genetic predisposition to schizophrenia. *Schizophrenia Bulletin,* 1977, *3,* 49–60.

Zarfas, D. E., & Wolf, L. C. Maternal age patterns and the incidence of Down's syndrome. *American Journal of Mental Deficiency,* 1979, *83,* 353–359.

Zax, M., Cowen, E. L., Rapoport, J., Beach, D. R., & Laird, J. D. Follow-up study of children identified early as emotionally disturbed. *Journal of Consulting and Clinical Psychology,* 1968, *32,* 369–374.

Zigler, E. Research in personality structure in the retardate. In N. R. Ellis (Ed.), *International review of research in mental retardation,* Vol. 1. New York: Academic Press, 1966.

Zigler, E. Familial mental retardation: A continuing dilemma. *Science,* 1967, *155,* 292–298.

Zigler, E. Developmental versus difference theories of mental retardation and the problem of motivation. *American Journal of Mental Deficiency,* 1969, *73,* 536–556.

Zigler, E., & Balla, D. Luria's verbal deficiency theory of mental retardation and performance on sameness, symmetry, and opposition tasks: A critique. *American Journal of Mental Deficiency,* 1971, *75,* 400–413.

Zilboorg, G., & Henry, G. W. *A history of medical psychology.* New York: Norton, 1941.

Zimbardo, P. G. Shy murderers. *Psychology Today,* November 1977, 68–76, 148.

Zubin, J., Eron, L. D., & Schumer, F. *An experimental approach to projective techniques.* New York: Wiley, 1965.

Zubin, J., & Spring, B. Vulnerability—A new view of schizophrenia. *Journal of Abnormal Psychology,* 1977, *86,* 103–126.

Zweig, S. *Mental healers: Franz Anton Mesmer, Mary Baker Eddy, Sigmund Freud.* New York: Frederick Unger, 1932.

Name Index

Subject Index